GO!

with Microsoft®

Access 2010

Comprehensive

**Shelley Gaskin,
Carolyn McLellan, and
Nancy Graviett**

M000121845

Prentice Hall

Boston   Columbus   Indianapolis   New York   San Francisco   Upper Saddle River
Amsterdam   Cape Town   Dubai   London   Madrid   Milan   Munich   Paris   Montreal   Toronto
Delhi   Mexico City   Sao Paulo   Sydney   Hong Kong   Seoul   Singapore   Taipei   Tokyo

Associate VP/Executive Acquisitions Editor, Print: Stephanie Wall

Editorial Project Manager: Laura Burgess

Editor in Chief: Michael Payne

Product Development Manager: Eileen Bien Calabro

Development Editor: Toni Ackley

Editorial Assistant: Nicole Sam

Director of Marketing: Kate Valentine

Marketing Manager: Tori Olson Alves

Marketing Coordinator: Susan Osterlitz

Marketing Assistant: Darshika Vyas

Senior Managing Editor: Cynthia Zonneveld

Associate Managing Editor: Camille Trentacoste

Production Project Manager: Mike Lackey

Operations Director: Alexis Heydt

Operations Specialist: Natacha Moore

Senior Art Director: Jonathan Boylan

Cover Photo: © Ben Durrant

Text and Cover Designer: Blair Brown

Manager, Cover Visual Research & Permissions: Karen Sanatar

Manager, Rights and Permissions: Zina Arabia

AVP/Director of Online Programs, Media: Richard Keaveny

AVP/Director of Product Development, Media: Lisa Strite

Media Project Manager, Editorial: Alana Coles

Media Project Manager, Production: John Cassar

Full-Service Project Management: PreMediaGlobal

Composition: PreMediaGlobal

Printer/Binder: Quad/Graphics-Taunton

Cover Printer: Lehigh-Phoenix Color

Text Font: Bookman Light

Credits and acknowledgments borrowed from other sources and reproduced, with permission, in this textbook appear on appropriate page within text.

Microsoft® and Windows® are registered trademarks of the Microsoft Corporation in the U.S.A. and other countries. Screen shots and icons reprinted with permission from the Microsoft Corporation. This book is not sponsored or endorsed by or affiliated with the Microsoft Corporation.

Many of the designations by manufacturers and seller to distinguish their products are claimed as trademarks. Where those designations appear in this book, and the publisher was aware of a trademark claim, the designations have been printed in initial caps or all caps.

Library of Congress Cataloging-in-Publication Data

Go! with Microsoft Access 2010 / Shelley Gaskin ... [et al.].

    p. cm.

Includes index.

ISBN-13: 978-0-13-800771-3

ISBN-10: 0-13-800771-3

1. Microsoft Office. 2. Business—Computer programs. I. Gaskin, Shelley.

HF5548.4.M525G6254 2011

005.5—dc22

                        2010019636

10 9 8 7 6 5 4 3 2

Prentice Hall
is an imprint of

www.pearsonhighered.com

ISBN 10: 0-13-800771-3

ISBN 13: 978-0-13-800771-3

Brief Contents

Contents

Access

Chapter 1   Getting Started with Access Databases 49

Chapter 2 Sort and Query a Database 115

Chapter 3 Forms, Filters, and Reports 183

Chapter 4   Enhancing Tables............................ 253

Chapter 5 Enhancing Queries 323

Chapter 6   Customizing Forms and Reports

Chapter 9 Integrating Access with Other Applications 599

GO! System Contributors

We thank the following people for their hard work and support in making the GO! System all that it is!

Instructor Resource Authors

Adickes, Erich	Parkland College	Holly, Terri	Indian River State College
Baray, Carrie	Ivy Tech Community College	Jacob, Sherry	Kentucky Community and Technical College
Bornstein, Abigail	City College of San Francisco		
Bowman, Valeria	National College	Landenberger, Toni	Southeast Community College-Nebraska
Callahan, Michael	Lone Star College		
Clausen, Jane	Western Iowa Tech Community College	Leinbach, Andrea	Harrisburg Area Community College
Cleary, Kevin	University at Buffalo	Lutz, Mary	Southwestern Illinois College
Colucci, William	Montclair State University	McMahon, Richard	University of Houston—Downtown
Crossley, Connie	Cincinnati State Technical and Community College	Miller, Abigail	Gateway Community and Technical College
Damanti, Lori		Miller, Sandra	Wenatchee Valley College
Edington, Barbara	St. Francis College	Monson, Shari	Black Hawk College
Emrich, Stefanie	Metropolitan Community College of Omaha, Nebraska	Neal, Ruth	Navarro College
		Niebur, Katherine	Dakota County Technical College
Faix, Dennis	Harrisburg Area Community College	Nowakowski, Anthony	Buffalo State
Hadden, Karen	Western Iowa Tech Community College	Pierce, Tonya	Ivy Tech Community College
		Reynolds, Mark	Lone Star College
Hammerle, Patricia	Indiana University/Purdue University at Indianapolis	Roselli, Diane	Harrisburg Area Community College
		Shing, Chen-Chi	Radford University
Hicks, Janette	Binghamton University/State University of New York	St. John, Steve	Tulsa Community College
		Sterr, Jody	Blackhawk Technical College
Hines, James	Tidewater Community College	Thompson, Joyce	Lehigh Carbon Community College
Holland, Susan	Southeast Community College-Nebraska	Tucker, William	Austin Community College
		Volker, Bonita	Tidewater Community College
Hollingsworth, Mary Carole	Georgia Perimeter College	Walters, Kari	Louisiana State University

Technical Editors

Matthew Bisi	Sarah Evans	Joyce Nielsen	Jan Snyder
Mary Corcoran	Adam Layne	Janet Pickard	Sam Stamport
Lori Damanti	Elizabeth Lockley	Sean Portnoy	Mara Zebest
Barbara Edington			

Student Reviewers

Albinda, Sarah Evangeline	Phoenix College	Frye, Alicia	Phoenix College
Allen, John	Asheville-Buncombe Tech Community College	Gadomski, Amanda	Northern Michigan University
		Gassert, Jennifer	Harrisburg Area Community College
Alexander, Steven	St. Johns River Community College		
Alexander, Melissa	Tulsa Community College	Gross, Mary Jo	Kirkwood Community College
Bolz, Stephanie	Northern Michigan University	Gyselinck, Craig	Central Washington University
Berner, Ashley	Central Washington University	Harrison, Margo	Central Washington University
Boomer, Michelle	Northern Michigan University	Hatt, Patrick	Harrisburg Area Community College
Busse, Brennan	Northern Michigan University		
Butkey, Maura	Central Washington University	Heacox, Kate	Central Washington University
Cates, Concita	Phoenix College	Hedgman, Shaina	Tidewater College
Charles, Marvin	Harrisburg Area Community College	Hill, Cheretta	Northwestern State University
		Hochstedler, Bethany	Harrisburg Area Community College Lancaster
Christensen, Kaylie	Northern Michigan University		
Clark, Glen D. III	Harrisburg Area Community College	Homer, Jean	Greenville Technical College
		Innis, Tim	Tulsa Community College
Cobble, Jan N.	Greenville Technical College	Jarboe, Aaron	Central Washington University
Connally, Brianna	Central Washington University	Key, Penny	Greenville Technical College
Davis, Brandon	Northern Michigan University	Klein, Colleen	Northern Michigan University
Davis, Christen	Central Washington University	Lloyd, Kasey	Ivy Tech Bloomington
De Jesus Garcia, Maria	Phoenix College	Moeller, Jeffrey	Northern Michigan University
Den Boer, Lance	Central Washington University	Mullen, Sharita	Tidewater Community College
Dix, Jessica	Central Washington University	Nelson, Cody	Texas Tech University
Downs, Elizabeth	Central Washington University	Nicholson, Regina	Athens Tech College
Elser, Julie	Harrisburg Area Community College	Niehaus, Kristina	Northern Michigan University
		Nisa, Zaibun	Santa Rosa Community College
Erickson, Mike	Ball State University	Nunez, Nohelia	Santa Rosa Community College

Oak, Samantha	Central Washington University	Rozelle, Lauren	Texas Tech University
Oberly, Sara	Harrisburg Area Community College Lancaster	Schmadeke, Kimberly	Kirkwood Community College
		Shafapay, Natasha	Central Washington University
Oertii, Monica	Central Washington University	Shanahan, Megan	Northern Michigan University
Palenshus, Juliet	Central Washington University	Sullivan, Alexandra Nicole	Greenville Technical College
Pohl, Amanda	Northern Michigan University	Teska, Erika	Hawaii Pacific University
Presnell, Randy	Central Washington University	Torrenti, Natalie	Harrisburg Area Community College
Reed, Kailee	Texas Tech University		
Ritner, April	Northern Michigan University	Traub, Amy	Northern Michigan University
Roberts, Corey	Tulsa Community College	Underwood, Katie	Central Washington University
Rodgers, Spencer	Texas Tech University	Walters, Kim	Central Washington University
Rodriguez, Flavia	Northwestern State University	Warren, Jennifer L.	Greenville Technical College
Rogers, A.	Tidewater Community College	Wilson, Kelsie	Central Washington University
Rossi, Jessica Ann	Central Washington University	Wilson, Amanda	Green River Community College
Rothbauer, Taylor	Trident Technical College	Wylie, Jimmy	Texas Tech University

Series Reviewers

Abraham, Reni	Houston Community College	Buehler, Lesley	Ohlone College
Addison, Paul	Ivy Tech Community College	Buell, C	Central Oregon Community College
Agatston, Ann	Agatston Consulting Technical College	Burns, Christine	Central New Mexico Community College
Akuna, Valeria, Ph.D.	Estrella Mountain Community College	Byars, Pat	Brookhaven College
Alexander, Melody	Ball Sate University	Byrd, Julie	Ivy Tech Community College
Alejandro, Manuel	Southwest Texas Junior College	Byrd, Lynn	Delta State University, Cleveland, Mississippi
Alger, David	Tidewater Community College Chesapeake Campus	Cacace, Richard N.	Pensacola Junior College
		Cadenhead, Charles	Brookhaven College
Allen, Jackie	Rowan-Cabarrus Community College	Calhoun, Ric	Gordon College
Ali, Farha	Lander University	Cameron, Eric	Passaic Community College
Amici, Penny	Harrisburg Area Community College	Canine, Jill	Ivy Tech Community College of Indiana
Anderson, Patty A.	Lake City Community College	Cannamore, Madie	Kennedy King
Andrews, Wilma	Virginia Commonwealth College, Nebraska University	Cannon, Kim	Greenville Technical College
		Carreon, Cleda	Indiana University—Purdue University, Indianapolis
Anik, Mazhar	Tiffin University		
Armstrong, Gary	Shippensburg University	Carriker, Sandra	North Shore Community College
Arnold, Linda L.	Harrisburg Area Community College	Casey, Patricia	Trident Technical College
		Cates, Wally	Central New Mexico Community College
Ashby, Tom	Oklahoma City Community College		
		Chaffin, Catherine	Shawnee State University
Atkins, Bonnie	Delaware Technical Community College	Chauvin, Marg	Palm Beach Community College, Boca Raton
Aukland, Cherie	Thomas Nelson Community College	Challa, Chandrashekar	Virginia State University
		Chamlou, Afsaneh	NOVA Alexandria
Bachand, LaDonna	Santa Rosa Community College	Chapman, Pam	Wabaunsee Community College
Bagui, Sikha	University of West Florida	Christensen, Dan	Iowa Western Community College
Beecroft, Anita	Kwantlen University College		
Bell, Paula	Lock Haven College	Clay, Betty	Southeastern Oklahoma State University
Belton, Linda	Springfield Tech. Community College		
		Collins, Linda D.	Mesa Community College
Bennett, Judith	Sam Houston State University	Cone, Bill	Northern Arizona University
Bhatia, Sai	Riverside Community College	Conroy-Link, Janet	Holy Family College
Bishop, Frances	DeVry Institute—Alpharetta (ATL)	Conway, Ronald	Bowling Green State University
Blaszkiewicz, Holly	Ivy Tech Community College/Region 1	Cornforth, Carol G.	WVNCC
		Cosgrove, Janet	Northwestern CT Community
Boito, Nancy	HACC Central Pennsylvania's Community College	Courtney, Kevin	Hillsborough Community College
Borger-Boglin, Grietje L.	San Antonio College/Northeast Lakeview College	Coverdale, John	Riverside Community College
		Cox, Rollie	Madison Area Technical College
Branigan, Dave	DeVry University	Crawford, Hiram	Olive Harvey College
Bray, Patricia	Allegany College of Maryland	Crawford, Sonia	Central New Mexico Community College
Britt, Brenda K.	Fayetteville Technical Community College		
		Crawford, Thomasina	Miami-Dade College, Kendall Campus
Brotherton, Cathy	Riverside Community College		
Brown, Judy	Western Illinois University	Credico, Grace	Lethbridge Community College

Crenshaw, Richard — Miami Dade Community College, North

Crespo, Beverly — Mt. San Antonio College

Crooks, Steven — Texas Tech University

Crossley, Connie — Cincinnati State Technical Community College

Curik, Mary — Central New Mexico Community College

De Arazoza, Ralph — Miami Dade Community College

Danno, John — DeVry University/Keller Graduate School

Davis, Phillip — Del Mar College

Davis, Richard — Trinity Valley Community College

Davis, Sandra — Baker College of Allen Park

Dees, Stephanie D. — Wharton County Junior College

DeHerrera, Laurie — Pikes Peak Community College

Delk, Dr. K. Kay — Seminole Community College

Denton, Bree — Texas Tech University

Dix, Jeanette — Ivy Tech Community College

Dooly, Veronica P. — Asheville-Buncombe Technical Community College

Doroshow, Mike — Eastfield College

Douglas, Gretchen — SUNYCortland

Dove, Carol — Community College of Allegheny

Dozier, Susan — Tidewater Community College, Virginia Beach Campus

Driskel, Loretta — Niagara Community College

Duckwiler, Carol — Wabaunsee Community College

Duhon, David — Baker College

Duncan, Mimi — University of Missouri-St. Louis

Duthie, Judy — Green River Community College

Duvall, Annette — Central New Mexico Community College

Ecklund, Paula — Duke University

Eilers, Albert — Cincinnati State Technical and Community College

Eng, Bernice — Brookdale Community College

Epperson, Arlin — Columbia College

Evans, Billie — Vance-Granville Community College

Evans, Jean — Brevard Community College

Feuerbach, Lisa — Ivy Tech East Chicago

Finley, Jean — ABTCC

Fisher, Fred — Florida State University

Foster, Nancy — Baker College

Foster-Shriver, Penny L. — Anne Arundel Community College

Foster-Turpen, Linda — CNM

Foszcz, Russ — McHenry County College

Fry, Susan — Boise State University

Fustos, Janos — Metro State

Gallup, Jeanette — Blinn College

Gelb, Janet — Grossmont College

Gentry, Barb — Parkland College

Gerace, Karin — St. Angela Merici School

Gerace, Tom — Tulane University

Ghajar, Homa — Oklahoma State University

Gifford, Steve — Northwest Iowa Community College

Glazer, Ellen — Broward Community College

Gordon, Robert — Hofstra University

Gramlich, Steven — Pasco-Hernando Community College

Graviett, Nancy M. — St. Charles Community College, St. Peters, Missouri

Greene, Rich — Community College of Allegheny County

Gregoryk, Kerry — Virginia Commonwealth State

Griggs, Debra — Bellevue Community College

Grimm, Carol — Palm Beach Community College

Guthrie, Rose — Fox Valley Technical College

Hahn, Norm — Thomas Nelson Community College

Haley-Hunter, Deb — Bluefield State College

Hall, Linnea — Northwest Mississippi Community College

Hammerschlag, Dr. Bill — Brookhaven College

Hansen, Michelle — Davenport University

Hayden, Nancy — Indiana University—Purdue University, Indianapolis

Hayes, Theresa — Broward Community College

Headrick, Betsy — Chattanooga State

Helfand, Terri — Chaffey College

Helms, Liz — Columbus State Community College

Hernandez, Leticia — TCI College of Technology

Hibbert, Marilyn — Salt Lake Community College

Hinds, Cheryl — Norfolk State University

Hines, James — Tidewater Community College

Hoffman, Joan — Milwaukee Area Technical College

Hogan, Pat — Cape Fear Community College

Holland, Susan — Southeast Community College

Holliday, Mardi — Community College of Philadelphia

Hollingsworth, Mary Carole — Georgia Perimeter College

Hopson, Bonnie — Athens Technical College

Horvath, Carrie — Albertus Magnus College

Horwitz, Steve — Community College of Philadelphia

Hotta, Barbara — Leeward Community College

Howard, Bunny — St. Johns River Community

Howard, Chris — DeVry University

Huckabay, Jamie — Austin Community College

Hudgins, Susan — East Central University

Hulett, Michelle J. — Missouri State University

Humphrey, John — Asheville Buncombe Technical Community College

Hunt, Darla A. — Morehead State University, Morehead, Kentucky

Hunt, Laura — Tulsa Community College

Ivey, Joan M. — Lanier Technical College

Jacob, Sherry — Jefferson Community College

Jacobs, Duane — Salt Lake Community College

Jauken, Barb — Southeastern Community

Jerry, Gina — Santa Monica College

Johnson, Deborah S. — Edison State College

Johnson, Kathy — Wright College

Johnson, Mary — Kingwood College

Johnson, Mary — Mt. San Antonio College

Jones, Stacey — Benedict College

Jones, Warren — University of Alabama, Birmingham

Jordan, Cheryl — San Juan College

Kapoor, Bhushan — California State University, Fullerton

Kasai, Susumu — Salt Lake Community College

Kates, Hazel — Miami Dade Community College, Kendall

Keen, Debby — University of Kentucky

Keeter, Sandy — Seminole Community College

Kern-Blystone, Dorothy Jean — Bowling Green State

Kerwin, Annette — College of DuPage

Keskin, Ilknur — The University of South Dakota

Kinney, Mark B.	Baker College	Marghitu, Daniela	Auburn University
Kirk, Colleen	Mercy College	Marks, Suzanne	Bellevue Community College
Kisling, Eric	East Carolina University	Marquez, Juanita	El Centro College
Kleckner, Michelle	Elon University	Marquez, Juan	Mesa Community College
Kliston, Linda	Broward Community College, North Campus	Martin, Carol	Harrisburg Area Community College
Knuth, Toni	Baker College of Auburn Hills	Martin, Paul C.	Harrisburg Area Community College
Kochis, Dennis	Suffolk County Community College	Martyn, Margie	Baldwin-Wallace College
Kominek, Kurt	Northeast State Technical Community College	Marucco, Toni	Lincoln Land Community College
Kramer, Ed	Northern Virginia Community College	Mason, Lynn	Lubbock Christian University
		Matutis, Audrone	Houston Community College
Kretz, Daniel	Fox Valley Technical College	Matkin, Marie	University of Lethbridge
Laird, Jeff	Northeast State Community College	Maurel, Trina	Odessa College
		May, Karen	Blinn College
Lamoureaux, Jackie	Central New Mexico Community College	McCain, Evelynn	Boise State University
		McCannon, Melinda	Gordon College
Lange, David	Grand Valley State	McCarthy, Marguerite	Northwestern Business College
LaPointe, Deb	Central New Mexico Community College	McCaskill, Matt L.	Brevard Community College
		McClellan, Carolyn	Tidewater Community College
Larsen, Jacqueline Anne	A-B Tech	McClure, Darlean	College of Sequoias
Larson, Donna	Louisville Technical Institute	McCrory, Sue A.	Missouri State University
Laspina, Kathy	Vance-Granville Community College	McCue, Stacy	Harrisburg Area Community College
Le Grand, Dr. Kate	Broward Community College	McEntire-Orbach, Teresa	Middlesex County College
Lenhart, Sheryl	Terra Community College	McKinley, Lee	Georgia Perimeter College
Leonard, Yvonne	Coastal Carolina Community College	McLeod, Todd	Fresno City College
		McManus, Illyana	Grossmont College
Letavec, Chris	University of Cincinnati	McPherson, Dori	Schoolcraft College
Lewis, Daphne L., Ed.D.	Wayland Baptist University	Meck, Kari	HACC
Lewis, Julie	Baker College-Allen Park	Meiklejohn, Nancy	Pikes Peak Community College
Liefert, Jane	Everett Community College	Menking, Rick	Hardin-Simmons University
Lindaman, Linda	Black Hawk Community College	Meredith, Mary	University of Louisiana at Lafayette
Lindberg, Martha	Minnesota State University		
Lightner, Renee	Broward Community College	Mermelstein, Lisa	Baruch College
Lindberg, Martha	Minnesota State University	Metos, Linda	Salt Lake Community College
Linge, Richard	Arizona Western College	Meurer, Daniel	University of Cincinnati
Logan, Mary G.	Delgado Community College	Meyer, Colleen	Cincinnati State Technical and Community College
Loizeaux, Barbara	Westchester Community College		
Lombardi, John	South University	Meyer, Marian	Central New Mexico Community College
Lopez, Don	Clovis-State Center Community College District	Miller, Cindy	Ivy Tech Community College, Lafayette, Indiana
Lopez, Lisa	Spartanburg Community College		
Lord, Alexandria	Asheville Buncombe Tech	Mills, Robert E.	Tidewater Community College, Portsmouth Campus
Lovering, LeAnne	Augusta Technical College		
Lowe, Rita	Harold Washington College	Mitchell, Susan	Davenport University
Low, Willy Hui	Joliet Junior College	Mohle, Dennis	Fresno Community College
Lucas, Vickie	Broward Community College	Molki, Saeed	South Texas College
Luna, Debbie	El Paso Community College	Monk, Ellen	University of Delaware
Luoma, Jean	Davenport University	Moore, Rodney	Holland College
Luse, Steven P.	Horry Georgetown Technical College	Morris, Mike	Southeastern Oklahoma State University
Lynam, Linda	Central Missouri State University	Morris, Nancy	Hudson Valley Community College
Lyon, Lynne	Durham College		
Lyon, Pat Rajski	Tomball College	Moseler, Dan	Harrisburg Area Community College
Macarty, Matthew	University of New Hampshire		
MacKinnon, Ruth	Georgia Southern University	Nabors, Brent	Reedley College, Clovis Center
Macon, Lisa	Valencia Community College, West Campus	Nadas, Erika	Wright College
		Nadelman, Cindi	New England College
Machuca, Wayne	College of the Sequoias	Nademlynsky, Lisa	Johnson & Wales University
Mack, Sherri	Butler County Community College	Nagengast, Joseph	Florida Career College
Madison, Dana	Clarion University	Nason, Scott	Rowan Cabarrus Community College
Maguire, Trish	Eastern New Mexico University		
Malkan, Rajiv	Montgomery College	Ncube, Cathy	University of West Florida
Manning, David	Northern Kentucky University	Newsome, Eloise	Northern Virginia Community College Woodbridge
Marcus, Jacquie	Niagara Community College		

Nicholls, Doreen — Mohawk Valley Community College
Nicholson, John R. — Johnson County Community College
Nielson, Phil — Salt Lake Community College
Nunan, Karen L. — Northeast State Technical Community College

O'Neal, Lois Ann — Rogers State University
Odegard, Teri — Edmonds Community College
Ogle, Gregory — North Community College
Orr, Dr. Claudia — Northern Michigan University South
Orsburn, Glen — Fox Valley Technical College
Otieno, Derek — DeVry University
Otton, Diana Hill — Chesapeake College
Oxendale, Lucia — West Virginia Institute of Technology

Paiano, Frank — Southwestern College
Pannell, Dr. Elizabeth — Collin College
Patrick, Tanya — Clackamas Community College
Paul, Anindya — Daytona State College
Peairs, Deb — Clark State Community College
Perez, Kimberly — Tidewater Community College
Porter, Joyce — Weber State University
Prince, Lisa — Missouri State University-Springfield Campus
Proietti, Kathleen — Northern Essex Community College
Puopolo, Mike — Bunker Hill Community College
Pusins, Delores — HCCC
Putnam, Darlene — Thomas Nelson Community College

Raghuraman, Ram — Joliet Junior College
Rani, Chigurupati — BMCC/CUNY
Reasoner, Ted Allen — Indiana University—Purdue
Reeves, Karen — High Point University
Remillard, Debbie — New Hampshire Technical Institute
Rhue, Shelly — DeVry University
Richards, Karen — Maplewoods Community College
Richardson, Mary — Albany Technical College
Rodgers, Gwen — Southern Nazarene University
Rodie, Karla — Pikes Peak Community College
Roselli, Diane Maie — Harrisburg Area Community College
Ross, Dianne — University of Louisiana in Lafayette
Rousseau, Mary — Broward Community College, South
Rovetto, Ann — Horry-Georgetown Technical College
Rusin, Iwona — Baker College
Sahabi, Ahmad — Baker College of Clinton Township
Samson, Dolly — Hawaii Pacific University
Sams, Todd — University of Cincinnati
Sandoval, Everett — Reedley College
Santiago, Diana — Central New Mexico Community College
Sardone, Nancy — Seton Hall University
Scafide, Jean — Mississippi Gulf Coast Community College
Scheeren, Judy — Westmoreland County Community College
Scheiwe, Adolph — Joliet Junior College
Schneider, Sol — Sam Houston State University
Schweitzer, John — Central New Mexico Community College
Scroggins, Michael — Southwest Missouri State University
Sedlacek, Brenda — Tidewater Community College
Sell, Kelly — Anne Arundel Community College
Sever, Suzanne — Northwest Arkansas Community College

Sewell, John — Florida Career College
Sheridan, Rick — California State University-Chico
Silvers, Pamela — Asheville Buncombe Tech
Sindt, Robert G. — Johnson County Community College
Singer, Noah — Tulsa Community College
Singer, Steven A. — University of Hawai'i, Kapi'olani Community College
Sinha, Atin — Albany State University
Skolnick, Martin — Florida Atlantic University
Smith, Kristi — Allegany College of Maryland
Smith, Patrick — Marshall Community and Technical College
Smith, Stella A. — Georgia Gwinnett College
Smith, T. Michael — Austin Community College
Smith, Tammy — Tompkins Cortland Community Collge
Smolenski, Bob — Delaware County Community College
Smolenski, Robert — Delaware Community College
Southwell, Donald — Delta College
Spangler, Candice — Columbus State
Spangler, Candice — Columbus State Community College
Stark, Diane — Phoenix College
Stedham, Vicki — St. Petersburg College, Clearwater
Stefanelli, Greg — Carroll Community College
Steiner, Ester — New Mexico State University
Stenlund, Neal — Northern Virginia Community College, Alexandria
St. John, Steve — Tulsa Community College
Sterling, Janet — Houston Community College
Stoughton, Catherine — Laramie County Community College
Sullivan, Angela — Joliet Junior College
Sullivan, Denise — Westchester Community College
Sullivan, Joseph — Joliet Junior College
Swart, John — Louisiana Tech University
Szurek, Joseph — University of Pittsburgh at Greensburg
Taff, Ann — Tulsa Community College
Taggart, James — Atlantic Cape Community College
Tarver, Mary Beth — Northwestern State University
Taylor, Michael — Seattle Central Community College
Terrell, Robert L. — Carson-Newman College
Terry, Dariel — Northern Virginia Community College
Thangiah, Sam — Slippery Rock University
Thayer, Paul — Austin Community College
Thompson, Joyce — Lehigh Carbon Community College
Thompson-Sellers, Ingrid — Georgia Perimeter College
Tomasi, Erik — Baruch College
Toreson, Karen — Shoreline Community College
Townsend, Cynthia — Baker College
Trifiletti, John J. — Florida Community College at Jacksonville
Trivedi, Charulata — Quinsigamond Community College, Woodbridge
Tucker, William — Austin Community College
Turgeon, Cheryl — Asnuntuck Community College
Turpen, Linda — Central New Mexico Community College
Upshaw, Susan — Del Mar College
Unruh, Angela — Central Washington University
Vanderhoof, Dr. Glenna — Missouri State University-Springfield Campus
Vargas, Tony — El Paso Community College
Vicars, Mitzi — Hampton University
Villarreal, Kathleen — Fresno
Vitrano, Mary Ellen — Palm Beach Community College

Vlaich-Lee, Michelle	Greenville Technical College	Willer, Ann	Solano Community College
Volker, Bonita	Tidewater Community College	Williams, Mark	Lane Community College
Waddell, Karen	Butler Community College	Williams, Ronald D.	Central Piedmont Community College
Wahila, Lori (Mindy)	Tompkins Cortland Community College	Wilms, Dr. G. Jan	Union University
Wallace, Melissa	Lanier Technical College	Wilson, Kit	Red River College
Walters, Gary B.	Central New Mexico Community College	Wilson, MaryLou	Piedmont Technical College
		Wilson, Roger	Fairmont State University
Waswick, Kim	Southeast Community College, Nebraska	Wimberly, Leanne	International Academy of Design and Technology
Wavle, Sharon M.	Tompkins Cortland Community College	Winters, Floyd	Manatee Community College
		Worthington, Paula	Northern Virginia Community College
Webb, Nancy	City College of San Francisco		
Webb, Rebecca	Northwest Arkansas Community College	Wright, Darrell	Shelton State Community College
		Wright, Julie	Baker College
Weber, Sandy	Gateway Technical College	Yauney, Annette	Herkimer County Community College
Weissman, Jonathan	Finger Lakes Community College	Yip, Thomas	Passaic Community College
Wells, Barbara E.	Central Carolina Technical College	Zavala, Ben	Webster Tech
Wells, Lorna	Salt Lake Community College	Zaboski, Maureen	University of Scranton
Welsh, Jean	Lansing Community College Nebraska	Zlotow, Mary Ann	College of DuPage
		Zudeck, Steve	Broward Community College, North
White, Bruce	Quinnipiac University	Zullo, Matthew D.	Wake Technical Community College

About the Authors

Shelley Gaskin, Series Editor, is a professor in the Business and Computer Technology Division at Pasadena City College in Pasadena, California. She holds a bachelor's degree in Business Administration from Robert Morris College (Pennsylvania), a master's degree in Business from Northern Illinois University, and a doctorate in Adult and Community Education from Ball State University. Before joining Pasadena City College, she spent 12 years in the computer industry where she was a systems analyst, sales representative, and Director of Customer Education with Unisys Corporation. She also worked for Ernst & Young on the development of large systems applications for their clients. She has written and developed training materials for custom systems applications in both the public and private sector, and has written and edited numerous computer application textbooks.

This book is dedicated to my students, who inspire me every day.

Carolyn McLellan is the Dean of the Division of Information Technology and Business at Tidewater Community College in Virginia Beach, Virginia. She has a master's degree in Secondary Education from Regent University and a bachelor's degree in Business Education from Old Dominion University. She taught for Norfolk Public Schools for 17 years in Business Education and served as a faculty member at Tidewater Community College for eight years teaching networking, where she developed over 23 new courses and earned the Microsoft Certified Trainer and Microsoft Certified System Engineer industry certifications. In addition to teaching, Carolyn loves to play volleyball, boogie board at the beach, bicycle, crochet, cook, and read.

This book is dedicated to my daughters, Megan and Mandy, who have my eternal love; to my mother, Jean, who always believes in me and encouraged me to become a teacher; to my sister Debbie, who was my first student and who inspires me with her strength in overcoming hardships; to my niece Jenna, for her bravery, composure, and beauty; to my grandsons, Damon and Jordan, who bring me happiness and a renewed joie de vie; and to the students and IT faculty at Tidewater Community College.

Nancy Graviett is a professor in the Business and Computer Science department at St. Charles Community College in Cottleville, Missouri, where she is the program coordinator for the Business Administrative Systems program and teaches within the program. Nancy is also very active with distance learning and teaches in face-to-face, hybrid, and online formats. She holds a master's degree from University of Missouri. Nancy holds Microsoft® Certified Application Specialist certification in multiple applications and provides training both on and off campus. In her free time, Nancy enjoys quilting and spending time with family and friends.

I dedicate this book to my husband, David, my children (Matthew and Andrea), and my parents, whose love and support I cherish more than they could ever know.

Teach the Course You Want in Less Time

A Microsoft® Office textbook designed for student success!

- **Project-Based** – Students learn by creating projects that they will use in the real world.

- **Microsoft Procedural Syntax** – Steps are written to put students in the right place at the right time.

- **Teachable Moment** – Expository text is woven into the steps—at the moment students need to know it—not chunked together in a block of text that will go unread.

- **Sequential Pagination** – Students have actual page numbers instead of confusing letters and abbreviations.

Student Outcomes and Learning Objectives – Objectives are clustered around projects that result in student outcomes.

Project Activities – A project summary stated clearly and quickly.

Project Files – Clearly shows students which files are needed for the project and the names they will use to save their documents.

Scenario – Each chapter opens with a story that sets the stage for the projects the student will create.

Project Results – Shows students how their final outcome will appear.

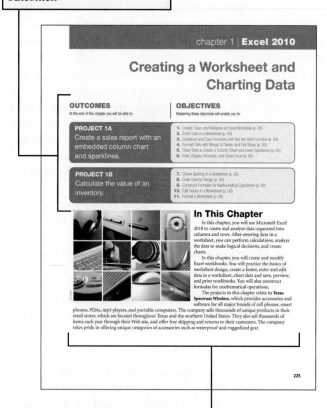

Key Feature

Microsoft Procedural Syntax – Steps are written to put the student in the right place at the right time.

Color Coding – Color variations between the two projects in each chapter make it easy to identify which project students are working on.

Objective 1 | Create, Save, and Navigate an Excel Workbook

On startup, Excel displays a new blank *workbook*—the Excel document that stores your data—which contains one or more pages called a *worksheet*. A worksheet—or *spreadsheet*—is stored in a workbook, and is formatted as a pattern of uniformly spaced horizontal rows and vertical columns. The intersection of a column and a row forms a box referred to as a *cell*.

Activity 1.01 | Starting Excel and Naming and Saving a Workbook

1 **Start** Excel. In the lower right corner of the window, if necessary, click the Normal button, and then to the right, locate the zoom—magnification—level.

Your zoom level should be 100%, although some figures in this textbook may be shown at a higher zoom level.

Another Way
Use the keyboard shortcut Ctrl+S to display the Save As dialog box.

2 In the upper left corner of your screen, click the **File tab** to display **Backstage** view, click **Save As**, and then in the **Save As** dialog box, navigate to the location where you will store your workbooks for this chapter.

3 In your storage location, create a new folder named **Excel Chapter 1** Open the new folder to display its folder window, and then in the **File name** box, notice that *Book1* displays as the default file name.

4 In the **File name** box, click *Book1* to select it, and then using your own name, type **Lastname_Firstname_1A_Quarterly_Sales** being sure to include the underscore (Shift + -) instead of spaces between words. Compare your screen with Figure 1.2.

Figure 1.2

Path to your new Excel Chapter 1 folder in address bar

File name with your name and underscores between words

Save button

Project 1A: Sales Report with Embedded Column Chart and Sparklines | Excel **227**

---

6 In the vertical scroll bar, click the **down scroll arrow** one time to move **Row 1** out of view.

A *row* is a horizontal group of cells. Beginning with number 1, a unique number identifies each row—this is the *row heading*, located at the left side of the worksheet. A single worksheet has 1,048,576 rows.

7 In the lower left corner, click the **Sheet1 tab**.

The first worksheet in the workbook becomes the active worksheet. By default, new workbooks contain three worksheets. When you save a workbook, the worksheets are contained within it and do not have separate file names.

8 Use the skills you just practiced to scroll horizontally to display **column A**, and if necessary, **row 1**.

Objective 2 | Enter Data in a Worksheet

Cell content, which is anything you type in a cell, can be one of two things: either a *constant value*—referred to simply as a *value*—or a *formula*. A formula is an equation that performs mathematical calculations on values in your worksheet. The most commonly used values are *text values* and *number values*, but a value can also include a date or a time of day.

Activity 1.03 | Entering Text and Using AutoComplete

A *text value*, also referred to as a *label*, usually provides information about number values in other worksheet cells. For example, a title such as First Quarter Accessory Sales gives the reader an indication that the data in the worksheet relates to information about sales of accessories during the three-month period January through March.

1 Click the **Sheet1 tab** to make it the active sheet. Point to and then click the cell at the intersection of **column A** and **row 1** to make it the *active cell*—the cell is outlined in black and ready to accept data.

The intersecting column letter and row number form the *cell reference*—also called the *cell address*. When a cell is active, its column letter and row number are highlighted. The cell reference of the selected cell, *A1*, displays in the Name Box.

2 With cell **A1** as the active cell, type the worksheet title **Texas Spectrum Wireless** and then press Enter. Compare your screen with Figure 1.7.

Text or numbers in a cell are referred to as *data*. You must confirm the data you type in a cell by pressing Enter or by some other keyboard movement, such as pressing Tab or an arrow key. Pressing Enter moves the selection to the cell below.

230 Excel

Key Feature

Sequential Pagination – Students are given actual page numbers to navigate through the textbook instead of confusing letters and abbreviations.

Key Feature

Teachable Moment – Expository text is woven into the steps—at the moment students need to know it—not chunked together in a block of text that will go unread.

End-of-Chapter

Content-Based Assessments – Assessments with defined solutions.

Objective List - Every project includes a listing of covered objectives from Projects A and B.

End-of-Chapter

Outcomes-Based Assessments – Assessments with open-ended solutions.

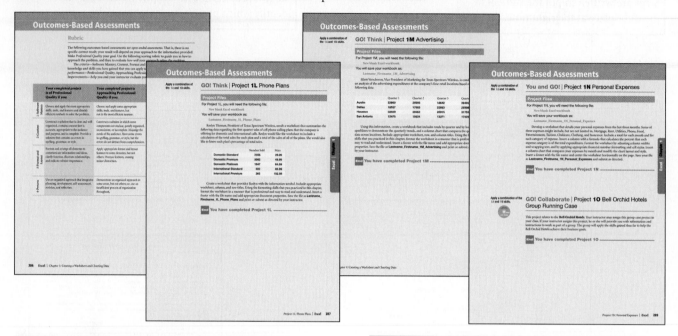

Task-Specific Rubric – A matrix specific to the **GO! Solve It** projects that states the criteria and standards for grading these defined-solution projects.

Outcomes Rubric – A matrix specific to the **GO! Think** projects that states the criteria and standards for grading these open-ended assessments.

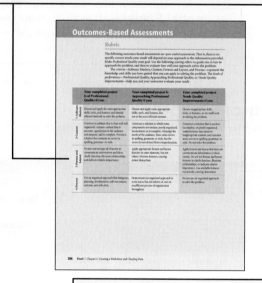

Student CD – All student data files readily available on a CD that comes with the book.

Student Videos – A visual and audio walk-through of every A and B project in the book (see sample images on following page).

Student Videos! –

Each chapter comes with two videos that include audio, demonstrating the objectives and activities taught in the chapter.

Instructor Materials

Annotated Instructor Edition - An instructor tool includes a full copy of the student textbook annotated with teaching tips, discussion topics, and other useful pieces for teaching each chapter.

Assignment Sheets – Lists all the assignments for the chapter. Just add in the course information, due dates, and points. Providing these to students ensures they will know what is due and when.

Scripted Lectures – Classroom lectures prepared for you.

Annotated Solution Files – Coupled with the assignment tags, these create a grading and scoring system that makes grading so much easier for you.

PowerPoint Lectures – PowerPoint presentations for each chapter.

Scoring Rubrics – Can be used either by students to check their work or by you as a quick check-off for the items that need to be corrected.

Syllabus Templates - For 8-week, 12-week, and 16-week courses.

Test Bank – Includes a variety of test questions for each chapter.

Companion Website – Online content such as the Online Study Guide, Glossary, and Student Data Files are all at **www.pearsonhighered.com/go**.

Using the Common Features of Microsoft Office 2010

OUTCOMES

At the end of this chapter you will be able to:

OBJECTIVES

Mastering these objectives will enable you to:

PROJECT 1A
Create, save, and print a Microsoft Office 2010 file.

1. Use Windows Explorer to Locate Files and Folders (p. 3)
2. Locate and Start a Microsoft Office 2010 Program (p. 6)
3. Enter and Edit Text in an Office 2010 Program (p. 9)
4. Perform Commands from a Dialog Box (p. 11)
5. Create a Folder, Save a File, and Close a Program (p. 13)
6. Add Document Properties and Print a File (p. 18)

PROJECT 1B
Use the Ribbon and dialog boxes to perform common commands in a Microsoft Office 2010 file.

7. Open an Existing File and Save It with a New Name (p. 22)
8. Explore Options for an Application (p. 25)
9. Perform Commands from the Ribbon (p. 26)
10. Apply Formatting in Office Programs (p. 32)
11. Use the Microsoft Office 2010 Help System (p. 43)
12. Compress Files (p. 44)

olly/Shutterstock

In This Chapter

In this chapter, you will use Windows Explorer to navigate the Windows folder structure, create a folder, and save files in Microsoft Office 2010 programs. You will also practice using the features of Microsoft Office 2010 that are common across the major programs that comprise the Microsoft Office 2010 suite. These common features include creating, saving, and printing files.

Common features also include the new Paste Preview and Microsoft Office Backstage view. You will apply formatting, perform commands, and compress files. You will see that creating professional-quality documents is easy and quick in Microsoft Office 2010, and that finding your way around is fast and efficient.

The projects in this chapter relate to **Oceana Palm Grill**, which is a chain of 25 casual, full-service restaurants based in Austin, Texas. The Oceana Palm Grill owners plan an aggressive expansion program. To expand by 15 additional restaurants in North Carolina and Florida by 2018, the company must attract new investors, develop new menus, and recruit new employees, all while adhering to the company's quality guidelines and maintaining its reputation for excellent service. To succeed, the company plans to build on its past success and maintain its quality elements.

Project 1A PowerPoint File

myitlab
Project 1A Training

In Activities 1.01 through 1.06, you will create a PowerPoint file, save it in a folder that you create by using Windows Explorer, and then print the file or submit it electronically as directed by your instructor. Your completed PowerPoint slide will look similar to Figure 1.1.

Project Files

For Project 1A, you will need the following file:

New blank PowerPoint presentation

You will save your file as:

Lastname_Firstname_1A_Menu_Plan

Project Results

Oceana Palm Grill Menu Plan

Prepared by Firstname Lastname
For Laura Hernandez

Figure 1.1
Project 1A Menu Plan

Objective 1 | Use Windows Explorer to Locate Files and Folders

A *file* is a collection of information stored on a computer under a single name, for example, a Word document or a PowerPoint presentation. Every file is stored in a *folder*—a container in which you store files—or a *subfolder*, which is a folder within a folder. Your Windows operating system stores and organizes your files and folders, which is a primary task of an operating system.

You *navigate*—explore within the organizing structure of Windows—to create, save, and find your files and folders by using the **Windows Explorer** program. Windows Explorer displays the files and folders on your computer, and is at work anytime you are viewing the contents of files and folders in a *window*. A window is a rectangular area on a computer screen in which programs and content appear; a window can be moved, resized, minimized, or closed.

Activity 1.01 | Using Windows Explorer to Locate Files and Folders

1 Turn on your computer and display the Windows *desktop*—the opening screen in Windows that simulates your work area.

> **Note | Comparing Your Screen with the Figures in This Textbook**
>
> Your screen will match the figures shown in this textbook if you set your screen resolution to 1024 × 768. At other resolutions, your screen will closely resemble, but not match, the figures shown. To view your screen's resolution, on the Windows 7 desktop, right-click in a blank area, and then click Screen resolution. In Windows Vista, right-click a blank area, click Personalize, and then click Display Settings. In Windows XP, right-click the desktop, click Properties, and then click the Settings tab.

2 In your CD/DVD tray, insert the **Student CD** that accompanies this textbook. Wait a few moments for an **AutoPlay** window to display. Compare your screen with Figure 1.2.

AutoPlay is a Windows feature that lets you choose which program to use to start different kinds of media, such as music CDs, or CDs and DVDs containing photos; it displays when you plug in or insert media or storage devices.

> **Note | If You Do Not Have the Student CD**
>
> If you do not have the Student CD, consult the inside back flap of this textbook for instructions on how to download the files from the Pearson Web site.

Figure 1.2

AutoPlay window

Close button

Windows desktop (yours may vary in color and arrangement)

3 In the upper right corner of the **AutoPlay** window, move your mouse over—*point* to—the **Close** button ![Close], and then *click*—press the left button on your mouse pointing device one time.

4 On the left side of the **Windows taskbar**, click the **Start** button ⬤ to display the **Start menu**. Compare your screen with Figure 1.3.

The *Windows taskbar* is the area along the lower edge of the desktop that contains the *Start button* and an area to display buttons for open programs. The Start button displays the *Start menu*, which provides a list of choices and is the main gateway to your computer's programs, folders, and settings.

Figure 1.3

Computer on Start menu

Start menu (your array of programs may vary)

Windows 7 taskbar

Start button

5 On the right side of the **Start menu**, click **Computer** to see the disk drives and other hardware connected to your computer. Compare your screen with Figure 1.4, and then take a moment to study the table in Figure 1.5.

The *folder window* for *Computer* displays. A folder window displays the contents of the current folder, *library*, or device, and contains helpful parts so that you can navigate within Windows.

In Windows 7, a library is a collection of items, such as files and folders, assembled from *various locations*; the locations might be on your computer, an external hard drive, removable media, or someone else's computer.

The difference between a folder and a library is that a library can include files stored in *different locations*—any disk drive, folder, or other place that you can store files and folders.

Figure 1.4

Back and Forward

Address bar

File list

Navigation pane

Folder window toolbar

Views button

Search box

Preview pane button

Details pane

Window Part	Use to:
Address bar	Navigate to a different folder or library, or go back to a previous one.
Back and Forward buttons	Navigate to other folders or libraries you have already opened without closing the current window. These buttons work in conjunction with the address bar; that is, after you use the address bar to change folders, you can use the Back button to return to the previous folder.
Details pane	Display the most common file properties—information about a file, such as the author, the date you last changed the file, and any descriptive *tags*, which are custom file properties that you create to help find and organize your files.
File list	Display the contents of the current folder or library. In Computer, the file list displays the disk drives.
Folder window for *Computer*	Display the contents of the current folder, library, or device. The Folder window contains helpful features so that you can navigate within Windows.
Folder window toolbar	Perform common tasks, such as changing the view of your files and folders or burning files to a CD. The buttons available change to display only relevant tasks.
Navigation pane	Navigate to, open, and display favorites, libraries, folders, saved searches, and an expandable list of drives.
Preview pane button	Display (if you have chosen to open this pane) the contents of most files without opening them in a program. To open the preview pane, click the Preview pane button on the toolbar to turn it on and off.
Search box	Look for an item in the current folder or library by typing a word or phrase in the search box.
Views button	Choose how to view the contents of the current location.

Figure 1.5

6 On the toolbar of the **Computer** folder window, click the **Views button arrow** 📊 ▾ — the small arrow to the right of the Views button—to display a list of views that you can apply to the file list. If necessary, on the list, click **Tiles**.

> The Views button is a *split button*; clicking the main part of the button performs a *command* and clicking the arrow opens a menu or list. A command is an instruction to a computer program that causes an action to be carried out.

> When you open a folder or a library, you can change how the files display in the file list. For example, you might prefer to see large or small *icons*—pictures that represent a program, a file, a folder, or some other object—or an arrangement that lets you see various types of information about each file. Each time you click the Views button, the window changes, cycling through several views—additional view options are available by clicking the Views button arrow.

Another Way
Point to the CD/DVD drive, right-click, and then click Open.

7 In the **file list**, under **Devices with Removable Storage**, point to your **CD/DVD Drive**, and then *double-click*—click the left mouse button two times in rapid succession— to display the list of folders on the CD. Compare your screen with Figure 1.6.

> When double-clicking, keep your hand steady between clicks; this is more important than the speed of the two clicks.

Figure 1.6

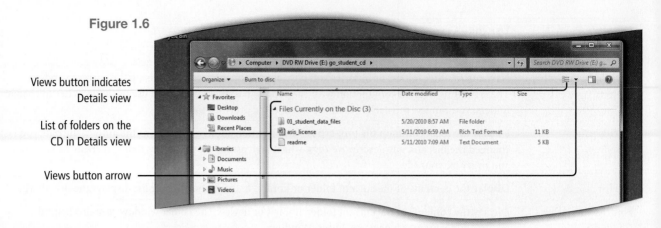

Views button indicates Details view

List of folders on the CD in Details view

Views button arrow

8 In the **file list**, point to the folder **01_student_data_files** and double-click to display the list of subfolders in the folder. Double-click to open the folder **01_common_ features**. Compare your screen with Figure 1.7.

The Student Resource CD includes files that you will use to complete the projects in this textbook. If you prefer, you can also copy the **01_student_data_files** folder to a location on your computer's hard drive or to a removable device such as a *USB flash drive*, which is a small storage device that plugs into a computer USB port. Your instructor might direct you to other locations where these files are located; for example, on your learning management system.

Figure 1.7

Address bar displays sequence of folders

One folder in the *01_common_features* folder

9 In the upper right corner of the **Computer** window, click the **Close** button to redisplay your desktop.

Objective 2 | Locate and Start a Microsoft Office 2010 Program

Microsoft Office 2010 includes programs, servers, and services for individuals, small organizations, and large enterprises. A *program*, also referred to as an *application*, is a set of instructions used by a computer to perform a task, such as word processing or accounting.

Activity 1.02 | Locating and Starting a Microsoft Office 2010 Program

1 On the **Windows taskbar**, click the **Start** button to display the **Start** menu.

2 From the displayed **Start** menu, locate the group of **Microsoft Office 2010** programs on your computer—the Office program icons from which you can start the program may be located on your Start menu, in a Microsoft Office folder on the **All Programs** list, on your desktop, or any combination of these locations; the location will vary depending on how your computer is configured.

> *All Programs* is an area of the Start menu that displays all the available programs on your computer system.

3 Examine Figure 1.8, and notice the programs that are included in the Microsoft Office Professional Plus 2010 group of programs. (Your group of programs may vary.)

> *Microsoft Word* is a word processing program, with which you create and share documents by using its writing tools.

> *Microsoft Excel* is a spreadsheet program, with which you calculate and analyze numbers and create charts.

> *Microsoft Access* is a database program, with which you can collect, track, and report data.

> *Microsoft PowerPoint* is a presentation program, with which you can communicate information with high-impact graphics and video.

> Additional popular Office programs include *Microsoft Outlook* to manage e-mail and organizational activities, *Microsoft Publisher* to create desktop publishing documents such as brochures, and *Microsoft OneNote* to manage notes that you make at meetings or in classes and to share notes with others on the Web.

> The Professional Plus version of Office 2010 also includes *Microsoft SharePoint Workspace* to share information with others in a team environment and *Microsoft InfoPath Designer and Filler* to create forms and gather data.

Figure 1.8

All Programs menu

Microsoft Office folder

Programs in Microsoft Office (your list may vary)

4 Click to open the program **Microsoft PowerPoint 2010**. Compare your screen with Figure 1.9, and then take a moment to study the description of these screen elements in the table in Figure 1.10.

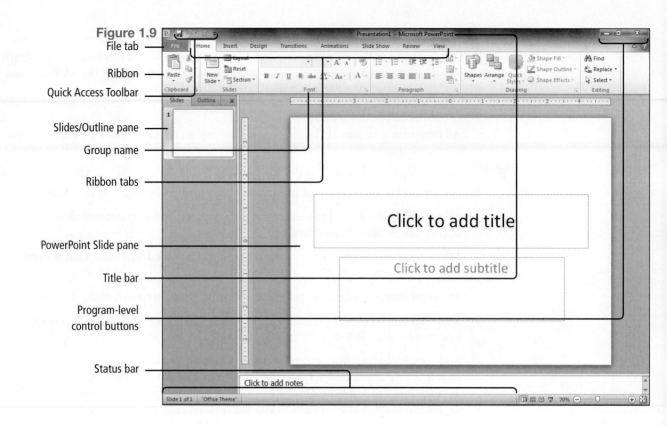

Figure 1.9

Figure 1.10

Screen Element	Description
File tab	Displays Microsoft Office Backstage view, which is a centralized space for all of your file management tasks such as opening, saving, printing, publishing, or sharing a file—all the things you can do *with* a file.
Group names	Indicate the name of the groups of related commands on the displayed tab.
PowerPoint Slide pane	Displays a large image of the active slide in the PowerPoint program.
Program-level control buttons	Minimizes, restores, or closes the program window.
Quick Access Toolbar	Displays buttons to perform frequently used commands and resources with a single click. The default commands include Save, Undo, and Redo. You can add and delete buttons to customize the Quick Access Toolbar for your convenience.
Ribbon	Displays a group of task-oriented tabs that contain the commands, styles, and resources you need to work in an Office 2010 program. The look of your Ribbon depends on your screen resolution. A high resolution will display more individual items and button names on the Ribbon.
Ribbon tabs	Display the names of the task-oriented tabs relevant to the open program.
Slides/Outline pane	Displays either thumbnails of the slides in a PowerPoint presentation (Slides tab) or the outline of the presentation's content (Outline tab). In each Office 2010 program, different panes display in different ways to assist you.
Status bar	Displays file information on the left and View and Zoom on the right.
Title bar	Displays the name of the file and the name of the program. The program window control buttons—Minimize, Maximize/Restore Down, and Close—are grouped on the right side of the title bar.

Objective 3 | Enter and Edit Text in an Office 2010 Program

All of the programs in Office 2010 require some typed text. Your keyboard is still the primary method of entering information into your computer. Techniques to **edit**—make changes to—text are similar among all of the Office 2010 programs.

Activity 1.03 | Entering and Editing Text in an Office 2010 Program

1 In the middle of the PowerPoint Slide pane, point to the text *Click to add title* to display the I pointer, and then click one time.

The **insertion point**—a blinking vertical line that indicates where text or graphics will be inserted—displays.

In Office 2010 programs, the mouse **pointer**—any symbol that displays on your screen in response to moving your mouse device—displays in different shapes depending on the task you are performing and the area of the screen to which you are pointing.

2 Type **Oceana Grille Info** and notice how the insertion point moves to the right as you type. Point slightly to the right of the letter *e* in *Grille* and click to place the insertion point there. Compare your screen with Figure 1.11.

Figure 1.11

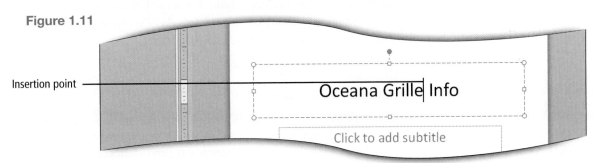

Insertion point

3 On your keyboard, locate and press the Backspace key to delete the letter *e*.

Pressing Backspace removes a character to the left of the insertion point.

4 Point slightly to the left of the *I* in *Info* and click one time to place the insertion point there. Type **Menu** and then press Spacebar one time. Compare your screen with Figure 1.12.

By **default**, when you type text in an Office program, existing text moves to the right to make space for new typing. Default refers to the current selection or setting that is automatically used by a program unless you specify otherwise.

Figure 1.12

Menu inserted

5 Press `Del` four times to delete *Info* and then type **Plan**

Pressing `Del` removes—deletes—a character to the right of the insertion point.

6 With your insertion point blinking after the word *Plan*, on your keyboard, hold down the `Ctrl` key. While holding down `Ctrl`, press `←` three times to move the insertion point to the beginning of the word *Grill*.

This is a ***keyboard shortcut***—a key or combination of keys that performs a task that would otherwise require a mouse. This keyboard shortcut moves the insertion point to the beginning of the previous word.

A keyboard shortcut is commonly indicated as `Ctrl` + `←` (or some other combination of keys) to indicate that you hold down the first key while pressing the second key. A keyboard shortcut can also include three keys, in which case you hold down the first two and then press the third. For example, `Ctrl` + `Shift` + `←` selects one word to the left.

7 With the insertion point blinking at the beginning of the word *Grill*, type **Palm** and press `Spacebar`.

8 Click anywhere in the text *Click to add subtitle*. With the insertion point blinking, type the following and include the spelling error: **Prepered by Annabel Dunham**

9 With your mouse, point slightly to the left of the *A* in *Annabel*, hold down the left mouse button, and then ***drag***—hold down the left mouse button while moving your mouse—to the right to select the text *Annabel Dunham*, and then release the mouse button. Compare your screen with Figure 1.13.

The ***Mini toolbar*** displays commands that are commonly used with the selected object, which places common commands close to your pointer. When you move the pointer away from the Mini toolbar, it fades from view.

To ***select*** refers to highlighting, by dragging with your mouse, areas of text or data or graphics so that the selection can be edited, formatted, copied, or moved. The action of dragging includes releasing the left mouse button at the end of the area you want to select. The Office programs recognize a selected area as one unit, to which you can make changes. Selecting text may require some practice. If you are not satisfied with your result, click anywhere outside of the selection, and then begin again.

Figure 1.13

Mini toolbar displays

Oceana Palm Grill Menu Plan

Annabel Dunham selected

Prepered by Annabel Dunham

10 With the text *Annabel Dunham* selected, type your own firstname and lastname.

In any Windows-based program, such as the Microsoft Office 2010 programs, selected text is deleted and then replaced when you begin to type new text. You will save time by developing good techniques to select and then edit or replace selected text, which is easier than pressing the [Del] key numerous times to delete text that you do not want.

11 Notice that the misspelled word *Prepered* displays with a wavy red underline; additionally, all or part of your name might display with a wavy red underline.

Office 2010 has a dictionary of words against which all entered text is checked. In Word and PowerPoint, words that are *not* in the dictionary display a wavy red line, indicating a possible misspelled word or a proper name or an unusual word—none of which are in the Office 2010 dictionary.

In Excel and Access, you can initiate a check of the spelling, but wavy red underlines do not display.

12 Point to *Prepered* and then ***right-click***—click your right mouse button one time.

The Mini toolbar and a ***shortcut menu*** display. A shortcut menu displays commands and options relevant to the selected text or object—known as ***context-sensitive commands*** because they relate to the item you right-clicked.

Here, the shortcut menu displays commands related to the misspelled word. You can click the suggested correct spelling *Prepared*, click Ignore All to ignore the misspelling, add the word to the Office dictionary, or click Spelling to display a ***dialog box***. A dialog box is a small window that contains options for completing a task. Whenever you see a command followed by an ***ellipsis*** (…), which is a set of three dots indicating incompleteness, clicking the command will always display a dialog box.

13 On the displayed shortcut menu, click **Prepared** to correct the misspelled word. If necessary, point to any parts of your name that display a wavy red underline, right-click, and then on the shortcut menu, click Ignore All so that Office will no longer mark your name with a wavy underline in this file.

More Knowledge | Adding to the Office Dictionary

The main dictionary contains the most common words, but does not include all proper names, technical terms, or acronyms. You can add words, acronyms, and proper names to the Office dictionary by clicking Add to Dictionary when they are flagged, and you might want to do so for your own name and other proper names and terms that you type often.

Objective 4 | Perform Commands from a Dialog Box

In a dialog box, you make decisions about an individual object or topic. A dialog box also offers a way to adjust a number of settings at one time.

Activity 1.04 | Performing Commands from a Dialog Box

1 Point anywhere in the blank area above the title *Oceana Palm Grill Menu Plan* to display the ⌖ pointer.

2 Right-click to display a shortcut menu. Notice the command *Format Background* followed by an ellipsis (…). Compare your screen with Figure 1.14.

Recall that a command followed by an ellipsis indicates that a dialog box will display if you click the command.

Figure 1.14

Shortcut menu ———

Ellipsis following command ———

3 Click **Format Background** to display the **Format Background** dialog box, and then compare your screen with Figure 1.15.

Figure 1.15

Fill selected ———

Format Background dialog box ———

Options related to the background fill ———

4 On the left, if necessary, click **Fill** to display the **Fill** options.

Fill is the inside color of an object. Here, the dialog box displays the option group names on the left; some dialog boxes provide a set of tabs across the top from which you can display different sets of options.

5 On the right, under **Fill**, click the **Gradient fill** option button.

The dialog box displays additional settings related to the gradient fill option. An *option button* is a round button that enables you to make one choice among two or more options. In a gradient fill, one color fades into another.

6 Click the **Preset colors arrow**—the arrow in the box to the right of the text *Preset colors*—and then in the gallery, in the second row, point to the fifth fill color to display the ScreenTip *Fog*.

A *gallery* is an Office feature that displays a list of potential results. A *ScreenTip* displays useful information about mouse actions, such as pointing to screen elements or dragging.

7 Click **Fog**, and then notice that the fill color is applied to your slide. Click the **Type arrow**, and then click **Rectangular** to change the pattern of the fill color. Compare your screen with Figure 1.16.

Figure 1.16

Gradient fill option button selected

Rectangular displays

Close button

8 At the bottom of the dialog box, click **Close**.

As you progress in your study of Microsoft Office, you will practice using many dialog boxes and applying dramatic effects such as this to your Word documents, Excel spreadsheets, Access databases, and PowerPoint slides.

Objective 5 | Create a Folder, Save a File, and Close a Program

A ***location*** is any disk drive, folder, or other place in which you can store files and folders. Where you store your files depends on how and where you use your data. For example, for your classes, you might decide to store primarily on a removable USB flash drive so that you can carry your files to different locations and access your files on different computers.

If you do most of your work on a single computer, for example your home desktop system or your laptop computer that you take with you to school or work, store your files in one of the Libraries—Documents, Music, Pictures, or Videos—provided by your Windows operating system.

Although the Windows operating system helps you to create and maintain a logical folder structure, take the time to name your files and folders in a consistent manner.

Activity 1.05 | Creating a Folder, Saving a File, and Closing a Program

A PowerPoint presentation is an example of a file. Office 2010 programs use a common dialog box provided by the Windows operating system to assist you in saving files. In this activity, you will create a folder on a USB flash drive in which to store files. If you prefer to store on your hard drive, you can use similar steps to store files in your My Documents folder in your Documents library.

1 Insert a USB flash drive into your computer, and if necessary, **Close** ☒ the **AutoPlay** dialog box. If you are not using a USB flash drive, go to Step 2.

> As the first step in saving a file, determine where you want to save the file, and if necessary, insert a storage device.

2 At the top of your screen, in the title bar, notice that *Presentation1 – Microsoft PowerPoint* displays.

> Most Office 2010 programs open with a new unsaved file with a default name—*Presentation1, Document1*, and so on. As you create your file, your work is temporarily stored in the computer's memory until you initiate a Save command, at which time you must choose a file name and location in which to save your file.

3 In the upper left corner of your screen, click the **File tab** to display **Microsoft Office Backstage** view. Compare your screen with Figure 1.17.

> Microsoft Office *Backstage view* is a centralized space for tasks related to *file* management; that is why the tab is labeled *File*. File management tasks include, for example, opening, saving, printing, publishing, or sharing a file. The *Backstage tabs*—*Info, Recent, New, Print, Save & Send*, and *Help*—display along the left side. The tabs group file-related tasks together.

> Above the Backstage tabs, *Quick Commands*—*Save, Save As, Open*, and *Close*—display for quick access to these commands. When you click any of these commands, Backstage view closes and either a dialog box displays or the active file closes.

> Here, the *Info tab* displays information—*info*—about the current file. In the center panel, various file management tasks are available in groups. For example, if you click the Protect Presentation button, a list of options that you can set for this file that relate to who can open or edit the presentation displays.

> On the Info tab, in the right panel, you can also examine the *document properties*. Document properties, also known as *metadata*, are details about a file that describe or identify it, such as the title, author name, subject, and keywords that identify the document's topic or contents. On the Info page, a thumbnail image of the current file displays in the upper right corner, which you can click to close Backstage view and return to the document.

More Knowledge | Deciding Where to Store Your Files

Where should you store your files? In the libraries created by Windows 7 (Documents, Pictures, and so on)? On a removable device like a flash drive or external hard drive? In Windows 7, it is easy to find your files, especially if you use the libraries. Regardless of where you save a file, Windows 7 will make it easy to find the file again, even if you are not certain where it might be.

In Windows 7, storing all of your files within a library makes sense. If you perform most of your work on your desktop system or your laptop that travels with you, you can store your files in the libraries created by Windows 7 for your user account—Documents, Pictures, Music, and so on. Within these libraries, you can create folders and subfolders to organize your data. These libraries are a good choice for storing your files because:

- From the Windows Explorer button on the taskbar, your libraries are always just one click away.
- The libraries are designed for their contents; for example, the Pictures folder displays small images of your digital photos.
- You can add new locations to a library; for example, an external hard drive, or a network drive. Locations added to a library behave just like they are on your hard drive.
- Other users of your computer cannot access your libraries.
- The libraries are the default location for opening and saving files within an application, so you will find that you can open and save files with fewer navigation clicks.

Figure 1.17

Save command

Information about the
file you are working on

Info tab selected

Backstage tabs,
Info tab active

Groups

Indicates unsaved file
with default name

Document Properties

Screen thumbnail

4 Above the **Backstage tabs**, click **Save** to display the **Save As** dialog box.

Backstage view closes and the Save As dialog box, which includes a folder window and an area at the bottom to name the file and set the file type, displays.

When you are saving something for the first time, for example a new PowerPoint presentation, the Save and Save As commands are identical. That is, the Save As dialog box will display if you click Save or if you click Save As.

Note | Saving Your File

After you have named a file and saved it in your desired location, the Save command saves any changes you make to the file without displaying any dialog box. The Save As command will display the Save As dialog box and let you name and save a new file based on the current one—in a location that you choose. After you name and save the new document, the original document closes, and the new document—based on the original one—displays.

---

5 In the **Save As** dialog box, on the left, locate the **navigation pane**; compare your screen with Figure 1.18.

By default, the Save command opens the Documents library unless your default file location has been changed.

Figure 1.18

Save As dialog box
Address bar

Default save location

Navigation pane

File list (yours will vary)

File name box

Save as type defaults to
PowerPoint Presentation

6 On the right side of the **navigation pane**, point to the **scroll bar**. Compare your screen with Figure 1.19.

A *scroll bar* displays when a window, or a pane within a window, has information that is not in view. You can click the up or down scroll arrows—or the left and right scroll arrows in a horizontal scroll bar—to scroll the contents up or down or left and right in small increments.

You can also drag the *scroll box*—the box within the scroll bar—to scroll the window in either direction.

Figure 1.19

Vertical scroll arrows

Vertical scroll box

Vertical scroll bar

Horizontal scroll bar

Horizontal scroll arrows

Horizontal scroll box

7 Click the **down scroll arrow** as necessary so that you can view the lower portion of the **navigation pane**, and then click the icon for your USB flash drive. Compare your screen with Figure 1.20. (If you prefer to store on your computer's hard drive instead of a USB flash drive, in the navigation pane, click Documents.)

Figure 1.20

Drive letter of your USB flash drive (yours will vary)

New folder button

File list on USB flash drive (yours may contain files or folders)

USB flash drive selected (yours will vary)

8 On the toolbar, click the **New folder** button.

In the file list, a new folder is created, and the text *New folder* is selected.

9 Type **Common Features Chapter 1** and press Enter. Compare your screen with Figure 1.21.

In Windows-based programs, the Enter key confirms an action.

Figure 1.21

New folder

10 In the **file list**, double-click the name of your new folder to open it and display its name in the **address bar**.

11 In the lower portion of the dialog box, click in the **File name** box to select the existing text. Notice that Office inserts the text at the beginning of the presentation as a suggested file name.

12 On your keyboard, locate the ⎯ key. Notice that the Shift of this key produces the underscore character. With the text still selected, type **Lastname_Firstname_1A_Menu_Plan** Compare your screen with Figure 1.22.

> You can use spaces in file names, however some individuals prefer not to use spaces. Some programs, especially when transferring files over the Internet, may not work well with spaces in file names. In general, however, unless you encounter a problem, it is OK to use spaces. In this textbook, underscores are used instead of spaces in file names.

Figure 1.22

File name box indicates your file name

Save as type box indicates *PowerPoint Presentation*

Save button

13 In the lower right corner, click **Save**; or press Enter. See Figure 1.23.

> Your new file name displays in the title bar, indicating that the file has been saved to a location that you have specified.

Figure 1.23

File name in title bar

14 In the text that begins *Prepared by*, click to position the insertion point at the end of your name, and then press Enter to move to a new line. Type **For Laura Hernandez**

15 Click the **File tab** to display **Backstage** view. At the top of the center panel, notice that the path where your file is stored displays. Above the Backstage tabs, click **Close** to close the file. In the message box, click **Save** to save the changes you made and close the file. Leave PowerPoint open.

> PowerPoint displays a message asking if you want to save the changes you have made. Because you have made additional changes to the file since your last Save operation, an Office program will always prompt you to save so that you do not lose any new data.

Objective 6 | Add Document Properties and Print a File

The process of printing a file is similar in all of the Office applications. There are differences in the types of options you can select. For example, in PowerPoint, you have the option of printing the full slide, with each slide printing on a full sheet of paper, or of printing handouts with small pictures of slides on a page.

Activity 1.06 | Adding Document Properties and Printing a File

> **Alert! | Are You Printing or Submitting Your Files Electronically?**
>
> If you are submitting your files electronically only, or have no printer attached, you can still complete this activity. Complete Steps 1-9, and then submit your file electronically as directed by your instructor.

1 In the upper left corner, click the **File tab** to display **Backstage** view. Notice that the **Recent tab** displays.

> Because no file was open in PowerPoint, Office applies predictive logic to determine that your most likely action will be to open a PowerPoint presentation that you worked on recently. Thus, the Recent tab displays a list of PowerPoint presentations that were recently open on your system.

2 At the top of the **Recent Presentations** list, click your **Lastname_Firstname_1A_ Menu_Plan** file to open it.

3 Click the **File tab** to redisplay **Backstage** view. On the right, under the screen thumbnail, click **Properties**, and then click **Show Document Panel**. In the **Author** box, delete the existing text, and then type your firstname and lastname. Notice that in PowerPoint, some variation of the slide title is automatically inserted in the Title box. In the **Subject** box, type your Course name and section number. In the **Keywords** box, type **menu plan** and then in the upper right corner of the **Document Properties** panel, click the **Close the Document Information Panel** button ☒.

> Adding properties to your documents will make them easier to search for in systems such as Microsoft SharePoint.

Another Way

Press Ctrl + P or Ctrl + F2 to display the Print tab in Backstage view.

4 Redisplay **Backstage** view, and then click the **Print tab**. Compare your screen with Figure 1.24.

> On the Print tab in Backstage view, in the center panel, three groups of printing-related tasks display—Print, Printer, and Settings. In the right panel, the *Print Preview* displays, which is a view of a document as it will appear on the paper when you print it.

> At the bottom of the Print Preview area, on the left, the number of pages and arrows with which you can move among the pages in Print Preview display. On the right, *Zoom* settings enable you to shrink or enlarge the Print Preview. Zoom is the action of increasing or decreasing the viewing area of the screen.

Figure 1.24

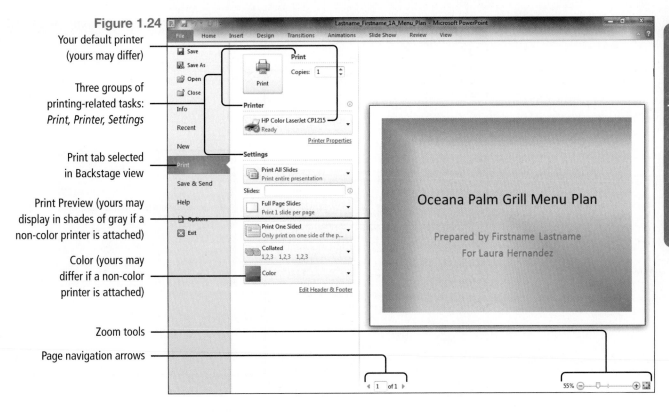

Your default printer
(yours may differ)

Three groups of
printing-related tasks:
Print, Printer, Settings

Print tab selected
in Backstage view

Print Preview (yours may
display in shades of gray if a
non-color printer is attached)

Color (yours may
differ if a non-color
printer is attached)

Zoom tools

Page navigation arrows

5 Locate the **Settings group**, and notice that the default setting is to **Print All Slides** and to print **Full Page Slides**—each slide on a full sheet of paper.

6 Point to **Full Page Slides**, notice that the button glows orange, and then click the button to display a gallery of print arrangements. Compare your screen with Figure 1.25.

Figure 1.25

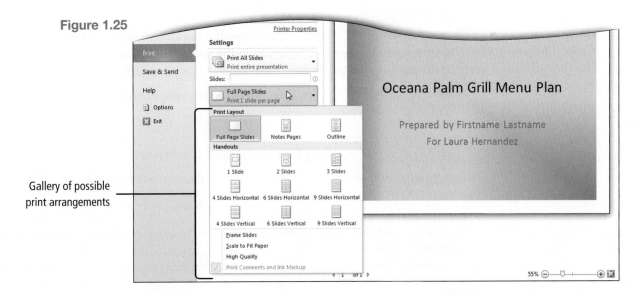

Gallery of possible
print arrangements

7 In the displayed gallery, under **Handouts**, click **1 Slide**, and then compare your screen with Figure 1.26.

The Print Preview changes to show how your slide will print on the paper in this arrangement.

Figure 1.26

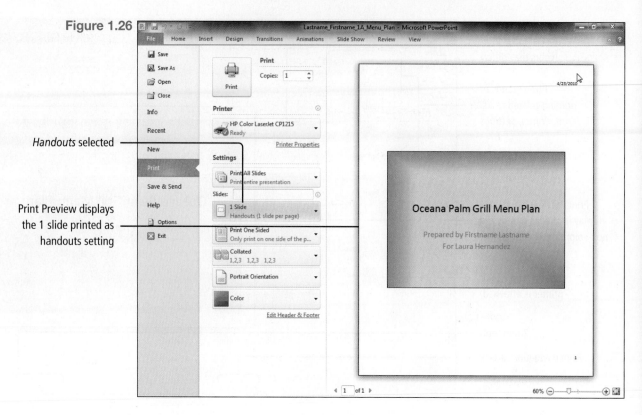

Handouts selected

Print Preview displays
the 1 slide printed as
handouts setting

8 To submit your file electronically, skip this step and move to Step 9. To print your slide, be sure your system is connected to a printer, and then in the **Print group**, click the **Print** button. On the Quick Access Toolbar, click **Save** 🔲, and then move to Step 10.

> The handout will print on your default printer—on a black and white printer, the colors will print in shades of gray. Backstage view closes and your file redisplays in the PowerPoint window.

9 To submit your file electronically, above the **Backstage tabs**, click **Close** to close the file and close **Backstage** view, click **Save** in the displayed message, and then follow the instructions provided by your instructor to submit your file electronically.

Another Way

In the upper right corner of your PowerPoint window, click the red Close button.

10 Display **Backstage** view, and then below the **Backstage tabs**, click **Exit** to close your file and close PowerPoint.

More Knowledge | Creating a PDF as an Electronic Printout

From Backstage view, you can save an Office file as a **PDF file. Portable Document Format** (PDF) creates an image of your file that preserves the look of your file, but that cannot be easily changed. This is a popular format for sending documents electronically, because the document will display on most computers. From Backstage view, click Save & Send, and then in the File Types group, click Create PDF/XPS Document. Then in the third panel, click the Create PDF/XPS button, navigate to your chapter folder, and then in the lower right corner, click Publish.

End **You have completed Project 1A** ————————————————

Project 1B Word File

Project Activities

In Activities 1.07 through 1.16, you will open, edit, save, and then compress a Word file. Your completed document will look similar to Figure 1.27.

Project Files

For Project 1B, you will need the following file:

cf01B_Cheese_Promotion

You will save your Word document as:

Lastname_Firstname_1B_Cheese_Promotion

Project Results

Memo

TO: Laura Mabry Hernandez, General Manager

FROM: Donna Jackson, Executive Chef

DATE: December 17, 2014

SUBJECT: Cheese Specials on Tuesdays

To increase restaurant traffic between 4:00 p.m. and 6:00 p.m., I am proposing a trial cheese event in one of the restaurants, probably Orlando. I would like to try a weekly event on Tuesday evenings where the focus is on a good selection of cheese.

I envision two possibilities: a selection of cheese plates or a cheese bar—or both. The cheeses would have to be matched with compatible fruit and bread or crackers. They could be used as appetizers, or for desserts, as is common in Europe. The cheese plates should be varied and diverse, using a mixture of hard and soft, sharp and mild, unusual and familiar.

I am excited about this new promotion. If done properly, I think it could increase restaurant traffic in the hours when individuals want to relax with a small snack instead of a heavy dinner.

The promotion will require that our employees become familiar with the types and characteristics of both foreign and domestic cheeses. Let's meet to discuss the details and the training requirements, and to create a flyer that begins something like this:

Oceana Palm Grill Tuesday Cheese Tastings

Lastname_Firstname_1B_Cheese_Promotion

Figure 1.27
Project 1B Cheese Promotion

Objective 7 | Open an Existing File and Save It with a New Name

In any Office program, use the Open command to display the *Open dialog box*, from which you can navigate to and then open an existing file that was created in that same program.

The Open dialog box, along with the Save and Save As dialog boxes, are referred to as *common dialog boxes*. These dialog boxes, which are provided by the Windows programming interface, display in all of the Office programs in the same manner. Thus, the Open, Save, and Save As dialog boxes will all look and perform the same in each Office program.

Activity 1.07 | Opening an Existing File and Saving it with a New Name

In this activity, you will display the Open dialog box, open an existing Word document, and then save it in your storage location with a new name.

1 Determine the location of the student data files that accompany this textbook, and be sure you can access these files.

> For example:
>
> If you are accessing the files from the Student CD that came with this textbook, insert the CD now.
>
> If you copied the files from the Student CD or from the Pearson Web site to a USB flash drive that you are using for this course, insert the flash drive in your computer now.
>
> If you copied the files to the hard drive of your computer, for example in your Documents library, be sure you can locate the files on the hard drive.

2 Determine the location of your **Common Features Chapter 1** folder you created in Activity 1.05, in which you will store your work from this chapter, and then be sure you can access that folder.

> For example:
>
> If you created your chapter folder on a USB flash drive, insert the flash drive in your computer now. This can be the same flash drive where you have stored the student data files; just be sure to use the chapter folder you created.
>
> If you created your chapter folder in the Documents library on your computer, be sure you can locate the folder. Otherwise, create a new folder at the computer at which you are working, or on a USB flash drive.

3 Using the technique you practiced in Activity 1.02, locate and then start the **Microsoft Word 2010** program on your system.

Another Way

In the Word (or other program) window, press Ctrl + F12 to display the Open dialog box.

4 On the Ribbon, click the **File tab** to display **Backstage** view, and then click **Open** to display the **Open** dialog box.

5 In the **navigation pane** on the left, use the scroll bar to scroll as necessary, and then click the location of your student data files to display the location's contents in the **file list**. Compare your screen with Figure 1.28.

> For example:
>
> If you are accessing the files from the Student CD that came with your book, under Computer, click the CD/DVD.
>
> If you are accessing the files from a USB flash drive, under Computer, click the flash drive name.
>
> If you are accessing the files from the Documents library of your computer, under Libraries, click Documents.

Figure 1.28

Open dialog box

Scroll bar in
navigation pane

Navigation pane

CD/DVD selected
(or location of your
student files)

Another Way
Point to a folder name,
right-click, and then
from the shortcut
menu, click Open.

6 Point to the folder **01_student_data_files** and double-click to open the folder. Point
to the subfolder **01_common_features**, double-click, and then compare your screen
with Figure 1.29.

Figure 1.29

File list displays
the contents of the
01_common_features folder

Another Way
Click one time to select
the file, and then press
[Enter] or click the Open
button in the lower
right corner of the
dialog box.

7 In the **file list**, point to the **chapter_01** subfolder and double-click to open it. In the
file list, point to Word file **cf01B_Cheese_Promotion** and then double-click to open
and display the file in the Word window. On the Ribbon, on the **Home tab**, in the
Paragraph group, if necessary, click the **Show/Hide** button [¶] so that it is active—
glowing orange. Compare your screen with Figure 1.30.

On the title bar at the top of the screen, the file name displays. If you opened the document
from the Student CD, (*Read-Only*) will display. If you opened the document from another
source to which the files were copied, (*Read-Only*) might not display. **Read-Only** is a property
assigned to a file that prevents the file from being modified or deleted; it indicates that you
cannot save any changes to the displayed document unless you first save it with a new name.

Figure 1.30

File name displays in the
title bar (*Read-only* will
display if opened from
the CD)

Show/Hide button active

Word document displays
in the Word window

Another Way

Press F12 to display the Save As dialog box.

8 Click the **File tab** to display **Backstage** view, and then click the **Save As** command to display the **Save As** dialog box. Compare your screen with Figure 1.31.

> The Save As command displays the Save As dialog box where you can name and save a *new* document based on the currently displayed document. After you name and save the new document, the original document closes, and the new document—based on the original one—displays.

Figure 1.31

Save As dialog box

Navigation pane

Current file name selected

Default type is *Word Document*

9 In the **navigation pane**, click the location in which you are storing your projects for this chapter—the location where you created your **Common Features Chapter 1** folder; for example, your USB flash drive or the Documents library.

10 In the **file list**, double-click the necessary folders and subfolders until your **Common Features Chapter 1** folder displays in the **address bar**.

11 Click in the **File name** box to select the existing file name, or drag to select the existing text, and then using your own name, type **Lastname_Firstname_1B_Cheese_Promotion** Compare your screen with Figure 1.32.

> As you type, the file name from your 1A project might display briefly. Because your 1A project file is stored in this location and you began the new file name with the same text, Office predicts that you might want the same or similar file name. As you type new characters, the suggestion is removed.

Figure 1.32

Your folder name in address bar

File name box displays your new file name

Save button

12 In the lower right corner of the **Save As** dialog box, click **Save**; or press Enter. Compare your screen with Figure 1.33.

The original document closes, and your new document, based on the original, displays with the name in the title bar.

Figure 1.33

New document name in title bar

Insertion point at beginning of document

Objective 8 | Explore Options for an Application

Within each Office application, you can open an *Options dialog box* where you can select program settings and other options and preferences. For example, you can set preferences for viewing and editing files.

Activity 1.08 | Viewing Application Options

1 Click the **File tab** to display **Backstage** view. Under the **Help tab**, click **Options**.

2 In the displayed **Word Options** dialog box, on the left, click **Display**, and then on the right, locate the information under **Always show these formatting marks on the screen**.

When you press Enter, Spacebar, or Tab on your keyboard, characters display to represent these keystrokes. These screen characters do not print, and are referred to as *formatting marks* or *nonprinting characters*.

3 Under **Always show these formatting marks on the screen**, be sure the last check box, **Show all formatting marks**, is selected—select it if necessary. Compare your screen with Figure 1.34.

Figure 1.34

Word Options dialog box

Display selected

Information about formatting marks

Check box selected

4 In the lower right corner of the dialog box, click **OK**.

Objective 9 | Perform Commands from the Ribbon

The *Ribbon*, which displays across the top of the program window, groups commands and features in a manner that you would most logically use them. Each Office program's Ribbon is slightly different, but all contain the same three elements: *tabs*, *groups*, and *commands*.

Tabs display across the top of the Ribbon, and each tab relates to a type of activity; for example, laying out a page. Groups are sets of related commands for specific tasks. Commands—instructions to computer programs—are arranged in groups, and might display as a button, a menu, or a box in which you type information.

You can also minimize the Ribbon so only the tab names display. In the minimized Ribbon view, when you click a tab the Ribbon expands to show the groups and commands, and then when you click a command, the Ribbon returns to its minimized view. Most Office users, however, prefer to leave the complete Ribbon in view at all times.

Activity 1.09 | Performing Commands from the Ribbon

1 Take a moment to examine the document on your screen.

This document is a memo from the Executive Chef to the General Manager regarding a new restaurant promotion.

2 On the Ribbon, click the **View tab**. In the **Show group**, if necessary, click to place a check mark in the **Ruler** check box, and then compare your screen with Figure 1.35.

> When working in Word, display the rulers so that you can see how margin settings affect your document and how text aligns. Additionally, if you set a tab stop or an indent, its location is visible on the ruler.

Figure 1.35

Quick Access Toolbar —
Ruler selected —
Button to minimize Ribbon —

Rulers —

3 On the Ribbon, click the **Home tab**. In the **Paragraph group**, if necessary, click the **Show/Hide** button so that it glows orange and formatting marks display in your document. Point to the button to display information about the button, and then compare your screen with Figure 1.36.

> When the Show/Hide button is active—glowing orange—formatting marks display. Because formatting marks guide your eye in a document—like a map and road signs guide you along a highway—these marks will display throughout this instruction. Many expert Word users keep these marks displayed while creating documents.

Figure 1.36

Show/Hide button glows orange —
Paragraph group —

ScreenTip for Show/Hide button —

Paragraph mark —

Tab mark —

4 In the upper left corner of your screen, above the Ribbon, locate the **Quick Access Toolbar**.

> The *Quick Access Toolbar* contains commands that you use frequently. By default, only the commands Save, Undo, and Redo display, but you can add and delete commands to suit your needs. Possibly the computer at which you are working already has additional commands added to the Quick Access Toolbar.

5 At the end of the Quick Access Toolbar, click the **Customize Quick Access Toolbar** button.

6 Compare your screen with Figure 1.37.

> A list of commands that Office users commonly add to their Quick Access Toolbar displays, including *Open*, *E-mail*, and *Print Preview and Print*. Commands already on the Quick Access Toolbar display a check mark. Commands that you add to the Quick Access Toolbar are always just one click away.
>
> Here you can also display the More Commands dialog box, from which you can select any command from any tab to add to the Quick Access Toolbar.

Figure 1.37

Customize Quick Access Toolbar

Popular commands to add

Existing commands checked

Displays *More Commands* dialog box

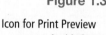

Another Way

Right-click any command on the Ribbon, and then on the shortcut menu, click Add to Quick Access Toolbar.

7 On the displayed list, click **Print Preview and Print**, and then notice that the icon is added to the **Quick Access Toolbar**. Compare your screen with Figure 1.38.

> The icon that represents the Print Preview command displays on the Quick Access Toolbar. Because this is a command that you will use frequently while building Office documents, you might decide to have this command remain on your Quick Access Toolbar.

Figure 1.38

Icon for Print Preview command added to Quick Access Toolbar

8 In the first line of the document, be sure your insertion point is blinking to the left of the *O* in *Oceana*. Press Enter one time to insert a blank paragraph, and then click to the left of the new paragraph mark (¶) in the new line.

> The *paragraph symbol* is a formatting mark that displays each time you press Enter.

9 On the Ribbon, click the **Insert tab**. In the **Illustrations group**, point to the **Clip Art** button to display its ScreenTip.

> Many buttons on the Ribbon have this type of *enhanced ScreenTip*, which displays more descriptive text than a normal ScreenTip.

10 Click the **Clip Art** button.

> The Clip Art *task pane* displays. A task pane is a window within a Microsoft Office application that enables you to enter options for completing a command.

11 In the **Clip Art** task pane, click in the **Search for** box, delete any existing text, and then type **cheese grapes** Under **Results should be:**, click the arrow at the right, if necessary click to *clear* the check mark for **All media types** so that no check boxes are selected, and then click the check box for **Illustrations**. Compare your screen with Figure 1.39.

Figure 1.39

Search term

Blank paragraph

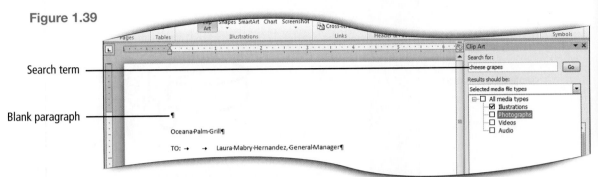

12 Click the **Results should be arrow** again to close the list, and then if necessary, click to place a check mark in the **Include Office.com content** check box.

> By selecting this check box, the search for clip art images will include those from Microsoft's online collections of clip art at www.office.com.

13 At the top of the **Clip Art** task pane, click **Go**. Wait a moment for clips to display, and then locate the clip indicated in Figure 1.40.

Figure 1.40

Check box selected

Locate this image

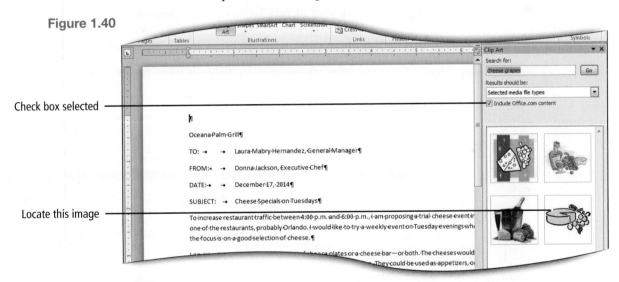

14 Click the image indicated in Figure 1.40 one time to insert it at the insertion point, and then in the upper right corner of the **Clip Art** task pane, click the **Close** ⊠ button.

Alert! | If You Cannot Locate the Image

If the image shown in Figure 1.40 is unavailable, select a different cheese image that is appropriate.

---

15 With the image selected—surrounded by a border—on the Ribbon, click the **Home tab**, and then in the **Paragraph group**, click the **Center** button ▤. Click anywhere outside of the bordered picture to *deselect*—cancel the selection. Compare your screen with Figure 1.41.

Figure 1.41

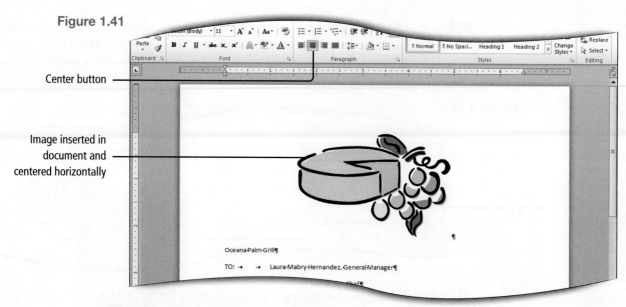

Center button

Image inserted in document and centered horizontally

Oceana·Palm·Grill¶

TO: →   → Laura·Mabry·Hernandez,·General·Manager¶

16 Point to the inserted clip art image, and then watch the last tab of the Ribbon as you click the image one time to select it.

> The *Picture Tools* display and an additional tab—the *Format* tab—is added to the Ribbon. The Ribbon adapts to your work and will display additional tabs—referred to as ***contextual tabs***—when you need them.

17 On the Ribbon, under **Picture Tools**, click the **Format tab**.

Alert! | **The Size of Groups on the Ribbon Varies with Screen Resolution**

Your monitor's screen resolution might be set higher than the resolution used to capture the figures in this book. In Figure 1.42 below, the resolution is set to 1024 × 768, which is used for all of the figures in this book. Compare that with Figure 1.43 below, where the screen resolution is set to 1280 × 1024.

At a higher resolution, the Ribbon expands some groups to show more commands than are available with a single click, such as those in the Picture Styles group. Or, the group expands to add descriptive text to some buttons, such as those in the Arrange group. Regardless of your screen resolution, all Office commands are available to you. In higher resolutions, you will have a more robust view of the commands.

Figure 1.42

Picture Styles group at 1024 x 768 resolution

Arrange group at 1024 x 768 resolution

Figure 1.43

More styles show

Picture Styles at 1280 x 1024

Arrange group at 1280 x 1024

Expanded buttons

---

18 In the **Picture Styles group**, point to the first style to display the ScreenTip *Simple Frame, White*, and notice that the image displays with a white frame.

19 Watch the image as you point to the second picture style, and then to the third, and then to the fourth.

This is *Live Preview*, a technology that shows the result of applying an editing or formatting change as you point to possible results—*before* you actually apply it.

20 In the **Picture Styles group**, click the fourth style—**Drop Shadow Rectangle**—and then click anywhere outside of the image to deselect it. Notice that the Picture Tools no longer display on the Ribbon. Compare your screen with Figure 1.44.

Contextual tabs display only when you need them.

Figure 1.44

Picture Tools no longer display on the Ribbon

Drop Shadow Rectangle picture style applied to image

21 In the upper left corner of your screen, on the Quick Access Toolbar, click the **Save** button to save the changes you have made.

Activity 1.10 | Minimizing and Using the Keyboard to Control the Ribbon

Instead of a mouse, some individuals prefer to navigate the Ribbon by using keys on the keyboard. You can activate keyboard control of the Ribbon by pressing the [Alt] key. You can also minimize the Ribbon to maximize your available screen space.

1 On your keyboard, press the [Alt] key, and then on the Ribbon, notice that small labels display. Press [N] to activate the commands on the **Insert tab**, and then compare your screen with Figure 1.45.

Each label represents a *KeyTip*—an indication of the key that you can press to activate the command. For example, on the Insert tab, you can press [F] to activate the Clip Art task pane.

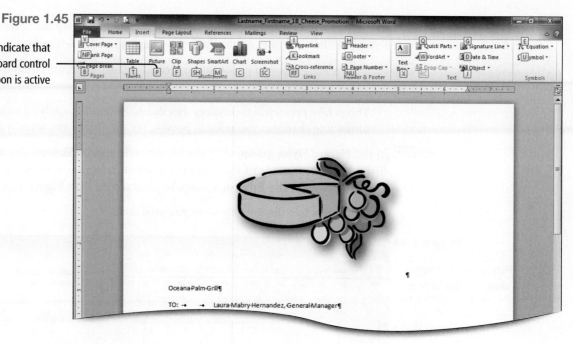

Figure 1.45

KeyTips indicate that
keyboard control
of the Ribbon is active

2 Press **Esc** to redisplay the KeyTips for the tabs. Then, press **Alt** again to turn off keyboard control of the Ribbon.

3 Point to any tab on the Ribbon and right-click to display a shortcut menu.

> **Another Way**
>
> Double-click the active tab; or, click the Minimize the Ribbon button at the right end of the Ribbon.

Here you can choose to display the Quick Access Toolbar below the Ribbon or minimize the Ribbon to maximize screen space. You can also customize the Ribbon by adding, removing, renaming, or reordering tabs, groups, and commands on the Ribbon, although this is not recommended until you become an expert Office user.

4 Click **Minimize the Ribbon**. Notice that only the Ribbon tabs display. Click the **Home tab** to display the commands. Click anywhere in the document, and notice that the Ribbon reverts to its minimized view.

> **Another Way**
>
> Double-click any tab to redisplay the full Ribbon.

5 Right-click any Ribbon tab, and then click **Minimize the Ribbon** again to turn the minimize feature off.

Most expert Office users prefer to have the full Ribbon display at all times.

6 Point to any tab on the Ribbon, and then on your mouse device, roll the mouse wheel. Notice that different tabs become active as your roll the mouse wheel.

You can make a tab active by using this technique, instead of clicking the tab.

Objective 10 | Apply Formatting in Office Programs

Formatting is the process of establishing the overall appearance of text, graphics, and pages in an Office file—for example, in a Word document.

Activity 1.11 | Formatting and Viewing Pages

In this activity, you will practice common formatting techniques used in Office applications.

1 On the Ribbon, click the **Insert tab**, and then in the **Header & Footer group**, click the **Footer** button.

Another Way

On the Design tab, in the Insert group, click Quick Parts, click Field, and then under Field names, click FileName.

2 At the top of the displayed gallery, under **Built-In**, click **Blank**. At the bottom of your document, with *Type text* highlighted in blue, using your own name type the file name of this document **Lastname_Firstname_1B_Cheese_Promotion** and then compare your screen with Figure 1.46.

Header & Footer Tools are added to the Ribbon. A *footer* is a reserved area for text or graphics that displays at the bottom of each page in a document. Likewise, a *header* is a reserved area for text or graphics that displays at the top of each page in a document. When the footer (or header) area is active, the document area is inactive (dimmed).

Figure 1.46

Design tab added

Header & Footer Tools active

Document area inactive (dimmed) when footer area is active

Close Header and Footer button

Your file name

Footer area displays

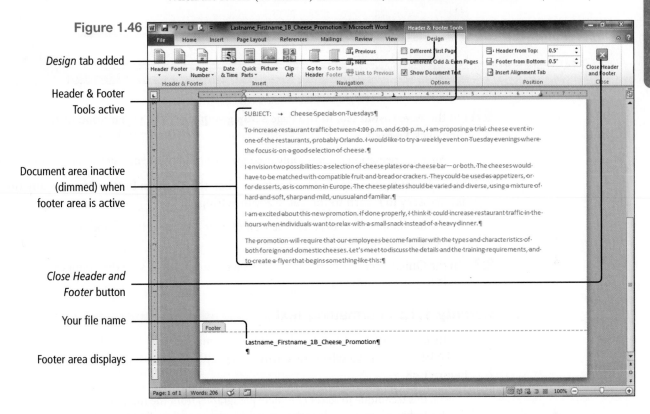

3 On the Ribbon, on the **Design tab**, in the **Close group**, click the **Close Header and Footer** button.

4 On the Ribbon, click the **Page Layout tab**. In the **Page Setup group**, click the **Orientation** button, and notice that two orientations display—*Portrait* and *Landscape*. Click **Landscape**.

In *portrait orientation*, the paper is taller than it is wide. In *landscape orientation*, the paper is wider than it is tall.

5 In the lower right corner of the screen, locate the **Zoom control** buttons.

To *zoom* means to increase or decrease the viewing area. You can zoom in to look closely at a section of a document, and then zoom out to see an entire page on the screen. You can also zoom to view multiple pages on the screen.

6 Drag the **Zoom slider** to the left until you have zoomed to approximately *60%*. Compare your screen with Figure 1.47.

Figure 1.47

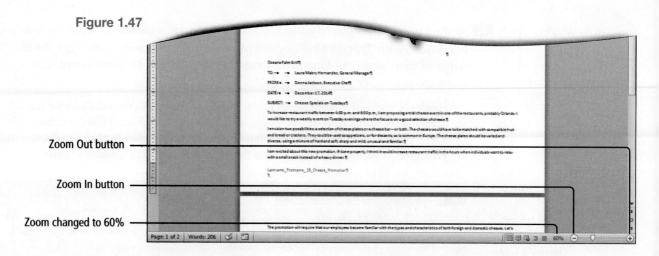

Zoom Out button

Zoom In button

Zoom changed to 60%

7 On the **Page Layout tab**, in the **Page Setup group**, click the **Orientation** button, and then click **Portrait**.

> Portrait orientation is commonly used for business documents such as letters and memos.

8 In the lower right corner of your screen, click the **Zoom In** button ⊕ as many times as necessary to return to the **100%** zoom setting.

> Use the zoom feature to adjust the view of your document for editing and for your viewing comfort.

9 On the Quick Access Toolbar, click the **Save** button 🖫 to save the changes you have made to your document.

Activity 1.12 | Formatting Text

1 To the left of *Oceana Palm Grill*, point in the margin area to display the 🔏 pointer and click one time to select the entire paragraph. Compare your screen with Figure 1.48.

> Use this technique to select complete paragraphs from the margin area. Additionally, with this technique you can drag downward to select multiple-line paragraphs—which is faster and more efficient than dragging through text.

Figure 1.48

Paragraph selected

2 On the Ribbon, click the **Home tab**, and then in the **Paragraph group**, click the **Center** button 🟰 to center the paragraph.

> *Alignment* refers to the placement of paragraph text relative to the left and right margins. *Center alignment* refers to text that is centered horizontally between the left and right margins. You can also align text at the left margin, which is the default alignment for text in Word, or at the right margin.

3 On the **Home tab**, in the **Font group**, click the **Font button arrow** `Calibri (Body) ▾`. At the top of the list, point to **Cambria**, and as you do so, notice that the selected text previews in the Cambria font.

A *font* is a set of characters with the same design and shape. The default font in a Word document is Calibri, which is a *sans serif* font—a font design with no lines or extensions on the ends of characters.

The Cambria font is a *serif* font—a font design that includes small line extensions on the ends of the letters to guide the eye in reading from left to right.

The list of fonts displays as a gallery showing potential results. For example, in the Font gallery, you can see the actual design and format of each font as it would look if applied to text.

4 Point to several other fonts and observe the effect on the selected text. Then, at the top of the **Font** gallery, under **Theme Fonts**, click **Cambria**.

A *theme* is a predesigned set of colors, fonts, lines, and fill effects that look good together and that can be applied to your entire document or to specific items.

A theme combines two sets of fonts—one for text and one for headings. In the default Office theme, Cambria is the suggested font for headings.

5 With the paragraph *Oceana Palm Grill* still selected, on the **Home tab**, in the **Font group**, click the **Font Size button arrow** `11 ▾`, point to **36**, and then notice how Live Preview displays the text in the font size to which you are pointing. Compare your screen with Figure 1.49.

Figure 1.49

Font Size button

Font button

Font Size list

Pointing to 36 pt font size

Oceana Palm Grill centered, Cambria font applied

6 On the displayed list of font sizes, click **20**.

Fonts are measured in *points*, with one point equal to 1/72 of an inch. A higher point size indicates a larger font size. Headings and titles are often formatted by using a larger font size. The word *point* is abbreviated as *pt*.

7 With *Oceana Palm Grill* still selected, on the **Home tab**, in the **Font group**, click the **Font Color button arrow** `A ▾`. Under **Theme Colors**, in the seventh column, click the last color—**Olive Green, Accent 3, Darker 50%**. Click anywhere to deselect the text.

8 To the left of *TO:*, point in the left margin area to display the ⌐ pointer, hold down the left mouse button, and then drag down to select the four memo headings. Compare your screen with Figure 1.50.

Use this technique to select complete paragraphs from the margin area—dragging downward to select multiple-line paragraphs—which is faster and more efficient than dragging through text.

Figure 1.50

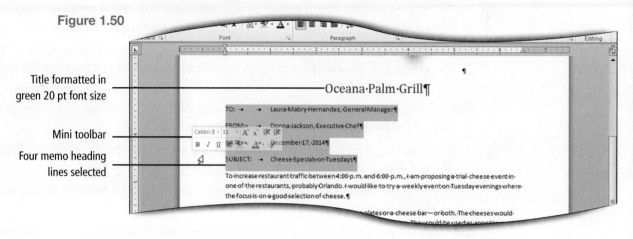

Title formatted in green 20 pt font size

Mini toolbar

Four memo heading lines selected

9 With the four paragraphs selected, on the Mini toolbar, click the **Font Color** button A⌐, which now displays a dark green bar instead of a red bar.

The font color button retains its most recently used color—Olive Green, Accent 3, Darker 50%. As you progress in your study of Microsoft Office, you will use other buttons that behave in this manner; that is, they retain their most recently used format.

The purpose of the Mini toolbar is to place commonly used commands close to text or objects that you select. By selecting a command on the Mini toolbar, you reduce the distance that you must move your mouse to access a command.

10 Click anywhere in the paragraph that begins *To increase*, and then *triple-click*—click the left mouse button three times—to select the entire paragraph. If the entire paragraph is not selected, click in the paragraph and begin again.

11 With the entire paragraph selected, on the Mini toolbar, click the **Font Color button arrow** A⌐, and then under **Theme Colors**, in the sixth column, click the first color—**Red, Accent 2**.

It is convenient to have commonly used commands display on the Mini toolbar so that you do not have to move your mouse to the top of the screen to access the command from the Ribbon.

12 Select the text *TO:* and then on the displayed Mini toolbar, click the **Bold** button B and the **Italic** button I.

Font styles include bold, italic, and underline. Font styles emphasize text and are a visual cue to draw the reader's eye to important text.

13 On the displayed Mini toolbar, click the **Italic** button I again to turn off the Italic formatting. Notice that the Italic button no longer glows orange.

A button that behaves in this manner is referred to as a *toggle button*, which means it can be turned on by clicking it once, and then turned off by clicking it again.

14 With *TO:* still selected, on the Mini toolbar, click the **Format Painter** button ☑. Then, move your mouse under the word *Laura*, and notice the ⬚I mouse pointer. Compare your screen with Figure 1.51.

> You can use the *Format Painter* to copy the formatting of specific text or of a paragraph and then apply it in other locations in your document.

> The pointer takes the shape of a paintbrush, and contains the formatting information from the paragraph where the insertion point is positioned. Information about the Format Painter and how to turn it off displays in the status bar.

Figure 1.51

Format Painter button on the Mini toolbar

Memo headings formatted in green

Mouse pointer

Paragraph formatted in red

Format Painter information in the status bar

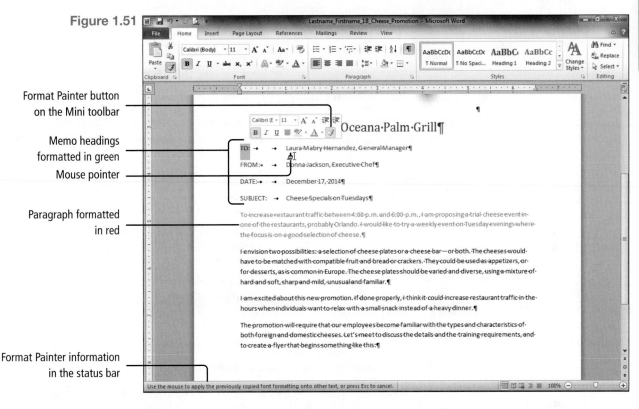

15 With the ⬚I pointer, drag to select the text *FROM:* and notice that the Bold formatting is applied. Then, point to the selected text *FROM:* and on the Mini toolbar, *double-click* the **Format Painter** button ☑.

16 Select the text *DATE:* to copy the Bold formatting, and notice that the pointer retains the ⬚I shape.

> When you *double-click* the Format Painter button, the Format Painter feature remains active until you either click the Format Painter button again, or press (Esc) to cancel it—as indicated on the status bar.

17 With Format Painter still active, select the text *SUBJECT:*, and then on the Ribbon, on the **Home tab**, in the **Clipboard group**, notice that the **Format Painter** button ☑ is glowing orange, indicating that it is active. Compare your screen with Figure 1.52.

Figure 1.52

Format Painter button on Ribbon glows orange

Memo headings formatted with Bold

SUBJECT: **still selected**

18 Click the **Format Painter** button 🖌 on the Ribbon to turn the command off.

19 In the paragraph that begins *To increase*, triple-click again to select the entire paragraph. On the displayed Mini toolbar, click the **Bold** button B and the **Italic** button I . Click anywhere to deselect.

20 On the Quick Access Toolbar, click the **Save** button 💾 to save the changes you have made to your document.

Activity 1.13 | Using the Office Clipboard to Cut, Copy, and Paste

The **Office Clipboard** is a temporary storage area that holds text or graphics that you select and then cut or copy. When you **copy** text or graphics, a copy is placed on the Office Clipboard and the original text or graphic remains in place. When you **cut** text or graphics, a copy is placed on the Office Clipboard, and the original text or graphic is removed—cut—from the document.

After cutting or copying, the contents of the Office Clipboard are available for you to **paste**—insert—in a new location in the current document, or into another Office file.

1 Hold down Ctrl and press Home to move to the beginning of your document, and then take a moment to study the table in Figure 1.53, which describes similar keyboard shortcuts with which you can navigate quickly in a document.

To Move	Press
To the beginning of a document	Ctrl + Home
To the end of a document	Ctrl + End
To the beginning of a line	Home
To the end of a line	End
To the beginning of the previous word	Ctrl + ←
To the beginning of the next word	Ctrl + →
To the beginning of the current word (if insertion point is in the middle of a word)	Ctrl + ←
To the beginning of a paragraph	Ctrl + ↑
To the beginning of the next paragraph	Ctrl + ↓
To the beginning of the current paragraph (if insertion point is in the middle of a paragraph)	Ctrl + ↑
Up one screen	PgUp
Down one screen	PageDown

Figure 1.53

Another Way

Right-click the selection, and then click Copy on the shortcut menu; or, use the keyboard shortcut Ctrl + C.

2 To the left of *Oceana Palm Grill*, point in the left margin area to display the 📄 pointer, and then click one time to select the entire paragraph. On the **Home tab**, in the **Clipboard group**, click the **Copy** button 📋.

Because anything that you select and then copy—or cut—is placed on the Office Clipboard, the Copy command and the Cut command display in the Clipboard group of commands on the Ribbon.

There is no visible indication that your copied selection has been placed on the Office Clipboard.

3 On the **Home tab**, in the **Clipboard group**, to the right of the group name *Clipboard*, click the **Dialog Box Launcher** button 🗗, and then compare your screen with Figure 1.54.

The Clipboard task pane displays with your copied text. In any Ribbon group, the *Dialog Box Launcher* displays either a dialog box or a task pane related to the group of commands.

It is not necessary to display the Office Clipboard in this manner, although sometimes it is useful to do so. The Office Clipboard can hold 24 items.

Figure 1.54

Copy button

Dialog Box Launcher in Clipboard group

Clipboard task pane displays

Selected text on the Office Clipboard

4 In the upper right corner of the **Clipboard** task pane, click the **Close** button ❌.

Another Way

Right-click, on the shortcut menu under Paste Options, click the desired option button.

5 Press Ctrl + End to move to the end of your document. Press Enter one time to create a new blank paragraph. On the **Home tab**, in the **Clipboard group**, point to the **Paste** button, and then click the *upper* portion of this split button.

The Paste command pastes the most recently copied item on the Office Clipboard at the insertion point location. If you click the lower portion of the Paste button, a gallery of Paste Options displays.

6 Click the **Paste Options** button ☐ that displays below the pasted text as shown in Figure 1.55.

> Here you can view and apply various formatting options for pasting your copied or cut text. Typically you will click Paste on the Ribbon and paste the item in its original format. If you want some other format for the pasted item, you can do so from the *Paste Options gallery*.

> The Paste Options gallery provides a Live Preview of the various options for changing the format of the pasted item with a single click. The Paste Options gallery is available in three places: on the Ribbon by clicking the lower portion of the Paste button—the Paste button arrow; from the Paste Options button that displays below the pasted item following the paste operation; or, on the shortcut menu if you right-click the pasted item.

Figure 1.55
Upper portion of Paste button
Paste button arrow on the Ribbon
Pasted text
Paste Options button
Paste Options gallery

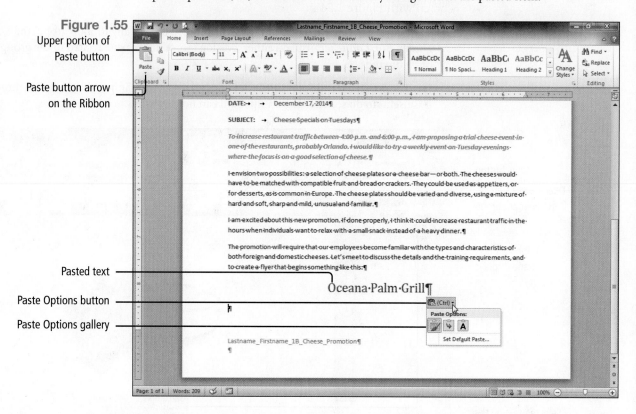

7 In the displayed **Paste Options** gallery, *point* to each option to see the Live Preview of the format that would be applied if you clicked the button.

> The contents of the Paste Options gallery are contextual; that is, they change based on what you copied and where you are pasting.

8 Press Esc to close the gallery; the button will remain displayed until you take some other screen action.

Another Way

On the Home tab, in the Clipboard group, click the Cut button; or, use the keyboard shortcut Ctrl + X.

---

9 Press Ctrl + Home to move to the top of the document, and then click the **cheese image** one time to select it. While pointing to the selected image, right-click, and then on the shortcut menu, click **Cut**.

> Recall that the Cut command cuts—removes—the selection from the document and places it on the Office Clipboard.

10 Press [Del] one time to remove the blank paragraph from the top of the document, and then press [Ctrl] + [End] to move to the end of the document.

11 With the insertion point blinking in the blank paragraph at the end of the document, right-click, and notice that the **Paste Options** gallery displays on the shortcut menu. Compare your screen with Figure 1.56.

Figure 1.56

Paste Options on shortcut menu

12 On the shortcut menu, under **Paste Options**, click the first button—**Keep Source Formatting**.

13 Click the picture to select it. On the **Home tab**, in the **Paragraph group**, click the **Center** button.

14 Above the cheese picture, click to position the insertion point at the end of the word *Grill*, press [Spacebar] one time, and then type **Tuesday Cheese Tastings** Compare your screen with Figure 1.57.

Figure 1.57

Heading

Picture inserted and centered

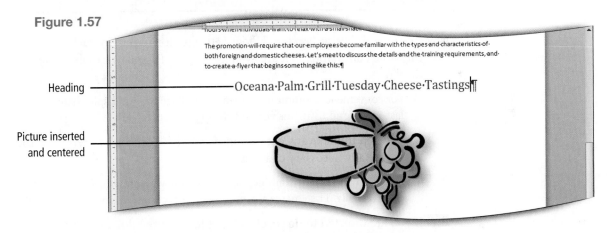

Activity 1.14 | Viewing Print Preview and Printing a Word Document

1 Press [Ctrl] + [Home] to move to the top of your document. Select the text *Oceana Palm Grill*, and then replace the selected text by typing **Memo**

2 Display **Backstage** view, on the right, click **Properties**, and then click **Show Document Panel**. Replace the existing author name with your first and last name. In the **Subject** box, type your course name and section number, and then in the **Keywords** box, type **cheese promotion** and then **Close** the **Document Information Panel**.

Another Way
Press Ctrl + F2 to display Print Preview.

3 On the Quick Access Toolbar, click **Save** 🖫 to save the changes you have made to your document.

4 On the Quick Access Toolbar, click the **Print Preview** button 🔍 that you added. Compare your screen with Figure 1.58.

Figure 1.58

Memo typed →

If no printer is attached to your system, OneNote is the default printer

Print tab active in Backstage view

Print Preview (if you have a non-color printer as your default printer, the preview may display in shades of gray)

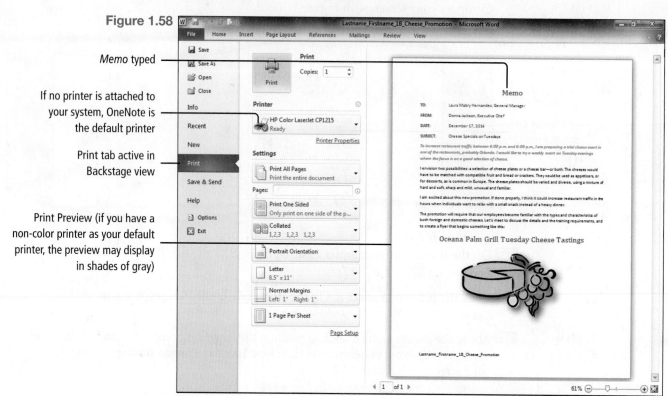

5 Examine the **Print Preview**. Under **Settings**, notice that in **Backstage** view, several of the same commands that are available on the Page Layout tab of the Ribbon also display.

> For convenience, common adjustments to Page Layout display here, so that you can make last-minute adjustments without closing Backstage view.

6 If you need to make any corrections, click the Home tab to return to the document and make any necessary changes.

> It is good practice to examine the Print Preview before printing or submitting your work electronically. Then, make any necessary corrections, re-save, and redisplay Print Preview.

7 If you are directed to do so, click Print to print the document; or, above the Info tab, click Close, and then submit your file electronically according to the directions provided by your instructor.

> If you click the Print button, Backstage view closes and the Word window redisplays.

8 On the Quick Access Toolbar, point to the **Print Preview icon** 🔍 you placed there, right-click, and then click **Remove from Quick Access Toolbar**.

> If you are working on your own computer and you want to do so, you can leave the icon on the toolbar; in a lab setting, you should return the software to its original settings.

9 At the right end of the title bar, click the program **Close** button ⊠.

10 If a message displays asking if you want the text on the Clipboard to be available after you quit Word, click **No**.

This message most often displays if you have copied some type of image to the Clipboard. If you click Yes, the items on the Clipboard will remain for you to use.

Objective 11 | Use the Microsoft Office 2010 Help System

Within each Office program, the Help feature provides information about all of the program's features and displays step-by-step instructions for performing many tasks.

Activity 1.15 | Using the Microsoft Office 2010 Help System in Excel

In this activity, you will use the Microsoft Help feature to find information about formatting numbers in Excel.

Another Way
Press F1 to display Help.

1 **Start** the **Microsoft Excel 2010** program. In the upper right corner of your screen, click the **Microsoft Excel Help** button ❓.

2 In the **Excel Help** window, click in the white box in upper left corner, type **formatting numbers** and then click **Search** or press Enter.

3 On the list of results, click **Display numbers as currency**. Compare your screen with Figure 1.59.

Figure 1.59

Excel Help window

Search term

Print button

Search button

Help information

Excel Help button

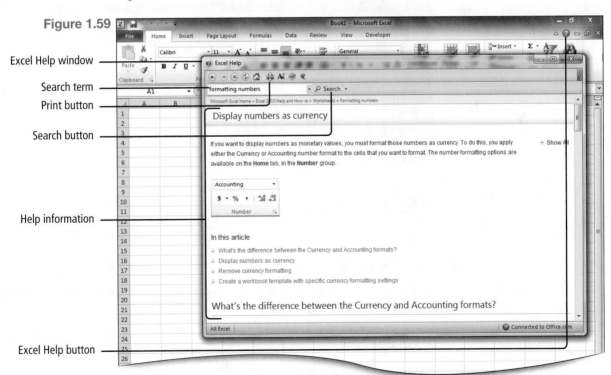

4 If you want to do so, on the toolbar at the top of the **Excel Help** window, click the Print 🖨 button to print a copy of this information for your reference.

5 On the title bar of the Excel Help window, click the **Close** button ![close]. On the right side of the Microsoft Excel title bar, click the **Close** button ![close] to close Excel.

Objective 12 | Compress Files

A *compressed file* is a file that has been reduced in size. Compressed files take up less storage space and can be transferred to other computers faster than uncompressed files. You can also combine a group of files into one compressed folder, which makes it easier to share a group of files.

Activity 1.16 | Compressing Files

In this activity, you will combine the two files you created in this chapter into one compressed file.

1 On the Windows taskbar, click the **Start** button ![start], and then on the right, click **Computer**.

2 On the left, in the **navigation pane**, click the location of your two files from this chapter—your USB flash drive or other location—and display the folder window for your **Common Features Chapter 1** folder. Compare your screen with Figure 1.60.

Figure 1.60

Address bar displays path

Your chapter files in file list (your name displays)

Folder window for your chapter folder

Location selected in navigation pane (your location may vary)

3 In the **file list**, click your **Lastname_Firstname_1A_Menu_Plan** file one time to select it.

4 Hold down [Ctrl], and then click your **Lastname_Firstname_1B_Cheese_Promotion** file to select both files. Release [Ctrl].

In any Windows-based program, holding down [Ctrl] while selecting enables you to select multiple items.

5 Point anywhere over the two selected files and right-click. On the shortcut menu, point to **Send to**, and then compare your screen with Figure 1.61.

Figure 1.61

Two files selected

Send to submenu

Shortcut menu
(yours may vary)

6 On the shortcut submenu, click **Compressed (zipped) folder**.

Windows creates a compressed folder containing a *copy* of each of the selected files. The folder name is the name of the file or folder to which you were pointing, and is selected—highlighted in blue—so that you can rename it.

7 Using your own name, type **Lastname_Firstname_Common_Features_Ch1** and press Enter.

The compressed folder is now ready to attach to an e-mail or share in some other electronic format.

8 Close ☒ the folder window. If directed to do so by your instructor, submit your compressed folder electronically.

More Knowledge | Extracting Compressed Files

Extract means to decompress, or pull out, files from a compressed form. When you extract a file, an uncompressed copy is placed in the folder that you specify. The original file remains in the compressed folder.

End You have completed Project 1B ————————————————

Content-Based Assessments

Summary

In this chapter, you used Windows Explorer to navigate the Windows file structure. You also used features that are common across the Microsoft Office 2010 programs.

Key Terms

Content-Based Assessments

Matching

Match each term in the second column with its correct definition in the first column by writing the letter of the term on the blank line in front of the correct definition.

_____ 1. A collection of information stored on a computer under a single name.

_____ 2. A container in which you store files.

_____ 3. A folder within a folder.

_____ 4. The program that displays the files and folders on your computer.

_____ 5. The Windows menu that is the main gateway to your computer.

_____ 6. In Windows 7, a window that displays the contents of the current folder, library, or device, and contains helpful parts so that you can navigate.

_____ 7. In Windows, a collection of items, such as files and folders, assembled from various locations that might be on your computer.

_____ 8. The bar at the top of a folder window with which you can navigate to a different folder or library, or go back to a previous one.

_____ 9. An instruction to a computer program that carries out an action.

_____ 10. Small pictures that represent a program, a file, a folder, or an object.

_____ 11. A set of instructions that a computer uses to perform a specific task.

_____ 12. A spreadsheet program used to calculate numbers and create charts.

_____ 13. The user interface that groups commands on tabs at the top of the program window.

_____ 14. A bar at the top of the program window displaying the current file and program name.

_____ 15. One or more keys pressed to perform a task that would otherwise require a mouse.

A Address bar
B Command
C File
D Folder
E Folder window
F Icons
G Keyboard shortcut
H Library
I Microsoft Excel
J Program
K Ribbon
L Start menu
M Subfolder
N Title bar
O Windows Explorer

Multiple Choice

Circle the correct answer.

1. A small toolbar with frequently used commands that displays when selecting text or objects is the:
   A. Quick Access Toolbar   B. Mini toolbar   C. Document toolbar

2. In Office 2010, a centralized space for file management tasks is:
   A. a task pane   B. a dialog box   C. Backstage view

3. The commands Save, Save As, Open, and Close in Backstage view are located:
   A. above the Backstage tabs   B. below the Backstage tabs   C. under the screen thumbnail

4. The tab in Backstage view that displays information about the current file is the:
   A. Recent tab   B. Info tab   C. Options tab

5. Details about a file, including the title, author name, subject, and keywords are known as:
   A. document properties   B. formatting marks   C. KeyTips

6. An Office feature that displays a list of potential results is:
   A. Live Preview   B. a contextual tab   C. a gallery

7. A type of formatting emphasis applied to text such as bold, italic, and underline, is called:

   A. a font style   **B.** a KeyTip   **C.** a tag

8. A technology showing the result of applying formatting as you point to possible results is called:

   A. Live Preview   **B.** Backstage view   **C.** gallery view

9. A temporary storage area that holds text or graphics that you select and then cut or copy is the:

   A. paste options gallery   **B.** ribbon   **C.** Office clipboard

10. A file that has been reduced in size is:

   A. a compressed file   **B.** an extracted file   **C.** a PDF file

Getting Started with Access Databases

OUTCOMES

At the end of this chapter you will be able to:

OBJECTIVES

Mastering these objectives will enable you to:

PROJECT 1A
Create a new database.

1. Identify Good Database Design (p. 51)
2. Create a Table and Define Fields in a New Database (p. 52)
3. Change the Structure of Tables and Add a Second Table (p. 64)
4. Create and Use a Query, Form, and Report (p. 74)
5. Save and Close a Database (p. 80)

PROJECT 1B
Create a database from a template.

6. Create a Database Using a Template (p. 82)
7. Organize Objects in the Navigation Pane (p. 86)
8. Create a New Table in a Database Created with a Template (p. 88)
9. Print a Report and a Table in a Database Created with a Template (p. 90)

Joy Brown/Shutterstock

In This Chapter

In this chapter, you will use Microsoft Access 2010 to organize a collection of related information. Access is a powerful program that enables you to organize, search, sort, retrieve, and present information in a professional-looking manner. You will create new databases, enter data into Access tables, and create a query, form, and report—all of which are Access objects that make a database useful. In this chapter, you will also create a database from a template provided with the Access program. The template creates a complete database that you can use as provided, or you can modify it to suit your needs. Additional templates are available from the Microsoft Online Web site. For your first attempt at a database, consider using a template.

The projects in this chapter relate to **Capital Cities Community College**, which is located in the Washington D. C. metropolitan area. The college provides high-quality education and professional training to residents in the cities surrounding the nation's capital. Its four campuses serve over 50,000 students and offer more than 140 certificate programs and degrees at the associate's level. CapCCC has a highly acclaimed Distance Education program and an extensive Workforce Development program. The college makes positive contributions to the community through cultural and athletic programs and partnerships with businesses and non-profit organizations.

Project 1A Contact Information Database with Two Tables

Project Activities

In Activities 1.01 through 1.17, you will assist Dr. Justin Mitrani, Vice President of Instruction at Capital Cities Community College, in creating a new database for tracking the contact information for students and faculty members. Your completed database objects will look similar to Figure 1.1.

Project Files

For Project 1A, you will need the following files:

New blank Access database
a01A_Students (Excel workbook)
a01A_Faculty (Excel workbook)

You will save your database as:

Lastname_Firstname_1A_Contacts

Project Results

Figure 1.1
Project 1A Contacts

Objective 1 | Identify Good Database Design

A *database* is an organized collection of *data*—facts about people, events, things, or ideas—related to a specific topic or purpose. *Information* is data that is organized in a useful manner. Your personal address book is a type of database, because it is a collection of data about one topic—the people with whom you communicate. A simple database of this type is called a *flat database* because it is not related or linked to any other collection of data. Another example of a simple database is a list of movie DVDs. You do not keep information about your DVDs in your address book because the data is not related to your addresses.

A more sophisticated type of database is a *relational database*, because multiple collections of data in the database are related to one another; for example, data about the students, the courses, and the faculty members at a college. Microsoft Access 2010 is a relational *database management system*—also referred to as a *DBMS*—which is software that controls how related collections of data are stored, organized, retrieved, and secured.

Activity 1.01 | Using Good Design Techniques to Plan a Database

The first step in creating a new database is to determine the information you want to keep track of, and then ask yourself, *What questions should this database be able to answer for me?* The purpose of a database is to store the data in a manner that makes it easy for you to get the information you need by asking questions. For example, in the Contacts database for Capital Cities Community College, the questions to be answered might include:

How many students are enrolled at Capital Cities Community College?

How many faculty members teach in the Accounting Department?

Which and how many students live in Arlington, Virginia?

Which and how many students have a balance owed?

Which and how many students are majoring in Information Systems Technology?

Tables are the foundation of an Access database because all of the data is stored in one or more tables. A table is similar in structure to an Excel worksheet; that is, data is organized into rows and columns. Each table row is a *record*—all of the categories of data pertaining to one person, place, thing, event, or idea. Each table column is a *field*—a single piece of information for every record. For example, in a table storing student contact information, each row forms a record for only one student. Each column forms a field for a single piece of information for every record; for example, the student ID number for all students.

When organizing the fields of information in your database, break each piece of information into its smallest useful part. For example, create three fields for the name of a student—one field for the last name, one field for the first name, and one field for the middle name or initial.

The *first principle of good database design* is to organize data in the tables so that *redundant*—duplicate—data does not occur. For example, record the contact information for students in only *one* table, because if the address for a student changes, the change can be made in just one place. This conserves space, reduces the likelihood of errors when recording the new data, and does not require remembering all of the different places where the address is stored.

The *second principle of good database design* is to use techniques that ensure the accuracy of data when it is entered into the table. Typically, many different people enter data into a database—think of all the people who enter data at your college. When entering a state in a contacts database, one person might enter the state as *Virginia* and another might enter the state as *VA*. Use design techniques to help those who enter data into a database do so in a consistent and accurate manner.

Normalization is the process of applying design rules and principles to ensure that your database performs as expected. Taking the time to plan and create a database that is well designed will ensure that you can retrieve meaningful information from the database.

The tables of information in a relational database are linked or joined to one another by a *common field*—a field in one or more tables that stores the same data. For example, the Student Contacts table includes the Student ID, name, and address of every student. The Student Activities table includes the name of each club, and the Student ID—but not the name or address—of each student in each club. Because the two tables share a common field—Student ID—you can create a list of names and addresses of all the students in the Photography Club. The names and addresses are stored in the Student Contacts table, and the Student IDs of the Photography Club members are stored in the Student Activities table.

Objective 2 | Create a Table and Define Fields in a New Blank Database

There are two methods to create a new Access database: create a new database using a *database template*—a preformatted database designed for a specific purpose—or create a new database from a blank database. A blank database has no data and has no database tools; you create the data and the tools as you need them.

Regardless of the method you use, you must name and save the database before you can create any *objects* in it. Objects are the basic parts of a database; you create objects to store your data and to work with your data. The most common database objects are tables, forms, and reports. Think of an Access database as a container for the objects that you will create.

Activity 1.02 | Starting with a New Database

1 **Start** Access. Take a moment to compare your screen with Figure 1.2 and study the parts of the Microsoft Access window described in the table in Figure 1.3.

From this Access starting point in Backstage view, you can open an existing database, create a new blank database, or create a new database from a template.

Figure 1.2

Available Templates panel
Title bar
Blank database selected
Blank database panel
New tab
Office.com online Templates (yours may differ)
Browse for a location button

Microsoft Access Opening Window

Window Part	Description
Available Templates panel	Displays alternative methods of creating a database.
Blank database	Starts a new blank database.
Blank database panel	Displays when *Blank database* button is selected under Available Templates.
Browse for location button	Enables you to select a storage location for the database.
New tab	Displays, when active in Backstage view, the various methods by which you can create a new database.
Office.com Templates	Displays template categories available from the Office.com Web site.
Title bar	Displays the Quick Access Toolbar, program name, and program-level buttons.

Figure 1.3

2 On the right, under **Blank database**, to the right of the **File Name** box, click the **Browse** button 📂. In the **File New Database** dialog box, navigate to the location where you are saving your databases for this chapter, create a new folder named **Access Chapter 1** and then notice that *Database1* displays as the default file name—the number at the end of your file name might differ if you have saved a database previously with the default name. In the **File New Database** dialog box, click **Open**.

3 In the **File name** box, replace the existing text with **Lastname_Firstname_1A_Contacts** Press Enter, and then compare your screen with Figure 1.4.

On the right, the name of your database displays in the File Name box, and the drive and folder where the database is stored displays under the File Name box. An Access database has the file extension *.accdb*.

Figure 1.4

File name with your name and underscores between words

Drive and folder where your database is stored (yours may differ)

Create button

.accdb file extension

4 Under the **File Name** box, click the **Create** button, compare your screen with Figure 1.5, and then take a moment to study the screen elements described in the table in Figure 1.6.

Access creates the new database and opens *Table1*. Recall that a table is an Access object that stores your data in columns and rows, similar to the format of an Excel worksheet. Table objects are the foundation of a database because tables store the actual data.

Figure 1.5

Ribbon with command groups arranged on tabs

Object tab

Table Tools active

Title bar with database name

Object window

Navigation Pane

Object window Close button

Status bar

Parts of the Access Database Window

Window Part	Description
Navigation Pane	Displays the database objects; from here you open the database objects to display in the object window at the right.
Object tab	Identifies and enables you to select the open object.
Object window	Displays the active or open object (table, query, or other object).
Object window Close button	Closes the active object (table, query, or other object).
Ribbon with command groups arranged on tabs	Groups the commands for performing related database tasks on tabs.
Status bar	Indicates the active view and the status of actions occurring within the database on the left; provides buttons to switch between Datasheet view and Design view on the right.
Table Tools	Provides tools for working with a table object; Table Tools are available only when a table is displayed.
Title bar	Displays the name of your database.

Figure 1.6

Activity 1.03 | Assigning the Data Type and Name to Fields

After you have saved and named your database, the next step is to consult your database plan, and then create the tables in which to enter your data. Limit the data in each table to *one* subject. For example, in this project, your database will have two tables— one for student contact information and one for faculty contact information.

Recall that each column in a table is a field and that field names display at the top of each column of the table. Recall also that each row in a table is a record—all of the data pertaining to one person, place, thing, event, or idea. Each record is broken up into its smallest usable parts—the fields. Use meaningful names to name fields; for example, *Last Name*.

1 Notice the new blank table that displays in Datasheet view, and then take a moment to study the elements of the table's object window. Compare your screen with Figure 1.7.

The table displays in *Datasheet view*, which displays the data as columns and rows similar to the format of an Excel worksheet. Another way to view a table is in *Design view*, which displays the underlying design—the *structure*—of the table's fields. The *object window* displays the open object—in this instance, the table object.

In a new blank database, there is only one object—a new blank table. Because you have not yet named this table, the object tab displays a default name of *Table1*. Access creates the first field and names it *ID*. In the ID field, Access assigns a unique sequential number—each number incremented by one—to each record as it is entered into the table.

Figure 1.7

Navigation Pane Close button

Field names row

New record row

Object tab with default table name

First field is *ID*

Navigation Pane

Fields tab on the Ribbon

2 In the **Navigation Pane**, click the **Open/Close** button ⟪ to collapse the **Navigation Pane** to a narrow bar on the left and to display more of the table.

The *Navigation Pane* is an area of the Access window that displays and organizes the names of the objects in a database. From the Navigation Pane, you can open objects for use.

Another Way
To the right of *Click to Add*, click the arrow.

3 In the field names row, click anywhere in the text *Click to Add* to display a list of data types. Compare your screen with Figure 1.8.

Data type is the characteristic that defines the kind of data that you can type in a field, such as numbers, text, or dates. A field in a table can have only one data type. Part of your database design should include deciding on the data type of each field. After you have selected the data type, you can name the field.

Figure 1.8

Click to display data types

Navigation Pane closed

List of data types

4 In the list of data types, click **Text**, and notice that in the second column, *Click to Add* changes to *Field1*, which is selected. Type **Last Name** and then press Enter.

The second column displays *Last Name* as the field name, and the data type list displays in the third column. The **Text data type** describes text, a combination of text and numbers, or numbers that are not used in calculations, such as a ZIP code.

Another Way
With the list of data types displayed, type *T* to select Text.

5 In the third field name box, click **Text**, type **First Name** and then press Enter. In the fourth field name box, click **Text**, type **Middle Initial** and then press Enter.

6 Using the technique you just practiced, create the remaining fields as follows by first selecting the data type, then typing the field name, and then pressing Enter. The field names in the table will display on one line.

The ZIP/Postal Code field is assigned a data type of Text because the number is never used in a calculation. The Amount Owed field is assigned a data type of Currency; the **Currency data type** describes monetary values and numeric data used in mathematical calculations involving data with one to four decimal places. Access automatically adds a U.S. dollar sign ($) and two decimal places to all of the numbers in the fields with a data type of *Currency*.

Data Type		Text	Text	Text	**Text**	**Text**	**Text**	**Text**	**Text**	**Text**	**Text**	**Currency**
Field Name	ID	Last Name	First Name	Middle Initial	**Address**	**City**	**State/ Region**	**ZIP/Postal Code**	**Phone Number**	**E-mail**	**Faculty Advisor ID**	**Amount Owed**

7 If necessary, by using the horizontal scroll bar at the bottom of the screen, scroll to the left to bring the first column into view. Compare your screen with Figure 1.9.

Access automatically created the ID field, and you created 11 additional fields in the table. The horizontal scroll bar indicates that there are additional fields that are not displayed on the screen—your screen width may vary.

Access | Chapter 1

Figure 1.9

Twelve fields created—scroll
to the left to display *ID* and
Last Name fields

Activity 1.04 | Renaming Fields and Changing Data Types in a Table

Another Way

Right-click the field
name, and then on the
shortcut menu, click
Rename Field.

1 Click anywhere in the text *ID*. In the **Properties group**, click the **Name & Caption** button. In the **Enter Field Properties** dialog box, in the **Name** box, change *ID* to **Student ID** and then click **OK**.

The field name *Student ID* is a better description of the data in this field. In the Enter Field Properties dialog box, the *Caption* property is used to display a name for a field other than that listed as the field name. Many database designers do not use spaces in field names; instead, they might name a field LastName—with no spaces—and then create a caption for that field so it displays with spaces in tables, forms, and reports. In the Enter Field Properties dialog box, you can also provide a description for the field if you want to do so.

2 In the **Formatting group**, notice that the **Data Type** for the **Student ID** field is *AutoNumber*. Click the **Data Type arrow**, click **Text**, and then compare your screen with Figure 1.10.

In the new record row, the Student ID field is selected. By default, Access creates an ID field for all new tables and sets the data type for the field to AutoNumber. The *AutoNumber data type* describes a unique sequential or random number assigned by Access as each record is entered. By changing the data type of this field from *AutoNumber* to *Text*, you can enter a custom student ID number.

When records in a database have *no* unique value, for example the names in your address book, the AutoNumber data type is a useful way to automatically create a unique number so that you have a way to ensure that every record is different from the others.

Figure 1.10

Field renamed

New record row—indicated
by asterisk

Selected field

Data type indicates *Text*

Activity 1.05 | Adding a Record to a Table

A new address book is not useful until you fill it with names, addresses, and phone numbers. Likewise, a new database is not useful until you *populate* it—fill one or more tables with data. You can populate a table with records by typing data directly into the table.

Another Way

Press Tab to move to the next field.

1 In the new record row, click in the **Student ID** field to display the insertion point, type **1238765** and then press Enter. Compare your screen with Figure 1.11.

The pencil icon [✎] in the *record selector box*—the small box at the left of a record in Datasheet view that, when clicked, selects the entire record—indicates that a record is being entered or edited.

Figure 1.11

Pencil icon indicates record being entered or edited

Record selector box

First student ID is *1238765*

Insertion point in Last Name field

2 With the insertion point positioned in the **Last Name** field, type **Fresch** and then press Enter.

> **Note | Correct Typing Errors**
>
> Correct typing errors by using the techniques you have practiced in other Office applications. For example, use Backspace to remove characters to the left, Del to remove characters to the right, or select the text you want to replace and type the correct information. Press Esc to exit out of a record that has not been completely entered.

3 In the **First Name** field, type **Michael** and then press Enter.

4 In the **Middle Initial** field, type **B** and then press Enter.

5 In the **Address** field, type **7550 Douglas Ln** and then press Enter.

Do not be concerned if the data does not completely display in the column. As you progress in your study of Access, you will adjust the column widths so that you can view all of the data.

6 Continue entering data in the fields as indicated below, pressing Enter to move to the next field.

City	State/Region	ZIP/Postal Code	Phone Number	E-mail	Faculty Advisor ID
Alexandria	**VA**	**22336**	**(571) 555-0234**	**mfresch@capccc.edu**	**FAC-2289**

> **Note | Format for Typing Telephone Numbers in Access**
>
> Access does not require any specific format for typing telephone numbers in a database. The examples in this project use the format of Microsoft Outlook. Using such a format facilitates easy transfer of Outlook information to and from Access.

7 In the **Amount Owed** field, type **150** and then press [Enter]. Compare your screen with Figure 1.12.

> Pressing [Enter] or [Tab] in the last field moves the insertion point to the next row to begin a new record. As soon as you move to the next row, Access saves the record—you do not have to take any specific action to save a record.

Figure 1.12

First record entered and saved

Insertion point blinking in first field of new record row

8 To give your table a meaningful name, on the Quick Access Toolbar, click the **Save** button. In the **Save As** dialog box, in the **Table Name** box, using your own name, replace the highlighted text by typing **Lastname Firstname 1A Students**

> Save each database object with a name that identifies the data that it contains. When you save objects within a database, it is not necessary to use underscores. Your name is included as part of the object name so that you and your instructor can identify your printouts or electronic files.

9 In the **Save As** dialog box, click **OK**, and then notice that the object tab displays the new table name you just typed.

> **More Knowledge | Renaming a Table**
>
> To change the name of a table, close the table, display the Navigation Pane, right-click the table name, and then on the shortcut menu, click Rename. Type the new name or edit as you would any selected text.

Activity 1.06 | Adding Additional Records to a Table

1 In the new record row, click in the **Student ID** field, and then enter the contact information for the following two additional students, pressing [Enter] or [Tab] to move from field to field. The data in each field will display on one line in the table.

Student ID	Last Name	First Name	Middle Initial	Address	City	State/ Region	ZIP/ Postal Code	Phone Number	E-mail	Faculty Advisor ID	Amount Owed
2345677	Ingram	Joseph	S	1 Casa Del Sol	Potomac	MD	20854	(240) 555-0177	jingram@ capccc.edu	FAC-2377	378.5
3456689	Bass	Amanda	J	1446 Yellow Rose Ln	Fairfax	VA	22030	(703) 555-0192	abass@ capccc.edu	FAC-9005	0

2 Compare your screen with Figure 1.13.

Figure 1.13

Records for three students entered

Some fields out of view—your screen may vary in number of columns displayed

Activity 1.07 | Importing Data from an Excel Workbook into an Existing Access Table

When you create a database table, you can type the records directly into a table. You can also ***import*** data from a variety of sources. Importing is the process of copying data from one source or application to another application. For example, you can import data from a Word table or an Excel worksheet into an Access database because the data is arranged in columns and rows, similar to a table in Datasheet view.

In this activity, you will ***append***—add on—data from an Excel spreadsheet to your *1A Students* table. To append data, the table must already be created, and it must be closed.

1 In the upper right corner of the table, below the Ribbon, click the **Object Close** ⊠ button to close your **1A Students** table. Notice that no objects are open.

2 On the Ribbon, click the **External Data tab**. In the **Import & Link group**, click the **Excel** button. In the **Get External Data - Excel Spreadsheet** dialog box, click the **Browse** button.

> **Another Way**
>
> Select the file name, and in the lower right area of the dialog box, click Open.

3 In the **File Open** dialog box, navigate to your student files, locate and double-click the Excel file **a01A_Students**, and then compare your screen with Figure 1.14.

The path to the ***source file***—the file being imported—displays in the File name box. There are three options for importing data from an Excel workbook—import the data into a *new* table in the current database, append a copy of the records to an existing table, or link the data from Excel to a linked table. A ***link*** is a connection to data in another file. When linking, Access creates a table that maintains a link to the source data.

Figure 1.14

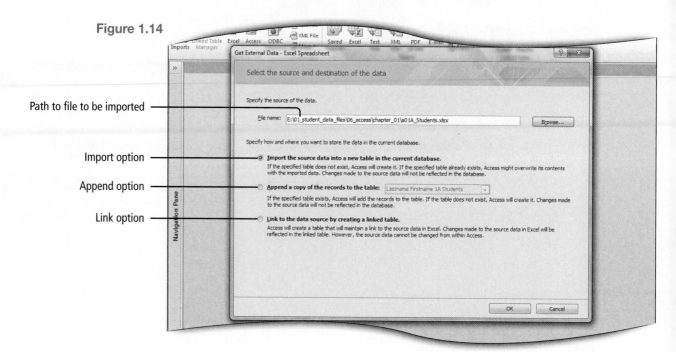

Path to file to be imported

Import option

Append option

Link option

4 Click the **Append a copy of the records to the table** option button, and then in the box to its right, click the **arrow**.

Currently your database has only one table, so no other tables display on the list. However, when a database has multiple tables, here you can select the table to which you want to append records. The table into which you import or append data is referred to as the *destination table*.

5 Press Esc to cancel the list, and then in the lower right corner of the dialog box, click **OK**. Compare your screen with Figure 1.15.

The first screen of the Import Spreadsheet Wizard displays, and the presence of scroll bars indicates that records and fields are out of view in this window. To append records from an Excel worksheet to an existing database table, the field names in the Excel worksheet must be identical to the field names in the table, and that is true in this table.

Figure 1.15

Field names in Excel sheet exactly match field names in Access table

Scroll bars indicate more data

6 In the lower right corner, click **Next**. Notice that the name of your table displays under **Import to Table**. In the lower right corner, click **Finish**.

7 In the **Get External Data - Excel Spreadsheet** dialog box, click **Close**, and then Open ⟫ the **Navigation Pane**.

8 Point to the right edge of the **Navigation Pane** to display the ⟷ pointer. Drag to the right to widen the pane to display the entire table name, and then compare your screen with Figure 1.16.

Figure 1.16

Table in the database

Width of Navigation Pane increased

Another Way

To open an object from the Navigation Pane, right-click the object name, and then on the shortcut menu, click Open.

9 In the **Navigation Pane**, double-click your **1A Students** table to open the table in Datasheet view, and then **Close** ⟪ the **Navigation Pane**.

10 At the bottom left corner of your screen, locate the navigation area, and notice that there are a total of **26** records in the table—you created three records and imported 23 additional records. Compare your screen with Figure 1.17.

The records from the Excel worksheet display in your table, and the first record is selected. The *navigation area* indicates the number of records in the table and contains controls (arrows) with which you can navigate among the records.

Figure 1.17

Three records you entered

26 total records

Navigation area

Current view indicated

Access | Chapter 1

Objective 3 | Change the Structure of Tables and Add a Second Table

Recall that the structure of a table is the underlying design, including field names and data types. You can create a table or modify a table in Datasheet view. To define and modify fields, many database experts prefer to work in Design view, where you have many additional options for defining the fields in a table.

Activity 1.08 | Deleting a Table Field in Design View

In this activity, you will delete the *Middle Initial* field from the table.

1 Click the **Home tab**, and then in the **Views group**, click the **View button arrow**.

There are four common views in Access, but two that you will use often are Datasheet view and Design view. On the displayed list, Design view is represented by a picture of a pencil, a ruler, and an angle. When one of these four icons is displayed on the View button, clicking the View button will display the table in the view represented by the icon. Datasheet view displays the table data in rows and columns.

2 On the list, click **Design View**, and then compare your screen with Figure 1.18.

Design view displays the underlying design—the structure—of the table and its fields. In Design view, you cannot view the data; you can view only the information about each field's characteristics. Each field name is listed, along with its data type. A column to add a Description—information about the data in the field—is provided.

In the Field Properties area, you can make additional decisions about how each individual field looks and behaves. For example, you can set a specific field size.

Figure 1.18

Delete Rows button

Data Type column

Field Name column

Row selector box for Middle Initial field

Space to add field description

Field Properties area

3 In the **Field Name** column, to the left of **Middle Initial**, point to the row selector box to display the ➡ pointer, and then click one time to select the entire row.

Another Way

Right-click the selected row and click Delete Rows.

4 On the **Design tab**, in the **Tools group**, click the **Delete Rows** button, read the message in the message box, and then click **Yes**.

Deleting a field deletes both the field and its data; you cannot undo this action. Thus, Access prompts you to be sure you want to proceed. If you change your mind after deleting a field, you must add the field back into the table and then reenter the data in that field for every record.

Activity 1.09 | Modifying a Field Size and Adding a Description

Typically, many individuals enter data into a table. For example, at your college many Registration Assistants enter and modify student and course information daily. Two ways to help reduce errors are to restrict what can be typed in a field and to add descriptive information.

1 With your table still displayed in **Design** view, in the **Field Name** column, click anywhere in the **State/Region** field name.

2 In the lower portion of the screen, under **Field Properties**, click **Field Size** to select the text *255*, type **2** and then compare your screen with Figure 1.19.

This action limits the size of the State/Region field to no more than two characters—the size of the two-letter state abbreviations provided by the United States Postal Service. *Field properties* control how the field displays and how data can be entered in the field. You can define properties for every field in the Field Properties area.

The default field size for a text field is 255. Limiting the field size property to 2 ensures that only two characters can be entered for each state. However, this does not prevent someone from entering two characters that are incorrect. Setting the proper data type for the field and limiting the field size are two ways to *help* to reduce errors.

Figure 1.19

State/Region field selected

Field Size indicates *2*

3 In the **State/Region** row, click in the **Description** box, type **Two-character state abbreviation** and then press Enter.

> Descriptions for fields in a table are optional. Include a description if the field name does not provide an obvious explanation of the field. Information typed in the description area displays on the left side of the status bar in Datasheet view when the field is active, providing additional information to individuals who are entering data.

> When you enter a description for a field, a Property Update Options button displays below the text you typed, which enables you to copy the description for the field to all other database objects that use this table as an underlying source.

4 Click in the **Student ID** field name box. Using the technique you practiced, in the **Field Properties** area, change the **Field Size** to **7**

> By limiting the field size to seven characters, which is the maximum number of characters in a Student ID, you help to ensure the accuracy of the data.

5 In the **Student ID** row, click in the **Description** box, and then type **Seven-digit Student ID number**

6 Click in the **Faculty Advisor ID** field name box. In the **Field Properties** area, change the **Field Size** to **8** In the **Description** box for this field, type **Eight-character ID of faculty member assigned as advisor** and then press Enter.

7 On the Quick Access Toolbar, click the **Save** button 🖫 to save the design changes to your table, and then notice the message.

> The message indicates that the field size property of one or more fields has changed to a shorter size. If more characters are currently present in the Student ID, State/Region, or Faculty Advisor ID than you have allowed, the data could be *truncated*—cut off or shortened—because the fields were not previously restricted to a specific number of characters.

8 In the message box, click **Yes**.

Activity 1.10 | Viewing a Primary Key in Design View

Primary key refers to the field in the table that uniquely identifies a record. For example, in a college registration database, your Student ID number uniquely identifies you—no other student at the college has your exact student number. In the 1A Students table, the Student ID uniquely identifies each student.

When you create a table using the Blank database command, by default Access designates the first field as the primary key field. It is good database design practice to establish a primary key for every table, because doing so ensures that you do not enter the same record more than once. You can imagine the confusion if another student at your college had the same Student ID number as you do.

1 With your table still displayed in Design view, in the **Field Name** column, click in the **Student ID** box. To the left of the box, notice the small icon of a key, as shown in Figure 1.20.

Access automatically designates the first field as the primary key field, but you can set any field as the primary key by clicking in the box to the left of the field name, and then clicking the Primary Key button.

Figure 1.20

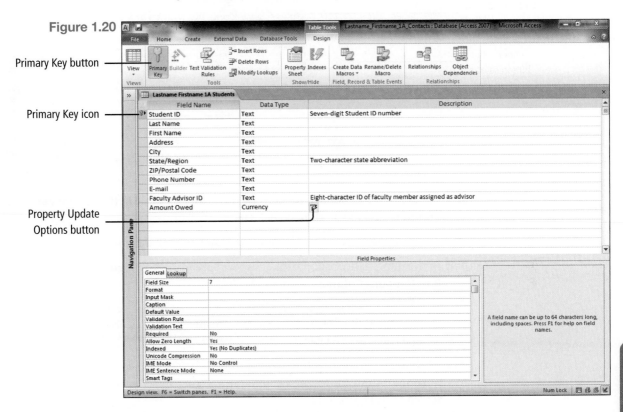

Primary Key button

Primary Key icon

Property Update Options button

2 On the **Design tab**, in the **Views group**, notice that the **View** button contains a picture of a Datasheet, indicating that clicking the button will return you to Datasheet view. Click the **View** button.

Activity 1.11 | Adding a Second Table to a Database by Importing an Excel Spreadsheet

Many Microsoft Office users track data in an Excel spreadsheet. The sorting and filtering capabilities of Excel are useful for a simple database where all the information resides in one large Excel spreadsheet. However, Excel is limited as a database management tool because it cannot *relate* the information in multiple spreadsheets in a way in which you could ask a question and get a meaningful result. Data in an Excel spreadsheet can easily become an Access table by importing the spreadsheet, because Excel's format of columns and rows is similar to that of an Access table.

1 On the Ribbon, click the **External Data tab**, and then in the **Import & Link group**, click the **Excel** button. In the **Get External Data – Excel Spreadsheet** dialog box, to the right of the **File name** box, click **Browse**.

2 In the **File Open** dialog box, navigate to your student files, and then double-click **a01A_Faculty**. Compare your screen with Figure 1.21.

Figure 1.21

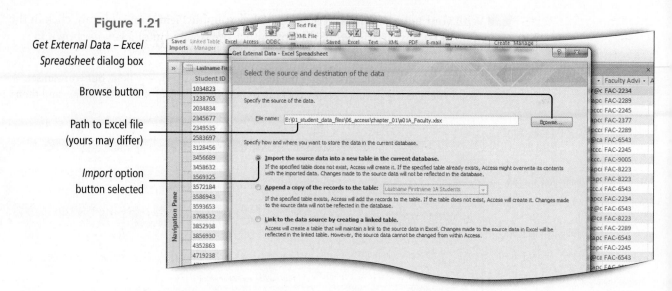

Get External Data – Excel Spreadsheet dialog box

Browse button

Path to Excel file (yours may differ)

Import option button selected

3 Be sure that the **Import the source data into a new table in the current database** option button is selected, and then click **OK**.

The Import Spreadsheet Wizard opens and displays the spreadsheet data.

4 In the upper left portion of the **Import Spreadsheet Wizard** dialog box, select the **First Row Contains Column Headings** check box.

The Excel data is framed, indicating that the first row of Excel column titles will become the Access table field names, and the remaining rows will become the individual records in the new Access table.

5 Click **Next**. Notice that the first column—*Faculty ID*—is selected, and in the upper portion of the Wizard, the **Field Name** and the **Data Type** display. Compare your screen with Figure 1.22.

Here you can review and change the field properties for each field (column). You can also identify fields in the spreadsheet that you do not want to import into the Access table by selecting the Do not import field (Skip) check box.

Figure 1.22

Import Spreadsheet Wizard dialog box

Excel column titles

Spreadsheet data—Excel rows become records

Next button

6 Click **Next**. In the upper portion of the Wizard, click the **Choose my own primary key** option button, and then be sure that **Faculty ID** displays.

> In the new table, Faculty ID will be the primary key. No two faculty members have the same Faculty ID. By default, Access selects the first field as the primary key, but you can click the arrow to select a different field.

7 Click **Next**. In the **Import to Table** box, type **Lastname Firstname 1A Faculty** and then click **Finish**.

8 In the **Get External Data – Excel Spreadsheet** dialog box, click **Close**, and then **Open** the **Navigation Pane**.

9 In the **Navigation Pane**, double-click your **1A Faculty** table to open it in Datasheet view, and then **Close** the **Navigation Pane**.

10 Click in the **ZIP/Postal Code** field, and then on the Ribbon, click the **Fields tab**. In the **Formatting group**, change the **Data Type** to **Text**. Compare your screen with Figure 1.23.

> The data from the *a01A_Faculty* worksheet displays in your *1A Faculty* table in the database. The navigation area indicates that there are 30 records in the table. Recall that if a field contains numbers that are not used in calculations, the data type should be set to Text. When you import data from an Excel spreadsheet, check the data types of all fields to ensure they are correct.

Figure 1.23

ZIP/Postal Code data type changed to Text

Table created by importing Excel spreadsheet

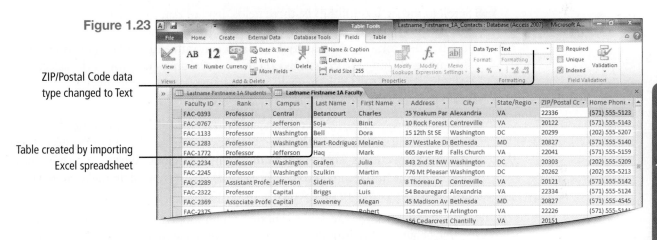

Activity 1.12 | Adjusting Column Widths

By using techniques similar to those you use for Excel worksheets, you can adjust the widths of Access fields that display in Datasheet view.

1 In the object window, click the **object tab** for your **1A Students** table.

> Clicking the object tabs along the top of the object window enables you to display open objects to work with them. All of the columns are the same width regardless of the amount of data in the field, the field size that was set, or the length of the field name. If you print the table as currently displayed, some of the data or field names will not fully print until you adjust the column widths.

2 In the field names row, point to the right edge of the **Address** field to display the ⬌ pointer, and then compare your screen with Figure 1.24.

Figure 1.24

Pointer positioned on right edge of Address field

3 With your ⬌ pointer positioned as shown in Figure 1.24, double-click the right edge of the **Address** field.

> The column width of the Address field widens to fully display the longest entry in the field. In this manner, the width of a column can be increased or decreased to fit its contents in the same manner as a column in an Excel worksheet. In Access this is referred to as *Best Fit*.

4 Point to the **Phone Number** field name to display the ⬇ pointer, right-click to select the entire column and display a shortcut menu, and then click **Field Width**. In the **Column Width** dialog box, click **Best Fit**.

5 Scroll to the right until the last three fields display. Point to the **E-mail** field name to display the ⬇ pointer, hold down the left mouse button, and then drag to the right to select this column, the **Faculty Advisor ID** column, and the **Amount Owed** column. By double-clicking the ⬌ pointer on the right boundary of any of the selected columns, or by displaying the Field Width dialog box from the shortcut menu, apply **Best Fit** to the selected columns.

6 Scroll all the way to the left to view the **Student ID** field. To the left of the *Student ID* field name, click the **Select All** button ⬜. Click the **Home tab**, and in the **Records group**, click the **More** button. Click **Field Width**, and in the **Column Width** dialog box, click **Best Fit**. In the first record, scroll to the right as necessary, click in the **Amount Owed** field, and then compare your screen with Figure 1.25.

> In this manner, you can adjust all of the column widths at one time. After applying Best Fit, be sure to click in any field to remove the selection from all of the records; otherwise, the layout changes will not be saved with the table. Adjusting the width of columns does not change the data in the table's records; it changes only the *display* of the data.

Figure 1.25

Select All button

More button

City	State/Region	ZIP/Postal Code	Phone Number	E-mail	Faculty Advisor ID	Amount Owed	Click to Add
Rockville	MD	20857	(301) 555-2320	jbarthmaier@capccc.edu	FAC-2234	$3,210.00	
Alexandria	VA	22336	(571) 555-0234	mfresch@capccc.edu	FAC-2289	$150.00	
Arlington	VA	22226	(571) 555-2017	ltelfer@capccc.edu	FAC-2245	$402.50	
Potomac	MD	20854	(240) 555-0177	jingram@capccc.edu	FAC-2377	$378.50	
Alexandria	VA	22336	(571) 555-0302	avohra@capccc.edu	FAC-2289	$0.00	
Alexandria	VA	22336	(571) 555-0305	cmcelaney@capccc.edu	FAC-6543	$15.15	
Vienna	VA	22180	(703) 555-2329	wwall@capccc.edu	FAC-2245	$0.00	
Fairfax	VA	22030	(703) 555-0192	abass@capccc.edu	FAC-9005	$0.00	
West Springfield	VA	22152	(703) 555-2330	scaputo@capccc.edu	FAC-8223	$0.00	
Alexandria	VA	22334	(703) 555-0301	cthomas@capccc.edu	FAC-8223	$0.00	
Fairfax	VA	22031	(571) 555-2026	creid@capccc.edu	FAC-6543	$1,232.00	
Washington	DC	20262	(202) 555-9360	jstavish@capccc.edu	FAC-2234	$26.25	
Alexandria	VA	22302	(703) 555-0301	ahernandez@capccc.edu	FAC-6543	$896.25	
Manassas			(703) 555-1017	ralexander@capccc.edu	FAC-8223	$0.00	
				amorris@capccc.edu	FAC-2289		

> **Note** | Adjusting Column Widths
>
> If you adjust column widths individually, scroll to the right and scroll down to be sure that all of the data displays in all of the fields. Access adjusts the column widths to fit the screen size based on the displayed data. If data is not displayed on the screen when you adjust a column width, the column may not be adjusted adequately to display all of the data in the field. For that reason, select all of the columns and apply Best Fit to be sure that all of the data displays when scrolling or printing. Click in any field after applying Best Fit to remove the selection, and then save the table before performing other tasks.

7 On the Quick Access Toolbar, click the **Save** button 🖫 to save the table design changes—changing the column widths.

> If you do not save the table after making design changes, Access will prompt you to save when you close the table.

Activity 1.13 | Printing a Table

Although a printed table does not look as professional as a printed report, there are times when you will want to print a table. For example, you may need a quick reference or want to proofread the data that has been entered.

1 On the Ribbon, click the **File tab** to display **Backstage** view, click the **Print** tab, click **Print Preview**, and then compare your screen with Figure 1.26.

Figure 1.26

Print Preview window

Navigation Pane

Next Page button

Page 1 displays

Navigation area—used to move from page to page

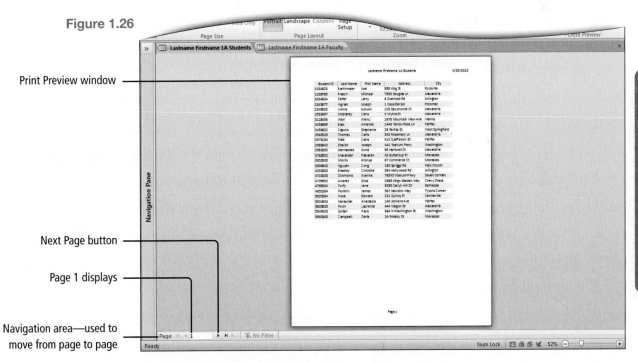

2 In the lower left corner, click the **Next Page** button ▶ two times. Point to the top of the page to display the 🔍 pointer, click one time to zoom in, and then compare your screen with Figure 1.27.

> The display enlarges, and the Zoom Out pointer displays. The third page of the table displays the last two field columns. The Next Page button is dimmed, indicating there are no more pages. The Previous Page button is darker, indicating that pages exist before this page.

Figure 1.27

Zoom Out pointer

Last two fields display
on a third page

Page 3 displays

Previous page button

Another Way
Click the 🔍 pointer
to zoom back to Fit to
Window view.

3 On the Ribbon, in the **Zoom group**, click the **Zoom** button to zoom back to Fit to
Window view.

4 In the **Page Layout group**, click the **Landscape** button. In the navigation area, click
the **Previous Page** button ◀ to display **Page 1**, and then compare your screen
with Figure 1.28.

The orientation of the printout changes, the table name and current date display at the
top of the page, and the page number displays at the bottom. The change in orientation
from portrait to landscape is not saved with the table. Each time you print, you must
check the margins, page orientation, and other print parameters to print as you intend.

Figure 1.28

Landscape button

First page displays in
landscape orientation

5 On the **Print Preview tab**, in the **Print group**, click the **Print** button. In the **Print** dialog box, under **Print Range**, verify that the **All** option button is selected. Under **Copies**, verify that the **Number of Copies** is **1**. Compare your screen with Figure 1.29.

Figure 1.29

Print dialog box

Default printer (yours may differ)

One copy

Print all pages

6 Determine how your instructor wants you to submit your work for this project—on paper or electronically. If submitting electronically, determine if, in addition to submitting your Access database, you are to create and submit electronic printouts of individual database objects.

7 To print on paper, in the **Print** dialog box, click **OK**, and then in the **Close Preview group**, click the **Close Print Preview** button. This printout will have two pages. To create an electronic PDF printout of this table object, in the Print dialog box, click Cancel, and then follow the steps in the following Note—or follow the specific directions provided by your instructor.

> **Note** | To Create a PDF Electronic Printout of an Access Object
>
> Display the object (table, report, and so on) in Print Preview and adjust margins and orientation as desired. On the Print Preview tab, in the Data group, click the PDF or XPS button. In the Publish as PDF or XPS dialog box, navigate to your chapter folder. Use the default file name, or follow your instructor's directions to name the object. In the lower right corner, click Publish—the default setting is PDF. If necessary, close the Adobe Acrobat/Reader window and the Export-PDF dialog box. Click the Close Print Preview button; your electronic printout is saved.

8 At the far right edge of the object window, click the **Close Object** button ☒ to close the **1A Students** table.

9 With your **1A Faculty** table displayed, to the left of the **Faculty ID** field name, click the **Select All** button ☐ to select all of the columns. On the **Home tab**, in the **Records group**, click the **More** button. Click **Field Width**, and in the **Column Width** dialog box, click **Best Fit**. Click in any field in the table to remove the selection, and then **Save** 🖫 the table.

Access | Chapter 1

10 Display the table in **Print Preview**. Change the **Orientation** to **Landscape**. If directed to do so by your instructor, create a paper or electronic printout, and then **Close Print Preview**—two pages result.

11 Click the **Close Object** button [×].

All of your database objects—the *1A Students* table and the *1A Faculty* table—are closed; the object window is empty.

Objective 4 | Create and Use a Query, Form, and Report

A *query* is a database object that retrieves specific data from one or more database objects—either tables or other queries—and then, in a single datasheet, displays only the data that you specify. Because the word *query* means *to ask a question*, think of a query as a question formed in a manner that Access can answer.

A *form* is an Access object with which you can enter data, edit data, or display data from a table or a query. In a form, the fields are laid out in an attractive format on the screen, which makes working with the database easier for those who must enter and look up data.

A *report* is a database object that displays the fields and records from a table or a query in an easy-to-read format suitable for printing. Create reports to *summarize* information in a database in a professional-looking manner.

Activity 1.14 | Using the Simple Query Wizard to Create a Query

A *select query* is one type of Access query. A select query, also called a *simple select query*, retrieves (selects) data from one or more tables or queries and then displays the selected data in a datasheet. A select query creates subsets of data to answer specific questions; for example, *Which students live in Arlington, VA?*

The objects from which a query selects its data are referred to as the query's *data source*. In this activity, you will create a simple select query using a *wizard*. A wizard is a feature in Microsoft Office programs that walks you step by step through a process. The process involves choosing the data source, and then indicating the fields you want to include in the query result. The query—the question that you want to ask—is *What is the name, complete mailing address, and Student ID of every student?*

1 Click the **Create tab**, and then in the **Queries group**, click the **Query Wizard** button. In the **New Query** dialog box, click **Simple Query Wizard**, and then click **OK**. Compare your screen with Figure 1.30.

Figure 1.30

Simple Query Wizard dialog box

Tables/Queries arrow

Add Field button

No database objects display in object window—all are closed

2 Click the **Tables/Queries arrow**, and then click your **Table: 1A Students**.

> To create a query, first choose the data source—the object from which to select data. The name and complete mailing address of every student is stored in the 1A Students table, so this table will be your data source.

3 Under **Available Fields**, click **Student ID**, and then click the **Add Field** button **>** to move the field to the **Selected Fields** list on the right. Point to the **Last Name** field, and then double-click to add the field to the **Selected Fields** list.

> Use either method to add fields to the Selected Fields list. Fields can be added in any order.

4 By using the **Add Field** button **>** or by double-clicking the field name, add the following fields to the **Selected Fields** list: **First Name**, **Address**, **City**, **State/Region**, and **ZIP/Postal Code**. Compare your screen with Figure 1.31.

> Choosing these seven fields will answer the question, *What is the Student ID, name, and address of every student?*

Figure 1.31

Data source—1A Students table

Seven fields added to Selected Fields list

Next button

5 Click **Next**. In the **Simple Query Wizard** dialog box, click in the **What title do you want for your query?** box. Edit as necessary so that the query name, using your own last and first name, is **Lastname Firstname 1A All Students Query** and then compare your screen with Figure 1.32.

Figure 1.32

Name of query

Open the query to view information option button selected

Finish button

6 Click **Finish**.

Access *runs* the query—performs the actions indicated in your query design by searching the records in the data source you selected, and then finding the records that match specified criteria. The records that match the criteria display in a datasheet. A select query *selects*—pulls out and displays—*only* the information from the data source that you requested, including the specified fields.

In the object window, Access displays every student record in Datasheet view, but displays *only* the seven fields that you moved to the Selected Fields list in the Simple Query Wizard dialog box.

7 If necessary, apply Best Fit to the columns and then Save the query. Display the query in **Print Preview**. Change the **Orientation** to **Landscape**, and then create a paper or electronic printout as instructed. **Close** the **Print Preview**.

8 In the object window, click the **Close Object** button [X] to close the query.

Activity 1.15 | Creating and Printing a Form

One type of Access form displays only one record in the database at a time. Such a form is useful not only to the individual who performs the data entry—typing in the actual records—but also to anyone who has the job of viewing information in a database. For example, when you visit the Records office at your college to obtain a transcript, someone displays your record on a screen. For the viewer, it is much easier to look at one record at a time, using a form, than to look at all of the student records in the database table.

The Form command on the Ribbon creates a form that displays all of the *fields* from the underlying data source (table)—one record at a time. You can use this new form immediately, or you can modify it. Records that you create or edit in a form are automatically added to or updated in the underlying table or tables.

1 **Open** >> the **Navigation Pane**. Increase the width of the **Navigation Pane** so that all object names display fully. Notice that a table displays a datasheet icon, and a query displays an icon of two overlapping datasheets. Right-click your **1A Students** table to display a menu as shown in Figure 1.33.

Figure 1.33

Navigation Pane Close button

Table icon

1A Students table

Query icon

Shortcut menu

2 On the shortcut menu, click **Open** to display the table in the object window, and then **Close** << the **Navigation Pane** to maximize your object space.

3 Scroll to the right, and notice that there are 11 fields in the table. On the **Create tab**, in the **Forms group**, click the **Form** button. Compare your screen with Figure 1.34.

Access creates a form based on the currently selected object—the 1A Students table. Access creates the form in a simple top-to-bottom format, with all 11 fields in the record lined up in a single column.

The form displays in *Layout view*—the Access view in which you can make changes to a form or to a report while the object is open. Each field displays the data for the first student record in the table—*Joel Barthmaier*.

Figure 1.34

Form object icon

First record, for *Joel Barthmaier*, displays

Layout View button active

Next record button

Total number of records is 26

Navigation buttons to move among records

Access | Chapter 1

4 At the right edge of the status bar, notice that the **Layout View** button ▤ is active, indicating that the form is displayed in Layout view.

Another Way

On the Home tab, in the Views group, click the View button, which displays an icon of a form.

5 At the right edge of the status bar, click the **Form View** button ▦.

In *Form view*, you can view the records, but you cannot change the layout or design of the form.

6 In the navigation area, click the **Next record** button ▶ three times. The fourth record—for *Joseph Ingram*—displays.

You can use the navigation buttons to scroll among the records to display any single record.

7 **Save** 💾 the form with the default name—*Lastname Firstname 1A Students*. Along the left edge of the record, under ▶, click anywhere in the narrow gray bar—the *record selector bar*—to select only the record for *Joseph Ingram*. Notice that the bar turns black, indicating that the record is selected.

8 To print the form for *Joseph Ingram* only, click the **File tab**, and then click **Print**—do *not* display Print Preview. Instead, click **Print**. In the **Print** dialog box, in the lower left corner, click **Setup**. Click the **Columns tab**, change the **Width** to **7.5** so that the form prints on one page, and then click **OK**. The maximum column width that you can enter is dependent upon the printer that is installed on your system. In the lower left corner of the **Print** dialog box, click the **Selected Record(s)** option button, and then click **OK**.

> **Note** | To Print a Single Form in PDF
>
> To create a PDF electronic printout of a single record in a form, change the column width to 7.5 as described in step 8 above, and then in the Print dialog box, click Cancel. On the left edge of the form, click the Record Selector bar so that it is black—selected. On the Ribbon click the External Data tab. In the Export group, click the PDF or XPS button. Navigate to your chapter folder, and then in the lower left corner of the dialog box, if necessary, select the Open file after publishing check box. In the lower right corner of the dialog box, click the Options button. In the Options dialog box, under Range, click the Selected records option button, click OK, and then click Publish. Close the Adobe Reader or Acrobat window.

9 **Close** ✕ the form. Notice that your **1A Students** table remains open.

Activity 1.16 | Creating, Modifying, and Printing a Report

1 **Open** ⟫ the **Navigation Pane**, and then open your **1A Faculty** table by double-clicking the table name or by right-clicking and clicking Open from the shortcut menu. **Close** ⟪ the **Navigation Pane**.

2 Click the **Create tab**, and then in the **Reports group**, click the **Report** button.

When you click the Report button, Access generates the report in Layout view and includes all of the fields and all of the records in the table, and does so in a format suitable for printing. Dotted lines indicate how the report would break across pages if you print it. In Layout view, you can make quick changes to the report layout.

Another Way

Right-click the field. From the shortcut menu, click Select Entire Column, and then press [Del].

3 Click the **Faculty ID** field name, and then on the Ribbon, click the **Arrange tab**. In the **Rows & Columns group**, click the **Select Column** button, and then press [Del]. Using the same technique, delete the **Rank** field.

The Faculty ID and Rank fields and data are deleted, and the report readjusts the fields.

4 Click the **Address** field name, and then use the scroll bar at the bottom of the screen to scroll to the right to display the **Mobile Phone** field; be careful not to click in the report. Hold down [Shift] and then click the **Mobile Phone** field name to select all of the fields from *Address* through *Mobile Phone*. With all the field names selected—surrounded by a colored border—in the **Row & Columns group**, click the **Select Column** button, and then press [Del].

Use this technique to select and delete multiple columns in Layout view.

5 Scroll to the left, and notice that you can see all of the remaining fields. In any record, click in the **E-mail** field. Point to the right edge of the field box to display the ↔ pointer. Drag to the right slightly to increase the width of the field so that all E-mail addresses display on one line.

6 Click the **Last Name** field name. On the Ribbon, click the **Home tab**. In the **Sort & Filter group**, click the **Ascending** button. Compare your screen with Figure 1.35.

By default, tables are sorted in ascending order by the primary key field, which is the Faculty ID field. You can change the default and sort any field in either ascending order or descending order. The sort order does not change in the underlying table, only in the report.

Figure 1.35
Ascending button selected

Four fields display in report

Report sorted by Last Name field

E-mail addresses display on one line

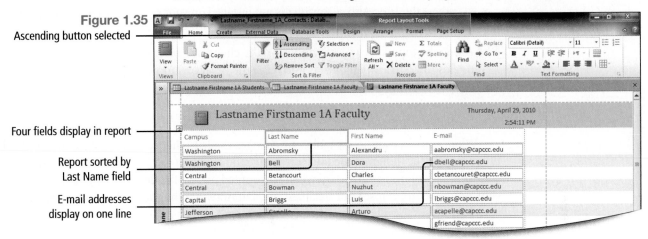

7 Click the **Save** button 🖫. In the **Report Name** box, add **Report** to the end of the suggested name, and then click **OK**.

8 Display the report in **Print Preview**. In the **Zoom group**, click the **Two Pages** button, and then compare your screen with Figure 1.36.

The report will print on two pages because the page number at the bottom of the report is located beyond the right margin of the report.

Figure 1.36

Two Pages button

Page number at bottom of second page

Access | Chapter 1

9 In the **Close Preview group**, click the **Close Print Preview button**. Scroll down to the bottom of the report, and then scroll to the right to display the page number. Click the page number—**Page 1 of 1**—and then press (Del).

10 Display the report in **Print Preview** and notice that the report will print on one page. In the **Zoom group**, click the **One Page** button. **Save** 🖫 the changes to the design of the report, and then create a paper or electronic printout as instructed. At the right end of the Ribbon, click the **Close Print Preview** button.

> The default margins of a report created with the Report tool are 0.25 inch. Some printers require a greater margin so your printed report may result in two pages—you will learn to adjust this later. Also, if a printer is not installed on your system, the report may print on two pages.

11 Along the top of the object window, right-click any object tab, and then click **Close All** to close all of the open objects and leave the object window empty.

Objective 5 | Save and Close a Database

When you close an Access table, any changes made to the records are saved automatically. If you change the design of the table or change the layout of the Datasheet view, such as adjusting the column widths, you will be prompted to save the design changes. At the end of your Access session, close your database and exit Access. If the Navigation Pane is open when you close Access, it will display when you reopen the database.

Activity 1.17 | Closing and Saving a Database

1 **Open** » the **Navigation Pane**. Notice that your report object displays with a green report icon. Compare your screen with Figure 1.37.

Figure 1.37

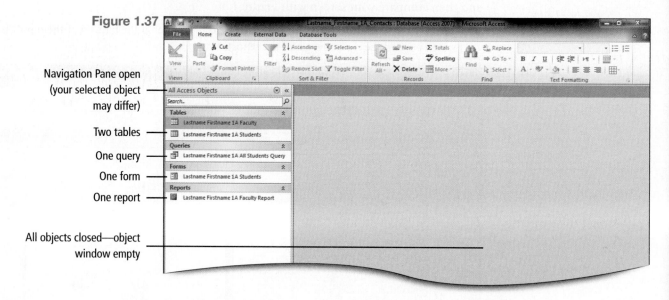

Navigation Pane open (your selected object may differ)

Two tables

One query

One form

One report

All objects closed—object window empty

> **Another Way**
> In the upper right corner of the window, click the Close button.

2 Display **Backstage** view, click **Close Database**, and then click **Exit**. As directed by your instructor, submit your database and the five paper or electronic printouts—two tables, one query, one form, and one report—that are the results of this project.

End You have completed Project 1A

Project 1B Student Workshops Database

myitlab
Project 1B Training

Project Activities

In Activities 1.18 through 1.23, you will assist Dr. Kirsten McCarty, Vice President of Student Services, by creating a database to store information about student workshops presented by Capital Cities Community College. You will use a database template that tracks event information, add workshop information to the database, and then print the results. Your completed report and table will look similar to Figure 1.38.

Project Files

For Project 1B, you will need the following files:

New Access database using the Events template
a01B_Workshops (Excel workbook)

You will save your database as:

Lastname_Firstname_1B_Student_Workshops

Project Results

Figure 1.38
Project 1B Student Workshops

Objective 6 | Create a Database Using a Template

A *database template* contains pre-built tables, queries, forms, and reports to perform a specific task, such as tracking a large number of events. For example, your college may hold events such as athletic contests, plays, lectures, concerts, and club meetings. Using a predefined template, your college Activities Director can quickly create a database to manage these events. The advantage of using a template to start a new database is that you do not have to create the objects—all you need to do is enter your data and modify the pre-built objects to suit your needs.

The purpose of the database in this project is to track the student workshops offered by Capital Cities Community College. The questions to be answered might include:

What workshops will be offered and when will they be offered?

In what rooms and campus locations will the workshops be held?

Which workshop locations have a computer projector for PowerPoint presentations?

Activity 1.18 | Creating a New Database Using a Template

1 **Start** Access. Under **Available Templates**, click **Sample templates**. If necessary, scroll down to locate and then click **Events**. Compare your screen with Figure 1.39.

> Sample templates are stored on your computer; they are included with the Access program.

Figure 1.39

Available Sample templates stored on computer

Events template

2 On the right side of the screen, to the right of the **File Name** box, click the **Browse** button, and then navigate to your **Access Chapter 1** folder.

3 At the bottom of the **File New Database** dialog box, select the text in the **File name** box. Using your own name, type **Lastname_Firstname_1B_Student_Workshops** and then press Enter.

4 In the lower right corner of your screen, click the **Create** button.

Access creates the *1B Student Workshops* database, and the database name displays in the title bar. A predesigned *form*—Event List—displays in the object window. Although you can enter events for any date, when you open the database in the future, the Event List will display only those events for the current date and future dates.

5 Under the Ribbon, on the **Message Bar**, a Security Warning displays. On the **Message Bar**, click the **Enable Content** button.

Databases provided by Microsoft are safe to use on your computer.

Activity 1.19 | Building a Table by Entering Records in a Multiple Items Form

The purpose of a form is to simplify the entry of data into a table—either for you or for others who enter data. In Project 1A, you created a simple form that enabled you to display or enter records in a table one record at a time. The Events template creates a *Multiple Items form*, a form that enables you to display or enter *multiple* records in a table, but still with an easier and simplified layout than typing directly into the table itself.

1 Click in the first empty **Title** field. Type **Your Cyber Reputation** and then press Tab. In the **Start Time** field, type **3/9/16 7p** and then press Tab.

Access formats the date and time. As you enter dates and times, a small calendar displays to the right of the field, which you can click to select a date instead of typing.

2 In the **End Time** field, type **3/9/16 9p** and then press Tab. In the **Description** field, type **Internet Safety** and then press Tab. In the **Location** field, type **Jefferson Campus** and then press Tab three times to move to the **Title** field in the new record row. Compare your screen with Figure 1.40.

Because the workshops have no unique value, Access uses the AutoNumber data type of the ID field to assign a unique, sequential number to each record. In the navigation area, each record is identified as a task, rather than a record or page.

Figure 1.40

Multiple items form named as *Event List*

AutoNumber data type creates a unique number

First record entered

Total line displays by default

Access formats date and time

3 Directly above the field names row, click **New Event**.

> A *single-record form* displays, similar to the simple form you created in Project 1A. A single-record form enables you to display or enter one record at a time into a table.

4 Using Tab to move from field to field, enter the following record—press Tab three times to move from the **End Time** field to the **Description** field. Compare your screen with Figure 1.41.

Title	Location	Start Time	End Time	Description
Writing a Research Paper	**Washington Campus**	**3/10/16 4p**	**3/10/16 6p**	**Computer Skills**

Figure 1.41

Save and New button

New Event button

Single-record form

Close button

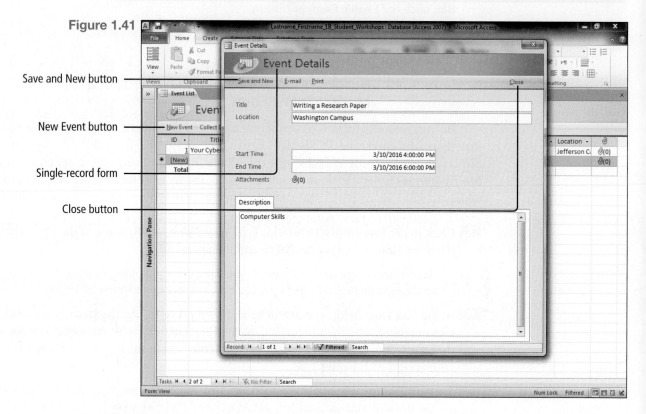

5 In the upper right corner of the single-record form, click **Close**, and notice that the new record displays in the Multiple Items form.

6 Using either the rows on the Multiple Items form or the New Event single-record form, enter the following records, and then compare your screen with Figure 1.42.

ID	Title	Start Time	End Time	Description	Location
3	**Resume Writing**	**3/18/16 2p**	**3/18/16 4p**	**Job Skills**	**Capital Campus**
4	**Careers in the Legal Profession**	**3/19/16 2p**	**3/19/16 4p**	**Careers**	**Central Campus**

> **Alert!** | **Does a Single Record Form Open?**
>
> In the Multiple Items form, pressing [Enter] three times at the end of a row to begin a new record may display the single-record New Event form. If you prefer to use the Multiple Items form, close the single-record form and continue entering records, using the [Tab] key to move from field to field.

Figure 1.42

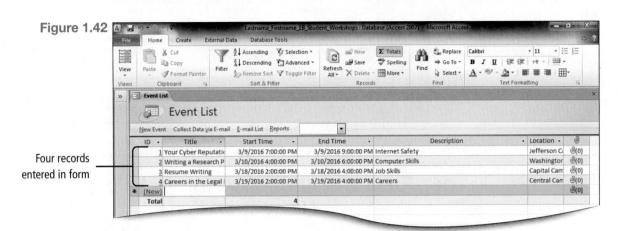

Four records entered in form

In the upper right corner of the object window, click **Close** [X] to close the **Event List** form.

On the Ribbon, click the **External Data tab**. In the **Import & Link group**, click the **Excel** button.

> Recall that you can populate a table by importing data from an Excel workbook.

In the **Get External Data – Excel Spreadsheet** dialog box, click the **Browse** button. Navigate to your student files, and then double-click **a01B_Workshops**.

Click the second option button—**Append a copy of the records to the table**—and then click **OK**.

Click **Next**, click **Finish**, and then **Close** the dialog box.

Open [»] the **Navigation Pane**. Double-click **Event List** to open the form that displays data stored in the Events table, and then **Close** [«] the **Navigation Pane**.

To the left of the **ID** field name, click the **Select All** button [ ] to select all of the columns.

> **Another Way**
>
> With the columns selected, in the field heading row, point to the right edge of any of the selected columns, and then double-click to apply Best Fit to all of the selected columns.

In the field names row, point to any of the selected field names, right-click, and then click **Field Width**. In the **Column Width** dialog box, click **Best Fit**. Notice that the widths of all of the columns are adjusted to accommodate the longest entry in the column.

In the first record, click in the **Title** field to deselect the columns. **Save** [ ] the form, and then compare your screen with Figure 1.43.

> Eight additional records display—those imported from the a01B_Workshops Excel workbook.

Figure 1.43

Eight additional records
imported from an
Excel workbook

Objective 7 | Organize Objects in the Navigation Pane

Use the Navigation Pane to organize database objects, to open them, and to perform common tasks like renaming an object.

Activity 1.20 | Organizing Database Objects in the Navigation Pane

The Navigation Pane groups and displays your database objects and can do so in predefined arrangements. In this activity, you will group your database objects using the *Tables and Related Views* category, which groups objects by the table to which they are related. This grouping is useful because you can easily determine the data source table of queries, forms, and reports.

1 Open [»] the **Navigation Pane**. At the top of the **Navigation Pane**, click the **Navigation arrow** [▼]. In the list, under **Navigate To Category**, click **Tables and Related Views**.

2 Confirm that *Events* displays in the bar under the Search box at the top of the **Navigation Pane**. Compare your screen with Figure 1.44.

The icons to the left of the objects listed in the Navigation Pane indicate that the Events template created a number of objects for you—among them, one table titled *Events*, one query, two forms, and five reports. The Event List Multiple Items form, which is currently displayed in the object window, is included in the Navigation Pane. All of the objects were created using the underlying data source, which is the Events table.

Figure 1.44

One table
One query
Two forms
Five reports

Another Way

Double-click the table name to open it in the object window.

→ **3** In the **Navigation Pane**, point to the **Events** *table*, right-click, and then click **Open**.

The Events table is the active object in the object window. Use the Navigation Pane to open objects for use. The 12 records that you entered using the Multiple Items *form* and by importing from an Excel workbook display in the *table*. Tables are the foundation of your database because your data must be stored in a table. You can enter records directly into a table or you can use a form to enter records.

4 In the object window, click the **Event List tab** to bring the form into view and make it the active object.

Recall that a form presents a more user-friendly screen for entering records into a table.

Another Way

Double-click the report name to open it.

→ **5** In the **Navigation Pane**, right-click the *report* (green icon) named **Current Events**, and then click **Open**. Compare your screen with Figure 1.45.

An advantage of using a template to begin a database is that many objects, such as attractively formatted reports, are already designed for you.

Figure 1.45

Three open objects

Current Events report preformatted and designed by the template

Current Events report in Navigation Pane

6 In the object window, **Close** ✕ the **Current Events** report.

7 From the **Navigation Pane**, open the **Events By Week** report.

In this predesigned report, the events are displayed by week. After entering records in the form or table, the preformatted reports are updated with the records from the table.

8 **Close** ✕ the **Events By Week** report, and then **Close** ✕ the remaining two open objects. **Close** « the **Navigation Pane**.

Access | Chapter 1

Objective 8 | Create a New Table in a Database Created with a Template

The Events database template created only one table—the *Events* table. Although the database was started from a template and contains other objects, you can add additional objects as needed.

Activity 1.21 | Creating a New Table and Changing Its Design

Dr. McCarty has information about the various locations where workshops are held. For example, for the Jefferson campus, she has information about the room, seating arrangements, number of seats, and audio-visual equipment. In the Events table, workshops are scheduled in rooms at each of the four campuses. It would not make sense to store information about the campus rooms multiple times in the same table. It is *not* considered good database design to have duplicate information in a table.

When data in a table becomes redundant, it is usually an indication that you need a new table to contain the information about the topic. In this activity, you will create a table to track the workshop locations and the equipment and seating arrangements in each location.

1 On the Ribbon, click the **Create tab**. In the **Tables group**, click the **Table** button.

2 Click the **Click to Add arrow**, click **Text**, type **Campus/Location** and then press Enter.

3 In the third column, click **Text**, type **Room** and then press Enter. In the fourth column, click **Text**, type **Seats** and then press Enter. In the fifth column, click **Text**, type **Room Arrangement** and then press Enter. In the sixth column, click **Text**, type **Equipment** and then press ↓.

The table has six fields. Access creates the first field in the table—the ID field—to ensure that every record has a unique value.

4 Right-click the **ID** field name, and then click **Rename Field**. Type **Room ID** and then press Enter. On the **Fields tab**, in the **Formatting group**, click the **Data Type arrow**, and then click **Text**. In the **Field Validation group**, notice that **Unique** is selected.

Recall that, by default, Access creates the ID field with the AutoNumber data type so that the field can be used as the primary key. Here, this field will store a unique room ID that is a combination of letters, symbols, and numbers, so it is appropriate to change the data type to Text. In Datasheet view, the primary key field is identified by the selection of the Unique check box.

5 In the new record row, click in the **Room ID** field, type **JEFF-01** and then press Tab. In the **Campus/Location** field, type **Jefferson Campus** and then press Tab. In the **Room** field, type **J123** and then press Tab. In the **Seats** field, type **150** and then press Tab. In the **Room Arrangement** field, type **Theater** and then press Tab. In the **Equipment** field, type **Computer Projector, Surround Sound, & Microphones** and then press Tab to move to the new record row. Compare your screen with Figure 1.46.

Recall that Access saves the record when you move to another row within the table. You can press either Tab or Enter to move to another field in a table.

Figure 1.46

New table
Renamed field
First record entered

Room ID field assigned data type of *Text*

Selected field—Room ID—indicated as primary key field

6 In the **Views group**, click the **View** button to switch to **Design** view. In the **Save As** dialog box, save the table as **Lastname Firstname 1B Workshop Locations** and then click **OK**.

7 In the **Field Name** column, to the left of the **Room ID** box, notice the key icon.

In Design view, the key icon indicates the field—Room ID—that is identified as the primary key.

8 In the **Views group**, click the **View** button to switch to **Datasheet** view.

9 Enter the following records in the table:

Room ID	Campus/Location	Room	Seats	Room Arrangement	Equipment
WASH-01	**Washington Campus**	**A15**	**35**	**Lecture/Classroom**	**Computer Projector**
CAP-01	**Capital Campus**	**C202**	**50**	**Lecture/Classroom**	**Smart Board**
CEN-01	**Central Campus**	**H248**	**20**	**U-shaped**	**White Board**
JEFF-02	**Jefferson Campus**	**A15**	**25**	**U-shaped**	**25 Computers, Projector**

10 To the left of the **Room ID** field name, click the **Select All** button ☐ to select all of the columns. On the **Home tab**, in the **Records group**, click the **More** button. Click **Field Width**, and in the **Column Width** dialog box, click **Best Fit**. Click in any field to remove the selection, and then **Save** 🖫 the changes to the table. In the object window, **Close** ☒ the **1B Workshop Locations** table.

11 Open ≫ the **Navigation Pane**, and then locate the name of your new table. Point to the right edge of the **Navigation Pane** to display the ↔ pointer. Drag to the right to display the entire table name, and then compare your screen with Figure 1.47.

Recall that as currently arranged, the Navigation Pane organizes the objects by Tables and Related Views. In Figure 1.47, the Events table is listed first, followed by its related objects, and then the Workshop Locations table is listed. In its current view, the tables are sorted in ascending order by name; therefore, your table may be listed before the Events table depending on your last name.

Figure 1.47

Navigation Pane
width increased

Section for Events table
and related objects

Section for Workshop
Locations table and
related objects
(your section and table
location may differ)

New table

Objective 9 | Print a Report and a Table in a Database Created with a Template

Recall that an advantage to starting a new database with a template, instead of from a blank database, is that many report objects are already created for you.

Activity 1.22 | Viewing and Printing a Report

1 From the **Navigation Pane**, open the **Event Details** *report* (not the form).

The pre-built Event Details report displays in an attractively arranged format.

2 **Close** ☒ the **Event Details** report. Open the **All Events** report. In the lower right corner of the status bar, click the **Layout View** button ⊞. At the top of the report, click on the text *All Events* to display a colored border, and then click to the left of the letter *A* to place the insertion point there. Using your own name, type **Lastname Firstname** and then press Spacebar. Press Enter, and then **Save** ⊟ the report.

Each report displays the records in the table in different useful formats.

Another Way

Right-click the object tab, and then click Print Preview.

3 Display **Backstage** view, click **Print**, and then click **Print Preview**. In the navigation area, notice that the navigation arrows are dimmed, which indicates that this report will print on one page.

4 Create a paper or electronic printout as instructed, **Close Print Preview**, and then **Close** ☒ the report.

Activity 1.23 | Printing a Table

When printing a table, use the Print Preview command to determine if the table will print on one page or if you need to adjust column widths, margins, or the orientation. Recall that there will be occasions when you want to print a table for a quick reference or for proofreading. For a more professional-looking format, and for more options to format the output, create and print a report.

1 From the **Navigation Pane**, open your **1B Workshop Locations** table. **Close** ⟪ the **Navigation Pane**. Display **Backstage** view, click **Print**, and then click **Print Preview**.

The table displays in the Print Preview window, showing how it will look when it is printed. The name of the table and the date the table is printed display at the top of the page. The navigation area displays *1* in the Pages box, and the right-pointing arrow—the Next Page arrow—is active. Recall that when a table is in the Print Preview window, the navigation arrows are used to navigate from one page to the next, rather than from one record to the next.

2 In the navigation area, click the **Next Page** button ▶.

The second page of the table displays the last field column. Whenever possible, try to print all of the fields horizontally on one page. Of course, if there are many records, more than one page may be needed to print all of the records.

3 On the **Print Preview tab**, in the **Page Layout group**, click the **Landscape** button, and then compare your screen with Figure 1.48. Notice that the entire table will print on one page.

Figure 1.48

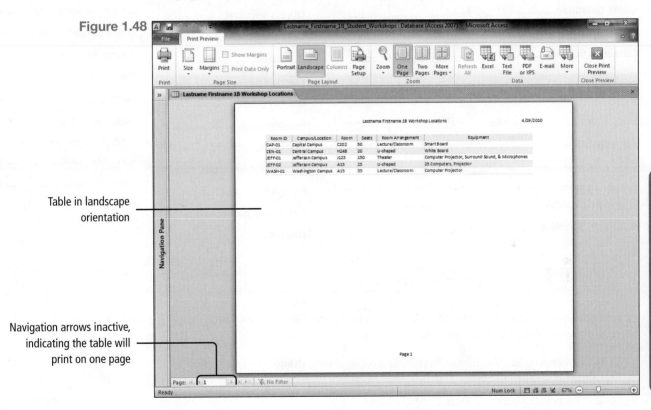

Table in landscape orientation

Navigation arrows inactive, indicating the table will print on one page

4 Create a paper or electronic printout if instructed to do so, and then **Close Print Preview**.

5 **Close** ✕ the **1B Workshop Locations** table. For the convenience of the next person opening the database, **Open** ≫ the **Navigation Pane**. In **Backstage** view, click **Close Database**, and then click **Exit** to close the Access program. As directed by your instructor, submit your database and the two paper or electronic printouts—one report and one table—that are the results of this project.

End **You have completed Project 1B** ————————————————

Content-Based Assessments

Summary

Microsoft Access 2010 is a database management system that uses various objects—tables, forms, queries, reports—to organize information. Data is stored in tables in which you establish fields, set the data type and field size, and create a primary key. Data from a database can be reported and printed.

Key Terms

Matching

Match each term in the second column with its correct definition in the first column by writing the letter of the term on the blank line in front of the correct definition.

_____ 1. An organized collection of facts about people, events, things, or ideas related to a specific topic.

_____ 2. Facts about people, events, things, or ideas.

_____ 3. Data that is organized in a useful manner.

_____ 4. A simple database file that is not related or linked to any other collection of data.

_____ 5. The database object that stores the data, and which is the foundation of an Access database.

_____ 6. A table row that contains all of the categories of data pertaining to one person, place, thing, event, or idea.

_____ 7. A single piece of information that is stored in every record and represented by a column in a table.

_____ 8. A principle stating that data is organized in tables so that there is no redundant data.

_____ 9. A principle stating that techniques are used to ensure the accuracy of data entered into a table.

A Common field

B Data

C Database

D Field

E First principle of good database design

F Flat database

G Information

H Navigation Pane

I Normalization

J Object window

K Objects

L Populate

M Record

N Second principle of good database design

O Table

Content-Based Assessments

_____ 10. The process of applying design rules and principles to ensure that a database performs as expected.

_____ 11. A field in one or more tables that stores the same data.

_____ 12. The basic parts of a database; for example tables, forms, queries, and reports.

_____ 13. The window area that organizes the database objects and from which you open objects.

_____ 14. The window area that displays each open object on its own tab.

_____ 15. The action of filling a database with records.

Multiple Choice

Circle the correct answer.

1. The Access view that displays data in columns and rows like an Excel worksheet is:
   - **A.** Datasheet view
   - **B.** Design view
   - **C.** Layout view

2. The characteristic that defines the kind of data you can enter into a field is the:
   - **A.** data source
   - **B.** data type
   - **C.** field property

3. The box at the left of a record in Datasheet view that you click to select an entire record is the:
   - **A.** link
   - **B.** navigation area
   - **C.** record selector box

4. To add on to the end of an object, such as to add records to the end of an existing table, is to:
   - **A.** append
   - **B.** import
   - **C.** run

5. Characteristics of a field that control how the field displays and how data is entered are:
   - **A.** data sources
   - **B.** data types
   - **C.** field properties

6. The field that uniquely identifies a record in a table is known as the:
   - **A.** attachments field
   - **B.** common field
   - **C.** primary key

7. The underlying design of a table is referred to as the:
   - **A.** caption
   - **B.** source file
   - **C.** structure

8. The object that retrieves specific data and then displays only the data that you specify is a:
   - **A.** form
   - **B.** query
   - **C.** report

9. The object that displays fields and records from a table or query in a printable format is a:
   - **A.** form
   - **B.** query
   - **C.** report

10. Information repeated in a database in a manner that indicates poor design is said to be:
    - **A.** relational
    - **B.** redundant
    - **C.** truncated

Apply 1A skills from these Objectives:

1 Identify Good Database Design

2 Create a Table and Define Fields in a New Database

3 Change the Structure of Tables and Add a Second Table

4 Create and Use a Query, Form, and Report

5 Save and Close a Database

Skills Review | Project 1C Work Study Students Database

In the following Skills Review, you will create a database to store information about the Work Study students and the divisions in which they are employed. Your completed database objects will look similar to Figure 1.49.

Project Files

For Project 1C, you will need the following files:

New blank Access database
a01C_Student_Workers (Excel workbook)
a01C_Divisions (Excel workbook)

You will save your database as:

Lastname_Firstname_1C_Student_Workers

Project Results

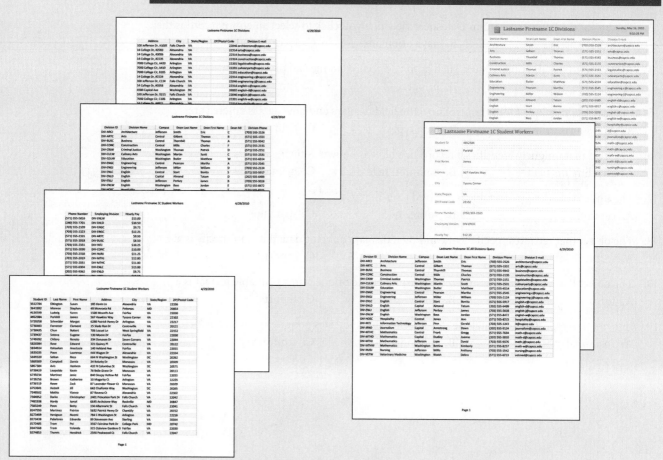

Figure 1.49

(Project 1C Work Study Students Database continues on the next page)

Content-Based Assessments

Skills Review | Project 1C Work Study Students Database (continued)

1 **Start** Access. Click **Blank database**, and then in the lower right corner, click the **Browse** button. In the **File New Database** dialog box, navigate to your **Access Chapter 1** folder, and then in the **File name** box, replace the existing text with **Lastname_Firstname_1C_Student_Workers** Press Enter, and then in the lower right corner, click **Create**.

a. **Close** the **Navigation Pane**. Click in the text *Click to Add*. Click **Text**, type **Last Name** and then press Enter.

b. In the third field name box, click **Text**, type **First Name** and then press Enter. In the fourth field name box, click **Text**, type **Middle Initial** and then press Enter. Create the remaining fields as shown in **Table 1**, pressing Enter after the last field name.

c. Scroll as necessary to view the first field. Click the **ID** field name. In the **Properties group**, click the **Name & Caption** button. In the **Enter Field Properties** dialog box, in the **Name** box, change *ID* to **Student ID** and then click **OK**. In the **Formatting group**, click the **Data Type arrow**, and then click **Text**.

d. In the first record row, click in the **Student ID** field, type **3512784** and press Enter. In the **Last Name** field, type **Elkington** In the **First Name** field, type **Susan** In the **Middle Initial** field, type **A** In the **Address** field, type **185 Kevin Ln**

e. Continue entering data in the fields as shown in **Table 2**, pressing Enter to move to the next field and to the next row.

f. Click **Save**, and then in the **Table Name** box, using your own name, replace the selected text by typing **Lastname Firstname 1C Student Workers** and then click **OK**.

2 Scroll, if necessary, to view the first field. In the new record row, click in the **Student ID** field, and then enter the information for two additional students as shown in **Table 3**, pressing Enter to move from field to field.

a. **Close** your **1C Student Workers** table. On the **External Data tab**, in the **Import & Link group**, click the **Excel** button. In the **Get External Data - Excel Spreadsheet** dialog box, click the **Browse** button. In the **File Open** dialog box, navigate to your student data files, and then double-click the **a01C_Student_Workers** Excel file.

b. **Append a copy of the records to the table**, and then click **OK**. Click **Next**, click **Finish**, and then click **Close**. **Open** the **Navigation Pane**, and then widen it so that you can view the entire table name. In the **Navigation Pane**, double-click your **1C Student Workers** table to open it, and then **Close** the **Navigation Pane**—30 total records display.

Table 1

Data Type					Text	Text	Text	Text	Text	Text	Currency
Field Name	ID	Last Name	First Name	Middle Initial	Address	City	State/Region	ZIP/Postal Code	Phone Number	Employing Division	Hourly Pay

(Return to Step 1-c)

Table 2

City	State/Region	ZIP/Postal Code	Phone Number	Employing Division	Hourly Pay
Alexandria	VA	22336	(571) 555-5816	DIV-ENLW	15

(Return to Step 1-f)

Table 3

Student ID	Last Name	First Name	Middle Initial	Address	City	State/Region	ZIP/Postal Code	Phone Number	Employing Division	Hourly Pay
3641892	Monroe	Stephen	D	48 Monrovia Rd	Potomac	MD	20854	(240) 555-7701	DIV-ENLD	10.5
4126598	Ludwig	Karen	E	1508 Moonlit Ave	Fairfax	VA	22030	(703) 555-2109	DIV-ENGC	9.75

(Return to Step 2-a)

(Project 1C Work Study Students Database continues on the next page)

Content-Based Assessments

3 Click the **Home tab**, and then in the **Views group**, click the **View** button to switch to **Design** view.

a. To the left of **Middle Initial**, point to the row selector box, and then click to select the entire row. On the **Design tab**, in the **Tools group**, click the **Delete Rows** button, and then click **Yes**.

b. Click anywhere in the **State/Region** field name, and then under **Field Properties**, set the **Field Size** to **2** In the **State/Region** row, click in the **Description** box, and then type **Two-character state abbreviation**

c. Click in the **Student ID** field name box, set the **Field Size** to **7** and in the **Description** box, type **Seven-digit Student ID** Then **Save** the design of your table; click **Yes**. On the **Design tab**, in the **Views group**, click the **View** button to switch to **Datasheet** view.

4 On the Ribbon, click the **External Data tab**, and then in the **Import & Link group**, click the **Excel** button. In the **Get External Data – Excel Spreadsheet** dialog box, click the **Browse** button. Navigate to your student data files, and then double-click **a01C_Divisions**. Be sure that the **Import the source data into a new table in the current database** option button is selected, and then click **OK**.

a. In the **Import Spreadsheet Wizard** dialog box, click to select the **First Row Contains Column Headings** check box, and then click **Next**.

b. Click **Next** again. Click the **Choose my own primary key** option button, and to the right, be sure that *Division ID* displays. Click **Next**. In the **Import to Table** box, type **Lastname Firstname 1C Divisions** and then click **Finish**. Click **Close**, **Open** the **Navigation Pane**, and then open your **1C Divisions** table. **Close** the **Navigation Pane**—22 records display.

c. At the top of the object window, click the **1C Student Workers tab**. To the left of the **Student ID** field name, click the **Select All** button. Click the **Home tab**, and in the **Records group**, click the **More** button. Click **Field Width**, and in the **Column Width** dialog box, click **Best Fit**. Click in any field, and then **Save** the table.

d. Display **Backstage** view, click **Print**, and then click **Print Preview**. In the **Page Layout group**, click the **Landscape** button. Create a paper or electronic printout as directed by your instructor; two pages result. Click **Close Print Preview**, and then **Close** your **1C Student Workers** table.

e. With your **1C Divisions** table displayed, to the left of the **Division ID** field name, click the **Select All** button, and then apply **Best Fit** to all of the columns. Click in any field, **Save** the table, and then display the table in **Print Preview**. Change the **Orientation** to **Landscape**. Create a paper or electronic printout as directed—two pages result. **Close Print Preview**, and then **Close** your **1C Divisions** table.

5 On the **Create tab**, in the **Queries group**, click the **Query Wizard** button. In the **New Query** dialog box, click **Simple Query Wizard**, and then click **OK**. Click the **Tables/Queries arrow**, and then be sure your **Table: 1C Divisions** is selected.

a. Under **Available Fields**, click **Division ID**, and then click the **Add Field** button to move the field to the **Selected Fields** list on the right. Using either the **Add Field** button or by double-clicking, add the following fields to the **Selected Fields** list: **Division Name, Campus, Dean Last Name, Dean First Name, Division Phone**, and **Division E-mail**. The query will answer the question, *What is the Division ID, Division Name, Campus, Dean's name, Division Phone number, and Division E-mail address of every division?*

b. Click **Next**. In the **Simple Query Wizard** dialog box, change the query title to **Lastname Firstname 1C All Divisions Query** and then click **Finish** to run the query.

c. Display the query in **Print Preview**. Change the **Orientation** to **Landscape**. In the **Page Size group**, click the **Margins** button, and then click **Normal**. Create a paper or electronic printout as directed—one page results. **Close Print Preview**, and then **Close** the query.

d. **Open** the **Navigation Pane**, open your **1C Student Workers** table, and then **Close** the **Navigation Pane**. The table contains 10 fields. On the **Create tab**, in the **Forms group**, click the **Form** button. Click **Save**, and then in the **Save As** dialog box, accept the default name for the form—*Lastname Firstname 1C Student Workers*—by clicking **OK**. In the navigation area, click the **Next record** button three times to display the record for *James Parkhill*. At the left edge of the form, click the gray **record selector bar** to select only this record. By using the instructions in Activity 1.15, print or create an electronic printout of this record as directed. **Close** the form object. Your **1C Student Workers** table object remains open.

(Project 1C Work Study Students Database continues on the next page)

Content-Based Assessments

Skills Review | Project **1C** Work Study Students Database (continued)

6 **Open** the **Navigation Pane**, open your **1C Divisions** table, and then **Close** the **Navigation Pane**. On the **Create tab**, in the **Reports group**, click the **Report** button. In the field names row at the top of the report, click the **Division ID** field name. On the Ribbon, click the **Arrange tab**. In the **Rows & Columns group**, click the **Select Column** button, and then press Del. Using the same technique, delete the **Campus** field.

a. Scroll to position the **Dean MI** field at the left of your screen, and click the field name **Dean MI**. Hold down Ctrl, and then click the field names for **Address**, **City**, **State/Region**, and **ZIP/Postal Code**. On the **Arrange tab**, in the **Rows & Columns group**, click the **Select Column** button, and then press Del.

b. Scroll to the left, and then click in the **Dean Last Name** field name. By using the ⟷ pointer, decrease the width of the field until there is about **0.25 inch** of space between the **Dean Last Name** field and the **Dean First Name** field. Decrease the widths of the **Dean First Name** and **Division Phone** fields in a similar manner. In the **Division E-mail** field, click in the first record—the data in the field displays on two lines. Increase the width of the field slightly so that each record's data in the field displays on one line. Be sure that the width of the report is within the dotted boundaries.

c. Click the **Division Name** field name. On the Ribbon, click the **Home tab**. In the **Sort & Filter group**, click the **Ascending** button to sort the report in alphabetic order by Division Name.

d. **Save** the report as **Lastname Firstname 1C Divisions Report** and then click **OK**. Display the report in **Print Preview**. In the **Zoom group**, click the **Two Pages** button, and notice that the report will print on two pages because the page number is beyond the right margin of the report. **Close Print Preview**. With the report displayed in **Layout** view, scroll down and to the right to display the page number— **Page 1 of 1**. Click the page number, press Del, and then **Save** the changes to the report.

e. Display the report in **Print Preview**, and notice that the report will print on one page. In the **Zoom group**, click the **One Page** button. Create a paper or electronic printout of the report as directed. Click **Close Print Preview**. Along the top of the object window, right click any **object tab**, and then click **Close All** to close all of the open objects, leaving the object window empty.

f. **Open** the **Navigation Pane**. If necessary, increase the width of the **Navigation Pane** so that all object names display fully. Display **Backstage** view, click **Close Database**, and then click **Exit**. As directed by your instructor, submit your database and the five paper or electronic printouts—two tables, one query, one form, and one report—that are the results of this project.

End **You have completed Project 1C**

Content-Based Assessments

Apply **1B** skills from these Objectives:

■ Create a Database Using a Template

■ Organize Objects in the Navigation Pane

■ Create a New Table in a Database Created with a Template

■ Print a Report and a Table in a Database Created with a Template

Skills Review | Project **1D** Benefits Events

In the following Skills Review, you will create a database to store information about Employee Benefit Events at Capital Cities Community College. Your completed report and table will look similar to Figure 1.50.

Project Files

For Project 1D, you will need the following files:

New Access database using the Events template
a01D_Benefits_Events (Excel workbook)

You will save your database as:

Lastname_Firstname_1D_Benefits_Events

Project Results

Figure 1.50

(Project 1D Benefits Events continues on the next page)

Content-Based Assessments

1 **Start** Access. Under **Available Templates**, click **Sample templates**, and then click **Events**. On the right, to the right of the **File Name** box, click the **Browse** button, and then navigate to your **Access Chapter 1** folder.

a. Select the text in the **File name** box, and then using your own information, type **Lastname_Firstname_1D_Benefits_Events** and then press Enter. In the lower right corner of your screen, click the **Create** button. If necessary, click Enable Content.

b. Click in the first empty **Title** field, type **Medical Plan** and then press Tab. In the **Start Time** field, type **5/2/16 8a** and then press Tab.

c. In the **End Time** field, type **5/2/16 1p** and then press Tab. In the **Description** field, type **Health Benefits** and then press Tab. In the **Location** field, type **Jefferson Campus** and then press Tab three times to move to the **Title** field in the new record row.

d. Directly above the field names row, click **New Event**, and then using Tab to move from field to field, enter the record shown in **Table 1** by using the single-record form, which is another way to enter records into a table.

e. **Close** the single-record form. Using either the rows on the Multiple Items form or the New Event single-record form, enter the records shown in **Table 2**.

f. **Close** the **Event List** form. On the Ribbon, click the **External Data tab**, and in the **Import & Link group**, click the **Excel** button. In the **Get External Data – Excel Spreadsheet** dialog box, click the **Browse** button. Navigate to your student data files, and then double-click **a01D_Benefits_Events**. Click the second option button—**Append a copy of the records to the table**—and then click **OK**.

g. Click **Next**, click **Finish**, and then **Close** the dialog box. **Open** the **Navigation Pane**, and then double-click **Event List** to open the form that displays data stored in the Events table—11 total records display.

2 At the top of the **Navigation Pane**, click the **Navigation arrow**. In the list, under **Navigate To Category**, click **Tables and Related Views**.

a. In the **Navigation Pane**, point to the **Events** *table*, right-click, and then click **Open** to display the records in the underlying table.

b. In the **Navigation Pane**, double-click the *report* named **Current Events** to view this predesigned report. From the **Navigation Pane**, open the **Events By Week** report to view this predesigned report.

c. **Close** the **Events By Week** report, and then **Close** the remaining three open objects. **Close** the **Navigation Pane**.

3 On the **Create tab**, in the **Tables group**, click the **Table** button.

a. Click the **Click to Add arrow**, click **Text**, type **Campus/Location** and then press Enter. In the third column, click **Text**, type **Room** and then press Enter. In the fourth column, click **Text**, type **Seats** and then press Enter. In the fifth column, click **Text**, type **Room Arrangement** and then press Enter. In the sixth column, click **Text**, type **Equipment** and then press ↓.

b. Right-click the **ID** field name, and then click **Rename Field**. Type **Room ID** and then press Enter. On the **Fields tab**, in the **Formatting group**, click the **Data Type arrow**, and then click **Text**.

c. In the new record row, click in the **Room ID** field, type **CAP-01** and then press Tab. In the **Campus/Location** field, type **Capital Campus** and then press Tab. In the **Room** field, type **C14** and then press Tab. In the **Seats** field, type **150** and then press Tab. In the **Room Arrangement** field, type **Theater** and then press Tab. In the **Equipment** field, type **Computer Projector, Surround Sound, & Microphones** and then press Tab to move to the new record row.

Table 1

Title	Location	Start Time	End Time	Description	
Eye Care Plan	Washington Campus	5/2/16 2p	5/2/16 4p	Health Benefits	---▶ (Return to Step 1-e)

Table 2

ID	Title	Start Time	End Time	Description	Location	
3	Prescription Plan	5/3/16 8a	5/3/16 10a	Health Benefits	Capital Campus	
4	Pension Plan	5/3/16 2p	5/3/16 4p	Retirement Benefits	Central Campus	---▶ (Return to Step 1-f)

(Project 1D Benefits Events continues on the next page)

Access | Chapter 1

Content-Based Assessments

d. In the **Views group**, click the **View** button to switch to **Design** view. In the **Save As** dialog box, save the table as **Lastname Firstname 1D Event Locations** and then click **OK**. Notice that the **Room ID** field is the **Primary Key**.

e. On the **Design tab**, in the **Views group**, click the **View** button to switch to **Datasheet** view. Enter the records in the table as shown in **Table 3**.

f. To the left of the **Room ID** field name, click the **Select All** button to select all of the columns. On the **Home tab**, in the **Records group**, click the **More** button. In the **Column Size** dialog box, click **Best Fit**.

g. Click in any record to cancel the selection of the columns, and then **Save** the table. **Open** the **Navigation Pane**, and then widen the pane to view the full names of all objects.

4 **Open** the **All Events** report, and then **Close** the **Navigation Pane**. In the lower right corner, click the **Layout View** button. At the top of the report, click the text *All Events* to surround the title with a colored border, and then click to the left of the letter *A* to place the insertion

point there. Using your own name, type **Lastname Firstname** and then press Spacebar and Enter. **Save** the report.

a. Display **Backstage** view, click **Print**, and then click **Print Preview**. Notice that the entire report will print on one page in portrait orientation. Create a paper or electronic printout if instructed to do so, and then click **Close Print Preview**. **Close** the **All Events** report.

b. With the **1D Event Locations** table open in **Datasheet** view, display **Backstage** view, click **Print**, and then click **Print Preview**. On the **Print Preview tab**, in the **Page Layout group**, click the **Landscape** button, and then notice that the entire table will print on one page.

c. Create a paper or electronic printout if instructed to do so, and then click **Close Print Preview**. **Close** the **1D Event Locations** table.

d. **Open** the **Navigation Pane**. Display **Backstage** view, click **Close Database**, and then click **Exit**. As directed by your instructor, submit your database and the two paper or electronic printouts—one report and one table—that are the results of this project.

Table 3

Room ID	Campus/Location	Room	Seats	Room Arrangement	Equipment
CEN-01	**Central Campus**	**H212**	**35**	**Lecture/Classroom**	**Computer Projector, 3 screens**
JEFF-01	**Jefferson Campus**	**J520**	**50**	**Lecture/Classroom**	**Smart Board**
WASH-01	**Washington Campus**	**A150**	**40**	**U-shaped**	**White Board & Computer Projector**
CEN-02	**Central Campus**	**C14**	**25**	**Computer Lab**	**25 Computers & Projector**

(Return to Step 3-f)

End **You have completed Project 1D**

Content-Based Assessments

1 Identify Good Database Design

2 Create a Table and Define Fields in a New Database

3 Change the Structure of Tables and Add a Second Table

4 Create and Use a Query, Form, and Report

5 Save and Close a Database

Mastering Access | Project **1E** Kiosk Inventory

In the following Mastering Access project, you will create a database to track information about the inventory of items for sale in the kiosk located on the quad at the Central Campus of Capital Cities Community College. Your completed database objects will look similar to those in Figure 1.51.

Project Files

For Project 1E, you will need the following files:

New blank Access database
a01E_Inventory (Excel workbook)
a01E_Inventory_Storage (Excel workbook)

You will save your database as:

Lastname_Firstname_1E_Inventory

Project Results

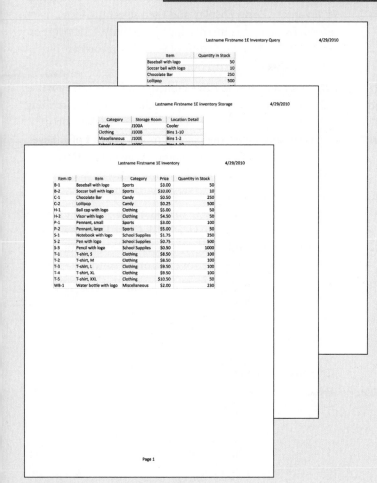

Figure 1.51

(Project 1E Kiosk Inventory continues on the next page)

Content-Based Assessments

Mastering Access | Project **1E** Kiosk Inventory (continued)

1 **Start** Access. Create a new **Blank database** in your **Access Chapter 1** folder. Name the database **Lastname_Firstname_1E_Inventory** and then **Close** the **Navigation Pane**. Create additional fields as shown in **Table 1**.

2 Change the **Data Type** of the **ID** field to **Text**, rename the field to **Item ID** and then enter the records as shown in **Table 2**.

3 **Save** the table as **Lastname Firstname 1E Inventory** and then **Close** the table. From your student data files, **Import** and then **Append** the **a01E_Inventory** Excel file to the **1E Inventory** table. Then, from the **Navigation Pane**, open your **1E Inventory** table—17 records display. Widen and then **Close** the **Navigation Pane**.

4 In **Design** view, delete the **Storage Location** field. Click in the **Category** field, change the **Field Size** to **25** and in the **Description** box, type **Enter the category of the Item** Click in the **Item ID** field, and then change the **Field Size** to **10 Save** the changes to the design of your table, click **Yes**, and then switch to **Datasheet** view. Apply **Best Fit** to all of the fields in the table, **Save** the table, and then display the table in **Print Preview**—one page results. Create a paper or electronic printout as directed by your instructor. **Close** the table.

5 From your student data files, **Import** the **a01E_Inventory_Storage** Excel file into the database as a new table; use the first row as the column headings and the **Category** field as the primary key. As the last step in the Wizard, name the table **Lastname Firstname 1E Inventory Storage** and then **Open** the **Navigation Pane**. **Open** your **1E Inventory Storage** table, and then **Close** the **Navigation Pane**. Display the new table in **Design** view, click in the **Location Detail** field, change the **Field Size** to

30 and then as the **Description**, type **Enter room and bin numbers or alternate location of inventory item**. In **Datasheet** view, apply **Best Fit** to all of the fields, **Save** the table, and then display the table in **Print Preview**. Create a paper or electronic printout as directed—one page results. **Close** the table.

6 **Create**, by using the **Query Wizard**, a **Simple Query** based on your **1E Inventory** table. Include only the fields that will answer the question *For all Items, what is the Quantity in Stock?* **Save** the query with the default name. Create a paper or electronic printout as directed and then **Close** the query.

7 Display the **1E Inventory** table, and then **Create** a **Form** for this table. **Save** the form as **Lastname Firstname 1E Inventory Form** Display and then select the fifth record. By using the instructions in Activity 1.15, print or create an electronic printout of only this record as directed. **Close** the form object.

8 With the **1E Inventory** table open, **Create** a **Report**. **Delete** the **Price** field, and then sort the records in **Ascending** order by the **Item ID** field. Scroll down to the bottom of the report and delete the page number—**Page 1 of 1**. **Save** the report as **Lastname Firstname 1E Inventory Report** and then create a paper or electronic printout as directed.

9 **Close All** open objects. **Open** the **Navigation Pane**. If necessary, widen the pane so that all of the object names display fully. In **Backstage** view, click **Close Database** and then click **Exit**. As directed by your instructor, submit your database and the five paper or electronic printouts—two tables, one query, one form, and one report—that are the results of this project.

Table 1

Data Type		Text	Text	Text	Currency	Number	
Field Name	ID	Item	Category	Storage Location	Price	Quantity in Stock	- - - ➤ (Return to Step 2)

Table 2

Item ID	Item	Category	Storage Location	Price	Quantity in Stock	
C-1	Chocolate Bar	Candy	J100A	.5	250	
C-2	Lollipop	Candy	J100A	.25	500	
T-1	T-shirt, S	Clothing	J100B	8.5	100	- - - ➤ (Return to Step 3)

End **You have completed Project 1E** ⎯⎯⎯⎯⎯⎯⎯⎯⎯⎯⎯⎯

Content-Based Assessments

Mastering Access | Project 1F Recruiting Events

In the following Mastering Access project, you will create a database to store information about the recruiting events that are scheduled to attract new students to Capital Cities Community College. Your completed report and table will look similar to those in Figure 1.52.

Project Files

For Project 1F, you will need the following files:

> New Access database using the Events template
> a01F_Recruiting_Events (Excel workbook)

You will save your database as:

> Lastname_Firstname_1F_Recruiting_Events

Project Results

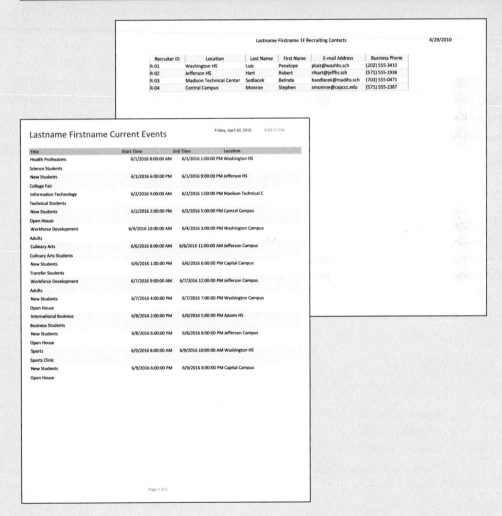

Figure 1.52

(Project 1F Recruiting Events continues on the next page)

Content-Based Assessments

Mastering Access | Project 1F Recruiting Events (continued)

1 **Start** Access, click **Sample templates**, and then click **Events**. In your **Access Chapter 1** folder, save the database as **Lastname_Firstname_1F_Recruiting_Events** If necessary, enable the content.

2 In the Multiple Items form or the New Event single-record form, enter the records shown in **Table 1** into the Events table.

3 **Close** the **Event List** form, and then click the **External Data tab**. **Import** and **Append** the **Excel** file **a01F_Recruiting_Events** to the **Events** table. **Open** the **Navigation Pane**, organize the objects by **Tables and Related Views**, and then **Open** your **Events** table to view 13 records. **Close** the **Navigation Pane**. Apply **Best Fit** to all of the fields, **Save** the table, and then **Close** the table.

4 **Create** a new table using the **Table** button. Click the **Click to Add arrow**, click **Text**, type **Location** and then press Enter. In the third column, click **Text**, type **Last Name** and then press Enter. In the fourth column, click **Text**, type **First Name** and then press Enter. In the fifth column, click **Text**, type **E-mail Address** and then press Enter. In the sixth column, click **Text**, type **Business Phone** and then press ↓.

5 Right-click the **ID** field name, and then **Rename** the field to **Recruiter ID** Change the **Data Type** to **Text**, and then enter the records as shown in **Table 2**.

6 Apply **Best Fit** to all of the columns. **Save** the table as **Lastname Firstname 1F Recruiting Contacts** and then **Close** the table.

7 From the **Navigation Pane**, open the **Current Events Report**. In the lower right corner of the status bar, click the **Layout View** button, click the title *Current Events*, and then click to position your insertion point to the left of *C*. Type your own name in the format **Lastname Firstname** Display the report in **Print Preview**, and then create a paper or electronic printout if instructed to do so. **Close** the **Print Preview**. **Close** the report and save the changes.

8 From the **Navigation Pane**, open your **1F Recruiting Contacts** table. Display the table in **Print Preview**, change to **Landscape** orientation, and then create a paper or electronic printout if instructed to do so. **Close** the **Print Preview**, and then **Close** the table. **Open** the **Navigation Pane** and, if necessary, increase the width of the pane so that your table name displays fully. From **Backstage** view, click **Close Database**, and then click **Exit**. As directed by your instructor, submit your database and the two paper or electronic printouts—one report and one table—that are the results of this project.

Table 1

ID	Title	Start Time	End Time	Description	Location
1	Health Professions	6/1/16 8a	6/1/16 1p	Science Students	Washington HS
2	New Students	6/1/16 6p	6/1/16 9p	College Fair	Jefferson HS
3	Information Technology	6/2/16 9a	6/2/16 1p	Technical Students	Madison Technical Center
4	New Students	6/2/16 2p	6/2/16 5p	Open House	Central Campus

(Return to Step 3)

Table 2

Recruiter ID	Location	Last Name	First Name	E-mail Address	Business Phone
R-01	Washington HS	Luiz	Penelope	pluiz@washhs.sch	(202) 555-3410
R-02	Jefferson HS	Hart	Robert	rlhart@jeffhs.sch	(571) 555-1938
R-03	Madison Technical Center	Sedlacek	Belinda	bsedlacek@madihs.sch	(703) 555-0471
R-04	Central Campus	Monroe	Stephen	smonroe@capccc.edu	(571) 555-2387

(Return to Step 6)

 End **You have completed Project 1F**

Content-Based Assessments

Apply **1A** and **1B** skills from these Objectives:

1. Identify Good Database Design
2. Create a Table and Define Fields in a New Database
3. Change the Structure of Tables and Add a Second Table
4. Create and Use a Query, Form, and Report
5. Save and Close a Database
6. Create a Database Using a Template
7. Organize Objects in the Navigation Pane
8. Create a New Table in a Database Created with a Template
9. Print a Report and a Table in a Database Created with a Template

Mastering Access | Project 1G Campus Expansion

In the following Mastering Access project, you will create one database to store information about the campus expansion for Capital Cities Community College and a second database to store information about the public events related to the expansion projects. Your completed database objects will look similar to Figure 1.53.

Project Files

For Project 1G, you will need the following files:

New blank Access database
a01G_Projects (Excel workbook)
a01G_Contractors (Excel workbook)
New Access database using the Events template

You will save your databases as:

Lastname_Firstname_1G_Campus_Expansion
Lastname_Firstname_1G_Public_Events

Project Results

Figure 1.53

(Project 1G Campus Expansion continues on the next page)

Access | Chapter 1

Content-Based Assessments

Mastering Access | Project 1G Campus Expansion (continued)

1 **Start** Access. Create a new **Blank database** in your **Access Chapter 1** folder. Name the database **Lastname_Firstname_1G_Campus_Expansion** and then **Close** the **Navigation Pane**. Create the additional fields shown in **Table 1**.

2 Change the **ID** field name to **Project ID** and change its **Data Type** to **Text**. Add the three records shown in **Table 2**.

3 **Save** the table as **Lastname Firstname 1G Projects** and then **Close** the table. **Import** and **Append** the **Excel** file **a01G_Projects** to the **1G Projects** table. Then, from the **Navigation Pane**, open your **1G Projects** table—8 records display. **Close** the **Navigation Pane**.

4 In **Design** view, click in the **Project ID** field, change the **Field Size** to **5** and as the **Description** type **Enter Project ID using the format P-###** Switch to **Datasheet** view, and save by clicking **Yes** two times. Apply **Best Fit** to all of the fields in the table, **Save** the table, and then display it in **Print Preview**. Set the orientation to **Landscape**—one page results. Create a paper or electronic printout as directed by your instructor, and then **Close** the table.

5 From the **External Data tab**, import the **Excel** file **a01G_Contractors** into the database as a new table; use the first row as the column headings and set the **ID** field as the primary key. In the final dialog box, name the table **Lastname Firstname 1G Contractors** and then **Open** the new table in **Datasheet** view. Apply **Best Fit** to all of the fields, **Save** the table, and then display the table in **Print Preview**. Set the orientation to **Landscape**—one page results. Create a paper or electronic printout as directed, and then **Close** the table.

6 **Create**, by using the **Query Wizard**, a **Simple Query** based on your **1G Projects** table. Include only the appropriate fields to answer the question *For every Building Project, what is the Budget Amount?* Save the query with the default name. Create a paper or electronic printout as directed, and then **Close** the query.

7 Open your **1G Projects** table, and then **Create** a **Form** for this table. Save the form as **Lastname Firstname 1G Projects Form** Display and select the seventh record, and then by using the instructions in Activity 1.15, print or create an electronic printout of this record as directed. **Close** the form object, saving changes to it.

8 With the **1G Projects** table open and active, **Create** a **Report**. **Delete** the **Project ID** field. Sort the records in **Descending** order by the **Budget Amount** field—Access automatically totals this field. Adjust the field widths on the left and right as necessary so that the fields display within the margins of the report. At the bottom of the report, delete the **page number**, and then delete the total that displays in the **Budget Amount** column. **Save** the report as **Lastname Firstname 1G Projects Report** and then create a paper or electronic printout as directed.

9 **Close All** open objects. If necessary, **Open** the **Navigation Pane** and widen the pane so that all object names display fully. Display **Backstage** view, and then click **Close Database**. Do *not* exit Access.

Table 1

Data Type		Text	Text	Text	Currency	
Field Name	ID	Building Project	Site	Contractor	Budget Amount	- - -▶ (Return to Step 2)

Table 2

Project ID	Building Project	Site	Contractor	Budget Amount
P-356	Student Center, 2-story	Jefferson Campus	Glenmore Construction	61450000
P-823	Student Center, multilevel	Central Campus	Glenmore Construction	41900000
P-157	Regional Health Center	Capital Campus	Wright Rosen Construction	42600000

(Return to Step 3)

(Project 1G Campus Expansion continues on the next page)

Content-Based Assessments

10 From **Sample templates**, create a new database using the **Events** template. **Save** the database in your **Access Chapter 1** folder as **Lastname_Firstname_1G_Public_ Events** If necessary, enable the content. Enter the records in **Table 3** by using the displayed Multiple Items Event List form or the single-record form, which is available by clicking New Event above the field names row.

11 **Close** the **Event List** form. Open the **Navigation Pane**, and then by using the **Navigation Pane arrow**, arrange the database objects by **Tables and Related Views**. Point to the **Events: Table** object, right-click, click **Rename**, and then using your own name, type **Lastname**

Firstname 1G Events Press [Enter] and then widen the Navigation Pane if necessary.

12 **Open** your **1G Events** table, **Close** the **Navigation Pane**, and then apply **Best Fit** to all of the columns. **Save** the table, display it in **Print Preview**, change the orientation to **Landscape**, set the **Margins** to **Normal**, and then create a paper or electronic printout as directed. **Close** all open objects. **Open** the **Navigation Pane**, display **Backstage** view, click **Close Database**, and then click **Exit**. As directed by your instructor, submit your database and the six paper or electronic printouts—three tables, one query, one form, and one report—that are the results of this project.

Table 3

ID	Title	Start Time	End Time	Description	Location
1	Groundbreaking	6/13/16 10a	6/13/16 11a	Student Center groundbreaking	Jefferson Campus
2	Dedication	8/26/16 12:30p	8/26/16 2p	Gymnasium building dedication	Washington Campus
3	Community Arts Expo	10/5/16 6p	10/5/16 9p	Book and Art Expo	Joint Use Library

(Return to Step 11)

End You have completed Project **1G**

Access | Chapter 1

Content-Based Assessments

GO! Fix It | Project **1H** Scholarships

Project Files

For Project 1H, you will need the following file:

> a01H_Scholarships

You will save your database as:

> Lastname_Firstname_1H_Scholarships

In this project, you will make corrections to and update an Access database that will store information about scholarships awarded to students. Start Access. In Backstage view, click Open, navigate to your student files, and then open the a01H_Scholarships file. With the database open, display Backstage view. Click Save Database As, and in the Save As dialog box, navigate to your Access Chapter 1 folder, name the file **Lastname_Firstname_1H_Scholarships** and then click Save. In the message bar, click the Enable Content button.

To complete the project you must find and correct errors in field names, data types, data design, and column widths. You should know:

- The table name should be renamed **Lastname Firstname 1H Scholarships**
- In the table, all of the data in the fields and the field names should display fully.
- Three fields in the table have incorrect data types.
- The field that represents the unique value for each record should be set as the primary key.
- In one of the records, there is a data entry error involving an athlete's name; after correcting the entry, be sure to click in another record so that the record you edit is saved.
- When open, the Navigation Pane should fully display the table name.
- A query should be created for the 1H Scholarships table that answers the question *What is the Amount, Sport, First Name, and Last Name of every athlete receiving a scholarship?* Apply Best Fit to the query results.
- Using the table, a report should be created that includes the Amount, Sport, Award Date, and the last and first name of the athlete. Sort the report in descending order by the amount and then adjust the column widths so that the fields display within the margins of the report. At the bottom of the report, delete the total for the Amount field, delete the page number, and then save the report with the default name.

If directed to do so, create a paper or electronic printout of the table, the query, and the report. The table should use Landscape orientation, and the query and report should use Portrait orientation. Be sure that the report prints on one page.

End **You have completed Project 1H** ———————————

Content-Based Assessments

GO! Make It | Project 1I Theater Events

Project Files

For Project 1I, you will need the following file:

New Access database using the Events template

You will save your database as:

Lastname_Firstname_1I_Theater_Events

Using the Events database template, create the table of theater events shown in Figure 1.54 that the Performing Arts department will present or host for April. Name the database **Lastname_Firstname_1I_Theater_Events** Arrange the Navigation Pane by Tables and Related Views, rename the Events table **Lastname Firstname 1I Theater Events** and then widen the Navigation Pane so that all object names display fully. Open the table, apply Best Fit to all the columns, save the table, and then create a paper or electronic printout of the table as directed by your instructor. Use Landscape orientation and Normal margins.

Project Results

Lastname Firstname 1I Theater Events   4/29/2010

ID	Title	Start Time	End Time	Location	Description	📎
1	Symphony Orchestra Concert	4/2/2016 7:30:00 PM	4/2/2016 10:00:00 PM	Jefferson Campus	Opera soprano Barbara Botillini	(0)
2	The Big Band Concert	4/4/2016 7:30:00 PM	4/4/2016 9:00:00 PM	Capital Campus	The Ruth Mystic Big Band Concert	(0)
3	Chaos in the House	4/6/2016 3:00:00 PM	4/6/2016 5:00:00 PM	Central Campus	Gospel Show	(0)
4	Tom Sawyer	4/7/2016 7:00:00 PM	4/7/2016 10:00:00 PM	Washington Campus	CapCCC Players	(0)
5	Tom Sawyer	4/8/2016 3:00:00 PM	4/8/2016 6:00:00 PM	Washington Campus	CapCCC Players	(0)
6	Virginia Arts Festival	4/16/2016 8:00:00 PM	4/16/2016 10:00:00 PM	Jefferson Campus	Anika Shankar	(0)
7	Virginia Arts Festival	4/17/2016 7:00:00 PM	4/17/2016 9:00:00 PM	Central Campus	Music from the Crooked Elbow	(0)
8	College Awards Ceremony	4/22/2016 1:00:00 PM	4/22/2016 4:00:00 PM	Washington Campus	CapCCC Faculty and Staff Awards	(0)
9	Virginia Arts Festival	4/23/2016 7:30:00 PM	4/23/2016 10:00:00 PM	Capital Campus	Russian Folk Dance Spectacular	(0)
10	Music in Motion Dance	4/29/2016 1:00:00 PM	4/29/2016 3:00:00 PM	Central Campus	Dancing to Modern Music	(0)

Page 1

Figure 1.54

End **You have completed Project 1I**

Content-Based Assessments

GO! Solve It | Project **1J** Student Activities

Project Files

For Project 1J, you will need the following files:

New Access database using the Events template
a01J_Student_Activities (Word document)

You will save your database as:

Lastname_Firstname_1J_Student_Activities

Create a new database from the Events database template and name the database **Lastname_Firstname_1J_Student_Activities** Using the data in the a01J_Student_Activities Word document, enter the data into the Multiple Items form. Each event begins at 7 p.m. and ends at 9 p.m. After entering the records, close the form, arrange the Navigation Pane by Tables and Related Views, rename the table that stores the records as **Lastname Firstname 1J Activities** and then widen the Navigation Pane so that all object names display fully. Open the table, apply Best Fit to the columns, and then save the table. Display the table in Print Preview, and then use the proper commands to be sure that the table prints on one page with the table name at the top of the page. Print the table or submit electronically as directed.

		Performance Level		
		Exemplary: You consistently applied the relevant skills	**Proficient:** You sometimes, but not always, applied the relevant skills	**Developing:** You rarely or never applied the relevant skills
Performance Elements	Create database and enter data	Database was created using the correct template and correct name. Data entered correctly.	Some but not all of the data was entered correctly.	Most of the data was entered incorrectly.
	Rename table and format table	Table named correctly and Best Fit applied to all columns.	Table named incorrectly and/or Best Fit not properly applied.	Incorrect table name and inadequate formatting applied to all columns.
	Create table printout	Printout displays on one page in Landscape orientation and the table name displays at the top.	The printout displays on two pages or the table name does not display at the top.	The printout displays on two pages and the table name does not display at the top of the page.

End **You have completed Project 1J** ———————

Content-Based Assessments

GO! Solve It | Project **1K** Media Contacts

Project Files

For Project 1K, you will need the following files:

New blank Access database
a01K_Media_Contacts (Excel workbook)

You will save your database as:

Lastname_Firstname_1K_Media_Contacts

Create a new blank database and name the database **Lastname_Firstname_1K_Media_Contacts** Close the default Table1. Create a table by importing the a01K_Media_Contacts Excel workbook, use the first row as the column headings, and use Media ID as the Primary Key. Name the table **Lastname Firstname 1K Media Contacts** Modify the table design by creating separate fields for the Contact's first name and last name, and then adjust the data accordingly. Apply Best Fit to the columns, and then save the table. Display the table in Print Preview, and then use the Page Layout commands to display the table on one page, being sure the table name prints at the top of the page. Print the table or submit electronically as directed.

Create a simple query that answers the following question: *What is the Publication name, first name, last name, and E-mail address for all of the media contacts?* Accept the default name, apply Best Fit to all of the columns, and then create a paper or electronic printout on one page as directed.

Create a report and delete the Media ID column. Adjust the widths of the remaining fields so that all of the data displays within the margins of the report. Sort the report in ascending order by the Publication field. In Layout View, select the report title, and then on the Format tab, in the Font group, change the font of the title of the report to 14. At the bottom of the report, delete the page number. Save the report as **Lastname Firstname 1K Media Contacts Report** and then create a paper or electronic printout as directed. Arrange the Navigation Pane by Tables and Related Views, and then widen the Navigation Pane so that all object names display fully.

	Performance Level		
	Exemplary: You consistently applied the relevant skills	**Proficient:** You sometimes, but not always, applied the relevant skills	**Developing:** You rarely or never applied the relevant skills
Create database, import data to create a table, and then modify the table design	Table created by importing from an Excel workbook, fields correctly modified, and primary key field identified.	Table created by importing from an Excel workbook, but fields are incorrect, or primary key field is incorrect.	Table created by importing from an Excel workbook, but both fields and primary key are incorrect.
Create query	Query created, named correctly, answers the question, formatted correctly.	Query created, but does not completely answer the question or formatted incorrectly.	Query does not answer the question and also includes errors in formatting.
Create report	Report created, Media ID field deleted, field sizes adjusted, sorted by Publication, correctly named, and formatted.	Report created with some errors in fields, report name, sorting, or formatting.	Report created with numerous errors in fields, report name, sorting, or formatting.

Performance Elements

End **You have completed Project 1K**

Outcomes-Based Assessments

Rubric

The following outcomes-based assessments are *open-ended assessments*. That is, there is no specific correct result; your result will depend on your approach to the information provided. Make *Professional Quality* your goal. Use the following scoring rubric to guide you in *how* to approach the problem, and then to evaluate *how well* your approach solves the problem.

The *criteria*—Software Mastery, Content, Format and Layout, and Process—represent the knowledge and skills you have gained that you can apply to solving the problem. The *levels of performance*—Professional Quality, Approaching Professional Quality, or Needs Quality Improvements—help you and your instructor evaluate your result.

	Your completed project is of Professional Quality if you:	Your completed project is Approaching Professional Quality if you:	Your completed project Needs Quality Improvements if you:
1-Software Mastery	Choose and apply the most appropriate skills, tools, and features and identify efficient methods to solve the problem.	Choose and apply some appropriate skills, tools, and features, but not in the most efficient manner.	Choose inappropriate skills, tools, or features, or are inefficient in solving the problem.
2-Content	Construct a solution that is clear and well organized, contains content that is accurate, appropriate to the audience and purpose, and is complete. Provide a solution that contains no errors in spelling, grammar, or style.	Construct a solution in which some components are unclear, poorly organized, inconsistent, or incomplete. Misjudge the needs of the audience. Have some errors in spelling, grammar, or style, but the errors do not detract from comprehension.	Construct a solution that is unclear, incomplete, or poorly organized; contains some inaccurate or inappropriate content; and contains many errors in spelling, grammar, or style. Do not solve the problem.
3-Format and Layout	Format and arrange all elements to communicate information and ideas, clarify function, illustrate relationships, and indicate relative importance.	Apply appropriate format and layout features to some elements, but not others. Overuse features, causing minor distraction.	Apply format and layout that does not communicate information or ideas clearly. Do not use format and layout features to clarify function, illustrate relationships, or indicate relative importance. Use available features excessively, causing distraction.
4-Process	Use an organized approach that integrates planning, development, self-assessment, revision, and reflection.	Demonstrate an organized approach in some areas, but not others; or, use an insufficient process of organization throughout.	Do not use an organized approach to solve the problem.

Outcomes-Based Assessments

Apply a combination of the **1A** and **1B** skills.

GO! Think | Project **1L** Student Clubs

Project Files

For Project 1L, you will need the following files:

> New blank Access database
> a01L_Clubs (Word file)
> a01L_Student_Clubs (Excel file)
> a01L_Club_Presidents (Excel file)

You will save your database as:

> Lastname_Firstname_1L_Student_Clubs

Kirsten McCarty, Vice President of Student Services, needs a database that tracks information about student clubs. The database should contain two tables, one for club information and one for contact information for the club presidents.

Create a new blank database and name it **Lastname_Firstname_1L_Student_Clubs** Using the information provided in the a01L_Clubs Word document, create the first table with two records to store information about the clubs. Then import 23 records from the a01L_Student_Clubs Excel file. Create a second table by importing 25 records from the a0lL_Club_Presidents Excel file. Name the tables appropriately and include your name. Be sure the data types are correct and the records are entered correctly. Apply Best Fit to all of the columns.

Create a simple query based on the Clubs table that answers the following question: *What is the Club Name, Meeting Day, Meeting Time, and Room ID for all of the clubs?* Based on the Clubs table, create a form. Create a report based on the Presidents of the clubs that lists the Last Name (in ascending order), First Name, and Phone number of every president. Print the two tables, the seventh record in Form view, the query, and the report being sure that each object prints on one page, or submit electronically as directed. Group objects on the Navigation Pane by Tables and Related Views. On the Navigation Pane, be sure that all object names display fully.

 You have completed Project 1L

Apply a combination of the **1A** and **1B** skills.

GO! Think | Project **1M** Faculty Training

Project Files

For Project 1M, you will need the following files:

> New Access database using the Events template
> a01M_Faculty_Training (Word file)

You will save your database as:

> Lastname_Firstname_1M_Faculty_Training

Use the information provided in the a01M_Faculty_Training Word file to create a database using the Events database template. Name the database **Lastname_Firstname_1M_Faculty_Training** Use the information in the Word file to enter the records. Training times begin at 11:30 a.m. and end at 1 p.m. Arrange the Navigation Pane by Tables and Related Views, and rename the Events table appropriately to include your name. Display the All Events report in Layout View and insert your Lastname Firstname in front of the report title *All Events*. Print the table and the All Events report or submit electronically as directed.

 You have completed Project 1M

Outcomes-Based Assessments

You and GO! | Project **1N** Personal Contacts

Project Files

For Project 1N, you will need the following file:

New blank Access database

You will save your database as:

Lastname_Firstname_1N_Personal_Contacts

Create a database that stores information about your personal contacts, such as friends and family members. Name the database **Lastname_Firstname_1N_Personal_Contacts** Include a field for a birthday. Enter at least 10 records in the table, and name the table **Lastname Firstname 1N Personal Contacts** Create a query that includes at least three of the fields in the table in the result; for example, a list of names and phone numbers. Create a report that includes the name and address for each contact. Print the table, query, and report, making sure that the data for each object prints on one page, or submit electronically as directed.

End You have completed Project 1N ──────────────────

Sort and Query a Database

OUTCOMES

At the end of this chapter you will be able to:

OBJECTIVES

Mastering these objectives will enable you to:

Brendan Fisher/Shutterstock

In This Chapter

In this chapter, you will sort Access database tables and create and modify queries. To convert data into meaningful information, you must manipulate your data in a way that you can answer questions. One question might be: *Which students have a grade point average of 3.0 or higher?* With such information, you could send information about scholarships or internships to selected students.

Questions can be answered by sorting the data in a table or by creating a query. Queries enable you to isolate specific data in database tables by limiting the fields that display and by setting conditions that limit the records to those that match specified conditions. You can also use a query to create a new field that is calculated by using one or more existing fields.

The projects in this chapter relate to **Capital Cities Community College**, which is located in the Washington D. C. metropolitan area. The college provides high-quality education and professional training to residents in the cities surrounding the nation's capital. Its four campuses serve over 50,000 students and offer more than 140 certificate programs and degrees at the associate's level. CapCCC has a highly acclaimed Distance Education program and an extensive Workforce Development program. The college makes positive contributions to the community through cultural and athletic programs and partnerships with businesses and non-profit organizations.

Project 2A Instructors and Courses Database

myitlab
Project 2A Training

Project Activities

In Activities 2.01 through 2.13, you will assist Carolyn Judkins, the Dean of the Business and Information Technology Division at the Jefferson Campus, in locating information about instructors and courses in the Division. Your results will look similar to Figure 2.1.

Project Files

For Project 2A, you will need the following file:

a02A_Instructors_Courses

You will save your database as:

Lastname_Firstname_2A_Instructors_Courses

Project Results

Figure 2.1
Project 2A Instructors and Courses

Objective 1 | Open an Existing Database

There will be instances in which you may want to work with a database and still keep the *original* version of the database. Like the other Microsoft Office 2010 applications, you can open a database file and save it with a new name.

Activity 2.01 | Opening and Renaming an Existing Database

1 **Start** Access. In **Backstage** view, click **Open**. Navigate to the student data files for this textbook, and then open the **a02A_Instructors_Courses** Access database.

2 Click the **File tab** to return to **Backstage** view, and then click **Save Database As.** In the **Save As** dialog box, navigate to the location where you are saving your databases for this chapter. Create a new folder named **Access Chapter 2** and then click **Open**.

3 In the **File name** box, select the file name, to which *1* has been added at the end. Edit as necessary to name the database **Lastname_Firstname_2A_Instructors_Courses** and then press Enter.

> Use this technique when you want to keep a copy of the original database file.

4 On the **Message Bar**, notice the **Security Warning**. In the **Navigation Pane**, notice that this database contains two table objects. Compare your screen with Figure 2.2.

Figure 2.2

Database name in title bar

Message Bar

2A Instructors table

2A Schedule table

Security Warning message

Activity 2.02 | Resolving Security Alerts and Renaming Tables

The *Message Bar* is the area below the Ribbon that displays information such as security alerts when there is potentially unsafe, active content in an Office document that you open. Settings that determine the alerts that display on your Message Bar are set in the Access *Trust Center*, which is an area of Access where you can view the security and privacy settings for your Access installation.

You may or may not be able to change the settings in the Trust Center, depending upon decisions made within your organization's computing environment. You can display the Trust Center from Options, which is available in Backstage view.

1 On the **Message Bar**, click the **Enable Content** button.

> When working with the student files that accompany this textbook, repeat these actions each time you see this security warning. Databases for this textbook are safe to use on your computer.

2 In the **Navigation Pane**, right-click the **2A Instructors** table, and then click **Rename**. With the table name selected and using your own name, type **Lastname Firstname 2A Instructors** and then press Enter to rename the table. Using the same technique, **Rename** the **2A Schedule** table to **Lastname Firstname 2A Schedule**

> Including your name in the table enables you and your instructor to easily identify your work, because Access includes the table name in the header of printed and PDF pages.

3 Point to the right edge of the **Navigation Pane** to display the ↔ pointer. Drag to the right to widen the pane until both table names display fully.

Objective 2 | Create Table Relationships

Access databases are relational databases because the tables in the database can relate—actually connect—to other tables through common fields. Recall that common fields are fields that contain the same data in more than one table.

After you have a table for each subject in your database, you must provide a way to connect the data in the tables when you need meaningful information. To do this, create common fields in related tables, and then define table relationships. A *relationship* is an association that you establish between two tables based on common fields. After the relationship is established, you can create a query, a form, or a report that displays information from more than one table.

Activity 2.03 | Creating Table Relationships and Enforcing Referential Integrity

In this activity, you will create a relationship between two tables in the database.

1 Double-click your **2A Instructors** table to open it in the object window and examine its contents. Then open your **2A Schedule** table and examine its contents.

> In the 2A Instructors table, *Instructor ID* is the primary key field, which ensures that each instructor will appear in the table only one time. No two instructors have the same Instructor ID.

> In the 2A Schedule table, *Schedule ID* is the primary key field. Every scheduled course section during an academic term has a unique Schedule ID. The 2A Schedule table includes the *Instructor ID* field, which is the common field between the 2A Schedule table and the 2A Instructors table.

2 In the **2A Schedule** table, scroll to the right to display the Instructor ID field, and then compare your screen with Figure 2.3.

> Because *one* instructor can teach *many* different courses, *one* Instructor ID number can be present *many* times in the 2A Schedule table. This relationship between each instructor and the courses is known as a *one-to-many relationship*. This is the most common type of relationship in Access.

Figure 2.3

Two table objects open in the object window; *2A Schedule* table active

Tables renamed

Navigation Pane width increased so that both table names are visible

Instructor teaches more than one course

3 In the upper right corner of the object window, click **Close** ☒ two times to close each table. Click the **Database Tools tab**, and then in the **Relationships group**, click the **Relationships** button. Compare your screen with Figure 2.4.

> The Show Table dialog box displays in the Relationships window. In the Show Table dialog box, the Tables tab displays all of the table objects in the database. Your two tables are listed.

Figure 2.4

Relationships window

Two tables in database

4 Point to the title bar of the **Show Table** dialog box, and then drag down and to the right slightly to move the **Show Table** dialog box away from the top of the **Relationships** window.

> Moving the Show Table dialog box enables you to see the tables as they are added to the Relationships window.

5 In the **Show Table** dialog box, click your **2A Instructors** table, and then at the bottom of the dialog box, click **Add**. In the **Show Table** dialog box, double-click your **2A Schedule** table to add the table to the **Relationships** window. In the **Show Table** dialog box, click **Close**, and then compare your screen with Figure 2.5.

> You can use either technique to add a table to the Relationships window. A *field list*—a list of the field names in a table—for each of the two table objects displays, and each table's primary key is identified. Although this database currently has only two tables, larger databases can have many tables. Scroll bars in a field list indicate that there are fields that are not currently in view.

Figure 2.5

Field list for 2A
Schedule table

Field list for 2A
Instructors table

Primary keys

Scroll bar indicates there
are fields out of view

Alert! | Are There More Than Two Field Lists in the Relationships Window?

If you double-click a table more than one time, a duplicate field list displays in the Relationships window. To remove a field list from the Relationships window, right-click the title bar of the field list, and then click Hide Table. Alternatively, click anywhere in the field list, and then on the Design tab, in the Relationships group, click the Hide Table button.

---

6 In the **2A Schedule** field list—the field list on the right—point to the title bar to display the 🖑 pointer. Drag the field list to the right until there are about 2 inches between the field lists.

7 In the **2A Instructors** field list—the field list on the left—point to the lower right corner of the field list to display the ⬊ pointer, and then drag down and to the right to increase the height and width of the field list until the entire name of the table in the title bar displays and all of the field names display.

This action enables you to see all of the available fields and removes the vertical scroll bar.

8 By using the same technique and the ⬊ pointer, resize the **2A Schedule** field list so that all of the field names and the table name display as shown in Figure 2.6.

Recall that *one* instructor can teach *many* scheduled courses. This arrangement of the tables on your screen displays the *one table* on the left side and the *many table* on the right side. Recall also that the primary key in each table is the field that uniquely identifies the record in each table. In the 2A Instructors table, each instructor is uniquely identified by the Instructor ID. In the 2A Schedule table, each scheduled course section is uniquely identified by the Schedule ID.

Figure 2.6

Table on *many* side
of relationship

Table on *one* side
of relationship

Instructor ID is common
field between the
two tables

Note | The Field That Is Highlighted Does Not Matter

After you rearrange the two field lists in the Relationships window, the highlighted field indicates the active field list, which is the list you moved last. This is of no consequence for completing the activity.

Another Way

On the Design tab, in the Tools group, click the Edit Relationships button. In the Edit Relationships dialog box, click Create New, and then in the Create New dialog box, designate the tables and fields that will create the relationship.

9 In the **2A Instructors** field list, point to **Instructor ID**, hold down the left mouse button, and then drag down and to the right into the **2A Schedule** field list until the 🖢 pointer's arrow is on top of **Instructor ID**. Then release the mouse button to display the **Edit Relationships** dialog box.

As you drag, a small graphic displays to indicate that you are dragging a field from one field list to another. A table relationship works by matching data in two fields—the common field. In these two tables, the common field has the same name—*Instructor ID*. Common fields are not required to have the same names; however, they must have the same data type and field size.

10 Point to the title bar of the **Edit Relationships** dialog box, and then drag the dialog box below the two field lists as shown in Figure 2.7.

Both tables include the Instructor ID field—the common field between the two tables. By dragging, you create the *one-to-many* relationship. In the 2A Instructors table, Instructor ID is the primary key. In the 2A Schedule table, Instructor ID is referred to as the **foreign key** field. The foreign key is the field in the related table used to connect to the primary key in another table. The field on the *one* side of the relationship is typically the primary key.

Figure 2.7

Edit Relationships dialog box

Instructor ID field common to both tables

One-To-Many indicated as Relationship Type

11 In the **Edit Relationships** dialog box, click to select the **Enforce Referential Integrity** check box.

Referential integrity is a set of rules that Access uses to ensure that the data between related tables is valid. Enforcing referential integrity ensures that an instructor cannot be added to the 2A Schedules table if the Instructor ID is *not* included in the 2A Instructors table. Similarly, enforcing referential integrity ensures that you cannot delete an instructor from the 2A Instructors table if there is a course listed in the 2A Schedule table for that instructor.

12 In the **Edit Relationships** dialog box, click the **Create** button, and then compare your screen with Figure 2.8.

A *join line*—the line joining two tables—displays between the two tables. On the join line, *1* indicates the *one* side of the relationship, and the infinity symbol (∞) indicates the *many* side of the relationship. These symbols display when referential integrity is enforced.

Figure 2.8

1 indicates *one* side of the relationship

Join line connects the two common fields, creating the relationship

∞ indicates *many* side of the relationship

Activity 2.04 | Printing a Relationship Report and Displaying Subdatasheet Records

The Relationships window provides a map of how your database tables are related, and you can print this information as a report.

1 With the **Relationships** window open, on the **Design tab**, in the **Tools group**, click the **Relationship Report** button to create the report and display it in Print Preview.

2 On the **Print Preview tab**, in the **Page Size group**, click the **Margins** button, and then click **Normal**. Compare your screen with Figure 2.9. If instructed to do so, create a paper or electronic printout of this relationship report.

Figure 2.9

Print Preview tab
Margins button

Database name and date (your date will differ)

Field lists with join lines

3 On the **Quick Access Toolbar**, click the **Save** button 🖫 to save the report. In the **Save As** dialog box, click **OK** to accept the default name.

The report name displays in the Navigation Pane under *Unrelated Objects*. Because the report is just a map of the relationships, and not a report containing actual records, it is not associated with any of the tables.

4 In the object window, **Close** ⊠ the report, and then **Close** ⊠ the **Relationships** window.

5 From the **Navigation Pane**, open your **2A Instructors** table, and then **Close** ⟨⟨⟩ the **Navigation Pane**. For the first record—*Instructor ID 1224567*—on the left side of the record, click the **plus sign** (+), and then compare your screen with Figure 2.10.

> Plus signs to the left of a record in a table indicate that *related* records exist in another table. Clicking the plus sign displays the related records in a **subdatasheet**. In the first record, for *Deborah Fresch*, you can see that related records exist in the 2A Schedule table—she is teaching five LGL courses that are listed in the schedule. The plus sign displays because you created a relationship between the two tables using the Instructor ID field—the common field.

Figure 2.10

Course sections from the 2A Schedule table for *Associate Professor Deborah Fresch*

Plus sign indicates that related records may exist in another table

6 For the first record, click the **minus sign** (−) to collapse the subdatasheet.

> **More Knowledge | Other Types of Relationships: One-to-One and Many-to-Many**
>
> There are other relationships you can create using the same process in the Relationships window. The type of relationship is determined by the placement of the primary key field. A one-to-one relationship exists between two tables when a record in one table is related to a single record in a second table. In this case, both tables use the same field as the primary key. This is most often used when data is placed in a separate table because access to the information is restricted.
>
> You can also create a many-to-many relationship between tables, where many records in one table can be related to many records in another table. For example, many students can enroll in many courses. To create a many-to-many relationship, you must create a third table that contains the primary key fields from both tables. These primary key fields are then joined to their related fields in the other tables. In effect, you create multiple one-to-one relationships.

Objective 3 | Sort Records in a Table

Sorting is the process of arranging data in a specific order based on the value in a field. For example, you can sort the names in your address book alphabetically by each person's last name, or you can sort your DVD collection by the date of purchase. Initially, records in an Access table display in the order they are entered into the table. When a primary key is established, the records display in order based on the primary key field.

Activity 2.05 | Sorting Records in a Table in Ascending or Descending Order

In the following activity, you will determine the departments of the faculty in the Business and Information Technology Division by sorting the data. You can sort data in either *ascending order* or *descending order*. Ascending order sorts text alphabetically (A to Z) and sorts numbers from the lowest number to the highest number. Descending order sorts text in reverse alphabetical order (Z to A) and sorts numbers from the highest number to the lowest number.

Access | Chapter 2

1 Notice that the records in the **2A Instructors** table are sorted in ascending order by **Instructor ID**, which is the primary key field.

Another Way

On the Home tab, in the Sort & Filter group, click the Ascending button.

2 In the field names row, click the **Department arrow**, click **Sort A to Z**, and then compare your screen with Figure 2.11.

To sort records in a table, click the arrow to the right of the field name in the column on which you want to sort, and then choose the sort order. After a field is sorted, a small arrow in the field name box indicates its sort order. The small arrow in the field name points up, indicating an ascending sort; and in the Ribbon, the Ascending button is selected.

The records display in alphabetical order by Department. Because the department names are now grouped together, you can quickly scroll the length of the table to see the instructors in each department. The first record in the table has no data in the Department field because the Instructor ID number *9999999* is reserved for Staff, a designation that is used until a scheduled course has been assigned to a specific instructor.

Figure 2.11

Ascending button selected

Small arrow indicates order by which the field is sorted

Records sorted alphabetically by Department

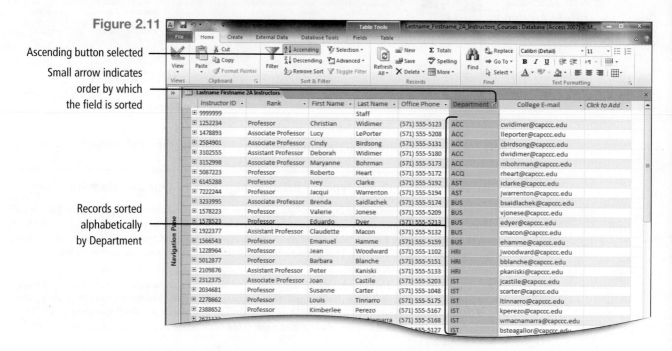

3 On the **Home tab**, in the **Sort & Filter group**, click the **Remove Sort** button to clear the sort and return the records to the default sort order, which is by the primary key field—*Instructor ID*.

4 Click the **Last Name arrow**, and then click **Sort Z to A**.

The records in the table are sorted by last name in reverse alphabetical order. The small arrow in the Field name box points down, indicating a descending sort. On the Ribbon, the Descending button is selected.

5 In the **Sort & Filter group**, click the **Remove Sort** button.

Activity 2.06 | Sorting Records in a Table on Multiple Fields

To sort a table on two or more fields, first identify the fields that will act as the *outermost sort field* and the *innermost sort field*. The outermost sort field is the first level of sorting, and the innermost sort field is the second level of sorting. For example, you might want to sort first by the Last Name field, which would be the outermost sort field, and then by the First Name field, which would be the innermost sort field. After you identify your outermost and innermost sort fields, sort the innermost field first, and then sort the outermost field.

In this activity, you will sort the records in descending order by the department name. Within each department name, you will sort the records in ascending order by last name.

1 In the **Last Name** field, click any record. In the **Sort & Filter group**, click the **Ascending** button.

The records are sorted in ascending alphabetical order by Last Name—the innermost sort field.

2 Point anywhere in the **Department** field, and then right-click. From the shortcut menu, click **Sort Z to A**. Compare your screen with Figure 2.12.

The records are sorted in descending alphabetical order first by Department—the *outermost* sort field—and then within a specific Department grouping, the sort continues in ascending alphabetical order by Last Name—the *innermost* sort field. The records are sorted on multiple fields using both ascending and descending order.

Figure 2.12

Small arrow indicates descending sort

Small arrow indicates ascending sort

Within each *Department*, *Last Name* sorted in ascending order

Records sorted in descending order by Department

3 Display **Backstage** view, click **Print**, and then click **Print Preview**. In the **Page Layout** group, click the **Landscape** button. In the **Zoom group**, click the **Two Pages** button, and notice that the table will print on two pages.

4 On the **Print Preview tab**, in the **Print group**, click the **Print** button. Under **Print Range**, click the **Pages** option button. In the **From** box, type **1** and then in the **To** box, type **1** to print only the first page. If directed to submit a paper copy, click OK or create an electronic copy as instructed. To create a PDF of only the first page, in the Data group, click PDF or XPS, click the Options button, and then indicate *Page 1 to 1*. In the **Close Preview group**, click the **Close Print Preview** button.

5 In the object window, **Close** ☒ the table. In the message box, click **Yes** to save the changes to the sort order.

6 **Open** ☒ the **Navigation Pane**, and then open the **2A Instructors** table. Notice the table was saved with the sort order you specified.

7 In the **Sort & Filter group**, click the **Remove Sort** button. **Close** ☒ the table, and in the message box, click **Yes** to save the table with the sort removed. **Close** ☒ the **Navigation Pane**.

Generally, tables are not stored with the data sorted. Instead, queries are created that sort the data; and then reports are created to display the sorted data.

Objective 4 | Create a Query in Design View

Recall that a *select query* is a database object that retrieves (selects) specific data from one or more tables and then displays the specified data in Datasheet view. A query answers a question such as *Which instructors teach courses in the IST department?* Unless a query has already been set up to ask this question, you must create a new query.

Database users rarely need to see all of the records in all of the tables. That is why a query is so useful; it creates a *subset* of records—a portion of the total records—according to your specifications and then displays only those records.

Activity 2.07 | Creating a New Select Query in Design View

Previously, you created a query using the Query Wizard. To create complex queries, use Query Design view. The table or tables from which a query selects its data is referred to as the *data source*.

1 On the Ribbon, click the **Create tab**, and then in the **Queries group**, click the **Query Design** button. Compare your screen with Figure 2.13.

A new query opens in Design view and the Show Table dialog box displays, which lists both tables in the database.

Figure 2.13

Query1 tab

Queries group

Query Design button

Show Table dialog box

Available tables

2 In the **Show Table** dialog box, double-click **2A Instructors**, and then **Close** the **Show Table** dialog box.

A field list for the 2A Instructors table displays in the upper area of the Query window. The Instructor ID field is the primary key field in this table. The Query window has two parts: the *table area* (upper area), which displays the field lists for tables that are used in the query, and the *design grid* (lower area), which displays the design of the query.

Alert! | Is There More Than One Field List in the Query Window?

If you double-click a table more than one time, a duplicate field list displays in the Query window. To remove a field list from the Query window, right-click the title bar of the field list, and then click Remove Table.

---

3 Point to the lower right corner of the field list to display the ⌐ pointer, and then drag down and to the right to expand the field list, displaying all of the field names and the table name. In the **2A Instructors** field list, double-click **Rank**, and then look at the design grid.

The Rank field name displays in the design grid in the Field row. You limit the fields that display when the query is run by placing only the desired field names in the design grid.

4 In the **2A Instructors** field list, point to **First Name**, hold down the left mouse button, and then drag down into the design grid until the ⌐ pointer displays in the **Field** row in the second column. Release the mouse button, and then compare your screen with Figure 2.14.

This is a second way to add field names to the design grid. As you drag the field, a small rectangular shape attaches to the mouse pointer. When you release the mouse button, the field name displays in the Field row.

Figure 2.14

2A Instructors field list expanded in table area

Two field names added to the Field row in design grid

5 In design grid, in the **Field** row, click in the third column, and then click the **arrow** that displays. From the list, click **Last Name** to add the field to the design grid, which is a third way to add a field to the design grid.

6 Using one of the techniques you just practiced, add the **Office Phone** field to the fourth column and the **Department** field to the fifth column in the design grid.

Activity 2.08 | Running, Saving, Printing, and Closing a Query

After you create a query, you *run* it to display the results. When you run a query, Access looks at the records in the table (or tables) you have included in the query, finds the records that match the specified conditions (if any), and displays only those records in a datasheet. Only the fields that you have added to the design grid display in the query results. The query always runs using the current table or tables, presenting the most up-to-date information.

Another Way

On the Design tab, in the Results group, click the View button to automatically start the Run command.

1 On the **Design tab**, in the **Results group**, click the **Run** button, and then compare your screen with Figure 2.15.

This query answers the question, *What is the Rank, First Name, Last Name, Office Phone number, and Department of all of the instructors in the 2A Instructors table?* A query is a subset of the records in one or more tables, arranged in Datasheet view, using the fields and conditions that you specify. The five fields that you specified in the design grid display in columns, and the records from the 2A Instructors table display in rows.

Figure 2.15

Five fields specified in design grid

Records displayed in rows

2 On the **Quick Access Toolbar**, click the **Save** button. In the **Save As** dialog box, type **Lastname Firstname 2A Instructors Query** and then click **OK**.

Save your queries if you are likely to ask the same question again; doing so will save you the effort of creating the query again to answer the same question.

Alert! | Does a Message Display After Entering a Query Name?

Query names are limited to 64 characters. For all projects, if you have a long last name or first name that results in your query name exceeding the 64-character limit, ask your instructor how you should abbreviate your name.

---

3 Display **Backstage** view, click **Print**, and then click **Print Preview**. Create a paper or electronic printout if instructed to do so, and then **Close Print Preview**.

Queries answer questions and gather information from the data in the tables. Queries are typically created as a basis for a report, but query results can be printed like any other table of data.

4 **Close** ☒ the query. **Open** ☒ the **Navigation Pane**, and then notice that the **2A Instructors Query** object displays under the **2A Instructors** table object.

> The new query name displays in the Navigation Pane under the table with which it is related—the 2A Instructors table. Only the design of the query is saved. The records still reside in the table object. Each time you open the query, Access runs it again and displays the results based on the data stored in the related table(s). Thus, the results of a query always reflect the latest information in the related table(s).

Objective 5 | Create a New Query from an Existing Query

You can create a new query from scratch or you can open an existing query, save it with new name, and modify the design to suit your needs. Using an existing query saves you time if your new query uses all or some of the same fields and conditions in an existing query.

Activity 2.09 | Creating a New Query from an Existing Query

1 From the **Navigation Pane**, open your **2A Instructors Query** by either double-clicking the name or by right-clicking and clicking Open.

> The query runs, opens in Datasheet view, and displays the records from the 2A Instructors table as specified in the query design grid.

2 Display **Backstage** view, and then click **Save Object As**. In the **Save As** dialog box, type **Lastname Firstname 2A Instructor IDs Query** and then click **OK**. Click the **Home tab**, and then in the **Views group**, click the **View** button to switch to **Design** view.

> A new query, based on a copy of the 2A Instructors Query, is created and displays in the object window and in the Navigation Pane under its data source—the 2A Instructors table.

3 **Close** ☒ the **Navigation Pane**. In the design grid, point to the thin gray selection bar above the **Office Phone** field name until the ⬇ pointer displays. Click to select the **Office Phone** column, and then press ⌜Del⌟.

> This action deletes the field from the query design only—it has no effect on the field in the underlying 2A Instructors table. The Department field moves to the left. Similarly, you can select multiple fields and delete them at one time.

4 From the gray selection bar, select the **First Name** column. In the selected column, point to the selection bar to display the ⬚ pointer, and then drag to the right until a dark vertical line displays on the right side of the **Last Name** column. Release the mouse button to position the **First Name** field in the third column.

> To rearrange fields in the query design, select the field to move, and then drag it to a new position in the design grid.

5 Using the technique you just practiced, move the **Department** field to the left of the **Rank** field.

6 From the field list, drag the **Instructor ID** field down to the first column in the design grid until the ⬚ pointer displays, and then release the mouse button. Compare your screen with Figure 2.16.

> The Instructor ID field displays in the first column, and the remaining four fields move to the right. Use this method to insert a field to the left of a field already displayed in the design grid.

Figure 2.16

New query created
by copying the 2A
Instructors Query

First Name in the
last column

Five fields in the
design grid

Instructor ID in the
first column

Department in the
second column

7 On the **Design tab**, in the **Results group**, click the **Run** button.

This query answers the question, *What is the Instructor ID, Department, Rank, Last Name, and First Name for every instructor in the 2A Instructors table?* The results of the query are a subset of the records contained in the 2A Instructors table. The records are sorted by the primary key field—Instructor ID.

8 From **Backstage** view, display the query in **Print Preview**. Create a paper or electronic printout if instructed to do so, and then **Close Print Preview**.

9 **Close** ☒ the query, and in the message box, click **Yes** to save the changes to the design—deleting a field, moving two fields, and adding a field. **Open** ≫ the **Navigation Pane**.

The query is saved and closed. The new query name displays in the Navigation Pane under the related table. Recall that when you save a query, only the *design* of the query is saved; the records reside in the related table object or objects.

Objective 6 | Sort Query Results

You can sort the results of a query in ascending or descending order in either Datasheet view or Design view. Use Design view if your query results should display in a specified sort order, or if you intend to use the sorted results in a report.

Activity 2.10 | Sorting Query Results

In this activity, you will save an existing query with a new name, and then sort the query results by using the Sort row in Design view.

1 On the **Navigation Pane**, click your **2A Instructor IDs Query**. Display **Backstage** view, and then click **Save Object As**. In the **Save As** dialog box, type **Lastname Firstname 2A Department Sort Query** and then click **OK**. Click the **Home tab**, and then drag the right edge of the **Navigation Pane** to the right to increase its width so that the names of the new query and the relationship report display fully.

Access creates a new query, based on a copy of your 2A Instructors ID Query; that is, the new query includes the same fields in the same order as the query on which it is based.

2 In the **Navigation Pane**, right-click your **2A Department Sort Query**, and then click **Design View. Close** ⟨«⟩ the **Navigation Pane**.

3 In the design grid, in the **Sort** row, click in the **Last Name** field to display the insertion point and an arrow. Click the **Sort arrow**, and then in the list, click **Ascending**. Compare your screen with Figure 2.17.

Figure 2.17

Sort row in design grid ⎯⎯⎯

Ascending sort added to Last Name field

4 On the **Design tab** in the **Results group**, click the **Run** button.

> In the query result, the records are sorted in ascending alphabetical order by the Last Name field, and two instructors have the same last name of *Widimer*.

5 On the **Home tab** in the **Views group**, click the **View** button to switch to **Design** view.

6 In the **Sort** row, click in the **First Name** field, click the **Sort arrow**, and then click **Ascending**. **Run** the query.

> In the query result, the records are sorted first by the Last Name field. If instructors have the same last name, then Access sorts those records by the First Name field. The two instructors with the last name of *Widimer* are sorted by their first names.

7 Switch to **Design** view. In the **Sort** row, click in the **Department** field, click the **Sort arrow**, and then click **Descending**. **Run** the query; if necessary, scroll down to display the last records, and then compare your screen with Figure 2.18.

> In Design view, fields with a Sort designation are sorted from left to right. That is, the sorted field on the left becomes the outermost sort field, and the sorted field on the right becomes the innermost sort field.

> Thus, the records are sorted first in descending alphabetical order by the Department field—the leftmost sort field. Then, within each same department name field, the Last Names are sorted in ascending alphabetical order. And, finally, within each same last name field, the First Names are sorted in ascending alphabetical order.

> If you run a query and the sorted results are not what you intended, be sure that the fields are displayed from left to right according to the groupings that you desire.

Figure 2.18

Department names sorted in descending order

Within each Department, Last Names sorted in ascending order

Within each Last Name, First Names sorted in ascending order

8 Display the query in **Print Preview**. Create a paper or electronic printout if instructed to do so, and then **Close Print Preview**. **Close** ☒ the query. In the message box, click **Yes** to save the changes to the query design.

> **More Knowledge | Sorting**
>
> If you add a sort order to the *design* of a query, it remains as a permanent part of the query design. If you use the sort buttons in the Datasheet view, they will override the sort order of the query design, and can be saved as part of the query. A sort order designated in Datasheet view does not display in the Sort row of the query design grid.

Objective 7 | Specify Criteria in a Query

Queries locate information in a database based on *criteria* that you specify as part of the query. Criteria are conditions that identify the specific records for which you are looking.

Criteria enable you to ask a more specific question; therefore, you will get a more specific result. For example, if you want to find out how many instructors are in the IST department, limit the results to that specific department, and then only the records that match the specified department will display.

Activity 2.11 | Specifying Text Criteria in a Query

In this activity, you will assist Dean Judkins by creating a query to answer the question *How many instructors are in the IST Department?*

1 Be sure that all objects are closed and that the **Navigation Pane** is closed. Click the **Create tab**, and then in the **Queries group**, click the **Query Design** button.

2 In the **Show Table** dialog box, **Add** the **2A Instructors** table to the table area, and then **Close** the **Show Table** dialog box.

3 Expand the field list to display all of the fields and the table name. Add the following fields to the design grid in the order given: **Department, Instructor ID, Rank, First Name**, and **Last Name**.

4 In the **Criteria** row of the design grid, click in the **Department** field, type **IST** and then press Enter. Compare your screen with Figure 2.19.

Access places quotation marks around the criteria to indicate that this is a *text string*—a sequence of characters. Use the Criteria row to specify the criteria that will limit the results of the query to your exact specifications. The criteria is not case sensitive; so you can type *ist* instead of IST.

Figure 2.19

Five fields added to the design grid

Criteria row in design grid

Criteria under Department—Access adds quotation marks

Note | Pressing Enter After Adding Criteria

If you press Enter or click in another column or row in the query design grid after you have added your criteria, you can see how Access alters the criteria so it can interpret what you have typed. Sometimes, there is no change, such as when you add criteria to a number or currency field. Other times, Access may capitalize a letter or add quotation marks or other symbols to clarify the criteria. Whether or not you press Enter after adding criteria has no effect on the query results. It is used here to help you see how the program behaves.

---

5 **Run** the query, and then compare your screen with Figure 2.20.

Thirteen records display that meet the specified criteria—records that have *IST* in the Department field.

Figure 2.20

Thirteen records match Department *IST* criteria

Alert! | Do Your Query Results Differ?

If you mistype the criteria, or enter it under the wrong field, or make some other error, the result will display no records. This indicates that there are no records in the table that match the criteria as you entered it. If this occurs, return to Design view and re-examine the query design. Verify that the criteria is typed in the Criteria row, under the correct field, and without typing errors. Then run the query again.

6 Save ⊟ the query as **Lastname Firstname 2A IST Query** and then display the query in **Print Preview**. Create a paper or electronic printout if instructed to do so, and then **Close Print Preview**.

7 Close ⊠ the query, **Open** ⊠ the **Navigation Pane**, and then notice that the **2A IST Query** object displays under the **2A Instructors** table—its data source.

Recall that queries in the Navigation Pane display an icon of two overlapping tables.

Activity 2.12 | Specifying Criteria Using a Field Not Displayed in the Query Results

So far, all of the fields that you included in the query design have also been included in the query results. It is not required to have every field in the query display in the results. In this activity, you will create a query to answer the question, *Which instructors have a rank of Professor?*

1 Close ⊠ the **Navigation Pane**. Click the **Create tab**, and then in the **Queries group**, click the **Query Design** button.

2 From the **Show Table** dialog box, **Add** the **2A Instructors** table to the table area, and then **Close** the dialog box. Expand the field list.

3 Add the following fields, in the order given, to the design grid: **Instructor ID**, **First Name**, **Last Name**, and **Rank**.

4 In the **Sort** row, in the **Last Name** field, click the **Sort arrow**; click **Ascending**.

5 In the **Criteria** row, click in the **Rank** field, type **professor** and then press ⏎. Compare your screen with Figure 2.21.

Recall that criteria is not case sensitive. As you start typing *professor*, a list of functions display, from which you can select if including a function in your criteria. When you press ⏎, the insertion point moves to the next criteria box and quotation marks are added around the text string that you entered.

Figure 2.21

Show row; check boxes selected for every field

Last Name field sorted in Ascending order

Criteria for Rank field

6 In the design grid, in the **Show** row, notice that the check box is selected for every field. **Run** the query to view the query results.

Nineteen records meet the criteria. In the Rank column each record displays *Professor*, and the records are sorted in ascending alphabetical order by the Last Name field.

7 Switch to **Design** view. In the design grid, under **Rank**, in the **Show** row, click to clear the check box.

Because it is repetitive and not particularly useful to have *Professor* display for each record in the query results, clear this check box so that the field does not display. However, you should run the query before clearing the Show check box to be sure that the correct records display.

8 **Run** the query, and then notice that the *Rank* field does not display.

The query results display the same 19 records, but the *Rank* field does not display. Although the Rank field is still included in the query criteria for the purpose of identifying specific records, it is not necessary to display the field in the results. When appropriate, clear the Show check box to avoid cluttering the query results with data that is not useful.

9 **Save** 🖫 the query as **Lastname Firstname 2A Professor Rank Query** and then display the query in **Print Preview**. Create a paper or electronic printout if instructed to do so, and then **Close Print Preview. Close** ✕ the query.

Activity 2.13 | Using *Is Null* Criteria to Find Empty Fields

Sometimes you must locate records where data is *missing*. You can locate such records by using *Is Null*—empty—as the criteria in a field. Additionally, you can display only the records where a value *has* been entered in a field by using *Is Not Null* as the criteria, which will exclude records where the specified field is empty. In this activity, you will design a query to find out *Which scheduled courses have no credits listed?*

1 Click the **Create tab**. In the **Queries group**, click the **Query Design** button. Add the **2A Schedule** table to the table area, **Close** the **Show Table** dialog box, and then expand the field list.

2 Add the following fields to the design grid in the order given: **Subject**, **Catalog#**, **Section**, **Course Name**, and **Credits**.

3 In the **Criteria** row, click in the **Credits** field, type **is null** and then press Enter.

Access capitalizes *is null*. The criteria *Is Null* examines the field and looks for records that do *not* have any values entered in the Credits field.

4 In the **Sort** row, click in the **Subject** field, click the **Sort arrow**, and then click **Ascending**. **Sort** the **Catalog#** field in **Ascending** order, and then **Sort** the **Section** field in **Ascending** order. Compare your screen with Figure 2.22.

Figure 2.22
Three fields sorted in ascending alphabetical order

Is Null criteria in Credits field

5 **Run** the query, and then compare your screen with Figure 2.23.

Five scheduled courses do not have credits listed—the Credits field is empty. The records are sorted in ascending order first by the Subject field, then by the Catalog # field, and then by the Section. Using the information displayed in the query results, a course scheduler can more easily locate the records in the table to enter the credits.

Figure 2.23

Credits field empty (null) for five courses

Sorted first by Subject

Within Subject, sorted by Catalog#

Within Catalog#, sorted by Section

6 **Save** 🖫 the query as **Lastname Firstname 2A No Credits Query** and then display the query in **Print Preview**. Create a paper or electronic printout if instructed to do so, and then **Close Print Preview**.

7 **Close** ☒ the query. **Open** 》 the **Navigation Pane**, and then notice that the **2A No Credits Query** object displays under the **2A Schedule** table object, which is the query's data source.

8 From **Backstage** view, click **Close Database**, and then click **Exit** to close the Access program. As directed by your instructor, submit your database and the eight paper or electronic printouts—relationship report, sorted table, and six queries—that are the results of this project.

End **You have completed Project 2A** —————————————————

Project 2B Athletic Scholarships Database

myitlab
Project 2B Training

Project Activities

In Activities 2.14 through 2.26, you will assist Randy Shavrain, Athletic Director for Capital Cities Community College, in developing and querying his Athletic Scholarships database. Your results will look similar to Figure 2.24.

Project Files

For Project 2B, you will need the following files:

  a02B_Athletes_Scholarships
  a02B_Athletes (Excel file)

You will save your database as:

  Lastname_Firstname_2B_Athletic_Scholarships

Project Results

Figure 2.24
Project 2B Athletic Scholarships

Access | Chapter 2

Objective 8 | Specify Numeric Criteria in a Query

Criteria can be set for fields containing numeric data. When you design your table, set the appropriate data type for fields that will contain numbers, currency, or dates so that mathematical calculations can be performed.

Activity 2.14 | Opening an Existing Database and Importing a Spreadsheet

In this activity, you will open, rename, and save an existing database, and then import an Excel spreadsheet that Mr. Shavrain wants to bring into Access as a new table.

1 **Start** Access. In **Backstage** view, click **Open**. From your student files, open **a02B_Athletes_Scholarships**.

2 From **Backstage** view, click **Save Database As**. In the **Save As** dialog box, navigate to your **Access Chapter 2** folder, and then in the **File name** box, type **Lastname_Firstname_2B_Athletic_Scholarships** and then press [Enter].

3 On the **Message Bar**, click the **Enable Content** button. In the **Navigation Pane**, **Rename 2B Scholarships Awarded** to **Lastname Firstname 2B Scholarships Awarded**, and then double-click to open the table. **Close** [«] the **Navigation Pane**, and then examine the data in the table. Compare your screen with Figure 2.25.

In this table, Mr. Shavrain tracks the names and amounts of scholarships awarded to student athletes. Students are identified only by their Student ID numbers, and the primary key is the Scholarship ID field.

Figure 2.25

Scholarship Name field

Amount field

Student ID numbers for students receiving scholarship

4 **Close** [×] the table. On the Ribbon, click the **External Data tab**, and then in the **Import & Link group**, click the **Excel** button. In the **Get External Data – Excel Spreadsheet** dialog box, to the right of the **File name** box, click **Browse**.

5 In the **File Open** dialog box, navigate to your student data files, and then double-click **a02B_Athletes**. Be sure that the **Import the source data into a new table in the current database** option button is selected, and then click **OK**.

The Import Spreadsheet Wizard opens and displays the spreadsheet data.

6 Click **Next**. In the upper left portion of the **Import Spreadsheet Wizard** dialog box, select the **First Row Contains Column Headings** check box. Click **Next**, and then click **Next** again.

7 In the upper portion of the Wizard, click the **Choose my own primary key** option button, and then be sure that **Student ID** displays.

> In the new table, Student ID will be the primary key. No two students have the same Student ID.

8 Click **Next**. In the **Import to Table** box, type **Lastname Firstname 2B Athletes** and then click **Finish**. In the **Get External Data – Excel Spreadsheet** Wizard, click **Close**, and then **Open** » the **Navigation Pane**. Widen the **Navigation Pane** so that the table names display fully.

9 **Open** the new **2B Athletes** table, and then on the **Home tab**, switch to **Design View**.

10 For the **Student ID** field, click in the **Data Type** box, click the **arrow**, and then click **Text**. For the **ZIP/Postal Code** field, change the **Data Type** to **Text**, and then set the **Field Size** to **5** Click in the **State/Region** field, set the **Field Size** to **2** and then switch back to **Datasheet View**, saving the changes.

> Recall that numeric data that will not be used in any calculations, such as the Student ID, should have a Data Type of *Text*.

11 In the message box, click **Yes**—no data will be lost. **Close** « the **Navigation Pane**. Take a moment to review the imported data. Using the **Select All** button ☐, apply **Best Fit** to all of the fields. Click in any field to cancel the selection, **Save** 🖫 the table, and then **Close** ☒ the table.

Activity 2.15 | Creating Table Relationships

In this activity, you will create a one-to-many relationship between the 2B Athletes table and the 2B Scholarships Awarded table by using the common field—*Student ID*.

1 Click the **Database Tools tab**, and then in the **Relationships group**, click the **Relationships** button.

2 In the **Show Table** dialog box, **Add** the **2B Athletes** table, and then **Add** the **2B Scholarships Awarded** table to the table area. **Close** the **Show Table** dialog box.

3 Move and resize the two field lists to display all of the fields and the entire table name, and then position the field lists so that there is approximately one inch of space between the two field lists.

> Resizing and repositioning the field lists is not required, but doing so makes it easier for you to view the field lists and the join line when creating relationships.

4 In the **2B Athletes** field list, point to the **Student ID** field. Hold down the left mouse button, drag into the **2B Scholarships Awarded** field list on top of the **Student ID** field, and then release the mouse button to display the **Edit Relationships** dialog box.

5 Point to the title bar of the **Edit Relationships** dialog box, and then drag it below the two field lists. In the **Edit Relationships** dialog box, be sure that **Student ID** is displayed as the common field for both tables.

> The two tables relate in a *one-to-many* relationship—*one* athlete can have *many* scholarships. The common field between the two tables is the Student ID field. In the 2B Athletes table, Student ID is the primary key. In the 2B Scholarships Awarded table, Student ID is the foreign key.

6 In the **Edit Relationships** dialog box, select the **Enforce Referential Integrity** check box. Click **Create**, and then compare your screen with Figure 2.26.

> The one-to-many relationship is established. The *1* and ∞ indicate that referential integrity is enforced, which ensures that a scholarship cannot be awarded to a student whose Student ID is not in the 2B Athletes table. Similarly, you cannot delete a student athlete from the 2B Athletes table if there is a scholarship listed for that student in the 2B Scholarships Awarded table.

Figure 2.26

Join line—symbols indicate referential integrity enforced

Primary key in the *one* table

Foreign key in the *many* table

7 On the **Design tab**, in the **Tools group**, click the **Relationship Report** button. Create a paper or electronic printout if instructed to do so.

8 Save ⊞ the report as **Lastname Firstname 2B Relationships** and then click **OK**. Close ✕ the report, and then **Close** ✕ the **Relationships** window.

9 Open » the **Navigation Pane**, open the **2B Athletes** table, and then **Close** « the **Navigation Pane**. On the left side of the table, in the first record, click the **plus sign** (+) to display the subdatasheet for the record.

> In the first record, for *Joel Barthmaier*, one related record exists in the 2B Scholarships Awarded table. The related record displays because you created a relationship between the two tables using Student ID as the common field.

10 Close ✕ the **2B Athletes** table.

Activity 2.16 | Specifying Numeric Criteria in a Query

Mr. Shavrain wants to know *Which scholarships are in the amount of $300, and for which sports?* In this activity, you will specify criteria in the query so that only the records of scholarships in the amount of $300 display.

1 Click the **Create tab**. In the **Queries group**, click the **Query Design** button.

2 In the **Show Table** dialog box, **Add** the **2B Scholarships Awarded** table to the table area, and then **Close** the **Show Table** dialog box. Expand the field list to display all of the fields and the entire table name.

3 Add the following fields to the design grid in the order given: **Scholarship Name**, **Sport**, and **Amount**.

4 In the **Sort** row, click in the **Sport** field. Click the **Sort arrow**, and then click **Ascending**.

5 In the **Criteria** row, click in the **Amount** field, type **300** and then press Enter. Compare your screen with Figure 2.27.

> When entering currency values as criteria, do not type the dollar sign. Include a decimal point only if you are looking for a specific amount that includes cents—for example 300.49. Access does not insert quotation marks around the criteria because the field's data type is Number.

Figure 2.27

Numeric criteria—no quotation marks

Sort in ascending order by *Sport*

6 On the **Design tab**, in the **Results group**, click the **Run** button to view the results.

Five scholarships were awarded in the exact amount of $300. In the navigation area, *1 of 5* displays to indicate the number of records that match the criteria.

7 On the **Home tab**, in the **Views group**, click the **View** button to switch to **Design** view.

Activity 2.17 | Using Comparison Operators

Comparison operators are symbols that evaluate each field value to determine if it is the same (=), greater than (>), less than (<), or in between a range of values as specified by the criteria.

If no comparison operator is specified, equal (=) is assumed. For example, in the previous activity, you created a query to display only records where the *Amount* is 300. The comparison operator of = was assumed, and Access displayed only records that had values equal to 300.

1 Be sure your query is displayed in **Design** view. In the **Criteria** row, click in the **Amount** field, delete the existing criteria, type **>300** and then press Enter.

2 On the **Design tab**, in the **Results group**, click the **Run** button.

Fourteen records have an Amount that is greater than $300. The results show the records for which the Amount is *greater than* $300, but do not display amounts that are *equal to* $300.

3 Switch to **Design** view. In the **Criteria** row, under **Amount**, delete the existing criteria. Type **<300** and then press Enter. **Run** the query.

Eleven records display and each has an Amount less than $300. The results show the records for which the Amount is *less than* $300, but does not include amounts that are *equal to* $300.

4 Switch to **Design** view. In the **Criteria** row, click in the **Amount** field, delete the existing criteria, type **>=300** and then press Enter.

5 **Run** the query, and then compare your screen with Figure 2.28.

Nineteen records display, including the records for scholarships in the exact amount of $300. The records include scholarships *greater than* or *equal to* $300. In this manner, comparison operators can be combined. This query answers the question, *Which scholarships have been awarded in the amount of $300 or more, and for which sports, with the Sport names in alphabetical order?*

Figure 2.28

Nineteen records with a scholarship amount of $300 or more

6 Save 🖫 the query as **Lastname Firstname 2B $300 or More Query** and then display the query in **Print Preview**. Create a paper or electronic printout if instructed to do so, and then **Close Print Preview**.

7 Close ☒ the query. Open ≫ the **Navigation Pane**, and notice that the new query displays under the table from which it retrieved the records—*2B Scholarships Awarded*.

Activity 2.18 | Using the Between ... And Comparison Operator

The *Between ... And operator* is a comparison operator that looks for values within a range. It is useful when you need to locate records that are within a range of dates; for example, scholarships awarded between August 1 and September 30. In this activity, you will create a new query from an existing query, and then add criteria to look for values within a range of dates. The query will answer the question *Which scholarships were awarded between August 1 and September 30?*

1 On the **Navigation Pane**, click the **2B $300 or More Query** object to select it. Display **Backstage** view and click **Save Object As**. In the **Save As** dialog box, type **Lastname Firstname 2B Awards Aug-Sep Query** and then click **OK**.

2 Click the **Home tab**. Open the **2B Awards Aug-Sep Query** object, **Close** ≪ the **Navigation Pane**, and then switch to **Design** view. From the **2B Scholarships Awarded** field list, add the **Award Date** as the fourth field in the design grid.

3 In the **Criteria** row, click in the **Amount** field, and then delete the existing criteria so that the query is not restricted by amount. In the **Criteria** row, click in the **Award Date** field, type **between 8/1/16 and 9/30/16** and then press Enter.

4 In the selection bar of the design grid, point to the right edge of the **Award Date** column to display the ⊞ pointer, and then double-click. Compare your screen with Figure 2.29.

The width of the Award Date column is increased to fit the longest entry, enabling you to see all of the criteria. Access places pound signs (#) around dates and capitalizes *between* and *and*. This criteria instructs Access to look for values in the Award Date field that begin with 8/1/16 and end with 9/30/16. Both the beginning and ending dates will be included in the query results.

Figure 2.29

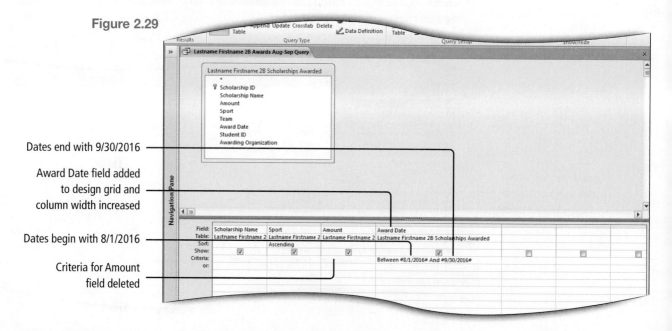

Dates end with 9/30/2016

Award Date field added to design grid and column width increased

Dates begin with 8/1/2016

Criteria for Amount field deleted

5 **Run** the query, and notice that three scholarships were awarded between 08/1/16 and 9/30/16.

6 Display the query in **Print Preview**, create a paper or electronic printout if instructed to do so, and then **Close Print Preview**.

7 **Close** ⊠ the query. In the message box, click **Yes** to save the changes to the query design. **Open** » the **Navigation Pane**, and notice that the new query displays under the table that is its data source—*2B Scholarships Awarded*.

Objective 9 | Use Compound Criteria

You can specify more than one condition—criterion—in a query; this is called *compound criteria*. Compound criteria use AND and OR *logical operators*. Logical operators enable you to enter criteria for the same field or different fields.

Activity 2.19 | Using AND Criteria in a Query

Compound criteria use an *AND condition* to display records in the query results that meet all parts of the specified criteria. In this activity, you will help Mr. Shavrain answer the question *Which scholarships over $500 were awarded for Football?*

1 **Close** « the **Navigation Pane**. On the Ribbon, click the **Create tab**. In the **Queries group**, click the **Query Design** button. **Add** the **2B Scholarships Awarded** table to the table area. **Close** the **Show Table** dialog box, and then expand the field list.

2 Add the following fields to the design grid in the order given: **Scholarship Name**, **Sport**, and **Amount**.

3 In the **Criteria** row, click in the **Sport** field, type **football** and then press Enter.

4 In the **Criteria** row, in the **Amount** field, type **>500** and then press Enter. Compare your screen with Figure 2.30.

You create the AND condition by placing the criteria for both fields on the same line in the Criteria row. The results will display only records that contain *Football* AND an amount greater than *$500*.

Figure 2.30

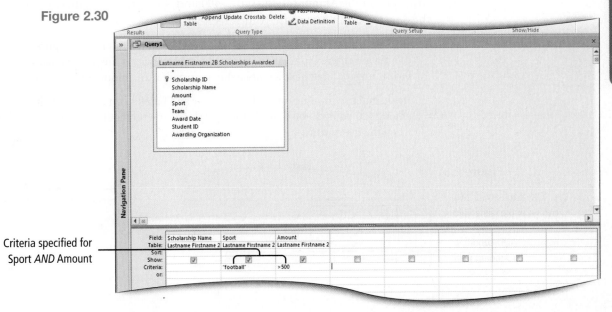

Criteria specified for Sport *AND* Amount

Access | Chapter 2

5 On the **Design tab**, in the **Results group**, click the **Run** button.

> Two records display that match both conditions—Football in the Sport field *and* greater than $500 in the Amount field.

6 Save 💾 the query as **Lastname Firstname 2B Football and Over $500 Query** and then click **OK** or press Enter. **Close** ☒ the query.

7 Open ≫ the **Navigation Pane**, and then click one time to select the **2B Football and Over $500 Query** object. Display the query in **Print Preview**, create a paper or electronic printout if instructed to do so, and then **Close Print Preview**.

> You can print any selected object from the Navigation Pane—the object does not have to be open to print.

8 Close ≪ the **Navigation Pane**.

Activity 2.20 | Using OR Criteria in a Query

Use the *OR condition* to specify multiple criteria for a single field, or multiple criteria for different fields when you want to display the records that meet any of the conditions. In this activity, you will help Mr. Shavrain answer the question *Which scholarships over $400 were awarded in the sports of Baseball or Swimming, and what is the award date of each?*

1 Click the **Create tab**. In the **Queries group**, click the **Query Design** button.

2 **Add** the **2B Scholarships Awarded** table. **Close** the dialog box, expand the field list, and then add the following four fields to the design grid in the order given: **Scholarship Name**, **Sport**, **Amount**, and **Award Date**.

3 In the **Criteria** row, click in the **Sport** field, and then type **baseball**

4 In the design grid, on the **or** row, click in the **Sport** field, type **swimming** and then press Enter. **Run** the query.

> The query results display seven scholarship records where the Sport is either Baseball *or* Swimming. Use the OR condition to specify multiple criteria for a single field.

5 Switch to **Design** view. In the **or** row, under **Sport**, delete *swimming*. In the **Criteria** row, under **Sport**, delete *baseball*. Type **swimming or baseball** and then in the **Criteria** row, click in the **Amount** field. Type **>400** and then press Enter. Increase the width of the **Sport** column. Compare your screen with Figure 2.31.

> This is an alternative way to use the OR compound operator in the Sport field. Because criteria are entered for two different fields, Access selects the records that are Baseball *or* Swimming *and* that have a scholarship awarded in an amount greater than $400.

> If you enter swimming on the Criteria row and baseball on the or row, then you must enter >400 on both the Criteria row and the or row so that the correct records display when the query runs.

Figure 2.31

OR condition for two criteria in the same field

AND condition for Amount field

6 **Run** the query to display the two records that match the conditions.

7 **Close** $\boxed{\times}$ the query. In the message box, click **Yes** to save changes to the query. In the **Save As** dialog box, type **Lastname Firstname 2B Swimming or Baseball Over $400 Query** and then click **OK**.

8 **Open** $\boxed{\gg}$ the **Navigation Pane**, increase the width of the **Navigation Pane** to display the full name of all objects, and then click one time to select the **2B Swimming or Baseball Over $400 Query** object. Display the query in **Print Preview**, create a paper or electronic printout if instructed to do so, and then **Close Print Preview**. Close $\boxed{\ll}$ the **Navigation Pane**.

Objective 10 | Create a Query Based on More Than One Table

In a relational database, you can retrieve information from more than one table. Recall that a table in a relational database contains all of the records about a single topic. Tables are joined by relating the primary key field in one table to a foreign key field in another table. This common field creates a relationship, so you can include data from more than one table in a query.

For example, the Athletes table contains all of the information about the student athletes—name, address, and so on. The Scholarships Awarded table includes the scholarship name, amount, and so on. When an athlete receives a scholarship, only the Student ID field is included with the scholarship to identify who received the scholarship. It is not necessary to include any other data about the athletes in the Scholarships Awarded table; doing so would result in redundant data.

Activity 2.21 | Creating a Query Based on More Than One Table

In this activity, you will create a query that selects records from two tables. This is possible because a relationship has been created between the two tables in the database. The query will answer the questions *What is the name, e-mail address, and phone number of athletes who have received swimming or tennis scholarships, and what is the name and amount of the scholarship?*

1 Click the **Create tab**. In the **Queries group**, click the **Query Design** button. **Add** the **2B Athletes** table and the **2B Scholarships Awarded** table to the table area, and then **Close** the **Show Table** dialog box. Expand the two field lists, and then drag the **2B Scholarships Awarded** field list to the right so that there is approximately one inch of space between the field lists.

The join line displays because you previously created a relationship between the tables. It indicates a *one-to-many* relationship—*one* athlete can have *many* scholarships.

2 From the **2B Athletes** field list, add the following fields to the design grid in the order given: **First Name**, **Last Name**, **College E-mail**, and **Home Phone**.

3 In the **Sort** row, click in the **Last Name** field. Click the **Sort arrow**, and then click **Ascending** to sort the records in alphabetical order by last name.

4 From the **2B Scholarships Awarded** field list, add the following fields to the design grid in the order given: **Scholarship Name**, **Sport**, and **Amount**.

5 In the **Criteria** row, click in the **Sport** field. Type **swimming or tennis** and then press Enter.

6 In the design grid, increase the width of the **Home Phone** and **Scholarship Name** columns to display the entire table name on the **Table** row. If necessary, scroll to the right to display the *Home Phone* and *Scholarship Name* fields in the design grid, and then compare your screen with Figure 2.32.

> When extracting data from multiple tables, the information on the Table row is helpful, especially when different tables include the same field names, such as address, but different data, such as a student's address or a coach's address.

Figure 2.32

Table row indicates data source —

Criteria entered for Sport field —

7 **Run** the query, and then compare your screen with Figure 2.33.

> Information for eight student athletes displays. The First Name and Last Name fields are included in the query results even though the common field—*Student ID*—is *not* included in the query design. Because Student ID is included in both tables, and a one-to-many relationship was created between the tables, the Student ID field is used to select the records in both tables by using one query. Two students—*Carla Reid* and *Florence Zimmerman*—received scholarships in both Swimming and Tennis. Recall that *one* student athlete can receive *many* scholarships.

Figure 2.33

Sport of *Tennis* or *Swimming* —

Students with scholarships in both sports —

8 Save 🖫 the query as **Lastname Firstname 2B Swimming or Tennis Query** and then display the query in **Print Preview**. Set the **Margins** to **Normal**, and then change the orientation to **Landscape**. Create a paper or electronic printout if instructed to do so, and then **Close Print Preview**.

9 **Close** ☒ the query, **Open** ≫ the **Navigation Pane**, and then compare your screen with Figure 2.34.

> Your new query—*2B Swimming or Tennis Query*—displays under both tables from which it retrieved records.

Figure 2.34

Query displays under data sources

Objective 11 | Use Wildcards in a Query

Wildcard characters serve as a placeholder for one or more unknown characters in the criteria. When you are unsure of the particular character or set of characters to include in criteria, use wildcard characters in place of the characters.

Activity 2.22 | Using a Wildcard in a Query

Use the asterisk (*) to represent one or more characters. For example, if you use the * wildcard in the criteria Fo*, the results will display Foster, Forrester, Forrest, Fossil, or any word beginning with *Fo*. In this activity, you will use the asterisk (*) wildcard in the criteria row to answer the question *Which athletes received scholarships from local Rotary Clubs, country clubs, or foundations?*

1 **Close** «« the **Navigation Pane**. On the Ribbon, click the **Create tab**. In the **Queries group**, click the **Query Design** button.

2 **Add** both tables to the table area, **Close** the **Show Table** dialog box, and then expand the field lists.

3 Add the following fields to the design grid in the order given: from the **2B Athletes** table, **First Name** and **Last Name**; from the **2B Scholarships Awarded** table, **Awarding Organization**.

4 In the **Sort** row, click in the **Last Name** field. Click the **arrow**, and then click **Ascending**.

5 In the **Criteria** row, under **Awarding Organization**, type **rotary*** and then press [Enter].

The wildcard character * is a placeholder to match one or more characters. After pressing [Enter], Access adds *Like* to the beginning of the criteria.

6 **Run** the query, and then compare your screen with Figure 2.35.

Three athletes received scholarships from Rotary Clubs. The results are sorted alphabetically by the Last Name field.

Access | Chapter 2

Figure 2.35

Awarding Organization
for all records
begins with *Rotary*

First Name	Last Name	Awarding Organization
Lan	Geng	Rotary Club of Alexandria
Eugene	Sotova	Rotary Club of Falls Church
Khrystyna	Tilson	Rotary Club of Arlington

7 Switch to **Design** view. On the **or** row, under **Awarding Organization**, type ***country club** and then press Enter.

> The * can be used at the beginning, middle, or end of the criteria. The position of the * wildcard character determines the location of the unknown characters. Here you will search for records that end in *Country Club*.

8 **Run** the query to display six records, and notice that three records begin with *Rotary*, and three records end with *Country Club*—sorted alphabetically by Last Name.

9 Switch to **Design** view. Under **Awarding Organization** and under **Like "*country club"**, type ***foundation*** and then press Enter. Compare your screen with Figure 2.36.

> The query will also display records that have the word *Foundation* anywhere—beginning, middle, or end—in the field. Three *OR* criteria have been entered for the Awarding Organization field—the query results will display students who have received scholarships from an organization name that begins with Rotary, *or* that ends in County Club, *or* that has Foundation anywhere in the middle of the name.

Figure 2.36

Three variations of
* wildcard placement

10 **Run** the query to display 28 records.

> Twenty-eight scholarships were from a Country Club, *or* a Rotary Club, *or* a Foundation.

11 **Save** 🖫 the query as **Lastname Firstname 2B Wildcard Query** and then display the results in **Print Preview**. Create a paper or electronic printout if instructed to do so, and then **Close Print Preview**.

12 **Close** ☒ the query, and then **Open** ⟫ the **Navigation Pane**.

> Because the 2B Wildcard Query object retrieved data from two tables, it displays below the 2B Scholarships Awarded table *and* the 2B Athletes table—the data sources.

More Knowledge | Search for a Single Unknown Character by Using the ? Wildcard

The question mark (?) is a wildcard that is used to search for unknown single characters. For each question mark included in criteria, any character can be inserted. For example, if you use *b?d* as a criteria, the query might locate bid, bud, bed, or any three-character word beginning with *b* and ending with *d*. If *b??d* is entered as the criteria, the results could include bind, bend, bard, or any four-character word beginning with *b* and ending with *d*.

Objective 12 | Use Calculated Fields in a Query

Queries can create calculated values that are stored in a *calculated field*. A calculated field stores the value of a mathematical operation. For example, you can multiply two fields together, such as Total Credit Hours and Tuition Per Credit Hour to get a Total Tuition Due amount for each student without having to include a specific field for this amount in the table, which reduces the size of the database and provides more flexibility.

There are two steps to produce a calculated field in a query. First, name the field that will store the calculated values. Second, write the *expression*—the formula—that performs the calculation. Each field name used in the calculation must be enclosed within its own pair of square brackets, and the new field name must be followed by a colon (:).

Activity 2.23 | Using Calculated Fields in a Query

For each scholarship received by student athletes, the Capital Cities Community College Alumni Association will donate an amount equal to 50 percent of each scholarship. In this activity, you will create a calculated field to determine the additional amount each scholarship is worth. The query will answer the question *What is the value of each scholarship if the Alumni Association makes a matching 50% donation?*

1 **Close** « the **Navigation Pane**, and then click the **Create tab**. In the **Queries group**, click the **Query Design** button.

2 **Add** the **2B Scholarships Awarded** table to the table area, **Close** the **Show Table** dialog box, and then expand the field list. Add the following fields to the design grid in the order given: **Student ID**, **Scholarship Name**, and **Amount**.

3 In the **Sort** row, click in the **Student ID** field; sort **Ascending**.

4 In the **Field** row, right-click in the first empty column to display a shortcut menu, and then click **Zoom**.

The Zoom dialog box gives you more working space so that you can see the entire calculation as you type it. The calculation can also be typed directly in the empty Field box in the column.

5 In the **Zoom** dialog box, type **Matching Donation:[Amount]*0.5** and then compare your screen with Figure 2.37.

The first element, *Matching Donation*, is the new field name where the calculated values will display. Following that is a colon (:), which separates the new field name from the expression. *Amount* is enclosed in square brackets because it is an existing field name in the 2B Scholarships Awarded table; it contains the numeric data on which the calculation will be performed. Following the right square bracket is an asterisk (*), which in math calculations signifies multiplication. Finally, the percentage (0.5 or 50%) displays.

Figure 2.37

Zoom dialog box ——

New field name for calculated value followed by a colon (:) ——

Expression—formula that calculates the value ——

6 In the **Zoom** dialog box, click **OK**, and then **Run** the query. Compare your screen with Figure 2.38.

> The query results display three fields from the 2B Scholarships Awarded table plus a fourth field—*Matching Donation*—in which a calculated value displays. Each calculated value equals the value in the Amount field multiplied by 0.5.

Figure 2.38

New field name

Values calculated (50% of value in Amount field)

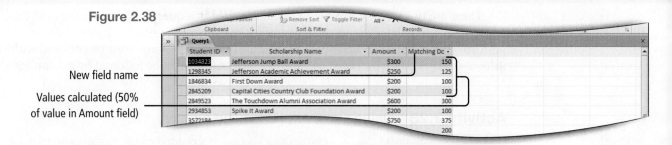

> **Alert! | Does Your Screen Differ?**
>
> If your calculations in a query do not work, switch to Design view and carefully check the expression you typed. Spelling or syntax errors prevent calculated fields from working properly.

7 Notice the formatting of the **Matching Donation** field—there are no dollar signs, commas, or decimal places; you will adjust this formatting later.

> When using a number, such as 0.5, in an expression, the values in the calculated field may not be formatted the same as in the existing field.

8 Switch to **Design** view. In the **Field** row, in the first empty column, right-click, and then click **Zoom**. In the **Zoom** dialog box, type **Total Scholarship:[Amount]+[Matching Donation]** and then compare your screen with Figure 2.39.

> Each existing field name—*Amount* and *Matching Donation*—must be enclosed in separate pairs of brackets.

Figure 2.39

New field name followed by a colon (:)

Expression with two existing field names in separate pairs of brackets

9 In the **Zoom** dialog box, click **OK**, and then **Run** the query to view the results.

Total Scholarship is calculated by adding together the Amount field and the Matching Donation field. The Total Scholarship column includes dollar signs, commas, and decimal points, which carried over from the Currency format in the Amount field.

10 Switch to **Design** view. In the **Field** row, click in the **Matching Donation** field box.

11 On the **Design tab**, in the **Show/Hide group**, click the **Property Sheet** button.

> **Another Way**
>
> Right-click the Matching Donation field name, and then click Properties.

The *Property Sheet* displays on the right side of your screen. A Property Sheet is a list of characteristics—properties—for fields in which you can make precise changes to each property associated with the field. The left column displays the Property name, for example, Description. To the right of the Property name is the Property setting box.

12 In the **Property Sheet**, on the **General tab**, click in the **Format** property setting box, and then click the **arrow** that displays. Compare your screen with Figure 2.40.

A list of formats for the Matching Donation field displays.

Figure 2.40

Property Sheet for Matching Donation field

Format arrow

List of formats for numeric field

13 In the list, click **Currency**. Click the next property, **Decimal Places**, click the **arrow**, and then click **0**.

14 In the design grid, in the **Field** row, click in the **Total Scholarship** field. On the **Property Sheet**, set the **Format** to **Currency** and the **Decimal Places** to **0**.

15 **Close** ⊠ the **Property Sheet**, and then **Run** the query. Select all of the columns and apply **Best Fit**.

The Matching Donation and Total Scholarship fields are formatted as Currency with 0 decimal places.

16 **Save** 🖫 the query as **Lastname Firstname 2B Matching Donations Query** and then display the query results in **Print Preview**. Change the **Orientation** to **Landscape**. Create a paper or electronic printout if instructed to do so, and then **Close Print Preview**. **Close** ⊠ the query.

Objective 13 | Calculate Statistics and Group Data in a Query

In Access queries, you can perform statistical calculations on a group of records. Calculations that are performed on a group of records are called *aggregate functions*.

Activity 2.24 | Using the MIN, MAX, AVG, and SUM Functions in a Query

In this activity, you will use the minimum, maximum, average, and sum functions in a query to examine the amounts of scholarships awarded. The last query will answer the question *What is the total dollar amount of all scholarships awarded?*

1 On the **Create tab**, in the **Queries group**, click the **Query Design** button.

2 **Add** the **2B Scholarships Awarded** table to the table area, **Close** the **Show Table** dialog box, and then expand the field list. Add the **Amount** field to the design grid.

> Include only the field you want to summarize in the query, so that the aggregate function (minimum, maximum, average, sum, and so forth) is applied to that single field.

3 On the **Design tab**, in the **Show/Hide group**, click the **Totals** button to add a **Total** row as the third row in the design grid. Notice that in the design grid, on the **Total** row, under **Amount**, *Group By* displays.

> Use the Total row to select the aggregate function that you want to use for the field.

4 In the **Total** row, under **Amount**, click in the **Group By** box, and then click the **arrow** to display the list of aggregate functions. Compare your screen with Figure 2.41, and take a moment to review the table in Figure 2.42.

Figure 2.41

Totals button in the Show/Hide group

Total row added to the design grid

List of aggregate functions

Aggregate Functions	
Function Name	**What It Does**
Sum	Totals the values in a field.
Avg	Averages the values in a field.
Min	Locates the smallest value in a field.
Max	Locates the largest value in a field.
Count	Counts the number of records in a field.
StDev	Calculates the Standard Deviation for the values in a field.
Var	Calculates the Variance for the values in a field.
First	Displays the First value in a field.
Last	Displays the Last value in a field.
Expression	Creates a calculated field that includes an aggregate function.
Where	Limits records to those that match a condition specified in the Criteria row.

Figure 2.42

5 From the list of functions, click **Min**, and then **Run** the query. Double-click the right edge of the column heading to apply Best Fit to the column.

> Access calculates the minimum (smallest) scholarship award—*$100.00*. The field name *MinOfAmount* displays for the calculation. This query answers the question, *What is the minimum (smallest) scholarship amount awarded?*

6 Switch to **Design** view. In the **Amount** field, in the **Total** row, select the **Max** function, and then **Run** the query.

> The maximum (largest) scholarship amount is *$750.00*.

7 Switch to **Design** view, select the **Avg** function, and then **Run** the query.

> The average scholarship amount awarded is *$358.33*.

8 Switch to **Design** view. Select the **Sum** function, and then **Run** the query.

> Access sums the Amount field for all records and displays a result of *$10,750.00*. The field name, *SumOfAmount*, displays. This query answers the question, *What is the total dollar amount of all the scholarships awarded?*

Activity 2.25 | Grouping Data in a Query

Aggregate functions can also be used to calculate totals by groups of data. For example, to group (summarize) the amount of scholarships awarded to each student, you include the Student ID field, in addition to the Amount field, and then group all of the records for each student together to calculate a total awarded to each student. Similarly, you can calculate how much is awarded for each sport.

1 Switch to **Design** view. Drag the **Student ID** field to the first column of the design grid—**Amount** becomes the second column. On the **Total** row, under **Student ID**, notice that *Group By* displays.

This query groups—summarizes—the records by StudentID and calculates a total Amount for each student.

2 **Run** the query, and then compare your screen with Figure 2.43.

The query calculates the total amount of all scholarships for each student.

Figure 2.43

Total scholarship amount awarded to each student

3 Switch to **Design** view. In the design grid, delete the **Student ID** field, and then drag the **Sport** field to the first column—**Amount** becomes the second column.

4 In the design grid, click in the **Amount** field, and then on the **Design tab**, in the **Show/Hide group**, click the **Property Sheet** button.

5 In the **Property Sheet**, set the **Format** to **Currency**, set the **Decimal Places** to **0**, and then **Close** ⊠ the **Property Sheet**.

6 **Run** the query, and then compare your screen with Figure 2.44.

Access summarizes the data by sport. Basketball scholarships are the largest total Amount—*$3,500*.

Figure 2.44

Total scholarship amount awarded for each sport

7 Save 🔲 the query as **Lastname Firstname 2B Total by Sport Query** and then display the query results in **Print Preview**. Create a paper or electronic printout if instructed to do so, and then **Close Print Preview**. **Close** ✕ the query.

Objective 14 | Create a Crosstab Query

A *crosstab query* uses an aggregate function for data that can be grouped by two types of information and displays data in a compact, spreadsheet-like format. A crosstab query always has at least one row heading, one column heading, and one summary field. Use a crosstab query to summarize a large amount of data in a small space that is easy to read.

Activity 2.26 | Creating a Crosstab Query Using One Table

In this activity, you will create a crosstab query that displays the total amount of scholarships awarded for each sport and for each team—women's or men's.

1 On the **Create tab**, in the **Queries group**, click the **Query Wizard** button. In the **New Query** dialog box, click **Crosstab Query Wizard**, and then click **OK**.

2 In the **Crosstab Query Wizard**, click **Table: 2B Scholarships Awarded** and then click **Next**.

3 To select the row headings, under **Available Fields**, double-click **Sport** to sort the scholarship amounts by the different sports. Click **Next**, and then compare your screen with Figure 2.45.

The sports are displayed as *row headings*; here you are prompted to select *column headings*.

Figure 2.45

Crosstab Query Wizard—select column heading

Sport names display as row headings

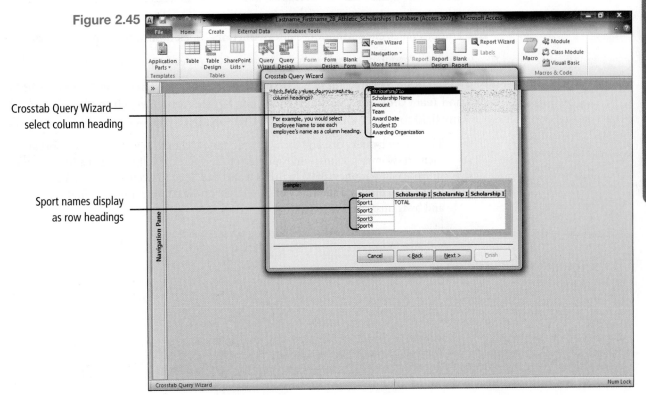

4 To select the column headings, in the field list, click **Team**. Click **Next**, and then compare your screen with Figure 2.46.

The teams will be listed as column headings; here you are prompted to select a field to summarize.

Figure 2.46

Teams display as column headings

5 Under **Fields**, click **Amount**. Under **Functions**, click **Sum**, and then click **Next**.

The crosstab query will sum the Amount field for each sport and team.

6 In the **What do you want to name your query?** box, type **Lastname Firstname 2B Sport and Team Crosstab Query** and then click **Finish**. Apply **Best Fit** to the columns, click in any field to cancel the selection, and then compare your screen with Figure 2.47.

The crosstab query displays the total amount of scholarships awarded by sport and also by men's or women's teams. For example, for the sport of Golf, a total of $700 was awarded in scholarship money; $500 to men's teams and $200 to women's teams. A crosstab query is useful to display a summary of data based on two different fields—in this case, by sport and by teams.

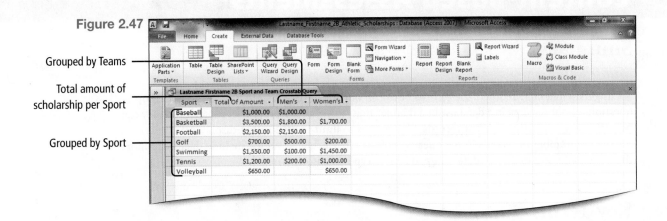

Figure 2.47

Grouped by Teams

Total amount of scholarship per Sport

Grouped by Sport

7 Display the query results in **Print Preview**. Create a paper or electronic printout if instructed to do so, and then **Close Print Preview**. **Close** ☒ the query, and click **Yes** to save changes to the query layout.

8 **Open** ☒ the **Navigation Pane**. In **Backstage** view, click **Close Database**, and then click **Exit**. As directed by your instructor, submit your database and the ten paper or electronic printouts—relationship report and nine queries—that are the results of this project.

More Knowledge | Creating a Crosstab Query Using Two Related Tables

To create a crosstab query using fields from more than one table, you must first create a select query with the fields from both tables that will be included in the crosstab query.

End **You have completed Project 2B** ——————————

Content-Based Assessments

Summary

Sorting data in a table reorders the records based on one or more fields. Use queries to ask complex questions about the data in a database in a manner that Access can interpret. Save queries so they can be run as needed against current records. Use queries to limit the fields that display, add criteria to restrict the number of records in the query results, create calculated values, include data from more than one table, and to display data grouped by two types of information.

Key Terms

Matching

Match each term in the second column with its correct definition in the first column by writing the letter of the term on the blank line in front of the correct definition.

_____ 1. The area below the Ribbon that displays information such as security alerts.

_____ 2. An area where you can view the security and privacy settings for your Access installation.

_____ 3. An association that you establish between two tables based on common fields.

_____ 4. A relationship between two tables where one record in the first table corresponds to many records in the second table.

_____ 5. A list of field names in a table.

_____ 6. The field that is included in the related table so the field can be joined with the primary key in another table for the purpose of creating a relationship.

_____ 7. A set of rules that ensures that the data between related tables is valid.

_____ 8. The line joining two tables that visually indicates the common fields and the type of relationship.

_____ 9. A format for displaying related records in a datasheet when you click the plus sign (+) next to a record in a table on the one side of a relationship.

_____ 10. The process of arranging data in a specific order based on the value in a field.

A Ascending

B Descending

C Field list

D Foreign key

E Innermost

F Join line

G Message Bar

H One-to-many relationship

I Outermost

J Referential integrity

K Relationship

L Select query

M Sorting

N Subdatasheet

O Trust Center

_____ 11. A sorting order that arranges text in alphabetical order (A to Z) or numbers from lowest to highest.

_____ 12. A sorting order that arranges text in reverse alphabetical order (Z to A) or numbers from highest to lowest.

_____ 13. When sorting on multiple fields in Datasheet view, the field that is used for the first level of sorting.

_____ 14. When sorting on multiple fields in Datasheet view, the field that is used for the second level of sorting.

_____ 15. A database object that retrieves (selects) specific data from one or more tables and then displays the results in Datasheet view.

Multiple Choice

Circle the correct answer.

1. The lower area of the Query window that displays the design of the query is the:
   A. design grid   B. property sheet   C. table area

2. The process in which Access searches the records in the table, finds the records that match specified criteria, and then displays the records in a datasheet is:
   A. select   B. run   C. sort

3. Conditions in a query that identify the specific records for which you are looking are known as:
   A. aggregate functions B. criteria   C. expressions

4. A criteria that searches for fields that are empty is:
   A. Is Empty   B. Is Not Null   C. Is Null

5. The symbols of =, >, and < are known as:
   A. aggregate functions B. comparison operators   C. logical operators

6. A comparison operator that looks for values within a range is:
   A. And   B. Between ... And   C. Or

7. The logical operator that requires all conditions to be met is:
   A. AND   B. Is Null   C. OR

8. A wildcard character that serves as a placeholder for one or more unknown characters is the:
   A. *   B. ?   C. /

9. A field that stores the value of a mathematical operation is:
   A. an aggregate field   B. a calculated field   C. an expression

10. A query that uses an aggregate function for data that can be grouped by two types of information is:
    A. an aggregate query B. a calculated query   C. a crosstab query

Access | Chapter 2

Content-Based Assessments

Apply **2A** skills from these Objectives:

1. Open an Existing Database
2. Create Table Relationships
3. Sort Records in a Table
4. Create a Query in Design View
5. Create a New Query from an Existing Query
6. Sort Query Results
7. Specify Criteria in a Query

Skills Review | Project **2C** Music Department

In the following Skills Review, you will assist Dr. William Jinkens, the Capital Cities Community College Music Director, in using his database to answer various questions about the instruments in the Music Department's inventory. Your results will look similar to Figure 2.48.

Project Files

For Project 2C, you will need the following file:

a02c_Music_Department

You will save your database as:

Lastname_Firstname_2C_Music_Department

Project Results

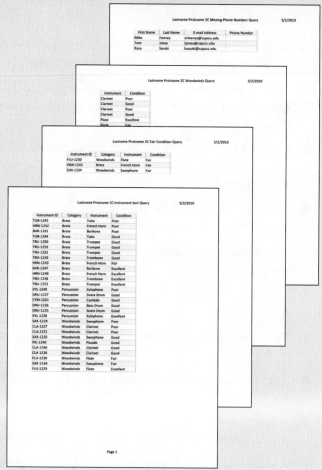

Figure 2.48

(Project 2C Music Department continues on the next page)

Content-Based Assessments

1 **Start** Access. In **Backstage** view, click **Open**. Navigate to the student files that accompany this textbook, and then open the **a02C_Music_Department** database.

a. Click the **File tab** to return to **Backstage** view, and then click **Save Database As**. In the **Save As** dialog box, navigate to your **Access Chapter 2** folder. In the **File name** box, select the file name, and then type **Lastname_Firstname_2C_Music_Department** and then press Enter. In the **Message Bar**, click **Enable Content**.

b. **Rename** the 2C Student Musicians table to **Lastname Firstname 2C Student Musicians** and then **Rename** the 2C Instruments Inventory to **Lastname Firstname 2C Instruments Inventory** Widen the **Navigation Pane** to display fully both table names.

2 **Open** both tables to examine the contents of each, **Close** the tables, and then **Close** the **Navigation Pane**.

a. Click the **Database Tools tab**, and in the **Relationships group** click the **Relationships** button. Drag the **Show Table** dialog box down into the lower right portion of your screen.

b. In the **Show Table** dialog box, click your **2C Student Musicians**, and then click **Add**. Double-click your **2C Instruments Inventory** to add the table to the **Relationships** window. In the **Show Table** dialog box, click **Close**.

c. Drag the **2C Instruments Inventory** field list—the field list on the right—to the right about 3 inches. In the **2C Student Musicians** field list—the field list on the left—position your mouse pointer over the lower right corner of the field list to display the ⬚ pointer, and then drag to the right to increase the width of the field list until the entire name of the table in the title bar displays and all of the field names display. Then use the ⬚ pointer to resize the **2C Instruments Inventory** field list so that all of the field names and the table name display.

d. In the **2C Student Musicians** field list, point to **Student ID**, hold down the left mouse button, and then drag down and to the right to the **2C Instruments Inventory** field list until your mouse pointer is on top of **Student ID**. Then release the mouse button. Drag the **Edit Relationships** dialog box to the lower portion of your screen. The relationship between the two tables is a one-to-many relationship; *one* student can play *many* instruments.

e. In the **Edit Relationships** dialog box, click to select the **Enforce Referential Integrity** check box, and then click the **Create** button. On the **Design tab**, in the **Tools group**, click the **Relationship Report** button. On the **Print Preview tab**, in the **Page Size group**, change the **Margins** to **Normal**, and then create a paper or electronic printout as directed.

f. **Save** the relationship report with the default name. **Close** the report, and then **Close** the **Relationships** window. From the **Navigation Pane**, open the 2C **Instruments Inventory** table, and then **Close** the **Navigation Pane**.

3 In the **Condition** field, click any record. On the **Home tab**, in the **Sort & Filter group**, click the **Descending** button to sort the records from *Poor* to *Excellent*. In the field names row, click the **Category arrow**, and then click **Sort A to Z** to sort the records first by *Category* and then by *Condition*.

a. Display **Backstage** view, click **Print**, and then click **Print Preview**. Create a paper or electronic copy as directed. **Close Print Preview**, **Close** the table, and then click **No**; you do not need to save the sort changes.

4 Click the **Create tab**, and then in the **Queries group**, click the **Query Design** button. In the **Show Table** dialog box, double-click your **2C Instruments Inventory** table, and then **Close** the **Show Table** dialog box. Expand the field list.

a. Double-click **Instrument ID** to add the field to the design grid. Point to the **Category** field, hold down the left mouse button, and then drag the field down into the design grid until you are pointing to the **Field** row in the second column. Release the mouse button.

b. In design grid, in the **Field** row, click in the third column, and then click the **arrow** that displays. From the list, click **Instrument** to add the field to the design grid. Using the technique of your choice, add the **Student ID** field to the fourth column and the **Condition** field to the fifth column in the design grid.

c. On the **Design tab**, in the **Results group**, click the **Run** button. This query answers the question, *What is the Instrument ID, Category, Instrument, Student ID, and Condition of all of the instruments in the 2C Instruments Inventory table?*

d. **Save** the query as **Lastname Firstname 2C All Instruments Query** and then click **OK**. Display the query in **Print Preview**, and then create a paper or electronic printout as directed. **Close Print Preview**.

(Project 2C Music Department continues on the next page)

Access | **Chapter 2**

5 Display **Backstage** view, click **Save Object As**. In the **Save As** dialog box, type **Lastname Firstname 2C Condition Query** and then click **OK** to create a new query based on an existing query. Click the **Home tab**, and then switch to **Design** view.

a. In the design grid, point to the thin gray selection bar above the **Student ID** field name until the ⬇ pointer displays. Click to select the **Student ID** column, and then press ⌈Del⌋.

b. In the gray selection bar, select the **Instrument ID** column. Point to the **selection bar** to display the ⬉ pointer, and then drag to the right until a dark vertical line displays on the right side of the **Condition** column. Release the mouse button to position the **Instrument ID** field in the fourth column.

c. **Run** the query. The query results display four fields. This query answers the question, *What is the Category, Instrument, Condition, and Instrument ID for every Instrument in the 2C Instruments Inventory table?*

d. Display the query in **Print Preview**, and then create a paper or electronic printout as directed. **Close Print Preview**, **Close** the query, and in the message box, click **Yes** to save the changes to the design—you moved two fields. **Open** the **Navigation Pane**.

6 **Open** your **2C All Instruments Query**. **Save** the query object as **Lastname Firstname 2C Instrument Sort Query** and then click the **Home tab**. **Close** the **Navigation Pane**. Switch to **Design** view.

a. In the design grid, delete the **Student ID** field. In the **Sort** row, click in the **Category** field. Click the **Sort arrow**, and then in the list, click **Ascending**. In the **Sort** row, click in the **Condition** field, click the **Sort arrow**, and then click **Descending**. **Run** the query. This query answers the question, *For every Instrument ID, within each Category (with Category sorted in ascending order), what Instruments are in the inventory and what is the instrument's Condition (with Condition sorted in descending order)?*

b. Display the query in **Print Preview**. Create a paper or electronic printout if instructed to do so, and then **Close Print Preview**. **Close** the query. In the message box, click **Yes** to save the changes to the query design.

7 Click the **Create tab**, and then in the **Queries group**, click the **Query Design** button. **Add** your **2C Instruments Inventory** table to the table area, and then **Close** the **Show Table** dialog box. Expand the field list. Add the following

fields to the design grid in the order given: **Instrument ID**, **Category**, **Instrument**, and **Condition**.

a. In the design grid, on the **Criteria** row, click in the **Condition** field, type **fair** and then press ⌈Enter⌋. **Run** the query; three records display that meet the specified criteria—records that have *fair* in the Condition field.

b. **Save** the query as **Lastname Firstname 2C Fair Condition Query** and then create a paper or electronic printout as directed. **Close Print Preview**, and then **Close** the query.

c. **Create** a new query in **Query Design** view. **Add** the **2C Instruments Inventory** table to the table area, and then expand the field list. Add the following fields, in the order given, to the design grid: **Category**, **Instrument**, and **Condition**.

d. In the **Criteria** row, click in the **Category** field, type **woodwinds** and then press ⌈Enter⌋. Under **Category**, in the **Show** row, click to clear the check box, and then **Run** the query. Ten instruments are categorized as woodwinds. Recall that if all results use the same criteria, such as *woodwinds*, it is not necessary to display the data in the query results.

e. **Save** the query as **Lastname Firstname 2C Woodwinds Query** and then create a paper or electronic printout as directed. **Close Print Preview**. **Close** the query.

f. **Create** a new query in **Query Design** view. **Add** the **2C Student Musicians** table to the table area, and then expand the field list. Add the following fields, in the order given, to the design grid: **First Name**, **Last Name**, **E-mail Address**, and **Phone Number**.

g. In the **Criteria** row, click in the **Phone Number** field, type **is null** and then press ⌈Enter⌋. In the **Sort** row, click in the **Last Name** field, click the **Sort arrow**, and then click **Ascending**. **Run** the query. Three student musicians do not have a phone number stored in the 2C Student Musicians table.

h. **Save** the query as **Lastname Firstname 2C Missing Phone Numbers Query** and then create a paper or electronic printout as directed. **Close Print Preview**, and then **Close** the query. **Open** the **Navigation Pane**.

i. Display **Backstage** view, click **Close Database**, and then click **Exit** to close the Access program. As directed by your instructor, submit your database and the eight paper or electronic printouts— relationship report, sorted table, and six queries— that are the results of this project.

End You have completed Project 2C

Content-Based Assessments

- **8** Specify Numeric Criteria in a Query
- **9** Use Compound Criteria
- **10** Create a Query Based on More Than One Table
- **11** Use Wildcards in a Query
- **12** Use Calculated Fields in a Query
- **13** Calculate Statistics and Group Data in a Query
- **14** Create a Crosstab Query

Skills Review | Project **2D** Concerts and Sponsors

In the following Skills Review, you will assist Dr. William Jinkens, the Capital Cities Community College Music Director, in answering questions about concerts, sponsors, box office receipts, dates, and concert locations. Your results will look similar to Figure 2.49.

Project Files

For Project 2D, you will need the following files:

a02D_Concerts_Sponsors
a02D_Sponsors (Excel file)

You will save your database as:

Lastname_Firstname_2D_Concerts_Sponsors

Project Results

Figure 2.49

(Project 2D Concerts and Sponsors continues on the next page)

Access | Chapter 2

Content-Based Assessments

1 **Start** Access. In the **Backstage** view, click **Open**. Navigate to the student files that accompany this textbook, and then open the **a02D_Concerts_Sponsors** database.

a. Click the **File tab** to return to **Backstage** view, and then click **Save Database As**. In the **Save As** dialog box, navigate to your **Access Chapter 2** folder. In the **File name** box, select the file name, and then type **Lastname_Firstname_2D_Concerts_Sponsors** and then press Enter. In the **Message Bar**, click **Enable Content**. **Rename** the **2D Concerts** table to **Lastname Firstname 2D Concerts** and then widen the **Navigation Pane** to display the entire table name.

b. Click the **External Data tab**, and then in the **Import & Link group**, click the **Excel** button. In the **Get External Data – Excel Spreadsheet** dialog box, click **Browse**. Navigate to your student files, and then double-click the Excel file **a02D_Sponsors**. Be sure that the **Import the source data into a new table in the current database** option button is selected, and then click **OK**.

c. In the **Import Spreadsheet Wizard**, select the **First Row Contains Column Headings** check box, and then click **Next**. Click **Next** again. Click the **Choose my own primary key** option button, and then be sure that **Sponsor ID** displays. Click **Next**. In the **Import to Table** box, type **Lastname Firstname 2D Sponsors** and then click **Finish**. In the Wizard, click **Close**. The imported Excel spreadsheet becomes the second table in the database.

d. From the **Navigation Pane**, open your **2D Sponsors** table. Apply **Best Fit** to all columns, and then **Close** the table, saving changes to the design. Click the **Database Tools tab**, and in the **Relationships group**, click the **Relationships** button. **Add** the **2D Sponsors** table, and then **Add** the **2D Concerts** table to the table area. **Close** the **Show Table** dialog box. Expand and move the field lists as necessary.

e. In the **2D Sponsors** field list, point to the **Sponsor ID** field, hold down the left mouse button, drag into the **2D Concerts** field list, position the mouse pointer on top of the **Sponsor ID** field, and then release the mouse button. In the **Edit Relationships** dialog box, select the **Enforce Referential Integrity** check box, and then click the **Create** button. A one-to-many relationship is established; *one* sponsor organization can sponsor *many* concerts.

f. On the **Design tab**, in the **Tools group**, click the **Relationship Report** button. Create a paper or electronic printout as directed, and then **Close** the report. In the message box, click **Yes**; and then in the **Save As** dialog box, click **OK** to save the report with the default name. **Close** the **Relationships** window, and then **Close** the **Navigation Pane**.

2 Click the **Create tab**, and then in the **Queries group**, click the **Query Design** button. **Add** the **2D Concerts** table to the table area, **Close** the **Show Table** dialog box, and then expand the field list.

a. Add the following fields to the design grid in the order given: **Concert Name**, **Box Office Receipts**, and **Concert Location**. Click in the **Sort** row under **Concert Location**, click the **Sort arrow**, and then click **Ascending**. In the **Criteria** row, under **Box Office Receipts**, type **>=800** press Enter, and then **Run** the query. Nine records meet the criteria. This query answers the question, *Which concerts had Box Office Receipts of $800 or more, and where was each concert held in alphabetical order by Concert Location?*

b. **Save** the query as **Lastname Firstname 2D $800 or More Query** and then create a paper or electronic printout as directed. **Close Print Preview**.

c. With the query still open, display **Backstage** view, click **Save Object As**, type **Lastname Firstname 2D Concerts Jan-Apr Query** and then click **OK**. Click the **Home tab**, and then switch to **Design** view. From the **2D Concerts** field list, add **Date** as the fourth field in the design grid.

d. In the **Criteria** row, under **Box Office Receipts**, delete the existing criteria so that the query is not restricted by receipts. Click in the **Sort** row under **Concert Location**, click the **Sort arrow**, and then click **(not sorted)**. Click in the **Sort** row under **Date**, click the **Sort arrow**, and then click **Ascending**.

e. Click in the **Criteria** row under **Date**, type **between 1/1/16 and 4/30/16** and then press Enter. **Run** the query. Five records meet the criteria. This query answers the question, *What is the Concert Name, Box Office Receipts, Concert Location, and Date, in chronological order between January 1, 2016, and April 30, 2016, of concerts held?* **Print** or submit electronically as directed. **Close Print Preview**, **Close** the query, and then click **Yes** to save the changes to the query design.

(Project 2D Concerts and Sponsors continues on the next page)

Content-Based Assessments

Skills Review | Project 2D Concerts and Sponsors (continued)

3 **Create** a query in **Query Design** view. **Add** the **2D Concerts** table to the table area, **Close** the **Show Table** dialog box, and then expand the field list. Add the following fields to the design grid in the order given: **Concert Name**, **Concert Location**, and **Box Office Receipts**.

a. In the **Criteria** row, under **Concert Location**, type **Virginia Community Theater** and then press Enter. In the **Criteria** row, under **Box Office Receipts**, type **<=1000** and then press Enter. In the **Concert Location** field, clear the **Show** check box. **Run** the query; two records display. This query answers the question, *Which concerts that were held at the Virginia Community Theater had Box Office Receipts of $1,000 or less?*

b. **Save** the query as **Lastname Firstname 2D VCT Low Box Office Receipts Query** and then create a paper or electronic printout as directed. **Close** the query.

c. **Create** a query in **Query Design** view. **Add** the **2D Concerts** table to the table area, **Close** the **Show Table** dialog box, and then expand the field list. Add the following fields to the design grid: **Concert Name**, **Concert Location**, **Box Office Receipts**, and **Date**.

d. In the **Criteria** row, under **Concert Location**, type **Virginia Community Theater or DC Events Center** and press Enter. In the **Criteria** row, under **Box Office Receipts**, type **>1000** and then press Enter. In the **Sort** row, under **Date**, click the **Sort arrow**, and then click **Ascending**.

e. **Run** the query. Four records display. This query answers the question, *Which concerts held at either the Virginia Community Theater or the DC Events Center had Box Office Receipts of more than $1,000 and on what dates, in chronological order, were the concerts held?*

f. **Save** the query as **Lastname Firstname 2D VCT or DC Over $1000 Query** and then create a paper or electronic printout as directed. **Close Print Preview**, and then **Close** the query.

4 **Create** a query in **Query Design** view, **Add** both tables to the table area, and then expand the field lists. Reposition the field lists so that **2D Sponsors** is on the left side. From the **2D Sponsors** field list, add the following fields to the design grid in the order given: **Sponsor Name** and **Web Address**. Click in the **Sort** row

under **Sponsor Name**, click the **Sort arrow**, and then click **Ascending**.

a. From the **2D Concerts** field list, add the following fields to the design grid in the order give: **Concert Name**, **Concert Location**, and **Box Office Receipts**.

b. In the **Criteria** row, under **Concert Location**, type **Virginia Community Theater** and then click in the **or** row, under **Concert Location**. Type **DC Events Center** and then press Enter.

c. In the design grid, select the **Box Office Receipts** field, and then drag it to the first field position in the grid. **Run** the query; 12 records display. This query answers the question, *What were the Box Office Receipts, Sponsor Name, sponsor Web Address, Concert Name, and Concert Location of all concerts held at either the Virginia Community Theater or the DC Events Center, sorted alphabetically by Sponsor Name?*

d. **Save** the query as **Lastname Firstname 2D Receipts and Sponsors VCT or DC Query** and then display the query results in **Print Preview**. Change the orientation to **Landscape**, change the **Margins** to **Normal**, and then create a paper or electronic printout as directed. **Close** the query.

5 **Create** a query in **Query Design** view, **Add** both tables to the table area, **Close** the **Show Table** dialog box, and then expand the field lists. Reposition the field lists so that **2D Sponsors** is on the left side.

a. From the **2D Sponsors** field list, add the **Sponsor Name** field to the design grid. From the **2D Concerts** field list, add the **Concert Name** field to the design grid.

b. In the **Criteria** row, under **Sponsor Name**, type ***radio*** and then press Enter. In the **Criteria** row, under **Concert Name**, type ***festival** and then press Enter.

c. **Run** the query; two records have the word *Radio* somewhere in the Sponsor Name and the word *Festival* at the end of the Concert Name. This query answers the question, *Which radio stations are sponsoring Festival-type concerts?* **Save** the query as **Lastname Firstname 2D Radio Festivals Query** and then create a paper or electronic printout as directed. **Close** the query.

6 **Create** a query in **Query Design** view. **Add** both tables to the table area, **Close** the **Show Table** dialog box, and then expand the field lists. If necessary, reposition the

(Project 2D Concerts and Sponsors continues on the next page)

Access | Chapter 2

Content-Based Assessments

field lists so that *2D Sponsors* is on the left side. From the field lists, add the following fields to the design grid in the order given: **Concert ID**, **Sponsor Name**, and **Box Office Receipts**. Click in the **Sort** row under **Concert ID**, click the **Sort arrow**, and then click **Ascending**.

a. Sponsors have indicated that they will donate an additional amount to the Music Department based on 50 percent of the Box Office Receipts. On the **Field** row, right-click in the first empty column to display a shortcut menu, and then click **Zoom**. In the **Zoom** dialog box, type **Matching Donation:[Box Office Receipts]*0.5** and then click **OK**.

b. **Run** the query to view the new field—*Matching Donation*. Switch to **Design** view. In the **Field** row, in the first empty column, right-click, and then click **Zoom**. In the **Zoom** dialog box, type **Total Receipts: [Box Office Receipts]+[Matching Donation]** and then click **OK**. **Run** the query to view the results.

c. Switch to **Design** view. In the field row, click in the **Matching Donations** field. In the **Show/Hide group**, click the **Property Sheet** button, and then set the **Format** to **Currency** and the **Decimal Places** to **2**. **Close** the **Property Sheet**.

d. **Run** the query. This query answers the question *In ascending order by Concert ID, assuming each sponsor makes a matching 50 percent donation based on each concert's Box Office Receipts, what is the Sponsor Name, Box Office Receipts, Matching Donation, and Total Receipts for each concert?*

e. Select all of the columns, and then apply **Best Fit**. **Save** the query as **Lastname Firstname 2D Matching Donation Query** and then display the query results in **Print Preview**. Change the orientation to **Landscape**, and then create a paper or electronic printout as directed. **Close** the query.

7 Create a query in **Query Design** view. **Add** the **2D Concerts** table to the table area, **Close** the **Show Table** dialog box, and then expand the field list. Add the **Box Office Receipts** field to the design grid.

a. On the **Design tab**, in the **Show/Hide group**, click the **Totals** button, which adds a *Total* row as the third row in the design grid. On the **Total** row, under **Box Office Receipts**, click in the **Group By** box. Click the **arrow**, and then click the **Sum** function.

b. With the field still selected, display the **Property Sheet**, set the **Decimal Places** to **0**, and then **Close** the **Property Sheet**. **Run** the query. The total Box Office Receipts for all the concerts was $*17,475*. Apply **Best Fit** to the **SumOfBox Office Receipts** column.

c. Switch to **Design** view. In the design grid, add the **Concert Location** field as the first field of the design grid. **Run** the query. This query answers the question *For each Concert Location, what are the total Box Office Receipts?*

d. **Save** the query as **Lastname Firstname 2D Total Receipts by Location Query** and then create a paper or electronic printout as directed. **Close** the query.

8 Create a query using the **Query Wizard**. In the **New Query** dialog box, click **Crosstab Query Wizard**, and then click **OK**. Be sure that **2D Concerts** is selected, and then click **Next**.

a. Under **Available Fields**, double-click **Sponsor ID** so that you can display Box Office Receipts by Sponsor ID, and then click **Next**. In the field list, click **Concert Location** to add the locations as column headings, and then click **Next**.

b. Under **Fields**, click **Box Office Receipts**. Under **Functions**, click **Sum**, and then click **Next**.

c. Name the query **Lastname Firstname 2D Sponsors and Locations Crosstab Query** and then click **Finish**. Click the **Home tab**, switch to **Design** view, click in the **Box Office Receipts** column, display the **Property Sheet**, and then set the **Decimal Places** to **0**. **Close** the **Property Sheet**, **Run** the query, and apply **Best Fit** to all of the columns. This query answers the question *By Sponsor ID, what are the total Box Office Receipts for each Concert Location?*

d. Display the query results in **Print Preview**. Change the orientation to **Landscape**, change the **Margins** to **Normal**, and then create a paper or electronic printout as directed—two pages result. **Close** the query, saving changes to the design.

e. **Open** the **Navigation Pane**. Increase the width of the **Navigation Pane** to display fully all of the object names. Display **Backstage** view, click **Close Database**, and then click **Exit**. As directed by your instructor, submit your database and the ten paper or electronic printouts—relationship report and nine queries—that are the results of this project.

 You have completed Project 2D

Content-Based Assessments

Apply 2A skills from these Objectives:

1. Open an Existing Database
2. Create Table Relationships
3. Sort Records in a Table
4. Create a Query in Design View
5. Create a New Query from an Existing Query
6. Sort Query Results
7. Specify Criteria in a Query

Mastering Access | Project 2E Grants and Organizations

In the following Mastering Access project, you will assist Susan Elkington, Director of Grants for the college, in using her database to answer questions about public and private grants awarded to the college departments. Your results will look similar to Figure 2.50.

Project Files

For Project 2E, you will need the following file:

    a02E_Grants_Organizations

You will save your database as:

    Lastname_Firstname_2E_Grants_Organizations

Project Results

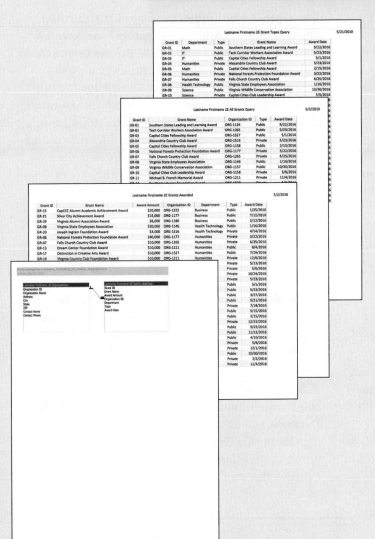

Figure 2.50

(Project 2E Grants and Organizations continues on the next page)

Access | Chapter 2

Content-Based Assessments

Mastering Access | Project 2E Grants and Organizations (continued)

1 **Start** Access. From your student files, open the **a02E_Grants_Organizations** database. Save the database in your **Access Chapter 2** folder as **Lastname_Firstname_2E_Grants_Organizations** and then enable the content. In the **Navigation Pane**, **Rename** the tables by adding **Lastname Firstname** to the beginning of each table name, and then widen the **Navigation Pane** to display fully both table names. **Open** both tables and examine their contents to become familiar with the data. **Close** both tables, and leave the **Navigation Pane** open.

2 Create a *one-to-many* relationship between the **2E Organizations** table and the **2E Grants Awarded** table based on the **Organization ID** field, and then **Enforce Referential Integrity**. *One* organization can award *many* grants. Create a **Relationship Report**, saving it with the default name. Create a paper or electronic printout as directed, and then **Close** all open objects, saving changes if prompted.

3 **Open** the **2E Grants Awarded** table, and then **Close** the **Navigation Pane**. **Sort** so that the records in the table are in alphabetical order by the **Department** and then in descending order by **Award Amount**. Create a paper or electronic printout as directed, being sure that the table prints on only one page by using **Landscape**, with **Normal** margins. **Close** the table, and do *not* save changes to the table.

4 **Create** a query in **Query Design** view, using the **2E Grants Awarded** table to answer the question, *What is the Grant ID, Grant Name, Award Amount, Type, and Award Date for all of the grants?* Display the fields in the order listed in the question. **Save** the query as **Lastname Firstname 2E All Grants Query** and then, with **Normal** margins, create a paper or electronic printout as directed. **Close Print Preview**, and leave the query open.

5 Use **2E All Grants Query** to create a new query. **Save** the **Object As Lastname Firstname 2E Grant Types Query** and then redesign the query to answer the question, *What is the Grant ID, Department, Type, Grant Name, and Award Amount for all grants?* Display the only the fields necessary to answer the question and in the order listed in the question. With **Normal** margins, create a paper or

electronic printout as directed. **Close** the query, saving the design changes.

6 From the **Navigation Pane**, open the **2E All Grants Query**, and then **Close** the **Navigation Pane**. **Save** the **Object As Lastname Firstname 2E Grant Sort Query** and then switch to **Design** view. Redesign the query to answer the question, *What is the Grant Name, Department, Award Amount, and Award Date for grants sorted first in alphabetical order by Department and then in descending order by Amount?* Display only the fields necessary to answer the question and in the order listed in the question. With **Normal** margins, create a paper or electronic printout as directed. **Close** the query, saving changes to the query design.

7 **Open** the **Navigation Pane**, open **2E Grant Sort Query**, and then **Close** the **Navigation Pane**. **Save** the **Object As Lastname Firstname 2E Private Grants Query** and then switch to **Design** view. Redesign the query to answer the question, *What is the Grant Name, Department, Award Amount, and Award Date for grants that have a Type of Private, sorted in alphabetical order by Grant Name?* Do *not* display the **Type** field in the query results; display the fields in the order listed in the question. With **Normal** margins, create a paper or electronic printout as directed. **Close** the query, saving changes to the query design.

8 **Create** a query in **Query Design** view, using the **2E Organizations** table to answer the question, *What is the Organization Name and Contact Name where the Contact Phone number is missing from the table, sorted in alphabetical order by the Organization Name?* Two records meet the criteria. **Save** the query as **Lastname Firstname 2E Missing Phone# Query** and then create a paper or electronic printout as directed. **Close** the query.

9 **Open** the **Navigation Pane** and widen it so that all object names display fully. In **Backstage** view, click **Close Database**, and then click **Exit**. As directed by your instructor, submit your database and the seven paper or electronic printouts—relationship report, sorted table, and five queries—that are the results of this project.

End **You have completed Project 2E**

Content-Based Assessments

8 Specify Numeric Criteria in a Query

9 Use Compound Criteria

10 Create a Query Based on More Than One Table

11 Use Wildcards in a Query

12 Use Calculated Fields in a Query

13 Calculate Statistics and Group Data in a Query

14 Create a Crosstab Query

Mastering Access | Project **2F** Events and Clients

In the following Mastering Access project, you will assist Hank Schwan, the Capital Cities Community College Facilities Manager, in using his database to answer questions about facilities that the college rents to community and private organizations at times when the facilities are not in use for college activities. Your results will look similar to Figure 2.51.

Project Files

For Project 2F, you will need the following files:

a02F_Events_Clients
a02F_Rental_Clients (Excel file)

You will save your database as:

Lastname_Firstname_2F_Events_Clients

Project Results

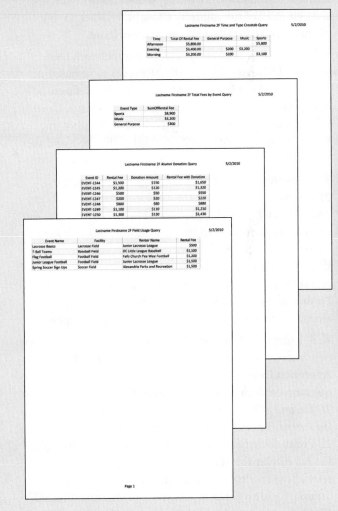

Figure 2.51

(Project 2F Events and Clients continues on the next page)

1 **Start** Access. From your student files, open the **a02F_Events_Clients** database. Save the database in your **Access Chapter 2** folder as **Lastname_Firstname_2F_Events_Clients** and then enable the content. In the **Navigation Pane**, **Rename** the table by adding **Lastname Firstname** to the beginning of the table name.

2 **Import** the **a02F_Rental_Clients** Excel spreadsheet from the student data files that accompany this textbook into the current database as a new table. Designate the first row of the spreadsheet as column headings. Select the **Rental Client ID** field as the primary key. Name the table **Lastname Firstname 2F Rental Clients** and then widen the **Navigation Pane** to display fully the two table names. **Open** both tables and examine their contents to become familiar with the data. In the **2F Rental Clients** table, apply **Best Fit** to all of the columns. **Close** both tables, saving changes, and then **Close** the **Navigation Pane**.

3 Create a *one-to-many* relationship between the **2F Rental Clients** table and the **2F Events** table based on the **Rental Client ID** field, and then **Enforce Referential Integrity**. *One* rental client can have *many* events. Create a **Relationship Report**, saving it with the default name. Create a paper or electronic printout as directed, and then **Close** all open objects, saving changes if prompted.

4 **Create** a query in **Query Design** view using the **2F Events** table to answer the question, *What is the Event Name, Rental Client ID, and Rental Fee for events with fees greater than or equal to $500, in ascending order by Rental Client ID, and in which Facility was the event held?* Display the fields in the order listed in the question. Eleven records meet the criteria. **Save** the query as **Lastname Firstname 2F Fees $500 or More Query** Create a paper or electronic printout as directed. Leave the query open.

5 Using the **2F Fees $500 or More Query** object, create a new query, and save it as **Lastname Firstname 2F Afternoon Events Query** Redesign the query to answer the questions, *Which Events were held in the Afternoon between 7/1/16 and 8/31/16, in chronological order by date, what was the Rental Fee, and what was the Event ID?* (Hint: Open the 2F Events table to see how the Time field data is stored.). Do *not* display the **Time** field in the results, and do *not* restrict the results by **Rental Fee**. Four records meet the criteria. Create a paper or electronic printout as directed, **Close** the query, and save changes to the design.

6 **Create** a query in **Query Design** view using the **2F Events** table to answer the question, *Which Events and Event Types were held in either the White Sands Music Hall or the Theater that had Rental Fees greater than $500?* Display the fields in the order listed in the question. Three records meet the criteria. **Save** the query as **Lastname Firstname 2F WS and Theater Over $500 Query** and then create a paper or electronic printout as directed. **Close** the query.

7 **Create** a query in **Query Design** view using both tables to answer the question, *Which Events were held on one of the sports fields, for which Renter Name, and what was the Rental Fee in order of lowest fee to highest fee?* (Hint: Use a wildcard with the word *Field*.) Display the fields in the order listed in the question. Five records meet the criteria. **Save** the query as **Lastname Firstname 2F Field Usage Query** and then with **Normal** margins, create a paper or electronic printout as directed. **Close** the query.

8 The college Alumni Association will donate money to the Building Fund in an amount based on 10 percent of total facility rental fees. **Create** a query in **Query Design** view to answer the question, *In ascending order by Event ID, what will be the total of each Rental Fee if the Alumni Association donates an additional 10% of each fee?* (Hint: First compute the amount of the donation, name the new field **Donation Amount** and run the query to view the results. Then calculate the new rental fee and name the new field **Rental Fee with Donation**) **Run** the query.

Switch back to **Design** view, change the properties of the new fields to display in **Currency** format with **0** decimal places, and then **Run** the query again. For *EVENT-1244*, the *Donation Amount* is *$150* and the *Rental Fee with Donation* is *$1,650*. Apply **Best Fit** to the columns in the query results. **Save** the query as **Lastname Firstname 2F Alumni Donation Query** and then create a paper or electronic printout as directed. **Close** the query.

9 **Create** a query in **Query Design** view using the **2F Events** table and the **Sum** aggregate function to answer the question, *In descending order by Rental Fee, what are the total Rental Fees for each Event Type?* Change the properties of the appropriate field to display **Currency** format with **0** decimal places, and then **Run** the query. For a *Sports* Event Type, Rental Fees total *$8,900*. Apply **Best Fit** to the columns in the query results. **Save** the query as **Lastname Firstname 2F Total Fees by Event Query** and then create a paper or electronic printout as directed. **Close** the query.

(Project 2F Events and Clients continues on the next page)

10 By using the **Query Wizard**, create a **Crosstab Query** based on the **2F Events** table. Select **Time** as the **row headings** and **Event Type** as the **column headings**. **Sum** the **Rental Fee** field. Name the query **Lastname Firstname 2F Time and Type Crosstab Query** Change the design to display **Currency** format with **0** decimal places in the appropriate column, and then apply **Best Fit** to all of the columns. This query answers the question *What are the total Rental Fees for each time of the day and for each Event Type?* Create

a paper or electronic printout as directed. **Close** the query, saving changes to the design.

11 **Open** the **Navigation Pane** and widen it so that all object names display fully. In **Backstage** view, click **Close Database**, and then click **Exit**. As directed by your instructor, submit your database and the eight paper or electronic printouts—relationship report and seven queries—that are the results of this project.

End **You have completed Project 2F**

Access | Chapter 2

Content-Based Assessments

Mastering Access | Project **2G** Students and Scholarships

In the following Mastering Access project, you will assist Thao Nguyen, Director of Academic Scholarships, in using her database to answer questions about scholarships awarded to students. Your results will look similar to Figure 2.52.

Project Files

For Project 2G, you will need the following file:

  a02G_Students_Scholarships

You will save your database as:

  Lastname_Firstname_2G_Students_Scholarships

Project Results

Figure 2.52

(Project 2G Students and Scholarships continues on the next page)

Mastering Access | Project **2G** Students and Scholarships (continued)

1 **Start** Access. From your student files, open the **a02G_Students_Scholarships** database. Save the database in your **Access Chapter 2** folder as **Lastname_Firstname_ 2G_Students_Scholarships** and then enable the content. **Rename** both tables by adding **Lastname Firstname** to the beginning of the table name, and then widen the **Navigation Pane** to display fully the object names.

2 Open the two database tables to become familiar with the data. **Close** the tables, and then create a *one-to-many* relationship between the **2G Students** table and the **2G Scholarships Awarded** table based on the **Student ID** field, and then **Enforce Referential Integrity**; *one* student can have *many* scholarships. Create the **Relationship Report**, and create a paper or electronic printout as directed, saving it with the default name. **Close** all open objects.

3 Open the **2G Scholarships Awarded** table, and then **Sort** the appropriate fields in **Ascending** order so that the records are sorted by the **Major** field. Within each Major, the records should be sorted by **Scholarship Name**. Create a paper or electronic printout, being sure to print the results on one page. **Close** the table, and do *not* save changes to the table design. **Close** the **Navigation Pane**.

4 **Create** a query in **Query Design** view using the **2G Scholarships Awarded** table to answer the question, *In alphabetical order by Scholarship Name, what is the Amount and Major for scholarships greater than or equal to $500?* Display the fields in the order listed in the question. Ten records meet the criteria. **Save** the query as **Lastname Firstname 2G Scholarships $500 or More Query** and create a paper or electronic printout as directed. **Close Print Preview**, and leave the query open.

5 Using the **2G Scholarships $500 or More Query**, create a query. **Save** the **Object As Lastname Firstname 2G Scholarships 1st Qtr Query** and then redesign the query to answer the question *Which scholarships were awarded, in chronological order by Award Date, between 1/1/16 and 3/31/16, for what Amount, and what was Student ID of the student?* Display the fields in the order listed in the question, display *only* the fields listed in the question, do *not* restrict the amount, and sort only by date. Eight records meet the criteria. Create a paper or electronic printout as directed. **Close** the query, saving changes.

6 **Create** a query in **Query Design** view using the **2G Scholarships Awarded** table to answer the question, *Which scholarships were awarded for either Nursing or CIS majors for Amounts of more than $100, listed in descending*

order by Amount? Display the fields in the order listed in the question. Four records meet the criteria. (Hint: If five records display, switch to **Design view** and combine the majors on one criteria line using OR.) **Save** the query as **Lastname Firstname 2G Nursing or CIS More Than $100 Query** and then create a paper or electronic printout as directed. **Close** the query.

7 **Create** a query in **Query Design** view. Use the **2G Students** table and a wildcard to answer the question, *In alphabetical order by City and in alphabetical order by Last Name, what are the Student ID, City, First Name, and Last Name of students from cities that begin with the letter A?* Display the fields in the order listed in the question. Four records meet the criteria. **Save** the query as **Lastname Firstname 2G Cities Query** Create a paper or electronic printout as directed. **Close** the query.

8 **Create** a query in **Query Design** view using the **2G Students** table and all of the table's fields to answer the question *For which students is the ZIP Code missing?* Three students are missing ZIP Codes. **Save** the query as **Lastname Firstname 2G Missing ZIP Query** and then with **Normal** margins, create a paper or electronic printout as directed. **Close** the query. Using the information that displays in the query results, an enrollment clerk can use a reference to look up the ZIP codes for the students and then enter the ZIP codes in the student records in the underlying table.

9 For each scholarship, the Board of Trustees of the college will donate an amount equal to 50 percent of each scholarship. **Create** a query in **Query Design** view. Use both tables and calculated fields to answer the question, *In alphabetical order by Scholarship Name, and including the first and last name of the scholarship recipient, what will the value of each scholarship be if the Board of Trustees makes a matching 50 percent donation?* (Hint: First compute the amount of the donation, naming the new field **Donation** and then calculate the new scholarship value, naming the new field **New Value**).

Run the query, switch back to **Design** view, and as necessary, change the properties of all the numeric fields to display in **Currency** format with **0** decimal places, and then **Run** the query. For the *Alexandria Historical Society Scholarship*, the *Donation* is *$150* and the *New Value* is *$450*. Apply **Best Fit** to the columns in the query results. **Save** the query as **Lastname Firstname 2G Trustee Donation Query** and then create a paper or electronic printout as directed, being sure to print the results on one page. **Close** the query.

(Project 2G Students and Scholarships continues on the next page)

Access | Chapter 2

Content-Based Assessments

10 **Create** a new query in **Query Design** view. Use the **2G Scholarships Awarded** table and the **Sum** aggregate function to answer the question *For each Major, in descending order by Amount, what are the total scholarship amounts?* Display the fields in the order listed in the question. Use the **Property Sheet** to display the sums in the **Currency** format with **0** decimal places. *History* majors received *$1,850* in scholarships. Apply **Best Fit** to the columns in the query results. **Save** the query as **Lastname Firstname 2G Total Scholarships by Major Query** and then create a paper or electronic printout as directed. **Close** the query.

11 **Create** a **Crosstab Query** using the **2G Scholarships Awarded** table. Use the **Student ID** field as row headings and the **Major** field as column headings to answer the

question *For each student or major, what is the total scholarship Amount awarded?* Name the query **Lastname Firstname 2G Student ID and Major Crosstab Query** In **Design** view, apply **0** decimal places to the appropriate fields. Apply **Best Fit** to the columns in the query results. **Save** the query, and then as directed, create a paper or electronic printout in **Landscape** orientation—the query results will print on two pages. **Close** the query.

12 **Open** the **Navigation Pane** and widen it to display all of the object names. In **Backstage** view, click **Close Database**, and then click **Exit**. As directed by your instructor, submit your database and the ten paper or electronic printouts—relationship report, sorted table, and eight queries—that are the results of this project.

End **You have completed Project 2G**

Content-Based Assessments

GO! Fix It | Project 2H Social Sciences Division

Project Files

For Project 2H, you will need the following file:

a02H_Social_Sciences

You will save your database as:

Lastname_Firstname_2H_Social_Sciences

In this project, you will correct query design errors in a database used by the Dean of Social Sciences. From the student files that accompany this textbook, open the file a02H_Social_Sciences, and then save the database in your Access Chapter 2 folder as **Lastname_Firstname_2H_Social Sciences**

To complete the project you must find and correct errors in relationships, query design, and column widths. In addition to errors that you find, you should know:

- A relationship should be created between the 2H Social Sciences Faculty table and the 2H Anthropology Dept Course Schedule table. A relationship report should be created and named **Lastname Firstname 2H Relationship Report** One faculty member can teach many courses.

- You should add your last name and first name to each query name; do *not* rename the tables.

- Several queries do not accurately reflect the result implied in the query name. Open each query and examine and correct the design of any queries that do not accurately reflect the query name.

- Be sure that all of the object names in the Navigation Pane display fully.

- Create a paper or electronic printout of the relationship report and the four queries as directed by your instructor.

End **You have completed Project 2H** ————————————

Content-Based Assessments

GO! Make It | Project 2I Faculty Awards

Project Files

For Project 2I, you will need the following file:

a02I_Faculty_Awards

You will save your database as:

Lastname_Firstname_2I_Faculty_Awards

Start Access, navigate to your student files, and then open the a02I_Faculty_Awards database file. Save the database in your Access Chapter 2 folder as **Lastname_Firstname_2I_Faculty Awards** Rename the two tables to include your name, create a relationship and relationship report. Then create two queries as shown in Figure 2.53. Create paper or electronic printouts as directed.

Project Results

Figure 2.53

Content-Based Assessments

GO! Solve It | Project **2J** Student Refunds

Project Files

For Project 2J, you will need the following file:

a02J_Student_Refunds

You will save your database as:

Lastname_Firstname_2J_Student_Refunds

Start Access, navigate to your student files and open the a02J_Student_Refunds database file. Save the database in your Access Chapter 2 folder as **Lastname_Firstname_2J_Student Refunds** Rename the tables by adding **Lastname Firstname** to the beginning of each table name. Create a relationship between the tables—one student can have many refunds—and then create a relationship report.

Create and save a query to answer the question, *What is the First Name and Last Name of the students who are eligible for a refund and who live in Alexandria or Falls Church sorted alphabetically by Last Name within City?* Create and save a query to answer the question, *What is the total Refund Amount for Full Time and Part Time Students?* Create and save a query to answer the question, *In ascending order by Refund Eligibility Date, what is the Last Name and First Name of students receiving a Refund of more than $50 between the dates of 8/1/16 and 12/31/16?* Apply Best Fit to all the query results, and then create paper or electronic printouts of the report and queries as directed.

	Performance Level		
	Exemplary: You consistently applied the relevant skills	**Proficient:** You sometimes, but not always, applied the relevant skills	**Developing:** You rarely or never applied the relevant skills
Create relationship and relationship report	Relationship and relationship report created correctly.	Relationship and relationship report created with one error.	Relationship and relationship report created with two or more errors, or missing entirely.
Create City query	Query created with correct name, fields, sorting, and criteria.	Query created with three elements correct and one incorrect.	Query created with two or more elements incorrect, or missing entirely.
Create Refund query	Query created with correct name, fields, and criteria.	Query created with two elements correct and one incorrect.	Query created with two or more elements incorrect, or missing entirely.
Create Refund Eligibility query	Query created with correct name, fields, sorting, and criteria.	Query created with three elements correct and one incorrect.	Query created with two or more two elements incorrect, or missing entirely.

Performance Element (left margin label)

End You have completed Project 2J ————————————

Content-Based Assessments

GO! Solve It | Project **2K** Leave

Project Files

For Project 2K, you will need the following file:

a02K_Leave

You will save your database as:

Lastname_Firstname_2K_Leave

Start Access, navigate to your student files, and then open the a02K_Leave database file. Save the database in your Access Chapter 2 folder as **Lastname_Firstname_2K_Leave** Rename the tables by adding **Lastname Firstname** to the beginning of each table name. Create a relationship between the tables—one employee can have many leave transactions—and a relationship report.

Create and save a query to answer the question, *Which employees, identified alphabetically by Last Name, have used Personal Leave?* Create and save a query to answer the question, *Which employees, identified alphabetically by Last Name, have no Phone Number?* Create and save a query to answer the question, *How many Leave Transactions were for Vacation leave grouped by the Employee# field?* (Hint: In the Total row of your query, use the Count function.) Create and save a crosstab query to answer the question, *What is the total number of leave transactions for each Employee # (row) by Leave Classification (column)?* Apply Best Fit to all of the query results, and then create paper or electronic printouts of the report and queries as directed by your instructor.

		Performance Level		
		Exemplary: You consistently applied the relevant skills	**Proficient:** You sometimes, but not always, applied the relevant skills	**Developing:** You rarely or never applied the relevant skills
Performance Element	Create relationship and relationship report	Relationship and relationship report created correctly.	Relationship and relationship report created with one error.	Relationship and relationship report created with two or more errors, or missing entirely.
	Create Personal Leave query	Query created with correct name, fields, sorting, and criteria.	Query created with three elements correct and one incorrect.	Query created with two or more elements incorrect, or missing entirely.
	Create Phone Number query	Query created with correct name, fields, and criteria.	Query created with two elements correct and one incorrect.	Query created with two or more elements incorrect, or missing entirely.
	Create Vacation Leave query	Query created with correct name, fields, grouping, and aggregate function.	Query created with three elements correct and one incorrect.	Query created with two or more elements incorrect, or missing entirely.
	Create Crosstab query	Query created with correct name, row headings, column headings, and aggregate function.	Query created with three elements correct and one incorrect.	Query created with two or more elements incorrect, or missing entirely.

End **You have completed Project 2K**

Outcomes-Based Assessments

Rubric

The following outcomes-based assessments are *open-ended assessments*. That is, there is no specific correct result; your result will depend on your approach to the information provided. Make *Professional Quality* your goal. Use the following scoring rubric to guide you in *how* to approach the problem and then to evaluate *how well* your approach solves the problem.

The *criteria*—Software Mastery, Content, Format and Layout, and Process—represent the knowledge and skills you have gained that you can apply to solving the problem. The *levels of performance*—Professional Quality, Approaching Professional Quality, or Needs Quality Improvements—help you and your instructor evaluate your result.

	Your completed project is of Professional Quality if you:	Your completed project is Approaching Professional Quality if you:	Your completed project Needs Quality Improvements if you:
1-Software Mastery	Choose and apply the most appropriate skills, tools, and features and identify efficient methods to solve the problem.	Choose and apply some appropriate skills, tools, and features, but not in the most efficient manner.	Choose inappropriate skills, tools, or features, or are inefficient in solving the problem.
2-Content	Construct a solution that is clear and well organized, contains content that is accurate, appropriate to the audience and purpose, and is complete. Provide a solution that contains no errors in spelling, grammar, or style.	Construct a solution in which some components are unclear, poorly organized, inconsistent, or incomplete. Misjudge the needs of the audience. Have some errors in spelling, grammar, or style, but the errors do not detract from comprehension.	Construct a solution that is unclear, incomplete, or poorly organized; contains some inaccurate or inappropriate content; and contains many errors in spelling, grammar, or style. Do not solve the problem.
3-Format and Layout	Format and arrange all elements to communicate information and ideas, clarify function, illustrate relationships, and indicate relative importance.	Apply appropriate format and layout features to some elements, but not others. Overuse features, causing minor distraction.	Apply format and layout that does not communicate information or ideas clearly. Do not use format and layout features to clarify function, illustrate relationships, or indicate relative importance. Use available features excessively, causing distraction.
4-Process	Use an organized approach that integrates planning, development, self-assessment, revision, and reflection.	Demonstrate an organized approach in some areas, but not others; or, use an insufficient process of organization throughout.	Do not use an organized approach to solve the problem.

Outcomes-Based Assessments

Apply a combination of
the **2A** and **2B** skills.

GO! Think | Project **2L** Coaches

Project Files

For Project 2L, you will need the following file:

> a02L_Coaches

You will save your database as:

> Lastname_Firstname_2L_Coaches

Use the skills you have practiced in this chapter to assist Randy Shavrain, the Athletic Director, in answering questions about the coaches in your **Lastname_Firstname_2L_Coaches** database. Create and save the relationship report with the default name, and save the queries you create with your name in the query title. Create paper or electronic printouts of the report and queries as directed by your instructor.

Mr. Shavrain needs to determine: 1) *In alphabetical order by Last Name, what is the Last Name and First Name of every coach involved with Dive activities? 2) In alphabetical order by Last Name, what is the Last Name and First Name of every coach involved with Basketball or Football activities? 3) In alphabetical order by Last Name, what is the Last Name and First Name of every coach with a Skill Specialty in Volleyball?*

 End **You have completed Project 2L** ——————————————————

Apply a combination of
the **2A** and **2B** skills.

GO! Think | Project **2M** Club Donations

Project Files

For Project 2M, you will need the following file:

> a02M_Club_Donations

You will save your database as:

> Lastname_Firstname_2M_Club_Donations

Use the skills you have practiced in this chapter to assist Dr. Kirsten McCarty, Vice President of Student Services, in answering questions about donations collected by students to support student services in your **Lastname_Firstname_2M_Club_Donations** database. Create and save the relationship report with the default name, and save the queries you create with your name in the query title. Create paper or electronic printouts of the report and queries as directed.

Dr. McCarty needs to determine: 1) *In ascending order by Last Name, what is the Last Name and First Name of donors who gave donations that are $25 or more? 2) What is the total of all donations grouped alphabetically by the Club Affiliation? 3) In alphabetical order by the student Last Name, and including the Donation ID#, what will the value of each donation be if the local sports store makes a matching 10 percent donation? 4) What are the total donations by Club Affiliation and Student ID?*

End **You have completed Project 2M** ——————————————————

Outcomes-Based Assessments

Apply a combination of the 2A and 2B skills.

You and GO! | Project 2N Personal Inventory

Project Files

For Project 2N, you will need the following file:

New blank Access database

You will save your database as:

Lastname_Firstname_2N_Personal_Inventory

Create a personal database containing a household inventory of your possessions. Name the new database **Lastname_Firstname_2N_Personal_Inventory** Create one or more tables with at least 10 records. Include fields such as item, room location, value, date of purchase. Your table should have items stored in several locations. Sort the table in descending order by the value of the item. Create a paper or electronic printout. Clear all sorts, and then close the table. Create at least three queries to answer specific questions about your inventory. Name the queries to reflect the question asked. Create paper or electronic printouts of your queries.

 You have completed Project 2N ————————————————

Access | Chapter 2

Forms, Filters, and Reports

Andresr/Shutterstock

In This Chapter

In this chapter, you will create forms to enter data and view data in database tables. Forms can display one record at a time, with fields placed in the same order to match a paper source document to make it easier to enter the new information or view existing information. Records in a form or table can be filtered to display only a portion of the total records based on matching specific values.

In this chapter, you will create reports that summarize data stored in a query or table in a professional-looking manner suitable for printing. After your report is created, you can modify the design so that the final report is laid out in a format that is useful to the person reading it.

The projects in this chapter relate to **Capital Cities Community College**, which is located in the Washington D. C. metropolitan area. The college provides high-quality education and professional training to residents in the cities surrounding the nation's capital. Its four campuses serve over 50,000 students and offer more than 140 certificate programs and degrees at the associate's level. CapCCC has a highly acclaimed Distance Education program and an extensive Workforce Development program. The college makes positive contributions to the community through cultural and athletic programs and partnerships with businesses and non-profit organizations.

Project 3A Students and Majors

Project Activities

In Activities 3.01 through 3.11, you will assist Juanita Ramirez, Director of Enrollment Services, in using an Access database to track new students and their major fields of study. Your completed forms will look similar to Figure 3.1.

Project Files

For Project 3A, you will need the following file:

a03A_Students_Majors

You will save your document as:

Lastname_Firstname_3A_Students_Majors

Project Results

Figure 3.1
Project 3A Students and Majors

Objective 1 | Create and Use a Form to Add and Delete Records

A *form* is an Access object you can use to enter new records into a table, or to edit, delete, or display existing records in a table. A form is useful to control access to the data. For example, you can design a form for college Registration Assistants who can see and enter the courses scheduled and fees paid by an individual student. However, they cannot see or enter grades in the student's record.

Some Access forms display only one record at a time; other forms display multiple records at the same time. A form that displays only one record at a time is useful not only to the individual who performs the *data entry*—typing the actual records—but also to anyone who has the job of viewing information in a database. For example, when you visit the Records Office at your college to obtain a transcript, someone displays your record on a screen. For the viewer, it is much easier to look at one record at a time, using a form, than to look at all of the student records in the database.

Activity 3.01 | Creating a Form

There are several ways to create a form in Access, but the fastest and easiest way is to use the *Form tool*. With a single mouse click, all fields from the underlying data source are placed on the form. You can use the new form immediately, or you can modify it in Layout view or in Design view.

The Form tool incorporates all of the information—both the field names and the individual records—from an existing table or query and then instantly creates the form for you. Records that you edit or create using a form automatically update the underlying table or tables. In this activity, you will create a form and then use it to add new student records to the database.

1 **Start** Access. In **Backstage** view, click **Open**. Navigate to the student data files for this textbook, and then open the **a03A_Students_Majors** database.

2 Display **Backstage** view, click **Save Database As**, and then in the **Save As** dialog box, navigate to the location where you are saving your databases for this chapter. Create a new folder named **Access Chapter 3** and then click **Open**.

3 In the **File name** box, select the file name, and then type **Lastname_Firstname_3A_Students_Majors** and then press Enter. On the **Message Bar**, click the **Enable Content** button. Notice that there are two tables in this database.

4 On the Ribbon, click the **Database Tools tab**. In the **Relationships group**, click the **Relationships** button. Compare your screen with Figure 3.2.

> *One* major is associated with *many* students. Thus, a one-to-many relationship has been established between the 3A Majors table and the 3A Students table using the Major ID# field as the common field.

Figure 3.2

Join line with symbols
indicating one-to-many
relationship and
referential integrity

Major ID# is common field

5 **Close** ☒ the **Relationships** window. From the **Navigation Pane**, open the **3A Students** table. Notice the ten fields—*Student ID#, First Name, MI, Last Name, Address, City, State, ZIP, Phone,* and *Major ID#*. **Close** ☒ the table.

6 In the **Navigation Pane**, be sure the **3A Students** table is selected. Click the **Create tab**, and then in the **Forms group**, click the **Form** button. **Close** « the **Navigation Pane**, and then compare your screen with Figure 3.3.

Access creates the form based on the currently selected object—the 3A Students table—and displays the form in *Layout view*. In Layout view, you can modify the form while it is displaying data. For example, you can adjust the size of the text boxes to fit the data.

Access creates the form in a simple top-to-bottom layout, with all ten fields in the table lined up in a single column. The data for the first record in the table displays.

Figure 3.3

Layout View button active

Dotted lines indicate
Layout view active

Form displays all
10 fields from the
3A Students table

New (blank) record button

Data for Record 1 of 101
displays in form

Navigation buttons

7 In the navigation area, click the **Next record** button ▶ four times. The fifth record—
Student ID 1298345—displays. In the navigation area, click the **Last record** button ▶|
to display the record for *Student ID 9583924*, and then click the **First record** button |◀
to display the record for *Student ID 1034823*.

You can use the navigation buttons to scroll among the records to display any single record.

8 Save 🖫 the form as **Lastname Firstname 3A Student Form** and then **Close** ✕ the
form object.

9 Open » the **Navigation Pane**, and then, if necessary, increase the width of the **Navigation
Pane** to display the entire form name. Notice that your new form displays under the table
with which it is related—the **3A Students** table.

10 In the **Navigation Pane**, click to select the **3A Majors** table. Click the **Create tab**, and
then in the **Forms group**, click the **Form** button. **Close** « the **Navigation Pane**, and
then compare your screen with Figure 3.4. Notice that *Major ID 105*, for *Diagnostic
Medical Sonography*, has five students selecting this major.

If a form's record has related records in another table, the related records display in the
form because of the established one-to-many relationship between the underlying tables.

Figure 3.4

3A Majors form

*Major ID# has related
records (students
declaring this major)*

11 Close ✕ the **3A Majors** form. In the message box, click **Yes**. In the **Save As** dialog box,
name the form **Lastname Firstname 3A Major Form** and then click **OK**.

Activity 3.02 | Adding Records to a Table by Using a Form

By using a single-record form to add and delete records, you can reduce the number
of data entry errors, because the individual performing the data entry is looking at
only one record at a time. Recall that your database is useful only if the information is
accurate—just like your personal address book is useful only if it contains accurate
addresses and phone numbers.

Forms are based on—also referred to as ***bound*** to—the table where the records are stored. When a record is entered in a form, the new record is added to the underlying table. The reverse is also true—when a record is added to a table, the new record can be viewed in the related form. In this activity, you will add a new record to the 3A Students table by using the form that you just created.

1 Open **»** the **Navigation Pane**, open your **3A Student Form** object, and then **Close** **«** the **Navigation Pane**. In the navigation area, click the **New (blank) record** button ▶︎ to display a new blank form.

Another Way

Press the Enter key, provided there are no special buttons on the form, such as a link to create a new form or a link to print the form.

2 In the **Student ID#** field, type **9712345** and then press Tab.

Use the Tab key to move from field to field in a form. This is known as ***tab order***—the order in which the insertion point moves from one field to the next when you press the Tab key. As you start typing, the pencil icon displays in the ***record selector bar*** at the left—the bar used to select an entire record. This icon displays when a record is created or edited.

3 Using your own first name and last name, continue entering the data as shown in the following table, and then compare your screen with Figure 3.5.

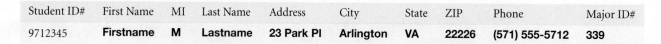

Student ID#	First Name	MI	Last Name	Address	City	State	ZIP	Phone	Major ID#
9712345	**Firstname**	**M**	**Lastname**	**23 Park Pl**	**Arlington**	**VA**	**22226**	**(571) 555-5712**	**339**

Figure 3.5

Pencil icon in record selector bar

Be sure you have typed your own name

New record entered using the form

4 With your insertion point in the last field, press Tab to save the record and display a new blank record. **Close** **×** the **3A Student Form** object.

5 Open **»** the **Navigation Pane**. Open the **3A Students** table. In the navigation area, click the **Last record** button ▶︎ to verify that the record you entered in the form is stored in the underlying table. **Close** **×** the **3A Students** table.

6 From the **Navigation Pane**, open the **3A Major Form** object. At the bottom of your screen, in the navigation area for the form—*not* the navigation area for the subdatasheet—click the **New (blank) record** button ▶. In the blank form, enter the information in the following table:

Major ID#	Major Name
339.555.22	**Network Security**

7 **Close** ✕ your **3A Major Form** object. From the **Navigation Pane**, open the **3A Majors** table, and then scroll down to verify that the new record for Major ID# *339.555.22 Network Security* displays in the table—records are sorted by the *Major ID#* field. **Close** ✕ the table.

Activity 3.03 | Deleting Records from a Table by Using a Form

You can delete records from a database table by using a form. In this activity, you will delete Major ID# 800.03 because the program has been discontinued.

Another Way
Press Ctrl + F.

1 From the **Navigation Pane**, open your **3A Major Form** object. On the **Home tab**, in the **Find group**, click the **Find** button to open the **Find and Replace** dialog box.

2 In the **Look In** box, notice that *Current field* displays. In the **Find What** box, type **800.03** and then click **Find Next**. Compare your screen with Figure 3.6, and confirm that the record for **Major ID# 800.03** displays.

Because you clicked in the Major ID# field before opening the dialog box, Access searches for the data in this field.

Figure 3.6

Record for *Major ID#* 800.03 displays

Find and Replace dialog box

Find What box

Look In box indicates that Access will search the Current field—*Major ID#*

3 **Close** ![x] the **Find and Replace** dialog box. On the **Home tab**, in the **Records group**, click the **Delete button arrow**, and then click **Delete Record** to delete the record for Major ID# 800.03.

> Access removes the record from the screen and displays a message alerting you that you are about to delete *1 record(s)*. If you click Yes to delete the record, you cannot use the Undo button to reverse the action. If you delete a record by mistake, you must re-create the record by reentering the data. Because no students are associated with this major, you can delete it from the table.

4 In the message box, click **Yes** to delete the record. In the navigation area for the form, notice that the number of records in the table is *70*. **Close** ![x] the form.

5 From the **Navigation Pane**, open the **3A Majors** table. Examine the table to verify that the *Major ID# 800.03* record no longer exists, and then **Close** ![x] the table.

> Adding and deleting records in a form updates the records stored in the underlying table.

Activity 3.04 | Printing a Form

Clicking the Print button while a form is displayed causes *all* of the records to print in the form layout. In this activity, you will print only *one* record.

1 From the **Navigation Pane**, open your **3A Student Form** object. Press Ctrl + F to display the **Find and Replace** dialog box. In the **Find What** box, type **9712345** and then click **Find Next** to display the record with your name. **Close** ![x] the **Find and Replace** dialog box.

2 Display **Backstage** view. Click the **Print tab**, and then in the **Print group**, click **Print**. In the **Print** dialog box, under **Print Range**, click the **Selected Record(s)** option button. In the lower left corner of the dialog box, click **Setup**.

3 In the **Page Setup** dialog box, click the **Columns tab**. Under **Column Size**, in the **Width** box, delete the existing text, and type **7.5** Compare your screen with Figure 3.7.

> Change the width of the column in this manner so that the form prints on one page. Forms are not typically printed, so the width of the column in a form may be greater than the width of the paper on which you are printing. The maximum column width that you can enter is dependent upon the printer that is installed on your system.

Figure 3.7

Column Width set to 7.5

Selected Record(s) option button selected

4 Click **OK** to close the **Page Setup** dialog box, and then, to create an electronic printout of this single form, see the instructions in the Note below. To print on paper, click **OK** to close the **Print** dialog box and to print only your record in the form layout.

> **Note** | To Print a Single Form in PDF
>
> To create a PDF electronic printout of a single record in a form, change the column width to 7.5 as described in step 3 above, and then in the Print dialog box, click Cancel. On the left edge of the form, click anywhere in the Record Selector bar so that it is black—selected. On the Ribbon, click the External Data tab. In the Export group, click the PDF or XPS button. In the Publish as PDF or XPS dialog box, navigate to the location where you are storing your files for this project. In the File name box, notice that your form name is automatically entered for you. Then, in the lower left corner of the dialog box, if necessary, select the Open file after publishing check box. In the lower right corner of the dialog box, click the Options button. In the Options dialog box, under Range, click the Selected records option button, click OK, and then click Publish. Close the Adobe Reader or Acrobat window, and then hold this file until you complete the project and submit it as directed by your instructor.

5 **Close** ☒ the **3A Student Form** object. Using the techniques you just practiced, open your **3A Major Form** object, display the record for the **Major ID#** of **339.555.22**, and then print only that record, or create an electronic printout of only that record. Then **Close** ☒ the **3A Major Form** object.

If there are no related records in the subdatasheet, the empty subdatasheet does not display in the printed form.

Objective 2 | Create a Form by Using the Form Wizard

The *Form Wizard* creates a form quickly like the Form tool, but gives you more flexibility in the design, layout, and number of fields. The design of the form should be planned for the individuals who use the form—either for entering new records or viewing records. For example, when your college counselor displays information, it may be easier for the counselor to view the information if the fields are arranged in a layout that differs from the manner in which the Form Tool arranges them.

Activity 3.05 | Creating a Form by Using the Form Wizard

At Capital Cities Community College, when a student changes his or her major, the student fills out a paper form. To make it easier to change the information in the database, you will create an Access form that matches the layout of the paper form. This will make it easier for the individual who changes the data in the database.

1 In the **Navigation Pane**, click to select the **3A Students** table. On the **Create tab**, in the **Forms group**, click the **Form Wizard** button.

The Form Wizard walks you step by step through the process of creating a form by asking questions. In the first Form Wizard dialog box, you select the fields to include on the form. The fields can come from more than one table or query.

2 Under **Tables/Queries**, in the text box, click the **arrow** to display a list of available tables and queries from which you can create the form.

There are two tables in the database from which you can create a new form. Because you selected the 3A Students table on the Navigation Pane, the 3A Students table is the selected table.

3 Click **Table: 3A Students**, and then compare your screen with Figure 3.8.

The field names from the 3A Students table display in the Available Fields list.

Figure 3.8

One Field button

3A Students table selected

Available Fields list

Field names in the 3A Students table

Selected Fields list

Another Way
Double-click the field name.

4 Use the **One Field** button > to move the following fields to the **Selected Fields** list: **First Name**, **Last Name**, and **Major ID#**. Compare your screen with Figure 3.9.

Three fields from the 3A Students table display in the Selected Fields list.

Figure 3.9

Three fields that will display in the form

5 Click **Next**. Be sure **Columnar** is selected as the layout, and then click **Next**. Under **What title do you want for your form?**, select the existing text, and then type **Lastname Firstname 3A Student Major Change Form** and then click **Finish** to close the wizard and create the form. If necessary, increase the width of the Navigation Pane to display the entire form name, and then compare your screen with Figure 3.10.

The form is saved and added to the Navigation Pane under its data source. The first record in the underlying table displays in *Form view*, which is used to view, add, delete, and modify records stored in a table.

Figure 3.10

Form created using Wizard

New form displays in the Navigation Pane under related table

First record in the 3A Students table displays in form

Objective 3 | Modify a Form in Layout View and in Design View

After you create a form, you can make changes to it. For example, you can group the fields, resize the fields, and change the style of the form.

Activity 3.06 | Grouping Controls and Applying a Theme to a Form in Layout View

Layout view enables you to make changes to the design of a form while displaying the data from the underlying table. Most changes to a form can be made in Layout view.

Another Way

On the Home tab, in the Views group, click the View button arrow, and then click Layout View; or, right-click the object tab, and then click Layout View.

1 **Close** « the **Navigation Pane** and be sure your **3A Student Major Change Form** object displays. In the lower right corner of your screen, on the status bar, click the **Layout View** button 🖫, and then compare your screen with Figure 3.11.

The field names and data for the first record display in *controls*—objects on a form that display data, perform actions, and let you view and work with information.

The data in the first record displays in *text box controls*. The most commonly used control is the text box control, which typically displays data from the underlying table. A text box control is a *bound control*—its source data comes from a table or query.

The field names—*First Name*, *Last Name*, and *Major ID#*—display in *label controls*. Access places a label control to the left of a text box control. A label control contains descriptive information that displays on the form, usually the field name. A control that does not have a source of data, for example a label that displays the title of the form, is an *unbound control*.

Figure 3.11

Label control, an unbound control

Label controls— field names

Text box controls— bound to data in table

Form displays in Layout view

2 Click the **First Name label control**. Hold down Shift, and then click the **Last Name label control**, the **Major ID# label control**, and the **three text box controls** to select all label and text box controls.

> **Alert! | Do Your Controls Change Order When Selecting?**
>
> If, when selecting controls, the controls change order, click Undo and select the controls again. Be careful not to drag the mouse when you are selecting multiple controls.

3 With all six controls selected—surrounded by a colored border—on the Ribbon, click the **Arrange tab**. In the **Table group**, click the **Stacked** button. Click the **First Name Label control** to deselect all of the controls and to surround the **First Name label control** with a colored border. Compare your screen with Figure 3.12.

This action groups the controls together in the *Stacked layout* format—a layout similar to a paper form, with labels to the left of each field. Grouping the controls enables you to easily move and edit controls as you redesign your form.

A dotted line forms a border around the field names and data. Above and to the left of the first field name—*First Name*—the *layout selector* ⊞ displays, with which you can select and move the entire group of controls.

Figure 3.12

Arrange tab

Stacked button

Layout selector

4 Click the **Design tab**, and then in the **Themes group**, click the **Themes** button. In the **Themes** gallery, locate and right-click the **Couture** theme. Click **Apply Theme to This Object Only**.

The *Themes* button enables you to apply a predefined format to all of the database objects or to the current object. Right-click a theme so that you can apply the theme to a single object within the database. Apply a theme before performing other formatting to the text in your form.

> **Note | Applying a Theme to an Object and Determining the Applied Theme**
>
> If you click a theme rather than right-clicking it and selecting an option, the theme is applied to all objects in the database. To determine the applied theme, in the Themes group, point to the Themes button. The ScreenTip displays the current theme.

5 Click anywhere in the title *3A Student Major Change Form* to select it. Click the **Format tab**. In the **Font group**, click the **Font Size arrow**, and then click **14**. Click the **Bold** button **B** to add bold emphasis to the text. Click the **Font Color button arrow**, and then under **Theme Colors**, in the last column, click the last color—**Brown, Accent 6, Darker 50%**.

Activity 3.07 | Modifying a Form in Design View

Design view presents a detailed view of the structure of your form. Because the form is not actually running when displayed in Design view, you cannot view the underlying data. However, some tasks, such as resizing sections, must be completed in Design view.

Another Way

On the Home tab, in the Views group, click the View button arrow, and then click Design View; or, right-click the object tab, and then click Design View.

1 On the status bar, click the **Design View** button 📐. Compare your screen with Figure 3.13.

This Design view of a form displays three sections—*Form Header*, *Detail*, and *Form Footer*—each designated by a *section bar* at the top of each section. The form header contains information, such as a form's title, that displays at the top of the screen in Form view and is printed at the top of the first page when records are printed as forms. The detail section displays the records from the underlying table, and the form footer displays at the bottom of the screen in Form view and is printed after the last detail section on the last page of a printout.

Figure 3.13

Form Header section bar

Detail section bar

Form Footer section bar

2 At the bottom of the form, point to the *lower* edge of the **Form Footer section bar** to display the ⊕ pointer, and then drag downward approximately **0.5 inch** to increase the height of the Form Footer section. Compare your screen with Figure 3.14.

Figure 3.14

Form Footer section height increased 0.5 inch

3 On the **Design tab**, in the **Controls group**, click the **Label** button [Aa]. Move the pointer into the **Form Footer** section, and then position the plus sign of the ⁺A pointer in the **Form Footer** section at approximately **0.25 inch on the horizontal ruler** and even with the lower edge of the **Form Footer section bar** as shown in Figure 3.15.

Figure 3.15

Button to create
a Label control

0.25 inch on
horizontal ruler

Label control pointer

4 Click one time. Using your own name, type **Created by Lastname Firstname** and then press Enter. With the label control selected, on the **Format tab**, in the **Font group**, click the **Bold** button B. Click the **Font Color arrow**, and then under **Theme Colors**, in the fourth column, click the first color—**Brown, Text 2**. If necessary, double-click the right edge of the label control to resize the control so that all of the data displays.

Another Way

On the Home tab, in the Views group, click the View button arrow, and then click Form View; or, right-click the object tab, and then click Form View.

5 On the right side of the status bar, click the **Form View** button 📖, and then compare your screen with Figure 3.16.

Form Footer text displays on the screen at the bottom of the form and prints only on the last page if all of the forms are printed as a group. In Form view, you can add, delete, or modify records stored in a table.

Figure 3.16

Title formatted,
Couture theme applied

Label control added and
formatted in Form
Footer section

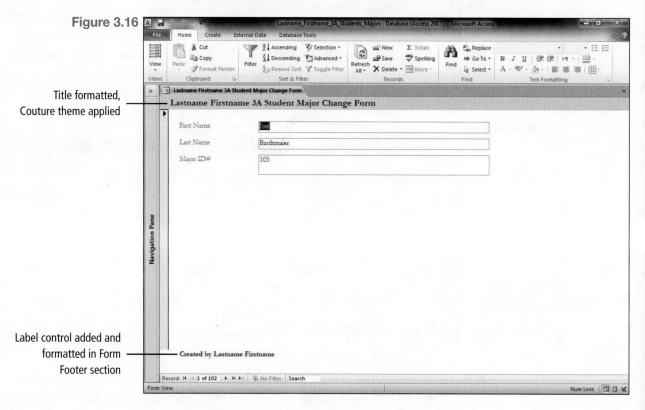

6 Save 💾 the changes you have made to the design of your form. Leave your **3A Student Major Change Form** open for the next activity.

Activity 3.08 | Adding, Resizing, and Moving Controls in Layout View

In Layout view, you can change the form's *control layout*—the grouped arrangement of controls.

1 At the right side of the status bar, click the **Layout View** button 📄.

Recall that the layout selector, which displays to the left and above the First Name label control, enables you to select and move the entire group of controls in Layout view.

2 On the **Design tab**, in the **Tools group**, click the **Add Existing Fields** button to display the **Field List** pane, which lists the fields in the underlying table—3A Students. Compare your screen with Figure 3.17.

Figure 3.17
Add Existing Fields button
Field List pane

3 In the **Field List** pane, click **Student ID#**, and then drag to the left until the 📄 pointer displays above the **First Name label control** and a colored line displays above the control. Release the mouse button, and then compare your screen with Figure 3.18. If you are not satisfied with the result, click Undo and begin again.

This action adds the Student ID# label and text box controls to the form above the First Name controls.

Figure 3.18
Student ID# label control
Text box control for *Student ID# field*

4 **Close** ☒ the **Field List** pane. Click the **Student ID# text box control**, which currently displays *1034823*, to surround it with a border and to remove the border from the label control.

5 Point to the right edge of the **text box control** until the ↔ pointer displays, and then drag to the left until all of the right edges of the text box controls align under the *C* in *Controls* in the Ribbon's **Controls group** above. Compare your screen with Figure 3.19.

All four text box controls are resized simultaneously. By decreasing the width of the text box controls, you have more space in which to rearrange the form controls. In Layout view, because you can see your data, you can determine visually that the space you have allotted is adequate to display all of the data in every field.

Figure 3.19

Right edges of text box
controls align under
C in Controls group

Horizontal resize pointer

Another Way

Drag the selected label
controls to the desired
location and then release
the mouse button.

6 Click the **Last Name text box control**, which currently displays *Barthmaier*. Click the **Arrange tab**, and then in the **Rows & Columns group**, click the **Select Row** button. In the **Move group**, click the **Move Up** button one time to move the controls above the **First Name label control** as shown in Figure 3.20.

Figure 3.20

Select Row button

Move Up button

Last Name controls moved
above *First Name* controls

7 **Save** 🖫 the changes you have made to the design of your form.

Activity 3.09 | Formatting and Aligning Controls in Layout View

Another Way

Click the first control,
hold down Shift, and
then click the last
control.

1 With the form displayed in Layout view, click in the **Student ID# text box control**, which displays *1034823*. On the **Arrange tab**, in the **Rows & Columns group**, click the **Select Column** button to select all four text box controls.

2 With the four text box controls selected, click the **Format tab**. In the **Font group**, click the **Background Color button arrow** 🎨▾. Under **Theme Colors**, in the fifth column, click the second color—**Brown, Accent 1, Lighter 80%**.

> The text box controls display a background color of light brown. This formatting does not affect the label controls on the left.

3 Click the **Student ID# label control**. On the **Arrange tab**, in the **Rows & Columns group**, click the **Select Column** button. Click the **Format tab**, change the **Font Color**—*not* the Background Color—to **Brown, Text 2**—in the fourth column, the first color—and then apply **Bold** 🅑. Click in a blank area of the screen to cancel the selection, and then compare your screen with Figure 3.21.

Figure 3.21

Text box controls—font size and background color changed

Label controls—font size and font color changed, bold applied

Another Way

Click any control, and then on the Arrange tab, in the Rows & Columns group, click the Select Layout button.

4 Click any **label control** to display the layout selector, and then click the **layout selector** ⊞ to select all of the controls.

Clicking the layout selector enables you to edit all of the controls at one time.

5 On the **Format tab**, in the **Font group**, click the **Font Size button arrow**, and then click **12** to change the font size of the text in all of the controls.

6 With all of the controls still selected, on the Ribbon, click the **Design tab**. In the **Tools group**, click the **Property Sheet** button. In the **Property Sheet** pane, if necessary, click the **Format tab**, and then compare your screen with Figure 3.22.

The *Property Sheet* for the selected controls displays. Each control has an associated Property Sheet where precise changes to the properties—characteristics—of selected controls can be made. At the top of the Property Sheet, to the right of *Selection type:*, *Multiple selection* displays because you have more than one control selected.

Figure 3.22

Property Sheet button

Selection type

Property Sheet for selected controls

Selected controls

7 In the **Property Sheet**, click the word **Height**, type **0.25** and then press Enter.

The height of each control changes to 0.25 inch.

8 Click the **Student ID# label control** to select only that label control. Click the **Arrange tab**, and then in the **Rows & Columns group**, click the **Select Column** button. In the **Property Sheet**, click **Width** to select its value to the right. Type **1.25** and then press Enter.

The width of each selected label control changes to 1.25 inches.

9 In the **Form Footer section**, click the **label control** with your name. Hold down Shift, and then in the **Form Header section**, click the **label control** that displays the title *3A Student Major Change Form*. With these two controls selected, in the **Property Sheet**, click **Left**. Type **0.5** and then press Enter to align the left edge of the selected label controls at 0.5 inch. Compare your screen with Figure 3.23.

> The left edges of the Form Header and Form Footer label controls align at 0.5 inch. In this manner, you can place a control in a specific location on the form.

Figure 3.23

Form Header label control left aligned at 0.5 inch

Height of all controls changed to 0.25 inch; width of label controls changed to 1.25 inches

Left property setting

Form Footer label control left aligned at 0.5 inch

10 **Close** ☒ the **Property Sheet**. On the right side of the status bar, click the **Form View** button 📧.

> The form displays in Form view, the view an individual uses when entering data in the form. By using these techniques, you can make a form attractive and easy to use for those who view and enter records.

11 **Save** 📄 the changes you made to your form's design. In the navigation area, click the **Last record** button ▶ to display the record containing your name.

12 Display **Backstage** view, click the **Print tab**, and then on the right, click **Print**. In the **Print** dialog box, under **Print Range**, click the **Selected Record(s)** option button. Create a paper or electronic printout as directed. To create an electronic printout, follow the directions given at the end of Activity 1.04.

> Because you decreased the width of the text box controls, you do *not* have to adjust the Column Size width in the Page Setup dialog box as you did with the form you created using the Form tool.

13 With the **3A Student Major Change Form** object displayed in **Form** view, in the navigation area, click the **First record** button ◀ to prepare for the next activity.

Objective 4 | Filter Records

Filtering records in a form is the process of displaying only a portion of the total records—a *subset*—based on matching specific values. Filters are commonly used to provide a quick answer, and the result is not generally saved for future use. For example, by filtering records in a form, you can quickly display a subset of records for students majoring in Information Systems Technology, which is identified by the Major ID# of 339.

One reason that you create a form is to provide a user interface for the database. For example, the Registration Assistants at your college may not, for security reasons, have access to the entire student database. Rather, by using a form, they can access and edit only some information—the information necessary for their jobs. Filtering records within a form provides individuals who do not have access to the entire database a way to ask questions of the database without constructing a query, and also to save a filter that is used frequently.

Activity 3.10 | Filtering Data by Selection of One Field

The counselor would like to see records for students who are majoring in Information Systems Technology. In a form, you can use the *Filter By Selection* command—which retrieves only the records that contain the value in the selected field and which temporarily removes the records that do *not* contain the value in the selected field.

1 With your **3A Student Major Change Form** object displayed in **Form** view, in the first record, click in the shaded **Major ID# text box control**. On the **Home tab**, in the **Find group**, click the **Find** button. In the **Find and Replace** dialog box, in the **Find What** box, type **339** If necessary, in the Match box, click the arrow, and then click Whole Field. Click **Find Next**, and then compare your screen with Figure 3.24.

This action finds and displays a record with 339—the Major ID# for Information Systems Technology—so that you can filter the records using the selected value.

Figure 3.24

First record with
Major ID# of *339*

339 is the *Major ID#*
for Information Systems
Technology

2 **Close** the **Find and Replace** dialog box. In the **Sort & Filter group**, click the **Selection** button, and then click **Equals "339"**. Compare your screen with Figure 3.25.

Seven records match the contents of the selected Student Major ID# field—*339*—the ID# for the Information Systems Technology major. In the navigation area, a *Filtered* button with a funnel icon displays next to the number of records. *Filtered* also displays on the right side of the status bar to indicate that a filter is applied. On the Home tab, in the Sort & Filter group, the Toggle Filter button is active.

Figure 3.25

Toggle Filter button active

Filtered indicated on status bar

Filtered button displays in navigation area

Seven records match the value *339*—the Major ID# for Information Systems Technology

Another Way

Click the Filtered button in the navigation area.

3 On the **Home tab**, in the **Sort & Filter group**, click the **Toggle Filter** button to remove the filter and display all 102 records. Notice the **Unfiltered** button in the navigation area, which indicates that no filter is active.

Note | Toggle Filter Button

On the Home tab, the Toggle Filter button is used to apply or remove a filter. If no filter has been created, the button is not active—it is not highlighted. After a filter is created, this button becomes active. Because it is a toggle button used to apply or remove filters, the ScreenTip that displays for this button alternates between Apply Filter—when a filter is created but is not currently applied—and Remove Filter—when a filter is applied.

---

4 Be sure that the first record—for *Joel Barthmaier*—displays. On the **Home tab**, in the **Sort & Filter group**, click the **Toggle Filter** button to reapply the filter. In the navigation area, click the **Last record** button to display the last of the seven records that match *339*.

The record for *Student ID# 9712345* displays—the record with your name. In this manner, you can toggle a filter on or off as needed.

5 In the **Sort & Filter group**, click the **Toggle Filter** button to remove the filter and display all of the records.

6 In the navigation area, click the **Next record** button two times to display **Record 3**. In the **Last Name** field, select the first letter—**E**—of *Eckert*. On the **Home tab**, in the **Sort & Filter group**, click the **Selection** button. Click **Begins with "E"**.

A new filter is applied that displays three records in which the *Last Name* begins with the letter *E*.

7 In the navigation area, click the **Filtered** button to remove the filter and display all of the records.

8 **Save** the changes to your form, and then **Close** the form.

The filter is saved with the form even though the filter is not currently applied.

Activity 3.11 | Using Filter By Form and Advanced Filter/Sort

Use the *Filter By Form* command to filter the records in a form based on one or more fields, or based on more than one value in the same field. The Filter By Form command offers greater flexibility than the Filter by Selection command and can be used to answer a question that requires matching multiple values.

In this activity, you will use filtering techniques to help Juanita Ramirez determine how many students live in Alexandria or Arlington. Then you will determine how many students live in Arlington who are majoring in Information Systems Technology.

1 **Open** ⏵ the **Navigation Pane**, open your **3A Student Form** object, and then **Close** ⏴ the **Navigation Pane**.

2 On the **Home tab**, in the **Sort & Filter group**, click the **Advanced** button, and then click **Filter By Form**. Compare your screen with Figure 3.26.

The Filter by Form window displays all of the field names, but without any data. In the empty text box for each field, you can type a value or choose from a list of available values. The *Look for* and *Or* tabs display at the bottom.

Figure 3.26

Filter by Form indicated

Advanced button

Look for and *Or* tabs

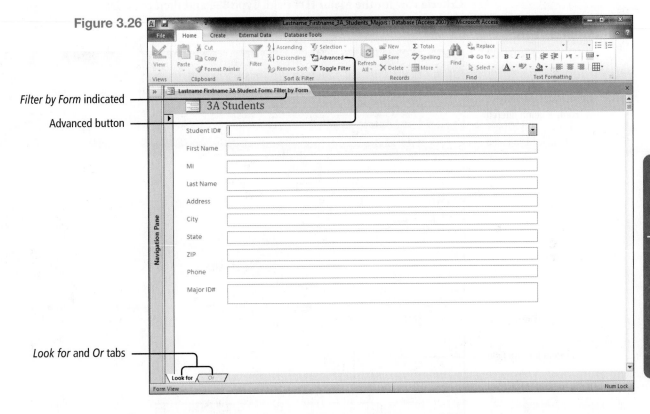

3 Click in the **City text box control**. At the right edge of the text box control, click the **arrow** that displays. In the list, click **Alexandria**. In the **Sort & Filter group**, click the **Toggle Filter** button.

As displayed in the navigation area, eight student records include *Alexandria* in the City field.

Another Way

Click in the text box control and type the criteria separated by the word *or*. For example, in the City text box control, type *Alexandria or Arlington*.

4 In the **Sort & Filter group**, click the **Advanced** button, and then click **Filter By Form**. At the bottom left of the window, click the **Or tab**. Click the **City text box control arrow**, and then click **Arlington**. In the **Sort & Filter group**, click the **Toggle Filter** button.

As displayed in the navigation area, eighteen student records include either Alexandria *or* Arlington in the City field. You have created an **OR condition**; that is, records display where, in this instance, either of two values—Alexandria *or* Arlington—is present in the selected field.

5 In the **Sort & Filter group**, click the **Advanced** button, and then click **Clear All Filters** to display all of the records.

6 Click the **Advanced** button again, and then from the list, click **Advanced Filter/Sort**. Expand the field list.

The Advanced Filter design grid displays. The design grid is similar to the query design grid.

7 From the **3A Students** field list, add the **City** field and then the **Major ID#** field to the design grid. In the **Criteria** row for the **City** field, type **Arlington** and then click in the **Criteria** row for the **Major ID#** field. Type **339** and then press Enter. Compare your screen with Figure 3.27.

Figure 3.27

Tab indicates *3A Student* Form is being filtered

Field list expanded

Design grid

Criteria for *City* field

Criteria for *Major ID#* field

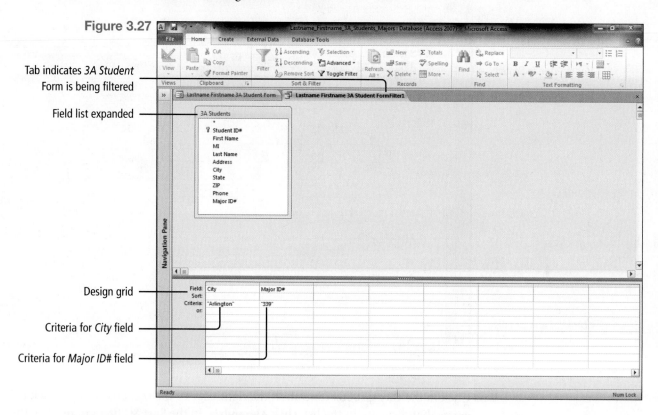

8 In the **Sort & Filter group**, click the **Toggle Filter** button.

Two records match the criteria. You have created an **AND condition**; that is, only records display where both values—Arlington *and* 339—are present in the selected fields. There are two Information Systems Technology majors who live in Arlington.

9 In the **Sort & Filter group**, click the **Toggle Filter** button to display all of the records.

In the navigation area, *Unfiltered* displays, which indicates that a filter was created for this form. Unless you Clear All Filters, the filter is saved with the form when the form is closed. When you reopen the form, you can click on the Toggle Filter button or the Unfiltered button to reapply the filter.

10 **Close** ☒ all open objects, and then **Open** ☒ the **Navigation Pane**. Display **Backstage** view, click **Close Database**, and then click **Exit**. As directed by your instructor, submit your database and the three paper or electronic printouts that are the results of this project.

More Knowledge | Using the Filter Button

You can filter a form in a manner similar to the way you filter records in a table. Click in the text box control of the field you wish to use for the filter. On the Home tab, in the Sort & Filter group, click the Filter button to display a shortcut menu. Select the (Select All) check box to clear the option, and then select the data by which you want to filter by clicking the check boxes preceding the data. To remove the filter, redisplay the menu, and then select the (Select All) check box.

End You have completed Project 3A ————————————

Project 3B Job Openings

Project Activities

In Activities 3.12 through 3.19, you will assist Damon Bass, Career Center Director for Capital Cities Community College, in using an Access database to track the employers and job openings advertised for the annual Career Fair. Your completed reports will look similar to Figure 3.28.

Project Files

For Project 3B, you will need the following file:

a03B_Job_Openings

You will save your database as:

Lastname_Firstname_3B_Job_Openings

Project Results

Figure 3.28
Project 3B Job Openings

Objective 5 | Create a Report by Using the Report Tool

A **report** is a database object that summarizes the fields and records from a query or from a table, in an easy-to-read format suitable for printing. A report consists of information extracted from queries or tables and also the report's design items, such as labels, headings, and graphics. The queries or tables that provide the underlying data for a report are referred to as the report's **record source**.

Activity 3.12 | Creating a Report by Using the Report Tool

The **Report tool** is the fastest way to create a report. This tool displays all of the fields and records from the record source that you select. You can use the Report tool to look at the underlying data quickly in an easy-to-read format, after which you can save the report and modify it in Layout view or in Design view. In this activity, you will use the Report tool to create a report from a query that lists all of the job openings with an annual salary of at least $40,000.

1 Start Access. In **Backstage** view, click **Open**. Navigate to the student data files for this textbook, and then open the **a03B_Job_Openings** database.

2 In **Backstage** view, click **Save Database As**. In the **Save As** dialog box, navigate to your **Access Chapter 3** folder. In the **File name** box, type **Lastname_Firstname_3B_Job_Openings** and then press [Enter]. On the **Message Bar**, click **Enable Content**. Notice that in this database, there are two tables and one query that uses both tables as its record source.

3 On the Ribbon, click the **Database Tools tab**. In the **Relationships group**, click the **Relationships** button. Compare your screen with Figure 3.29. If your relationships do not display, in the Relationships group, click the All Relationships button.

One employer is associated with *many* job openings. Thus, a one-to-many relationship has been established between the 3B Employers table and the 3B Job Openings table by using the Employer ID# field as the common field.

Figure 3.29

Employer ID# is common field

Join line indicating a one-to-many relationship and referential integrity

4 **Close** ☒ the **Relationships** window. Open both tables, and look at the fields and data in each table. Open the query to examine the data, and then switch to **Design** view to examine the design grid. When you are finished, **Close** ☒ all objects.

> The query answers the question *What is the Job#, Position, Employer Name, and # of Openings for jobs that have an Annual Salary of $40,000 or more?*

5 In the **Navigation Pane**, click to select the **3B Salary $40,000 or More** query. Click the **Create tab**, and then in the **Reports group**, click the **Report** button. **Close** ☒ the **Navigation Pane**, and then compare your screen with Figure 3.30.

> Access creates the 3B Job Openings report and displays it in Layout view. The report includes all of the fields and all of the records in the query. In Layout view, you can see the margins and page breaks in the report.

Figure 3.30

Dotted lines indicate margins

All fields from query display in report

All records from query display in report

Activity 3.13 | Modifying a Report in Layout View and Printing a Report

1 On the **Design tab**, in the **Themes group**, click the **Themes** button. From the gallery of themes, scroll down, locate, and then right-click the **Waveform** theme. Click **Apply Theme to This Object Only**.

> Recall that right-clicking a theme enables you to apply a predefined format to the active object only, which is another way to give a professional look to a report. Apply a theme before performing other formatting to the text in your report.

2 Click the **Job#** field name, and then click the **Arrange tab**. In the **Rows & Columns group**, click the **Select Column** button to select both the field name and the data in the field, and then press `Del` to remove the field from the report.

> The Job# field is deleted, and the remaining fields move to the left. No fields extend beyond the right margin of the report.

3 Notice that for several fields, there is an extra blank line in the record. In the **Employer Name** field, click in the **text box control** that displays *Monroe Heating & Air Conditioning*. Point to the right edge of the text box control to display the ⟷ pointer. Drag to the right slightly until the data in the text box control displays on one line. Scroll down to view the entire report to be sure that you have widened the column enough to accommodate all records on a single line.

> You should scroll down through the report to find the text box control that displays the most text and adjust the field width using that text box control. In this manner, you can be certain that all of the data in every text box control displays on one line.

4 Click the **Position** field name, and then click the **Home tab**. In the **Sort & Filter group**, click the **Ascending** button to sort the records in the report alphabetically by Position.

5 Scroll down to the bottom of the report, and then click the **Annual Salary calculated control**, which displays a total that is truncated at the bottom. Press Del to remove this total.

> Access automatically adds a calculated control to sum any field that is formatted as currency. Here, the total is not a useful number and this can be deleted.

6 At the top of the report, click the **# Openings** field name. Click the **Design tab**. In the **Grouping & Totals group**, click the **Totals** button, and then click **Sum**.

7 Scroll down to display the last line of the report. Click in the **# Openings calculated control**, point to the bottom edge of the control to display the ↕ pointer, and then double-click to resize the control. Compare your screen with Figure 3.31.

> The total number of job openings for positions with a salary equal to or greater than $40,000 is 100. Use Layout view to make quick changes to a report created with the Report tool. The Report tool is not intended to create a perfectly formatted formal report, but it is a way to summarize the data in a table or query quickly in an easy-to-read format suitable for printing and reading.

Figure 3.31

Waveform theme applied ——

Position field sorted in ascending order ——

Openings field summed ——

Calculated control removed from *Annual Salary* field ——

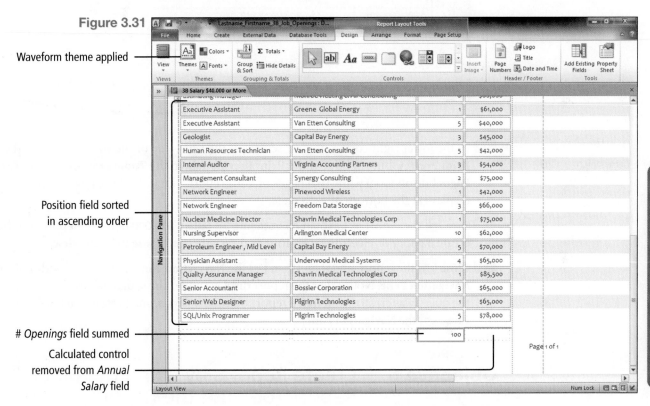

Executive Assistant	Greene Global Energy	1	$61,000
Executive Assistant	Van Etten Consulting	5	$40,000
Geologist	Capital Bay Energy	3	$45,000
Human Resources Technician	Van Etten Consulting	5	$42,000
Internal Auditor	Virginia Accounting Partners	3	$54,000
Management Consultant	Synergy Consulting	2	$75,000
Network Engineer	Pinewood Wireless	1	$42,000
Network Engineer	Freedom Data Storage	3	$66,000
Nuclear Medicine Director	Shavrin Medical Technologies Corp	1	$75,000
Nursing Supervisor	Arlington Medical Center	10	$62,000
Petroleum Engineer , Mid Level	Capital Bay Energy	5	$70,000
Physician Assistant	Underwood Medical Systems	4	$65,000
Quality Assurance Manager	Shavrin Medical Technologies Corp	1	$85,500
Senior Accountant	Bossier Corporation	3	$65,000
Senior Web Designer	Pilgrim Technologies	1	$65,000
SQL/Unix Programmer	Pilgrim Technologies	5	$78,000
		100	

Page 1 of 1

8 At the bottom of the report, notice that the **Page Number control** does not fit entirely within the margins. Click the **Page Number control** that displays *Page 1 of 1*, and then drag the ⟦⬚⟧ pointer to the left until the page number control is visually centered between the margins of the report.

> Always look at the headers and footers to determine if the data will print on one page.

9 Scroll up to display the top of the report. In the **Report Header** section, click the label control that displays *3B Salary $40,000 or More*. Click the **Format tab**, and then in the **Font group**, change the **Font Size** to **14**. Click the **label control** again so that you can edit the title. Using your own name, add **Lastname Firstname** to the beginning of the title, and then press Enter. If necessary, point to the right edge of the label control to display the ⟷ pointer, and then double-click to fit the width of the text in the control.

10 Click any field in the report. In the upper left corner of the report, click the **layout selector** ⊞, and then drag it slightly downward and to the right until the columns are visually centered between the margins of the report. If your columns rearrange, on the Quick Access Toolbar, click Undo and begin again. Compare your screen with Figure 3.32.

Using the layout selector, you can move the entire layout of the label controls and text box controls to horizontally center the records on the page. It is easier to control this movement if you drag downward slightly while moving the selector to the right.

Figure 3.32

Fields visually centered within margins

Your name displays in Report Header; Font Size of 14

Layout selector

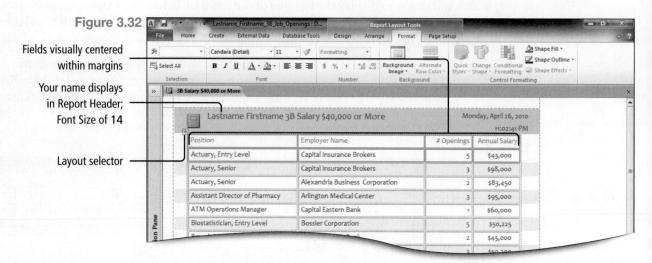

Another Way

In the object window, right-click the object tab, and then click Print Preview.

11 In the lower right corner of your screen, at the right side of the status bar, click the **Print Preview** button 🔍. On the **Print Preview tab**, in the **Zoom group**, click the **Two Pages** button to view the two pages of your report. Notice that the page number displays at the bottom of each page.

12 Save 🖫 the report as **Lastname Firstname 3B Salary $40,000 or More Report** and then create a paper or electronic printout as directed. Then **Close Print Preview**.

13 Close ☒ the report, and then **Open** ≫ the **Navigation Pane**. Expand the width of the **Navigation Pane**. Notice that the report displays under the source tables from which the query was created, and that a report object displays a small green notebook icon. **Close** ≪ the **Navigation Pane**.

Objective 6 | Create Reports by Using the Blank Report Tool and the Report Wizard

Use the **Blank Report tool** to create a report without predefined labels and fields. This is an efficient way to create a report, especially if you plan to include only a few fields in your report.

Activity 3.14 | Creating a Report by Using the Blank Report Tool

In this activity, you will build a report that lists only the Employer Name, Contact First Name, Contact Last Name, and Phone fields, which Mr. Bass will use as a quick reference for phoning the employers to verify the details of their Career Fair participation.

1 On the **Create tab**, in the **Reports group**, click the **Blank Report** button.

A blank report displays in Layout view, and the Field List pane displays.

2 In the **Field List** pane, click **Show all tables**, and then click the **plus sign** (+) next to **3B Employers** to display the field names in the table. Compare your screen with Figure 3.33.

Figure 3.33

Field List pane

Field list for *3B Employers* table expanded

3 In the **Field List** pane, point to the **Employer Name** field, right-click, and then click **Add Field to View**.

The Employer Name field and its data display as the first column of the report. Using the Report tool, you build the report field by field in the order that you want the fields to display.

4 From the **Field List** pane, drag the **Contact First Name** field into the blank report—anywhere to the right of *Employer Name*. Double-click the **Contact Last Name** field to add it as the third field in the report. Use any technique that you just practiced to add the **Phone** field as the fourth field in the report, and then compare your screen with Figure 3.34.

Figure 3.34

Four fields added to the report

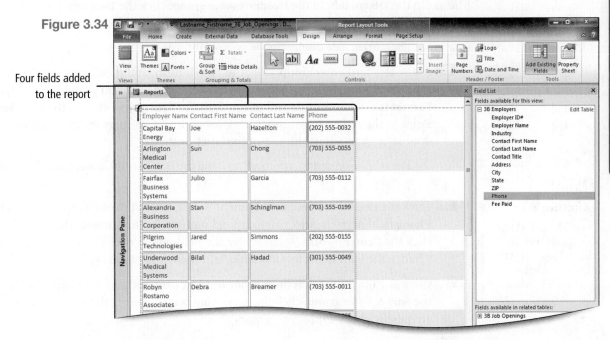

5 **Close** the **Field List** pane. On the **Design tab**, in the **Themes group**, click the **Themes** button. Right-click the **Equity** theme, and then click **Apply Theme to This Object Only**.

Recall that you should select a theme before making other formatting changes.

6 Under **Employer Name**, click in the **text box control** that displays *Monroe Heating & Air Conditioning*. Point to the right edge of the text box control to display the ↔ pointer, and then drag to the right until the data in the text box control displays on one line and there is a small amount of space between the name and the next column. Compare your screen with Figure 3.35.

Figure 3.35

All of the records display on one line

7 On the **Design tab**, in the **Header/Footer group**, click the **Date and Time** button. In the **Date and Time** dialog box, clear the **Include Time** check box, and then click **OK**.

> The current date displays in the upper right corner of the report.

8 In the **Header/Footer group**, click the **Title** button, and then using your own name, type **Lastname Firstname 3B Employer Phone List** and then press Enter. Click the **Format tab**. With the title still selected, in the **Font group**, change the **Font Size** to **14**. Point to the right edge of the title's label control to display the ↔ pointer, and then double-click to adjust the size of the label control.

> The title's label control width adjusts, and the Date control moves to the left within the margin.

Another Way

Click the first field name, and then click the Arrange tab. In the Rows & Columns group, click the Select Row button.

9 Click the **Employer Name** field name to select it. Hold down Shift, and then click the **Phone** field name to select all four field names. On the **Format tab**, in the **Font group**, click the **Center** button ≡ to center the field names over the data in the columns. Change the **Font Color** to **Automatic**, and then apply **Bold B**.

10 Click any one of the **Employer Name text box controls**, and then click the **Home tab**. In the **Sort & Filter group**, click the **Ascending** button to sort the records in the report alphabetically by Employer Name.

11 In the upper left corner of the report, click the **layout selector** ⊞, and then drag it downward slightly and to the right to visually center the fields between the margins. Compare your screen with Figure 3.36.

> Recall that it is easier to control this movement if you drag down slightly while moving the layout selector.

Figure 3.36

Field names formatted and centered over data

Report title added and formatted

Layout visually centered between the margins

Equity Theme applied

Date added (yours will vary)

12 Save 🖫 the report as **Lastname Firstname 3B Employer Phone List** and then on the status bar, click the **Print Preview** button 🔍. Create a paper or electronic printout as directed.

13 **Close Print Preview**, and then **Close** ✕ the report. **Open** 》 the **Navigation Pane**, and notice that the report displays below the *3B Employers* table—the underlying data source. **Close** 《 the **Navigation Pane**.

Activity 3.15 | Creating a Report by Using the Report Wizard

Use the **Report Wizard** when you need flexibility and want to control the report content and design. The Report Wizard enables you to specify how the data is grouped and sorted. You can use fields from more than one table or query, assuming you have created the appropriate relationships between the tables. The Report Wizard is similar to the Form Wizard; it creates a report by asking you a series of questions and then designs the report based on your answers.

In this activity, you will prepare a report for Mr. Bass that displays the employers, grouped by industry, and the total fees paid by employers for renting a booth at the Career Fair.

1 Click the **Create tab**, and then in the **Reports group**, click the **Report Wizard** button.

Here you select the tables or queries from which you want to extract information, and then select the fields to include in the report. You can also select more than one table or query.

2 Click the **Tables/Queries arrow**, and then click **Table: 3B Employers**. Move the following fields to the **Selected Fields** list in the order given: **Industry**, **Employer Name**, and **Fee Paid** (scroll down as necessary to locate the *Fee Paid* field). Compare your screen with Figure 3.37.

Figure 3.37

Report Wizard dialog box

Fields selected from *3B Employers* table

Three fields selected

3 Click **Next**, and notice that in this dialog box, you can add grouping levels. A preview of the grouping level displays on the right side of the dialog box.

Grouping data helps to organize and summarize the data in your report.

4 With **Industry** selected, click the **One Field** button ⊳ , and then compare your screen with Figure 3.38.

The preview window displays how the data will be grouped in the report. Grouping data in a report places all of the records that have the same data in a field together as a group—in this instance, each *Industry* will display as a group.

Figure 3.38

Report will be grouped by *Industry* names

5 Click **Next**, and then click the **1** box **arrow**. Click **Employer Name**, and then compare your screen with Figure 3.39.

> Here you indicate how you want to sort and summarize the information. You can sort on up to four fields. The Summary Options button displays because the data is grouped and contains numerical or currency data. The records in the report will sort alphabetically by Employer Name within Industry. Sorting records in a report presents a more organized report.

Figure 3.39

Sort order

Field that will be sorted

Summary options button
displays because report
contains numeric or
currency fields

6 In the **Report Wizard** dialog box, click the **Summary Options** button, and then compare your screen with Figure 3.40.

> The Summary Options dialog box displays. The Fee Paid field can be summarized by selecting one of four options—Sum, Avg, Min, or Max. You can also choose to display only summary information or to display both details—each record—and the summary information.

Figure 3.40

Aggregate functions
for *Fee Paid* field

Show options

7 To the right of **Fee Paid**, select the **Sum** check box. Under **Show**, be sure that the **Detail and Summary** option button is selected, click **OK**, and then click **Next**.

Here you select the layout and the page orientation. A preview of the layout displays on the left.

8 Click each **Layout** option button, noticing the changes in the preview box, and then click the **Stepped** option button to select it as the layout for your report. Under **Orientation**, be sure that **Portrait** is selected. At the bottom, be sure that the **Adjust the field width so all fields fit on a page** check box is selected, and then click **Next**.

9 In the **What title do you want for your report?** box, select the existing text, type **Lastname Firstname 3B Booth Fees by Industry Report** and then click **Finish**. Compare your screen with Figure 3.41.

The report is saved and displays in Print Preview. Each of the specifications you defined in the Report Wizard is reflected in the report. The records are grouped by Industry, and then within each Industry, the Employer Names are alphabetized. Within each Industry grouping, the Fee Paid is summed or totaled—the word *Sum* displays at the end of each grouping.

Figure 3.41

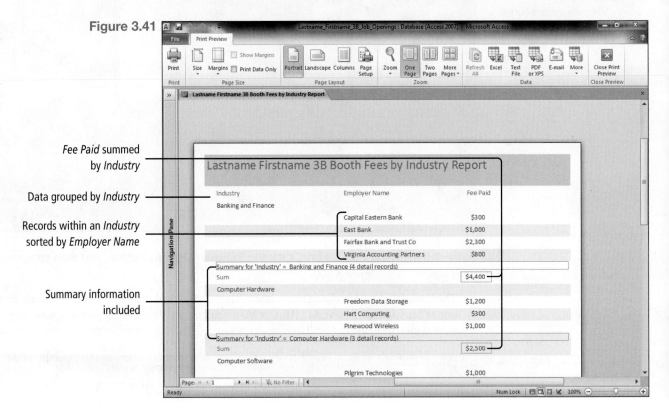

Fee Paid summed by *Industry*

Data grouped by *Industry*

Records within an *Industry* sorted by *Employer Name*

Summary information included

10 **Close Print Preview**. On the status bar, click the **Layout View** button .

Objective 7 | Modify the Design of a Report

After you create your report, you can modify its design by using tools and techniques similar to those you used to modify the design of a form. You can change the format of controls, add controls, remove controls, or change the placement of controls in the report. Most report modifications can be made in Layout view.

Activity 3.16 | Formatting and Deleting Controls in Layout View

1 With your **3B Booth Fees by Industry** report in **Layout** view, on the **Design tab**, in the **Themes group**, click the **Themes** button. In the **Themes gallery**, scroll down, and right-click the **Opulent** theme. Click **Apply Theme to This Object Only**.

2 Click the title—**3B Booth Fees by Industry Report**—to display a border around the label control, and then click the **Format tab**. In the **Font group**, change the **Font Size** to **14**, and then apply **Bold** **B**.

3 Within each *Industry* grouping, notice the **Summary for 'Industry'** information.

Access includes a summary line that details what is being summarized (in this case, summed) and the number of records that are included in the summary total. Now that Mr. Bass has viewed the report, he has decided this information is not necessary and can be removed.

4 Click any one of the **Summary for 'Industry' controls**.

> **Another Way**
> Right-click any of the selected controls, and then click Delete.

The control that you clicked is surrounded by a dark border, and all of the related controls are surrounded by paler borders to indicate that all are selected.

5 Press Del to remove the controls from the report. Compare your screen to Figure 3.42.

Figure 3.42

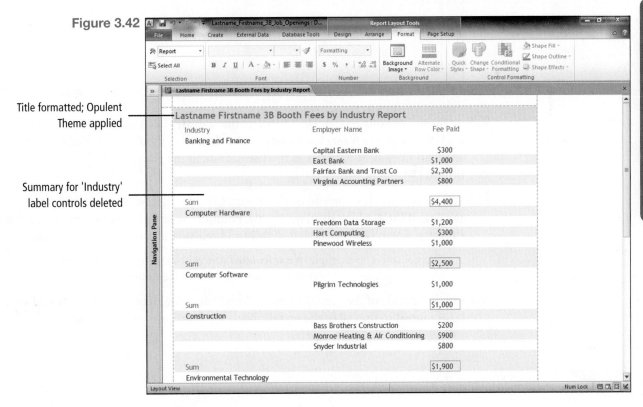

Title formatted; Opulent Theme applied

Summary for 'Industry' label controls deleted

6 **Save** the changes you have made to the report.

Access | Chapter 3

Activity 3.17 | Modifying Controls in Layout View

In this activity, you will modify the text in controls, move controls, resize controls, and add a control to the report, all of which is easily accomplished in Layout view.

1 On the left side of the report, click one of the **Sum label controls** to select all of the controls, and then double-click to select the text. Type **Total Fees by Industry** and then press Enter. Compare your screen with Figure 3.43.

The new text more clearly states what is being summed.

Figure 3.43

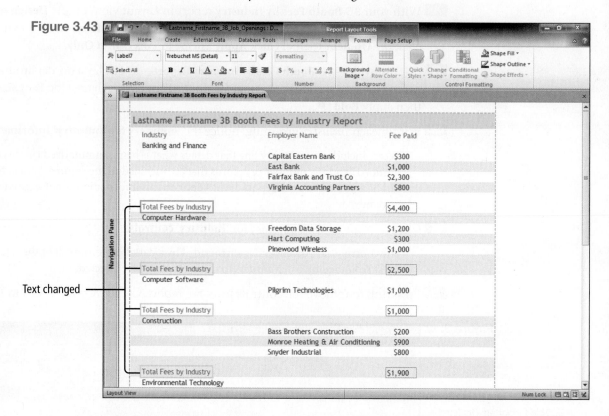

Text changed

2 At the top of your report, click to select the **Industry label control**. Hold down Shift, click the **Employer Name label control**, and then click the **Fee Paid label control** to select all three field names. On the **Format tab**, in the **Font group**, click the **Bold** button **B**.

3 Scroll down to view the end of the report. Click to select the **calculated control** for the **Grand Total**, which displays *20,400*. Point to the left edge of the control to display the ↔ pointer. Drag to the left slightly and release the mouse to display **$20,400**.

This control is an example of a *calculated control*—a control that contains an expression, often a formula—that uses one or more fields from the underlying table or query.

4 On the left side of the report, increase the width of the right edge of the **Grand Total label control** so that all of the text displays, and then **Save** 🖫 the report.

Activity 3.18 | Aligning Controls in Design View

Design view gives you a more detailed view of the structure of your report. You can see the header and footer sections for the report, for the page, and for groups. In Design view, your report is not actually running, so you cannot see the underlying data while you are working. In the same manner as forms, you can add labels to the Page Footer section or increase the height of sections. Some tasks, such as aligning controls, can also be completed in Design view.

1 On the status bar, click the **Design View** button 🖾, and then compare your screen with Figure 3.44.

The Design view for a report is similar to the Design view for a form. You can modify the layout of the report in this view, and use the dotted grid pattern to align controls. This report contains a **Report Header**, a **Page Header**, a **Group Header**, which in this instance is the *Industry* grouping, a Detail section that displays the data, a **Group Footer** (*Industry*), a **Page Footer**, and a **Report Footer**.

The Report Header displays information at the top of the *first page* of a report. The Page Header displays information at the top of *every page* of a report. The Group Header and Group Footer display the field label by which the data has been grouped—*Industry* in this instance. If you do not group data in a report, the Group Header does not display. Similarly, if you do not summarize data, the Group Footer does not display.

Figure 3.44

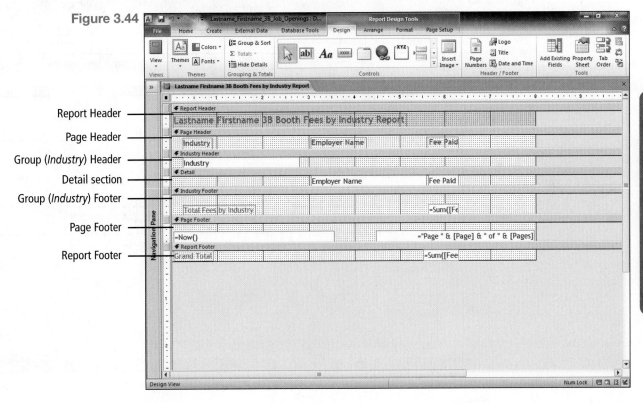

Report Header
Page Header
Group (*Industry*) Header
Detail section
Group (*Industry*) Footer
Page Footer
Report Footer

Access | Chapter 3

2 In the **Page Footer** section of the report, examine the two controls in this section.

The Page Footer displays information at the bottom of *every page* in the report, including the page number and the current date inserted by those controls.

The *date control* on the left side, displayed as *=Now( )*, inserts the current date each time the report is opened. The *page number control* on the right side, displayed as *="Page " & [Page] & " of " & [Pages]*, inserts the page number, for example Page 1 of 2, in the report when the report is displayed in Print Preview or when printed. Both of these are examples of functions that are used by Access to create controls in a report.

3 In the **Industry Footer** section, click the **Total Fees by Industry label control**. Hold down Shift. In the **Report Footer** section, click the **Grand Total label control** to select both controls.

4 On the **Arrange tab**, in the **Sizing & Ordering group**, click the **Align** button, and then click **Left. Save** 🖫 the report, and then compare your screen with Figure 3.45.

The left edge of the Grand Total label control is aligned with the left edge of the Total Fees by Industry label control. When using the Align Left feature, Access aligns the left edges of controls with the control that is farthest to the left in the report. Similarly, when using the Align Right feature, Access aligns the right edges of controls with the control that is farthest to the right in the report.

Figure 3.45

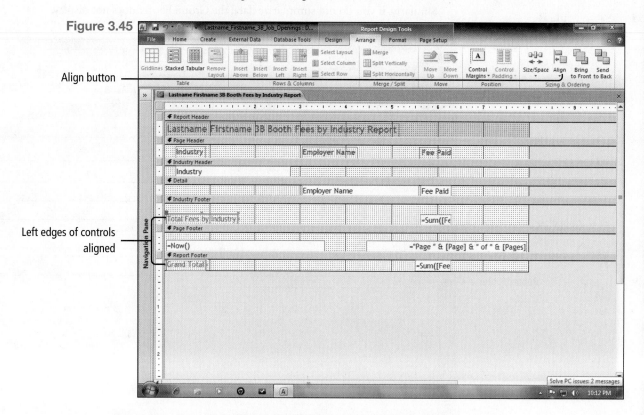

Align button

Left edges of controls aligned

5 Switch to **Layout** view to display the underlying data in the controls. Scroll down, and notice that the **Total Fees by Industry label controls** and the **Grand Total label control** are left aligned.

Objective 8 | Print a Report and Keep Data Together

Before you print a report, examine the preview of the report to ensure that all of the labels and data display fully and to make sure that all of the data is properly grouped. Sometimes a page break occurs in the middle of a group of data, leaving the labels on one page and the data or totals on another page.

Activity 3.19 | Keeping Data Together and Printing a Report

It is possible to keep the data in a group together so it does not break across a page unless, of course, the data itself exceeds the length of a page.

1 On the status bar, click the **Print Preview** button 🔍. If necessary, in the **Zoom group**, click the **Two Pages** button, and then compare your screen with Figure 3.46.

This report will print on two pages. One record and the summary data for the *Hotel and Food Service* group display at the top of page 2, which is separated from the rest of the grouping.

Figure 3.46

Top of second page—one record and summary data

Bottom of first page—*Industry* grouping name and two records

2 Click the **Close Print Preview** button to return to **Layout** view. On the **Design tab**, in the **Grouping & Totals group**, click the **Group & Sort** button.

At the bottom of the screen, the *Group, Sort, and Total pane* displays. Here you can control how information is grouped, sorted, or totaled. Layout view is the preferred view in which to accomplish such tasks, because you can see how the changes affect the display of the data.

3 In the **Group, Sort, and Total** pane, on the **Group on Industry bar**, click **More**. To the right of **do not keep group together on one page**, click the **arrow**, and then compare your screen with Figure 3.47.

The *keep whole group together on one page* command keeps each industry group together, from the name in the group header through the summary in the group footer. Next to *Group on Industry, with A on top* indicates that the industry names display in ascending sort order. The default setting is *do not keep group together on one page*.

Figure 3.47

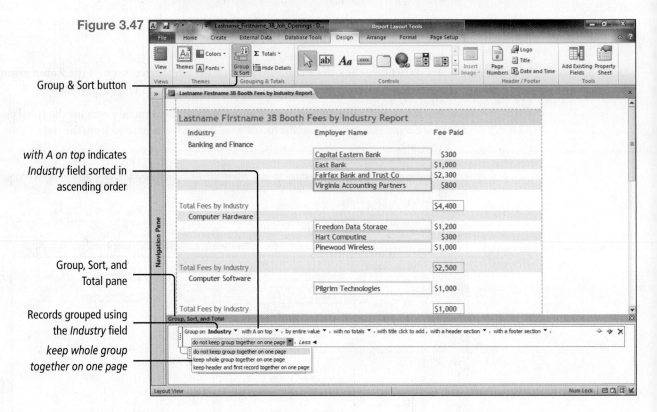

Group & Sort button

with A on top indicates *Industry* field sorted in ascending order

Group, Sort, and Total pane

Records grouped using the *Industry* field

keep whole group together on one page

4 Click **keep whole group together on one page**. In the **Grouping & Totals group**, click the **Group & Sort** button to close the **Group, Sort, and Total** pane. On the status bar, click the **Print Preview** button 🔍. If necessary, in the Zoom group, click the Two Pages button. Compare your screen with Figure 3.48.

All the records in the *Hotel and Food Service* industry group—the group header, the three records, and the summary information—display together at the top of page 2.

Figure 3.48

Entire industry group displays together

5 Save 💾 the report. Create a paper or electronic copy of the report as directed.

6 **Close Print Preview**, and then **Close** ☒ the report. **Open** » the **Navigation Pane**, and, if necessary, increase the width of the pane so that all object names display fully.

7 Display **Backstage** view, click **Close Database**, and then click **Exit**. As directed by your instructor, submit your database and the three paper or electronic printouts that are the results of this project.

End **You have completed Project 3B** _____

Content-Based Assessments

Summary

A form is an object for either entering or viewing information in a database—it creates a user interface for people using the database. A form is easy to use, because it can display one record at a time. Reports summarize the data in a database in a professional-looking manner suitable for printing. There are several tools for creating forms and reports, and you can modify forms and reports in Layout view or Design view.

Key Terms

Matching

Match each term in the second column with its correct definition in the first column by writing the letter of the term on the blank line in front of the correct definition.

_____ 1. The Access view in which you can make changes to a form or report while viewing the data.

_____ 2. The term used to describe objects and controls that are based on data that is stored in tables.

_____ 3. An Access view that displays the detailed structure of a query, form, or report.

_____ 4. Information, such as a form's title, that displays at the top of the screen in Form view and is printed at the top of the first page when records are printed as forms.

_____ 5. The section of a form or report that displays the records from the underlying table or query.

_____ 6. Information at the bottom of the screen in Form view that prints after the last detail section on the last page.

_____ 7. A gray bar in a form or report that identifies and separates one section from another.

_____ 8. An object on a form or report that displays data, performs actions, and lets you work with information.

_____ 9. The graphical object on a form or report that displays the data from the underlying table or query.

A Bound

B Bound control

C Calculated control

D Control

E Control layout

F Date control

G Design view

H Detail section

I Form footer

J Form header

K Label control

L Layout view

M Section bar

N Text box control

O Unbound control

_____ 10. A control that retrieves its data from an underlying table or query.

_____ 11. A control on a form or report that contains descriptive information, typically a field name.

_____ 12. A control that does not have a source of data, such as a title in a form or report.

_____ 13. The grouped arrangement of controls on a form or report.

_____ 14. A control that contains an expression, often a formula, that uses one or more fields from the underlying table or query.

_____ 15. A control on a form or report that inserts the current date each time the form or report is opened.

Multiple Choice

Circle the correct answer.

1. An Access object to enter new records into a table, edit or delete existing records in a table, or display existing records is a:
   A. bound control   B. form   C. report

2. The order that the insertion point moves from one field to another in a form when you press Tab is the:
   A. data entry order   B. control order   C. tab order

3. A small symbol that displays in the upper left corner of a selected control layout in a form or report that is displayed in Layout view and that is used to move an entire group of controls is the:
   A. control layout   B. label control   C. layout selector

4. A list of characteristics for controls on a form or report in which you can make precise changes to each property associated with the control is the:
   A. bound control   B. control layout   C. Property Sheet

5. The process of displaying only a portion of the total records (a subset) based on matching a specific value is:
   A. filtering   B. reporting   C. zooming

6. An Access command that filters the records in a form based on one or more fields, or based on more than one value in the field is Filter by:
   A. Form   B. Selection   C. Subset

7. A condition in which records that match at least one of the specified values are displayed is:
   A. AND   B. BOTH   C. OR

8. A database object that summarizes the fields and records from a table or query in an easy-to-read format suitable for printing is a:
   A. control   B. form   C. report

9. Information printed at the end of each group of records and that is used to display summary information for the group is called a:
   A. group footer   B. group header   C. Group, Sort, and Total pane

10. A predefined format that can be applied to the entire database or to individual objects in the database is called a:
    A. group header   B. subset   C. theme

Apply **3A** skills from these Objectives:

- ◼ Create and Use a Form to Add and Delete Records
- ◼ Create a Form by Using the Form Wizard
- ◼ Modify a Form in Layout View and in Design View
- ◼ Filter Records

Skills Review | Project **3C** Student Advising

In the following Skills Review, you will assist Gerald Finn, the Dean of Information Technology, in using an Access database to track students and their faculty advisors. Your completed forms will look similar to Figure 3.49.

Project Files

For Project 3C, you will need the following file:

a03C_Student_Advising

You will save your database as:

Lastname_Firstname_3C_Student_Advising

Project Results

Figure 3.49

(Project 3C Student Advising continues on the next page)

Content-Based Assessments

1 **Start** Access. In **Backstage** view, click **Open**, and then from your student files open the **a03C_Student_Advising** database. In **Backstage** view, click **Save Database As**. Save the database in your **Access Chapter 3** folder as **Lastname_Firstname_3C_Student_Advising** On the **Message Bar**, click the **Enable Content** button.

a. On the **Database Tools tab**, in the **Relationships group**, click the **Relationships** button. Notice the one-to-many relationship between the 3C Faculty Advisors table and the 3C Students table using the Faculty ID and Faculty Advisor ID fields as the common fields. *One* faculty member can advise *many* students. Recall that common fields do not need to have the same name; they must have the same data type. **Close** the **Relationships** window.

b. In the **Navigation Pane**, select the **3C Students** table. Click the **Create tab**, and then in the **Forms group**, click the **Form** button. **Save** the form as **Lastname Firstname 3C Student Form** and then **Close** the form object.

c. In the **Navigation Pane**, select the **3C Faculty Advisors** table. Click the **Create tab**, and then in the **Forms group**, click the **Form** button. **Close** the **Navigation Pane**, and then notice that *Faculty ID FAC-2877*, for *Professor Treiman*, has been assigned one student for advising.

d. **Close** the form, saving it as **Lastname Firstname 3C Faculty Advisor Form**

2 **Open** the **Navigation Pane**, and increase the width to display fully the object names. Open your **3C Student Form** object, and then **Close** the **Navigation Pane**. In the navigation area, click the **New (blank) record** button. In the **Student ID#** field, type **9898123** and then press [Tab].

a. Using your own name, continue entering the data as shown in **Table 1**.

b. In the last field, press [Tab] to save the record and display a new blank record. **Close** the **3C**

Student Form object, and then **Open** the **Navigation Pane**.

c. **Open** your **3C Faculty Advisor Form** object, and then **Close** the **Navigation Pane**. Notice that in the first record, your record displays in the subdatasheet for Professor Treiman. At the bottom of your screen, in the navigation area for the form—not the navigation area for the related records in the form itself—click the **New (blank) record** button. In the blank form, using your own name, enter the information in **Table 2**, being sure to press [Tab] after entering the data in the last field.

d. In the navigation area, click the **First record** button. Click in the **Last Name** field, and then on the **Home tab**, in the **Find group**, click the **Find** button to open the **Find and Replace** dialog box. In the **Find What** box, type **Holland** and then click **Find Next**. **Close** the **Find and Replace** dialog box.

e. On the **Home tab**, in the **Records group**, click the **Delete button arrow**, and then click **Delete Record** to delete the record for Professor Holland—because Professor Holland has no student advisees assigned, he can be deleted from the table. In the message box, click **Yes** to delete the record. In the navigation area for the form, notice that the number of records in the table is *18*.

f. Use the **Find** button to display the form for the **Faculty ID** of **FAC-1001** Display **Backstage** view. Click the **Print tab**, and then in the right panel, click **Print**. In the **Print** dialog box, under **Print Range**, click the **Selected Record(s)** option button, and then click **Setup**. In the **Page Setup** dialog box, click the **Columns tab**. Under **Column Size**, in the **Width** box, delete the existing text, type **7.5** and then click **OK** two times to print only your record in the form layout, or create an electronic printout. **Close** the **3C Faculty Advisor Form** object, and then **Open** the **Navigation Pane**.

Table 1

Student ID#	Last Name	First Name	Phone Number	E-mail	Concentration	Faculty Advisor ID
9898123	**Lastname**	**Firstname**	**(703) 555-1257**	**ns0001@capccc.edu**	**Network Security**	**FAC-2877**

(Return to Step 2-b)

Table 2

Faculty ID	Rank	Last Name	First Name	Office Phone	E-mail	Concentration
FAC-1001	**Professor**	**Lastname**	**Firstname**	**(703) 555-2844**	**nfac@capccc.edu**	**Database**

(Return to Step 2-d)

(Project 3C Student Advising continues on the next page)

Access | Chapter 3

g. Open your **3C Student Form** object, and then **Close** the **Navigation Pane**. Click in the **Last Name** field. Press Ctrl + F to display the **Find and Replace** dialog box. Enter the information to find the record where the **Last Name** field contains your **Lastname** and then **Print** only the selected record, changing the **Column Size Width** to **7.5** or create an electronic printout. **Close** the **3C Student Form** object, and then **Open** the **Navigation Pane**.

3 In the **Navigation Pane**, click to select the **3C Students** table. On the **Create tab**, in the **Forms group** click the **Form Wizard** button.

a. Under **Tables/Queries**, be sure that **Table: 3C Students** displays. Using the **One Field** button or by double-clicking, move the following fields to the **Selected Fields** list in the order specified: **First Name**, **Last Name**, and **Faculty Advisor ID**.

b. Click **Next**. Be sure **Columnar** is selected as the layout, and then click **Next**. In the box **What title do you want for your form?**, select the existing text, and then type **Lastname Firstname 3C Advisor Assignment Form** and then click **Finish** to close the wizard and create the form.

4 **Close** the **Navigation Pane**. Be sure your **3C Advisor Assignment Form** displays. In the lower right corner of your screen, click the **Layout View** button. Click the **First Name label control**. Hold down Shift, and then click the **Last Name label control**, the **Faculty Advisor ID label control**, and the **three text box controls** to select all of the controls. On the Ribbon, click the **Arrange tab**. In the **Table group**, click the **Stacked** button to group the controls. Click the **First Name label control** to deselect all of the controls and to surround the label control with a colored border.

a. On the **Design tab**, in the **Themes group**, click the **Themes** button. Right-click the **Couture** theme, and then click **Apply Theme to This Object Only**.

b. Click anywhere in the title *3C Advisor Assignment Form* to select it. On the **Format tab**, in the **Font group**, click the **Font Size button arrow**, and then click **16**. Click the **Bold** button. Click the **Font Color button arrow**, and then under **Theme Colors**, in the last column, click the last color—**Brown, Accent 6, Darker 50%**.

c. On the status bar, click the **Design View** button. Point to the *lower* edge of the **Form Footer section**

bar to display the ⬍ pointer, and then drag downward approximately **0.5 inch**. On the **Design tab**, in the **Controls group**, click the **Label** button. Position the plus sign of the ⁺A pointer in the **Form Footer** section at **0.25 inch on the horizontal ruler** and even with the lower edge of the Form Footer section bar. Click one time.

d. Using your own name, type **Created by Lastname Firstname** and then press Enter. Click the **Format tab**. With the label control selected, in the **Font group**, click the **Bold** button, and then change the **Font Color** to **Brown, Text 2**—in the fourth column, the first color. Point to a sizing handle to display one of the resize pointers, and then double-click to fit the control to the text you typed.

5 **Save** the form, and then switch to **Layout** view. On the **Design tab**, in the **Tools group**, click the **Add Existing Fields** button. In the **Field List** pane, point to **Student ID#**, and then drag to the left until the pointer is above the *First Name* label control and a thick colored line displays above the control. Release the mouse button to add the Student ID# controls to the form.

a. **Close** the **Field List** pane. Click the **Last Name text box control**, which currently displays *Barthmaier*, to surround it with a border. Point to the right edge of the **text box control** until the pointer displays, and then drag to the left until there is approximately **1"** of space between *Barthmaier* and the right edge of the text box control.

b. On the **Arrange tab**, in the **Rows & Columns** group, click the **Select Row** button. In the **Move group**, click the **Move Up** button one time to move the **Last Name controls** above the **First Name controls**. **Save** the form.

6 Click the **Student ID# text box control**, which displays *1034823*. In the **Rows & Columns group**, click the **Select Column** button to select all four text box controls. On the **Format tab**, in the **Font group**, click the **Background Color button arrow**. Under **Theme Colors**, in the fifth column, click the second color—**Brown, Accent 1, Lighter 80%**.

a. Click the **Student ID# label control**. On the **Arrange tab**, in the **Rows & Columns group**, click the **Select Column** button to select all four label controls. Click the **Format tab**, change the **Font Color**—*not* the Background Color—to **Brown, Text 2**—in the fourth column, the first color. Then apply **Bold**.

(Project 3C Student Advising continues on the next page)

Content-Based Assessments

b. Click the **layout selector** ⊞ to select all of the controls. Change the **Font Size** to **12**. On the Ribbon, click the **Design tab**, and then in the **Tools group**, click the **Property Sheet** button. In the **Property Sheet**, click the word **Height**, type **0.25** and then press Enter to adjust the height of all of the controls.

c. Click the **Student ID# label control** to select only that label. Click the **Arrange tab**, and then in the **Rows & Columns group**, click the **Select Column** button. In the **Property Sheet**, click **Width**, type **1.5** and then press Enter.

d. In the **Form Footer section**, click the label control with your name. Hold down Shift, and then in the **Form Header section**, in the **label control** that displays *3C Advisor Assignment Form*, click to select both controls. In the **Property Sheet**, change the **Left** property to **0.5** and then press Enter. **Save** the form.

e. **Close** the **Property Sheet**, and then switch to **Form** view. In the navigation area, click the **Last record** button to display the record containing your name. Display **Backstage** view, click the **Print tab**, and then click **Print**. In the **Print** dialog box, under **Print Range**, click the **Selected Record(s)** option button. Create a paper or electronic printout as directed, and then **Close Print Preview**.

7 With the form displayed in **Form** view, click the **First record** button, click the **Faculty Advisor ID label control** to select the text in the text box control. On the **Home tab**, in the **Find group**, click the **Find** button. In the **Find and Replace** dialog box, in the **Find What** box, type **FAC-9119** and then click **Find Next** to find and display the record for *Amanda Bass*. **Close** the **Find and Replace** dialog box. In

the **Sort & Filter group**, click the **Selection** button, and then click **Equals "FAC-9119"**. In the navigation area, notice that two students have been assigned to the faculty member with the *FAC-9119* advisor number.

a. In the **Sort & Filter group**, click the **Toggle Filter** button to remove the filter and display all 27 records. **Close** the form, and save changes.

b. **Open** the **Navigation Pane**, open your **3C Student Form** object, and then **Close** the **Navigation Pane**. On the **Home tab**, in the **Sort & Filter group**, click the **Advanced** button, and then click **Filter By Form**. Click in the **Concentration text box control**. At the right edge of the text box control, click the **arrow** that displays. In the list, click Programming. In the **Sort & Filter group**, click the **Toggle Filter** button, and notice that two students have a *Concentration* of *Programming*.

c. In the **Sort & Filter group**, click the **Advanced** button, and then click **Filter By Form**. At the bottom left side of the window, click the **Or tab**. Click the **Concentration text box control arrow**, and then click **Networking**. In the **Sort & Filter group**, click the **Toggle Filter** button. Seven students have a Concentration of *Programming* or *Networking*. In the **Sort & Filter group**, click the **Toggle Filter** button to display all of the records. **Save** and then **Close** the form.

d. **Open** the **Navigation Pane**; be sure all object names display fully. Display **Backstage** view, click **Close Database**, and then click **Exit**. As directed by your instructor, submit your database and the three paper or electronic printouts that are the results of this project.

End **You have completed Project 3C** ———————————

Access | Chapter 3

Content-Based Assessments

5 Create a Report by
Using the Report
Tool

6 Create Reports by
Using the Blank
Report Tool and the
Report Wizard

7 Modify the Design
of a Report

8 Print a Report and
Keep Data Together

Skills Review | Project **3D** Workshop Rooms

In the following Skills Review, you will assist Michelina Cortez, the Director of Workforce
Development, in using an Access database to track the details about workshops offered by
community members for the public and for students at the Washington Campus of Capital Cities
Community College. Your completed reports will look similar to Figure 3.50.

Project Files

For Project 3D, you will need the following file:

> a03D_Workshop_Rooms

You will save your database as:

> Lastname_Firstname_3D_Workshop_Rooms

Project Results

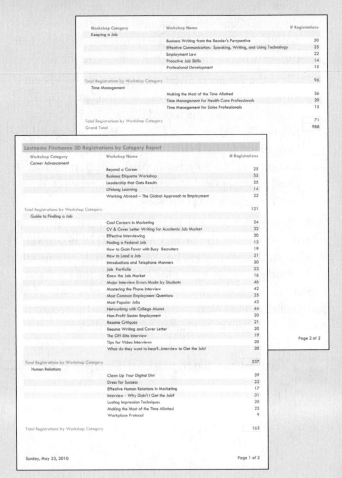

Figure 3.50

(Project 3D Workshop Rooms continues on the next page)

Content-Based Assessments

Skills Review | Project **3D** Workshop Rooms (continued)

1 **Start** Access. In **Backstage** view, click **Open**. From your student files, open the **a03D_Workshop_Rooms** database. In **Backstage** view, save the database in your **Access Chapter 3** folder as **Lastname_Firstname_3D_ Workshop_Rooms** and then in the **Message Bar**, click the **Enable Content** button. On the Ribbon, click the **Database Tools tab**, and then click the **Relationships** button. If your relationships do not display, in the Relationships group, click the All Relationships button. *One* room is associated with *many* workshops. Thus, a one-to-many relationship has been established between the 3D Rooms table and the 3D Workshops table using Room ID# as the common field. **Close** the **Relationships** window.

a. Open the two tables to examine the data, and then open the query in **Design** view to examine the design grid. This query answers the question *What is the Room ID#, Workshop Name, Workshop Category, and # Registrations for workshops that have wireless Internet connections available?* **Close** all open objects. In the **Navigation Pane**, select the **3D Workshops with Wireless Connection** query. Click the **Create tab**, and then in the **Reports group**, click the **Report** button. **Close** the **Navigation Pane**.

b. On the **Design tab**, in the **Themes group**, click the **Themes** button, right-click the **Waveform** theme, and then click **Apply Theme to This Object Only**.

c. Click the **Workshop Category** field name. Click the **Arrange tab**, and then in the **Rows & Columns group**, click the **Select Column** button. Press Del to remove the field from the report.

d. Click the **Room ID#** field name, and then drag the right edge of the control to the left until there is approximately **0.5** inch of space between the room number and the right edge of the field. Scroll down the report, and then in the **Workshop Name** field—second column—click in the **text box control** that displays *What do they want to hear? . . . Interview to Get the Job!* Drag the right edge of the control to the right until the data in the control displays on one line. With the **Workshop Name** field selected, click the **Home tab**. In the **Sort & Filter group**, click the **Ascending** button.

e. Scroll down to the bottom of the report, and notice that Access counted the number of records in the report—*26* displays under the Room ID# field. Click this **calculated control**, and then press Del. At the top of the report, click the **# Registrations** field name. On the **Design tab**, in the **Grouping & Totals group**, click the **Totals** button, and then click **Sum**. Scroll down to the bottom of the report, and then click the calculated control. Point to the bottom edge of the control to display the ↕ pointer, and then double-click to resize the control. The total number of registrations for the workshops that have a wireless connection is *641*.

f. Click the **Page number control**, and then drag the control to the left until the control is visually centered between the left and right margins of the report. At the top of the report, in the **Report Header** section, click the text *3D Workshops with Wireless Connection*. On the **Format tab**, in the **Font group**, change the **Font Size** to **14**, and then click the **label control** again to position the insertion point in the title. Using your own name, add **Lastname Firstname** to the beginning of the title. Click any field in the report. Above and to the left of the **Room ID#** field name, click the **layout selector** ⊞, and then drag it down slightly and to the right until the fields are visually centered between the margins of the report. **Save** the report as **Lastname Firstname 3D Workshops with Wireless Connection Report**

g. On the status bar, click the **Print Preview** button. On the **Print Preview tab**, in the **Zoom group**, click the **Two Pages** button, and notice that the report will print on one page. Create a paper or electronic printout as directed, and then **Close Print Preview**.

h. **Close** the report, and then **Open** the **Navigation Pane**. If necessary, increase the width of the **Navigation Pane** to display the entire report name, and then **Close** the **Navigation Pane**.

2 Click the **Create tab**, and then in the **Reports group**, click the **Blank Report** button. If the Field List pane does not display, on the Design tab, in the Tools group, click the Add Existing Fields button. In the **Field List** pane, click **Show all tables**, and then click the **plus sign** (+) next to **3D Rooms**. Point to the **Room ID#** field, right-click, and then click **Add Field to View**. From the **Field List** pane, drag the **Equipment** field into the blank report— anywhere to the right of *Room ID#*. Double-click the **Internet** field to add it as the third field in the report, and then **Close** the **Field List** pane.

a. On the **Design tab**, in the **Themes group**, click the **Themes** button, and then right-click the **Equity** theme. Click **Apply Theme to This Object Only**.

(Project 3D Workshop Rooms continues on the next page)

Under the **Equipment** field name, click in any **text box control** that displays *Overhead Projector*. Point to the right edge of the control to display the ⟷ pointer, and then drag to the right until the text in the control displays on one line and there is a small amount of space between the text and the next column.

b. On the **Design tab**, in the **Header/Footer group**, click the **Date and Time** button. Clear the **Include Time** check box, and then click **OK**. In the **Header/Footer group**, click the **Title** button. Using your own name, type **Lastname Firstname 3D Equipment List** and then press Enter.

c. With the title still selected, on the **Format tab**, in the **Font group**, change the **Font Size** to **14**. On the right edge of the **label control** for the title, double-click to resize the title's label control.

d. Click the **Room ID#** field name to select it. Hold down Shift, and then click the **Internet** field name to select all three field names. On the **Format tab**, in the **Font group**, click the **Center** button to center the field names over the data in the fields. Change the **Font Color** to **Automatic**, and then apply **Bold**. Click the **layout selector** ⊞, and then drag it down slightly and to the right to visually center the fields between the margins. **Save** the report as **Lastname Firstname 3D Equipment List**

e. On the status bar, click the **Print Preview** button. Create a paper or electronic printout as directed, and then **Close Print Preview**. **Close** the report.

3 Click the **Create tab**, and then in the **Reports group**, click the **Report Wizard** button. Click the **Tables/Queries arrow**, and then click **Table: 3D Workshops**. Double-click the following fields in the order given to move them to the **Selected Fields** list: **Workshop Category**, **Workshop Name**, and **# Registrations**. Click **Next**.

a. With **Workshop Category** selected, click the **One Field** button to group the report by this field, and then click **Next**. Click the **1 box arrow**, and then click **Workshop Name** to sort the records within each Workshop Category by the Workshop Name. Click the **Summary Options** button. To the right of **# Registrations**, select the **Sum** check box. Under **Show**, be sure that the **Detail and Summary** option button is selected, click **OK**, and then click **Next**.

b. Under **Layout**, be sure that the **Stepped** option button is selected. Under **Orientation**, be sure that **Portrait** is selected, and at the bottom of the **Report Wizard** dialog box, be sure that the **Adjust the field width so all fields fit on a page** check box is selected. Click **Next**, In the **What title do you want for your report?** box, select the existing text, type **Lastname Firstname 3D Registrations by Category Report** and then click **Finish**. **Close Print Preview**, and then on the status bar, click the **Layout View** button.

4 On the **Design tab**, in the **Themes group**, click the **Themes** button, right-click the **Median** theme, and then click **Apply Theme to This Object Only**. Click the title of the report. On the **Format tab**, in the **Font group**, change the **Font Size** to **14**, and then apply **Bold**. Click one of the **Summary for 'Workshop Category' controls**, and then press Del.

a. On the left side of the report, click one of the **Sum label controls**, and then double-click to select the text inside the control. Type **Total Registrations by Workshop Category** and then press Enter.

b. At the top of your report, click the **Workshop Category label control**. Hold down Shift, click the **Workshop Name label control**, and then click the **# Registrations label control** to select all three field names. On the **Format tab**, in the **Font group**, click the **Bold** button.

c. On the status bar, click the **Design View** button. In the **Report Footer section**, click the **Grand Total label control**. Hold down Shift, and in the **Workshop Category Footer section**, click the **Total Registrations by Workshop Category label control** to select both controls. On the **Arrange tab**, in the **Sizing & Ordering group**, click the **Align** button, and then click **Left** to align the left edges of the two controls.

5 On the status bar, click the **Print Preview** button. In the **Zoom group**, click the **Two Pages** button to view how your report is currently laid out. Notice that at the bottom of Page 1 and the top of Page 2, the records in the **Keeping a Job** category are split between the two pages. Click **Close Print Preview**. On the status bar, click the **Layout View** button.

(Project 3D Workshop Rooms continues on the next page)

Content-Based Assessments

Skills Review | Project **3D** Workshop Rooms (continued)

a. On the **Design tab**, in the **Grouping & Totals group**, click the **Group & Sort** button. In the **Group, Sort, and Total** pane, on the **Group on Workshop Category bar**, click **More**. Click the **do not keep group together on one page arrow**, and then click **keep whole group together on one page**. On the **Design tab**, in the **Grouping & Totals group**, click the **Group & Sort** button to close the **Group, Sort, and Total** pane. **Save** the report.

b. On the status bar, click the **Print Preview** button. Notice that the entire **Workshop Category** grouping of **Keeping a Job** displays together at the top of Page 2. Create a paper or electronic printout as directed, and then **Close Print Preview**. **Save**, and then **Close** the report. **Open** the **Navigation Pane**, and if necessary, increase the width of the Navigation Pane so that all object names display fully. In **Backstage** view, click **Close Database**, and then click **Exit**. As directed by your instructor, submit your database and the three paper or electronic printouts that are the results of this project.

End **You have completed Project 3D** ————————————————————

Content-Based Assessments

Apply **3A** skills from
these Objectives:

1. Create and Use a
   Form to Add and
   Delete Records
2. Create a Form by
   Using the Form
   Wizard
3. Modify a Form in
   Layout View and in
   Design View
4. Filter Records

Mastering Access | Project **3E** Raffle Sponsors

In the following Mastering Access project, you will assist Alina Ngo, Dean of Student Services at the Central Campus of Capital Cities Community College, in using her database to track raffle items and sponsors for the New Student Orientation sessions. Your completed forms will look similar to Figure 3.51.

Project Files

For Project 3E, you will need the following file:

    a03E_Raffle_Sponsors

You will save your database as:

    Lastname_Firstname_3E_Raffle_Sponsors

Project Results

Lastname Firstname 3E Sponsor Form		
Sponsor ID#	SP-1211	
Sponsor	Arlington Sweets	

3E Raffle Items

Raffle Item ID#	RAFF-31
Item Description	Lastname Firstname Software Game
Sponsor ID#	SP-1210
Provider Item Code	TG-79044
Category	Electronics
Retail Value	$35

Figure 3.51

(Project 3E Raffle Sponsors continues on the next page)

Content-Based Assessments

Mastering Access | Project 3E Raffle Sponsors (continued)

1 **Start** Access. From your student data files, **Open** the a03E_Raffle_Sponsors database. Save the database in your **Access Chapter 3** folder as **Lastname_Firstname_ 3E_Raffle_Sponsors** and then enable the content. View the relationship between the 3E Sponsors table and the 3E Raffle Items table. *One* sponsor can provide *many* raffle items for the New Student Orientation sessions.

2 Based on the **3E Raffle Items** table, use the **Form** tool to create a form. **Save** the form as **Lastname Firstname 3E Raffle Item Form** and then switch to **Form** view. Add the new record as shown in **Table 1**, using your own name in the **Item Description** field.

3 Display the first record, and, if necessary, click in the Raffle Item ID# field. Use the **Find** button to display the record for the **Raffle Item ID#** of **RAFF-06**, and then **Delete** the record. Display the record you entered for **RAFF-31**, and then **Print** the **Selected Record**, changing the column width to **7.5"** or create an electronic printout. **Close** the form, saving changes if prompted.

4 Based on the **3E Sponsors** table, use the **Form Wizard** tool to create a form. Include the following fields in the order given: **Sponsor**, **Contact Last Name**, **Contact First Name**, and **Phone Number**. Use a **Columnar** layout, and as the title type **Lastname Firstname 3E Sponsor Form**

5 In **Layout** view, apply the **Stacked** layout to all of the controls, and then apply the **Couture** theme to this object only. For the title of the form, change the **Font Size** to **16**, apply **Bold**, and change the **Font Color** to **Brown, Accent 6, Darker 50%**. In **Design** view, increase the height of the **Form Footer** section to approximately **0.5 inch**. In the **Form Footer** section and using your own name, add a **label control** that displays **Created by Lastname Firstname** For the **label control**, change the **Font Color** to **Brown, Text 2**, apply **Bold**, and then adjust the control to fit the text in the control.

6 **Save** the form, and then switch to **Layout** view. Display the **Field List** pane, and then add the **Sponsor ID#** field to the form above the **Sponsor** field. **Close** the **Field List** pane, and then move the **Contact First Name** controls directly above the **Contact Last Name** controls. Display **Record 5**—this record's Sponsor name is the longest entry of all records. Decrease the width of the **Sponsor text box control** until there is approximately **1 inch** between *Inc* and the right edge of the control. **Save** the form.

7 Select all five **text box controls**, set the **Background Color** to **Brown, Accent 1, Lighter 80%**. Select all of the **label controls**, set the **Font Color** to **Brown, Text 2**, and then apply **Bold**. With the controls selected, display the **Property Sheet**. For the **label controls**, set the **Width** to **1.75** Select all of the **label controls** and **text box controls**, set the **Font Size** to **12**, and the **Height** property to **0.25** In the **Form Header** and **Form Foote**r sections, select the **label controls** with the title and your name. Set the **Left** property to **0.5**

8 **Close** the **Property Sheet**, **Save** the form, and then switch to **Form** view. Using your first name and last name, add the record as shown in **Table 2**, being sure to use the (Tab) key to move among fields and to save the record.

9 Display the record you just added and then **Print** the **Selected Record**, or create an electronic printout as directed. **Close** the form.

10 Open your **3E Raffle Item Form** object. Using the **Advanced Filter/Sort** tool, create a filter that displays eight records with a **Category** of **Clothing** or **Dining** After verifying that eight records display, use the **Toggle Filter** button to display all 30 records. **Save** the form.

11 **Close** all open objects. **Open** the **Navigation Pane**, and, if necessary, increase the width of the **Navigation Pane** to display fully all of the object names. Display **Backstage** view. Click **Close Database**, and then click **Exit**. As directed by your instructor, submit your database and the two paper or electronic printouts that are the results of this project.

Table 1

Raffle Item ID#	Item Description	Sponsor ID#	Provider Item Code	Category	Retail Value
RAFF-31	Lastname Firstname Software Game	SP-1210	TG-79044	Electronics	35

(Return to Step 3)

Table 2

Sponsor ID#	Sponsor	Contact First Name	Contact Last Name	Phone Number
SP-1211	Arlington Sweets	Firstname	Lastname	(703) 555-5355

- - - ► (Return to Step 9)

End **You have completed Project 3E**

Content-Based Assessments

Apply 3B skills from these Objectives:

- ⑤ Create a Report by Using the Report Tool
- ⑥ Create Reports by Using the Blank Report Tool and the Report Wizard
- ⑦ Modify the Design of a Report
- ⑧ Print a Report and Keep Data Together

Mastering Access | Project 3F Contractor Services

In the following Mastering Access project, you will assist Roger Lockheart, Director of Facilities at the Jefferson Campus of Capital Cities Community College, in using a database to track facility and contractor services for an open house for prospective college students. Your completed reports will look similar to Figure 3.52.

Project Files

For Project 3F, you will need the following file:

  a03F_Contractor_Services

You will save your database as:

  Lastname_Firstname_3F_Contractor_Services

Project Results

Figure 3.52

(Project 3F Contractor Services continues on the next page)

Mastering Access | Project **3F** Contractor Services (continued)

1 **Start** Access. From your student files, **Open** the **a03F_Contractor_Services** database. Save the database in your **Access Chapter 3** folder as **Lastname_Firstname_3F_Contractor_Services** and then enable the content. View the relationship between the 3F Contractors table and the 3F Facility Services table. *One* contractor can provide *many* facility services. **Close** the **Relationships** window. Based on the **3F Setup and Tear Down Job Costs** query, use the **Report** tool to create a report, and then **Close** the **Navigation Pane**. This query answers the question *What is the Date, Job ID, Contractor ID, Contractor Last Name, Contractor First Name, Category, and Job Cost of setup and tear down jobs?*

2 Apply the **Waveform** theme to this object only. **Delete** the **Job ID** and **Contractor ID** fields from the report. Decrease the widths of the **Contractor Last Name**, **Contractor First Name**, and **Category** fields until there is approximately **0.25 to 0.5 inch** of space between the longest entry in each field—including the field name—and the right edge of each control. Be sure that there is enough space for *Tear Down* to display on one line. **Sort** the **Date** field in ascending order.

Scroll down to the bottom of the report, and increase the height of the **calculated control** that displays $4,440. Drag the **page number control** to the left to visually center it between the margins of the report. For the title, change the **Font Size** to **16**, and then using your last name and first name, add **Lastname Firstname** to the beginning of the title. Using the **layout selector** ⊞, visually center fields between the left and right margins. **Save** the report as **Lastname Firstname 3F Setup and Tear Down Job Costs Report** and then create a paper or electronic printout as directed—two pages will print. **Close** the report. **Open** the **Navigation Pane**, and increase the width of the **Navigation Pane** to display the entire report name. **Close** the **Navigation Pane.**

3 Use the **Blank Report** tool to create a report based on the **3F Contractors** table. Add the fields to the report in the order given: **Contractor Last Name, Contractor First Name**, and **Phone Number. Close** the **Field List** pane. Apply the **Equity** theme to this object only. Increase the width of the **Contractor Last Name** field so that the field name displays fully. Add the **Date** to the Report Header section—do not include the time. Add a **Title** of **Lastname Firstname 3F Contractors Phone List** to the report, and change the **Font Size** to **14**. Decrease the width of the

title's **label control** to fit the text and to move the date control to the left within the right margin. Apply **Bold** to the three field names. **Sort** the **Contractor Last Name** field in **Ascending** order. Using the **layout selector** ⊞, visually center the fields between the report margins. **Save** the report as **Lastname Firstname 3F Contractors Phone List** and then create a paper or electronic printout as directed. **Close Print Preview**, and then **Close** the report.

4 Use the **Report Wizard** to create a report based on the **3F Facility Services** table. Select the following fields in the order given: **Category, Service Description**, and **Job Cost. Group** the report by **Category, Sort** by **Service Description**, and **Sum** the **Job Cost** field. Select the **Stepped** layout and **Portrait** orientation. For the report title, type **Lastname Firstname 3F Job Cost by Category Report** and then switch to **Layout** view.

5 Apply the **Median** theme to this object only. For the title, change the **Font Size** to **14**, and apply **Bold. Delete** the **Summary for 'Category' controls**. Scroll down to the bottom of the report, and click the **text box control** that displays *Wireless network for laptop lane*. Decrease the width of the control until there is approximately **0.25 inch** of space between the end of the word *lane* and the right edge of the label control. At the bottom of the report, for the last record *Wireless network for laptop lane*, to the right, click the **text box control** that displays #—the number or pound sign displays because the text box control is not wide enough to display the entire value. Hold down Shift, and immediately below the selected control, click the **Sum calculated control**, and then under that, click the **Grand Total calculated control**. Drag the left edge of the three selected controls to the left approximately **0.5 inch** to display the amounts fully. **Save** the report.

6 Change the text in the **Sum label control** to **Total Job Cost by Category** and then at the top of the report, select the three **field names**, and apply **Bold. Save** the report.

7 Switch to **Design** view. Click the **label control** that displays *Total Job Cost by Category*, and then align the left edge of the control with the left edge of the **label control** that displays *Grand Total*. **Save** the report.

8 Display the report in **Print Preview** in the **Two Pages** arrangement, examine how the groupings break across pages, **Close Print Preview**, and then switch to **Layout** view. Display the **Group, Sort, and Total** pane, and then select **keep whole group together on one page**. Close the

(Project 3F Contractor Services continues on the next page)

Mastering Access | Project **3F** Contractor Services (continued)

Group, **Sort, and Total** pane. Display the report in **Print Preview** in the **Two Pages** arrangement, and then notice that the entire **Tear Down** grouping displays on Page 2. **Save** the report.

 Create a paper or electronic printout as directed, **Close Print Preview**, and then **Close** the report. **Open**

the **Navigation Pane**, and then display **Backstage** view. Click **Close Database**, and then click **Exit**. As directed by your instructor, submit your database and the three paper or electronic printouts that are the results of this project.

End **You have completed Project 3F** ────────────

Content-Based Assessments

Apply 3A and 3B skills from these Objectives:

- **1** Create and Use a Form to Add and Delete Records
- **2** Create a Form by Using the Form Wizard
- **3** Modify a Form in Layout View and in Design View
- **4** Filter Records
- **5** Create a Report by Using the Report Tool
- **6** Create Reports by Using the Blank Report Tool and the Report Wizard
- **7** Modify the Design of a Report
- **8** Print a Report and Keep Data Together

Mastering Access | Project **3G** Career Books

In the following Mastering Access project, you will assist Teresa Johnson, Head Librarian at the Capital Campus of Capital Cities Community College, in using a database to track publishers and book titles to assist students in finding employment. Your completed forms and reports will look similar to Figure 3.53.

Project Files

For Project 3G, you will need the following file:

a03G_Career_Books

You will save your database as:

Lastname_Firstname_3G_Career_Books

Project Results

Figure 3.53

(Project 3G Career Books continues on the next page)

Content-Based Assessments

Mastering Access | Project 3G Career Books (continued)

1 **Start** Access. From your student files, open the **a03G_Career_Books** database. Save the database in your **Access Chapter 3** folder as **Lastname_Firstname_3G_Career_Books** and then enable the content. Review the relationship between the 3G Publishers table and the 3G Career Book Titles table. *One* publisher can publish *many* books.

2 Based on the **3G Career Book Titles** table, use the **Form** tool to create a form. Switch to **Form** view, and then using your own name, add the record as shown in **Table 1**.

3 **Save** the form as **Lastname Firstname 3G Career Book Form** and then display the first record. Use the **Find** button to display the record for the **Title ID** of **T-18**, and then **Delete** the record. Display the record you entered for **T-34**, and then **Print** the **Selected Record**, changing the column width to **7.5"** or create an electronic printout. **Close** the form, saving changes if prompted.

4 Use the **Form Wizard** to create a form based on the **3G Publishers** table. Include the following fields: **Company Name**, **Rep Last Name**, **Rep First Name**, **Job Title**, and **Phone Number**. Use a **Columnar** layout, and as the title, type **Lastname Firstname 3G Publisher Form**

5 In **Layout** view, select all of the controls, and then apply the **Stacked** layout. Apply the **Couture** theme to this object only. For the title, change the **Font Size** to **16**, apply **Bold**, and change the **Font Color** to **Brown, Accent 6, Darker 50%**—in the last column, the last color. In **Design** view, increase the height of the **Form Footer** section approximately **0.5 inch**. In the **Form Footer** section, add a **label control** that displays **Created by Lastname Firstname** and then change the **Font Color** to **Brown, Text 2**—in the fourth column, the first color. Apply **Bold**, and then adjust the control to fit the data in the control. **Save** the form.

6 In **Layout** view, display the **Field List** pane, and then add the **Publisher ID** field to the form above the **Company Name** field. **Close** the **Field List** pane. Move the **Rep First Name** field directly above the **Rep Last Name** field. Click the **Job Title text box control**, and then drag the right edge of the control to the left until there is approximately **1 inch** of space between *Representative* and the right edge of the control. **Save** the form.

7 Select all of the **text box controls**, set the **Background Color** to **Brown, Accent 1, Lighter 80%**—in the fifth column, the second color. Select all of the **label controls**. Set the **Font Color** to **Brown, Text 2**, apply **Bold**, and then set the **Width** property to **1.5** Select all of the **label controls** and **text box controls**, set the **Font Size** to **12**, and then set the **Height** property to **0.25** For the **form header label control** and the **form footer label control**, set the **Left** property to **0.5**

8 **Close** the **Property Sheet**, **Save** the form, and switch to **Form** view. Using your own name, add a new record as shown in **Table 2**.

9 Display the record you just added and then **Print** the **Selected Record** or create an electronic printout as directed. **Close** the form.

10 **Open** your **3G Career Book Form** object. Using the **Filter By Form** tool, filter the records to display the **Category** of **Resumes** or **Job Search**. Twenty books meet the criteria. Click the **Toggle Filter** button to display all 31 records. **Save** the form, and then **Close** the form.

11 Use the **Report** tool to create a report based on the **3G Resume or Interview Books** query. Apply the **Waveform** theme to this object only. **Delete** the **Publisher ID**, **Category**, and **Company Name** fields from the report.

Table 1

Title ID	Title	Author Last Name	Author First Name	Publisher ID	Category	Copies On Hand	Value of Books
T-34	Effective Networking	Lastname	Firstname	PUB-100	Job Search	6	180

(Return to Step 3)

Table 2

Publisher ID	Company Name	Rep First Name	Rep Last Name	Job Title	Phone Number
PUB-111	Associated Publishers	Firstname	Lastname	Sales Associate	(703) 555-0857

(Return to Step 9)

(Project 3G Career Books continues on the next page)

Content-Based Assessments

Decrease the widths of the **Author Last Name** and **Author First Name** fields so that there is approximately **0.5 inch** between the word *Name* in the field name and the right edge of the label controls. Increase the width of the **Title** field until each title displays on one line. **Sort** the **Title** field in **Ascending** order.

Click the **Title** field name, and then on the **Design tab**, click the **Totals** button. Add a control that counts the number of records, and then increase the height of the control so that *14* displays fully in the calculated control. Drag the **page number control** to the left to visually center it between the report margins. For the title of the report, change the **Font Size** to **14**, and then using your own name, add **Lastname Firstname** to the beginning of the title. Using the **layout selector** ⊞, visually center the fields between the left and right margins. **Save** the report as **Lastname Firstname 3G Resume or Interview Books Report** and then create a paper or electronic printout as directed. **Close** the report.

12 Use the **Blank Report** tool to create a report based on the **3G Publishers** table. Add the following fields to the report in the order listed: **Company Name**, **Rep First Name**, **Rep Last Name**, and **Phone Number**. **Close** the **Field List** pane, and then apply the **Equity** theme to this object only. Increase the width of the **Company Name** field so that the text in each record displays on one line. Add the **Date** to the report, add a **Title** of **Lastname Firstname 3G Reps Phone List** For the title, change the **Font Size** to **14**, and then adjust the width of the title's label control, being sure that the date displays within the right margin of the report. Apply **Bold** to all of the field names, and then **Center** the field names over the data. **Sort** the **Company Name** field in **Ascending** order. Using the **layout selector**, visually center the fields between the left and right margins. **Save** the report as **Lastname Firstname 3G Reps Phone List** and then create a paper or electronic printout as directed. **Close** the report.

13 Use the **Report Wizard** to create a report based on the **3G Career Book Titles** table, Select the following fields: **Category**, **Title**, and **Value of Books**. **Group** the report by **Category**, **Sort** by **Title**, and **Sum** the **Value of Books** field. Select the **Stepped** layout, and **Portrait** orientation as the report title, type **Lastname Firstname 3G Book Values by Category Report** and then switch to **Layout** view.

14 Apply the **Opulent Theme** to this object only. For the title of the report, change the **Font Size** to **14** and then apply **Bold**. **Delete** the **Summary for 'Category'** controls. Scroll down to the bottom of the report, and in the **Title** field, click the **text box control** that displays *Interview Techniques and Resume Tips*, which is the longest entry in the field. Point to the right edge of the **text box control**, and then drag the pointer to the left until there is approximately **0.25 inch** between *Tips* and the right edge of the text box control. Scroll to the top of the report, and then click in the **Value of Books label control**. Double-click the left edge of the **label control** to increase the width of the label control and to display fully the text in the label control. **Save** the report.

15 Scroll down to the bottom of the report, and then on the right side of the report, increase the width of the **Sum calculated controls** and the **Grand Total calculated control** so that the entire figure, including the dollar sign, displays— the Grand Total is *$8,810*. Change the text in the **Sum label controls** to **Total Value of Books by Category** and then increase the width of the **Grand Total label control** to display fully the text in the control. **Save** the report.

16 At the top of the report, apply **Bold** to the three field names. Select any of the **Title text box controls**. Display the **Property Sheet**, set the **Height to 0.25**. **Close** the **Property Sheet**. In **Design** view, align the left edge of the **label control** that displays *Total Value of Books by Category* with the left edge of the **label control** that displays *Grand Total*. **Save** the report.

17 Display the report in **Print Preview** in the **Two Pages** arrangement, examine how the groupings break across pages, and then **Close Print Preview**. In **Layout** view, display the **Group, Sort, and Total** pane, and then click **keep whole group together on one page**. Close the **Group, Sort, and Total** pane. **Save** the report. Display the report in **Print Preview** in the **Two Pages** arrangement, and then notice that the entire **Resumes** grouping displays on Page 2. Create a paper or electronic printout as directed, and then **Close Print Preview**.

18 **Close** the report, and then **Open** the **Navigation Pane**. If necessary, increase the width of the Navigation Pane to display all of the object names fully. In **Backstage** view, click **Close Database**, and then click **Exit**. As directed by your instructor, submit your database and the five paper or electronic printouts that are the results of this project.

End **You have completed Project 3G**

Content-Based Assessments

GO! Fix It | Project **3H** Resume Workshops

Project Files

For Project 3H, you will need the following file:

a03H_Resume_Workshops

You will save your database as:

Lastname_Firstname_3H_Resume_Workshops

In this project, you will make corrections to and update an Access database that stores information about resume workshops that are scheduled for students. Start Access, navigate to the student files that accompany this textbook, and then open the a03H_Resume_Workshops database. Save the database in your Access Chapter 3 folder as **Lastname_Firstname_3H_Resume_Workshops** and enable the content.

To complete the project, you should know that:

- In the Participant Form object, all the field heights should be the same, and your name and 3H should display in the title. Create a filter that finds records where the Workshop Fee is $35—five records meet the criteria. Toggle the filter off, and then save the form. In the first record, enter your first name and last name in the appropriate fields. Then, as directed, create a paper or electronic printout of only this record.

- In the Resume Workshop Form object, in the header, change Lastname Firstname to your own last name and first name. Add a label control to the Form Footer section. Using your own name, type **Created by Lastname Firstname** and then bold the text. Save the form. Find the record for Workshop ID# R-002, and then, as directed, create a paper or electronic printout of only this record.

- In the Participant Input Form object, you should adjust the height and width of the controls so that the text in the controls displays on one line. The font sizes for the label controls and text box controls should match. Add your name and 3H to the title, and be sure that the title displays on one line. For the title, change the font size so that the title does not extend to the right of the text box controls beneath it. In the Form Footer section, create a label typing **Created by Lastname Firstname** and then bold the text in the label. Add a light blue background color to the text box controls, and then save the form. Display the record with your name and then, as directed, create a paper or electronic printout of only this record.

- For the Participant Fees Report, apply the Opulent theme to this object only. Add a title to the report that includes your name and 3H. Adjust the font size and the width of the label control, and be sure that the date control displays within the right margin of the report. Center the data in the Workshop ID text box controls. Center the layout between the margins, and add a total for the Workshop Fee column that sums the fees. Sort the Date Fee Received field in ascending order. Save the report, and then create a paper or electronic printout as directed.

- In the Participants by Workshop Name report, apply the Equity theme to this object only. Add your name and 3H to the title, and reduce the Font Size. Adjust controls so that all of the data displays fully. Delete the Summary for 'Workshop ID#' control. Change the text in the Sum label controls so that they reflect what is being summed. Align the left edges of the Sum and Grand Total label controls. Add the date to the Report Header section. Be sure that the groupings are kept together when printed. Create a paper or electronic printout as directed.

End You have completed Project 3H

Content-Based Assessments

GO! Make It | Project 3I Study Abroad

Project Files

For Project 3I, you will need the following file:

a03I_Study_Abroad

You will save your database as:

Lastname_Firstname_3I_Study_Abroad

From the student files that accompany this textbook, open the a03I_Study_Abroad database, and then save the database in your Access Chapter 3 folder as **Lastname_Firstname_3I_Study_Abroad** Using the Blank Report tool, create the report shown in Figure 3.54. Apply the Slipstream theme, and then create a paper or electronic printout as directed.

Project Results

Lastname Firstname 3I Trip Dates and Cost Report

Destination	Cost of Trip	Departure Date	Return Date
Costa Rica	$3,000	2/15/2016	2/25/2016
Egypt	$4,300	2/16/2016	2/26/2016
Great Britain	$6,000	3/22/2016	4/4/2016
Greece	$6,000	5/5/2016	5/15/2016
Ireland	$5,000	5/23/2016	6/2/2016
Italy	$4,500	5/1/2016	5/8/2016
Mexico	$2,000	2/8/2016	2/18/2016
Panama	$2,900	4/30/2016	5/5/2016
Paris	$7,580	5/6/2016	5/17/2016
Rome	$7,250	5/2/2016	5/12/2016
Singapore	$5,000	4/12/2016	4/20/2016
South Africa	$4,780	3/3/2016	3/10/2016
Switzerland	$5,400	2/25/2016	3/3/2016
Tokyo	$4,950	3/4/2016	3/12/2016
Tuscan Valley	$5,600	2/4/2016	2/14/2016

Figure 3.54

End You have completed Project 3I —————

Content-Based Assessments

GO! Solve It | Project 3J Job Offers

Project Files

For Project 3J, you will need the following file:

a03J_Job_Offers

You will save your database as:

Lastname_Firstname_3J_Job_Offers

From the student files that accompany this textbook, open the a03J_Job_Offers database file, save the database in your Access Chapter 3 folder as **Lastname_Firstname_3J_Job_Offers** and then enable the content.

Kevin Bodine, coordinator of the Student Employment Office, would like one form and two reports created from the Job Offers database. Using the skills you have practiced in this chapter, create an attractive form that can be used to update student candidate records. Using your own information, add a new record as Student ID# **9091246** with a College Major of **Business** and a Phone Number of **(703) 555-9876** Leave the Internship Completed field blank. Save the form as **Lastname Firstname 3J Candidate Update Form** and then create a paper or electronic printout of only your record.

Mr. Bodine wants an attractive report listing the Organization Name and the Offer Amount of each job offered to a student, grouped by the Student ID#, sorted in ascending order by the Organization Name. The Offer Amount field should display the maximum amount offered. Create and save the report as **Lastname Firstname 3J Job Offers by Student ID# Report** and then create a paper or electronic printout as directed.

Mr. Bodine also wants an attractive report of the names, college majors, and phone numbers of the student candidates, grouped by college majors and then sorted by the Last Name field. Save the report as **Lastname Firstname 3J Student Candidates by Major Report** and then create a paper or electronic printout as directed.

		Performance Level		
		Exemplary You consistently applied the relevant skills	**Proficient** You sometimes, but not always, applied the relevant skills	**Developing** You rarely or never applied the relevant skills
Performance Criteria	Create 3J Candidate Update Form	Form created with correct fields in easy-to-follow format and record entered for student.	Form created with no more than two missing elements.	Form created with more than two missing elements.
	Create 3J Job Offers by Student ID# Report	Report created with correct fields, grouped and sorted correctly, and in an attractive format.	Report created with no more than two missing elements.	Report created with more than two missing elements.
	Create 3J Student Candidates by Major Report	Report created with correct fields, grouped and sorted correctly, and in an attractive format.	Report created with no more than two missing elements.	Report created with more than two missing elements.

End **You have completed Project 3J** —————————————

Content-Based Assessments

Apply a combination of the 3A and 3B skills.

GO! Solve It | Project 3K Financial Aid

Project Files

For Project 3K, you will need the following file:

a03K_Financial_Aid

You will save your database as:

Lastname_Firstname_3K_Financial_Aid

From the student files that accompany this textbook, open the a03K_Financial_Aid database file, and then save the database in your Access Chapter 3 folder as **Lastname_Firstname_3K_Financial_Aid**

Marguerite Simons, the Financial Aid Director, wants an attractive, easy-to-follow form that can be used to update the Financial Aid Students table. Using your first name and last name, add a new record with the following information:

Student ID#	Financial Aid ID	Home Phone#	College E-mail
1472589	FA-07	(703) 555-3874	ns589@capccc.edu

Save the form as **Lastname Firstname 3K FA Student Update Form** and then create a paper or electronic printout of only your record.

Ms. Simons also wants an attractively formatted report listing the Award Name, the Student ID# and the Award Amount for financial aid offered to students, grouped by the Award name and sorted in ascending order by the Student ID# field (Hint: Use data from both tables). The Award Amount should be summed. Save the report as **Lastname Firstname 3K Amount by Award Name Report** and then create a paper or electronic printout of the report.

	Performance Level		
	Exemplary You consistently applied the relevant skills	**Proficient** You sometimes, but not always, applied the relevant skills	**Developing** You rarely or never applied the relevant skills
Create 3K FA Student Update Form	Form created with correct fields in easy-to-follow format and record entered for student.	Form created with no more than two missing elements.	Form created with more than two missing elements.
Create 3K Amount by Award Name Report	Report created with correct fields, grouped and sorted correctly, and in an attractive format.	Report created with no more than two missing elements.	Report created with more than two missing elements.

Performance Criteria

End **You have completed Project 3K** ⎯⎯⎯⎯⎯⎯⎯⎯⎯

Access | Chapter 3

Outcomes-Based Assessments

Rubric

The following outcomes-based assessments are *open-ended assessments*. That is, there is no specific correct result; your result will depend on your approach to the information provided. Make *Professional Quality* your goal. Use the following scoring rubric to guide you in *how* to approach the problem, and then to evaluate *how well* your approach solves the problem.

The *criteria*—Software Mastery, Content, Format and Layout, and Process—represent the knowledge and skills you have gained that you can apply to solving the problem. The *levels of performance*—Professional Quality, Approaching Professional Quality, or Needs Quality Improvements—help you and your instructor evaluate your result.

	Your completed project is of Professional Quality if you:	Your completed project is Approaching Professional Quality if you:	Your completed project Needs Quality Improvements if you:
1-Software Mastery	Choose and apply the most appropriate skills, tools, and features and identify efficient methods to solve the problem.	Choose and apply some appropriate skills, tools, and features, but not in the most efficient manner.	Choose inappropriate skills, tools, or features, or are inefficient in solving the problem.
2-Content	Construct a solution that is clear and well organized, contains content that is accurate, appropriate to the audience and purpose, and is complete. Provide a solution that contains no errors in spelling, grammar, or style.	Construct a solution in which some components are unclear, poorly organized, inconsistent, or incomplete. Misjudge the needs of the audience. Have some errors in spelling, grammar, or style, but the errors do not detract from comprehension.	Construct a solution that is unclear, incomplete, or poorly organized; contains some inaccurate or inappropriate content; and contains many errors in spelling, grammar, or style. Do not solve the problem.
3-Format and Layout	Format and arrange all elements to communicate information and ideas, clarify function, illustrate relationships, and indicate relative importance.	Apply appropriate format and layout features to some elements, but not others. Overuse features, causing minor distraction.	Apply format and layout that does not communicate information or ideas clearly. Do not use format and layout features to clarify function, illustrate relationships, or indicate relative importance. Use available features excessively, causing distraction.
4-Process	Use an organized approach that integrates planning, development, self-assessment, revision, and reflection.	Demonstrate an organized approach in some areas, but not others; or, use an insufficient process of organization throughout.	Do not use an organized approach to solve the problem.

Outcomes-Based Assessments

GO! Think | Project **3L** Food Services

Project Files

For Project 3L, you will need the following file:

> a03L_Food_Services

You will save your database as:

> Lastname_Firstname_3L_Food_Services

Use the skills you have practiced in this chapter to assist Luciano Perez, the Hospitality Director, in creating a form and a report to assist him with the staff scheduling of food services for a two-day student orientation workshop. Create an attractive form that he can use to update the 3L Staff table saving the form as **Lastname Firstname 3L Staff Update Form** Using your own name, add a new record with the following information:

> Staff ID: **STAFF-1119**   Phone Number: **(703) 555-0845** Title: **Server**

Create a paper or electronic printout of only your record. Create an attractive, easy-to-read report for calling staff members when the schedule changes. Name the report **Lastname Firstname 3L Staff Phone List** and then create a paper or electronic printout of the report as directed.

End You have completed Project 3L ————————————————

GO! Think | Project **3M** Donors and Gifts

Project Files

For Project 3M, you will need the following file:

> a03M_Donors_Gifts

You will save your database as:

> Lastname_Firstname_3M_Donors_Gifts

Use the skills you have practiced in this chapter to assist the Dean of Information Technology in using her database to create attractive forms and reports. The Dean would like an attractive form that would enable her work study student to enter the information in the Donors table. Create and save a form naming it **Lastname Firstname 3M Donor Update Form** Using your own name, add a new record with the following information:

> Donor ID: **DNR-1212**   Donor: **Lastname Foundation** Phone Number: **(703) 555-6091**

Create a paper or electronic printout of only your record. Create a donor list with the donor, contact names, and phone numbers so that the Dean can call the donors to thank them for donating gifts that will be distributed during the high school recruitment tours. Save the report as **Lastname Firstname 3M Donor Phone List** and then create a paper or electronic printout as directed.

Create a report grouped by Category and sorted by Item Description that includes the Retail Value totals and a Grand Total of the Retail Value of the gift items. Create a page footer control that displays **Created by Lastname Firstname** and then save the report as **Lastname Firstname 3M Gift Amounts by Category Report** and then create a paper or electronic printout as directed.

End You have completed Project 3M ————————————————

You and GO! | Project **3N** Personal Inventory

Project Files

For Project 3N, you will need the following file:

> Lastname_Firstname_2N_Personal_Inventory (your file from Chapter 2)

You will save your database as:

> Lastname_Firstname_3N_Personal_Inventory

If you have your database from Project 2N, save it in your Access Chapter 3 folder as **Lastname_Firstname_3N_Personal_Inventory** If you do not have the database from Project 2N, create a new database, saving it in your Access Chapter 3 folder with the same name given above. In the database, create one table with at least 18 records. Include fields such as item, room location, value, and date of purchase. Your table should have items stored in several locations.

Using the table, create an attractive form, naming it **Lastname Firstname 3N Inventory Update Form** Using the form, enter at least three records and then create a paper or electronic printout of one of the new records. Using the table, create an attractive report including fields for the room location, item name, and value or purchase price of the item—you may add more fields if you desire. Group the report by the room location, and sort by the value or purchase price of the item, summarizing the values. Name the report **Lastname Firstname 3N Room Values Report** and then create a paper or electronic printout as directed.

End You have completed Project 3N ————————————

Business Running Case

Razvan CHIRNOAGA/Shutterstock

This project relates to **Front Range Action Sports**, which is one of the country's largest retailers of sports gear and outdoor recreation merchandise. The company has large retail stores in Colorado, Washington, Oregon, California, and New Mexico, in addition to a growing online business. Major merchandise categories include fishing, camping, rock climbing, winter sports, action sports, water sports, team sports, racquet sports, fitness, golf, apparel, and footwear.

In this project, you will apply skills you practiced from the Objectives in Access Chapters 1 through 3. You will create a database for Frank Osei, Vice President of Finance, that contains inventory and supplier information. In addition, you will create queries that answer specific questions relating to the inventory items and suppliers, forms for entering and updating information, and reports. Your printed results will look similar to Figure 1.1.

Project Files

For Project BRC1, you will need the following files:

You will save your database as:

Lastname_Firstname_BRC1_Inventory_Suppliers

New blank Access database
aBRC1_Inventory (Excel workbook)
aBRC1_Suppliers (Excel workbook)

Project Results

Figure 1.1

Business Running Case

Front Range Action Sports

1 **Start** Access to create a new **Blank database**. In the location where you are storing your projects, create a new folder named **Front Range Action Sports** or navigate to this folder if you have already created it. **Save** the database as **Lastname_Firstname_BRC1_Inventory_Suppliers**

a. Rename the **ID** field to **Item ID#** and change the **Data Type** to **Text**. Then create the fields as shown in **Table 1**.

b. Enter the two records as shown in **Table 2**.

c. **Close** the table, **Save** it as **Lastname Firstname BRC1 Inventory** and then increase the width of the **Navigation Pane** to display the entire table name. On the **External Data tab**, in the **Import & Link group**, click the **Excel** button. Navigate to your student files, double-click **aBRC1_Inventory**, and then **Append a copy of the records** to the **BRC1 Inventory** table. From the **Navigation Pane**, open the **BRC1 Inventory** table and verify that there are 116 records in the table. Apply **Best Fit** to all of the fields—scroll down to be sure that all of the data in the **Item Name** field displays. Display the table in **Print Preview**, and then create a paper or electronic printout of the first page. **Close Print Preview**, **Close** the table, and **Save** changes to the layout of the table.

d. On the **External Data tab**, in the **Import & Link group**, click the **Excel** button. Navigate to your student files, double-click **aBRC1_Suppliers**, and then **Import the source data into a new table in the current database**. Click **First Row Contains Column Headings** and set the primary key to **Supplier ID**. Name the table **Lastname Firstname BRC1 Suppliers** and then **Open** the table. **Delete** the **Fax Number** field, and then apply **Best Fit** to all of the fields. Display the table in **Print Preview**, change the orientation to **Landscape**, change the **Margins** to **Normal**, and then create a paper or electronic printout as directed. **Close Print Preview**, **Close**

the table, and save changes to the layout of the table. On the **Navigation Pane**, click the **Navigation Pane arrow**, and then click **Tables and Related Views**.

e. Click the **Database Tools tab**, and then in the **Relationships group**, click the **Relationships** button. In the **Show Table** dialog box, double-click **BRC1 Suppliers**, double-click **BRC1 Inventory**, and then **Close** the dialog box. Expand the field lists, and then in the **BRC1 Suppliers** field list, point to **Supplier ID**. Drag to the right into the **BRC1 Inventory** field list on top of the **Supplier ID** field, release the mouse button, click **Enforce Referential Integrity**, and then click **Create**. *One* supplier can supply *many* inventory items. Create a **Relationship Report**, **Save** the report with the default name, and then create a paper or electronic printout as directed. **Close Print Preview**, and then **Close** any open objects. Increase the width of the **Navigation Pane** to display the entire report name, and then **Close** the **Navigation Pane**.

2 Create a query in **Query Design** view, based on the **BRC1 Inventory** table to answer the question, *What is the Item Name (in alphabetical order), Retail Price, and Category for the Sport of Hiking?* Do not display the **Sport** field in the query results. Forty records meet the criteria. **Save** the query as **Lastname Firstname BRC1 Hiking Query** and then create a paper or electronic printout as directed. **Close Print Preview**, and then **Close** the query.

a. Create a copy of the **BRC1 Hiking Query**, saving the object as **Lastname Firstname BRC1 Hiking or Biking Shoes Query** Redesign the query to answer the question, *What is the Sport, Item Name, Retail Price, and Supplier ID for the Category of Shoes where the Sport is Hiking or Biking?* **Sort** the records by the **Sport** field and by the **Item Name** field. Do not display the **Category** field in the query results. Nine records meet the criteria. Create a paper or electronic

Table 1

Data Type	Text	Text	Currency	Text	Text	Text
Field Name	Item ID#	Item Name	Retail Price	Category	Sport	Supplier ID

(Return to Step 1-b)

Table 2

Item#	Item Name	Retail Price	Category	Sport	Supplier ID#
106555	Snowboard	256.99	Equipment	Skiing	SUPP-06
106556	Wool Socks	12.59	Socks and Gloves	Skiing	SUPP-04

(Business Running Case: Front Range Action Sports continues on the next page)

(Return to Step 1-c)

250 **Business Running Case**

printout as directed. **Close Print Preview**, and **Close** the query.

b. Create a query in **Query Design** view, based on the **BRC1 Suppliers** table and the **BRC1 Inventory** table to answer the question, *What is the Item Name, Category, Company, and Business Phone for Categories that begin with the letter S, and sorted by Category, for the Sport of Fitness?* Do not display the **Sport** category in the query results. Eighteen records meet the criteria. **Save** the query as **Lastname Firstname BRC1 S Category Query** and then create a paper or electronic printout as directed. **Close Print Preview**, and **Close** the query.

c. Create a query in **Query Design** view, based on the **BRC1 Suppliers** table and the **BRC1 Inventory** table to answer the question, *What is the Company, Item Name, Category, Sport, and Retail Price for items that have a retail price of $100 or greater sorted in ascending order by Sport and then in descending order by Retail Price?* Twenty records meet the criteria. **Save** the query as **Lastname Firstname BRC1 Price $100 or Over Query** and then create a paper or electronic printout as directed, changing the margins to **Normal**. **Close Print Preview**, and **Close** the query.

d. Create a query in **Query Design** view, based on the **BRC1 Inventory** table to answer the question, *For Supplier ID of SUPP-01, for each Item Name and Retail Price, what is the markup of each item if marked up 10%, and what is the final price?* All numeric fields should be formatted as **Currency, 2 Decimal** places. Apply **Best Fit** to all of the fields, **Save** the query as **Lastname Firstname BRC1 10 Percent Markup Query** and then create a paper or electronic printout as directed. **Close Print Preview**, and then **Close** the query.

3 Based on the **BRC1 Suppliers** table, use the **Form** tool to create a form. Switch to **Form** view, and then using your own first name and last name for the **Company** field, add a new record as shown in **Table 3**.

a. Save the form as **Lastname Firstname BRC1 Supplier Form** and then create a paper or electronic printout of only the record you just created in the form, changing the **Column Width** to **7.5"** **Close Print Preview**, and then **Close** the form.

4 Based on the **BRC1 Suppliers** table, use the **Report** tool to create a new report. **Delete** the following fields from the report: **Supplier ID**, **Address**, **City**, **State**, and **ZIP**. Apply the **Paper** theme to this object only. **Sort** the **Company** field in **Ascending** order. Decrease the width of the **Business Phone** field to accommodate the longest entry in the field. **Bold** the field names, and **Center** the **Company** and **E-mail Address** field names over the data. Use the **layout selector** to visually center the layout between the left and right margins, and then visually center the **page number control** between the left and right margins. (Hint: scroll to the right to display the control.) **Save** the report as **Lastname Firstname BRC1 Suppliers Contact List** Display the report in **Print Preview**, and then create a paper or electronic printout as directed. **Close Print Preview**, and then **Close** the report.

5 Using the **Report Wizard**, create a report based on the **BRC1 Inventory** table. Add the following fields to the report: **Category**, **Item Name**, and **Retail Price**. **Group** by **Category**. **Sort** in **Ascending** order by **Item Name**. Find the **Average** of the **Retail Price** field. Select the **Stepped Layout**, and then as the report title, type **Lastname Firstname BRC1 Avg Price by Category Report**

a. In **Print Preview**, display the report by **Two Pages** and notice how the groupings are split between pages, that the **Retail Price** field name displays only *Price*, and that the prices in the text box and calculated controls display ###. **Close Print Preview**, and then switch to **Layout** view. Apply the **Oriel** theme to the report and no other objects.

b. Click the **Item Name** field name, hold down Shift, and then click the **text box control** that displays *Snowboard*. Decrease the width of the field until there is approximately **2** inches between **Item Name** and the right edge of the text box control. Scroll down the

Table 3

Supplier ID	Company	E-mail Address	Business Phone	Address	City	State	ZIP
SUPP-12	Lastname Firstname Inc	info@watersports.biz	(305) 555-6543	14 South Beach Rd	Miami	FL	33125

(Business Running Case: Front Range Action Sports continues on the next page)

(**Return to Step 3-a**)

Business Running Case

Front Range Action Sports (continued)

report to be sure that all Item Names display fully. Scroll to the top of the report, and then click the **Retail Price** field name, which displays only a portion of the word *Price*. Hold down (Shift), click the **text box control** below the field name, which displays ###, and then click the **calculated control** that also displays ###. Increase the width of the controls by pointing to the left edge of any one of the selected controls and dragging it to the left until the entire field name— **Retail Price**—displays as the field name.

c. Delete the **Summary for 'Category' label controls**. Change the text in the **Avg label control** from *Avg* to **Average Retail Price Per Category** and then move the **label control** to the right until the right edge of the control is approximately **0.25 inch** from the left edge of its associated calculated control.

d. Click in the **title** of the report, and then change the **Font Size** to **16**. Visually center the title between the left and right margins of the report. Select all of the field names, and then apply **Bold** and **Italic**.

e   On the **Design tab**, in the **Grouping & Totals** group, click the **Group & Sort** button. In the **Group, Sort, and Total** pane, click **More**. Click the **do not keep group together on one page arrow**, and then click **keep whole group together on one page**. In the **Grouping & Totals group**, click the **Group & Sort** button to close the **Group, Sort, and Total** pane. **Save** the report.

f. Display the report in **Print Preview** by **Two Pages**, and notice how the groupings are kept together on one page. On the **Print Preview tab**, in the **Print group**, click the **Print** button. In the **Print** dialog box, under **Print Range**, click **Pages**. In the **From** box, type **1** and in the **To** box, type **2** and then click **OK** to create a paper printout—or create an electronic printout as directed. **Close Print Preview**, and then **Close** the report.

6 **Open** the **Navigation Pane**, and if necessary, widen the pane to display fully all object names. Display **Backstage** view, click **Close Database**, and then click **Exit**.

End **You have completed Business Running Case 1** ———————

Enhancing Tables

TebNad/Shutterstock

In This Chapter

In this chapter, you will enhance tables and improve data accuracy and data entry. You will begin by identifying secure locations where databases will be stored and by backing up existing databases to protect the data. You will edit existing tables and copy data and table design across tables. You will create a new table in Design view and determine the best data type for each field based on its characteristics. You will use the field properties to enhance the table and to improve data accuracy and data entry, including looking up data in another table and attaching an existing document to a record.

Westland Plains, Texas, is a city of approximately 800,000 people in the western portion of the second-most populous state in the United States. The city's economy is built around the oil industry, a regional airport serving western Texas and eastern New Mexico, a multi-location medical center, and a growing high-tech manufacturing industry. Westland Plains has a rich cultural history that is kept alive by a number of civic organizations and museums; new culture and traditions are encouraged through the city's arts council. City residents of all ages enjoy some of the finest parks, recreation areas, and sports leagues in the state.

Project 4A City Directory

Project Activities

In Activities 4.01 through 4.12, you will redesign the tables and edit and proofread data, taking advantage of table relationships to avoid entering and storing redundant data. Joaquin Alonzo, the new City Manager of Westland Plains, has a database of city directory information. This database has three tables that have duplicate information in them. Your completed tables and relationships will look similar to Figure 4.1.

Project Files

For Project 4A, you will need the following files:

    a04A_City_Directory
    a04A_City_Employees

You will save your files as:

    Lastname_Firstname_4A_City_Directory
    Lastname_Firstname_4A_City_Directory_2015-10-30 (date will vary)
    Lastname_Firstname_4A_City_Employees

Project Results

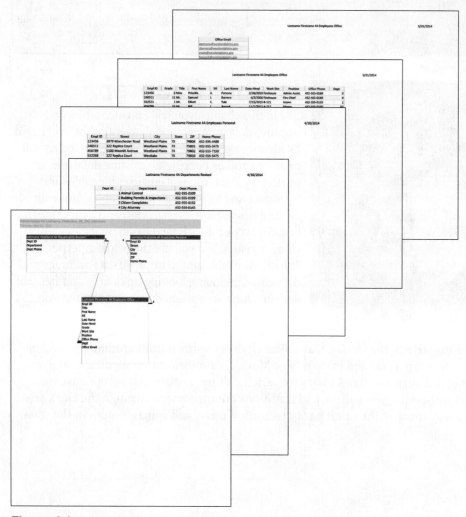

Figure 4.1
Project 4A City Directory

Objective 1 | Manage Existing Tables

A database is most effective when the data is maintained accurately and efficiently. It is important to back up your database often to be sure you can always obtain a clean copy if the data is corrupted or lost. Maintaining the accuracy of the field design and data is also critical to have a useful database; regular reviews and updates of design and data are necessary. It is also helpful to avoid rekeying data that already exists in a database; using copy/paste or appending records reduces the chances for additional errors as long as the source data is accurate.

Activity 4.01 | Backing Up a Database

Before modifying the structure of an existing database, it is important to *back up* the database so that a copy of the original database will be available if you need it. It is also important to back up databases regularly to avoid losing data.

1 **Start** Access. Navigate to the student data files for this textbook. Locate and open the **a04A_City_Directory** file and enable the content.

2 Display **Backstage** view, click **Save & Publish**, and then, under **Save Database As**, double-click **Back Up Database**. In the **Save As** dialog box, navigate to the drive on which you will be saving your folders and projects for this chapter. Create a new folder named **Access Chapter 4** and then compare your screen with Figure 4.2.

Access appends the date to the file name as a suggested name for the backed-up database. Having the date as part of the file name assists you in determining the copy that is the most current.

Figure 4.2

Your date may differ

Default name for backed-up database

3 In the **File name** box, before the file name, type **Lastname_Firstname_** and remove **a0** from the name. In the **Save As** dialog box, click **Save**. In the title bar, notice that the original database file—not the backed-up file—is open.

4 Click the **Start** button , click **Computer**, and then navigate to the location of your **Access Chapter 4** folder. Open the folder to verify that the backed-up database exists, but do not open the file. **Close** ☒ Windows Explorer.

5 Save 🔲 the database as **Lastname_Firstname_4A_City_Directory** in your **Access Chapter 4** folder.

This is another method of making a copy of a database. The original file exists with the original name—the date is not appended to the database name, and the newly saved file is open.

Activity 4.02 | Adding File Locations to Trusted Locations

In this activity, you will add the location of your database files for this chapter and the location of the student data files to the *Trust Center*—a security feature that checks documents for macros and digital signatures. When you open any database from a location displayed in the Trust Center, no security warning will display. You should not designate the My Documents folder as a trusted location because others may try to gain access to this known folder.

1 Display **Backstage** view, and click the **Enable Content** button. Click **Advanced Options** to display the **Microsoft Office Security Options** dialog box. In the lower left corner, click **Open the Trust Center**.

2 In the **Trust Center** window, in the left pane, click **Trusted Locations**. Compare your screen with Figure 4.3.

The right pane displays the locations that are trusted sources. A *trusted source* is a person or organization that you know will not send you databases with malicious code. Under Path and User Locations, there is already an entry. A *path* is the location of a folder or file on your computer or storage device.

Figure 4.3

Location on computer for Access Wizard databases

Trusted Locations

Information about selected path

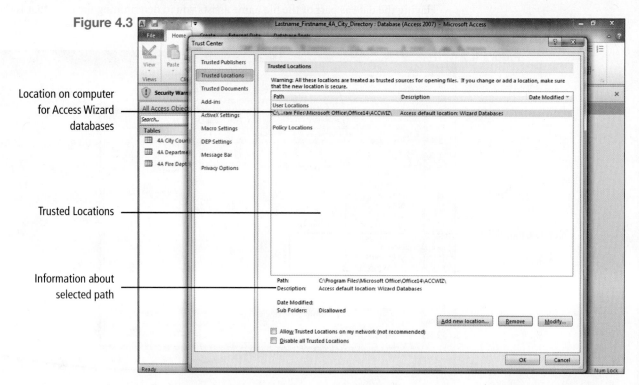

3 In the **Trusted Locations** pane, at the lower right, click **Add new location**. In the **Microsoft Office Trusted Location** dialog box, click **Browse**. In the **Browse** dialog box, navigate to where you saved your *Access Chapter 4* folder, double-click **Access Chapter 4**, and then click **OK**. Compare your screen with Figure 4.4.

The Microsoft Office Trusted Location dialog box displays the path to a trusted source of databases. Notice that you can trust any subfolders in the *Access Chapter 4* folder by checking that option.

Figure 4.4

Path to Access Chapter 4
folder—yours may differ

Check box to trust
subfolders within
this folder

4 In the **Microsoft Office Trusted Location** dialog box, under **Description**, using your own first and last name, type **Databases created by Firstname Lastname** and then click **OK**.

> The Trusted Locations pane displays the path of the *Access Chapter 4* folder. You will no longer receive a security warning when you open databases from this location.

5 Using the technique you just practiced, add the location of your student data files to the Trust Center. For the description, type **Student data files created for GO! Series**

> Only locations that you know are secure should be added to the Trust Center. If other people have access to the databases and can change the information in the database, the location is not secure.

6 At the lower right corner of the **Trust Center** dialog box, click **OK**. In the displayed **Microsoft Office Security Options** dialog box, click **OK**.

> The message bar no longer displays—you opened the database from a trusted location.

7 Display **Backstage** view, and then click **Close Database**. Open **Lastname_Firstname_ 4A_City_Directory**.

> The database opens, and the message bar with the Security Alert does not display. Using the Trust Center button is an efficient way to open databases that are saved in a safe location.

More Knowledge | Remove a Trusted Location

Display Backstage view, and then click the Options button. In the Access Options dialog box, in the left pane, click Trust Center. In the right pane, click the Trust Center Settings button, and then click Trusted Locations. Under Path, click the trusted location that you want to remove, and then click the Remove button. Click OK to close the dialog box.

Activity 4.03 | Copying a Table and Modifying the Structure

In this activity, you will copy the *4A Departments* table, modify the structure by deleting fields and data that are duplicated in other tables, and then designate a primary key field.

1 In the Navigation Pane, click **4A Departments**. On the **Home tab**, in the **Clipboard group**, click the **Copy** button. In the **Clipboard group**, click the **Paste** button.

Copy sends a duplicate version of the selected table to the Clipboard, leaving the original table intact. The *Clipboard* is a temporary storage area in Windows. Office can store up to 24 items in the Clipboard. *Paste* moves the copy of the selected table from the Clipboard into a new location. Because two tables cannot have the same name in a database, you must rename the pasted version.

2 In the displayed **Paste Table As** dialog box, under **Table Name**, type **Lastname Firstname 4A Departments Revised** and then compare your screen with Figure 4.5.

Under Paste Options, you can copy the structure only, including all the items that are displayed in Design view—field names, data types, descriptions, and field properties. To make an exact duplicate of the table, click Structure and Data. To copy the data from the table into another existing table, click Append Data to Existing Table.

Figure 4.5

Table name

Copies fields, data types, field descriptions, and field properties only

Copies structure from above and the data

Adds the data in the table to an existing table

Another Way

There are two other methods to copy and paste selected tables:
- In the Navigation Pane, right-click the table, and from the displayed list, click Copy. To paste the table, right-click the Navigation Pane, and click Paste from the options listed.
- In the Navigation Pane, click the table, hold down Ctrl, and then press C. To paste the table, point to the Navigation Pane, hold down Ctrl, and then press V.

3 Under **Paste Options**, be sure that the **Structure and Data** option button is selected, and then click **OK**. Notice that the copied table displays in the **Navigation Pane**. Open the **4A Departments Revised** table in **Datasheet** view. **Close** ⟪ the **Navigation Pane**.

The *4A Departments Revised* table is an exact duplicate of the *4A Departments* table. Working with a duplicate table ensures that the original table will be available if needed.

4 Point to the **Dept Head** field name until the ↓ pointer displays. Drag to the right to the **Admin Asst** field name to select both fields. On the **Home tab**, in the **Records group**, click the **Delete** button. In the displayed message box, click **Yes** to permanently delete the fields and the data.

The names of the employees are deleted from this table to avoid having employee data in more than one table. Recall that a table should store data about one subject—this table now stores only departmental data. In addition to removing duplicate data, the fields that you deleted were also poorly designed. They combined both the first and last names in the same field, limiting the use of the data to entire names only.

5 Switch to **Design** view. To the left of **Department**, click the row selector box. On the **Design tab**, in the **Tools group**, click the **Insert Rows** button to insert a blank row (field) above the *Department* field.

6 Under **Field Name**, click in the blank field name box, type **Dept ID** and then press Tab. In the **Data Type** box, type **a** and then press Tab. Alternatively, click the Data Type arrow, and then select the AutoNumber data type. In the **Tools group**, click the **Primary Key** button, and then compare your screen with Figure 4.6.

Recall that a primary key field is used to ensure that each record is unique. Because each department has a unique name, you might question why the Department field is not the primary key field. Primary key fields should be data that does not change often. When companies are reorganized, department names are often changed.

Figure 4.6

Field added to the table

Primary key field

7 Switch to **Datasheet** view, and in the displayed message box, click **Yes** to save the table.

Because the *Dept ID* field has a data type of AutoNumber, each record is sequentially numbered. The data in this field cannot be changed because it is generated by Access.

8 In the datasheet, next to **Department**, click the **Sort and Filter arrow**, and then click **Sort A to Z**.

Sorting the records by the department name makes it easier to locate a department.

9 **Save** the table. **Close** the table. **Open** the **Navigation Pane**.

More Knowledge | Clipboard Size Limitations

Access tables can be very large, depending on the number of fields and records in the table. Although the Office Clipboard can store up to 24 selected items, you might find that you cannot add more items to the Clipboard even if there are fewer than 24 stored items. Access will prompt you to clear items from the Clipboard if there is not enough storage space.

Activity 4.04 | Appending Records to a Table

In this activity, you will copy the *4A City Council Members* table to use as the basis for a single employees table. You will then copy the data in the *4A Fire Dept Employees* table and *append*—add on—the data to the new employees table.

1 Using the technique you practiced in Activity 4.03, copy and paste the structure and data of the **4A City Council Members** table, and then **Save** the pasted table as **Lastname Firstname 4A Employees**

An exact duplicate of the *4A City Council Members* table is created. The *4A Employees* table will be used to build a table of all employees.

2 Open the **4A Employees** table, and notice the records that were copied from the *4A City Council Members* table.

3 **Copy** the **4A Fire Dept Employees** table, and then click the **Paste** button. In the **Paste Table As** dialog box, under **Table Name**, type **Lastname Firstname 4A Employees** Under **Paste Options**, click the **Append Data to Existing Table** option button, and then click **OK**. With the **4A Employees table** active, in the **Records group**, click the **Refresh All** button, and then compare your screen with Figure 4.7.

The table to which you are appending the records must exist before using the Append option. Clicking the Refresh All button causes Access to refresh or update the view of the table, displaying the newly appended records. The *4A Employees* table then displays the two records for the fire department employees—last names of *Barrero* and *Parsons*— and the records are arranged in ascending order by the first field. The records still exist in the *4A Fire Dept Employees* table. If separate tables existed for the employees in each department, you would repeat these steps until every employee's record is appended to the *4A Employees* table.

Figure 4.7

Barrero and Parsons records appended to the table

Alert! | Does a Message Box Display?

If a message box displays stating that the Microsoft Office Access database engine could not find the object, you probably mistyped the name of the table in the Paste Table As dialog box. In the Navigation Pane, note the spelling of the table name to which you are copying the records. In the message box, click OK, and then in the Paste Table As dialog box, under Table Name, correctly type the table name.

---

4 **Close** the table.

More Knowledge | Appending Records

Access appends all records from the *source table*—the table from which you are copying records—into the *destination table*—the table to which the records are appended—as long as the field names and data types are the same in both tables. Exceptions include:

- If the source table does not have all of the fields that the destination table has, Access will still append the records, leaving the data in the missing fields empty in the destination table.

- If the source table has a field name that does not exist in the destination table or the data type is incompatible, the append procedure will fail.

  Before performing an append procedure, carefully analyze the structure of both the source table and the destination table.

Activity 4.05 | Splitting a Table into Two Tables

The *4A Employees* table stores personal data and office data about the employees. Although the table contains data about one subject—employees—you will split the table into two separate tables to keep the personal information separate from the office information.

1 Using the technique you practiced, copy and paste the structure and data of the **4A Employees** table, naming the pasted table **Lastname Firstname 4A Employees Personal** Repeat the procedure for the **4A Employees** table, naming the pasted table **Lastname Firstname 4A Employees Office**

Access creates two exact duplicates of the *4A Employees* table. These tables will be used to split the *4A Employees* table into two separate tables, one storing personal data and the other storing office data.

2 Open the **4A Employees Personal** table, widening the navigation pane as necessary. **Close** « the **Navigation Pane**. Scroll to the right, if needed, to display the **Date Hired**, **Office Phone**, **Position**, and **Office Email** fields. Select all four fields. On the **Home tab**, in the **Records group**, click the **Delete** button. In the displayed message box, click **Yes** to permanently delete the fields and data.

> Because these fields contain office data, they are deleted from the *4A Employees Personal* table. These fields will be stored in the *4A Employees Office* table.

3 Select the **Title**, **First Name**, **MI**, and **Last Name** fields, and then delete the fields. **Save** 🖫 the table.

> These fields you deleted are stored in the *4A Employees Office* table. You have deleted redundant data from the *4A Employees Personal* table.

4 **Open** » the **Navigation Pane**. Open the **4A Employees Office** table. **Close** « the **Navigation Pane**. Point to the **Street** field name until the ↓ pointer displays. Click and drag to the right to the **Home Phone** field name, and then compare your screen with Figure 4.8.

> Five fields are selected and will be deleted from this table. This is duplicate data that exists in the *4A Employees Personal* table. The *Empl ID* field will be the common field between the two tables.

Figure 4.8

Duplicate data—stored in 4A Employees Personal table

Common field—4A Employees Office table and 4A Employees Personal table

5 **Delete** the selected fields and data from the table.

> The *4A Employees Office* table now stores only office data about the employees and can be linked to the *4A Employees Personal* table through the common field, *Empl ID*.

6 Click the **Position** field name. Under **Table Tools**, click the **Fields tab**. In the **Add & Delete group**, click the **Number** button.

> A blank field is inserted between the *Position* field and the *Office Email* field, and it holds numeric data. Because this field will be used to link to the *4A Departments Revised* Dept ID field, which has a data type of AutoNumber, this field must use a data type of Number, even though it will not be used in a calculation.

7 The default name *Field1* is currently selected; type **Dept** to replace it and name the new field. Press ⏎.

8 **Open** » the **Navigation Pane**. Open the **4A Departments Revised** table.

> The *4A Departments Revised* table opens in Datasheet view, and the records are sorted in ascending order by the *Department* field.

9 Locate the **Dept ID** for the **Fire Administration** department. On the **tab row**, click the **4A Employees Office tab** to make the table active. In the record for Samuel Barrero, enter the Fire Administration Dept ID, **9,** in the **Dept** field. Press ↓ two times. In the third record for **Empl ID—Priscilla Parsons**—type **9**

10 Using the techniques you just practiced, find the **Dept ID** for the **City Council** department, and then enter that number in the **Dept** field for the second and fourth records in the **4A Employees Office** table. Compare your screen with Figure 4.9.

The *Dept* field is a common field with the *Dept ID* field in the *4A Departments Revised* table and will be used to link or join the two tables.

Figure 4.9

Common field for two tables

Dept ID for Fire Administration Department

Dept ID for City Council Department

11 On the **tab row**, right-click any table tab, and then click **Close All**.

Activity 4.06 | Appending Records from Another Database

Additional employee records are stored in another database. In this activity, you will open a second database to copy and paste records from tables in the second database to tables in the *4A_City_Directory* database.

1 On the taskbar, click the **Start** button, and then **open** a second instance of **Access**. Navigate to the location where the student data files for this textbook are saved. Locate and open the **a04A_City_Employees** file. Display **Backstage view**, click **Save Database As**, and save the database as **Lastname_Firstname_4A_City_Employees** in your **Access Chapter 4** folder.

2 In the **4A_City_Employees** database window, in the **Navigation Pane**, right-click **4A Office**, and then click **Copy**. Click the Access icon in the taskbar to see two instances of Access open. Compare your screen with Figure 4.10.

Each time you start Access, you open an *instance* of it. Two instances of Access are open, and each instance displays in the taskbar.

You cannot open multiple databases in one instance of Access. If you open a second database in the same instance, Access closes the first database. You can, however, open multiple instances of Access that display different databases. The number of times you can start Access at the same time is limited by the amount of your computer's available RAM.

Figure 4.10

Current database—4A_
City_Employees

4A_City_Directory
database

Two instances
of Access open

3 Point to each thumbnail to display the ScreenTip, and then click the button for the **4A_City_Directory** database. In the **4A_City_Directory** database window, right-click the **Navigation Pane**, and then click **Paste**—recall that you copied the *4A Office* table. In the **Paste Table As** dialog box, under **Table Name**, type **Lastname Firstname 4A Employees Office** being careful to type the table name exactly as it displays in the Navigation Pane. Under **Paste Options**, click the **Append Data to Existing Table** option button, and then click **OK**.

> The records from the *4A Office* table in the source database—*4A_City_Employees*—are copied and pasted into the *4A Employees Office* table in the destination database—*4A_City_Directory*.

4 Using the techniques you just practiced, append the records from the **4A Personal** table in the **4A_City_Employees** database to the **Lastname Firstname 4A Employees Personal** table in the **4A_City_Directory** database.

5 Make the **4A_City_Employees** database active, and on the title bar for the **4A_City_Employees** database window, click the **Close** button.

6 If the **4A_City_Directory** database is not active, on the taskbar, click the **Microsoft Access** button. Open the **4A Employees Personal** table, and then open the **4A Employees Office** table. **Close** ⟪ the **Navigation Pane**.

7 If necessary, on the tab row, click the **4A Employees Office tab** to make the table active, and then compare your screen with Figure 4.11.

> In addition to appending records, you can copy a single record or data in a field from a table in the source database file to a table in the destination database file. Now that you have finished restructuring the database, you can see that it is wise to plan your database before creating the tables and entering data.

Access | Chapter 4

Figure 4.11

Three appended records

8 On the **tab row**, right-click any table tab, and then click **Close All**.

Objective 2 | Modify Existing Tables

Data in a database is usually **dynamic**—changing. Records can be created, deleted, and edited in a table. It is important that the data is always up-to-date and accurate in order for the database to provide useful information.

Activity 4.07 | Finding and Deleting Records

1 **Open** 》 the **Navigation Pane**. Open the **4A Departments Revised** table. **Close** 《 the **Navigation Pane**. In the datasheet, next to Dept ID, click the **Sort and Filter arrow**, and then click **Sort Smallest to Largest**.

Sorting the records by the department ID returns the data to its primary key order.

2 In the table, in the **Department** field, click in the record containing the City Teasurer—Record 8. On the **Home tab**, in the **Find group**, click the **Find** button. Alternatively, hold down Ctrl, and then press F. The Find and Replace dialog box displays with the Find tab active.

3 In the **Find and Replace** dialog box, in the **Find What** box, type **City Assessor**

The Look In box displays *Current field,* which refers to the Department field because you clicked in that field before you clicked the Find button.

4 In the **Find and Replace** dialog box, click the **Look in box arrow**. Notice that Access can search for the data in the entire Departments table instead of only the Department field. Leaving the entry as **Current field**, click the **Look in box arrow** one time to close the list, and then click the **Find Next** button. Compare your screen with Figure 4.12.

If Access did not locate Record 5, ensure that you typed *City Assessor* correctly in the Find What box. If you misspelled *City Assessor* in the table, type the misspelled version in the Find What box. This is an example of how important accuracy is when entering data in your tables.

Figure 4.12

Search term found

Access will search
for *City Assessor*

Field to search
(Department)

5 In the **Find and Replace** dialog box, click **Cancel** to close the dialog box.

> The table displays with *City Assessor* selected in Record 5. Even though you can locate this record easily in the table because there are a limited number of records, keep in mind that most database tables contain many more records. Using the Find button is an efficient way to locate a record in the table.

6 Point to the **Record Selector** box for the *City Assessor* record until the → pointer displays. Click one time to ensure that the entire record is selected, and then compare your screen with Figure 4.13.

Figure 4.13

Record selector box

Selected record

Another Way

There are three other methods to delete selected records in a table:
- On the Home tab, in the Records group, click the Delete button arrow, and then click Delete Record.
- On the selected record, right-click, and then click Delete Record.
- From the keyboard, press [Del].

7 On the **Home tab**, in the **Records group**, click the **Delete** button, and then compare your screen with Figure 4.14. Notice that Access displays a message stating that you are about to delete one record and will be unable to undo the Delete operation.

Figure 4.14

Delete arrow

Delete button

Record with Dept ID 5 is NOT displayed

Warning message

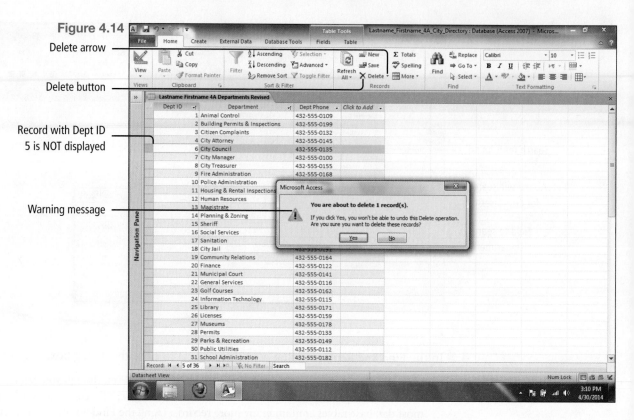

8 In the message box, click **Yes** to confirm the deletion.

The record holding information for *City Assessor* no longer displays in the table, has been permanently deleted from the table, and will no longer display in any other objects that were created using the Contacts table. The record number of Dept ID 6—City Council— is now record 5 and is the current record.

> **More Knowledge | Why the Dept ID Field Data Did Not Renumber Sequentially**
>
> You added the Dept ID field with an Autonumber data type. Because of this, when data is entered into the table, Dept ID is automatically numbered sequentially, and those numbers are not changed as records are added, deleted, or modified.

Activity 4.08 | Finding and Modifying Records

When data needs to be changed or updated, you must locate and modify the record with the data. Recall that you can move among records in a table using the navigation buttons at the bottom of the window and that you can use Find to locate specific data. Other navigation methods include using keys on the keyboard and using the Search box in the navigation area.

1 Take a moment to review the table in Figure 4.15, which lists the key combinations you can use to navigate within an Access table.

Key Combinations for Navigating a Table

Keystroke	Movement
↑	Moves the selection up one record at a time.
↓	Moves the selection down one record at a time.
Page Up	Moves the selection up one screen at a time.
PageDown	Moves the selection down one screen at a time.
Ctrl + Home	Moves the selection to the first field in the table or the beginning of the selected field.
Ctrl + End	Moves the selection to the last field in the table or the end of the selected field.
Tab	Moves the selection to the next field in the table.
Shift + Tab	Moves the selection to the previous field in the table.
Enter	Moves the selection to the next field in the table.

Figure 4.15

2 On the keyboard, press ↓ to move the selection down one record. Record 6—*City Manager*—is now the current record.

3 On the keyboard, hold down Ctrl, and then press Home to move to the first field of the first record in the table—Dept ID *1*.

4 In the navigation area, click the **Next record** button five times to navigate to Record 6—Dept ID *7*.

5 On the keyboard, hold down Ctrl, and then press End to move to the last field in the last record in the table—Dept Phone *432-555-0162*.

6 On the keyboard, hold down Shift, and then press Tab to move to the previous field in the same record in the table—*City Mayor* in the Department field.

7 In the navigation area at the bottom of the screen, click in the **Search** box, and type **b**

> Record 2 is selected, and the letter *B* in *Building Permits & Inspections* is highlighted. Search found the first occurrence of the letter *b*. It is not necessary to type capital letters in the Search box; Access will locate the words regardless of capitalization.

8 In the **Search** box, replace the b with **sa**

> Record 16 is selected, and the letters *Sa* in *Sanitation* are highlighted. Search found the first occurrence of the letters *sa*. This is the record that needs to be modified. It is not necessary to type an entire word in the Search box to locate a record containing that word.

9 In the field box, double-click the word *Sanitation* to select it. Type **Trash Pickup** to replace the current entry. The Small Pencil icon in the Record Selector box means that the record is being edited and has not yet been saved. Press ↓ to move to the next record and save the change.

> If you must edit part of a name, drag through letters or words to select them. You can then type the new letters or words over the selection to replace the text without having to press Del or Backspace.

10 **Save** 🖫 and **Close** the table. **Open** » the **Navigation Pane**.

Activity 4.09 | Adding and Moving Fields in Design View and Datasheet View

In this activity, you will add and move fields in Design view and in Datasheet view.

1 Right-click the **4A Employees Office** table to display a shortcut menu, and click **Design View** to open the table in Design view. Alternatively, double-click the table name in the **Navigation Pane** to open the table in Datasheet view, and click the **View** button to switch to Design view. **Close** [«] the **Navigation Pane**.

2 In the **Field Name** column, locate the **Office Phone** field name, and then click anywhere in the box.

3 On the **Design tab**, in the **Tools group**, click the **Insert Rows** button. Alternatively, right-click, and then from the shortcut menu, click Insert Rows.

A new row is inserted above the *Office Phone* field. Recall that a row in Design view is a field.

4 In the empty **Field Name** box, type **Grade** and then press [Tab] to move to the **Data Type** column. Click the **Data Type arrow** to display the list of data types, and then click **Number** to set the data type for this field. Compare your screen with Figure 4.16.

A new field has been created in the *Lastname Firstname_4A Employees Office* table. An advantage of adding a field in the Design view is that you name the field and set the data type when you insert the field.

Figure 4.16

Number data type assigned to Grade

New field named Grade added between Date Hired and Office Phone fields

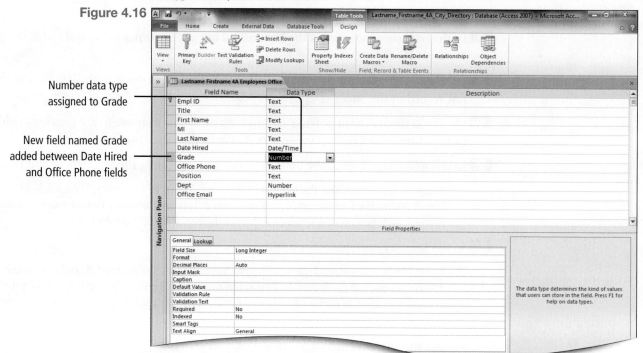

5 Switch the **4A Employees Office** table to **Datasheet** view. In the displayed message box, click **Yes** to save the design change.

The *Grade* field displays to the left of the *Office Phone* field.

6 Point to **Grade** until the [↓] pointer displays, and click one time to select the column. Drag the field left until you see a dark horizontal line between *Empl ID* and *Title*, and then release the mouse button. Compare your screen with Figure 4.17.

The *Grade* field is moved after the *Empl ID* field and before the *Title* field. If you move a field to the wrong position, select the field again, and then drag it to the correct position. Alternatively, on the Quick Access Toolbar, click the Undo button to place the field back in its previous position.

Figure 4.17

Grade field moved between Empl ID and Title fields

7 Select the **Office Phone** column. On the **Fields** tab, in the **Add & Delete** group, click **Text**. Alternatively, right-click the selected field and, from the shortcut menu, click **Insert Column**. A new column is inserted to the right of *Office Phone*.

8 If necessary, double-click **Field1**—the name of your field may differ if you have been experimenting with adding fields—to select the field name. Type **Work Site** and press Enter to save the field name. On the first record, click in the first empty **Work Site** field box. On the **Fields** tab, in the **Formatting group**, verify that the **Data Type** is **Text**.

9 In the first record—248311—click in the **Grade** field. Using the techniques you have practiced, enter the grade for each record shown in the following list, pressing ↓ after each entry to move to the next record. Repeat the process for the **Work Site** field.

Empl ID	Grade	Work Site
248311	11	Firehouse
456789	15	A-212
532268	8	B-121
589426	6	A-214
589764	6	Firehouse
689444	8	A-210
786531	12	A-214

10 Switch to **Design** view. Scroll the field list until the **Office Phone** and **Dept** fields both display, if necessary. In the **Field Name** column, locate **Office Phone**, and then click the **Row Selector** box to select the field. Point to the **Row Selector** box to display the → pointer. Drag the field down until you see a dark horizontal line following *Position*, and then release the mouse button. **Save** 🖫 the table.

11 Switch to **Datasheet** view. Notice that the **Office Phone** field is moved to the right of **Position**.

Activity 4.10 | Checking Spelling

In this exercise, you will use the spelling checker to find spelling errors in your data. It is important to realize that this will not find all data entry mistakes, so you will need to use additional proofreading methods to ensure the accuracy of the data.

1 In the first record—248311—click in the **Empl ID** field. On the **Home tab**, in the **Records group**, click the **Spelling** button. Alternatively, press F7. Compare your screen with Figure 4.18.

The Spelling dialog box displays, and *Barrero* is highlighted because it is not in the Office dictionary. Many proper names will be *flagged*—highlighted—by the spelling checker. Take a moment to review the options in the Spelling dialog box; these are described in the table in Figure 4.19.

Figure 4.18

Word NOT in dictionary

Suggested alternatives

Spelling Dialog Box Buttons

Button	Action
Ignore 'Last Name' Field	Ignores any words in the selected field.
Ignore	Ignores this one occurrence of the word but continues to flag other instances of the word.
Ignore All	Discontinues flagging any instance of the word anywhere in the table.
Change	Changes the identified word to the word highlighted under Suggestions.
Change All	Changes every instance of the word in the table to the word highlighted under Suggestions.
Add	Adds the word to a custom dictionary, which can be edited. This option does not change the built-in Office dictionary.
AutoCorrect	Adds the flagged word to the AutoCorrect list, which will subsequently correct the word automatically if misspelled in any objects typed in the future.
Options	Displays the Access Options dialog box.
Undo Last	Undoes the last change.

Figure 4.19

2 In the **Spelling** dialog box, click the **Ignore 'Last Name' Field** button.

Present, which displays in the Position field, is flagged by the spelling checker. In the Spelling dialog box under Suggestions, *President* is highlighted.

3 In the **Spelling** dialog box, click the **Change** button to change the word from *Present* to *President*.

When the spelling checker has completed checking the table and has found no other words missing from its dictionary, a message displays stating *The spelling check is complete.*

4 In the message box, click **OK**.

5 **Close** the table.

Objective 3 | Create and Modify Table Relationships

Recall that Access databases are ***relational databases***—the tables a database can relate to or connect to other tables through common fields. A relational database avoids redundant data, helps to reduce errors, and saves space. To create a relationship, the common fields must have the same data type and same field size, but they do not need to have the same field name. Table relationships work by matching data using the common fields in the tables. For example, you could have four tables relating to employees—one table for personal data, one table for office data, one table for benefits data, and one table for training data. All of these tables are connected to one another through a common field—the employee ID.

Activity 4.11 | Creating Table Relationships and Testing Referential Integrity

You should create relationships before creating other database objects, such as queries, forms, and reports, because when you create another object, Access displays all of the available tables and fields. For example, if you create a query on a stand-alone table—one that is not related to other tables—you cannot access relevant information in other tables. You must add the tables to the query and then establish a relationship. In this activity, you will create relationships between the tables in the *4A City Directory* database.

1 On the Ribbon, click the **Database Tools tab**. In the **Relationships group**, click the **Relationships** button. If the Show Table dialog box does not display, on the **Relationship Tools Design tab**, in the **Relationships** group, click the **Show Table** button or right-click an empty area in the **Relationships** window and then click **Show Table**.

> The Show Table dialog box displays, and the Tables tab is active. The Tables tab displays all of the tables in the database, including the hidden tables.

2 In the **Show Table** dialog box, click **4A Departments Revised**. Holding down Ctrl, click **4A Employees Office**, and then click **4A Employees Personal**. Notice that three tables are selected. Click **Add**, and then click **Close**.

> The three tables are added to the Relationships window. If you have any extra tables in the Relationship window, right-click the *title bar* of the table, and select *Hide Table* from the list. Three field lists display all of the field names. The *4A Employees Office* field list displays a vertical scroll bar, indicating that there are more fields than those displayed.

3 Expand the field list box for the **4A Employees Office** table by dragging the bottom border downward and to the right until the table name and all of the field names display fully. Expand the field list box for the other two tables so the table names display fully. Point to the title bar of the middle field list box, and drag down to move the field list below the other two.

4 In the **4A Departments Revised** field list, click **Dept ID**, and then drag it on top of **Dept** in the **4A Employees Office** field list. Release the mouse button.

Alert! | Are the Wrong Field Names Displayed in the Edit Relationships Dialog Box?

If you released the mouse button on a field other than Dept in the 4A Employees Office field list, that field name will be displayed in the Edit Relationships dialog box. To correct this, in the Edit Relationships dialog box, click Cancel, and then re-create the relationship.

---

5 In the displayed **Edit Relationships** dialog box, select the **Enforce Referential Integrity** check box, and then click **Create**.

> Recall that *referential integrity* is a set of rules Access uses to ensure that the data between related tables is valid. Enforcing referential integrity prevents *orphan records*—records that reference deleted records in a related table.

6 In the **4A Employees Office** field list, click **Empl ID**, drag it on top of **Empl ID** in the **4A Employees Personal** field list, and then release the mouse button. In the displayed **Edit Relationships** dialog box, verify that **4A Employees Office** appears on the left side of the box, and then select the **Enforce Referential Integrity** check box. Notice the Relationship Type—One-to-One—and then click **Create**.

A join line displays between the two field lists, indicating a one-to-one relationship between the two tables. By enforcing referential integrity in a *one-to-one relationship*, each record in the first table—*4A Employees Office*—can have only one matching record in the second table—*4A Employees Personal*—and each record in the second table can have only one matching record in the first table. A one-to-one relationship can be used to divide a table with many fields, to isolate part of the table for security reasons, or to store a part of the main table.

7 Close the Relationships tab. Click **Yes** to save changes to the layout of Relationships. On the **Design tab**, in the **Tools group**, click the **Relationship Report** button. If you are instructed to submit this result, create a paper or electronic printout. On the **Print Preview** tab, in the **Close Preview** group, click **Close Print Preview**. Close the Design view, saving changes.

8 **Open** >> the **Navigation Pane**. Open the **4A Departments Revised** table, and then open the **4A Employees Office** table. **Close** << the **Navigation Pane**.

Both tables open in Datasheet view. Make the *4A Employees Office* table the active table if it is not already. Recall that enforcing referential integrity in a one-to-many table relationship ensures that a department for an employee cannot be added to the *4A Employees Office* table if that department does not exist in the *4A Departments Revised* table. Also, you will be unable to delete a department from the *4A Departments Revised* table if an employee who works in that department is stored in the *4A Employees Office* table. In this activity, you will test these two integrity protection features.

Note | Check the Order of the Fields

If the fields are not in the order displayed, return to Design view to reorder them. Save the changes before moving to Step 9.

---

9 In the **4A Employees Office** table, add a new record by using the following information.

Empl ID	Grade	Title	First Name	MI	Last Name	Date Hired	Work Site	Position	Office Phone	Dept	Office Email
332521	1	Mr.	Elliott	C.	Yale	7/15/15	B-121	Intern	432-555-0133	50	eyale@westlandplains.gov

10 Press Tab to move to the next record, and then compare your screen with Figure 4.20.

A message box displays indicating that you cannot add or change this record because a related record—a record for Dept 50—is required in the *4A Departments Revised* table. Enforcing referential integrity prevents you from creating this record because there is no related record for the department.

Figure 4.20

Referential integrity prevents the addition of this record

Related table must have record entered before creating this record

11 In the displayed message box, click **OK**. In the new record, under Dept, select **50** and then type **1**—the Department ID for Animal Control. **Close** the table.

> The *4A Employees Office* table closes, and the *4A Departments Revised* table is active.

12 In the **4A Departments Revised** table, point to the record selector box for the fifth record—**City Council**—and then click to select the record. On the **Home tab**, in the **Records group**, click the **Delete** button.

> A message displays stating that the record cannot be deleted or changed because of related records in the *4A Employees Office* table. Referential integrity protects an individual from deleting a record in one table that has related records in another table.

13 In the displayed message box, click **OK**. View the table in **Print Preview**. If you are instructed to submit this result, create a paper or electronic printout. **Close** the **4A Departments Revised** table.

Activity 4.12 | Setting and Testing Cascade Options

There might be a time that you need to make a change to the primary key field in a table on the *one* side of a relationship. For example, the employee ID may have been incorrectly entered into the database, and it needs to be changed for all records. You also may need to delete a record that has a related record in another table. When referential integrity is enforced, you cannot make these changes. For that reason, Access provides *cascade options*—options that update records in related tables when referential integrity is enforced. This enables you to complete these tasks even when referential integrity is enforced. To use Cascade Options, referential integrity must be enforced.

1 On the Ribbon, click the **Database Tools tab**. In the **Relationships group**, click the **Relationships** button. Click the **join line** between the **4A Employees Office** field list and the **4A Employees Personal** field list. On the **Design tab**, in the **Tools group**, click the **Edit Relationships** button. Alternatively, right-click the join line, and then click Edit Relationships; or double-click the join line.

2 In the displayed **Edit Relationships** dialog box, select the **Cascade Update Related Fields** check box, and then click **OK**. **Close** the Relationships object, saving changes, and then **Open** [»] the **Navigation Pane**.

3 **Open** the **4A Employees Office** table. Recall that this table has a one-to-one relationship with the *4A Employees Personal* table. **Close** [«] the **Navigation Pane**.

4 Locate the record for **Empl ID 589764**. Between the record selector box and the Empl ID field, click the plus sign (+), and then compare your screen with Figure 4.21.

> After you create a relationship between two tables, in Datasheet view, plus signs display next to every record of the table that is the one side of the relationship. Clicking the plus sign displays the *subdatasheet*—record or records from the related table—and changes the plus sign to a minus sign (–). Clicking the minus sign collapses the subdatasheet.

Figure 4.21

Click to display
subdatasheet

Click to collapse
subdatasheet

Subdatasheet from 4A
Employees Personal table

5 Click the minus sign (–) to collapse the related record. In the **Empl ID** field, select **589764**, type **123456** and then press ↓.

6 Open ⧉ the **Navigation Pane**. Open the **4A Employees Personal** table. Notice that the first record—the **Empl ID**—is now **123456**.

The *Cascade Update* option enables an individual to change a primary key field, and updates automatically follow in the records in the related tables.

7 Close ⧉ the **Navigation Pane**. In the **4A Employees Personal** table, click the plus sign (+) for the first record.

Because this table and the *4A Employees Office* table are joined with a one-to-one relationship, each table displays the subdatasheet for the other table. If tables are joined with a one-to-many relationship, the subdatasheet can be displayed only in the table on the *one* side of the relationship.

8 Collapse the subdatasheet for the first record, and then close the open tables. Click the **Database Tools tab**, and then in the **Relationships group**, click the **Relationships** button. Double-click the **join line** between the **4A Employees Office** field list and the **4A Employees Personal** field list to display the **Edit Relationships** dialog box.

To edit relationships, the tables must be closed.

Alert! | Is the Edit Relationships Dialog Box Empty?

If the names of the tables and fields do not display in the Edit Relationships dialog box, you may not have clicked the join line—instead, you probably clicked near the join line. Click Cancel and then begin again.

---

9 In the displayed **Edit Relationships** dialog box, select the **Cascade Delete Related Records** check box, and then click **OK**. **Close** the **Relationships tab**. Open ⧉ the **Navigation Pane**. Open the **4A Employees Personal** table, and then open the **4A Employees Office** table. **Close** ⧉ the **Navigation Pane**.

10 In the **4A Employees Office** table, locate the record for the **Empl ID** of **589426**, and then select the record. Delete the record—do not click a button in the displayed message box. Compare your screen with Figure 4.22.

A message displays stating that deleting this record in this table will cause records in the related tables to also be deleted.

Figure 4.22

Cascade Delete Records causes this message to display

Note | Record Must Be Deleted in Correct Table for Cascade Update or Delete to Work

When the Cascade Delete option is selected, the record must be deleted from the table that is listed on the one side of the Edit Relationships dialog box. Deleting the record from the table listed on the many side of the Edit Relationships dialog box deletes the record from that table only. If the tables are joined in a one-to-one relationship, the record must be deleted from the table listed on the left primary key side in the Edit Relationships dialog box.

---

11 In the displayed message box, click **Yes**. Click the **4A Employees Personal** table to make it active. On the **Home tab**, in the **Records group**, click the **Refresh All** button.

> Recall that if a table is open and changes are made to fields or records in a related object, the changes are not immediately displayed. Clicking the Refresh All button updates the view of the table, removing the deleted record—the record for Marla Fernando.

> The *Cascade Delete* option enables you to delete a record in a table and delete all of the related records in related tables.

12 For the **4A Employees Personal** and **4A Employees Office** tables, adjust all column widths, ensuring that all of the field names and all of the data displays. View each table in **Print Preview**, and then change the orientation to **Landscape**. As necessary, adjust the margins to display each table on one page. If you are instructed to submit this result, create a paper or electronic printout.

13 **Close** all open objects. Display **Backstage** view, **Close** the database, and then **Exit** Access.

More Knowledge | Delete a Table Relationship

To remove a table relationship, you must delete the join line in the Relationships window. Right-click the join line, and from the shortcut menu, click Delete. Alternatively, click the join line to select it, and then press Del. When you delete a relationship, you also delete referential integrity between the tables.

End **You have completed Project 4A**

Project 4B IT Tasks

myitlab
Project 4B Training

Project Activities

In Activities 4.13 through 4.24, you will create a table in Design view that stores records about assigned tasks, modify its properties, and customize its fields. Matthew Shoaf, Director of the Information Technology Department, has created a table to keep track of tasks that he has assigned to the employees in his department. You will add features to the database table that will help to reduce data entry errors and that will make data entry easier, and you will add attachments to records. Your completed table will look similar to Figure 4.23.

Project Files

For Project 4B, you will need the following files:

 a04B_IT_Tasks
 a04B_WorkOrder_1.docx
 a04B_WorkOrder_2.docx

You will save your database as:

 Lastname_Firstname_4B_IT_Tasks

Project Results

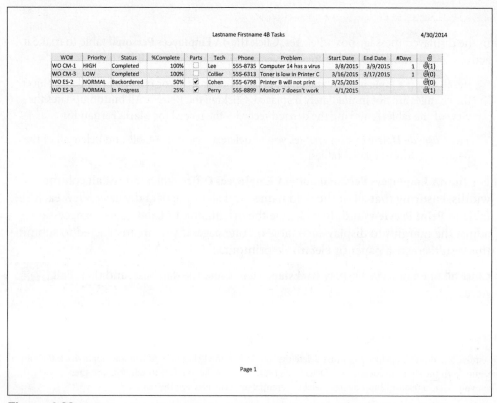

Figure 4.23
Project 4B IT Tasks

Objective 4 | Create a Table in Design View

In this activity, you will create a second table in a database using Design view.

Activity 4.13 | Creating a Table in Design View

In this activity, you will create a table to keep track of the tasks that the IT department will be completing. Creating a table in Design view gives you the most control over the characteristics of the table and the fields. Most database designers use Design view to create tables, setting the data types and formats before entering any records. Design view is a good way to create a table when you know exactly how you want to set up your fields.

1 **Start** Access. Navigate to the location where the student data files for this textbook are saved. Locate and open the **a04B_IT_Tasks** file. **Save** 🖫 the database in your **Access Chapter 4** folder as **Lastname_Firstname_4B_IT_Tasks**

2 If you did not add the Access Chapter 4 folder to the Trust Center, enable the content. In the **Navigation Pane**, under **Tables**, rename **4B Employees** by adding **Lastname Firstname** to the beginning of the table name. **Close** « the **Navigation Pane**.

3 On the Ribbon, click the **Create tab**. In the **Tables group**, click the **Table Design** button to open an empty table in Design view, and then compare your screen with Figure 4.24.

Figure 4.24

4 In the first **Field Name box**, type **WO#**, press Tab, and then on the **Design tab**, in the **Tools** group, click the **Primary Key** button. Press Tab.

5 Click the **Data Type arrow** to display a list of data types, as shown in Figure 4.25. Take a moment to study the table in Figure 4.26 that describes all 12 possible data types.

In Design view, all the data types are displayed. In Datasheet view, the list depends on the data entered in the field and does not display Lookup Wizard.

Figure 4.25

List of data types

Data Types

Data Type	Description	Example
Text	Text or combinations of text and numbers; also, numbers that are not used in calculations. Limited to 255 characters or length set on field, whichever is less. Access does not reserve space for unused portions of the text field. This is the default data type.	An inventory item, such as towels, or a phone number or postal code that is not used in calculations and that may contain characters other than numbers.
Memo	Lengthy text or combinations of text and numbers that can hold up to 65,535 characters depending on the size of the database.	A description of a product.
Number	Numeric data used in mathematical calculations with varying field sizes.	A quantity, such as 500.
Date/Time	Date and time values for the years 100 through 9999.	An order date, such as 11/10/2012 3:30 p.m.
Currency	Monetary values and numeric data that can be used in mathematical calculations involving data with one to four decimal places. Accurate to 15 digits on the left side of the decimal separator and to 4 digits on the right side. Use this data type to store financial data and when you do not want Access to round values.	An item price, such as $8.50.
AutoNumber	Available in Design view. A unique sequential or random number assigned by Access as each record is entered that cannot be updated.	An inventory item number, such as 1, 2, 3, or a randomly assigned employee number, such as 3852788.
Yes/No	Contains only one of two values—Yes/No, True/False, or On/Off. Access assigns 1 for all Yes values and 0 for all No values.	Whether an item was ordered—Yes or No.
OLE Object	An object created by programs other than Access that is linked to or embedded in the table. *OLE* is an abbreviation for *object linking and embedding*, a technology for transferring and sharing information among programs. Stores up to two gigabytes of data (the size limit for all Access databases). Must have an OLE server registered on the server that runs the database. Should usually use Attachment data type instead.	A graphics file, such as a picture of a product, a sound file, a Word document, or an Excel spreadsheet stored as a bitmap image.
Hyperlink	Web or e-mail addresses.	An e-mail address, such as dwalker@ityourway.com, or a Web page, such as http://www.ityourway.com.
Attachment	Any supported type of file—images, spreadsheet files, documents, or charts. Similar to e-mail attachments.	Same as OLE Object.
Calculated	Available in Design view. Opens the Expression Builder to create an expression based on existing fields or numbers. Field must be designated as a Calculated field when it is inserted into the table; the expression can be editing in the Field Properties.	Adding two existing fields such as [field1]+[field2], or performing a calculation with a field and a number such as [field3]*5.
Lookup Wizard	Available in Design view. Not really a data type, but will display in the list of data types. Links to fields in other tables to display a list of data instead of having to manually type the data.	Link to another field in the same or another table.

Figure 4.26

6 From the displayed list, click **Text**, and then press `Tab` to move to the **Description** box. In the **Description** box, type **Identification number assigned to task reported on work order form**

> Field names should be short; use the description box to display more information about the contents of the field.

7 Press `F6` to move to the **Field Properties** pane at the bottom of the screen. In the **Field Size** box, type **8** to replace the 255. Compare your screen with Figure 4.27.

> Pressing `F6` while in the Data Type column moves the insertion point to the first field property box in the Field Properties pane. Alternatively, click in the Field Size property box.

> Recall that a field with a data type of Text can store up to 255 characters. You can change the field size to limit the number of characters that can be entered into the field to promote accuracy. For example, if you use the two-letter state abbreviations for a state field, limit the size of the field to two characters. When entering a state in the field, you will be unable to type more than two characters.

Figure 4.27

Field Properties for a Text field

Field Size reduced from the default (255)

8 Click in the second **Field Name** box, type **Priority** and then press `Tab` twice to move to the **Description** box. Type **Indicate the priority level for this task** Press `F6` to move to the **Field Properties** pane at the bottom of the screen. Click in the **Format** box and type **>**

> Because Text is the default data type, you do not have to select it if it is the correct data type for the field.

> A greater than symbol (>) in the Format property box in a Text field converts all entries in the field to uppercase. Using a less than symbol (<) would force all entries to be lowercase.

9 In the third **Field Name** box, type **Status** and then press `Tab` three times to move to the next Field Name box.

> If the field name is descriptive enough, the Description box is optional.

10 In the fourth **Field Name** box, type **%Complete** Press `Tab` twice to move to the **Description** box, and type **Percentage of the task that has been completed**

11 In the fifth **Field Name** box, type **Parts** Press Tab to move to the **Data Type** box, and click **Yes/No**. Press Tab to move to the **Description** box. Type **Click the field to indicate parts have been ordered to complete the task**

> The data type of Yes/No is appropriate for this field because there are only two choices, parts are on order (yes) or parts are not on order (no). In **Datasheet view,** click the check box to indicate yes with a checkmark.

12 In the sixth **Field Name** box, type **Tech** and then press Tab three times to move to the next Field Name box.

13 In the seventh **Field Name** box, type **Phone** Press Tab two times to move to the **Description** box, type **Enter as ###-####** and then change the **Field Size** property to **8**

14 Click in the eighth **Field Name** box, and then type **Problem** Press Tab twice to move to the **Description** box, and then type **Description of the IT problem**

15 Click in the ninth **Field Name** box, and then type **Start Date** Press Tab to move to the **Data Type** box, and click **Date/Time**.

> The data type of Date/Time is appropriate for this field since it will only display date information. Because Date/Time is a type of number, this field can be used in calculations.

16 Click in the tenth **Field Name** box and then type **End Date** Press Tab to move to the **Data Type** box, and click **Date/Time**.

17 Click in the eleventh **Field Name** box and then type **#Days** Press Tab to move to the **Data Type** box, and click **Calculated**; the **Expression Builder** dialog box appears. In the **Expression Builder** dialog box, type **[End Date]-[Start Date]** and compare your screen to Figure 4.28.

> The data type of Calculated is appropriate for this field because the entry is calculated with an expression—subtracting *Start Date* from *End Date.* The *# Days* field will remain blank if the task has not yet been completed; nothing can be entered in the field.

> An expression can be entered using field names or numbers where the only spaces included are those that separate words in field names. Any time a field name is used in the expression, it should be enclosed in square brackets if the field name includes spaces. An existing field cannot be changed to a Calculated data type; it must be assigned when the field is added to the table. The expression can be edited in the Field Properties.

Figure 4.28

Expression Builder dialog box

Expression used to calculate # Days

18 Click **OK.** In the **Description** box, type **Number of days necessary to complete the task** Press F6 to move to the **Field Properties** pane at the bottom of the screen. Click in the **Result Type** property, and select **Integer.** Click in the **Format** property, and select **Fixed.** Click in the **Decimal Places** property, and select **0.**

19 Display **Backstage** view, click **Save** to display the **Save As** dialog box. Under **Table Name**, type **Lastname Firstname 4B Tasks** and then click **OK.** Switch to **Datasheet** view to view the table you have just created; there are no records in the table yet.

Objective 5 │ Change Data Types

Before creating a table, it is important to decide on the data types for the fields in the table. Setting a specific data type helps to ensure that the proper data will be entered into a field; for example, it is not possible to enter text into a field with a Currency data type. It is also important to choose a number data type when it is appropriate to avoid problems with calculations and sorting.

Activity 4.14 │ Changing Data Types

Once data is entered into a field, caution must be exercised when changing the data type—existing data may not be completely visible or may be deleted. You can change the data type in either Datasheet view or Design view.

1 With the **4B Tasks** table open, switch to **Design** view. Change the **Data Type** for the **%Complete** field to **Number.** Press F6 to move to the **Field Properties** pane at the bottom of the screen. Click in the **Field Size**, and select **Single.** Click in the **Format** property and select **Percent.** Set the **Decimal Places** property to **0.**

The data type of Number is more appropriate for this field since it will display only the amount of a task that has been completed. Defining the number as a percent with zero decimal places further restricts the entries. This will allow the field to be accurately used in calculations, comparisons, and sorts.

2 Change the data type for the **Problem** field to **Memo.**

The data type of Memo is more appropriate for this field since it may require more than 255 characters and spaces to effectively describe the IT problem that needs attention.

3 **Save** the changes, and then compare your screen with Figure 4.29.

Figure 4.29

Access │ Chapter 4

Objective 6 | Create a Lookup Field

Creating a *lookup field* can restrict the data entered in a field because the person entering data selects that data from a list retrieved from another table, query, or list of entered values. The choices can be displayed in a *list box*—a box containing a list of choices—or a *combo box*—a box that is a combination of a list box and a text box. You can create a lookup field by using the Lookup Wizard or manually by setting the field's lookup field properties. Whenever possible, use the Lookup Wizard because it simplifies the process, ensures consistent data entry, automatically populates the associated field properties, and creates the needed table relationships.

Activity 4.15 | Creating a Lookup Field Based on a List of Values

In this activity, you will create a lookup field for the Status field.

1 With the **4B Tasks** table open in **Design** view, in the **Status** field, click in the **Data Type** box, and then click the **arrow**. From the displayed list of data types, click **Lookup Wizard**. If a Windows Access Security Notice displays, click **Open**.

2 In the first **Lookup Wizard** dialog box, click the **I will type in the values that I want** option button, and then click **Next**. Compare your screen with Figure 4.30.

> The first step of the Lookup Wizard enables you to choose whether you want Access to locate the information from another table or query or whether you would like to type the information to create a list.

> The second step enables you to select the number of columns you want to include in the lookup field. The values are typed in the grid, and you can adjust the column width of the displayed list.

Figure 4.30

Lookup Wizard dialog box

Type first item here

Number of columns to display in the lookup field

3 Be sure the number of columns is **1**. Under **Col1**, click in the first row, type **Not Started** and then press Tab or ↓ to save the first item.

> If you mistakenly press Enter, the next dialog box of the wizard displays. If that happens, click the Back button.

4 Type the following data, and then compare your screen with Figure 4.31.

> **In Progress**
>
> **Completed**
>
> **Deferred to someone else**

Figure 4.31

Data to be displayed in
Status lookup field

5 Double-click the right edge of **Col1** to adjust the column width so all entries display, and then click **Next**. In the final dialog box, click **Finish**. With the **Status** field selected, under **Field Properties**, click the **Lookup tab**.

The Lookup Wizard populates the Lookup property boxes. The *Row Source Type* property indicates that the data is retrieved from a Value List, a list that you created. The *Row Source* property displays the data you entered in the list. The *Limit to List* property displays No, so you can type alternative data in the field.

6 **Save** the changes, and switch to **Datasheet** view. Click the **Status** field in the first record, and then click the drop-down arrow to view the lookup list. Press Esc to return to a blank field.

Alert! | Is the Last Item in the List Truncated?

If the last item in the list—Deferred to someone else—is truncated, switch to Design view. Select the field. Under Field Properties, on the Lookup tab, click in the List Width box, and then increase the width of the list box by typing a larger number than the one displayed.

Activity 4.16 | Creating a Lookup Field Based on Data in Another Table

In this activity, you will create a lookup field for the Assigned to field.

1 In the **4B Tasks** table, switch to **Design** view. In the **Tech** field, click in the **Data Type** box, and then click the **Data Type arrow**. From the displayed list of data types, click **Lookup Wizard**.

2 In the first **Lookup Wizard** dialog box, be sure that the **I want the lookup field to get the values from another table or query** option button is selected.

3 Click **Next**. The **4B Employees table** is selected.

4 Click **Next** to display the third **Lookup Wizard** dialog box. Under **Available Fields**, click **Last Name**, and then click the **Add Field** (>) button to move the field to the **Selected Fields** box. Move the **First Name** and **Job Title** fields from the **Available Fields** box to the **Selected Fields** box. Compare your screen with Figure 4.32.

Because there might be several people with the same last name, the First Name field and the Job Title field are included.

Figure 4.32

Fields from 4B Employees table

5 Click **Next** to display the fourth **Lookup Wizard** dialog box. In the **1** box, click the **arrow**, and then click **Last Name**. In the **2** box, click the **arrow**, and then click **First Name**. In the **3** box, click the **arrow**, and then click **Job Title**. Leave all three sort orders as **Ascending**.

> The list will first display last names in ascending order. If there are duplicate last names, then the duplicate last names will then be sorted by the first name in ascending order. If there are duplicate last names and first names, then those names will be sorted in ascending order by the job title.

6 Click **Next** to display the fifth **Lookup Wizard** dialog box. This screen enables you to change the width of the lookup field and to display the primary key field. Be sure the **Hide key column (recommended)** check box is selected, and then click **Next** to display the sixth and final **Lookup Wizard** dialog box.

> The actual data that is stored in the lookup field is the data in the primary key field.

7 Under **What label would you like for your lookup field?**, leave the default of **Tech** and be sure that **Allow Multiple Values** is *not* selected.

> Because you have already named the field, the default name is appropriate. If you were creating a new field that had not yet been named, a label would be entered on this screen. If you want to allow the selection of more than one last name when the lookup field displays and then store the multiple values, select the Allow Multiple Values check box, which changes the lookup field to a multivalued field. A *multivalued field* holds multiple values, such as a list of people to whom you have assigned the same task.

8 Click **Finish**. A message displays stating that the table must be saved before Access can create the needed relationship between the *4B Tasks* table and the *4B Employees* table. Click **Yes**.

9 With the **Tech** field selected, under **Field Properties**, click the **Lookup tab**.

> The Lookup Wizard populates the Lookup properties boxes. The *Row Source Type* property indicates that the data is retrieved from a Table or Query. The *Row Source* property displays the SQL statement that is used to retrieve the data from the fields in the *4B Employees* table. The *Limit to List* property displays Yes, which means you must select the data from the list and cannot type data in the field.

10 Click the **General tab** to display the list of general field properties.

Objective 7 | Set Field Properties

A *field property* is an attribute or characteristic of a field that controls the display and input of data. You previously used field properties to change the size of a field and to specify a specific format for data types. When you click in any of the property boxes, a description of the property displays to the right. Available field properties depend upon the data type of each field.

Activity 4.17 | Creating an Input Mask Using the Input Mask Wizard

An *input mask* is a field property that determines the data that can be entered, how the data displays, and how the data is stored. For example, an input mask can require individuals to enter telephone numbers in a specific format like (757) 555-1212. If you enter the telephone number without supplying an area code, you will be unable to save the record until the area code is entered. Input masks provide *data validation*—rules that help prevent individuals from entering invalid data—and help ensure that individuals enter data in a consistent manner. By default, you can apply input masks to fields with a data type of Text, Number, Currency, and Date/Time. The Input Mask Wizard can be used to apply input masks to fields with a data type of Text or Date/Time only.

1 Under **Field Name**, click **Phone**. Under **Field Properties**, click in the **Input Mask** box. At the right side of the Field Properties, notice the description given for this property. In the **Input Mask** box, click the **Build** button. If a Windows Access Security Notice displays, click **Open**. Compare your screen with Figure 4.33.

The Build button displays after you click in a field property box so you can further define the property. The Input Mask Wizard starts, which enables you to create an input mask using one of several standard masks that Access has designed, such as Phone Number, Social Security Number, Zip Code, and so on. Clicking in the Try It box enables you to enter data to test the input mask.

Figure 4.33

Example displayed for corresponding input mask

Build button

Input Mask box

Description of Input Mask property

2 In the displayed **Input Mask Wizard** dialog box, with **Phone Number** selected, click **Next**, and then compare your screen with Figure 4.34. In the **Input Mask Wizard** dialog box, notice the entry in the **Input Mask** box.

A *0* indicates a required digit; a *9* indicates an optional digit or space. The area code is enclosed in parentheses, and a hyphen (-) separates the three-digit prefix from the four-digit number. The exclamation point (!) causes the input mask to fill in from left to right. The Placeholder character indicates that the field will display an underscore character (_) for each digit before data is entered in Datasheet view.

Figure 4.34

0s indicate required digits

9s indicate optional digits or spaces

! causes the input mask to fill in from left to right

Placeholder character

3 In the **Input Mask Wizard** dialog box, click **Back**, and then click **Edit List**.

The Customize Input Mask Wizard dialog box displays, which enables you to edit the default input mask or add an input mask.

4 In the **Customize Input Mask Wizard** dialog box, in the navigation area, click the **New (blank) record** button. In the **Description** box, type **Local Phone Number** In the **Input Mask** box, type **!000-0000** Click in the **Placeholder** box, and change _ to # Click in the **Sample Data** box, select the data, and then type **555-1212** Compare your screen with Figure 4.35.

Because tasks are assigned to local personnel, the area code is unnecessary. Instead of displaying an underscore as the placeholder in the field, the number sign (#) displays.

Figure 4.35

New input mask for local phone numbers

Placeholder changed to #

5 In the **Customize Input Mask Wizard** dialog box, click **Close**.

The newly created input mask for Local Phone Number displays below the input mask for Password.

6 Under **Input Mask**, click **Local Phone Number**, and then click **Next**. Click the **Placeholder character arrow** to display other symbols that can be used as placeholders. Be sure that # is displayed as the placeholder character, and then click **Next**.

After creating an input mask to be used with the Input Mask Wizard, you can change the placeholder character for individual fields.

7 The next wizard screen enables you to decide how you want to store the data. Be sure that the **Without the symbols in the mask, like this** option button is selected, as shown in Figure 4.36.

Saving the data without the symbols makes the database size smaller.

Figure 4.36

Be sure this is selected ——

8 Click **Next**. In the final wizard screen, click **Finish**. Notice that the entry in the **Input Mask** box displays as **!000\-0000;;#**. **Save** the table.

Recall that the exclamation point (!) fills the input mask from left to right, and the 0s indicate required digits. The two semicolons (;) are used by Access to separate the input mask into three sections. This input mask has data in the first section—the 0s—and in the third section—the placeholder of #.

The second and third sections of an input mask are optional. The second section, which is not used in this input mask, determines whether the literal characters—in this case, the hyphen (-)—are stored with the data. A *0* in the second section will store the literal characters; a *1* or leaving it blank stores only the characters entered in the field. The third section of the input mask indicates the placeholder character—in this case, the # sign. If you want to leave the fill-in spaces blank instead of using a placeholder, type " "—there is a space between the quotation marks—in the third section.

9 Take a moment to study the table shown in Figure 4.37, which describes the characters that can be used to create a custom input mask.

Most Common Input Mask Characters

Character	Description
0	Required digit (0 through 9).
9	Optional digit or space.
#	Optional digit, space, plus sign, or minus sign; blank positions are converted to spaces.
L	Required letter (A through Z).
?	Optional letter.
A	Required digit or letter.
a	Optional digit or letter.
&	Any character or space; required.
C	Any character or space; optional.
<	All characters that follow are converted to lowercase.
>	All characters that follow are converted to uppercase.
!	Characters typed into the mask are filled from left to right. The exclamation point can be included anywhere in the input mask.
\	Character that follows is displayed as text. This is the same as enclosing a character in quotation marks.
Password	Creates a password entry box that displays asterisks (*) as you type. Access stores the characters.
" "	Used to enclose displayed text.
.	Decimal separator.
,	Thousands separator.
: ; - /	Date and time separators. Character used depends on your regional settings.

Figure 4.37

Activity 4.18 | Creating an Input Mask Using the Input Mask Properties Box

In addition to using the wizard, input masks can be created directly in the Input Mask Properties box. In this activity, you will use the Input Mask Properties box to create a mask that will ensure the Work Order # is entered according to departmental policy. An example of a work order number used by the Information Technology department is WO CM-46341. WO is an abbreviation for Work Order. CM represents the initials of the person entering the work order data. A hyphen separates the initials from a number assigned to the work order.

1 With the **4B Tasks** table displayed in **Design** view, click in the **WO#** field. Under **Field Properties**, click in the **Input Mask** box, type **WO**, press Spacebar, type **>LL-99** and then compare your screen with Figure 4.38.

The letters *WO* and a space will display at the beginning of every Work Order # (WO#). The greater than (>) sign converts any text following it to uppercase. Each *L* indicates that a letter (not a number) is required. A hyphen (-) follows the two letters, and the two 9s indicate optional numbers.

Take a moment to study the examples of input masks shown in Figure 4.39.

Figure 4.38

Space after WO

Input mask for WO# field

Examples of Input Masks

Input Mask	Sample Data	Description
(000) 000-0000	(206) 555-5011	Must enter an area code because of the 0s enclosed in parentheses.
(999) 000-0000!	(206) 555-6331 ( )555-6331	Area code is optional because of the 9s enclosed in parentheses. Exclamation point causes mask to fill in from left to right.
(000) AAA-AAAA	(206) 555-TELE	Enables you to substitute the last seven digits of a U.S.–style phone number with letters. Area code is required.
#999	-20 2009	Can accept any positive or negative number of no more than four characters and no thousands separator or decimal places.
>L????L?000L0	GREENGR339M3 MAY R 452B7	Allows a combination of required (L) and optional (?) letters and required numbers (0). The greater than (>) sign changes letters to uppercase.
00000-9999	23703- 23703-5100	Requires the five-digit postal code (0) and optional plus-four section (9).
>L<?????????????	Elizabeth Rose	Enables up to 15 letters in which the first letter is required and is capitalized; all other letters are lowercase.
ISBN 0-&&&&&&&&&-0	ISBN 0-13-232762-7	Allows a book number with text of ISBN, required first and last digits, and any combination of characters between those digits.
>LL00000-0000	AG23703-0323	Accepts a combination of two required letters, both uppercase, followed by five required numbers, a hyphen, and then four required numbers. Could be used with part or inventory numbers.

Figure 4.39

2 Click in the **Start Date** field to make the field active. Under **Field Properties**, click in the **Format** box, and then click the **arrow**. From the displayed list, click **Short Date**. Also set the format of **End Date** to **Short Date**.

> **More Knowledge | The Differences Between Input Masks and Display Formats**
>
> You can define input masks to control how data is entered into a field and then apply a separate display format to the same data. For example, you can require individuals to enter dates in a format such as 30 Dec. 2016 by using an input mask of DD MMM. YYYY. By using the Format property, you can specify a format of Short Date, which will display the data as 12/30/2016, regardless of how the data was entered.

3 Switch to **Datasheet** view, click **Yes** to save the table. In the **WO#** field in the first record, type **cm1** and then press Tab or Enter to go to the next field.

> The input mask adds the WO and a space. The cm is automatically capitalized, and the hyphen is inserted before the 1.

4 In the **Priority** field, type **High** and then press Tab or Enter to go to the next field.

5 In the **Status** field, type **C** to display the **Completed** item in the lookup list, and then press Tab or Enter to move to the next field.

6 In the **%Complete** field, type **100** and then press Tab or Enter three times to bypass the **Parts** and **Tech** fields.

> Leaving the Yes/No field blank assigns a No value in the Parts field, so parts are not on order for this task.

7 In the **Phone**# field, type 5558735 and then press Tab or Enter to move to the next field.

8 In the **Problem** field, type **Computer 14 has a virus** and then press Tab or Enter to move to the next field.

9 In the **Start Date** field, type **3/8/2015** and then press Tab or Enter to move to the next field.

10 In the **End Date** field, type **3/9/15** and then press Tab or Enter to move to the **#Days** field. Notice the calculated field now displays a 1.

11 Switch to **Design** view. The data entry is automatically saved when the record is complete.

Activity 4.19 | Specifying a Required Field

Recall that if a table has a field designated as the primary key field, an entry for the field is *required*; it cannot be left empty. You can set this requirement on other fields in either Design view or Datasheet view. In this activity, you will require an entry in the Status and Tech fields. Use the Required field property to ensure that a field contains data and is not left blank.

1 Click in the **Status** field, and then under **Field Properties**, click in the **Required** box. Click the **Required arrow**, and then compare your screen with Figure 4.40.

> Only Yes and No options display in the list.

Figure 4.40

Description of Required property

Required box

2 Click **Yes** to require an individual to enter the status for each record. **Save** the changes to the table.

A message displays stating that data integrity rules have been changed and that existing data may not be valid for the new rules. This message displays when you change field properties where data exists in the field. Clicking Yes requires Access to examine the field in every record to see if the existing data meets the new data validation rule. For each record Access finds where data does not meet the new validation rule, a new message displays that prompts you to keep testing with the new setting. You also can revert to the prior validation setting and continue testing or cancel testing of the data.

3 If the message is displayed, click **No**. Switch to **Datasheet** view. Click in the **Status** field. On the **Fields tab**, in the **Field Validation** group, notice that the **Required** check box is selected.

4 In the table, click in the **Tech** field, and then on the **Fields tab**. In the **Field Validation** group, click the **Required** check box. Compare your screen with Figure 4.41.

A message displays stating that the existing data violates the Required property for the Tech field because the field is currently blank.

Figure 4.41

Warning message

Access | Chapter 4

5 In the message box, click **Cancel**. Click the **arrow** at the right of the **Tech** field and select **Matthew Lee**.

> **More Knowledge** | Allowing Blank Data in a Required Text or Memo Field
>
> By default, all fields except the primary key field can be empty—null. If the Required property for a field is set to Yes, a value must be entered into the field. If data is required, Access will not save the record until a value is entered; however, you may not have the data to enter into a text or memo field where the Required property is set to Yes. To allow for this situation, you can set the Allow Zero Length property for the field to Yes. A *zero-length string* is created by typing two quotation marks with no space between them (""), which indicates that no value exists for a required text or memo field.

Activity 4.20 | Setting Default Values for Fields

You can use the Default Value field property to display a value in a field for new records. As you enter data, you can change the *default value* in the field to another value within the parameters of any validation rules. Setting a default value for fields that contain the same data for multiple records increases the efficiency of data entry. For example, if all of the employees in the organization live in Texas, set the default value of the state field to TX. If most of the employees in your organization live in the city of Westland Plains, set the default value of the city field to Westland Plains. If an employee lives in another city, type the new value over the displayed default value.

1 Switch to **Design** view. Under **Field Name**, click the **Priority** field. Under **Field Properties**, click in the **Default Value** box, and then type **Low** Switch to **Datasheet** view, and then **Save** 🖫 changes to the table. Notice that the **Priority** field displays *LOW* in the New Record row.

> Setting a default value does not change the data in saved records; the default value will display in new records and will be saved only if nothing else is typed in the field.

2 Switch back to **Design** view. Using the technique you just practiced, for the **Status** field, set the **Default Value** property to **Not Started** For the **%Complete** field, set the **Default Value** property to **0**

3 For the **Start Date** field, set the **Default Value** to **1/1/10** Switch to **Datasheet** view, and then **Save** 🖫 changes to the table. Compare your screen with Figure 4.42.

> The Status field shows a default value of *Not "Started"*. *Not* is an Access logical operator; therefore, Access excluded the word *Not* from the text expression.

Figure 4.42

Default values

Not is a reserved word

4 Switch to **Design** view. Click in the **Status** field. Under **Field Properties**, in the **Default Value** box, select the text, and then type **"Not Started"** Click in the **Start Date** field, and notice that in the **Default Value** box, Access displays the date as **#1/1/2010#**. Switch to **Datasheet** view, **Save** 🖫 changes to the table, and then view the default value in the **Status** field.

> Inserting quotation marks around *Not Started* informs Access that both words are part of the text expression.

> **More Knowledge** | Using the Current Date as a Default Value
>
> To use the current date as the default value for a Date/Time field, in the Default Value box, type date().

Activity 4.21 | Indexing Fields in a Table

An *index* is a special list created in Access to speed up searches and sorting—such as the index at the back of a book. The index is visible only to Access and not to you, but it helps Access find items much faster. You should index fields that you search frequently, fields that you sort, or fields used to join tables in relationships. Indexes, however, can slow down the creation and deletion of records because the data must be added to or deleted from the index.

1 Switch to **Design** view. Under **Field Name**, click **WO#**. Under **Field Properties**, locate the **Indexed** property box, and notice the entry of **Yes (No Duplicates)**.

By default, primary key fields are indexed. Because WO# is the primary key field, the field is automatically indexed, and no duplicate values are permitted in this field.

2 Under **Field Name**, click **Tech**. Under **Field Properties**, click in the **Indexed** property box, and then click the displayed **arrow**. Compare your screen with Figure 4.43.

Three options display for the Indexed property—No, Yes (Duplicates OK), and Yes (No Duplicates).

Figure 4.43

Description of Indexed property

Indexed property options

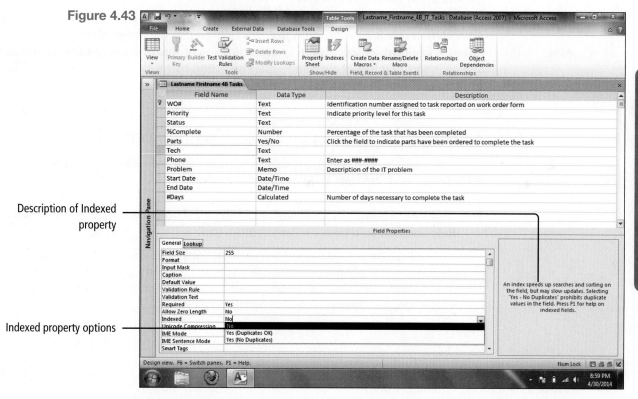

3 Click **Yes (Duplicates OK)**.

By adding an index to the field and allowing duplicates, you create faster searches and sorts on this field, while allowing duplicate data. Because a person may be assigned more than one task, allowing duplicate data is appropriate.

4 **Save** 🖫 the table design.

5 On the **Design tab**, in the **Show/Hide group**, click the **Indexes** button.

> An Indexes dialog box displays the indexes in the current table. Opening the Indexes dialog box is an efficient way to determine the fields that have been indexed in a table.

6 In the **Indexes: 4B Tasks** dialog box, click the **Close** button.

More Knowledge | **About the Caption Property**

The Caption property is used to give a name to fields used on forms and reports. Many database administrators create field names in tables that are short and abbreviated. In a form or report based on the table, a more descriptive name is desired. The value in the Caption property is used in label controls on forms and reports instead of the field name. If the Caption property is blank, the field name is used in the label control. A caption can contain up to 2,048 characters.

Objective 8 | Create Data Validation Rules and Validation Text

You have practiced different techniques to help ensure that data entered into a field is valid. Data types restrict the type of data that can be entered into a field. Field sizes control the number of characters that can be entered into a field. Field properties further control how data is entered into a field, including the use of input masks to require individuals to enter data in a specific way.

Another way to ensure the accuracy of data is by using the Validation Rule property. A *validation rule* is an expression that precisely defines the range of data that will be accepted in a field. An *expression* is a combination of functions, field values, constants, and operators that brings about a result. *Validation text* is the error message that displays when an individual enters a value prohibited by the validation rule.

Activity 4.22 | Creating Data Validation Rules and Validation Text

In this activity, you will create data validation rules and validation text for the %Complete field, the Start Date field, and the Priority field.

1 Under **Field Name**, click **%Complete**. Under **Field Properties**, click in the **Validation Rule** box, and then click the **Build** button 📖.

> The Expression Builder dialog box displays. The *Expression Builder* is a feature used to create formulas (expressions) in query criteria, form and report properties, and table validation rules. Take a moment to study the table shown in Figure 4.44, which describes the operators that can be used in building expressions.

Operators Used in Expressions

Operator	Function	Example
Not	Tests for values NOT meeting a condition.	**Not** > 10 (the same as <=10)
In	Tests for values equal to existing members in a list.	**In** ("High","Normal","Low")
Between...And	Tests for a range of values, including the vales on each end.	**Between** 0 **And** 100 (the same as >=0 **And** <=100)
Like	Matches pattern strings in Text and Memo fields.	**Like** "Car*"
Is Not Null	Requires individuals to enter values in the field. If used in place of the Required field, you can create Validation Text that better describes what should be entered in the field.	**Is Not Null** (the same as setting Required property to Yes)
And	Specifies that all of the entered data must fall within the specified limits.	>=#01/01/2014# **And** <=#03/01/2014# (Date must be between 01/01/2014 and 03/01/2014) Can use And to combine validation rules. For example, **Not** "USA" **And Like** "U*"
Or	Specifies that one of many entries can be accepted	"High" **Or** "Normal" **Or** "Low"
<	Less than.	<100
<=	Less than or equal to.	<=100
>	Greater than.	>0
>=	Greater than or equal to.	>=0
=	Equal to.	=Date()
<>	Not equal to.	<>#12/24/53#

Figure 4.44

Another Way

When using the Expression Builder to create an expression, you can either type the entire expression or, on the small toolbar in the dialog box, click an existing button, such as the > button, to insert operators in the expression.

2 In the upper box of the **Expression Builder** dialog box, type **>=0 and <=1** Alternatively, type the expression in the **Validation Rule** property box. In the **Expression Builder** dialog box, click **OK**.

The %Complete field has a data type of Number and is formatted as a percent. Recall that the Format property changes the way the stored data displays. To convert the display of a number to a percent, Access multiplies the value by 100 and appends the percent sign (%). Therefore, 100% is stored as 1—Access multiples 1 by 100, resulting in 100. A job that is halfway completed—50%—has the value stored as .5 because .5 times 100 equals 50.

3 Click in the **Validation Text** box, and then type **Enter a value between 0 and 100** so that the percentages are reflected accurately. Compare your screen with Figure 4.45.

Figure 4.45

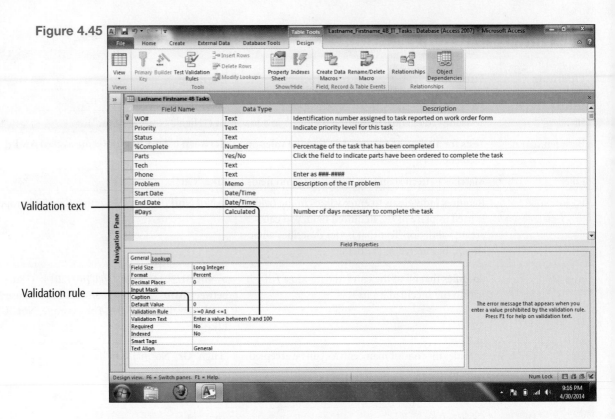

Validation text

Validation rule

4 Under **Field Name**, click **Start Date** to make the field active. Under **Field Properties**, click in the **Validation Rule** box, and then type **>=1/1/2010** Click in the **Validation Text** box, and then type **Enter a date 1/1/2010 or after** Compare your screen with Figure 4.46.

In expressions, Access inserts a number or pound sign (#) before and after a date. This validation rule ensures that the person entering data cannot enter a date prior to 1/1/2010.

Figure 4.46

Validation text

Validation rule—Access inserts # symbol before and after date

5 Under **Field Name**, click **Priority**. Under **Field Properties**, click in the **Validation Rule** box, and then type **in ("High","Normal","Low")** Click in the **Validation Text** box, and then type **You must enter High, Normal, or Low** Compare your screen with Figure 4.47.

The operators are not case sensitive; Access will capitalize the operators when you click in another property box. With the *In* operator, the members of the list must be enclosed in parentheses, and each member must be enclosed in quotation marks and separated from each other by commas. Another way to specify the same validation rule is: "High" Or "Normal" Or "Low".

Figure 4.47

The values that can be entered into the Priority field

Validation text

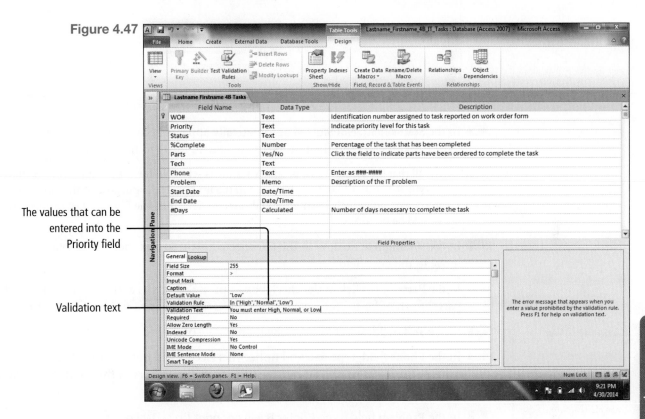

6 **Save** ⊟ the changes to the table. Switch to **Datasheet** view.

A message displays stating that data integrity rules have changed. Even though you have clicked No in previous message boxes, click **Yes**. In a large database, you should click Yes to have Access check the data in all of the records before moving on.

Activity 4.23 | Testing Table Design and Field Properties

In this activity, you will add additional records to the *4B Tasks* table to test the design and field properties.

1 With the **4B Tasks** table open in **Datasheet** view, in the second record in the **WO#** field, type **es2** and then press Tab or Enter to go to the next field.

2 In the **Priority** field, type **Medium** to replace the default entry *Low*, and then press Tab or Enter to go to the next field. The message *You must enter High, Normal, or Low* appears on your screen because the validation rule limits the entry in this field. Compare your screen with Figure 4.48. Click OK and type **Normal** in the **Priority** field to replace *Medium*. Press Tab or Enter to go to the next field.

Figure 4.48

Validation rule prohibits
entry of medium

3 In the **Status** field, **Not Started** automatically appears because it is the default entry. Type **Backordered** and then press [Tab] or [Enter] to move to the next field.

> Recall that the Limit to List property setting is set to No for the lookup field, enabling you to type data other than that displayed in the list box. If the purpose of the lookup field is to restrict individuals to entering only certain data, then the Limit to List property setting should be set to Yes.

4 In the **%Complete** field, with the **0%** selected, type **50** and then press [Tab] or [Enter] to move to the next field

5 In the **Parts** field, click in the check box or press [Spacebar] to add a checkmark to indicate parts are on order to complete the task. Press [Tab] or [Enter] to move to the next field.

Another Way

You can locate an entry in a long list faster if you type the first letter of the data for which you are searching. For example, if you are searching for a last name that begins with the letter *M*, when the list displays, type *m* or *M*. The selection will move down to the first entry that begins with the letter.

6 In the **Tech** field, select **Susan Cohen**. Press [Tab] or [Enter] to move to the next field.

7 In the **Phone** field, type **aaa** and notice that Access will not allow a letter entry because the input mask you just created requires numbers in this field. Type **5556798** and then press [Tab] or [Enter] to move to the next field.

8 In the **Problem** field, type **Printer B will not print** Press [Tab] or [Enter] to move to the next field.

9 In the **Start Date** field, type **3/25/2015** Press [Tab] or [Enter] three times to move past **#Days** and move to the next record.

> Notice the calendar icon that appears to the right of the date fields. Clicking the icon enables you to choose a date from a calendar.
>
> End Date is not a required field, so it accepts a blank entry. Because End Date is blank, there is nothing to calculate in the Task Duration field.

10 In the third record, in the **WO#** field, type **cm3** and then press [Tab] or [Enter] twice to move to the **Status** field.

11 In the **Status** field, select **Completed**. Press [Tab] or [Enter] to move to the next field.

12 In the **%Complete** field, with the *0%* selected, type **110** and then press [Tab] or [Enter] to move to the next field.

> A message, *Enter a value between 0 and 100*, appears on your screen because the validation rule limits the entry in this field.

13 Select the *110%* and type **100** Press [Tab] or [Enter] twice move to the **Tech** field.

14 In the **Tech** field, type **Rukstad** Press Tab or Enter to move to the next field. Compare your screen with Figure 4.49.

A message *The text you entered isn't an item in the list* appears on your screen. Recall that the Limit to List property setting is set to Yes for the lookup field, which restricts you from entering anything that is not on the list.

Figure 4.49

Lookup list prohibits entries not on the list

15 Click **OK** and select **Roberta Collier** from the lookup list. Press Tab or Enter to move to the next field.

16 In the **Phone#** field, type **5556313** Press Tab or Enter to move to the next field. In the **Problem** field, type **Toner is low in Printer C** Press Tab or Enter to move to the next field.

17 In the **Start Date** field, type **3/16/2015** Press Tab or Enter to move to the next field. In the **End Date** field, type **3/17/2015** Press Tab or Enter to move to the next field.

Objective 9 | Attach Files to Records

The attachment data type can be used to add one or more files to the records in a database. For example, if you have a database for an antique collection, you can attach a picture of each antique and a Word document that contains a description of the item. Access stores the attached files in their native formats—if you attach a Word document, it is saved as a Word document. By default, fields contain only one piece of data; however, you can attach more than one file by using the attachment data type. As you attach files to a record, Access creates one or more *system tables* to keep track of the multiple entries in the field. You cannot view or work with these system tables.

Activity 4.24 | Attaching a Word Document to a Record

In this activity, you will attach a Work Order Report that was created in Word to records in the *4B Tasks* table.

1 Switch to **Design** view, click in the empty field name box under **#Days**, type **Work Order** and then press Tab to move to the **Data Type** box. Click the **Data Type arrow**, click **Attachment**, and then press F6. Under **Field Properties**, on the **General tab**, and notice that only two field properties—**Caption** and **Required**—are displayed for an Attachment field.

Access | Chapter 4

2 Switch to **Datasheet** view, saving changes to the table. If necessary, scroll to the right to display the newly created Attachment field. Notice that the field name of *Work Order* does not display; instead, a paper clip symbol displays. In the first record, *(0)* displays after the paper clip symbol, indicating that there are no attachments for this record.

Because multiple files can be attached to a record, the name of the field displays the paper clip symbol.

3 In the first record, double-click in the **Attachment** field. In the displayed **Attachments** dialog box, click **Add**. Navigate to the location where the student data files for this textbook are saved. In the **Choose File** dialog box, double-click **a04B_WorkOrder_1**, and then compare your screen with Figure 4.50.

The Word document is added to the Attachments dialog box. You can attach multiple files to the same record.

Figure 4.50

Attachment field

Word document that will be attached to the first record

Indicates number of attachments for this record

4 In the **Attachments** dialog box, click **OK**. Notice that the **Attachment** field now indicates there is **1** attachment for the first record.

5 In the first record, double-click in the **Attachment** field. In the **Attachments** dialog box, click **a04B_WorkOrder_1.docx**, and then click **Open**.

Word opens, and the document displays. You can make changes to the document, and then save it in the database.

6 Close [X] Word. In the **Attachments** dialog box, click **OK**.

> **Note** | Saving Changes to an Attached File
>
> When you open an attached file in the program that was used to create it, Access places a temporary copy of the file in a temporary folder on the hard drive of your computer. If you change the file and save changes, Access saves the changes in the temporary copy. Closing the program used to view the attachment returns you to Access. When you click OK to close the Attachments dialog box, Access prompts you to save the attached file again. Click Yes to save the changes to the attached file in the database, or click No to keep the original, unedited version in the database.
>
> To find the location of your temporary folder, start Internet Explorer. On the Tools menu, click Internet Options. On the General tab, in the Browsing History section, click Settings. In the Settings dialog box, the temporary folder path displays in the Current location section.

7 Enter the following data for **Record 4**—a new record. Do not enter any data in the **End Date** field. The attachment is located in the student data files.

WO#	Priority	Status	%Complete	Parts	Tech	Phone#	Problem	Start Date	End Date	Attachment
es3	Normal	In Progress	25	Yes	Jennifer Perry	5558899	Monitor 7 doesn't work	4/1/15		a04B_ WorkOrder_2

8 Adjust all column widths, ensuring that all of the field names and all of the field data display. View the table in **Print Preview**, and then change the orientation to **Landscape**. Adjust the margins to display the table on one page, and be sure that the table name, date, and page number display. If you are instructed to submit this result, create a paper or electronic printout.

9 **Close** the table, saving changes. **Open** ⟫ the **Navigation Pane**. **Close** the database, and **Exit** ❌ Access.

End **You have completed Project 4B** ————————————

Content-Based Assessments

Summary

Database security is in important part of database maintenance. Create regular back-up files and add secure locations to the Trust Center to protect a database. Using existing tables as the basis to create new ones eliminates the chances of mistakes in table design. Use the Find feature to efficiently locate data in a table to edit or modify records. Establishing relationships between the database tables along with setting referential integrity and cascade options reduce data redundancy and increase data entry accuracy.

Create a table in Design view to control the field characteristics. Choose the best data type for each field based on the information it tracks, and set the appropriate field properties to minimize the chance for errors in data entry.

Key Terms

Matching

Match each term in the second column with its correct definition in the first column by writing the letter of the term on the blank line in front of the correct definition.

_____ 1. To make a copy of the original database for use if data is lost or becomes corrupt.

_____ 2. A security feature that checks documents for macros and digital signatures.

_____ 3. A temporary storage area in Windows.

_____ 4. A record that references a deleted record in a related table.

_____ 5. Options that update records in related tables when referential integrity is enforced.

_____ 6. A good way to create a table when you know exactly how fields will be set up.

_____ 7. An attribute or characteristic of a field that controls the display and input of data.

_____ 8. Determines the data that can be entered and how the data displays.

_____ 9. Rules that help prevent individuals from entering invalid data and help ensure that individuals enter data in a consistent manner.

_____ 10. A special list created in Access to speed up searches and sorting.

_____ 11. An expression that precisely defines a range of data that will be accepted in a field.

_____ 12. The error message that displays when an individual enters a value prohibited by the validation rule.

A Back up

B Cascade options

C Clipboard

D Data validation

E Design view

F Expression Builder

G Field property

H Index

I Input mask

J Multivalued field

K Orphan records

L System tables

M Trust Center

N Validation rule

O Validation text

____ 13. A feature used to create formulas in query criteria, form and report properties, and table validation rules.

____ 14. A field that holds multiple values, such as a list of people to whom you have assigned the same task.

____ 15. A table that is used to keep track of the multiple entries in a field but cannot be viewed or worked with.

Multiple Choice

Circle the correct answer.

1. Opening a database from a location in the Trust Center avoids the appearance of a(n):
   A. security warning   B. error message   C. error warning

2. Which option sends a duplicate version of the selected table to the Clipboard, leaving the original table intact?
   A. Cut   B. Paste   C. Copy

3. To add one or more records from a source table to a destination table is to:
   A. attach records   B. erase records   C. append records

4. The tables in a database can relate to or connect to other tables through common fields because Access databases are:
   A. dynamic   B. relational   C. linked

5. Which option should be used to ensure that orphan records are not left in the database?
   A. Cascade Update   B. Cascade Join   C. Cascade Delete

6. To apply an attribute or characteristic to a field that controls the display and input of data, use:
   A. Field Description   B. Field Properties   C. Data Properties

7. Which data type should be used to enter an expression that will compute the entry displayed?
   A. Expression   B. Calculated   C. Equation

8. Which field property is used to ensure that a field contains data and is not left empty?
   A. Default value   B. Required   C. Validated

9. Which field property is used to display a value in a field for all new records?
   A. Default value   B. Required   C. Validated

10. Which data type should be used to add one or more files to the records in a database?
    A. Document   B. Attachment   C. Add-on

Access | Chapter 4

Content-Based Assessments

Apply **4A** skills from these Objectives:

1. Manage Existing Tables
2. Modify Existing Tables
3. Create and Modify Table Relationships

Skills Review | Project **4C** Industries

Joaquin Alonzo, the City Manager of Westland Plains, has a database of the city's industry information. This database has five tables. The Industries table contains summary information from the other four tables. Each update to an individual industry table would require updates to the summary table. In the following Skills Review, you will redesign the tables, taking advantage of table relationships to avoid entering and storing redundant data. Your completed tables and relationships will look similar to Figure 4.51.

Project Files

For Project 4C, you will need the following file:

a04C_Industries

You will save your files as:

Lastname_Firstname_4C_Industries
Lastname_Firstname_a04C_Industries_2016-10-30 (date will vary)

Project Results

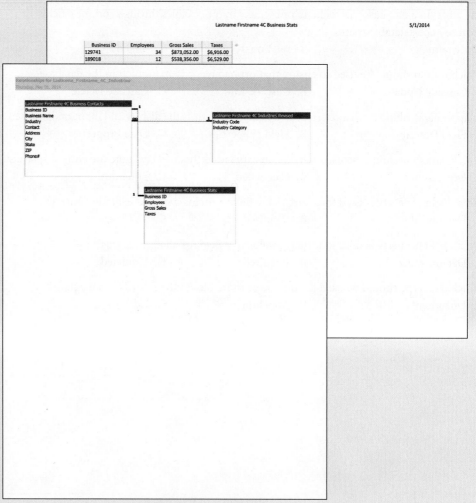

Figure 4.51

(Project 4C Industries continues on the next page)

Content-Based Assessments

1 **Start** Access. Locate and open the **a04C_Industries** file.

a. Display **Backstage** view, click on **Save & Publish**, and then double-click **Back Up Database**. In the **Save As** dialog box, navigate to your Access Chapter 4 folder, and then click **Save** to accept the default name.

b. **Save** the database in your **Access Chapter 4** folder as **Lastname_Firstname_4C_Industries**

2 In the **Navigation Pane**, double-click **4C Industries**. Take a moment to review the contents of the table, and then **Close** the table.

a. On the **Home tab**, in the **Clipboard group**, click the **Copy** button.

b. In the **Clipboard group**, click the **Paste** button.

c. In the displayed **Paste Table As** dialog box, under **Table Name**, type **Lastname Firstname 4C Industries Revised** Under **Paste Options**, be sure that the **Structure and Data** option button is selected, and then click **OK**.

3 Double-click **4C Industries Revised** to open the table in **Datasheet** view. Close the **Navigation Pane**.

a. Point to the **Business #5** field name until the pointer displays. Drag to the left to the **Business #1** field name to select the five fields. On the **Home tab**, in the **Records group**, click the **Delete** button. In the displayed message box, click **Yes** to permanently delete the fields and the data.

b. Switch to **Design** view. To the left of **Industry Code**, click the **row selector** box, and then in the **Tools group**, click the **Primary Key** button. **Close** the table, saving any changes. Open the **Navigation Pane**.

c. Using the technique you just practiced, copy and paste the structure and data of the **4C Airports** table, and then **Save** the pasted table as **Lastname Firstname 4C Business Contacts.**

4 In the Navigation Pane, click **4C High-Tech Manufacturing**.

a. On the **Home tab**, in the **Clipboard group**, click the **Copy** button, and then click the **Paste** button.

b. In the **Paste Table As** dialog box, under **Table Name**, type **Lastname Firstname 4C Business Contacts** Under **Paste Options**, click the **Append Data to Existing Table** option button, and then click **OK**.

c. Using the same procedure, append the **4C Medical Centers** table and the **4C Oil Companies** table to the **Lastname Firstname 4C Business Contacts** table.

5 Repeat the procedure, copying and pasting the structure and data of the **4C Business Contacts** table, and then naming the pasted table **Lastname Firstname 4C Business Stats** One table will contain only contact information, and the other table will contain only statistical information.

6 Open the **4C Business Contacts** table, and then close the **Navigation Pane**.

a. Select the **Employees**, **Gross Sales**, and **Taxes** fields. On the **Home tab**, in the **Records group**, click the **Delete** button. In the displayed message box, click **Yes** to permanently delete the fields and data.

b. Click the **Business Name** field name. On the Ribbon, click the **Fields tab**. In the **Add & Delete group**, click the **Text** button. Type **Industry** to replace **Field1,** and then press Enter. **Save** your work.

c. Open the **Navigation Pane**, and then open the **4C Industries Revised** table. Under **Industry Category**, locate the record for the **Airports**, and notice the **Industry Code** of AIR.

d. On the **tab row**, click the **4C Business Contacts tab** to make the table active. In the **Business ID** of **189018**, in the **Industry** field, type **AIR** Locate the **Business ID** of **675234**, and then in the **Industry Code** field, type **AIR** Locate the **Business ID** of **234155**, and then type **AIR**

e. Using the techniques you just practiced, locate the **Industry** for the **High-Tech Manufacturing, Medical Center,** and **Oil Company** Industry Categories. In Business IDs **258679, 399740, 479728, 927685,** and **966657**, type **HTM** In Business IDs **252479, 295738, 362149,** and **420879**, type **MED** and then in Business IDs **129741, 329718, 420943,** and **462296**, type **OIL**

f. Switch the **4C Business Contacts** table to **Design** view. With the insertion point in the **Business ID** field, in the **Tools group**, click the **Primary Key** button. **Save** the changes.

7 Open the **4C Business Stats** table, and then close the **Navigation Pane**.

a. Select the **Business Name** field, and then press Del. Click **Yes** to delete the field and data. Scroll to the

(Project 4C Industries continues on the next page)

right to display the **Address**, **City**, **State**, **ZIP**, **Contact,** and **Phone#** fields. Select all six fields, and then press ⌈Del⌉ Click **Yes** to delete the fields and data.

b. Switch the **4C Business Stats** table to **Design** view, set the **Business ID** field as the primary key field, and then **Save** the changes. Switch to **Datasheet** view.

c. In the **4C Business Stats** table, click in the **Employees** field in the first record. On the **Home tab**, in the **Find group**, click the **Find** button. In the **Find What** box, type **17** Click **Find Next** to select the next occurrence in the table. Click **Cancel** in the **Find and Replace** dialog box.

d. Click the **Record Selector** box to select the record containing *17*. On the **Home tab**, in the **Records group**, click the **Delete** button. In the displayed message box, click **Yes** to permanently delete the record.

8 Click on the **4C Business Contacts** tab to make it active. Switch to the **Datasheet** view. In the **Search** box in the navigation area at the bottom of the window, type **adv** Click at the end of AdventuCom. Press the ⌈Spacebar⌉ and type **Resources**

a. Switch to **Design** view. To the left of **Contact**, click the **row selector** box. Drag the field up until you see a dark horizontal line between *Industry Code* and *Business Name*, and then release the mouse button. **Save** the changes.

b. Switch to **Datasheet** view. On the **Home tab**, in the **Records group**, click the **Spelling** button. When it selects *Airpot*, **Change** the spelling to *Airport*. Ignore the other names selected. On the **tab row**, right-click any tab, and then click **Close All**.

9 On the Ribbon, click the **Database Tools tab**. In the **Relationships group**, click the **Relationships** button. If the Show Table dialog box does not display, on the **Design tab**, in the **Relationships** group, click the **Show Table** button. From the **Show Table** dialog box, add the **4C Industries Revised**, **4C Business Contacts**, and the **4C Business Stats** tables, and then click **Close**.

a. Expand the field lists to fully display the table name and field names, moving the center table down as necessary. In the **4C Industries Revised** field list, drag the **Industry Code** field to the **4C Business Contacts** field list until the pointer points to **Industry**, and then release the mouse button.

b. In the **Edit Relationships** dialog box, select the **Enforce Referential Integrity**, **Cascade Update Related Fields**, and **Cascade Delete Related Records** check boxes. In the **Edit Relationships** dialog box, click **Create**.

c. In the **4C Business Contacts** field list, drag the **Business ID** field to the **4C Business Stats** field list until the pointer points to **Business ID**, and then release the mouse button.

d. In the displayed **Edit Relationships** dialog box, select the **Enforce Referential Integrity** check box. Click **Create**.

e. On the **Design tab**, in the **Tools group**, click the **Relationship Report** button. If you are instructed to submit this result, create a paper or electronic printout. On the **Close Preview** group of the **Print Preview** tab, click **Close Print Preview**. The report is displayed in **Design** view. Close the relationships report, and then click **Yes** to save the design of Report 1. In the displayed **Save As** dialog box, click **OK** to accept the default report name.

f. Click the **join line** between the **4C Business Contacts** field list and the **4C Business Stats** field list. On the **Design tab**, in the **Tools group**, click the **Edit Relationships** button. In the **Edit Relationships** dialog box, select the **Cascade Update Related Fields** and **Cascade Delete Related Records** check boxes, and then click **OK**. **Close** the Relationships window. **Open** the **Navigation Pane**.

10 Open the **4C Business Contacts** table. Locate the record for **Business ID 927685**. In the **Business ID** field, select **927685**, type **987654** Locate the record for the **Business ID** of **420943**. Click in the record selector box to select the record. On the **Home tab**, in the **Records group**, click the **Delete** button. In the displayed message box, click **Yes**.

11 Open the **4C Business Stats** table to view the changes. For each table, adjust all column widths to view the field names and data. View the table in **Print Preview**, and then change the orientation to **Landscape**. If you are instructed to submit the results, create a paper or electronic printout.

12 **Close** the tables, **Close** the database, and then **Exit** Access.

 You have completed Project 4C ⸻⸻⸻⸻⸻⸻⸻⸻⸻⸻⸻

Content-Based Assessments

4 Create a Table in Design View

5 Change Data Types

6 Create a Lookup Field

7 Set Field Properties

8 Create Data Validation Rules and Validation Text

9 Attach Files to Records

Skills Review | Project **4D** Airport Employees

Joaquin Alonzo, City Manager of Westland Plains, Texas, has created a table to keep track of airport personnel. In the following Skills Review, you will add a table that stores records about the employees and modify the properties and customize the fields in the table. You will add features to the database table that will help to reduce data entry errors and that will make data entry easier. You will add attachments to records. Your completed table will look similar to Figure 4.52.

Project Files

For Project 4D, you will need the following files:

a04D_Airport_Employees
a04D_Service_Award
A new blank Word document

You will save your files as:

Lastname_Firstname_4D_Airport_Employees
Lastname_Firstname_4D_Screens

Project Results

Figure 4.52

(Project 4D Airport Employees continues on the next page)

1 **Start** Access. Locate and open the **a04D_Airport_Employees** file. **Save** the database in your **Access Chapter 4** folder as **Lastname_Firstname_4D_Airport_Employees**

2 Close the **Navigation Pane.** On the Ribbon, click the **Create tab.** In the **Tables group**, click the **Table Design** button to open an empty table in Design view.

a. In the first **Field Name** box, type **Empl ID** and press [Tab]. On the **Design tab** in the **Tools group**, click the **Primary Key** button. Press [Tab] three times to move to the next field.

b. In the second **Field Name** box, type **Vacation** Press [Tab] to move to the **Data Type** box, and click **Number.** Press [Tab] to move to the **Description** box. Type **Indicate how many weeks of vacation the employee receives per year** Press [Tab] or [Enter] to move to the next field.

c. In the third **Field Name** box, type **Coverage** and then press [Tab] twice to move to the **Description** box. Type **Indicate the type of insurance coverage the employee has selected** Press [F6] to move to the **Field Properties** pane at the bottom of the screen. In the **Field Size** box, type **10** to replace the 255.

d. Click in the fourth **Field Name** box, type **401K** Press [Tab], and select a **Yes/No** data type. Press [Tab] to move to the **Description** box. Type **Indicate whether or not the employee participates in the 401K plan**

e. Save the table as **Lastname Firstname 4D Employee Benefits** Switch to **Datasheet** view and enter these records:

Empl ID	Vacation	Coverage	401K
589764	3	Emp	Yes
976458	2	None	No
564897	2	Emp + C	Yes
248311	4	Fam	Yes

If you are instructed to submit this result, create a paper or electronic printout of the **4D Employee Benefits** table. **Close** the table.

3 In the **Navigation Pane**, under **Tables**, rename the **4D Employees** table by adding your **Lastname Firstname** to the beginning of the table name. Double-click **4D Employees** to open the table. Close the **Navigation Pane.**

a. Switch to **Design** view. Change the data type for the **Date Hired** field to **Date/Time.** Change the data type

for the **Annual Salary** field to **Currency.** Change the data type for the **Office E-mail** field to **Hyperlink.** **Save** your work. You will see message boxes warning that some data may be lost. Click **Yes** to continue.

b. In the **Title** field, click in the **Data Type** box, and then click the **arrow.** From the displayed list of data types, click **Lookup Wizard.**

c. In the first **Lookup Wizard** dialog box, click **I will type in the values that I want** option button, and then click **Next.** Be sure the number of columns is **1.** Click in the first row under **Col1**, type **Mr.** and then press [Tab] or [↓] to save the first item. Type the following data: **Mrs.** and **Miss** and **Ms.** and then click **Next.** In the final dialog box, click **Finish.**

d. In the **Position** field, click in the **Data Type** box, and then click the **arrow.** From the displayed list of data types, click **Lookup Wizard.**

e. In the first **Lookup Wizard** dialog box, be sure that **I want the lookup field to get the values from another table or query** is selected. Click **Next.** Select the **4D Positions** table. Click **Next.** Under **Available Fields**, click **Position**, and then click the **Add Field** button to move the field to the **Selected Fields** box. Click **Next.** In the **1** box, click the **arrow**, and then click **Position.** Leave the sort order as **Ascending.** Click **Next** twice to display the final **Lookup Wizard** dialog box. Under **What label would you like for your lookup field?**, leave the default of **Position** and be sure that **Allow Multiple Values** is *not* selected. Click **Finish.** Click **Yes.** If necessary, in the message box, click **Yes** to test the existing data with the new rules.

f. Under **Field Name**, click **Office Phone.** Under **Field Properties**, click in the **Input Mask** box and then click the **Build** button.

g. In the **Input Mask** dialog box, scroll down, click **Phone Number with Extension**, and then click **Next.** Change the placeholder from # to _ and then click **Next.** The next wizard screen enables you to decide how you want to store the data. Be sure that the **Without the symbols in the mask, like this** option button is selected, and then click **Next.** In the final wizard screen, click **Finish.**

h. Click in the **Date Hired** field. Under **Field Properties**, click in the **Format** box, and then click the **Format arrow.** From the displayed list, click **Medium Date.** Click in the **Required** box. Click the

(Project 4D Airport Employees continues on the next page)

Content-Based Assessments

Skills Review | Project **4D** Airport Employees (continued)

Required arrow, and then click **Yes**. Click in the **Monthly Earn** field. Under **Field Properties**, click in the **Expression** box, and edit the expression to read **[Annual Salary]/12** Click the **Format arrow**, and select **Currency** from the displayed list.

i. Under **Field Name**, click **State**. Under **Field Properties**, click in the **Format** box, and then type **>** Click in the **Default Value** box, and then type **tx**

j. Using the same technique, set the **Default Value** of the **City** field to **Westland Plains**

k. Under **Field Name**, click **Last Name**. Under **Field Properties**, click in the **Indexed** property box, and then click the displayed **arrow**. Click **Yes (Duplicates OK)**. **Save** your work. In the message box, click **Yes** to test the existing data with the new rules.

4 On the **Design tab**, in the **Show/Hide group**, click the **Indexes** button. Hold down [Alt], and then press [PrtScr]. Start **Word 2010**. Type your first and last names, and press [Enter]. Type **Project 4D Step 4** and press [Enter]. Press [Ctrl] + [V]. **Save** the document in your **Access Chapter 4** folder as **Lastname_Firstname_4D_Screens**. Leave the Word document open. Return to Access. **Close** Indexes.

5 Under **Field Name**, click **Date Hired**. Under **Field Properties**, click in the **Validation Rule** box, and then click the **Build** button.

a. In the upper box of the **Expression Builder** dialog box, type **<=now( )** and then click OK. Click in the **Validation Text** box, and then type **You cannot enter a date later than today** Hold down [Alt], and then press [PrtScr].

b. In the Word document, press [Enter], and then press [Ctrl] + [Enter] to insert a page break. Type your first and last names, press [Enter], and then type **Project 4D Step 5b** Press [Enter]. Press [Ctrl] + [V] and **Save** the document. If you are instructed to submit this result, create a paper or electronic printout. **Exit** Word.

6 With the **4D Employees** table open in **Design** view, click in the first blank field name box type **Service Award** Press [Tab] to move to the **Data Type** box, and click **Attachment**.

a. Switch to **Datasheet** view, saving changes to the table. In the message box, click **No** to test the existing data with the new rules.

b. In the first record, double-click in the **Attachment** field. In the **Attachments** dialog box, click **Add**. Navigate to the location where the student data files for this textbook are stored, and double-click **a04D_ Service_Award**. Click **OK**.

c. Click the **New (blank) record** button. Type the following data:
Empl ID: **543655**
Title: **Mr.**
First Name: **Mark**
Last Name: **Roberts**
Street: **1320 Woodbriar Ln.**
City: **Westland Plains**
State: **tx**
Postal Code: **79803**
Position: **Finance Director**
Date Hired: **5/09/10**
Salary: **87000**
Office Phone: **(432) 555-0167 X101**
Office E-mail: **mroberts@westlandplains.gov**

d. If you are instructed to submit this result, create a paper or electronic printout of the **4D Employees** table in **Landscape** orientation. This table will print on two pages. **Close 4D Employees**. If you are to submit your work electronically, follow your instructor's directions.

7 Open the **Navigation Pane**. **Close** the **Object Definition** window. **Close** the database, and **Exit** Access.

End **You have completed Project 4D** ——————————————

Content-Based Assessments

Mastering Access | Project **4E** Arts Council

In the following Mastering Access project, you will manage and modify tables and create relationships for the database that contains cultural information about the city of Westland Plains. The database will be used by the arts council. Your completed tables and report will look similar to Figure 4.53.

Project Files

For Project 4E, you will need the following file:

a04E_Arts_Council

You will save your database as:

Lastname_Firstname_4E_Arts_Council

Project Results

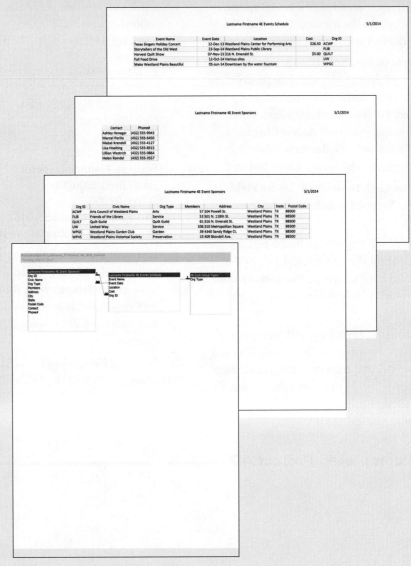

Figure 4.53

(Project 4E Arts Council continues on the next page)

Content-Based Assessments

Mastering Access | Project 4E Arts Council (continued)

1 **Start** Access. Locate and open the **a04E_Arts_ Council** file. **Save** the database in your **Access Chapter 4** folder as **Lastname_Firstname_4E_Arts_Council**

2 Right-click the **4E Cultural Events** table. Select **Copy**, and then in the clear area of the **Navigation Pane**, right-click and select **Paste**. In the **Paste Table As** dialog box, in the **Table Name** box, type **Lastname Firstname 4E Events Schedule** The **Paste Options** should include **Structure and Data**. Click **OK**.

3 Make a second copy of the **4E Cultural Events** table. Name the table **Lastname Firstname 4E Event Sponsors** and paste the **Structure and Data** from the source table.

4 Open the **4E Event Sponsors** table in **Datasheet** view. Select the first four columns beginning with the **Event Name** field through the **Cost** field. Press Del, and then click **Yes** to delete the fields and data. Switch to **Design** view, and then make the **Org ID** field the **Primary Key** field. Switch to **Datasheet** view, saving the changes. If you are instructed to submit this result, create a paper or electronic printout of the **4E Event Sponsors** table in **Landscape** orientation. It will print on two pages. **Close** the table.

5 Open the **4E Events Schedule** table in **Datasheet** view. Close the **Navigation Pane**. Select and delete the following fields: **Civic Name, Org Type, Members, Address, City, State, Postal Code, Contact**, and **Phone#**. **Save** the table.

6 Using **Find**, find **1876** in the **Event Name** field; in the **Match** field, select **Any Part of Field**. Select and delete the record.

7 In the navigation area at the bottom of the window, search for *v* in the records. When it stops at *Harvest Time*

Quilt Show, delete the word **Time** and the space following the word from the Event Name.

8 Switch to **Design** view. Select the **Event Date** field, and drag it up until it is between **Event Name** and **Location**. Release the mouse button. Switch to **Datasheet** view, saving the changes.

9 On the **Home tab**, click **Spelling** in the **Records** group. Make any spelling corrections necessary in the table. If you are instructed to submit this result, create a paper or electronic printout of the **4E Events Schedule** table in **Landscape** orientation. **Close** the table.

10 Create a relationship between the **4E Event Sponsors** and the **4E Events Schedule** tables using **Org ID** as the common field. Select **Enforce Referential Integrity**, **Cascade Update Related Fields**, and **Cascade Delete Related Records**.

11 Create a relationship between the **4E Civic Group Types** table and the **4E Event Sponsors** table using **Org Type** as the common field. Check **Enforce Referential Integrity**, **Cascade Update Related Fields**, and **Cascade Delete Related Records**. Adjust all field lists so that all table names and field names display.

12 Create a **Relationship Report**. Accept the default name for the report. If you are instructed to submit this result, create a paper or electronic printout. **Close** the **Relationships** window.

13 **Close** the database, and **Exit** Access.

End **You have completed Project 4E** ────────────

Apply **4B** skills from these
Objectives:

4 Create a Table in Design View

5 Change Data Types

6 Create a Lookup Field

7 Set Field Properties

8 Create Data Validation Rules and Validation Text

9 Attach Files to Records

Mastering Access | Project **4F** Library Programs

Joaquin Alonzo, City Manager, has asked Ron Singer, Database Manager for the city, to improve the library database. In the following Mastering Access project, you will create a table that stores records about the Westland Plains Library in Design view and then modify the properties and customize the fields in the table. You will add features to the database table that will help to reduce data entry errors and that will make data entry easier. You will add attachments to records. Your completed table will look similar to Figure 4.54.

Project Files

For Project 4F, you will need the following files:

a04F_Library_Programs
a04F_Photo_1.jpg
a04F_Photo_2.jpg
a04F_Photo_3.jpg

You will save your database as:

Lastname_Firstname_4F_Library_Programs

Project Results

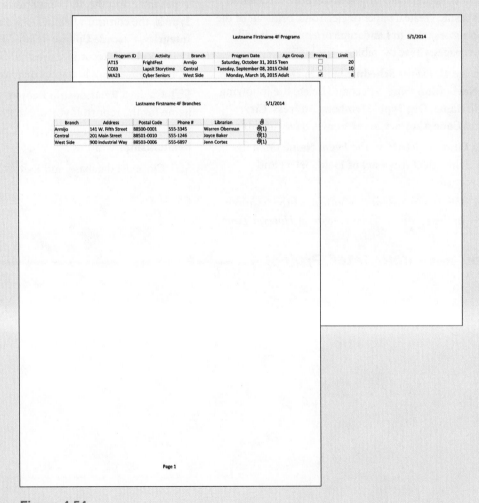

Figure 4.54

(Project 4F Library Programs continues on the next page)

Content-Based Assessments

Mastering Access | Project **4F** Library Programs (continued)

1 **Start** Access. Locate and open the **a04F_Library_ Programs** file. **Save** the database in your **Access Chapter 4** folder as **Lastname_Firstname_4F_Library_Programs** Rename the table by adding your **Lastname Firstname** to the beginning of the table name. Close the **Navigation Pane**.

2 Create a table in **Design** view. In the first **Field Name** box, type **Program ID** and press Tab twice. Make it the Primary Key field. Change the **Field size** to **5** and the format to all caps.

3 In the second **Field Name** box, type **Activity** and press Tab twice. In the **Field Properties**, click the **Indexed down arrow**, and then select **Yes (Duplicates OK)**. Make it a **Required** field.

4 In the third **Field Name** box, type **Branch** and press Tab to move to the **Data Type** box. Select **Lookup Wizard**. Be sure that **I want the lookup field to get the values from another table or query** is selected. Click **Next**. There is only one other table in this database from which to choose—*4F Branches*—and it is selected. Click **Next**. Under **Available Fields**, click **Branch**, and then click the **Add Field** button. Click **Next**. In the **1** box, click the **arrow**, and then click **Branch**. Leave the sort order as **Ascending**. Click **Next** two times. Under **What label would you like for your lookup field?**, accept the default of **Branch**, and then be sure that **Allow Multiple Values** is *not* selected. Click **Finish**.

5 **Save** the table as **Lastname Firstname 4F Programs**

6 In the fourth **Field Name** box, type **Program Date**, and press Tab to move to the **Data Type** box. Select **Date/ Time**. Click in the **Format** box, and select **Long Date**.

7 In the fifth **Field Name** box, type **Age Group** and press Tab twice. In the **Validation Rule** box, type **"Child" OR "Teen" OR "Adult"** For the **Validation Text**, type **Entry must be Child, Teen, or Adult**

8 Click in the sixth **Field Name** box, and type **Prereq** Press Tab to move to the **Data Type** box. Click **Yes/No**. Press Tab to move to the **Description** box, and then type **Click if there is a prerequisite required before enrolling in this activity**

9 Click in the seventh **Field Name** box, type **Limit** and press Tab to move to the **Data Type** box. Click **Number** and change the **Field Size** to **Integer**. In the **Validation Rule** box, type **<=20** In the **Validation Text** box, type **Participation is limited to a maximum of 20**

10 Switch to **Datasheet** view, saving the changes to the design. Populate the table with the data in **Table 1**.

11 Adjust the column widths so all data is visible. **Close** the table, saving the changes.

12 Open the **Navigation Pane**, and then open the **4F Branches** table in **Design** view. Add a **Photo ID** field at the bottom of the field list using an **Attachment** data type.

13 In the **Postal Code** field, under **Input Mask**, click the **Build** button. **Save** the table. From the **Input Mask Wizard**, under **Input Mask**, select **Zip Code**, and then click **Next**. Accept the default "_" as the placeholder character. Click **Next**. Store the data without the symbols in the mask, click **Next**, and then click **Finish**.

14 Switch to **Datasheet** view, saving the changes to the table design. Update the data for each branch.

Branch	Postal Code	Attachment
Armijo	88500-0001	a04F_Photo_1.jpg
Westside	88501-0010	a04F_Photo_2.jpg
Central	88503-0006	a04F_Photo_3.jpg

15 Adjust column widths as needed to display all of the data and field names in each table. **Save** the tables. If you are instructed to submit this result, create a paper or electronic printout of both tables. **Close** the tables.

16 **Close** the database, and **Exit** Access.

Table 1

Program ID	Activity	Branch	Program Date	Age Group	Prereq	Limit
WA23	Cyber Seniors	West Side	3/16/15	Adult	Yes	8
AT15	FrightFest	Armijo	10/31/15	Teen	No	20
CC63	Lapsit Storytime	Central	9/8/15	Child	No	10

--→ (Return to Step 11)

End **You have completed Project 4F**

Content-Based Assessments

Apply 4A and 4B skills
from these Objectives:

■ Manage Existing
   Tables
■ Create and Modify
   Table Relationships
■ Change Data Types
■ Set Field Properties
■ Attach Files to
   Records

Mastering Access | Project 4G Parks and Recreation

Yvonne Guillen is the Chair of the Parks & Recreation Commission for Westland Plains, Texas. The database she is using has separate tables that should be combined. In the following Mastering Access project, you will combine these tables into a facilities table. You will modify the existing tables, set field properties to ensure more accurate data entry, and add driving directions to the facilities as an attached document. Your completed work will look similar to Figure 4.55.

Project Files

For Project 4G, you will need the following files:

> A new blank Word document
> a04G_Parks_and_Recreation.docx
> a04G_Harris_Park.docx
> a04G_Northwest_Rec.docx

You will save your files as:

> Lastname_Firstname_4G_Parks_and_Recreation
> Lastname_Firstname_4G_Screen

Project Results

Figure 4.55

(Project 4G Parks and Recreation continues on the next page)

Mastering Access | Project **4G** Parks and Recreation (continued)

1 **Start** Access. Locate and open the **a04G_Parks_and_Recreation** file. **Save** the database in your **Access Chapter 4** folder as **Lastname_Firstname_4G_Parks_and_Recreation** Rename all tables by adding your **Lastname Firstname** to the beginning of each table name.

2 Select the **4G Community Centers** table. **Copy** and **Paste** the table. Name the table **Lastname Firstname 4G Facilities** In the **Paste Table As** dialog box, be sure the **Structure and Data** option is selected. Click **OK**.

3 Select the **4G Parks** table, click the **Copy** button, and then click **Paste**. In the **Table Name** box, type **Lastname Firstname 4G Facilities** Under **Paste Options**, select **Append Data to Existing Table**, and then click **OK** to create one table that contains all of the facility information for the Parks & Recreation Department.

4 From the **Database Tools tab**, in the **Relationships group**, click **Relationships**. Select the **4G Facilities** and **4G Activities** tables. Create a one-to-many relationship between the **4G Facilities** table **Facility Name** field and the **4G Activities** table **Facility** field. Be sure to check **Enforce Referential Integrity**, **Cascade Update Related Fields**, and **Cascade Delete Related Records**. Adjust the size and position of the field lists so the full table names are visible.

5 Create a **Relationship Report**. If you are instructed to submit this result, create a paper or electronic printout. **Save** the report using the default name. **Close** the report, and then **Close** the Relationships window.

6 Open the **4G Facilities** table in **Design** view. Delete the **Activities** field. This field is no longer needed in this table because the relationship is established.

7 Change the data type for the **Entry Fee** field to **Currency**. In the **Contact** field, change the field size to **20**.

8 Below the **Phone#** field add a new **Directions** field to the table and use a data type of **Attachment**. In the description box, type **How to get there**

9 Add a new **Monthly Pass** field between the **Entry Fee** and **Contacts** fields, and use a data type of **Calculated.** In the **Expression Builder** dialog box, type **[Entry Fee]*15** Change the **Result Type** to **Currency**.

10 Select the **Phone#** field. In the **Input Mask** box, type **!000-0000** Change the field size to **8** Set the **Field Property** of **Required** to **Yes**. Using the Clipboard and Word, submit a printed copy of the **Phone#** Field Properties if you are requested to do so. **Save** the document as **Lastname_Firstname_4G_Screen** Switch to **Datasheet** view. Save your changes. You will see a message box warning that some data may be lost. Click **Yes** to continue. You will also see a message explaining that data integrity rules have changed; click **No** to testing the data with the new rules.

11 In the **Harris Park** record, in the **Attachment** field, double-click, and then from the student data files, attach **a04G_Harris_Park**. Click **OK**.

12 Using the same technique, for the **Northwest Recreational Center**, add the directions that are in the **a04G_Northwest_Rec** file.

13 If you are instructed to submit this result, create a paper or electronic printout of the **4G Activities** table and the **4G Facilities** table. Be sure that all field names and data display.

14 **Close** the tables, **Close** the database, and **Exit** Access.

End **You have completed Project 4G**

Content-Based Assessments

GO! Fix It | Project **4H** Application Tracking

Project Files

For Project 4H, you will need the following file:

a04H_Application_Tracking

You will save your database as:

Lastname_Firstname_4H_Application Tracking

In this project, you will correct table design errors in a database used by the City Manager to track the application and permit process for the citizens of Westland Plains. From the student files that accompany this textbook, open the file a04H_Application_Tracking, and then save the database in your Access Chapter 4 folder as **Lastname_Firstname_4H_Application_Tracking** Rename all tables by adding your Lastname Firstname to the beginning of each table name.

To complete the project, you must find and correct errors in table design. In addition to the errors that you find, you should know:

- There are several spelling mistakes in the Application Types table. Make the necessary corrections.

- In the Applicants table, the order in which the fields are presented is disorganized. Reorder the fields so they display information about the file and the application in an orderly fashion. Add fields to hold the city and state for each applicant. Position the fields in an orderly fashion within the list. The state field should always be represented in all capital letters and allow for only two characters. Do not populate the fields.

- In the Applications table, many fields are not assigned accurate data types. Review the field names and descriptions to make appropriate changes. Change the field size for the Reviewer field to 3.

- Be sure that all applications are reviewed by an authorized reviewer; those are currently ROD, JDD, and NDH.

- All applications must include a submitted date.

- All relationships should be edited to enforce referential integrity and both cascade options.

Create a paper or electronic printout, as directed, of your updated Application Types table, Applicants table design, and relationship report.

End **You have completed Project 4H** ———————————————

Content-Based Assessments

GO! Make It | Project 4I Health Services

Project Files

For Project 4I, you will need the following files:

    a04I_Health_Services

    a04I_Badge

You will save your database as:

    Lastname_Firstname_4I_Health_Services

From the student files that accompany this textbook, open the a04I_Health_Services database file, and then save the database in your Access Chapter 4 folder as **Lastname_Firstname_4I_ Health_Services** Copy the Services table and paste it as **Lastname Firstname 4I Directors Personal** Modify the table design for the new table so the table appears as shown in Figure 4.56. Create a paper or electronic printout as directed.

Project Results

Figure 4.56

End **You have completed Project 4I**

Access | Chapter 4

Content-Based Assessments

GO! Solve It | Project **4J** Fire Department

Project Files

For Project 4J, you will need the following file:

a04J_Fire_Department

You will save your files as:

Lastname_Firstname_4J_Fire_Department

Lastname_Firstname_4J_Fire_Department_2015-10-30 (date will vary)

Samuel Barrero, the Fire Chief for Westland Plains, Texas, realizes that the Fire Department database is not designed efficiently. From the student files that accompany this textbook, open the a04J_Fire_Department database file, and then save the database in your Access Chapter 4 folder as **Lastname_Firstname_4J_Fire_Department** Make a backup copy of the original file before you make any changes.

Mr. Barrero has noticed that the 4J Administration Staff Directory, 4J Aircraft Rescue Staff Directory, and 4J Fire Prevention Staff Directory all contain the same fields. Use the copy and append techniques to create a combined table called **Lastname Firstname 4J Fire Department Directory**

Mr. Barrero sees some data type errors in the directory that need correcting. Change data types to match the data and descriptions, set field sizes, and apply input masks to assist with data entry. Utilize other tables in the database as the information source where possible.

Mr. Barrero also wants to see a relationships report where all relationships enforce referential integrity.

If you are instructed to submit this result, create a paper or electronic printout of your table design and relationship report.

	Performance Level		
	Exemplary: You consistently applied the relevant skills	**Proficient:** You sometimes, but not always, applied the relevant skills	**Developing:** You rarely or never applied the relevant skills
Create backup copy of database	Entire database was backed up correctly with a file name that describes it as a backup.	Database was backed up with no more than two missing elements.	Database was not backed up correctly.
Create 4J Fire Department Directory	Table was created with correct fields and appended records in easy-to-follow format.	Table was created with no more than two missing elements.	Table was created with more than two missing elements.
Edit data types in 4J Fire Department Directory	All data type errors have been corrected, field sizes set, and input masks and lookup fields have been used where possible.	No more than two corrections were missed.	More than two corrections were not made.
Create 4J relationship report	Report was created with correct tables and fields; referential integrity options are all selected.	Report was created with no more than two missing elements.	Report was created with more than two missing elements.

(Performance Elements)

End **You have completed Project 4J**

Content-Based Assessments

GO! Solve It | Project **4K** City Zoo

Project Files

For Project 4K, you will need the following files:

a04K_City_Zoo
a04K_Butterfly.jpg

You will save your database as:

Lastname_Firstname_4K_City_Zoo

Amanda Hartigan, Deputy City Manager for the Quality of Life Division of Westland Plains, Texas, and City Manager Joaquin Alonzo are meeting with the Mayor, Bill J. Aycock, to discuss the funding for the city zoo. The Corporate and Foundation Council provides citizens and corporations with a partnering opportunity to support the city zoo. Amanda has outlined a database to organize the sponsorships.

From the student files that accompany this textbook, open the a04K_City_Zoo database file, and then save the database in your Access Chapter 4 folder as **Lastname_Firstname_4K_City_Zoo**

In this project, you will open the a04K_City_Zoo database and examine the tables. Rename the tables by adding your **Lastname Firstname** to the beginning of each table name. Modify the 4K Sponsored Events table to eliminate redundancy between it and the 4K Sponsors table. Also, change data types and adjust field sizes to match the data. In the 4K Sponsors table, create data validation for sponsor type; it must be Individual, Family, or Corporate. In the 4K Sponsors table, use the 4K Sponsor Levels table as a lookup field. Apply an input mask to the Phone# field. To the 4K Sponsor Levels table, add **Logo** as an attachment field. Add the a04K_Butterfly file from the student data files to the appropriate record. Create a relationship between the 4K Sponsors table and the 4K Sponsored Events table, enforcing referential integrity. Create a relationship report. If you are instructed to submit this result, create a paper or electronic printout of the tables, and the relationship report.

	Performance Level		
	Exemplary: You consistently applied the relevant skills	**Proficient:** You sometimes, but not always, applied the relevant skills	**Developing:** You rarely or never applied the relevant skills
Modify the 4K Sponsored Events table to eliminate redundancy	Table was modified with correct fields in easy-to-follow format.	Table was modified with no more than two missing elements.	Table was modified with more than two missing elements.
Change data types and field properties in the 4K Sponsors table	Data types and field properties were assigned effectively for the data that each field will hold.	Data types and field properties were assigned with no more than two missing or incorrect elements.	Data types and field properties were assigned with more than two missing or incorrect elements.
Add field to 4K Sponsor Levels and populate field	Field was added with correct data type and correct data was added to the table.	Field was added with no more than two missing or incorrect elements.	Field was added with more than two missing or incorrect elements.
Create relationships and relationship report	Report was created with correct tables and fields; referential integrity options are all selected.	Report was created with no more than two missing elements.	Report was created with more than two missing elements.

Performance Elements

End **You have completed Project 4K** —————

Outcomes-Based Assessments

Rubric

The following outcomes-based assessments are *open-ended assessments*. That is, there is no specific correct result; your result will depend on your approach to the information provided. Make *Professional Quality* your goal. Use the following scoring rubric to guide you in *how* to approach the problem and then to evaluate *how well* your approach solves the problem.

The *criteria*—Software Mastery, Content, Format and Layout, and Process—represent the knowledge and skills you have gained that you can apply to solving the problem. The *levels of performance*—Professional Quality, Approaching Professional Quality, or Needs Quality Improvements—help you and your instructor evaluate your result

	Your completed project is of Professional Quality if you:	Your completed project is Approaching Professional Quality if you:	Your completed project Needs Quality Improvements if you:
1-Software Mastery	Choose and apply the most appropriate skills, tools, and features and identify efficient methods to solve the problem.	Choose and apply some appropriate skills, tools, and features, but not in the most efficient manner.	Choose inappropriate skills, tools, or features, or are inefficient in solving the problem.
2-Content	Construct a solution that is clear and well organized, contains content that is accurate, appropriate to the audience and purpose, and is complete. Provide a solution that contains no errors in spelling, grammar, or style.	Construct a solution in which some components are unclear, poorly organized, inconsistent, or incomplete. Misjudge the needs of the audience. Have some errors in spelling, grammar, or style, but the errors do not detract from comprehension.	Construct a solution that is unclear, incomplete, or poorly organized; contains some inaccurate or inappropriate content; and contains many errors in spelling, grammar, or style. Do not solve the problem.
3-Format and Layout	Format and arrange all elements to communicate information and ideas, clarify function, illustrate relationships, and indicate relative importance.	Apply appropriate format and layout features to some elements, but not others. Overuse features, causing minor distraction.	Apply format and layout that does not communicate information or ideas clearly. Do not use format and layout features to clarify function, illustrate relationships, or indicate relative importance. Use available features excessively, causing distraction.
4-Process	Use an organized approach that integrates planning, development, self-assessment, revision, and reflection.	Demonstrate an organized approach in some areas, but not others; or, use an insufficient process of organization throughout.	Do not use an organized approach to solve the problem.

Outcomes-Based Assessments

Apply a combination of the **4A** and **4B** skills.

GO! Think | Project **4L** Street Repairs

Project Files

For Project 4L, you will need the following files:

a04L_Street_Repairs
a04L_Request_Form.docx

You will save your database as:

Lastname_Firstname_4L_Street_Repairs

In this project, you will examine the database that has been created to help the Deputy City Manager of Infrastructure Services organize and track the constituent work requests for the city street repairs. Rename all of the tables by adding your **Lastname Firstname** to the beginning of each table name. Modify the design of the 4L Work Requests table. Set the Work Order # field as the primary key field, and then create an input mask to match the data for that field in the first record. For the Type field, create a lookup table using the 4L Repair Types table. In the Repair Team field, create a Lookup Wizard data type using the 4L Repair Teams table. In the Priority field, set the Required property to Yes, and then create a validation rule requiring an entry of 1, 2, or 3. Explain this rule with appropriate validation text. Open a04L_Request_Form, and then use the data to add information to the first record in the table. Use today's date as the start date. Add an attachment field to the table, and then add a04L_Request_Form as the attachment. Save the database as **Lastname_Firstname_4L_Street_Repairs** If you are instructed to submit this result, create a paper or electronic printout of the 4L Work Requests table.

 You have completed Project 4L —————————————————

Apply a combination of the **4A** and **4B** skills.

GO! Think | Project **4M** Police Department

Project Files

For Project 4M, you will need the following file:

a04M_Police_Department

You will save your files as:

Lastname_Firstname_4M_Police_Department
Lastname_Firstname_4M_Police_Department_2015_05_01 (your date will vary)

The City Manager of Westland Plains City, Texas, Joaquin Alonzo, is the governing official over the police department. He has reviewed the database that contains the information about the force and the individual officers. In this project, you will update the database to be more efficient. Before you begin this project, back up the original database. The database contains one table of many fields. Your job is to separate the table into two smaller tables that can be related—personal and professional information joined by the Badge ID. The first and last name fields should appear only in the 4M Police Force Professional table.

Change the field sizes and set data types as appropriate. Create validation rules, and then select field properties that will decrease the number of data entry errors. Enter your own information as the first record in each table. All Badge IDs will follow the same format as yours: **WP-321** You may choose a Regional Command from the following: Central, Northeast, Southside, or Westside. Choices for Precinct include First, Second, Third, or Fourth. The rank must be Commander, Sergeant, or Lieutenant. You were hired the second Monday of last month. Save the modified database as **Lastname_Firstname_4M_Police_Department** If you are instructed to submit this result, create a paper or electronic printout of the tables and the relationship report.

 You have completed Project 4M —————————————————

Access | Chapter 4

Outcomes-Based Assessments

Apply a combination of the 4A and 4B skills.

You and GO! | Project **4N** Club Directory

Project Files

For Project 4N, you will need the following file:

New blank Database

You will save your database as:

Lastname_Firstname_4N_Club_Directory

Create a database that stores information about a club or group with which you are involved. It might be through your school, community, or employer. Name the database **Lastname_Firstname_4N_Club_Directory** The database should include two related tables. The 4N Activities table will list the activities your organization has planned for the rest of the school year, and the 4N Directory table will be a directory of the members of the group.

The 4N Activities table should include the activity name, date, cost, location, and attached directions to each event. Be sure to assign a primary key, choose correct data types, and apply field properties for effective management of data. The 4N Directory table should include each member's name, address, phone number, e-mail, and an activity that they are planning. Be sure to assign a primary key, choose correct data types, and apply field properties for effective management of data. Every member should be planning one event. You should include at least five data types across the two tables. Enter at least six records in the 4N Activities table and twelve in the 4N Directory table. Establish a relationship between the two tables enforcing referential integrity. Create a backup copy of this database. If you are instructed to submit this result, create a paper or electronic printout of the tables and the relationship report.

You will be using this database in future chapters. Be sure to make corrections to your tables as necessary to prepare for the next chapter.

 You have completed Project 4N ——————————————————

Enhancing Queries

OUTCOMES

At the end of this chapter you will be able to:

PROJECT 5A
Create special-purpose queries.

PROJECT 5B
Create action queries and modify join types.

OBJECTIVES

Mastering these objectives will enable you to:

1. Create Calculated Fields in a Query (p.325)
2. Use Aggregate Functions in a Query (p.331)
3. Create a Crosstab Query (p.335)
4. Find Duplicate and Unmatched Records (p.339)
5. Create a Parameter Query (p.342)

6. Create a Make Table Query (p.347)
7. Create an Append Query (p.350)
8. Create a Delete Query (p.355)
9. Create an Update Query (p.358)
10. Modify the Join Type (p.361)

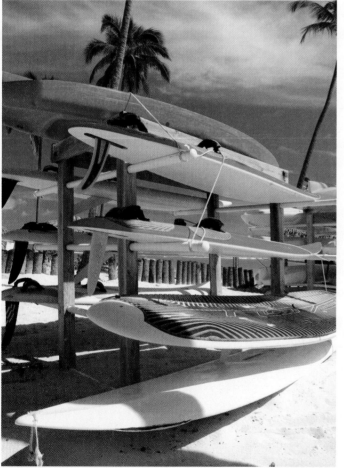

Nikolay Okhitin/Shutterstock

In This Chapter

Queries can do more than extract data from tables and other queries. You can create queries to perform special functions, such as calculate numeric fields and summarize numeric data. Queries can also be used to find duplicate and unmatched records in tables, which is useful for maintaining data integrity. If you want more flexibility in the data that the query extracts from underlying tables, you can create a parameter query, where an individual is prompted for the criteria. Queries can create additional tables in the database, append records to an existing table, delete records from a table, and modify data in a table. This is useful when you do not want to directly modify the data in the tables.

College classmates Mary Connolly and J.D. Golden grew up in the sun of Orange County, California, but they also spent time in the mountain snow. After graduating with business degrees, they combined their business expertise and their favorite sports to open **4Ever Boarding**, a snowboard and surf shop. The store carries top brands of men's and women's apparel, goggles and sunglasses, and boards and gear. The surfboard selection includes both classic boards and the latest high-tech boards. Snowboarding gear can be purchased in packages or customized for the most experienced boarders. Connolly and Golden are proud to count many of Southern California's extreme sports games participants among their customers.

Project 5A Inventory

Project Activities

In Activities 5.01 through 5.10, you will help Ally Mason, Purchasing Manager of 4Ever Boarding Surf and Snowboard Shop, create special-purpose queries to calculate data, summarize and group data, display data in a spreadsheet-like format, and find duplicate and unmatched records. You will also create a query that prompts individuals to enter the criteria. Your completed queries will look similar to Figure 5.1.

Project Files

For Project 5A, you will need the following file:

> a05A_Inventory

You will save your database as:

> Lastname_Firstname_5A_Inventory

Project Results

Figure 5.1
Project 5A Inventory

Objective 1 | Create Calculated Fields in a Query

Queries can be used to create a *calculated field*—a field that obtains its data by performing a calculation or computation, using a formula. For example, to determine the profit that will be made from the sale of an item, subtract the cost of the item from the sale price of the item. Another example is to create a calculated field that computes the gross pay for an employee. There are two steps needed to produce a calculated field in a query. First, in the design grid of the query, in a blank column, type the name of the field that will store the results of the calculated field—the name must be followed by a colon (:). Second, type the *expression*—the formula—that will perform the calculation. *Each field name* used in the expression must be enclosed within *its own pair* of square brackets, []. If you are using a number in the expression—for example, a percentage—type only the percentage; do not enclose it in brackets.

Activity 5.01 | Creating a Calculated Field Based on Two Existing Fields

In this activity, you will create a calculated field to determine the profit for each item in the inventory database.

1 **Start** Access. Navigate to the location where the student data files for this textbook are saved. Locate and open the **a05A_Inventory** file. Display **Backstage** view, and click **Save Database As**. In the **Save As** dialog box, navigate to the drive on which you will be saving your folders and projects for this chapter. Create a new folder named **Access Chapter 5** and then save the file as **Lastname_Firstname_5A_Inventory** in the folder.

2 If necessary, enable the content or add the Access Chapter 5 folder to the Trust Center. In the **Navigation Pane**, rename each table by adding **Lastname Firstname** to the beginning of each table name.

3 In the **Navigation Pane**, double-click **5A Inventory**. If the Field List pane opens, close it. Take a moment to study the fields in the table.

Snowboarding items have a catalog number beginning with *8*; surfing items have a catalog number beginning with *9*. The *Category* field is a Lookup column. If you click in the Category field, and then click the arrow, a list of category numbers and their descriptions display. The *Supplier* field identifies the supplier numbers with descriptions. *Cost* is the price the company pays to a supplier for each item. *Selling Price* is what the company will charge its customers for each item. *On Hand* refers to the current inventory for each item.

4 Switch to **Design** view, and then take a moment to study the data structure. Notice the Category field has a data type of Number; this reflects the autonumber field (ID field) in the Category table used in the Lookup field. When you are finished, **Close** ☒ the table, and then **Close** ☒ the **Navigation Pane**.

5 On the Ribbon, click the **Create tab**. In the **Queries group**, click the **Query Design** button. In the **Show Table** dialog box, double-click **5A Inventory** to add the table to the Query design workspace, and then click **Close**. Expand the list so the table name and all fields are visible.

If you add the wrong table to the workspace or have two copies of the same table, right-click the extra table, and click Remove Table.

6 From the **5A Inventory** field list, add the following fields, in the order specified, to the design grid: **Catalog#**, **Item**, **Cost**, and **Selling Price**. Recall that you can double-click a field name to add it to the design grid, or you can drag the field name to the field box on the design grid. You can also click in the field box, click the arrow, and click the field name from the displayed list.

7 On the **Design tab**, in the **Results group**, click the **Run** button to display the four fields used in the query, and then compare your screen with Figure 5.2.

Figure 5.2

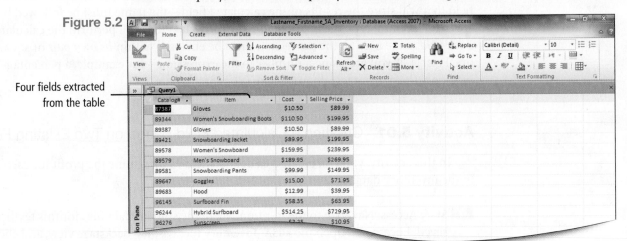

Four fields extracted from the table

8 Switch to **Design** view. In the **Field row**, right-click in the field cell in the first empty column—the fifth column—to display a shortcut menu, and then click **Zoom**. *Arithmetic operators* are mathematical symbols used to build expressions in calculated fields. Take a moment to study the arithmetic operators as described in Figure 5.3.

The Zoom dialog box gives you working space so that you can see the expression—formula—as you enter it. The expression can also be entered directly in the empty Field box.

Operator	Description	Example	Result
+	Addition	Cost:[Price]+[Tax]	Adds the value in the Price field to the value in the Tax field and displays the result in the Cost field.
−	Subtraction	Cost:[Price]– [Markdown]	Subtracts the value in the Markdown field from the value in the Price field and displays the result in the Cost field.
*	Multiplication	Tax:[Price]*.05	Multiplies the value in the Price field by .05 (5%) and displays the result in the Tax field. (Note: This is an asterisk, not an *x*.)
/	Division	Average:[Total]/3	Divides the value in the Total field by 3 and displays the result in the Average field.
∧	Exponentiation	Required:2∧[Bits]	Raises 2 to the power of the value in the Bits field and stores the result in the Required field.
\	Integer division	Average:[Children]\ [Families]	Divides the value in the Children field by the value in the Families field and displays the integer portion—the digits to the left of the decimal point—in the Average field.

Figure 5.3

9 In the **Zoom** dialog box, type **Profit Per Item:[Selling Price]-[Cost]** and then compare your screen with Figure 5.4.

> The first element of the calculated field—*Profit Per Item*—is the new field name that will display the calculated value. The field name must be unique for the table being used in the query. Following the new field name is a colon (:). A colon in a calculated field separates the new field name from the expression. *Selling Price* is enclosed in square brackets because it is an existing field name from the *5A Inventory* table and contains data that will be used in the calculation. Following *[Selling Price]* is a hyphen (-), which, in math calculations, signifies subtraction. Finally, *Cost*, an existing field in the *5A Inventory* table, is enclosed in square brackets. This field also contains data that will be used in the calculation.

Figure 5.4

New field name followed by a colon (:)

Existing field names

Note | Using Square Brackets Around Field Names in Expressions

Square brackets are not required around a field name in an expression if the field name is only one word. For example, if the field name is *Cost*, it is not necessary to type brackets around it—Access will automatically insert the square brackets. If a field name has a space in it, however, you must type the square brackets around the field name. Otherwise, Access will display a message stating that the expression you entered contains invalid syntax.

---

10 In the **Zoom** dialog box, click **OK**, and then **Run** the query. Compare your screen with Figure 5.5.

> A fifth column—the calculated field—with a field name of *Profit Per Item* displays. For each record, the value in the *Profit Per Item* field is calculated by subtracting the value in the *Cost* field from the value in the *Selling Price* field.

Figure 5.5

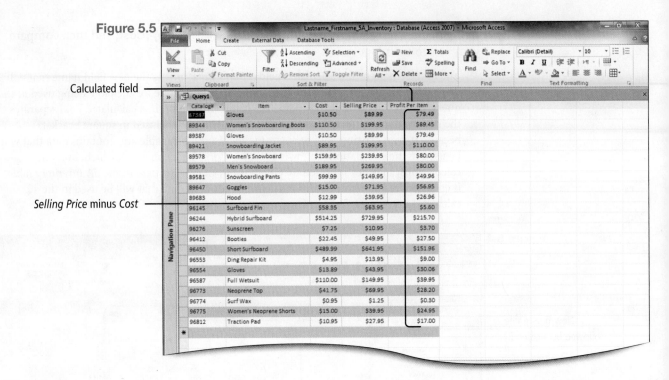

Calculated field

Selling Price minus Cost

Alert! | Does your screen differ?

If a calculation in a query does not work, carefully check the expression you typed. Common errors include spelling or spacing the existing field name incorrectly, not enclosing each existing field name in square brackets, using an existing field name from a table that is not included in the Query workspace, enclosing numbers in square brackets, and forgetting to type the colon after the new field name.

11 Adjust the column width of the *Profit Per Item* field. On the **tab row**, right-click the **Query1 tab**, and then click **Save**. In the **Save As** dialog box, under **Query Name**, type **Lastname Firstname 5A Profit Per Item** and then click **OK**. View the query in **Print Preview**, ensuring that the query prints on one page; if you are instructed to submit this result, create a paper or electronic printout. **Close** ✕ the query.

Activity 5.02 | Creating a Calculated Field Based on One Existing Field and a Number

In this activity, you will calculate the sale prices of each snowboarding item for the annual sale. During this event, all snowboarding supplies are discounted by 20 percent.

1 On the Ribbon, click the **Create tab**. In the **Queries group**, click the **Query Design** button. Add the **5A Inventory** table to the Query design workspace, and then **Close** the **Show Table** dialog box. Expand the field list.

2 From the **5A Inventory** field list, add the following fields, in the order specified, to the design grid: **Catalog#**, **Item**, and **Selling Price**.

3 In the **Field row**, right-click in the field cell in the first empty column—the fourth column—to display a shortcut menu, and then click **Zoom**. In the **Zoom** dialog box, type **Discount:[Selling Price]*.20** and then compare your screen with Figure 5.6.

The value in the *Discount* field is calculated by multiplying the value in the *Selling Price* field by .20—20%. Recall that only field names are enclosed in square brackets.

Figure 5.6

Field name followed by colon (:)

Existing field name in square brackets

20%

4 In the **Zoom** dialog box, click **OK**, and then **Run** the query.

The *Discount* field displays the results of the calculation. The data is not formatted with a dollar sign, and the first record displays a discount of 17.998. When using a number in an expression, the values in the calculated field may not be formatted the same as in the existing field.

5 Switch to **Design** view. On the **Design tab**, in the **Show/Hide group**, click the **Table Names** button.

In the design grid, the Table row no longer displays. If all of the fields in the design grid are from one table, you can hide the Table row. The Table Names button is a toggle button; if you click it again, the Table row displays in the design grid.

6 In the **Field row**, click in the **Discount** field box. On the **Design tab**, in the **Show/Hide group**, click the **Property Sheet** button. Alternatively, right-click in the field box and click Properties, or hold down [Alt] and press [Enter].

The Property Sheet for the selected field—*Discount*—displays on the right side of the screen. In the Property Sheet, under the title of *Property Sheet*, is the subtitle—*Selection type: Field Properties*.

Alert! | Does the Property Sheet Display a Subtitle of Selection Type: Query Properties?

To display the Property Sheet for a field, you must first click in the field; otherwise, the Property Sheet for the query might display. If this occurs, in the Field row, click the Discount field box to change the Property Sheet to this field.

---

7 In the **Property Sheet**, on the **General tab**, click in the **Format** box, and then click the displayed **arrow**. Compare your screen with Figure 5.7.

Figure 5.7

Title bar

Property Sheet for
the Discount field

List of possible formats

Format arrow

8 In the list of formats, click **Currency**. On the **Property Sheet** title bar, click the **Close** button. **Run** the query to display the results.

The values in the Discount field now display with a dollar sign, and the first record's discount—$18.00—displays with two decimal places.

9 Switch to **Design** view. In the **Field row**, right-click in the first empty column, and then click **Zoom**. In the **Zoom** dialog box, type **Sale Price:[Selling Price]-[Discount]** and then click **OK**. **Run** the query to display the results.

The *Sale Price* for Catalog #8737, Gloves, is *$71.99.* The value in the *Sale Price* field is calculated by subtracting the value in the *Discount* field from the value in the *Selling Price* field. The field names are not case sensitive—you can type a field name in lower case, such as *[selling price].* Because you used only existing fields in the expression that were formatted as currency, the values in the *Sale Price* field are formatted as currency.

10 Switch to **Design** view. In the design grid, under **Catalog#**, click in the **Criteria** box, type **8*** and then press Enter.

Recall that the asterisk (*) is a wildcard. In this criteria, Access will extract those records where the catalog number begins with *8* followed by one or more characters. Also, recall that Access formats the criteria. For example, you typed *8*,* and Access formatted the criteria as *Like "8*".*

11 **Run** the query. Notice that only the records with a **Catalog#** beginning with an **8** display—snowboarding items.

12 **Save** the query as **Lastname Firstname 5A Snowboarding Sale** View the query in **Print Preview**, ensuring that the query prints on one page. If you are instructed to submit this result, create a paper or electronic printout. **Close** the query.

Objective 2 | Use Aggregate Functions in a Query

In Access queries, you can use *aggregate functions* to perform a calculation on a column of data and return a single value. Examples are the Sum function, which adds a column of numbers, and the Average function, which adds a column of numbers, ignoring null values, and divides by the number of records with values. Access provides two ways to use aggregate functions in a query—you can add a total row in Datasheet view or create a totals query in Design view.

Activity 5.03 | Adding a Total Row to a Query

In this activity, you will create and run a query. In Datasheet view, you will add a Total row to insert an aggregate function in one or more columns without having to change the design of the query.

1 Create a new query in **Query Design**. Add the **5A Inventory** table to the Query design workspace, and then **Close** the **Show Table** dialog box. Expand the field list. From the **5A Inventory** field list, add the following fields, in the order specified, to the design grid: **Catalog#**, **Item**, **Cost**, and **On Hand**.

2 In the **Field row**, right-click in the first empty column, and then click **Zoom**. In the **Zoom** dialog box, type **Total Cost On Hand:[Cost]*[On Hand]**

> The value in the *Total Cost On Hand* field is calculated by multiplying the value in the *Cost* field by the value in the *On Hand* field. This field will display the cost of all of the inventory items, not just the cost per item.

3 In the **Zoom** dialog box, click **OK**, and then **Run** the query to display the results in Datasheet view. Adjust the column width of the newly calculated field to display the entire field name, and then compare your screen with Figure 5.8.

> If the *Total Cost On Hand* for Catalog #8937, Gloves, is not *$525.00*, switch to **Design** view and edit the expression you entered for the calculated field.

Figure 5.8

New field name

Result of Cost*On Hand

4 On the **Home tab**, in the **Records group**, click the **Totals** button. If necessary, scroll down until the newly created Total row displays. In the **Total row**, under **Total Cost On Hand**, click in the empty box to display an arrow at the left edge. Click the **arrow**, and then compare your screen with Figure 5.9. Take a moment to study the aggregate functions that can be used with both the Total row and the design grid as described in the table in Figure 5.10.

> The Total row displays after the New record row. The first field in a Total row contains the word *Total*. The Total row is not a record. The list of aggregate functions displayed will vary depending on the data type for each field or column; for example, number types display a full list of functions, whereas a text field will display only the *Count* function.

Figure 5.9

Totals button—
a toggle button

List of aggregate
functions that can be
used with this field

Record navigator bar
displays Totals

Total row

Function	Description	Can Be Used with Data Type(s)
Sum	Adds the values in a column.	Currency, Decimal, Number
Average	Calculates the average value for a column, *ignoring null values.*	Currency, Date/Time, Decimal, Number
Count	Counts the number of items in a column, *ignoring null values.*	All data types, except complex repeating scalar data, such as a column of multivalued lists
Maximum	Displays the item with the highest value. Can be used with text data only in Design view. With text data, the highest value is *Z*. Case and null values are ignored.	Currency, Date/Time, Decimal, Number, Text
Minimum	Displays the item with the lowest value. Can be used with text data only in Design view. For text data, the lowest value is *A*. Case and null values are ignored.	Currency, Date/Time, Decimal, Number, Text
Standard Deviation	Measures how widely values are dispersed from the mean value.	Currency, Decimal, Number
Variance	Measures the statistical variance of all values in the column. If the table has less than two rows, a null value is displayed.	Currency, Decimal, Number

Figure 5.10

5 From the displayed list, click **Sum**, and then compare your screen with Figure 5.11.

A sum of $65,919.00 displays, which is the total of all the data in the Total Cost On Hand field.

Figure 5.11

Summed column

Total row

Note | Applying Aggregate Functions to Multiple Fields

You can apply aggregate functions to more than one field by clicking in the Total row for the field, clicking the arrow, and then clicking the function. The functions for multiple fields can be different functions.

---

6 Save 🖫 the query as **Lastname Firstname 5A Total Cost of Inventory** View the query in **Print Preview**, ensuring that the query prints on one page; if you are instructed to submit this result, create a paper or electronic printout. **Close** the query.

More Knowledge | Removing the Aggregate Function and Removing the Total Row

To remove an aggregate function from a column, on the Total row under the field, click the arrow and then click None. To remove the Total row, on the Home tab, in the Records group, click the Totals button. You cannot cut or delete a Total row; you can only turn it on or off. You can copy a Total row and paste it into another file—for example, an Excel worksheet or a Word document.

Activity 5.04 | Creating a Totals Query

In this activity, you will create a *totals query*—a query that calculates subtotals across groups of records. For example, to subtotal the number of inventory items by suppliers, use a totals query to group the records by the supplier and then apply an aggregate function to the On Hand field. In the previous activity, you created a Total row, which applied an aggregate function to one column—field—of data. A totals query is used when you need to apply an aggregate function to some or all of the records in a query. A totals query can then be used as a source for another database object, such as a report.

1 Create a new query in **Query Design**. Add the **5A Suppliers** table and the **5A Inventory** table to the Query design workspace, and then **Close** the **Show Table** dialog box. Expand both field lists. Notice that there is a one-to-many relationship between the tables—*one* supplier can supply *many* items. From the **5A Inventory** field list, add **On Hand** to the first field box in the design grid.

2 On the **Design tab**, in the **Show/Hide group**, click the **Totals** button.

Like the Totals button on the Home tab, this button is a toggle button. In the design grid, a Total row displays under the Table row; and *Group By* displays in the box.

3 In the design grid, in the **Total row**, under **On Hand**, click in the box displaying *Group By* to display the arrow. Click the **arrow**, and then compare your screen with Figure 5.12.

A list of aggregate functions displays. This list displays more functions than the list in Datasheet view, and the function names are abbreviated.

Figure 5.12

Toggle button

Total row

List of aggregate functions

4 From the displayed list, click **Sum**. **Run** the query, and then compare your screen with Figure 5.13.

When you run a totals query, the result—*1160*—of the aggregate function is displayed; the records are not displayed. The name of the function and the field used are displayed in the column heading.

More Knowledge | Changing the Name of the Totals Query Result

To change the name from the combination aggregate function and field name to something more concise and descriptive, in Design view, in the Field row, click in the On Hand field box. On the Design tab, in the Show/Hide group, click the Property Sheet button. In the Property Sheet, on the General tab, click in the Caption box, and type the new name for the result.

Figure 5.13

Field name displays the function used—Sum

Only the sum is displayed in the totals query

5 Adjust the width of the column to display the entire field name, and then switch to **Design** view. In the **5A Inventory** field list, double-click **Item** to insert the field in the second column in the design grid. In the design grid, under **Item**, click in the **Total row** box, click the displayed **arrow**, and then click **Count**. **Run** the query. Adjust the width of the second column to display the entire field name.

> The number of records—*21*—displays. You can include multiple fields in a totals query, but each field in the query must have an aggregate function applied to it. If you include a field but do not apply an aggregate function, the query results will display every record and will not display a single value for the field or fields. The exception to this is when you group records by a category, such as supplier name.

6 Switch to **Design** view. From the **5A Suppliers** field list, drag **Company** to the design grid until the field is on top of **On Hand**.

> *Company* is inserted as the first field, and the *On Hand* field moves to the right. In the *Total* row under *Company*, *Group By* displays.

7 **Run** the query. If necessary, adjust column widths to display all of the field names and all of the data under each field, and then compare your screen with Figure 5.14.

> The results display the total number of inventory items on hand from each supplier and the number of individual items purchased from each supplier. By using this type of query, you can identify the supplier that provides the most individual items—Wetsuit Country— and the supplier from whom the company has the most on-hand inventory items—Dave's Sporting Shop.

Figure 5.14

Summed On Hand field for each Supplier

Number of inventory items for each Supplier

8 **Save** the query as **Lastname Firstname 5A Total On Hand By Supplier** View the query in **Print Preview**, ensuring that the query prints on one page. If you are instructed to submit this result, create a paper or electronic printout. **Close** the query.

Objective 3 | Create a Crosstab Query

A *crosstab query* uses an aggregate function for data that is grouped by two types of information and displays the data in a compact, spreadsheet-like format. A crosstab query always has at least one row heading, one column heading, and one summary field. Use a crosstab query to summarize a large amount of data in a small space that is easy to read.

Activity 5.05 | Creating a Select Query as the Source for the Crosstab Query

In this activity, you will create a select query displaying suppliers, the category of the inventory item, the inventory item, and the cost per item paid to the supplier. Recall that a select query is the most common type of query, and it extracts data from one or more tables or queries, displaying the results in a datasheet. After creating the select query, you will use it to create a crosstab query to display the data in a format that is easier to analyze. Because most crosstab queries extract data from more than one table or query, it is best to create a select query containing all of the fields necessary for the crosstab query.

1 Create a new query in **Query Design**. Add the following tables, in the order specified, to the Query design workspace: **5A Category**, **5A Inventory**, and **5A Suppliers**. In the **Show Table** dialog box, click **Close**. Expand the field lists.

2 In the **5A Suppliers** field list, double-click **Company** to add it to the first field box in the design grid. In the **5A Category** field list, double-click **CatName** to add it to the second field box in the design grid. In the **5A Inventory** field list, double-click **Cost** to add it to the third field box in the design grid. In the design grid, under **Company**, click in the **Sort** box. Click the **arrow**, and then click **Ascending**. Sort the **CatName** field in **Ascending** order.

3 On the **Design tab**, in the **Show/Hide group**, click the **Totals** button. In the design grid, notice a **Total row** displays under the **Table row**. Under **Cost**, click in the **Total** box, click the **arrow**, and then click **Sum**. Compare your screen with Figure 5.15.

Figure 5.15

Three fields added to design grid

First two fields sorted

Aggregate function—sums Cost field

4 **Run** the query. In the datasheet, adjust all column widths to display the entire field name and the data for each record, and then compare your screen with Figure 5.16.

The select query groups the totals vertically by company and then by category.

Figure 5.16

Sum of cost per item
sold by the company
within the category

Grouped first
by company

Grouped second
by category

5 Switch to **Design** view. On the **Design tab**, in the **Show/Hide group**, click the **Totals** button to remove the **Total row** from the design grid.

This select query will be used to create the crosstab query. When you create a crosstab query, you will be prompted to use an aggregate function on a field, so it should not be summed prior to creating the query.

6 **Save** the query as **Lastname Firstname 5A Cost Per Company and Category** and then **Close** the query.

Activity 5.06 | Creating a Crosstab Query

In this activity, you will create a crosstab query using the 5A Cost Per Company and Category query as the source for the crosstab query.

1 On the Ribbon, click the **Create tab**. In the **Queries group**, click the **Query Wizard** button. In the **New Query** dialog box, click **Crosstab Query Wizard**, and then click **OK**.

In the first Crosstab Query Wizard dialog box, you select the table or query to be used as the source for the crosstab query.

2 In the middle of the dialog box, under **View**, click the **Queries** option button. In the list of queries, click **Query: 5A Cost Per Company and Category**, and then click **Next**.

In the second Crosstab Query Wizard dialog box, you select the fields with data that you want to use as the row headings.

3 Under **Available Fields**, double-click **Company**, and then compare your screen with Figure 5.17.

Company displays under Selected Fields. At the bottom of the dialog box, in the Sample area, a preview of the row headings displays. Each company name will be listed on a separate row in the first column.

Figure 5.17

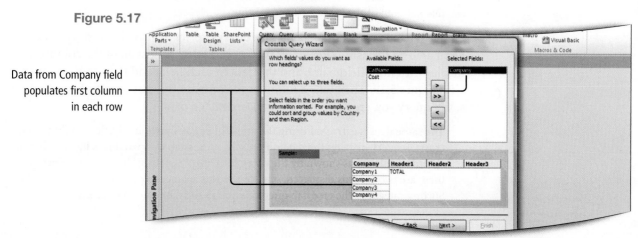

Data from Company field
populates first column
in each row

> **Note** | Selecting Multiple Fields for Row Headings
>
> You can select up to three fields for row headings in a crosstab query. An example would be sorting first by state, then by city, and then by Postal code. State would be the first row heading, city would be the second row heading, and Postal code would be the third row heading. Regardless of the number of fields used for row headings, at least two fields must remain available to complete the crosstab query.

4 In the **Crosstab Query Wizard** dialog box, click **Next**.

> In the third dialog box, you select the fields with data that you want to use as column headings.

5 In the displayed list of fields, **CatName** is selected; notice in the sample area that the category names display in separate columns. Click **Next**. Under **Functions**, click **Sum**, and then compare your screen with Figure 5.18.

> This dialog box enables you to apply an aggregate function to one or more fields. The function will add the cost of every item sold by each company for each category. Every row can also be summed.

Figure 5.18

Cost of items summed per company, per category

Each row will be summed

Categories— Snowboarding, Surfing, Miscellaneous

6 On the left side of the **Crosstab Query Wizard** dialog box, above the **Sample** area, clear the **Yes, include row sums** check box, and then click **Next**.

> If the check box is selected, a column will be inserted between the first and second column that sums all of the numeric data per row.

7 Under **What do you want to name your query?**, select the existing text, type **Lastname Firstname 5A Crosstab Query** and then click **Finish**. Adjust all of the column widths to display the entire field name and the data in each field, and then compare your screen with Figure 5.19. Then take a moment to compare this screen with Figure 5.16, the select query you created with the same extracted data.

> The same data is extracted using the select query as shown in Figure 5.16; however, the crosstab query displays the data differently. A crosstab query reduces the number of records displayed as shown by the entry for Dave's Sporting Shop. In the select query, there are two records displayed, one for the Miscellaneous category and one for the Surfing category. The crosstab query combines the data into one record.

Figure 5.19

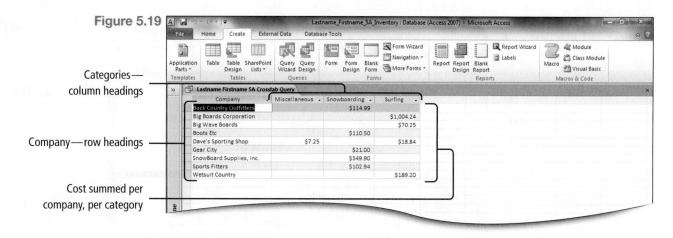

Categories—
column headings

Company—row headings

Cost summed per
company, per category

Note | Including Row Sums

If you include row sums in a crosstab query, the sum will display in a column following the column for the row headings. In this activity, the row sums column would display following the Company column. For Dave's Sporting Shop, the row sum would be $26.09—$7.25 plus $18.84.

8 View the query in **Print Preview**, ensuring that the query prints on one page. If you are instructed to submit this result, create a paper or electronic printout. **Close** the query, saving changes—you adjusted the column widths.

Objective 4 | Find Duplicate and Unmatched Records

Even when a table contains a primary key, it is still possible to have duplicate records in a table. For example, the same inventory item can be entered with different catalog numbers. You can use the *Find Duplicates Query Wizard* to locate duplicate records in a table. As databases grow, you may have records in one table that have no matching records in a related table; these are *unmatched records*. For example, there may be a record for a supplier in the Suppliers table, but no inventory items are ordered from that supplier. You can use the *Find Unmatched Query Wizard* to locate unmatched records.

Activity 5.07 | Finding Duplicate Records

In this activity, you will find duplicate records in the *5A Inventory* table by using the Find Duplicates Query Wizard.

1 On the **Create tab**, in the **Queries group**, click the **Query Wizard** button. In the **New Query** dialog box, click **Find Duplicates Query Wizard**, and then click **OK**.

2 In the first **Find Duplicates Query Wizard** dialog box, in the list of tables, click **Table: 5A Inventory**, and then click **Next**.

The second dialog box displays, enabling you to select the field or fields that may contain duplicate data. If you select all of the fields, then every field must contain the same data, which cannot be the case for a primary key field.

3 Under **Available fields**, double-click **Item** to move it under **Duplicate-value fields**, and then click **Next**.

The third dialog box displays, enabling you to select one or more fields that will help you distinguish duplicate from nonduplicate records.

4 Under **Available fields**, add the following fields, in the order specified, to the **Additional query fields** box: **Catalog#**, **Category**, **Supplier**, **Cost**, and **Selling Price**. Compare your screen with Figure 5.20.

Figure 5.20

Fields to help identify
duplicate records

5 Click **Next**. Click **Finish** to accept the suggested query name—*Find duplicates for Lastname Firstname 5A Inventory*—and then compare your screen with Figure 5.21.

> Three records display with a duplicate value in the *Item* field. Using the displayed fields, you can determine that the second and third records are duplicates; the *Catalog#* was entered incorrectly for one of the records. By examining the *5A Inventory* table, you can determine that Category 1 is Snowboarding and Category 2 is Surfing. You must exercise care when using the Find Duplicates Query Wizard. If you do not include additional fields to help determine whether the records are duplicates or nonduplicates, you might mistakenly determine that they are duplicates.

Figure 5.21

Different data in
primary key field

Duplicate records

6 Adjust all column widths, as needed. View the query in **Print Preview**, ensuring that the query prints on one page. If you are instructed to submit this result, create a paper or electronic printout. **Close** the query, saving changes.

> Normally, you would delete the duplicate record, but your instructor needs to verify that you have found the duplicate record by using a query.

More Knowledge | Removing Duplicate Records

If you choose to delete duplicate records, you must first deal with existing table relationships. If the record you want to delete exists in the table on the *many* side of the relationship, you can delete the record without taking additional steps. If the record exists in the table on the *one* side of the relationship, you must first delete the relationship, and then delete the record. You should then re-create the relationship between the tables. You can either manually delete the duplicate records or create a delete query to remove the duplicate records.

Activity 5.08 | Finding Unmatched Records

In this activity, you will find unmatched records in related tables—*5A Suppliers* and *5A Inventory*—by using the Find Unmatched Query Wizard.

1 On the **Create tab**, in the **Queries group**, click the **Query Wizard** button. In the **New Query** dialog box, click **Find Unmatched Query Wizard**, and then click **OK**.

2 In the first **Find Unmatched Query Wizard** dialog box, in the list of tables, click **Table: 5A Suppliers**, and then click **Next**.

The second dialog box displays, enabling you to select the related table or query that you would like Access to compare to the first table to find unmatched records.

3 In the list of tables, click **Table: 5A Inventory**, and then click **Next**.

The third dialog box displays, enabling you to select the matching fields in each table.

4 Under **Fields in '5A Suppliers'**, if necessary, click **ID**. Under **Fields in 5A Inventory**, if necessary, click **Supplier**. Between the two fields columns, click the button that displays <=>, and then compare your screen with Figure 5.22.

At the bottom of the dialog box, Access displays the matching fields of ID and Supplier.

Figure 5.22

Common field in 5A Inventory table

Links common fields

Common field in 5A Suppliers table

Matching fields

5 Click **Next**. Under **Available fields**, double-click **ID**, and then double-click **Company** to move the field names under **Selected fields**. Notice that these fields will display in the query results. Click **Next**.

6 In the last dialog box, under **What would you like to name your query?**, type **Lastname Firstname 5A Find Unmatched Query** and then click **Finish**. Compare your screen with Figure 5.23.

The query results display one company—*Winter Sports Club*—that has no inventory items in the *5A Inventory* table. Normally, you would either delete the Winter Sports Club record from the *5A Suppliers* table or add inventory items in the related *5A Inventory* for the Winter Sports Club, but your instructor needs to verify that you have located an unmatched record by using a query.

Figure 5.23

Supplier with no inventory items

7 Adjust all column widths. View the query in **Print Preview**, ensuring that the query prints on one page. If you are instructed to submit this result, create a paper or electronic printout. **Close** the query, saving changes.

> **More Knowledge** | Finding Unmatched Records in a Table with Multivalued Fields
>
> You cannot use the Find Unmatched Query Wizard with a table that has *multivalued fields*—fields that appear to hold multiple values. If your table contains multivalued fields, you must first create a query, extracting all of the fields except the multivalued fields, and then create the query to find unmatched records.

Objective 5 | Create a Parameter Query

A *parameter query* prompts you for criteria before running the query. For example, if you had a database of snowboarding events, you might need to find all of the snowboarding events in a particular state. You can create a select query for a state, but when you need to find information about snowboarding events in another state, you must open the original select query in Design view, change the criteria, and then run the query again. With a parameter query, you can create one query—Access will prompt you to enter the state and then display the results based upon the criteria you enter in the dialog box.

Activity 5.09 | Creating a Parameter Query Using One Criteria

In this activity, you will create a parameter query to display a specific category of inventory items. You can enter a parameter anywhere you use text, number, or date criteria.

1 Open » the **Navigation Pane**. Under **Tables**, double-click **5A Inventory** to open the table in **Datasheet** view. In any record, click in the **Category** field, and then click the **arrow** to display the list of categories. Take a moment to study the four categories used in this table. Be sure you do not change the category for the selected record. **Close** the table, and **Close** « the **Navigation Pane**.

2 Create a new query in **Query Design**. Add the **5A Category** table, the **5A Inventory** table, and the **5A Suppliers** table to the Query design workspace, and then **Close** the **Show Table** dialog box. Expand the field lists. From the **5A Category** field list, add **CatName** to the first column in the design grid. From the **5A Inventory** field list, add **Catalog#** and **Item** to the second and third columns in the design grid. From the **5A Suppliers** field list, add **Company** to the fourth column in the design grid.

3 In the **CatName** field, in the **Criteria row**, type **[Enter a Category]** and then compare your screen with Figure 5.24.

The brackets indicate a *parameter*—a value that can be changed—rather than specific criteria. When you run the query, a dialog box will display, prompting you to Enter a Category. The category you type will be set as the criteria for the query. Because you are prompted for the criteria, you can reuse this query without resetting the criteria in Design view.

Figure 5.24

Parameter entered in Criteria row

4 **Run** the query. In the **Enter Parameter Value** dialog box, type **Snowboarding** and then compare your screen with Figure 5.25.

Figure 5.25

Type *Snowboarding* as the criteria— spell it correctly

Alert! | **Does Your Screen Differ?**

If the Enter Parameter Value dialog box does not display, you may have typed the parameter incorrectly in the design grid. Common errors include using parentheses or curly braces instead of square brackets around the parameter text, causing Access to interpret the text as specific criteria. When you run the query, there are no records displayed. If you use curly braces, the query will not run. To correct, display the query in Design view, and then correct the parameter entered in the criteria row.

5 In the **Enter Parameter Value** dialog box, click **OK**.

Nine records display where the CatName field is Snowboarding.

6 Adjust all column widths, and **Save** the query as **Lastname Firstname 5A Category Parameter Query Close** the query, and then **Open** » the **Navigation Pane**.

7 In the **Navigation Pane**, under **Queries**, double-click **5A Category Parameter Query**. In the **Enter Parameter Value** dialog box, type **Surfing** and then click **OK**.

Eleven items categorized as Surfing display. Recall that when you open a query, Access runs the query so that the most up-to-date data is extracted from the underlying table or query. When you have entered a parameter as the criteria, you will be prompted to enter the criteria every time you open the query.

8 Switch to **Design** view. Notice that the parameter—[Enter a Category]—is stored with the query. Access does not store the criteria entered in the Enter Parameter Value dialog box.

9 **Run** the query, and in the **Enter Parameter Value** dialog box, type **Miscellaneous** being careful to spell it correctly. Click **OK** to display one record. Adjust all column widths.

10 View the query in **Print Preview**, ensuring that the query prints on one page. If you are instructed to submit this result, create a paper or electronic printout. **Close** the query, saving changes, and then **Close** « the **Navigation Pane**.

More Knowledge | Parameter Query Prompts

When you enter the parameter in the criteria row, make sure that the prompt—the text enclosed in the square brackets—is not the same as the field name. For example, if the field name is *Category*, do not enter *[Category]* as the parameter. Because Access uses field names in square brackets for calculations, no prompt will display. If you want to use the field name by itself as a prompt, type a question mark at the end of the prompt; for example, *[Category?]*. You cannot use a period, exclamation mark (!), square brackets ([]), or the ampersand (&) as part of the prompt.

Activity 5.10 | Creating a Parameter Query Using Multiple Criteria

In this activity, you will create a parameter query to display the inventory items that fall within a certain range in the On Hand field.

1 Create a new query in **Query Design**. Add the **5A Suppliers** table and the **5A Inventory** table to the Query design workspace, and then **Close** the **Show Table** dialog box. Expand the field lists. From the **5A Inventory** field list, add **Item** and **On Hand** to the first and second columns in the design grid. From the **5A Suppliers** field list box, add **Company** to the third column in the design grid.

2 In the **Criteria row**, right-click in the **On Hand** field, and then click **Zoom**. In the **Zoom** dialog box, type **Between [Enter the lower On Hand number] And [Enter the higher On Hand number]** and then compare your screen with Figure 5.26.

The Zoom dialog box enables you to see the entire parameter. The parameter includes *Between* and *And*, which will display a range of data. Two dialog boxes will display when you run the query. You will be prompted first to enter the lower number and then the higher number.

Figure 5.26

Zoom dialog box

Parameter with two prompts

3 After verifying that you have entered the correct parameter, in the **Zoom** dialog box, click **OK**, and then **Run** the query. In the first **Enter Parameter Value** dialog box, type **10** and then click **OK**. In the second **Enter Parameter Value** dialog box, type **20** and then click **OK**. Compare your screen with Figure 5.27.

> Two records have On Hand items in the range of 10 to 20. These might be inventory items that need to be ordered.

Figure 5.27

In the range of 10 to 20

4 Adjust all column widths, and **Save** the query as **Lastname Firstname 5A On Hand Parameter Query**

5 View the query in **Print Preview**, ensuring that the query prints on one page. If you are instructed to submit this result, create a paper or electronic printout. **Close** the query.

6 Open >> the **Navigation Pane**. **Close** the database, and **Exit** Access.

More Knowledge | Creating a Parameter Query Using Multiple Criteria

When you create a query using more than one field with parameters, the individual sees the prompts in the order that the fields are arranged from left to right in the design grid. When you create a query using more than one parameter in a single field, the individual sees the prompts in the order displayed, from left to right, in the criteria box. If you want the prompts to display in a different order, on the Design tab, in the Show/Hide group, click the Parameters button.

In the Parameter column, type the prompt for each parameter exactly as it was typed in the design grid. Enter the parameters in the order you want the dialog boxes to display when the query is run. In the Data type column, next to each entered parameter, specify the data type by clicking the arrow and displaying the list of data types. Click OK, and then run the query.

 You have completed Project 5A

Project 5B Orders

Project Activities

In Activities 5.11 through 5.19, you will help Miko Adai, Sales Associate for 4Ever Boarding Surf and Snowboard Shop, keep the tables in the database up to date and ensure that the queries display pertinent information. You will create action queries that will create a new table, update records in a table, append records to a table, and delete records from a table. You will also modify the join type of relationships to display different subsets of the data when the query is run. Your completed queries will look similar to Figure 5.28.

Project Files

For Project 5B, you will need the following files:

    a05B_Orders
    a05B_Potential_Customers

You will save your databases as:

    Lastname_Firstname_5B_Orders
    Lastname_Firstname_5B_Potential_Customers

Project Results

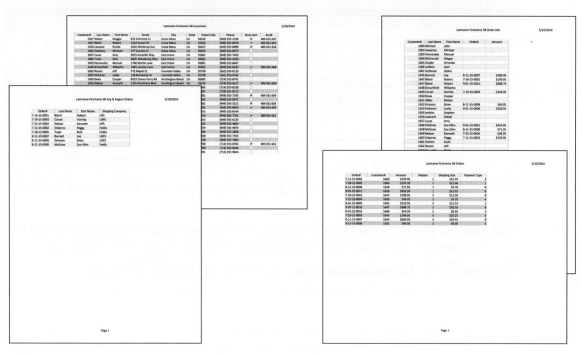

Figure 5.28
Project 5B Orders

Objective 6 | Create a Make Table Query

An ***action query*** enables you to create a new table or change data in an existing table. A ***make table query*** is an action query that creates a new table by extracting data from one or more tables. Creating a new table from existing tables is useful when you need to copy or back up data. For example, you may wish to create a table that displays the orders for the past month. You can extract that data and store it in another table, using the new table as a source for reports or queries. Extracting data and storing it in a new table reduces the time to retrieve ***static data***—data that does not change—and creates a convenient backup of the data.

Activity 5.11 | Creating a Select Query

In this activity, you will create a select query to extract the fields you wish to store in the new table.

1 **Start** Access. Navigate to the location where the student data files for this textbook are saved. Locate and open the **a05B_Orders** file. **Save** the database in your **Access Chapter 5** folder as **Lastname_Firstname_5B_Orders**

2 If you did not add the Access Chapter 5 folder to the Trust Center, enable the content. In the **Navigation Pane**, under **Tables**, rename the four tables by adding **Lastname Firstname** to the beginning of each table name. Take a moment to open each table and observe the data in each. In the **5B Orders** table, make a note of the data type for the **Order#** field and the pattern of data entered in the field. When you are finished, close all of the tables, and **Close** ⟨⟨ the **Navigation Pane**.

> In the *5B Orders* table, the first record contains an Order# of 7-11-15-0002. The first section of the order number is the month of the order, the second section is the day of the month, and the third section is the year. The fourth section is a sequential number. Records with orders for July, August, and September are contained in this table.

Alert! | **Action Queries and Trusted Databases**

To run an action query, the database must reside in a trusted location, or you must enable the content. If you try running an action query and nothing happens, check the status bar for the following message: *This action or event has been blocked by Disabled Mode.* Either add the storage location to Trusted Locations or enable the content. Then, run the query again.

---

3 **Create** a new query in **Query Design**. From the **Show Table** dialog box, add the following tables to the Query design workspace: **5B Customers**, **5B Orders**, and **5B Shippers**. **Close** the **Show Table** dialog box, and then expand the field lists. Notice the relationships between the tables.

> The *5B Customers* table has a one-to-many relationship with the *5B Orders* table—*one* customer can have *many* orders. The *5B Shippers* table has a one-to-many relationship with the *5B Orders* table—*one* shipper can ship *more* than one order.

4 From the **5B Orders** field list, add **Order#** to the first column of the design grid. From the **5B Customers** field list, add **Last Name** and **First Name**, in the order specified, to the second and third columns of the design grid. From the **5B Shippers** field list, add **Shipping Company** to the fourth column of the design grid.

5 In the design grid, under **Order#**, click in the **Criteria row**, type **7*** and then compare your screen with Figure 5.29.

Recall that the asterisk is a wildcard that stands for one or more characters—Access will extract the records where the Order# starts with a 7, and it does not matter what the following characters are. The first section of the Order# contains the month the order was placed without any regard for the year; all July orders will display whether they were placed in 2014, 2015, or any other year. You do not need criteria in a select query to convert it to a make table query.

Figure 5.29

Field added from 5B Shippers table

Fields added from 5B Customers table

Field added from 5B Orders table

Criteria for month of July

> **Note** | Using Expressions and Aggregate Functions in a Make Table Query
>
> In addition to using criteria in a select query upon which a make table query is based, you can use expressions to create a calculated field; for example, *Total Price:[Unit Price]*[On Hand]*. You can also use aggregate functions; for example, you may want to sum the *On Hand* field.

---

6 **Run** the query, and notice that five orders were placed in July.

The select query displays the records that will be stored in the new table.

Activity 5.12 | Converting a Select Query to a Make Table Query

In this activity, you will convert the select query you just created to a make table query.

1 Switch to **Design** view. On the **Design tab**, in the **Query Type group**, click the **Make Table** button. Notice the dark exclamation point (!) in several of the buttons in the Query Type group—these are action queries. In the **Make Table** dialog box, in the **Table Name** box, type **Lastname Firstname 5B July Orders** and then compare your screen with Figure 5.30.

The table name should be a unique table name for the database in which the table will be saved. If it is not, you will be prompted to delete the first table before the new table can be created. You can save a make table query in the current database or in another existing database.

Figure 5.30

Dark exclamation point designates action query type

New table name

Where to save new table

2 In the **Make Table** dialog box, be sure that **Current Database** is selected, and then click **OK**. **Run** the query.

A message displays indicating that *You are about to paste 5 row(s) into a new table* and that you cannot use the Undo command.

3 In the displayed message box, click **Yes**. **Close** the query, click **Yes** in the message box prompting you to save changes, and then name the query **Lastname Firstname 5B Make Table Query**

4 Open » the **Navigation Pane**. Notice that under **Tables**, the new table you created— **5B July Orders**—is displayed. Under **Queries**, the **5B Make Table Query** is displayed.

5 In the **Navigation Pane**, click the title—**All Access Objects**. Under **Navigate To Category**, click **Tables and Related Views**, widen the **Navigation Pane**, and then compare your screen with Figure 5.31.

The Navigation Pane is grouped by tables and related objects. Because the 5B Make Table Query extracted records from three tables—*5B Customers*, *5B Orders*, and *5B Shippers*—it is displayed under all three tables. Changing the grouping in the Navigation Pane to Tables and Related Views enables you to easily determine which objects are dependent upon other objects in the database.

Figure 5.31

Icon for Make Table query

Query extracted records from three tables

Table created with Make Table query

6 In the **Navigation Pane**, double-click **5B July Orders** to open the table in **Datasheet** view. Notice that the data in the **Order#** field does not display as it did in the **5B Orders** table. Switch to **Design** view.

If you click the category title instead of the table, the category will close—if that happens, double-click the category title to redisplay the table, and then double-click the table.

7 Notice that the **Order#** field does not have an input mask associated with it and that there is no **Primary Key** field for this table.

> When using a make table query to create a new table, the data in the new table does not inherit the field properties or the Primary Key field setting from the original table.

8 Switch to **Datasheet** view, and then adjust all column widths. **Close** the table, saving changes.

Note | Updating a Table Created with a Make Table Query

The data stored in a table created with a make table query is not automatically updated when records in the original tables are modified. To keep the new table up to date, you must run the make table query periodically to be sure the information is current.

Objective 7 | Create an Append Query

An *append query* is an action query that adds new records to an existing table by adding data from another Access database or from a table in the same database. An append query can be limited by criteria. Use an append query when the data already exists and you do not want to manually enter it into an existing table. Like the make table query, you first create a select query and then convert it to an append query.

Activity 5.13 | Creating an Append Query for a Table in the Current Database

In this activity, you will create a select query to extract the records for customers who have placed orders in August and then append the records to the *5B July Orders* table.

1 **Close** « the **Navigation Pane**. Create a new query in **Query Design**. From the **Show Table** dialog box, add the following tables to the Query design workspace: **5B Customers**, **5B Orders**, and **5B Shippers**. **Close** the **Show Table** dialog box, and then expand the field lists.

2 From the **5B Customers** field list, add **First Name** and **Last Name**, in the order specified, to the first and second columns of the design grid. From the **5B Orders** field list, add **Order#** and **Shipping Cost**, in the order specified, to the third and fourth columns of the design grid. From the **5B Shippers** field list, add **Shipping Company** to the fifth column of the design grid.

3 In the design grid, under **Order#**, click in the **Criteria row**, type **8*** and then press ↓. Compare your screen with Figure 5.32.

Figure 5.32

Five fields added to
the design grid

Criteria for orders in
August

4 **Run** the query, and notice that three customers placed orders in August.

5 Switch to **Design** view. On the **Design tab**, in the **Query Type group**, click the **Append** button. In the **Append** dialog box, click the **Table Name arrow**, and from the displayed list, click **Lastname Firstname 5B July Orders**, and then click **OK**. Compare your screen with Figure 5.33.

In the design grid, Access inserts an *Append To* row above the Criteria row. Access compares the fields in the query with the fields in the ***destination table***—the table to which you are appending the fields—and attempts to match fields. If a match is found, Access adds the name of the destination field to the Append To row in the query. If no match is found, Access leaves the destination field blank. You can click the box in the Append To row and select a destination field.

Figure 5.33

No matching field in 5B
Orders table

Matching field names in
5B Orders table

Append To row inserted

Criteria for orders placed
in August

6 **Run** the query. In the displayed message box, click **Yes** to append the three rows to the *5B July Orders* table.

7 **Close** the query, and then save it as **Lastname Firstname 5B Append August Orders**

8 **Open** » the **Navigation Pane**. Notice that **5B Append August Orders** displays under the three tables from which data was extracted.

9 In the **Navigation Pane**, click the title—**All Tables**. Under **Navigate To Category**, click **Object Type** to group the Navigation Pane objects by type. Under **Queries**, notice the icon that displays for **5B Append August Orders**. Recall that this icon indicates the query is an action query.

10 Under **Tables**, double-click **5B July Orders** to open the table in **Datasheet** view, and then compare your screen with Figure 5.34.

Three orders for August are appended to the *5B July Orders* table. Because there is no match in the *5B July Orders* table for the Shipping Cost field in the 5B Append August Orders query, the field is ignored when the records are appended.

Figure 5.34

Three rows appended

11 **Close** the table. In the **Navigation Pane**, under **Tables**, right-click **5B July Orders**, and then click **Rename**. **Rename** the table as **Lastname Firstname 5B July & August Orders**

12 With **5B July & August Orders** selected, display **Backstage** view and view the table in **Print Preview**. If you are instructed to submit this result, create a paper or electronic printout of the table, and then **Close** the Print Preview window.

Activity 5.14 | Creating an Append Query for a Table in Another Database

Miko Adai recently discovered that the marketing manager has been keeping a database of persons who have requested information about the 4Ever Boarding Surf and Snowboard Shop. These names need to be added to the *5B Customers* table so those potential clients can receive catalogs when they are distributed. In this activity, you will create an append query to add the records from the marketing manager's table to the *5B Customers* table.

1 On the Access window title bar, click the **Minimize** button. Click the **Start** button, and then open **Access**. Navigate to the location where the student data files for this textbook are saved. Locate and open the **a05B_Potential_Customers** file. **Save** the database in your **Access Chapter 5** folder as **Lastname_Firstname_5B_Potential_Customers**

2 If you did not add the Access Chapter 5 folder to the Trust Center, enable the content. In the **Navigation Pane**, under **Tables**, rename the table by adding **Lastname Firstname** to the beginning of **5B Potential Customers**. Take a moment to open the table, noticing the fields and field names. When you are finished, **Close** the table, and **Close** « the **Navigation Pane**.

The *5B Potential Customers* table in this database contains similar fields to the *5B Customers* table in the 5B_Orders database.

3 Create a new query in **Query Design**. From the **Show Table** dialog box, add the **5B Potential Customers** table to the Query design workspace, and then **Close** the **Show Table** dialog box. Expand the field list.

4 In the **5B Potential Customers** field list, click **Customer#**, hold down Shift, and then click **Phone** to select all of the fields. Drag the selection down into the first column of the design grid.

> Although you could click the asterisk (*) in the field list to add all of the fields to the design grid, it is easier to detect which fields have no match in the destination table when the field names are listed individually in the design grid.

5 On the **Design tab**, in the **Query Type group**, click the **Append** button. In the **Append** dialog box, click the **Another Database** option button, and then click the **Browse** button. Navigate to your **Access Chapter 5** folder, and then double-click **5B Orders**.

> The 5B Orders database contains the destination table.

6 In the **Append** dialog box, click the **Table Name arrow**, click **5B Customers**, and then compare your screen with Figure 5.35.

> Once you select the name of another database, the tables contained in that database display.

Figure 5.35

Destination table

Destination database

7 Click **OK**. In the design grid, notice that in the **Append To row**, Access found field name matches for all fields, except **LName** and **FName**.

8 In the design grid, under **LName**, click in the **Append To row**, click the **arrow**, and then compare your screen with Figure 5.36.

> A list displays the field names contained in the *5B Customers* table. If the field names are not exactly the same in the source and destination tables, Access will not designate them as matched fields. A *source table* is the table from which records are being extracted.

Figure 5.36

Unmatched field names

Source table

Destination table

Field names in destination table

9 In the displayed list, click **Last Name**. Under **FName**, click in the **Append To row**, and then click the **arrow**. In the displayed list, click **First Name**.

10 Save 🖫 the query as **Lastname Firstname 5B Append to 5B Customers** and then **Run** the query, clicking **Yes** to append 8 rows. **Close** the query, and then **Open** ≫ the **Navigation Pane. Close** the database, and then **Exit** ❌ this instance of Access.

Alert! | To Trust or Not to Trust? That Is the Question!

When you allow someone else to run an action query that will modify a table in your database, be sure that you can trust that individual. One mistake in the action query could destroy your table. A better way of running an action query that is dependent upon someone else's table is to obtain a copy of the table, place it in a database that you have created, and examine the table for malicious code. Once you are satisfied that the table is safe, you can create the action query to modify the data in your tables. Be sure to make a backup copy of the destination database before running action queries.

---

11 On the taskbar, click the button for your **5B_Orders** database. If you mistakenly closed the 5B_Orders database, reopen it. In the **Navigation Pane**, under **Tables**, double-click **5B Customers** to open the table in **Datasheet** view. **Close** ≪ the **Navigation Pane**. Compare your screen with Figure 5.37.

The first eight records—Customer#'s 1000 through 1007—have been appended to the *5B Customers* table. The last two fields—Store Acct and Acct#—are blank since there were no corresponding fields in the *5B Potential Customers* table.

Figure 5.37

No matching fields in source table

Eight records appended from another table in the database

More Knowledge | Running the Same Append Query a Second Time

If you run the same append query a second time with the same records in the source table and no primary key field is involved in the appending of records, you will have duplicate records in the destination table. If a primary key field is part of the record being duplicated, a message will display stating that Access cannot append all of the records due to one of several rule violations. If new records were added to the source table that were not originally appended to the destination table, clicking Yes in the message dialog box will enable those records to be added without adding duplicate records.

Objective 8 | Create a Delete Query

A **delete query** is an action query that removes records from an existing table in the same database. When information becomes outdated or is no longer needed, the records should be deleted from your database. Recall that one method you can use to find unnecessary records is to create a Find Unmatched query. Assuming outdated records have a common criteria, you can create a select query, convert it to a delete query, and then delete all of the records at one time rather than deleting the records one by one. Use delete queries only when you need to remove many records quickly. Before running a delete query, you should back up the database.

Activity 5.15 | Creating a Delete Query

A competing store has opened in Santa Ana, and the former customers living in that city have decided to do business with that store. In this activity, you will create a select query and then convert it to a delete query to remove records for clients living in Santa Ana.

1 With the **5B Customers** table open in **Datasheet** view, under **City**, click in any row. On the **Home tab**, in the **Sort & Filter group**, click the **Descending** button to arrange the cities in descending alphabetical order.

2 At the top of the datasheet, in the record for **Customer# 1660**, click the **plus (+) sign** to display the subdatasheet. Notice that this customer has placed an order that has been shipped.

3 Display the subdatasheets for the four customers residing in **Santa Ana**, and then compare your screen with Figure 5.38.

The four customers residing in Santa Ana have not placed orders.

Figure 5.38

Customer with order

Santa Ana customers with no orders

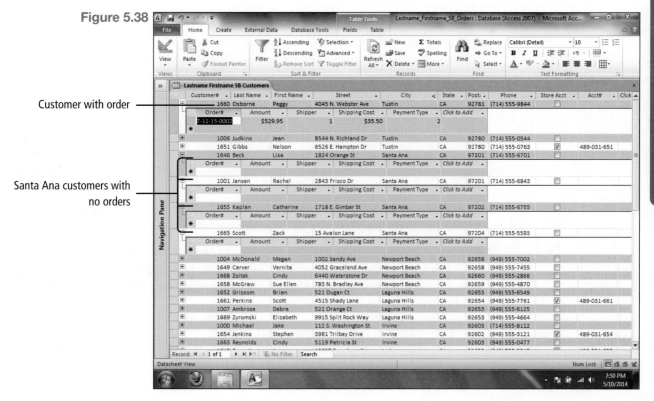

4 Collapse all of the subdatasheets by clicking each **minus (–) sign**.

5 On the Ribbon, click the **Database Tools tab**. In the **Relationships group**, click the **Relationships** button. On the **Design tab**, in the **Relationships group**, click the **All Relationships** button. Expand the field lists and rearrange the field lists to match the layout displayed in Figure 5.39.

> The *5B Customers* table has a one-to-many relationship with the *5B Orders* table, and referential integrity has been enforced. By default, Access will prevent the deletion of records from the table on the *one* side of the relationship if related records are contained in the table on the *many* side of the relationship. Because the records for the Santa Ana customers do not have related records in the related table, you will be able to delete the records from the *5B Customers* table, which is on the *one* side of the relationship.

> To delete records from the table on the *one* side of the relationship that have related records in the table on the *many* side of the relationship, you must either delete the relationship or enable Cascade Delete Related Records. If you need to delete records on the *many* side of the relationship, you can do so without changing or deleting the relationship.

Figure 5.39

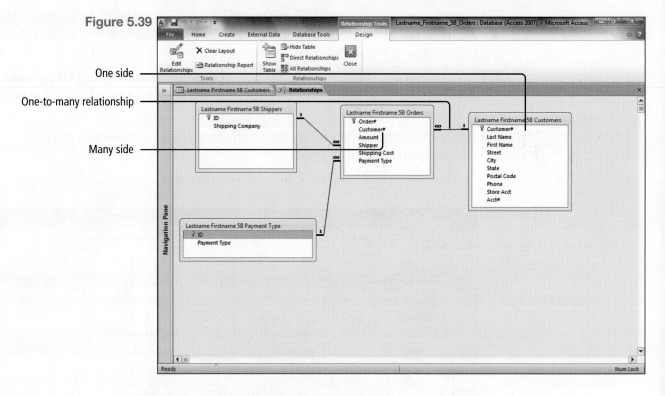

One side
One-to-many relationship
Many side

6 On the **tab row**, right-click any tab, and then click **Close All**, saving changes to the table and to the layout of the Relationships window.

7 Create a new query in **Query Design**. Add the **5B Customers** table to the Query design workspace, and then **Close** the **Show Table** dialog box. Expand the field list. From the field list, add **Customer#** and **City**, in the order specified, to the first and second columns in the design grid.

> Since you are deleting existing records based on criteria, you need to add only the field that has criteria attached to it—the City field. However, it is easier to analyze the results if you include another field in the design grid.

8 In the design grid, under **City**, click in the **Criteria** row, type **Santa Ana** and then press ↓.

> Access inserts the criteria in quotation marks because this is a Text field.

9 **Run** the query, and then compare your screen with Figure 5.40.

> Four records for customers in Santa Ana are displayed. If your query results display an empty record, switch to Design view and be sure that you typed the criteria correctly.

Figure 5.40

Customers living in Santa Ana

10 Switch to **Design** view. In the Query design workspace, to the right of the field list, right-click in the empty space. From the displayed shortcut menu, point to **Query Type**, and click **Delete Query**. Compare your screen with Figure 5.41. Alternatively, on the **Design** tab, in the **Query Type** group, click the **Delete** button.

> In the design grid, a Delete row is inserted above the Criteria row with the word *Where* in both columns. Access will delete all records *Where* the City is Santa Ana. If you include all of the fields in the query using the asterisk (*), Access inserts the word *From* in the Delete row, and all of the records will be deleted.

Figure 5.41

Delete query

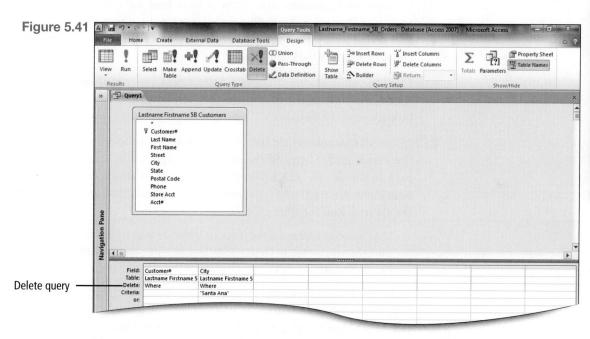

11 **Save** the query as **Lastname Firstname 5B Delete Santa Ana Customers** and then **Run** the query. In the message box stating that *You are about to delete 4 row(s) from the specified table*, click **Yes**.

12 **Close** the query, and then **Open** ![»] the **Navigation Pane**. Under **Queries**, notice the icon that is associated with a delete query—**5B Delete Santa Ana Customers**. Under **Tables**, open the **5B Customers** table in **Datasheet** view. Notice that the records are still in descending order by the **City** field, and notice that the four records for customers living in **Santa Ana** have been deleted from the table.

13 **Close** ![«] the **Navigation Pane**, leaving the table open for the next activity. On the **Home tab**, in the **Sort & Filter group**, click the **Remove Sort** button to clear all sorts from the **City** field.

Objective 9 | Create an Update Query

An *update query* is an action query that is used to add, change, or delete data in fields of one or more existing records. Combined with criteria, an update query is an efficient way to change data for a large number of records at one time, and you can change records in more than one table at a time. If you need to change data in a few records, you can use the Find and Replace dialog box. You are unable to use update queries to add or delete records in a table; use an append query or delete query as needed. Because you are changing data with an update query, you should back up your database before running one.

Activity 5.16 | Creating an Update Query

The postal codes are changing for all of the customers living in Irvine or East Irvine to a consolidated postal code. In this activity, you will create a select query to extract the records from the *5B Customers* table for customers living in these cities and then convert the query to an update query so that you change the postal codes for all of the records at one time.

1 With the **5B Customers** table open in **Datasheet** view, click in the **City** field in any row. Sort the **City** field in **Ascending** order. Notice that there are four customers living in **East Irvine** with postal codes of **92650** and five customers living in **Irvine** with postal codes of **92602**, **92603**, and **92604**.

2 **Close** the table, saving changes. Create a new query in **Query Design**. Add the **5B Customers** table to the Query design workspace, and then close the **Show Table** dialog box. Expand the field list.

3 In the **5B Customers** field list, double-click **City** to add the field to the first column of the design grid. Then add the **Postal Code** field to the second column of the design grid. In the design grid, under **City**, click in the **Criteria row**, and then type **Irvine or East Irvine** Alternatively, type **Irvine** in the Criteria row, and then type **East Irvine** in the **Or** row. **Run** the query.

> Nine records display for the cities of Irvine or East Irvine. If your screen does not display nine records, switch to Design view and be sure you typed the criteria correctly. Then run the query again.

4 Switch to **Design** view, and then notice how Access changed the criteria under the **City** field, placing quotation marks around the text and capitalizing *or*. On the **Design tab**, in the **Query Type group**, click the **Update** button.

> In the design grid, an Update To row is inserted above the Criteria row.

5 In the design grid, under **Postal Code**, click in the **Update To** row, type **92601** and then compare your screen with Figure 5.42.

Figure 5.42

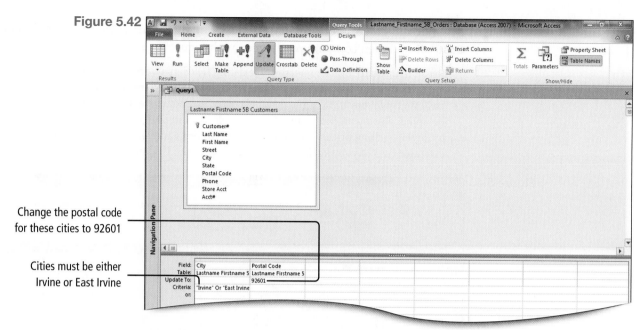

Change the postal code for these cities to 92601

Cities must be either Irvine or East Irvine

---

6 **Save** 🖫 the query as **Lastname Firstname 5B Update Postal Codes** and then **Run** the query. In the message box stating that *You are about to update 9 row(s)*, click **Yes**.

7 **Close** the query, and then **Open** » the **Navigation Pane**. Under **Queries**, notice the icon that is associated with an update query—**5B Update Postal Codes**. Under **Tables**, open the **5B Customers** table in **Datasheet** view. Notice that the nine records for customers living in **East Irvine** and **Irvine** have **Postal** codes of **92601**.

8 View the table in **Print Preview**. Change the orientation to **Landscape**, and, if necessary, change the margins to ensure that the table prints on one page. If you are instructed to submit this result, create a paper or electronic printout, and then **Close** the Print Preview window. **Close** the table.

Activity 5.17 | Creating an Update Query with an Expression

There was a computer problem, and customers were overcharged for items shipped FedEx. In this activity, you will create an update query to correct the field to reflect an accurate shipping cost. Any item shipped FedEx will be discounted 12 percent.

1 Open the **5B Orders** table in **Datasheet** view, and **Close** « the **Navigation Pane**. Click the right side of the **Shipper** field to see the lookup list. Notice an entry of **1** means the order was shipped using FedEx. Press [Esc] to return to the field box. Sort the **Shipper** field from **Smallest to Largest**. Notice that there are four orders that were shipped using FedEx. Make note of the shipping cost for each of those items.

2 **Close** the table, saving changes. Create a new query in **Query Design**. From the **Show Table** dialog box, add the **5B Shippers** table and the **5B Orders** table to the Query design workspace, and then **Close** the **Show Table** dialog box. Expand the field lists.

3 From the **5B Shippers** field list, add **Shipping Company** to the design grid. From the **5B Orders** field list, add **Shipping Cost** to the design grid. In the **Criteria row,** under **Shipping Company**, type **FedEx** Run the query.

> Four records display for FedEx. If your screen does not display four records, switch to Design view and be sure you typed the criteria correctly. Then run the query again.

4 Switch to **Design** view. On the **Design tab**, in the **Query Type group**, click the **Update** button.

> In the design grid, an Update To row is inserted above the Criteria row.

5 In the design grid, under **Shipping Cost**, click in the **Update To row**, type [**Shipping Cost**]*.88 and then compare your screen with Figure 5.43.

Recall that square brackets surround existing fields in an expression, and numbers do not include any brackets. This expression will reduce the current shipping cost by 12%, so the customers will pay 88% of the original cost. Currency, Date/Time, and Number fields can be updated using an expression. For example, a selling price field can be increased by 15% by keying [selling price]*1.15 in the Update To box, and an invoice due date can be extended by 3 days by keying [invoice date]+3 in the Update To box.

Figure 5.43

Expression to update shipping cost

Criteria for records to be updated

6 Save 🖫 the query as **Lastname Firstname 5B Update FedEx Shipping Costs** and then **Run** the query. In the message box stating that *You are about to update 4 row(s)*, click **Yes**.

The update query runs every time the query is opened, unless it is opened directly in Design view. To review or modify the query, right-click the query name, and then click Design view.

7 **Close** the query, and then **Open** 🔲 the **Navigation Pane**. Under **Tables**, open the **5B Orders** table in **Datasheet** view. Notice that the four records for orders shipped FedEx have lower shipping costs than they did prior to running the query, 88 percent of the original cost.

8 View the table in **Print Preview**. Change the orientation to **Landscape**, and, if necessary, change the margins to ensure that the table prints on one page. If you are instructed to submit this result, create a paper or electronic printout and then **Close** the Print Preview window. **Close** the **5B Orders** table.

More Knowledge | Restrictions for Update Queries

It is not possible to run an update query with these types of table fields:

- Calculated fields, created in a table or in a query.
- Fields that use total queries or crosstab queries as their source.
- AutoNumber fields, which can change only when you add a record to a table.
- Fields in union queries.
- Fields in unique-values or unique-records queries.
- Primary key fields that are common fields in table relationships, unless you set Cascade Update Related Fields.

You cannot cascade updates for tables that use a data type of AutoNumber to generate the primary key field.

Objective 10 | Modify the Join Type

When multiple tables are included in a query, a *join* helps you extract the correct records from the related tables. The relationship between the tables, based upon common fields, is represented in a query by a join, which is displayed as the join line between the related tables. When you add tables to the Query design workspace, Access creates the joins based on the defined relationships. If you add queries to the Query design workspace or tables where the relationship has not been defined, you can manually create joins between the objects by dragging a common field from one object to the common field in the second. Joins establish rules about records to be included in the query results and combine the data from multiple sources on one record row in the query results.

Activity 5.18 | Viewing the Results of a Query Using an Inner Join

The default join type is the *inner join*, which is the most common type of join. When a query with an inner join is run, only the records where the common field exists in both related tables are displayed in the query results. All of the queries you have previously run have used an inner join. In this activity, you will view the results of a query that uses an inner join.

1 **Close** [«] the **Navigation Pane**. On the Ribbon, click the **Database Tools tab**, and then in the **Relationships group** click the **Relationships** button. Notice the relationship between the **5B Customers** table and the **5B Orders** table.

> Because referential integrity has been enforced, it is easy to determine that the *5B Customers* table is on the *one* side of the relationship, and the *5B Orders* table is on the *many* side of the relationship. *One* customer can have *many* orders. The common field is Customer#.

2 In the **Relationships** window, double-click the **join line** between the **5B Customers** table and the **5B Orders** table. Alternatively, right-click the join line, and then click **Edit Relationship**, or click the line, and then in the **Tools** group, click the **Edit Relationships** button. Compare your screen with Figure 5.44.

> The Edit Relationships dialog box displays, indicating that referential integrity has been enforced and that the relationship type is *One-to-Many*. Because the relationship has been established for the tables, you can view relationship properties in the Relationships window.

Figure 5.44

Click here to display the join type

Referential integrity is enforced

Relationship type

3 In the **Edit Relationships** dialog box, click **Join Type**, and then compare your screen with Figure 5.45. In the displayed **Join Properties** dialog box, notice that option **1** is selected—*Only include rows where the joined fields from both tables are equal.*

> Option 1 is the default join type, which is an inner join. Options 2 and 3 are outer join types.

Figure 5.45

Default join type—inner join

Outer join types

4 In the **Join Properties** dialog box, click **Cancel**. In the **Edit Relationships** dialog box, click **Cancel**. **Close** the Relationships window.

> Because the relationships have been established and saved in the database, you should not change the join properties in the Relationships window. You should only change join properties in the Query design workspace.

5 **Open** » the **Navigation Pane**. In the **Navigation Pane**, open the **5B Orders** table and the **5B Customers** table, in the order specified, and then **Close** « the **Navigation Pane**.

6 With the **5B Customers** table active, on the **Home tab**, in the **Sort & Filter group**, click the **Remove Sort** button to remove the ascending sort from the **City** field. Notice that the records are now sorted by the **Customer#** field—the primary key field.

7 In the first record, click the **plus (+) sign** to expand the subdatasheet—the related record in the *5B Orders* table—and then notice that **Jake Michael** has no related records—he has not placed any orders. Click the **minus (–) sign** to collapse the subdatasheet.

8 Expand the subdatasheet for **Customer# 1645**, and then notice that **Joe Barnett** has one related record in the *5B Orders* table—he has placed one order. Collapse the subdatasheet.

9 Expand the subdatasheet for **Customer# 1647**, and then notice that **Robert Bland** has two related records in the *5B Orders* table—he has placed *many* orders. Collapse the subdatasheet.

10 On the **tab row**, click the **5B Orders tab** to make the datasheet active, and then notice that **12** orders have been placed. On the **tab row**, right-click any tab, and then click **Close All**, saving changes, if prompted.

11 Create a new query in **Query Design**. From the **Show Table** dialog box, add the **5B Customers** table and the **5B Orders** table to the Query design workspace, and then close the **Show Table** dialog box. Expand both field lists.

12 From the **5B Customers** field list, add **Customer#**, **Last Name**, and **First Name**, in the order specified, to the design grid. In the design grid, under **Customer#**, click in the **Sort row**, click the **arrow**, and then click **Ascending**. **Run** the query, and then compare your screen with Figure 5.46. There is no record for **Jake Michael**, there is one record for **Customer# 1645**—Joe Barnett—and there are two records for **Customer# 1647**—Robert Bland.

Because the default join type is an inner join, the query results display records only where there is a matching Customer#—the common field—in both related tables, even though you did not add any fields from the *5B Orders* table to the design grid. All of the records display for the table on the *many* side of the relationship—*5B Orders*. For the table on the *one* side of the relationship—*5B Customers*—only those records that have matching records in the related table display. Recall that there were 29 records in the *5B Customers* table and 12 records in the *5B Orders* table.

Figure 5.46

Common field

One corresponding record in 5B Orders table

Many corresponding records in 5B Orders table

13 Switch to **Design** view. From the **5B Orders** field list, add **Order#** to the fourth column of the design grid, and then add **Amount** to the fifth column of the design grid. **Run** the query to display the results.

The same 12 records display but with two additional fields.

Activity 5.19 | Changing the Join Type to an Outer Join

An *outer join* is typically used to display records from both tables, regardless of whether there are matching records. In this activity, you will modify the join type to display all of the records from the *5B Customers* table, regardless of whether the customer has placed an order.

1 Switch to **Design** view. In the Query design workspace, double-click the **join line** to display the **Join Properties** dialog box. Alternatively, right-click the join line, and then click **Join Properties**. Compare your screen with Figure 5.47.

The Join Properties dialog box displays the tables used in the join and the common fields from both tables. Option 1—inner join type—is selected by default. Options 2 and 3 are two different types of outer joins.

Option 2 is a *left outer join*. Select a left outer join when you want to display all of the records on the *one* side of the relationship, whether or not there are matching records in the table on the *many* side of the relationship. Option 3 is a *right outer join*. Selecting a right outer join will display all of the records on the *many* side of the relationship, whether or not there are matching records in the table on the *one* side of the relationship. This should not occur if referential integrity has been enforced because all orders should have a related customer.

Figure 5.47

Many side of the relationship
One side of the relationship
Common fields
Inner join
Left outer join
Right outer join

2 In the **Join Properties** dialog box, click the option button next to **2**, and then click **OK**. **Run** the query, and then compare your screen with Figure 5.48.

Thirty-two records display. There are 29 records in the *5B Customers* table; however, three customers have two orders, so there are two separate records for each of these customers. If a customer does not have a matching record in the *5B Orders* table, the Order# and Amount fields are left empty in the query results.

Figure 5.48

Fields blank because there
are no matching records
in 5B Orders table

Two orders for this
customer

Number of records in
query results

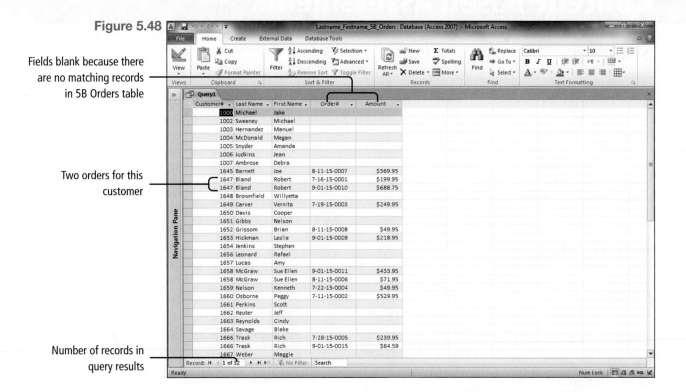

3 Save 🖫 the query as **Lastname Firstname 5B Outer Join** View the query in **Print Preview**, ensuring that the table prints on one page. If you are instructed to submit this result, create a paper or electronic printout.

4 **Close** the query, and then **Open** 》 the **Navigation Pane**. **Close** the database, and then **Exit** ⊠ Access.

More Knowledge | Other Types of Joins

There are two other types of joins: *cross joins* and *unequal joins*. A cross join is not explicitly set in Access 2010. In a cross join, each row from one table is combined with each row in a related table. Cross joins are usually created unintentionally when you do not create a join line between related tables. In fact, the results of the query will probably not make much sense. In the previous query, you would create a cross join by deleting the join line between the *5B Customers* table and the *5B Orders* table. A cross join produces many records; depending on the number of records in both tables, the cross join can take a long time to run. A cross join using the aforementioned tables would result in 348 displayed records when the query is run (29 customers × 12 orders = 348 records).

An unequal join is used to combine rows from two data sources based on field values that are not equal. The join can be based on any comparison operator, such as greater than (>), less than (<), or not equal to (<>). The results in an unequal join using the not equal to comparison operator are difficult to interpret and can display as many records as those displayed in a cross join. Unequal joins cannot be created in Design view; they can be created only in SQL view.

End **You have completed Project 5B** ⎯⎯⎯⎯⎯⎯⎯⎯⎯⎯⎯⎯⎯

Content-Based Assessments

Summary

Queries are powerful database objects that can be created to do more than just extract data from tables and other queries. In this chapter, you created queries for special purposes, such as creating calculated fields, summarizing and grouping data, displaying the data in a spreadsheet-like format for easier analysis, finding duplicate records and unmatched records that might cause problems with the database, and creating prompts to use in dynamic queries. You created action queries to create new tables, append records to tables, delete records from tables, and update data in tables. Finally, you examined the query results based upon the default inner join and an outer join.

Key Terms

Matching

Match each term in the second column with its correct definition in the first column by writing the letter of the term on the blank line in front of the correct definition.

_____ 1.   A formula that performs a calculation.

_____ 2.   Performs a calculation on a column of data to return a single value.

_____ 3.   A query that calculates subtotals across groups of records.

_____ 4.   A query that uses an aggregate function for data that is grouped by two types of information and then displays the data in a compact, spreadsheet-like format.

_____ 5.   Used to perform a query that locates duplicate records in a table.

_____ 6.   Records in one table that have no matching records in a related table.

_____ 7.   A query that prompts you for criteria before running it.

_____ 8.   A query that enables you to create a new table or change data in an existing table.

_____ 9.   An action query that creates a new table by extracting data from one or more tables.

_____ 10.   Data that does not change.

_____ 11.   An action query that adds new records to an existing table by adding data from another Access database or from a table in the same database.

_____ 12.   An action query that removes records from an existing table in the same database.

A Action query

B Aggregate function

C Append query

D Crosstab query

E Delete query

F Expression

G Find Duplicates Query Wizard

H Inner join

I Make table query

J Outer join

K Parameter query

L Static data

M Totals query

N Unmatched records

O Update query

_____ 13. An action query that is used to add, change, or delete data in fields of one or more existing records.

_____ 14. The type of join in which only the records where the common field exists in both related tables are displayed in the query results.

_____ 15. A join that is typically used to display records from both tables, regardless of whether there are matching records.

Multiple Choice

Circle the correct answer.

1. Symbols such as +, −, *, and / that are used to build expressions are known as:
   A. symbolic arguments   B. arithmetic arguments   C. arithmetic operators

2. In Access queries, you can use aggregate functions in the Datasheet view by adding a:
   A. Total row   B. Group by row   C. Zoom row

3. Which function should be used to add a column of numbers and return a single value?
   A. Sum   B. Average   C. Count

4. What type of query has to include at least one row heading, one column heading, and one summary field?
   A. Parameter query   B. Totals query   C. Crosstab query

5. Which Query Wizard is used to locate records in one table that do not have related records in a related table?
   A. Find Duplicates   B. Find Unmatched   C. Find Unrelated Records

6. A criteria value in a query that can be changed is called a:
   A. multivalue   B. parameter   C. duplicate

7. When creating an append query, the table to which you are appending the fields is called the:
   A. source table   B. destination table   C. navigation table

8. When creating an append query, the table from which records are being extracted is called the:
   A. source table   B. destination table   C. navigation table

9. Which expression would be used to update the current hourly wage by $.50?
   A. hourly wage+.5   B. [hourly wage]+[.5]   C. [hourly wage]+.5

10. What is used to help a query return only the records from each table you want to see, based on how those tables are related to other tables in the query?
    A. Join   B. Relationship   C. Properties

Content-Based Assessments

Apply 5A skills from these Objectives:

1. Create Calculated Fields in a Query
2. Use Aggregate Functions in a Query
3. Create a Crosstab Query
4. Find Duplicate and Unmatched Records
5. Create a Parameter Query

Skills Review | Project 5C Payroll

Lee Kawano, Lead Sales Associate of 4Ever Boarding Surf and Snowboard Shop, has a database containing employee data and payroll data. In the following Skills Review, you will create special-purpose queries to calculate data, summarize and group data, display data in a spreadsheet-like format, and find duplicate and unmatched records. You will also create a query that prompts an individual to enter the criteria. Your completed queries will look similar to Figure 5.49.

Project Files

For Project 5C, you will need the following file:

a05C_Payroll

You will save your database as:

Lastname_Firstname_5C_Payroll

Project Results

Figure 5.49

(Project 5C Payroll continues on the next page)

Content-Based Assessments

1 **Start** Access. Locate and open the **a05C_Payroll** file. Display **Backstage** view. **Save** the database in your **Access Chapter 5** folder as **Lastname_Firstname_5C_Payroll**

a. If necessary, enable the content or add the Access Chapter 5 folder to the Trust Center.

b. Rename the tables by adding **Lastname Firstname** to the beginning of each table name. **Close** the **Navigation Pane**.

2 On the Ribbon, click the **Create tab**. In the **Queries group**, click the **Query Design** button. In the **Show Table** dialog box, select the following three tables—**5C Employees**, **5C Payroll**, and **5C Timecard**. **Add** the tables to the Query design workspace, and then click **Close**. Expand the field lists.

a. From the **5C Employees** field list, add the following fields, in the order specified, to the design grid: **EmpID**, **Last Name**, and **First Name**.

b. From the **5C Payroll** field list, add the **Pay Rate** field.

c. From the **5C Timecard** field list, add the **Timecard Date** and the **Hours** field in this order. In the **Timecard Date** field **Criteria row**, type **6/29/2015**

d. In the **Field row**, right-click in the first cell in the first empty column to display a shortcut menu, and then click **Zoom**. In the **Zoom** dialog box, type **Gross Pay:[Pay Rate]*[Hours]** and then click **OK**. Press Enter. Run the query. Return to **Design** view.

e. If the **Gross Pay** does not show as currency, click in the **Gross Pay** field that you just added. On the **Design tab**, in the **Show/Hide group**, click the **Property Sheet** button. In the **Property Sheet**, on the **General tab**, click in the **Format** box, and then click the displayed **arrow**. In the list of formats, click **Currency**. On the **Property Sheet** title bar, click the **Close** button.

f. In the **Field row**, right-click in the first cell in the first empty column to display a shortcut menu, and then click **Zoom**. In the **Zoom** dialog box, type **Social Security:[Gross Pay]*0.062** and then click **OK**. Using the technique you just practiced, set a **Currency** format for this field if necessary. **Close** the Property Sheet.

g. In the **Field row**, right-click in the first cell in the first empty column to display a shortcut menu, and then click **Zoom**. In the **Zoom** dialog box, type **Net**

Pay:[Gross Pay]-[Social Security] and then click **OK**. **Run** the query to display the payroll calculations.

h. In the **Records group**, click the **Totals** button. In the **Total row**, under **Net Pay**, click in the empty box, and then click the **arrow** at the left edge. From the displayed list, click **Sum**.

i. Adjust column widths to display all field names and all data under each field. On the **tab row**, right-click the **Query1 tab**, and then click **Save**. In the **Save As** dialog box, under **Query Name**, type **Lastname Firstname 5C Net Pay** and then click **OK**. View the query in **Print Preview**, ensuring that the query prints on one page. If you are instructed to submit this result, create a paper or electronic printout. **Close** the query.

3 Create a new query in **Query Design**. Add the **5C Employees** table and the **5C Sales** table to the Query design workspace, and then **Close** the **Show Table** dialog box. Expand both field lists.

a. From the **5C Employees** field list, add **Last Name** to the first field box in the design grid. From the **5C Sales** table, add **Sales** to both the second and third field boxes.

b. On the **Design tab**, in the **Show/Hide group**, click the **Totals** button. In the design grid, in the **Total row**, under the first **Sales** field, click in the box displaying *Group By* to display the arrow, and then click the **arrow**. From the displayed list, click **Count**.

c. Under the second **Sales** field, click in the box displaying *Group By* to display the arrow, and then click the **arrow**. From the displayed list, click **Sum**.

d. In the design grid, in the **Sort row**, under **Last Name**, click in the box to display the arrow, and then click the **arrow**. From the displayed list, click **Ascending**. **Run** the query to display the total number of sales and the total amount of the sales for each associate.

e. If necessary, adjust column widths to display all field names and all data under each field. **Save** the query as **Lastname Firstname 5C Sales by Employee** View the query in **Print Preview**, ensuring that the query prints on one page. If you are instructed to submit this result, create a paper or electronic printout. **Close** the query.

(Project 5C Payroll continues on the next page)

Access | Chapter 5

4 **Create** a new query in **Query Design**. Add the following tables to the Query design workspace: **5C Employees** and **5C Sales**. In the **Show Table** dialog box, click **Close**. Expand the field lists.

a. From the **5C Employees** table, add the **Last Name** and **First Name** fields. From the **5C Sales** table, add the **Timecard Date** and **Sales** fields. **Run** the query to display the sales by date. **Save** the query as **Lastname Firstname 5C Sales by Date** and then **Close** the query.

b. On the Ribbon, click the **Create tab**. In the **Queries group**, click the **Query Wizard** button. In the **New Query** dialog box, click **Crosstab Query Wizard**, and then click **OK**. In the middle of the dialog box, under **View**, click the **Queries** option button. In the list of queries, click **Query: 5C Sales by Date**, and then click **Next**.

c. Under **Available Fields**, double-click **Last Name** and **First Name**, and then click **Next**. In the displayed list of fields, double-click **Timecard Date**. Select an interval of **Date**. Click **Next**. Under **Functions**, click **Sum**. On the left side of the **Crosstab Query Wizard** dialog box, above the **Sample** area, clear the **Yes, include row sums** check box, and then click **Next**.

d. Under **What do you want to name your query?**, select the existing text, type **Lastname Firstname 5C Crosstab** and then click **Finish**. Adjust all of the column widths to display the entire field name and the data in each field. The result is a spreadsheet view of total sales by employee by payroll date. View the query in **Print Preview**, ensuring that the query prints on one page. If you are instructed to submit this result, create a paper or electronic printout. **Close** the query, saving changes.

5 On the **Create tab**, in the **Queries group**, click the **Query Wizard** button. In the **New Query** dialog box, click **Find Duplicates Query Wizard**, and then click **OK**.

a. In the first **Find Duplicates Query Wizard** dialog box, in the list of tables, click **Table: 5C Payroll**, and then click **Next**. Under **Available fields**, double-click **EmpID** to move it under **Duplicate-value fields**, and then click **Next**.

b. Under **Available fields**, add all of the fields to the **Additional query fields** box. Click **Next**. Click **Finish** to accept the suggested query name—*Find duplicates*

for *Lastname Firstname 5C Payroll*. Adjust all column widths. View the query in **Print Preview**, ensuring that the query prints on one page. If you are instructed to submit this result, create a paper or electronic printout. **Close** the query, saving changes.

c. Open the **5C Payroll** table. Locate the second record for **EmpID**, **13**. Click the row selector, and then press ⌐Del⌐. Click **Yes** to confirm the deletion. The employee with *EmpID 13* is now in the *5C Payroll* table only one time. **Close** the table.

6 On the **Create tab**, in the **Queries group**, click the **Query Wizard** button. In the **New Query** dialog box, click **Find Unmatched Query Wizard**, and then click **OK**.

a. In the first **Find Unmatched Query Wizard** dialog box, in the list of tables, click **Table: 5C Employees**, and then click **Next**. In the list of tables, click **Table: 5C Payroll**, and then click **Next**. Under **Fields in '5C Employees'**, if necessary, click **EmpID**. Under **Fields in 5C Payroll**, if necessary, click **EmpID**. Click the **<=>** button. Click **Next**.

b. Under **Available fields**, double-click **EmpID**, **Last Name**, and **First Name** to move the field names under **Selected fields**. Click **Next**. In the last dialog box, under **What would you like to name your query?**, type **Lastname Firstname 5C Find Unmatched** and then click **Finish**. The query results display one employee—*Michael Gottschalk*—who took unpaid time off during this pay period.

c. Adjust all column widths. View the query in **Print Preview**, ensuring that the query prints on one page. If you are instructed to submit this result, create a paper or electronic printout. **Close** the query, saving changes if necessary.

7 **Create** a new query in **Query Design**. Add the **5C Employees** table and the **5C Timecard** table to the Query design workspace, and then **Close** the **Show Table** dialog box. Expand the field lists.

a. From the **5C Employees** field list, add **Last Name** and **First Name** to the first and second columns in the design grid. From the **5C Timecard** field list, add **Timecard Date** and **Hours** to the third and fourth columns in the design grid.

b. In the **Criteria row**, in the **Timecard Date** field, type **[Enter Date]**

(Project 5C Payroll continues on the next page)

Skills Review | Project 5C Payroll (continued)

c. In the **Criteria row**, right-click in the **Hours** field, and then click **Zoom**. In the **Zoom** dialog box, type **Between [Enter the minimum Hours] And [Enter the maximum Hours]** and then click **OK**.

d. **Run** the query. In the **Enter Parameter Value** dialog box, type **6/29/15** and then click **OK**. Type **60** and then click **OK**. Type **80** and then click **OK**. Three employees have worked between 60 and 80 hours during the pay period for 6/29/15. They have earned vacation hours.

e. Adjust all column widths, and **Save** the query as **Lastname Firstname 5C Parameter** View the query in **Print Preview**, ensuring that the query prints on one page. If you are instructed to submit this result, create a paper or electronic printout. **Close** the query.

8 Open the **Navigation Pane**, **Close** the database, and then **Exit** Access.

End You have completed Project 5C ——————————————————————

Content-Based Assessments

Apply 5B skills from these Objectives:

Apply 5B skills from these Objectives:

- **6** Create a Make Table Query
- **7** Create an Append Query
- **8** Create a Delete Query
- **9** Create an Update Query
- **10** Modify the Join Type

Skills Review | Project 5D Clearance Sale

Ally Mason, Purchasing Manager for 4Ever Boarding Surf and Snowboard Shop, must keep the tables in the database up to date and ensure that the queries display pertinent information. Two of the suppliers, Wetsuit Country and Boots Etc, will no longer provide merchandise for 4Ever Boarding Surf and Snowboard Shop. This merchandise must be moved to a new discontinued items table. In the following Skills Review, you will create action queries that will create a new table, update records in a table, append records to a table, and delete records from a table. You will also modify the join type of relationships to display different subsets of the data when the query is run. Your completed queries will look similar to Figure 5.50.

Project Files

For Project 5D, you will need the following files:

    a05D_Clearance_Sale
    a05D_Warehouse_Items

You will save your databases as:

    Lastname_Firstname_5D_Clearance_Sale
    Lastname_Firstname_5D_Warehouse_Items

Project Results

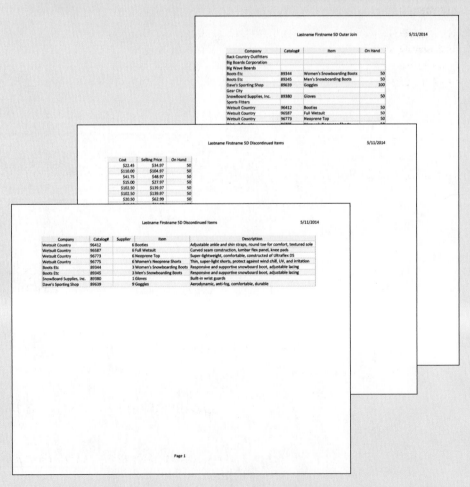

Figure 5.50

(Project 5D Clearance Sale continues on the next page)

Content-Based Assessments

1 **Start** Access. Locate and open the a05D_Clearance_Sale file. Display **Backstage** view. **Save** the database in your **Access Chapter 5** folder as Lastname_Firstname_5D_Clearance_Sale

a. If necessary, enable the content or add the Access Chapter 5 folder to the Trust Center.

b. Rename the tables by adding your **Lastname Firstname** to the beginning of each table name. **Close** the **Navigation Pane**.

2 Create a new query in **Query Design**. From the **Show Table** dialog box, add the following tables to the Query design workspace: **5D Suppliers** and **5D Inventory**. **Close** the **Show Table** dialog box, and then expand the field lists.

a. From the **5D Suppliers** field list, add **Company** to the first column of the design grid. From the **5D Inventory** field list, double-click each field to add them all to the design grid.

b. In the design grid, under **Supplier**, click in the **Criteria** row, type **6** and then **Run** the query. Notice that four items are supplied by *Wetsuit Country*.

c. Switch to **Design** view. On the **Design tab**, in the **Query Type group**, click the **Make Table** button. In the **Make Table** dialog box, in the **Table Name** box, type **Lastname Firstname 5D Discontinued Items** In the **Make Table** dialog box, be sure that **Current Database** is selected, and then click **OK**. **Run** the query. In the displayed message box, click **Yes** to paste the rows to the new table.

d. **Close** the query, click **Yes** in the message box asking if you want to save changes, and then name the query **Lastname Firstname 5D Wetsuit Country Items**

3 Create a new query in **Query Design**. From the **Show Table** dialog box, add the following tables, in the order specified, to the Query design workspace: **5D Suppliers** and **5D Inventory**. **Close** the **Show Table** dialog box, and then expand the field lists.

a. From the **5D Suppliers** field list, add **Company** to the first column of the design grid. From the **5D Inventory** field list, add all fields in the field list to the design grid.

b. In the design grid, under **Supplier**, click in the **Criteria** row, type **3** and then **Run** the query. Notice that one item is supplied by *Boots Etc*

c. Switch to **Design** view. On the **Design tab**, in the **Query Type group**, click the **Append** button. In the

Append dialog box, click the **Table Name arrow**, and from the displayed list, click **Lastname Firstname 5D Discontinued Items**, and then click **OK**.

d. **Run** the query. In the displayed message box, click **Yes** to append one row. **Close** the query, and then save it as **Lastname Firstname 5D Append1**

4 On the Access window title bar, click the **Minimize** button. **Start** a second instance of Access. Navigate to the location where the student data files for this textbook are saved. Locate and open the **a05D_Warehouse_Items** file. Save the database in your **Access Chapter 5** folder as **Lastname_Firstname_5D_Warehouse_Items** If necessary, enable the content or add the Access Chapter 5 folder to the Trust Center.

5 Create a new query in **Query Design**. From the **Show Table** dialog box, add the **5D Suppliers** table and the **5D Discontinued Items** table to the Query design workspace, and then close the **Show Table** dialog box. Expand the field lists. From the **5D Suppliers** field list, add **Company** to the first column of the design grid. From the **5D Discontinued Items** field list, add all of the fields to the design grid in the order listed.

a. On the **Design tab**, in the **Query Type group**, click the **Append** button. In the **Append** dialog box, click the **Another Database** option button, and then click the **Browse** button. Navigate to your **Access Chapter 5** folder, and then double-click **Lastname_Firstname_5D_Clearance_Sale**.

b. In the **Append** dialog box, click the **Table Name arrow**, click **5D Discontinued Items**, and then click **OK**. **Save** the query as **Lastname Firstname 5D Append2** and then **Run** the query. In the displayed message box, click **Yes** to append 3 rows. **Close** the query. **Close** the database, and then **Exit** this instance of Access.

c. From the Windows taskbar, click the **5D_Clearance_Sale** database. Verify that the **5D Discontinued Items** table now contains 8 rows. Create a new query in **Query Design**. Add the **5D Inventory** table to the Query design workspace, and then **Close** the **Show Table** dialog box.

d. Expand the field list. From the field list, add **Catalog#** and **On Hand**, in this order, to the first and second columns in the design grid. In the design grid, under **On Hand**, click in the **Criteria** row, type **0** and then **Run** the query.

(Project 5D Clearance Sale continues on the next page)

Access | Chapter 5

e. Switch to **Design** view. In the Query design workspace, right-click in the empty space. From the displayed shortcut menu, point to **Query Type**, and then click **Delete Query**.

f. **Save** the query as **Lastname Firstname 5D Delete Zero Inventory** and then **Run** the query. In the message box stating that *You are about to delete 1 row(s) from the specified table*, click **Yes**. **Close** the query. You have removed this item from the inventory.

6 Create a new query in **Query Design**. Add the **5D Discontinued Items** table to the Query design workspace, and then **Close** the **Show Table** dialog box. Expand the field list.

a. In the **5D Discontinued Items** field list, double-click **Catalog#** to add the field to the first column of the design grid. Then add the **Selling Price** field to the second column of the design grid.

b. On the **Design tab**, in the **Query Type group**, click the **Update** button. In the design grid, under **Selling Price**, click in the **Update To row**, and then type **[Selling Price]*0.7**

c. **Save** the query as **Lastname Firstname 5D Discounted Selling Prices** and then **Run** the query. In the message box stating that *You are about to update 8 row(s)*, click **Yes**. **Close** the query.

d. Open the **Navigation Pane**, and then double-click the **5D Discontinued Items** table to open it in **Datasheet** view. Close the **Navigation Pane**. Adjust all column widths. View the table in **Print Preview**. If you are instructed to submit this result, create a

paper or electronic printout in **Landscape** orientation. **Close** the table, saving changes.

7 Create a new query in **Query Design**. From the **Show Table** dialog box, add the **5D Suppliers** table and the **5D Discontinued Items** table to the Query design workspace, and then **Close** the **Show Table** dialog box.

a. Expand both field lists. From the **5D Suppliers** table, drag the **ID** field to the **5D Discontinued Items** table **Supplier** field to create a join between the tables.

b. From the **5D Suppliers** field list, add **Company** to the first column in the design grid. From the **5D Discontinued Items** field list, add **Catalog#**, **Item**, and **On Hand**, in this order, to the design grid. In the design grid, under **Company**, click in the **Sort row**, click the **arrow**, and then click **Ascending**. **Run** the query.

c. Switch to **Design** view. Verify that the **5D Suppliers** table appears on the left, and the **5D Discontinued Items** table is on the right. Correct as necessary. In the Query design workspace, double-click the **join line** to display the **Join Properties** dialog box. Click the option button next to **2**, and then click **OK**. **Run** the query. This query displays all of the supplier companies used by the shop, not just those with discontinued items.

d. **Save** the query as **Lastname Firstname 5D Outer Join** View the query in **Print Preview**, ensuring that the table prints on one page. If you are instructed to submit this result, create a paper or electronic printout. **Close** the query.

8 Open the **Navigation Pane**, **Close** the database, and then **Exit** Access.

End **You have completed Project 5D**

Content-Based Assessments

Apply 5A skills from these Objectives:

1. Create Calculated Fields in a Query
2. Use Aggregate Functions in a Query
3. Create a Crosstab Query
4. Find Duplicate and Unmatched Records
5. Create a Parameter Query

Mastering Access | Project **5E** Surfing Lessons

Mary Connolly, one of the owners of 4Ever Boarding Surf and Snowboard Shop, has a database containing student, instructor, and surfing lesson data. In the following Mastering Access project, you will create special-purpose queries to calculate data, summarize and group data, display data in a spreadsheet-like format, and find duplicate and unmatched records. You will also create a query that prompts an individual to enter the criteria. Your completed queries will look similar to Figure 5.51.

Project Files

For Project 5E, you will need the following file:

a05E_Surfing_Lessons

You will save your database as:

Lastname_Firstname_5E_Surfing_Lessons

Project Results

Figure 5.51

(Project 5E Surfing Lessons continues on the next page)

Access | Chapter 5

1 **Start** Access. Locate and open the **a05E_Surfing_Lessons** file. Display **Backstage** view. Save the database in in your **Access Chapter 5** folder as **Lastname_Firstname_5E_Surfing_Lessons** If necessary, enable the content or add the Access Chapter 5 folder to the Trust Center. Rename the tables by adding your **Lastname Firstname** to the beginning of each table name.

2 **Create** a query in **Query Design** using the **5E Surfing Lessons** table and the **5E Students** table. From the **5E Surfing Lessons** table, add the **Instructor** field, the **Lesson Time** field, and the **Duration** field to the first, second, and third columns of the design grid. From the **5E Students** table, add the **Last Name** and **First Name** fields to the fourth and fifth columns.

3 In the sixth column of the design grid, add a calculated field. In the field name row, type **End Time: [Duration]/24+[Lesson Time]** Display the field properties sheet, and then format this field as **Medium Time**. This field will display the time the lesson ends.

4 In the first blank column, in the field name row, add the calculated field **Fees:[Duration]*75** From the field properties sheet, select the **Format** of **Currency**. Surfing lessons cost $75.00 an hour.

5 In the **Instructor** field, in the **Sort row**, click **Ascending**. In the **Lesson Time** field, in the **Sort row**, click **Ascending**. **Run** the query.

6 On the **Home tab**, in the **Records group**, click the **Totals** button. In the **Fees column**, in the **Total row**, click the **down arrow**, and then click **Average**. Adjust field widths as necessary.

7 **Save** the query as **Lastname Firstname 5E Student Lessons** View the query in **Print Preview**, ensuring that the query prints on one page. If you are instructed to submit this result, create a paper or electronic printout. **Close** the query.

8 **Create** a new query using the **Crosstab Query Wizard**. Select the **Query: 5E Student Lessons**. Click **Next**. From the **Available Fields**, add **Instructor** to the **Selected Fields** column. Click **Next**. Double-click **Lesson Time**, and then click **Date**. Click **Next**. From the **Fields column**, select **Duration**, and then from **Functions**, select **Sum**. Clear the **Yes, include row sums** check box.

9 Click **Next**. Name the query **Lastname Firstname 5E Crosstab** Select **View the query**, and then click **Finish**. This query displays the instructor and the number of hours he or she taught by date. Adjust field widths as necessary.

10 View the query in **Print Preview**, ensuring that the query prints on one page. If you are instructed to submit this result, create a paper or electronic printout. **Close** the query, saving changes.

11 Click the **Query Wizard** button. In the **New Query** dialog box, click **Find Duplicates Query Wizard**. Search the **Table: 5E Surfing Lessons**, and select the **Lesson Time** field for duplicate information. Click **Next**. From **Available fields**, add the **Instructor** and **Duration** fields to the **Additional query fields** column. Accept the default name for the query. Click **Finish**. The query results show that there are duplicate lesson times. Adjust field widths as necessary.

12 View the query in **Print Preview**, ensuring that the query prints on one page. If you are instructed to submit this result, create a paper or electronic printout. **Close** and **Save** the query.

13 Click the **Query Wizard** button. In the **New Query** dialog box, click **Find Unmatched Query Wizard**. Select **Table: 5E Surfing Instructors**. From the **Which table or query contains the related records?** dialog box, click **Table: 5E Surfing Lessons**. Click **Instructor** as the **Matching** field. Display the one field **Instructor** in the query results. Name the query **Lastname Firstname 5E Unmatched** and then click **Finish**. Jack is the only instructor who has no students.

14 View the query in **Print Preview**, ensuring that the query prints on one page. If you are instructed to submit this result, create a paper or electronic printout. **Close** the query.

15 **Create** a query in **Design** view using the **5E Surfing Lessons** table and the **5E Students** table. From the **5E Surfing Lessons** table, add the **Instructor** field. From the **5E Students** table, add the **Last Name**, **First Name**, and **Phone#** fields in that order to the design grid. In the **Instructor** field, in the **Criteria row**, type **[Enter Instructor's First Name]**

16 **Run** the query. In the **Enter Parameter Value** dialog box, type **Andrea** and then press Enter. The query displays Andrea's students and their phone numbers.

17 **Save** the query as **Lastname Firstname 5E Parameter** Adjust field widths as necessary.

18 View the query in **Print Preview**, ensuring that the query prints on one page. If you are instructed to submit this result, create a paper or electronic printout. **Close** the query.

19 Open the **Navigation Pane**, **Close** the database, and then **Exit** Access.

 End **You have completed Project 5E**

Content-Based Assessments

Apply 5B skills from these Objectives:

- **6** Create a Make Table Query
- **7** Create an Append Query
- **8** Create a Delete Query
- **9** Create an Update Query
- **10** Modify the Join Type

Mastering Access | Project 5F Gift Cards

Karen Walker, Sales Associate for 4Ever Boarding Surf and Snowboard Shop, has decided to offer gift cards for purchase at the shop. She has a database of the employees and the details of the cards they have sold. In the following Mastering Access project, you will create action queries that will create a new table, update records in a table, append records to a table, and delete records from a table. You will also modify the join type of the relationship to display a different subset of the data when the query is run. Your completed queries will look similar to Figure 5.52.

Project Files

For Project 5F, you will need the following file:

a05F_Gift_Cards

You will save your database as:

Lastname_Firstname_5F_Gift_Cards

Project Results

Figure 5.52

(Project 5F Gift Cards continues on the next page)

Content-Based Assessments

Mastering Access | Project **5F** Gift Cards (continued)

1 **Start** Access. Locate and open the **a05F_Gift_Cards** file. Display **Backstage** view. Save the database in your **Access Chapter 5** folder as **Lastname_Firstname_5F_Gift_Cards** If necessary, enable the content or add the Access Chapter 5 folder to the Trust Center. Rename the tables by adding your **Lastname Firstname** to the beginning of each table name.

2 Create a new query in **Query Design**. To the Query design workspace, add the **5F Employees**, **5F Sales**, and the **5F Inventory** tables. From the **5F Employees** table, add the **First Name** and **Last Name** fields to the first and second columns of the design grid. From the **5F Sales** table, add the following fields to the design grid in the order specified: **Sales Date** and **Quantity**. From the **5F Inventory** table, add the **Item** and **Cost** fields.

3 In the **Item** field column, in the **Criteria row**, type **Gift Cards** In the **Cost** field column, in the **Criteria row**, type **10 Or 50 Sort** the **Last Name** field in **Ascending** order.

4 On the **Design tab**, click the **Make Table** button. Name the table **Lastname Firstname 5F $10 or $50 Gift Cards** Select **Current Database**, click **OK**, and then **Run** the query. **Close** the query, saving it as **Lastname Firstname 5F Make Table** Open the **5F $10 or $50 Gift Cards** table to display the two gift card purchases. **Close** the table.

5 Create a new query in **Query Design**. To the Query design workspace, add the **5F Employees**, **5F Sales**, and the **5F Inventory** tables. From the **5F Employees** table, add the **First Name** and **Last Name** fields to the first and second columns of the design grid. From the **5F Sales** table, add the following fields to the design grid in the following order: **Sales Date** and **Quantity**. From the **5F Inventory** table, add the **Item** and **Cost** fields.

6 In the **Item** field column, in the **Criteria row**, type **Gift Cards** In the **Cost** field column, in the **Criteria row**, type **100 Or 500 Sort** the **Last Name** field in **Ascending** order.

7 Click the **Append** button, and then append the records to the **5F $10 or $50 Gift Cards** table. Click **OK**. **Run** the query. Click **Yes** to append two rows. **Close** the query, saving it as **Lastname Firstname 5F Append** Open the **5F $10 or $50 Gift Cards** table to display all gift card purchases. **Close** the table, and then rename it **Lastname Firstname 5F Gift Cards**

8 View the table in **Print Preview**, ensuring that the table prints on one page. If you are instructed to submit this result, create a paper or electronic printout. **Close** the table.

9 Create a new query in **Query Design**. Add the **5F Inventory** table to the Query design workspace. From the **5F Inventory** table, add the **Catalog#** and **Item** fields to the first and second columns of the design grid. In the design grid, under **Item**, click in the **Criteria row**, and then type **Gift Cards**

10 **Run** the query to view the results. Switch to **Design** view, click the **Query Type: Delete** button, and then **Run** the query. Click **Yes** to delete the gift cards from the **5F Inventory** table. The gift cards are not to be counted as inventory items. **Close** and **Save** the query, naming it **Lastname Firstname 5F Delete**

11 Open the **5F Inventory** table. If you are instructed to submit this result, create a paper or electronic printout in **Landscape** orientation. **Close** the table.

12 Create a new query in **Query Design**. Add the **5F Employees** table to the Query design workspace. From the **5F Employees** table, add **Postal Code** to the first column of the design grid. In the design grid, under **Postal Code**, click in the **Criteria row**, and then type **972* Run** the query to view the results. Switch to **Design** view. Click the **Query Type: Update** button.

13 In the design grid, under **Postal Code**, click in the **Update To row**, and then type **92701**

14 **Run** the query. Click **Yes** to update two rows. **Close** the query, saving it as **Lastname Firstname 5F Update** Open the **5F Employees** table. View the table in **Print Preview**, ensuring that the table prints on one page. If you are instructed to submit this result, create a paper or electronic printout. **Close** the table.

15 Create a new query in **Query Design**. Add the **5F Employees** and **5F Gift Cards** tables to the Query design workspace. From the **5F Employees** field list, add **First Name** and **Last Name** to the first two columns of the design grid. From the **5F Gift Cards** field list, add **Cost** and **Quantity** field, in this order, to the design grid.

16 From the **5F Employees** field list, click **Last Name**, and then drag to the **5F Gift Cards Last Name** field. Double-click the **join line**, and then select option **2**. **Run**

(Project 5F Gift Cards continues on the next page)

Mastering Access | Project **5F** Gift Cards (continued)

the query to display the results, which include all 14 employees and not just gift card sellers. **Save** the query as **Lastname Firstname 5F Modified Join**

17 View the table in **Print Preview**, ensuring that the table prints on one page. If you are instructed to submit this result, create a paper or electronic printout. **Close** the query.

18 **Close** the database, and then **Exit** Access.

End You have completed Project 5F —————————————————————

Content-Based Assessments

1 Create Calculated Fields in a Query

2 Use Aggregate Functions in a Query

3 Create a Crosstab Query

9 Create an Update Query

Mastering Access | Project **5G** Advertisements

J.D. Golden, one of the owners of 4Ever Boarding Surf and Snowboard Shop, is responsible for all of the advertising for the business. In the following Mastering Access project, you will create special-purpose queries to calculate data, and then summarize and group data for advertising cost analysis. You will also create a query that prompts an individual to enter the criteria for a specific type of advertisement media. Your completed queries will look similar to Figure 5.53.

Project Files

For Project 5G, you will need the following file:

a05G_Advertisements

You will save your database as:

Lastname_Firstname_5G_Advertisements

Project Results

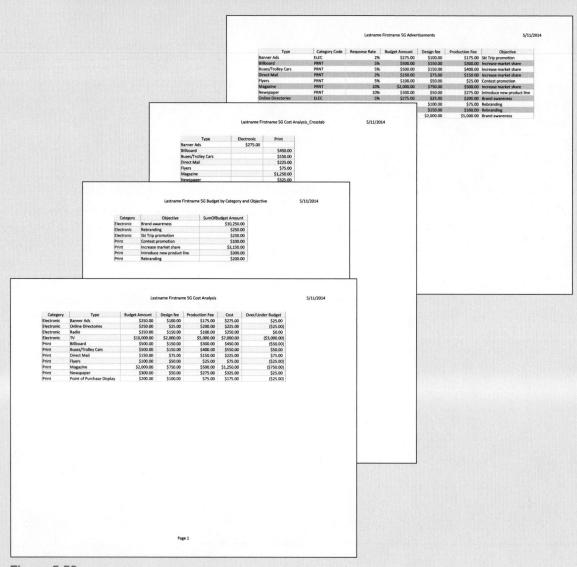

Figure 5.53

(Project 5G Advertisements continues on the next page)

Content-Based Assessments

Mastering Access | Project 5G Advertisements (continued)

1 **Start** Access. Locate and open the **a05G_Advertisements** file. Display **Backstage** view. Save the database in your **Access Chapter 5** folder as **Lastname_Firstname_5G_ Advertisements** If necessary, enable the content or add the Access Chapter 5 folder to the Trust Center. Rename the table by adding your **Lastname Firstname** to the beginning of the table names. Close the **Navigation Pane**.

2 Create a new query in **Query Design**. From the **5G Categories** table, add the **Category** field to the design grid. From the **5G Advertisements** table, add the **Type**, **Budget Amount**, **Design Fee**, and **Production Fee** fields to the design grid in this order.

3 In the first blank field column, add a calculated field. Type **Cost:[Design Fee]+[Production Fee]** In the next blank field column, add a second calculated field: **Over/Under Budget: [Cost]-[Budget Amount]**

4 **Run** the query. Save it as **Lastname Firstname 5G Cost Analysis**. View the results in **Print Preview**, ensuring that it fits on one page. If you are instructed to submit this result, create a paper or electronic printout. **Close** the query.

5 Create a new query in **Query Design**. From the **5G Categories** table, add the **Category** field to the design grid. From the **5G Advertisements** table, add the **Objective** and **Budget Amount** fields to the design grid. On the **Design tab**, in the **Show/Hide group**, click the **Totals** button. In the design grid, in the **Total row**, under **Budget Amount**, click **Sum**.

6 **Run** the query. Save it as **Lastname Firstname 5G Budget by Category and Objective** View the results in **Print Preview**, ensuring that it on one page. If you are

instructed to submit this result, create a paper or electronic printout. **Close** the query.

7 Create a new crosstab query using the Query Wizard. Select the **Query: 5G Cost Analysis**. For row headings, use **Type**, and for column headings, use **Category**. Select **Cost** for the calculated field, using the **Sum** function. Do not summarize each row. Accept the default name for this query.

8 Click **Finish** to view the cost in relation to the response rate for each type of advertisement.

9 View the query in **Print Preview**, ensuring that the query prints on one page. If you are instructed to submit this result, create a paper or electronic printout. **Close** the query.

10 Create a new query in **Query Design**. From the **5G Categories** table, add the **Category** field to the design grid. From the **5G Advertisements** table, add the **Budget Amount** field to the design grid. In the design grid, under **Category** field, click in the **Criteria row**, and then type **Electronic**

11 Click the **Query Type: Update** button. In the design grid, under **Budget Amount**, click in the **Update To row**, and then type **[Budget Amount]*1.10**

12 **Run** the query. Click **Yes** to update four rows. **Close** the query, saving it as **Lastname Firstname 5G Update** Open the **Navigation Pane**. Open the **5G Advertisements** table. View the table in **Print Preview**, ensuring that the table prints on one page. If you are instructed to submit this result, create a paper or electronic printout. **Close** the table.

13 **Close** the database, and then **Exit** Access.

End You have completed Project 5G ——————————

GO! Fix It | Project **5H** Contests

Project Files

For Project 5H, you will need the following files:

a05H_Snowboarding_Contests
a05H_Online_Registration

You will save your databases as:

Lastname_Firstname_5H_Snowboarding_Contests
Lastname_Firstname_5H_Online_Registration

In this project, you will correct query design errors in a database used to manage snowboarding contests for children, teenagers, and adults. To complete the project you must find and correct errors in relationships, query design, and column widths.

- In the **5H Snowboarding Contests** database, you should add your last name and first name to the beginning of each query name; do *not* rename the tables.

- All registration information should be kept in a table of its own. Use the 5H Contestants query to create the 5H Registration table. Append the customers that registered online; their information is found in the **5H Online Registration** database.

- Nelson Gibbs forgot to turn in his date of birth (DOB). Create a query to update his date of birth to 8/27/1990. He is registered for two contests.

- 5H Contestant Ages on Event Date only includes the customers that registered in the store. Update the design to reflect data from the correct table. Be sure that the contestant's full name, event date, and DOB are displayed in the results. The age is represented in days; update the expression to show the age in years only.

- Several queries do not accurately reflect the result implied in the query name. Open each query and examine and correct the design; modify them to accurately reflect the query name.

End **You have completed Project 5H** ——————————

Content-Based Assessments

GO! Make It | Project 5I Ski Trips

Project Files

For Project 5I, you will need the following file:

a05I_Ski_Trips

You will save your database as:

Lastname_Firstname_5I_Ski_Trips

From the student files that accompany this textbook, open the **a05I_Ski_Trips** database file. Save the database in your Access Chapter 5 folder as **Lastname_Firstname_5I_Ski_Trips** In Query Design, create a query to display the following fields from existing tables: **Ski Trips**: **Depart Date, Return Date, Resort, Price, Rentals, Lift**; **Ski Trip Captains**: **First Name** and **Last Name** in **Ascending** order. Add a calculated field to display the **#Days** included in the trip and the **Total Cost** including **Price, Rentals**, and **Lift**. Compare your results to those shown in Figure 5.54. Create a paper or electronic printout as directed.

Project Results

Lastname Firstname 5I Trip Details   5/11/2014

Depart Date	Return Date	#Days	Resort	Price	Rentals	Lift	Total Cost	First name	Last Name
12/28/2015 10:00:00 AM	1/1/2016 10:00:00 PM	4.50	Timber Ridge	$619	$0.00	$0.00	$619.00	Ashley	Henegar
12/12/2015 6:00:00 AM	12/13/2015 6:00:00 PM	1.50	Valley Lodge	$300	$15.00	$20.00	$335.00	Ashley	Henegar
1/8/2016 5:00:00 AM	1/9/2016 5:00:00 PM	1.50	Snow Time	$250	$0.00	$0.00	$250.00	Ashley	Henegar
12/11/2015 6:00:00 AM	12/12/2015 6:00:00 AM	1.00	Valley Lodge	$200	$15.00	$20.00	$235.00	Kenneth	Pliecher
12/20/2015 4:00:00 AM	12/21/2015 4:00:00 PM	1.00	Winter Haven	$125	$20.00	$25.00	$170.00	Kenneth	Pliecher
11/25/2015 6:00:00 AM	11/26/2015 6:00:00 AM	1.00	Valley Lodge	$200	$15.00	$20.00	$235.00	Kenneth	Pliecher
12/30/2015 7:30:00 PM	1/1/2016 7:30:00 PM	2.00	Timber Ridge	$519	$0.00	$0.00	$519.00	Kenneth	Pliecher
2/1/2016 7:30:00 PM	2/5/2016 7:30:00 PM	4.00	Timber Ridge	$449	$0.00	$0.00	$449.00	Kenneth	Pliecher
1/22/2016 5:00:00 AM	1/24/2016 5:00:00 PM	2.50	Snow Time	$375	$0.00	$0.00	$375.00	Kenneth	Pliecher
1/3/2016 8:00:00 PM	1/5/2016 8:00:00 PM	2.00	Chile Andes	$1,849	$0.00	$0.00	$1,849.00	Helen	Reindel
12/19/2015 4:00:00 PM	12/20/2015 4:00:00 PM	1.00	Winter Haven	$125	$20.00	$25.00	$170.00	Helen	Reindel
1/27/2016 7:00:00 PM	2/3/2016 1:00:00 PM	6.25	Switzerland	$1,699	$0.00	$0.00	$1,699.00	Helen	Reindel
12/26/2015 7:00:00 PM	1/1/2016 7:00:00 PM	6.00	Italy	$1,689	$0.00	$0.00	$1,689.00	Helen	Reindel
12/29/2015 4:00:00 AM	12/30/2015 4:00:00 PM	1.50	Winter Haven	$185	$20.00	$25.00	$230.00	Mitch	Taccaro
1/6/2016 2:00:00 PM	1/13/2016 8:00:00 PM	7.25	Canada	$1,349	$0.00	$0.00	$1,349.00	Mitch	Taccaro
11/27/2015 6:00:00 AM	11/28/2015 6:00:00 PM	1.50	Valley Lodge	$300	$15.00	$20.00	$335.00	Mitch	Taccaro

Page 1

Figure 5.54

End **You have completed Project 5I**

Content-Based Assessments

GO! Solve It | Project **5J** Applicant

Project Files

For Project 5J, you will need the following file:

a05J_Job_Applicants

You will save your database as:

Lastname_Firstname_5J_Job_Applicants

The owners of 4Ever Boarding Surf and Snowboard Shop, Mary Connolly and J.D. Golden, will be hiring more employees for the busy season. In this project, you will create special function queries to assist with their selection process. From the student files that accompany this textbook, open the **a05J_Job_Applicants** database file, and then save the database in your Access Chapter 5 folder as **Lastname_Firstname_5J_Job_Applicants**

Create a find unmatched records query to show all fields for applicants that have not been scheduled for an interview. Create a parameter query to locate a particular applicant and display all of his or her data. Use an aggregate function in a query that will count the number of applicants grouped by position. Save your queries by using your last and first names followed by the query type. View the queries in Print Preview, ensuring that the queries each print on one page. If you are instructed to submit this result, create a paper or electronic printout. Close the queries. Save and close the database.

Performance Element		Performance Level		
		Exemplary: You consistently applied the relevant skills	**Proficient:** You sometimes, but not always, applied the relevant skills	**Developing:** You rarely or never applied the relevant skills
	Create 5J Unmatched Records Query	Query created to identify applicants without an interview scheduled.	Query created with no more than two missing elements.	Query created with more than two missing elements.
	Create 5J Parameter Query	Query created to display a particular applicant's data.	Query created with no more than two missing elements.	Query created with more than two missing elements.
	Create 5J Totals Query	Query created to count the applicants for each position.	Query created with no more than two missing elements.	Query created with more than two missing elements.

End You have completed Project 5J

Content-Based Assessments

GO! Solve It | Project **5K** Ski Apparel

Project Files

For Project 5K, you will need the following file:

a05K_Ski_Apparel

You will save your database as:

Lastname_Firstname_5K_Ski_Apparel

Ally Mason is the Purchasing Manager for the 4Ever Boarding Surf and Snowboard Shop. It is her responsibility to keep the clothing inventory current and fashionable. You have been asked to help her with this task. From the student files that accompany this textbook, open the **a05K_Ski_Apparel** database file, and then save the database in your **Access Chapter 5** folder as **Lastname_Firstname_5K_Ski_Apparel**

The database consists of a table of ski apparel for youth, women, and men. Create a query to identify the inventory by status of the items (promotional, in stock, and discontinued clothing). Count how many items are in each category. Update the selling price of the discontinued items to 90 percent of the cost. Use a make table query to separate the promotional clothing into its own table and a delete query to remove those items from the 5K Ski Apparel table. Save your queries using your last and first names followed by the query type . View the queries in Print Preview, ensuring that the queries print on one page. If you are instructed to submit this result, create a paper or electronic printout. Close the queries, and then close the database.

	Performance Level		
	Exemplary: You consistently applied the relevant skills	Proficient: You sometimes, but not always, applied the relevant skills	Developing: You rarely or never applied the relevant skills
Create 5K Totals Query	Query created to display the inventory by status.	Query created with no more than two missing elements.	Query created with more than two missing elements.
Create 5K Update Query	Query created to update clearance sale prices.	Query created with no more than two missing elements.	Query created with more than two missing elements.
Create 5K Make Table Query	Query created to make a table for promotional clothing.	Query created with no more than two missing elements.	Query created with more than two missing elements.
Create 5K Delete Query	Query created to delete promotional clothing from the Ski Apparel table.	Query created with no more than two missing elements.	Query created with more than two missing elements.

Performance Element

End You have completed Project 5K ————————————————

Outcomes-Based Assessments

Rubric

The following outcomes-based assessments are *open-ended assessments*. That is, there is no specific correct result; your result will depend on your approach to the information provided. Make *Professional Quality* your goal. Use the following scoring rubric to guide you in *how* to approach the problem and then to evaluate *how well* your approach solves the problem.

The *criteria*—Software Mastery, Content, Format and Layout, and Process—represent the knowledge and skills you have gained that you can apply to solving the problem. The *levels of performance*—Professional Quality, Approaching Professional Quality, or Needs Quality Improvements—help you and your instructor evaluate your result.

	Your completed project is of Professional Quality if you:	Your completed project is Approaching Professional Quality if you:	Your completed project Needs Quality Improvements if you:
1-Software Mastery	Choose and apply the most appropriate skills, tools, and features and identify efficient methods to solve the problem.	Choose and apply some appropriate skills, tools, and features, but not in the most efficient manner.	Choose inappropriate skills, tools, or features, or are inefficient in solving the problem.
2-Content	Construct a solution that is clear and well organized, contains content that is accurate, appropriate to the audience and purpose, and is complete. Provide a solution that contains no errors in spelling, grammar, or style.	Construct a solution in which some components are unclear, poorly organized, inconsistent, or incomplete. Misjudge the needs of the audience. Have some errors in spelling, grammar, or style, but the errors do not detract from comprehension.	Construct a solution that is unclear, incomplete, or poorly organized; contains some inaccurate or inappropriate content; and contains many errors in spelling, grammar, or style. Do not solve the problem.
3-Format and Layout	Format and arrange all elements to communicate information and ideas, clarify function, illustrate relationships, and indicate relative importance.	Apply appropriate format and layout features to some elements, but not others. Overuse features, causing minor distraction.	Apply format and layout that does not communicate information or ideas clearly. Do not use format and layout features to clarify function, illustrate relationships, or indicate relative importance. Use available features excessively, causing distraction.
4-Process	Use an organized approach that integrates planning, development, self-assessment, revision, and reflection.	Demonstrate an organized approach in some areas, but not others; or, use an insufficient process of organization throughout.	Do not use an organized approach to solve the problem.

Outcomes-Based Assessments

GO! Think | Project **5L** Surfboards

Project Files

For Project 5L, you will need the following file:

   a05L_Surfboards

You will save your database as:

   Lastname_Firstname_5L_Surfboards

Ally Mason, Purchasing Manager for 4Ever Boarding Surf and Snowboard Shop, is stocking the shop with a variety of surfboards and accessories for the upcoming season.In this project, you will open the **5L_Surfboards** database and create queries to perform special functions. Save the database as **Lastname_Firstname_5L_Surfboards** Create a query to display the item, cost, selling price, on hand, and two calculated fields: Profit Per Item by subtracting the cost from the selling price and Inventory Profit by multiplying Profit Per Item by the number on hand for each item. Include a sum for the Inventory Profit column at the bottom of the query results. Check the supplier against the inventory using a find unmatched records query. Create a query to show the company that supplies each item, their e-mail address, and then the item and on hand fields for each item in the inventory. Before running the query, create an outer join query using the *5L Suppliers* table and the *5L Inventory* table. Save your queries using your last and first names followed by the query type. View the queries in Print Preview, ensuring that the queries print on one page. If you are instructed to submit this result, create a paper or electronic printout. Close the queries.

End You have completed Project 5L ————————

GO! Think | Project **5M** Shop Promotions

Project Files

For Project 5M, you will need the following file:

   a05M_Shop_Promotions

You will save your database as:

   Lastname_Firstname_5M_Shop_Promotions

The owners of 4Ever Boarding Surf and Snowboard Shop have invited some of Southern California's best extreme sports game participants to the shop to promote certain lines of clothing and gear. These participants will be on hand to answer questions, give demonstrations, and distribute prizes to customers. In this project, you will enhance the database by creating queries to perform special functions.

Open the **5M_Shop_Promotions** database. Save the database as **Lastname_Firstname_5M_Shop_Promotions** Use the Find Duplicates Query Wizard to find any events that may have been scheduled at the same time for the same day. The shop must be closed for remodeling. Use an update query to select only those events that are scheduled between July 31, 2015, and August 30, 2015, and reschedule those events for 30 days later than each original date. Create a parameter query to display the events by activity; run the query to display giveway activities. Save your queries using your last and first names followed by the query type. View the queries in Print Preview, ensuring that the queries print on one page. If you are instructed to submit this result, create a paper or electronic printout. Close the queries.

End You have completed Project 5M ————————

Outcomes-Based Assessments

You and GO! | Project **5N** Club Directory

Project Files

For Project 5N, you will need the following file:

> Lastname_Firstname_4N_Club_Directory (your file from Chapter 4)

You will save your database as:

> Lastname_Firstname_5N_Club_Directory

Create a personal database containing information about a club and its activities, if you do not already have one from Project 4N. Name the new database **Lastname_Firstname_5N_Club_Directory** If you do not have the database from Project 4N, create two related tables, one that lists the activities your organization has planned and the other to serve as the directory of the group. The Activities table should include information about the name (primary key field), date, cost, and location of the activity. The dates must all occur next year, and consider attaching directions to the event to the table. The Directory table should include full name, address, phone number, e-mail, and an activity they are planning. If you have the database from Project 4N, make any necessary corrections before saving it in your Access Chapter 5 folder.

Using the Activities table, create a query to determine the total and average cost of the activities they are planning. Also using the Activities table, create a list of all of the activities and the location for all activities that are free (you might not have any results). Create a query to display each activity along with how many students are working on the event. Create a query to display a list of events, along with the location and price; sort the query by date in ascending order. Create a parameter query to display all student information based on an activity. View the queries in Print Preview, ensuring that the queries print on one page. If you are instructed to submit this result, create a paper or electronic printout. Save the database as **Lastname_Firstname_5N_Club_Directory**

You will be using this database in future chapters. Be sure to make corrections to your tables as necessary to prepare for the next chapter.

End **You have completed Project 5N** ————————————————

Customizing Forms and Reports

OUTCOMES

At the end of this chapter you will be able to:

OBJECTIVES

Mastering these objectives will enable you to:

PROJECT 6A
Customize forms.

1. Create a Form in Design View (p. 391)
2. Change and Add Controls (p. 395)
3. Format a Form (p. 401)
4. Make a Form User Friendly (p. 407)

PROJECT 6B
Customize reports.

5. Create a Report Based on a Query Using a Wizard (p. 416)
6. Create a Report in Design View (p. 419)
7. Add Controls to a Report (p. 422)
8. Group, Sort, and Total Records in Design View (p. 427)

Nayashkova Olga/Shutterstock

In This Chapter

Forms provide you with a way to enter, edit, and display data from underlying tables. You have created forms using the Form button and the Form Wizard. Forms can also be created in Design view. Access provides tools that can enhance the visual appearance of forms, for example, adding color, backgrounds, borders, or instructions to the person using the form. Forms can also be used to manipulate data from multiple tables if a relationship exists between the tables.

Reports display data in a professional-looking format. Like forms, reports can also be created using a wizard or in Design view, and they can all be enhanced using Access tools. Reports can be based on tables or queries

Sand Dollar Cafe is a "quick, casual" franchise restaurant chain with headquarters in Palm Harbor, Florida. The founders wanted to create a restaurant where the flavors of the Caribbean islands would be available at reasonable prices in a bright, comfortable atmosphere. The menu features fresh food and quality ingredients in offerings like grilled chicken skewers, wrap sandwiches, fruit salads, mango ice cream, smoothies, and coffee drinks. All 75 outlets offer wireless Internet connections, making Sand Dollar Cafe the perfect place for groups and people who want some quiet time.

Project 6A Franchises

myitlab
Project 6A Training

Project Activities

In Activities 6.01 through 6.10, you will help Linda Kay, President, and James Winchell, Vice President of Franchising, create robust forms to match the needs of Sand Dollar Cafe. For example, the forms can include color and different types of controls and can manipulate data from several tables. You will customize your forms to make them easier to use and more attractive. Your completed form will look similar to Figure 6.1.

Project Files

For Project 6A, you will need the following files:

> a06A_Franchises
> a06A_Logo
> a06A_Background

You will save your database as:

> Lastname_Firstname_6A_Franchises

Project Results

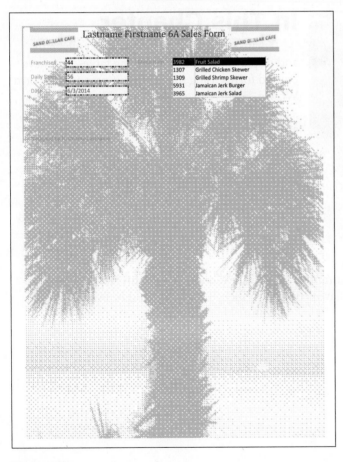

Figure 6.1
Project 6A Franchises

Objective 1 | Create a Form in Design View

You usually create a form using the Form tool or the Form Wizard and then modify the form in Design view to suit your needs. Use Design view to create a form when these tools do not meet your needs, or if you want more control in the creation of a form. Creating or modifying a form in Design view is a common technique when additional controls, such as combo boxes or images, need to be added to the form.

Activity 6.01 | Creating a Form in Design View

In this activity, you will create a form in Design view that will enable employees to enter the daily sales data for each franchise of Sand Dollar Cafe.

1 **Start** Access. Navigate to the location where the student data files for this textbook are saved. Locate and open the **a06A_Franchises** file. Display **Backstage** view, and click **Save Database As**. In the **Save As** dialog box, navigate to the drive on which you will be saving your folders and projects for this chapter. Create a new folder named **Access Chapter 6** and then save the database as **Lastname_Firstname_6A_Franchises** in the folder.

2 Enable the content or add the Access Chapter 6 folder to the Trust Center.

3 In the **Navigation Pane**, double-click **6A Sales** to open the table in **Datasheet** view. Take a moment to examine the fields in the table. In any record, click in the **Franchise#** field, and then click the **arrow**. This field is a Lookup field—the values are looked up in the *6A Franchises* table. The Menu Item field is also a Lookup field—the values are looked up in the *6A Menu Items* table.

4 **Close** ☒ the table, and then **Close** « the **Navigation Pane**. On the Ribbon, click the **Create tab**. In the **Forms group**, click the **Form Design** button.

The design grid for the Detail section displays.

5 On the **Design tab**, in the **Tools group**, click the **Property Sheet** button. Compare your screen with Figure 6.2. Notice that the *Selection type* box displays *Form*—this is the Property Sheet for the entire form.

Every object on a form, including the form itself, has an associated **Property Sheet** that can be used to further enhance the object. **Properties** are characteristics that determine the appearance, structure, and behavior of an object. This Property Sheet displays the properties that affect the appearance and behavior of the form. The left column displays the property name, and the right column displays the property setting. Some of the text in the property setting boxes may be truncated.

Figure 6.2

Property Sheet for form
Property Sheet tabs

Property

Property setting

Design grid

Another Way

On the Property Sheet for the form, click the Data tab. In the Record Source property setting box, click the Build button, which displays a Query Builder window and the Show Table dialog box. Add the objects from the Show Table dialog box, and then drag the appropriate fields down into the design grid. A query will be created that is used in the form.

---

6 If necessary, on the **Property Sheet**, click the **Format tab**, and then scroll down to display the **Split Form Orientation** property box. Point to the left edge of the **Property Sheet** until the pointer displays. Drag to the left until the setting in the **Split Form Orientation** property box—**Datasheet on Top**—displays entirely.

7 On the **Property Sheet**, click the **Data tab**. Click the **Record Source property setting box arrow**, and then click **6A Sales**.

The *Record Source property* enables you to specify the source of the data for a form or a report. The property setting can be a table name, a query name, or an SQL statement.

8 **Close** the **Property Sheet**. On the **Design tab**, in the **Tools group**, click the **Add Existing Fields** button, and then compare your screen with Figure 6.3.

The Field List for the record source—6A Sales—displays.

Figure 6.3

Field List for 6A Sales

Another Way

In the Field List, double-click each field name to add the fields to the form. It is not possible to select all the fields and then double-click. Alternatively, in the Field List, right-click a field name, and then click Add Field to View.

9 In the **Field List**, click **Franchise#**. To select multiple fields, hold down ⇧Shift, and then click **Date**. Drag the selected fields onto the design grid until the top of the arrow of the pointer is **three dots** below the bottom edge of the **Detail section bar** and aligned with the **1.5-inch mark on the horizontal ruler** as shown in Figure 6.4, and then release the mouse button.

Drag the fields to where the text box controls should display. If you drag to where the label controls should display, the label controls and text box controls will overlap. If you move the controls to an incorrect position, click the Undo button before moving them again.

Figure 6.4

1.5-inch mark

Detail section bar

10 Close ☒ the **Field List**.

11 On the Ribbon, click the **Arrange tab**. With all controls selected, in the **Table group**, click the **Stacked** button.

When you create a form in Design view, the controls are not automatically grouped in a stacked or tabular layout. Grouping the controls makes it easier to format the controls and keeps the controls aligned.

12 Save 🖫 the form as **Lastname Firstname 6A Sales Form**

> **More Knowledge | Horizontal and Vertical Spacing Between Controls**
>
> If the controls on a form are not grouped in a tabular or stacked layout, you can change the spacing between the controls. With the controls selected, click the Arrange tab. In the Sizing & Ordering group, click the Size/Space button, and then click the appropriate button to control spacing. Spacing options include Equal Horizontal, Increase Horizontal, Decrease Horizontal, Equal Vertical, Increase Vertical, and Decrease Vertical.

Activity 6.02 | Adding Sections to the Form

The only section that is automatically added to a form when it is created in Design view is the Detail section. In this activity, you will add a Form Header section and a Form Footer section.

1 Switch to **Form** view, and notice that the form displays only the data. There is no header section with a logo or name of the form.

2 Switch to **Design** view. Click the **Design tab.** In the **Header/Footer group**, click the **Logo** button. Navigate to the location where the student data files for this textbook are saved. Locate and double-click **a06A_Logo** to insert the logo in the Form Header section.

> Two sections—the Form Header and the Form Footer—are added to the form along with the logo. Sections can be added only in Design view.

3 On the selected logo, point to the right middle sizing handle until the pointer ↔ displays. Drag to the right until the right edge of the logo is aligned with the **1.5-inch mark on the horizontal ruler**.

4 In the **Header/Footer group**, click the **Title** button to insert the title in the Form Header section. Compare your screen with Figure 6.5.

> The name of the form is inserted as a title into the Form Header section, and the label control is the same height as the logo.

Figure 6.5

Logo button
Title button
Form Header section
Logo
Title

5 Scroll down until the **Form Footer** section bar displays. Point to the top of the **Form Footer** section bar until the pointer ↔ displays. Drag upward until the top of the Form Footer section bar aligns with the **2-inch mark on the vertical ruler**.

> The height of the Detail section is decreased. Extra space at the bottom of the Detail section will cause blank space to display between records if the form is printed.

6 In the **Controls group**, click the **Label** button *Aa*. Point to the **Form Footer** section until the plus sign (+) of the pointer aligns with the bottom of the **Form Footer** section bar and with the left edge of the **Date label control** in the Detail section. Drag downward to the bottom of the **Form Footer** section and to the right to **3 inches on the horizontal ruler**. Using your own first name and last name, type **Designed by Firstname Lastname** Press [Enter], and then compare your screen with Figure 6.6.

Figure 6.6

Label button

Label control

---

7 With the label control in the Form Footer section selected, hold down ⇧Shift, and then click each of the label controls in the Detail section. On the Ribbon, click the **Arrange tab**. In the **Sizing & Ordering group**, click the **Align** button, and then select **Left**. **Save** 🖫 the form, and then switch to **Form** view.

> The Form Header section displays the logo and the title of the form. The Form Footer section displays the label control that is aligned with the label controls in the Detail section. Both the Form Header and Form Footer sections display on every form page.

Objective 2 | Change and Add Controls

A **control** is an object, such as a label or text box, in a form or report that enables you to view or manipulate information stored in tables or queries. You have worked with label controls, text box controls, and, earlier in the chapter, logo controls, but there are more controls that can be added to a form. By default, when you create a form, Access uses the same field definitions as those in the underlying table or query. More controls are available in Design view than in Layout view.

Activity 6.03 | Changing Controls on a Form

In this activity, you will change a combo box control to a list box control.

1 Click the **Menu Item field arrow**.

> Because the underlying table—*6A Sales*—designated this field as a lookup field, Access inserted a combo box control for this field instead of a text box control. The Franchise# field is also a combo box control. A **combo box** enables individuals to select from a list or to type a value.

2 Switch to **Design** view. In the **Detail** section, click the **Menu Item label control**, hold down Shift, and then click the **Menu Item combo box control**. On the Ribbon, click the **Arrange tab**, and then in the **Table group**, click the **Remove Layout** button.

The Remove Layout button is used to remove a field from a stacked or tabular layout—it does not delete the field or remove it from the form. If fields are in the middle of a stacked layout column and are removed from the layout, the remaining fields in the column will display over the removed field. To avoid the clutter, first move the fields that you want to remove from the layout to the bottom of the column.

3 Click the **Undo** ↻ button. Point to the **Menu Item label control** until the pointer displays. Drag downward until a thin orange line displays on the bottom edges of the **Date** controls.

Alert! | Did the Control Stay in the Same Location?

In Design view, the orange line that indicates the location where controls will be moved is much thinner than—and not as noticeable as—the line in Layout view. If you drag downward too far, Access will not move the selected fields.

---

4 In the **Table group**, click the **Remove Layout** button to remove the Menu Item field from the stacked layout. Point to the selected controls, and then drag to the right and upward until the **Menu Item label control** is aligned with the **Franchise#** controls and with the **3-inch mark on the horizontal ruler**. Compare your screen with Figure 6.7.

Figure 6.7

3-inch mark ——

Combo box control ——

Text box control ——

5 With the **Menu Item controls** selected, in the **Table group**, click the **Stacked** button. Click anywhere in the **Detail** section to deselect the second column.

The Menu Item controls display in the second column and are grouped in a stacked layout. Recall that a stacked layout keeps the controls aligned and makes it easier to edit and move the controls.

6 Right-click the **Menu Item combo box control**. From the shortcut menu, point to **Change To**, and then click **List Box**.

A *list box* enables individuals to select from a list but does not enable individuals to type anything that is not in the list. Based on the data in the underlying table or query, Access displays the control types to which you can change a field. The control type can be changed in Design view only.

7 Save the form, and then switch to **Form** view. Notice the **Menu Item list box control** is not wide enough to display both columns and that there are horizontal and vertical scroll bars to indicate there is more data. To display another problem, click the **Franchise# combo box arrow**, and then notice that some of the city names are truncated. Press Esc.

8 Switch to **Design** view. Click the **Franchise# combo box**, and then point to the right edge of the control until the pointer ↔ displays. Drag to the right until the right edge of the control aligns with the **2.75-inch mark on the horizontal ruler** to resize all three controls in the column. Switch to **Form** view, click the **Franchise# arrow**, and then be sure that all of the city names display—if they do not, return to Design view and increase the width of the combo box control.

9 Switch to **Layout** view. Click the **Menu Item list box control**. Point to the right edge of the control until the pointer ↔ displays. Drag to the right until all of the Menu Item *1307* displays. Release the mouse button to display the resized list box.

10 Save the form, and switch to **Design** view.

More Knowledge | **Validate or Restrict Data in Forms**

When you design tables, set field properties to ensure the entry of valid data by using input masks, validation rules, and default values. Any field in a form created with a table having these properties inherits the validation properties from the underlying table. Setting these properties in the table is the preferred method; however, you can also set the properties on controls in the form. If conflicting settings occur, the setting on the bound control in the form will override the field property setting in the table.

Activity 6.04 | Adding Controls to a Form

In this activity, you will add an image control and button controls to the form. An *image control* enables individuals to insert an image into any section of a form or report. A *button control* enables individuals to add a command button to a form or report that will perform an action when the button is clicked.

1 On the **Design tab**, in the **Controls group**, click the **Insert Image** button, and then click Browse. In the displayed **Insert Picture** dialog box, navigate to the location where the student data files for this textbook are saved and double-click **a06A_Logo**. Align the plus sign (+) of the pointer with the bottom of the **Form Header** section bar at **5.5-inches on the horizontal ruler**, as shown in Figure 6.8.

Figure 6.8

Insert Image button

5.5-inch mark

Mouse pointer

2 Drag the pointer downward to the bottom of the **Form Header** section and to the right to **6.5 inches on the horizontal ruler**. Release the mouse button to insert the picture in the Form Header section.

> Using the logo control inserts a picture in a predetermined location—the left side—of the Form Header section. The image control is used to insert a picture anywhere in the form. There is a second image control in the Controls gallery on the Design tab.

3 Click the **title's label control**. Point to the right edge of the label control until the pointer [ ] displays. Drag to the left until there is **one dot** between the right edge of the label control and the left edge of the image control. On the **Format tab**, in the **Font group**, click the **Center** button [ ]. Switch to **Form** view, and then compare your screen with Figure 6.9.

> The title is centered between the logo on the left and the image on the right, but the logo and the image are not the same size.

Figure 6.9

Title centered

Image added to Form Header section

4 Switch to **Design** view, and then click the **image control**—the Sand Dollar Cafe image on the right side in the Form Header section. On the **Design tab**, in the **Tools group**, click the **Property Sheet** button. If necessary, on the **Property Sheet**, click the **Format tab**, and then compare your screen with Figure 6.10. Notice the **Width** and **Height** property settings.

> The Width property setting is 1 inch—yours may differ. The Height property setting is 0.375 inches—yours may differ.

Figure 6.10

Property Sheet for selected image control—image number may differ

Image control

Width property setting—yours may differ

Height property setting—yours may differ

5 If necessary, change the **Width** property setting to **1.25** and then change the **Height** property setting to **0.625** In the **Form Header** section, on the left side, click the **logo control**, and then notice that the Property Sheet for the logo control displays. On the **Property Sheet**, change the **Width** property setting to **1.25** and then change the **Height** property setting to **0.625**

> The width and height of the two controls are now the same.

6 On the Ribbon, click the **Arrange tab**. With the logo control selected, hold down Shift, and then click the **image control**. In the **Sizing & Ordering group**, click the **Align** button, click **Bottom**. Click the **title's label control**. In the **Table group**, click **Remove Layout**, and then point to the left middle sizing handle until the pointer ↔ displays. Drag to the right until there is **one dot** between the right edge of the logo control and the left edge of the title's label control.

> The logo control and the image control are aligned at the bottom, and the title's label control is resized.

7 **Close** ⊠ the **Property Sheet**. On the Ribbon, click the **Design tab**, click the **More** button ⊽ at the right edge of the **Controls gallery**, and be sure that the **Use Control Wizards** option is active. Click the **Button** button ▦. Move the mouse pointer down into the **Detail** section. Align the plus sign (+) of the pointer at **1.5 inches on the vertical ruler** and **1.5 inches on the horizontal ruler**, and then click. Compare your screen with Figure 6.11.

> The Command Button Wizard dialog box displays. The first dialog box enables you to select an action for the button based on the selected category.

Access | Chapter 6

Figure 6.11

Button control button

Command Button
Wizard dialog box

8 Take a moment to click the different categories to display the actions associated with the category. When you are finished, under **Categories**, click **Record Navigation**. Under **Actions**, click **Go To Previous Record**, and then click **Next**.

> The second Command Button Wizard dialog box displays, which enables you to select what will display on the button—either text or a picture. If you select picture, you can navigate to a location on your computer where pictures are saved, and then select any picture. If you select text, accept the default text or type new text. A preview of the button displays on the left side of the dialog box.

9 Next to **Picture**, be sure **Go to Previous** is selected, and then click **Next**.

> The third Command Button Wizard dialog box displays, which enables you to name the button. If you need to refer to the button later—usually in creating macros—a meaningful name is helpful. The buttons created with the Command Button Wizard are linked to macros—programs—that cannot be run or edited in previous versions of Access.

10 In the text box, type **btnPrevRecord** and then click **Finish**.

> When creating controls that can later be used in programming, it is a good idea to start the name of the control with an abbreviation of the type of control—btn—and then a descriptive abbreviation of the purpose of the control.

11 Using the techniques you have just practiced, add a **button control** about **1 inch** to the right of the **Previous Record button control**. Under **Categories**, click **Record Navigation**. Under **Actions**, click **Go to Next Record**. For **Picture**, click **Go to Next**, and then name the button **btnNextRecord** Do not be concerned if the button controls are not exactly aligned.

12 With the **Next Record button control** selected, hold down (Shift), and then click the **Previous Record button control**. Click the **Arrange tab**, and then in the **Sizing & Ordering group**, click the **Align** button, and then **Top**. Click the **Size/Space** button, and then click either **Increase Horizontal Spacing** button or **Decrease Horizontal Spacing** until there is approximately **1 inch** of space between the two controls. Compare your screen with Figure 6.12.

Figure 6.12

Size/Space button

Next record button control

Previous record button control

Approximately 1 inch of space between button controls

13 Save 💾 the form, and then switch to **Form** view. Experiment by clicking the **Next Record** button and the **Previous Record** button, and notice in the record navigator that you are displaying different records.

14 Switch to **Design** view. On the **Design tab**, in the **Controls group**, click the **Button** button ⬛. Align the plus sign (+) of the pointer at **1.5 inches on the vertical ruler** and at **5 inches on the horizontal ruler**, and then click.

15 In the **Command Button Wizard** dialog box, under **Categories**, click **Form Operations**. Under **Actions**, click **Print Current Form**, and then click **Next**. Click the **Text** option button to accept *Print Form*, and then click **Next**. Name the button **btnPrtForm** and then click **Finish**.

You will use this button to print one form when you are finished formatting the form.

16 Save 💾 the form.

Objective 3 | Format a Form

There are several methods you can use to modify the appearance of a form. Each section and control on a form has properties. Some properties can be modified by using buttons in the groups on a tab or by changing the property setting on the Property Sheet.

Activity 6.05 | Adding a Background Color

In this activity, you will modify the background color of the Form Header section, the Form Footer section, and the Detail section of the *6A Sales Form*. The background color is a property setting for each section; there is no background color property setting for the entire form. Property settings can also be changed in Layout view.

1 With **6A Sales Form** open in **Design** view, click the **Form Header** section bar.

The darkened bar indicates that the entire Form Header section of the form is selected.

Access | Chapter 6

2 On the **Format tab**, in the **Font group**, click the **Background Color button arrow** . Under **Theme Colors**, on the fourth row, click the seventh color—**Olive Green, Accent 3, Lighter 40%**.

> The background color for the Form Header section changes to a light shade of olive green.

3 Double-click the **Form Footer** section bar to display the Property Sheet for the Form Footer section. On the **Property Sheet**, click the **Format tab**, and then click in the **Back Color** property setting box—it displays Background 1. Click the **Build** button.

> The color palette displays. Background 1 is a code used by Access to represent the color white. You can select an Access Theme Color, a Standard Color, a Recent Color, or click More Colors to select shades of colors.

4 Click **More Colors**. In the displayed **Colors** dialog box, click the **Custom tab**.

> All colors use varying shades of Red, Green, and Blue.

5 In the **Colors** dialog box, click **Cancel**. On the **Property Sheet**, click the **Back Color property setting arrow**.

> A list of color schemes display. These colors also display on the color palette under Access Theme Colors.

Another Way

Open the form in Layout view. To select a section, click in an empty area of the section. On the Home tab, in the Text Formatting group, click the Background Color button.

6 From the displayed list, experiment by clicking on different color schemes and viewing the effects of the background color change. You will have to click the property setting arrow each time to select another color scheme. When you are finished, click the **Build** button. Under **Theme Colors**, on the fourth row, click the seventh color—**Olive Green, Accent 3, Lighter 40%**—and then press Enter.

> You can change the background color either by using the Background Color button in the Font group or by changing the Back Color property setting on the Property Sheet.

7 Using one of the techniques you have just practiced, change the background color of the **Detail** section to **Olive Green, Accent 3, Lighter 40%**. Switch to **Form** view, and then compare your screen with Figure 6.13.

Figure 6.13

Background color set to Olive Green, Accent 3, Lighter 40%

8 Save 🖫 the form, and then switch to **Design** view. **Close** the **Property Sheet**.

More Knowledge | Adding a Background Color to Controls

You can also add background colors to controls. First, click the control or controls to which you want to add a background color. If you want to use color schemes, open the Property Sheet, and then click the Back Color property setting arrow. If you want to use the color palette, in Design view, click the Format tab. In the Font group, click the Background Color button.

Activity 6.06 | Adding a Background Picture to a Form

In this activity, you will add a picture to the background of *6A Sales Form*.

1 With **6A Sales Form** open in **Design** view, locate the **Form selector**, as shown in Figure 6.14.

The *Form selector* is the box where the rulers meet, in the upper left corner of a form in Design view. Use the Form selector to select the entire form.

Figure 6.14

Form Selector ——

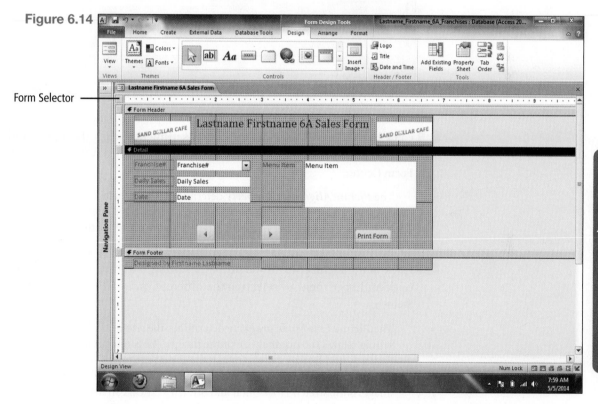

Access | Chapter 6

2 Double-click the **Form selector** to open the **Property Sheet** for the form.

3 On the **Property Sheet**, on the **Format tab**, click in the **Picture** property setting box. Click the **Build** button. Navigate to the location where the student data files for this textbook are saved. Locate and double-click **a06A_Background** to insert the picture in the form, and then compare your screen with Figure 6.15.

Figure 6.15

Centered picture

4 Click in the **Picture Alignment** property setting box, click the **arrow**, and then experiment by clicking the different alignment options. When you are finished, click **Form Center**.

The *Picture Alignment property* determines where the background picture for a form displays on the form. Center places the picture in the center of the page when the form is printed. Form Center places the picture in the center of the form data when the form is printed

5 Click in the **Picture Size Mode** property setting, and then click the **arrow** to display the options. Experiment by selecting the different options. When you are finished, click **Stretch**.

The *Picture Size Mode property* determines the size of the picture in the form. The Clip setting retains the original size of the image. The Stretch setting stretches the image both vertically and horizontally to match the size of the form—the image may be distorted. The Zoom setting adjusts the image to be as large as possible without distorting the image. Both Stretch Horizontal and Stretch Vertical can distort the image. If you have a background color and set the Picture Type property setting to Stretch, the background color will not display.

6 **Close** the **Property Sheet**, **Save** the form, and then switch to **Layout** view. Compare your screen with Figure 6.16.

Figure 6.16

Background color

Background picture

Activity 6.07 | Modifying the Borders of Controls

In this activity, you will modify the borders of some of the controls on *6A Sales Form*. There are related property settings on the Property Sheet.

1 With **6A Sales Form** open in **Layout** view, click the **Franchise#** combo box control. Holding down ⇧Shift, click the **Daily Sales** text box control, and then click the **Date** text box control. On the **Format tab**, in the **Control Formatting group**, click **Shape Outline**. Notice the options that are used to modify borders—Colors, Line Thickness, and Line Type. Compare your screen with Figure 6.17.

Figure 6.17

Line Color options

Selected controls

Line Thickness button

Line Type button

Chapter 6

Access

2 Point to **Line Type** and point to each line type to display the **ScreenTip**. The second line type—**Solid**—is the default line type. Click the last line type—**Dash Dot Dot**—and then switch to **Form** view to display the results. Notice that the borders of the three controls display a line type of Dash Dot Dot. Switch to **Layout** view.

> You can review the results in Layout view, but you would have to deselect the three controls.

3 With the three controls still selected, on the **Format tab**, in the **Control Formatting group**, click the **Shape Outline** button. Point to **Line Thickness** and point to each line thickness to display the **ScreenTip**. The first line thickness—**Hairline**—is the default line thickness. Click the third line type—**2 pt**.

4 In the **Control Formatting group**, **click** the **Shape Outline** button. Under **Theme Colors**, point to each color to display the **ScreenTip**, and then on the first row, click the fourth color—**Dark Blue, Text 2**. Switch to **Form** view to display the results.

> The borders of the three controls display a line thickness of 2 points, and the color of the borders is a darker shade. A *point* is 1/72 of an inch.

5 Switch to **Layout** view. With the three controls still selected, on the **Design tab**, in the **Tools group**, click the **Property Sheet** button, and then compare your screen with Figure 6.18. Notice the properties that are associated with the buttons on the Ribbon with which you changed the borders of the selected controls.

> Because multiple items on the form are selected, the Property Sheet displays *Selection type: Multiple selection*. You changed the property settings of the controls by using buttons, and the Property Sheet displays the results of those changes. You can also select multiple controls, open the Property Sheet, and make the changes to the properties. The Property Sheet displays more settings than those available through the use of buttons.

Figure 6.18

Border Style—related to Line Type button

Border Width—related to Line Thickness button

Border Color—related to the Line Color options

6 **Close** the **Property Sheet**, and then **Save** the form. Switch to **Form** view.

More Knowledge | **Adding Borders to Label Controls**

By default, the border style—line style—of a Label control is transparent, effectively hiding the border from the display. Because borders display around bound controls that contain data, it is recommended that you do not add borders to label controls so that individuals can easily distinguish the control that holds data.

Objective 4 | Make a Form User Friendly

To make forms easy to use, you can add instructions that display on the status bar while data is being entered and custom *ControlTips* that display when an individual pauses the mouse pointer over a control on a form. Additionally, you can change the tab order of the fields on a form. *Tab order* refers to the order in which the fields are selected when the Tab key is pressed. By default, the tab order is created based on the order in which the fields are added to the form.

Activity 6.08 | Adding a Message to the Status Bar

When you created tables, you may have added a description to the field, and the description displayed in the status bar of the Access window. If a description is included for a field in the underlying table of a form, the text of the description will also display in the status bar when an individual clicks in the field on the form. In this activity, you will add a description to the Daily Sales field in the *6A Sales* table, and then *propagate*—disseminate or apply—the changes to *6A Sales Form*. You will also add status bar text to a field on a form using the Property Sheet of the control.

1 With **6A Sales Form** open in **Form** view, click in the **Daily Sales** field. On the left side of the status bar, *Form View* displays—there is no text that helps an individual enter data.

2 **Close** the form, and then **Open** ⟩⟩ the **Navigation Pane**. Under **Tables**, right-click **6A Sales**, and then from the shortcut menu, click **Design View**. In the **Daily Sales** field, click in the **Description** box. Type **How many items were sold?** and then press Enter. Compare your screen with Figure 6.19.

A *Property Update Options button* displays in the Description box for the Date field. When you make changes to the design of a table, Access displays this button, which enables individuals to update the Property Sheet for this field in all objects that use this table as the record source.

Figure 6.19

Description entered

Property Update Options button

3 Click the **Property Update Options** button, and then click **Update Status Bar Text everywhere Daily Sales is used**. In the displayed **Update Properties** dialog box, under **Update the following objects?**, notice that only one object—*Form: 6A Sales Form*—displays, and it is selected. In the **Update Properties** dialog box, click **Yes**.

> The changes in the Description field in the table will be propagated to *6A Sales Form*. If multiple objects use the *6A Sales* table as the underlying object, you can propagate the change to all of the objects.

4 **Close** the table, saving changes, and then open the **6A Sales** table in **Datasheet** view. On any record, click in the **Daily Sales** field, and then notice the text—*How many items were sold?*—that displays on the left side of the status bar.

5 **Close** the table. In the **Navigation Pane**, under **Forms**, double-click **6A Sales Form** to open it in **Form** view. Close ⟪ the **Navigation Pane**. Click in the **Daily Sales** field, and then notice that on the left side of the status bar, *How many items were sold?* displays.

> Access propagated the change made in the underlying table to the form.

6 Switch to **Design** view. Click the **Daily Sales text box control**. On the **Design tab**, in the **Tools group**, click the **Property Sheet** button.

7 On the **Property Sheet**, click the **Other tab**. Locate the **Status Bar Text** property, and notice the setting *How many items were sold?*

> When Access propagated the change to the form, it populated the Status Bar Text property setting. The *Status Bar Text property* enables individuals to add descriptive text that will display in the status bar for a selected control.

8 In the **Detail** section, click the **Date text box control**, and then notice that the **Property Sheet** changes to display the properties for the **Date** text box control. Click in the **Status Bar Text** property setting box, type **Enter date of sales report** and then Press Enter.

> You do not have to enter a description for the field in the underlying table for text to display in the status bar when a field is selected in a form. Access does not display a Property Update Options button to propagate changes to the underlying table, and the text will not be added to the Description box for the field in the table.

9 **Save** 🖫 the form, and then switch to **Form** view. Click in the **Date** field, and then compare your screen with Figure 6.20.

> The status bar displays the text you entered in the Status Bar Text property setting box.

Figure 6.20

10 Switch to **Design** view.

> **More Knowledge | Conflicting Field Description and Status Bar Text Property Setting**
>
> When you create a form, the fields inherit the property settings from the underlying table. You can change the Status Bar Text property setting for the form, and it will override the setting that is inherited from the table. If you later change field properties in Table Design view, the Property Update Options button displays—you must manually propagate those changes to the table's related objects; propagation is not automatic. An exception to this is entering Validation Rules—changes are automatically propagated.

Activity 6.09 | Creating Custom ControlTips

Another way to make a form easier to use is to add custom ControlTips to objects on the form. A ControlTip is similar to a ScreenTip and temporarily displays descriptive text while the mouse pointer is paused over the control. This method is somewhat limited because most individuals press Tab or Enter to move from field to field and thus do not see the ControlTip. However, a ControlTip is a useful tool in a training situation when an individual is learning how to use the data entry form. In this activity, you will add a ControlTip to the Print Form button control.

1 With **6A Sales Form** open in **Design** view and the **Property Sheet** displayed, click the **Print Form** button. If necessary, click the **Other tab** to make it active. Notice the **Property Sheet** displays *Selection type: Command Button* and the Selection type box displays *btnPrtForm*, the name you gave to the button when you added it to the form.

2 Click in the **ControlTip Text** property setting box, and type **Prints the selected record** and then press Enter. Compare your screen with Figure 6.21.

Figure 6.21

Property Sheet for selected button

ControlTip property setting

3 **Close** the **Property Sheet**, **Save** 💾 the form, and then switch to **Form** view. Point to the **Print Form** button, and then compare your screen with Figure 6.22.

A ControlTip displays the message you typed for the ControlTip Text property setting.

Figure 6.22

ControlTip

Activity 6.10 | Changing the Tab Order

You can customize the order in which you enter data on a form by changing the tab order. Recall that tab order refers to the order in which the fields are selected each time Tab is pressed. As you press Tab, the *focus* of the form changes from one control to another control. Focus refers to the object that is selected and currently being acted upon.

1 With **6A Sales Form** open in **Form** view, in the record navigator, click the **New (blank) record** button. If necessary, click in the **Franchise#** combo box. Press ⎀Tab⎀ three times, and then notice that the insertion point moves from field to field, ending with the **Date** text box. Press ⎀Tab⎀ three more times, and then notice the **Print form** button is the focus. The button displays with a darker border. Press ⎀Enter⎀.

> Because the focus is on the Print Form button, the Print dialog box displays.

2 In the **Print** dialog box, click **Cancel**. Switch to **Design** view.

3 On the Ribbon, click the **Design tab**. In the **Tools group**, click the **Tab Order** button, and then compare your screen with Figure 6.23.

> The Tab Order dialog box displays. Under Section, Detail is selected. Under Custom Order, the fields and controls display in the order they were added to the form. To the left of each field name or button name is a row selector button.

> As you rearrange fields on a form, the tab order does not change from the original tab order. This can make data entry chaotic because the focus is changed in what appears to be an illogical order. The Auto Order button will change the tab order based on the position of the controls in the form from left to right and top to bottom.

Figure 6.23

Field names
Row selector box
Button names
Auto Order button

4 To the left of **Menu Item**, click the **row selector** box. Point to the **row selector** box, and then drag downward until a dark horizontal line displays between **Date** and **btnPrevRecord**.

> The Menu Item field will now receive the focus after the Date field.

Alert! | Did the Field Stay in the Same Location?

You must point to the row selector box before dragging the field. If you point to the field name, the field will not be moved.

---

5 In the **Tab Order** dialog box, click **OK**. Save ☐ the form, and then switch to **Form** view. In the record navigator, click the **Last Record** button. When the Menu Item field has the focus, it is easier to see it on a blank record. In the record navigator, click the **New (blank) record** button.

The insertion point displays in the Franchise# field.

6 Press ⎀ three times. Even though it is difficult to see, the focus changes to the **Menu Item** list box. Press ⎀ again, and then notice that the focus changes to the **btnPrevRecord** button.

Before allowing individuals to enter data into a form, you should always test the tab order to ensure that the data will be easy to enter.

7 Switch to **Design** view. In the **Detail** section, right-click the **Date text box control**, click **Properties**. If necessary, click the **Other** tab, and then compare your screen with Figure 6.24.

Text box controls have three properties relating to tab order: Tab Index, Tab Stop, and Auto Tab. Combo box controls and list box controls do not have an Auto Tab property.

Figure 6.24

Property Sheet for Date text box control

Tab Index property

Tab Stop property

Auto Tab property

8 On the **Property Sheet**, click in the **Tab Index** property setting box, which displays *2*. Click the **Build** button.

Tab Index settings begin with 0. Franchise# has a Tab Index setting of 0, which indicates that this field has the focus when the form is opened. Daily Sales has a Tab Index setting of 1—it will receive the focus when Tab is pressed one time. Date has a Tab Index setting of 2—it will receive the focus when Tab is pressed a second time. Menu Item has a Tab Index setting of 3—it will receive the focus when Tab is pressed a third time.

9 In the **Tab Order** dialog box, click **Cancel**. On the **Property Sheet**, notice that the **Tab Stop** property setting is **Yes**, which means individuals can Press ⎡Tab⎤ to move to this field.

The Auto Tab property setting is No. It should be changed to Yes only when a text field has an input mask. Recall that an input mask controls how the data is entered into a field; for example, the formatting of a phone number.

10 In the **Detail** section, click the **Franchise# combo box control**, and then on the **Property Sheet**, notice the settings for the **Tab Index** and **Tab Stop** properties.

The Tab Index setting is 0, which means this field has the focus when the form page is displayed—it is first on the tab order list. The Tab Stop setting is Yes. Because an input mask cannot be applied to a combo box, there is no Auto Tab property. The Auto Tab property applies only to a text box control.

11 In the **Detail** section, click the **Previous Record** button control. On the **Property Sheet**, click in the **Tab Stop** property setting box, click the **arrow**, and then click **No**.

Changing the Tab Stop property setting to No means that the focus will not be changed to the button by pressing Tab.

12 **Save** 🖫 the form, and then switch to **Form** view. In the record navigator, click the **Last record** button. Press ⎡Tab⎤ two times, watching the focus change from the **Franchise#** field to the **Date** field. Press ⎡Tab⎤ two more times, and then compare your screen with Figure 6.25.

Because the Tab Stop property setting for the Previous Record button control was changed to No, the button does not receive the focus by pressing the Tab key.

Figure 6.25

Focus is on Next Record button

Button not accessed using Tab key

13 In the **Detail** section, click the **Previous Record** button.

The previous record displays—you can still use the button by clicking on it.

14 Switch to **Design** view. Using the techniques you have just practiced, for the **Next Record** button and the **Print Form** button, change the **Tab Stop** property setting to **No**.

15 **Close** the **Property Sheet**. **Save** 🖫 the form, and then switch to **Form** view. Test the tab order by pressing Tab , making sure that the focus does not change to the **Next Record** button or the **Print Form** button.

> When the focus is on the Date field, pressing the Tab key moves the focus to the Franchise# field in the next record.

16 Navigate to **Record 5**—Franchise# 44. Unless you are required to submit your database electronically, in the **Detail** section, click the **Print Form** button. In the **Print** dialog box under **Print Range**, click **Selected Record(s)**, and then click **OK**. If you are instructed to submit this result as an electronic printout, select the record using the selector bar, and then from **Backstage** view, click **Save & Publish**. Click the **Save Object As** button, and click **PDF or XPS**. Navigate to the folder where you store your electronic printouts. Click the **Options** button, click **Selected records**, and then click **OK**. Click **Publish**.

17 **Close** the form, and then **Open** ⏩ the **Navigation Pane**. **Close** the database, and then **Exit** Access.

End **You have completed Project 6A** ——————————————————

Project 6B SDC

Project Activities

In Activities 6.11 through 6.18, you will create customized reports. The corporate office of Sand Dollar Cafe (SDC) maintains a database about the franchises, including daily sales of menu items per franchise, the franchise owners, and franchise fees and payments. Reports are often run to summarize data in the tables or queries. Creating customized reports will help the owners and officers of the company view the information in the database in a meaningful way. Your completed reports will look similar to Figure 6.26.

Project Files

For Project 6B, you will need the following files:

a06B_SDC
a06B_Logo

You will save your database as:

Lastname_Firstname_6B_SDC

Project Results

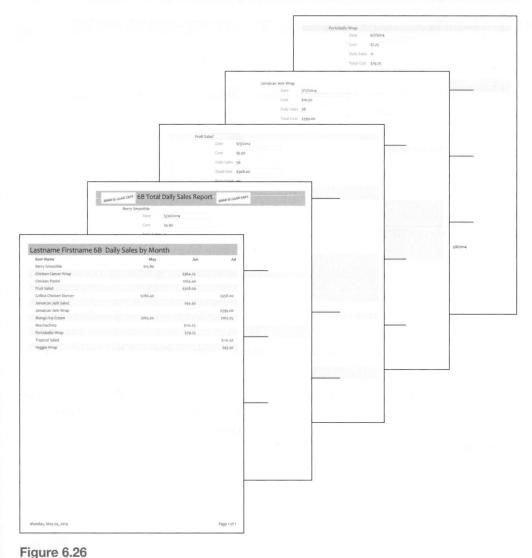

Figure 6.26
Project 6B SDC

Objective 5 | Create a Report Based on a Query Using a Wizard

A report wizard is a more efficient way to start a report, although Design view does offer you more control as you create your report. Once the report has been created, its appearance can be modified in Design or Layout view.

Activity 6.11 | Creating a Report Using a Wizard

In this activity, you will use a wizard to create a report for Sand Dollar Cafe that displays the data from the 6B Total Daily Sales Crosstab Query.

1 **Start** Access. Navigate to the location where the student data files for this textbook are saved. Locate and open the **a06B_SDC** file. Save the database in your **Access Chapter 6** folder as **Lastname_Firstname_6B_SDC**

2 If you did not add the Access Chapter 6 folder to the Trust Center, enable the content. In the **Navigation Pane**, under **Queries**, double-click **6B Total Daily Sales Crosstab Query**. Take a moment to study the data in the query, as shown in Figure 6.27.

The data is grouped by Item Name and Month. The sum function calculates the total daily sales for each item per month.

Figure 6.27

Data grouped by Months
Data grouped by Item Name

Aggregate function sums total daily sales for each item

3 **Close** the query. With **6B Total Daily Sales Crosstab Query** still selected, **Close** the **Navigation Pane**.

4 On the Ribbon, click the **Create tab**. In the **Reports group**, click the **Report Wizard** button.

5 Because the crosstab query was selected in the Navigation Pane, in the **Report Wizard** dialog box, in the **Tables/Queries** box, **Query: 6B Total Daily Sales Crosstab Query** displays. If it does not display, click the **Tables/Queries** arrow, and then click **Query: 6B Total Daily Sales Crosstab Query**.

6 Under **Available Fields**, notice there are more months than those that were displayed in 6B Total Daily Sales Crosstab Query.

> Because there was data for the months of May, June, and July only, the other months were hidden from the display in the query. To hide a column in Datasheet view, right-click the column header, and then from the shortcut menu, click Hide Fields.

7 Under **Available Fields**, double-click each field name, in the order specified, to add the field names to the Selected Fields box: **Item Name**, **May**, **Jun**, and **Jul**.

8 In the **Report Wizard** dialog box, click **Next**. Because no grouping levels will be used, click **Next**.

9 To sort the records within the report by Item Name, click the **arrow** next to the **1** box. From the displayed list, click **Item Name**. Leave the sort order as **Ascending**, and then click **Next**.

10 Under **Layout**, be sure the **Tabular** option button is selected. Under **Orientation**, be sure the **Portrait** option button is selected, and then click **Next**.

11 For the title of the report, type **Lastname Firstname 6B Daily Sales by Month** and then click **Finish**.

> The report displays in Print Preview. Because this report uses a crosstab query as the record source, it displays calculated data grouped by two different types of information.

Activity 6.12 | Modifying a Report Created Using a Wizard

In this activity, you will modify controls in the report to change its appearance. Although the report was created using a wizard, its appearance can be modified in Design view and Layout view.

1 On the **Print Preview tab**, in the **Close Preview group**, click the **Close Print Preview** button. If the **Field List** or **Property Sheet** displays, **Close** it.

2 On the Ribbon, click the **Design tab**. In the **Themes group**, click the **Themes** button to display a list of available themes. Under **Built-In**, on the tenth row, click the fourth theme—**Waveform**.

> *Themes* simplify the process of creating professional-looking objects within one program or across multiple programs. A theme includes theme colors and theme fonts that will be applied consistently throughout the objects in the database. It is a simple way to provide professional, consistent formatting in a database.

3 If necessary, click anywhere in an empty area of the report to deselect the **Item Name** column. Click the **Report title text box control**. On the **Format tab**, in the **Font group**, click the **Font Color button arrow** . Under **Theme Colors**, on the first row, click the fourth color—**Dark Blue, Text 2**.

4 Select all of the controls in the **Page Header** section by pointing to the top left of the **Page Header** section, holding down your mouse button, dragging the mouse across the Page Header controls and to the bottom of the Page Header section, and then releasing the mouse button. Use the techniques you have practiced to change the font color to **Dark Blue, Text 2**.

> Any group of controls can be selected using this lasso method. It can be more efficient than holding down Shift while clicking each control.

5 **Save** the report, and then switch to **Layout** view.

6 In the **Item Name** column, select any **text box control**. Point to the right edge of the control until the ↔ pointer displays. Drag to the left until the box is approximately **1.5 inches** wide; be sure none of the data in the column is cut off.

7 To select all of the text box controls, in the **May** column, click **15.8**. Holding down Shift, in the **Jun** and **Jul** columns, click a **text box control**. Compare your screen with Figure 6.28.

Figure 6.28

Selected text box controls

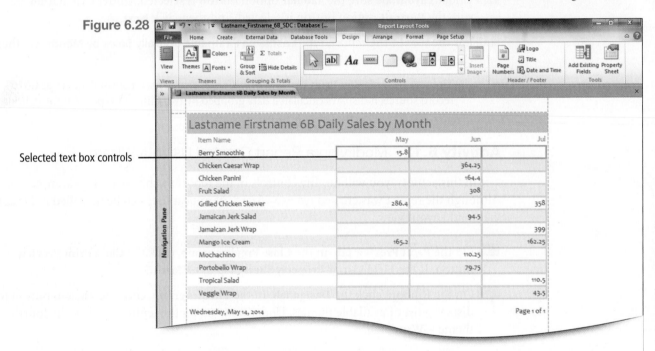

8 On the Ribbon, click the **Design tab**. In the **Tools group**, click the **Property Sheet** button. Notice that the selection type is *Multiple selection*.

9 On the **Property Sheet**, click the **Format tab**. Click the **Format property setting arrow**. From the displayed list, select **Currency**. Click the **Border Style property setting arrow**, and click **Sparse Dots**. **Close** the **Property Sheet**.

10 **Save** the report, and then switch to **Print Preview** view. If you are instructed to submit this result, create a paper or electronic printout. On the **Print Preview tab**, in the **Close Preview group**, click the **Close Print Preview** button.

11 **Close** the report, and then **Open** ▸▸ the **Navigation Pane**.

Objective 6 | Create a Report in Design View

You usually create a report using the Report tool, the Blank Report tool, or the Report Wizard, and then modify the report in Design view to suit your needs. Use Design view to create a report when these tools do not meet your needs or if you want more control in the creation of a report. Creating or modifying a report in Design view is a common technique when additional controls, such as calculated controls, need to be added to the report or properties need to be changed.

Activity 6.13 | Creating a Report in Design View

Creating a report with the Report tool, the Blank Report tool, or the Report Wizard is the easiest way to start the creation of a customized report, but you can also create a report from scratch in Design view. Once you understand the sections of a report and how to manipulate the controls within the sections, it is easier to modify a report that has been created using the report tools.

1 In the **Navigation Pane**, open **6B Total Daily Sales Query**. Switch to **Design** view, and then notice the underlying tables that were used in the creation of the query. Notice the calculated field—*Total Cost*.

Recall that a calculated field contains the field name, followed by a colon, and then an expression. In the expression, the existing field names must be enclosed in square brackets. The Total Cost was calculated by multiplying the value in the Cost field by the value in the Daily Sales field.

2 When you are finished, **Close** the query, and **Close** «| the **Navigation Pane**. On the Ribbon, click the **Create tab**. In the **Reports group**, click the **Report Design** button. When the design grid displays, scroll down to display all of the report sections.

Three sections are included in the blank design grid: the Page Header section, the Detail section, and the Page Footer section. A page header displays at the top of every printed page, and a page footer displays at the bottom of every printed page.

3 Select the report using the report selector. On the **Design tab**, in the **Tools group**, click the **Property Sheet** button. On the **Property Sheet**, click the **Data tab**. Click the **Record Source property setting box arrow**, and then compare your screen with Figure 6.29. If necessary, increase the width of the Property Sheet.

As with forms, the Record Source property setting is used to select the underlying table or query for the report.

Figure 6.29

Property Sheet for report

Record Source property

Tables and queries that
can be used as the
Record Source for report

4 From the displayed list of tables and queries, click **6B Total Daily Sales Query**, and then **Close** the **Property Sheet**.

6B Total Daily Sales Query is the record source—underlying query—for this report.

5 On the **Design tab**, in the **Tools group**, click the **Add Existing Fields** button to display the fields in 6B Total Daily Sales Query.

6 If all tables display in the field list, click **Show only fields in the current record source** at the bottom of the Field List box. In the **Field List**, click **Date**. Hold down Shift, and then click **Franchise#** to select all of the fields.

7 Drag the selected fields into the **Detail** section of the design grid until the top of the arrow of the pointer is **one dot** below the bottom edge of the **Detail** section bar and aligned with the **3-inch mark on the horizontal ruler**, and then compare your screen with Figure 6.30.

As with forms, drag the fields to where the text box controls should display.

Figure 6.30

3-inch mark

Text box controls

Label controls

8 With the label controls and text box controls for the fields selected, on the Ribbon, click the **Arrange tab**. In the **Table group**, click the **Stacked** button to group the fields together for easier formatting.

> **More Knowledge** | Using the Tabular Arrangement
>
> When you want your data to display efficiently in a report, in the Table group, on the Arrange tab, click the Tabular button. This will place the labels in the Page Header and the data in the Detail section for a table-like appearance.

9 On the Ribbon, click the **Design tab**. In the **Themes group**, click the **Themes** button. Under **In This Database**, notice the theme used in this database—**Waveform**. Press (Esc) to close the gallery.

10 **Close** the **Field List**, and then **Save** 🖫 the report as **Lastname Firstname 6B Total Daily Sales Report**

Activity 6.14 | Modifying the Sections of a Report

By default, a report created in Design view includes a Page Header section and a Page Footer section. Reports can also include a Report Header section and a Report Footer section. In this activity, you will add the Report Header and Report Footer sections and hide the Page Header section. Recall that a Report Header displays at the top of the first printed page of a report, and the Report Footer displays at the bottom of the last printed page of a report.

1 Right-click in the **Detail** section of the report, and click **Report Header/Footer**. Notice that the **Report Header** section displays at the top of the design grid. Scroll down to display the **Report Footer** section.

2 Scroll up to display the **Report Header** section. On the **Design tab**, in the **Header/Footer group**, click the **Logo** button. Locate and double-click **a06B_Logo** to insert the logo in the Report Header section. On the selected logo, point to the right middle sizing handle until the pointer ↔ displays. Drag to the right until the right edge of the logo is aligned with the **1.5-inch mark on the horizontal ruler**.

3 On the **Design tab**, in the **Header/Footer group**, click the **Title** button. In the **title's label control**, click to the left of your **Lastname**, delete your **Lastname Firstname** and the space, and then press (Enter). On the **title's label control**, point to the right middle sizing handle until the pointer ↔ displays, and then double-click to adjust the size of the label control to fit the text. Alternatively, drag the right middle sizing handle to the left.

4 Scroll down until the **Page Footer** section bar displays. Point to the top edge of the **Page Footer** section bar until the pointer ✚ displays. Drag upward until the top of the **Page Footer** section bar aligns with the **2.25-inch mark on the vertical ruler**.

This prevents extra blank space from printing between the records.

5 Scroll up until the **Report Header** section displays. Point to the top edge of the **Detail** section bar until the pointer ⊕ displays. Drag upward until the top edge of the **Detail** section bar aligns with the bottom edge of the **Page Header** section bar, and then compare your screen with Figure 6.31.

> The Page Header and Page Footer sections are paired together. Likewise, the Report Header and Report Footer sections are paired together. You cannot remove only one section of the pair. If you wish to remove one section of a paired header/footer, decrease the height of the section. Alternatively, set the Height property for the section to 0. Because there is no space in the Page Header section, nothing will print at the top of every page. To remove both of the paired header/footer sections, right click in the Detail section, and click the Page Header/Footer to deselect it.

Figure 6.31

Height of 0″

Paired sections

Report Header section
with logo and title

Paired sections

Label control sized
to fit text

6 Drag the right edge of the design grid to the left until it aligns with the **6.5-inch mark on the horizontal ruler. Save** 🖫 the report.

> The width of the report page is decreased, which will enable the report to fit within the margins of paper in portrait orientation.

Objective 7 │ Add Controls to a Report

Reports are not used to manipulate data in the underlying table or query, so they contain fewer types of controls. You can add label controls, text box controls, images, hyperlinks, or calculated controls to a report.

Activity 6.15 │ Adding Label and Text Box Controls to a Report

In this activity, you will add controls to the report that will contain the page number, the date, and your first name and last name.

1 On the **Design tab**, in the **Header/Footer group**, click the **Page Numbers** button. In the displayed **Page Numbers** dialog box, under **Format**, click **Page N of M**. Under **Position**, click **Bottom of Page [Footer]**. Alignment should remain **Center**; click **OK**.

> A text box control displays in the center of the Page Footer section. The control displays an expression that will display the page number. Every expression begins with an equal sign (=). "Page" is enclosed in quotation marks. Access interprets anything enclosed in quotation marks as text and will display it exactly as it is typed within the quotation marks, including the space. The & symbol is used for *concatenation*—linking or joining—of strings. A *string* is a series of characters. The word *Page* followed by a space will be concatenated—joined—to the string that follows the & symbol. [Page] is a reserved name that retrieves the current page number. This is followed by another & symbol that concatenates the page number to the next string—" of ". The & symbol continues concatenation of [Pages], a reserved name that retrieves the total number of pages in the report.

2 Save 🔲 the report. On the **Design tab**, in the **Views group**, click the **View button arrow**, and then click **Print Preview**. On the **Print Preview tab**, in the **Zoom group**, click the **Two Pages** button. Notice at the bottom of each page the format of the page number.

3 In the **Close Preview group**, click the **Close Print Preview** button.

4 On the **Design tab**, in the **Controls group**, click the **Label** button Aa. Point to the **Report Footer** section until the plus sign (+) of the pointer aligns with the bottom edge of the **Report Footer** section bar and with the left edge of the **Report Footer** section. Drag downward to the bottom of the **Report Footer** section and to the right to the **2.5-inch mark on the horizontal ruler**. Using your own first name and last name, type **Submitted by Firstname Lastname** and then compare your screen with Figure 6.32.

Figure 6.32

Label button
Text box control for page number
Label control

5 Click away from the label box, and then **Save** 🔲 the report. On the **Design tab**, in the **Header/Footer group**, click the **Date and Time** button. In the **Date and Time** dialog box, under **Include Date**, click the third option button, which displays the date as mm/dd/yyyy. Clear the **Include Time** check box, and then click **OK**.

> A text box control with an expression for the current date displays in the Report Header section. It may display over the Report title.

6 In the **Report Header**, click the **Date text box control** to select it. On the Ribbon, click the **Arrange tab**. In the **Table group**, click the **Remove Layout** button so the **Date text box control** can be moved. Right-click the selected control, and click **Cut**. Point to the **Report Footer** section bar, right-click, and then click **Paste**. Drag the text box control until the right edge of the text box control aligns with the **6.25-inch mark on the horizontal ruler**. Click the **Title label control** to select it, point to the right middle sizing handle until the pointer ↔ displays, and then drag to the right until the right edge of the text box control aligns with the **4.5-inch mark on the horizontal ruler**.

7 Save 🖫 the report, and then switch to **Layout** view. Notice that, for the first record, the data for the **Item Name** field does not fully display. Click the **Item Name text box control**, which partially displays *Berry Smoothie*. Point to the right edge of the **Item Name text box control** until the pointer ✛ displays. Drag to the right approximately **1 inch**. Because no ruler displays in Layout view, you will have to estimate the distance to drag.

Because the controls are in a stacked layout, the widths of all of the text box controls are increased.

8 Scroll down, observing the data in the **Item Name** field. Ensure that all of the data displays. If the data is not all visible in a record, use the technique you just practiced to increase the width of the text box control until all of the data displays.

9 Switch to **Design** view. Point to the right edge of the design grid until the pointer ↔ displays. If necessary, drag to the left until the right edge of the design grid aligns with the **6.5-inch mark on the horizontal ruler**. **Save** 🖫 the report.

The width of the report page will change with the addition of more text boxes, making it necessary to readjust the width so the report will fit within the margins of paper in portrait orientation.

More Knowledge | Adding a Hyperlink to a Report

Add a hyperlink to a report in Design view by clicking the Insert Hyperlink button in the Controls group and then specifying the complete URL. To test the hyperlink, in Design view, right-click the hyperlink, click Hyperlink, and then click Open Hyperlink. The hyperlink is active—jumps to the target—in Design view, Report view, and Layout view. The hyperlink is not active in Print Preview view. If the report is exported to another Office application, the hyperlink is active when it is opened in that application. An application that can *export* data can create a file in a format that another application understands, enabling the two programs to share the same data.

Activity 6.16 | Adding an Image Control and a Line Control to a Report

1 In **Design** view, in the **Report Header** section, right-click the **logo control**. From the displayed shortcut menu, click **Copy**. Right-click anywhere in the **Report Header** section, and then from the shortcut menu, click **Paste**.

> A copy of the image displays on top and slightly to the left of the original logo control.

2 Point to the selected logo until the pointer displays. Drag to the right until the left edge of the outlined control is the same distance from the title as the logo control on the left. Point to the top edge of the **Page Header** section bar until the pointer displays. Drag upward until the top of the **Page Header** section bar aligns with the **0.5-inch mark on the vertical ruler**.

> Recall that when you created a form in Design view, you clicked the Insert Image button and selected the location in the header section. You then had to change the properties of the image to match the size of the image in the logo control. Because you copied the original image from the logo, the images are the same size.

3 With the image control on the right selected, hold down Shift, and then click the **logo control**. On the Ribbon, click the **Arrange tab**. In the **Sizing & Ordering group**, click the **Align button**, and select **Bottom**. Compare your screen with Figure 6.33.

> Both the logo control and the image control are aligned along the bottom edges.

Figure 6.33

Logo control

Image control

4 On the Ribbon, click the **Design tab**. In the **Controls group**, click the More button, and then click the **Line** button. Point to the **Detail** section until the middle of the plus sign (+) of the pointer aligns at **2 inches on the vertical ruler** and **0 inches on the horizontal ruler**, as shown in Figure 6.34.

> A *line control* enables an individual to insert a line in a form or report.

Figure 6.34

Line button

0-inch mark

Line control pointer

2-inch mark

5 Hold down Shift, drag to the right to **6.5 inches on the horizontal ruler**, and then release the mouse button.

> An orange line control displays. Holding down the Shift key ensures that the line will be straight.

6 On the **Format tab**, in the **Control Formatting group**, click the **Shape Outline** button. Point to **Line Thickness** and then click the third line—**2 pt**. In the **Control Formatting group**, click the **Shape Outline** button. Under **Theme Colors**, on the fifth row, click the sixth color—**Blue, Accent 2, Darker 25%**.

7 **Save** the report, and then switch to **Report** view. Compare your screen with Figure 6.35. Notice the horizontal line that displays between the records.

Figure 6.35

Horizontal line between records

8 Switch to **Design** view.

Objective 8 | Group, Sort, and Total Records in Design View

Although it is much easier to create a report that is grouped and sorted using the Report Wizard, the same tasks can be completed in Design view. If a report has been created that was not grouped, you can modify the report in Design view to include grouping and summary data. Calculated controls are often added to reports to display summary information in reports with grouped records.

Activity 6.17 | Adding a Grouping and Sort Level to a Report

In this activity, you will add a grouping and sort order to the report, and then move a control from the Detail section to the Header section.

1 On the **Design tab**, in the **Grouping & Totals group**, click the **Group & Sort** button, and then compare your screen with Figure 6.36.

The Group, Sort, and Total Pane displays at the bottom of the screen. Because no grouping or sorting has been applied to the report, two buttons relating to these functions display in the Group, Sort, and Total Pane.

Figure 6.36

Group & Sort button

Group, Sort, and Total pane

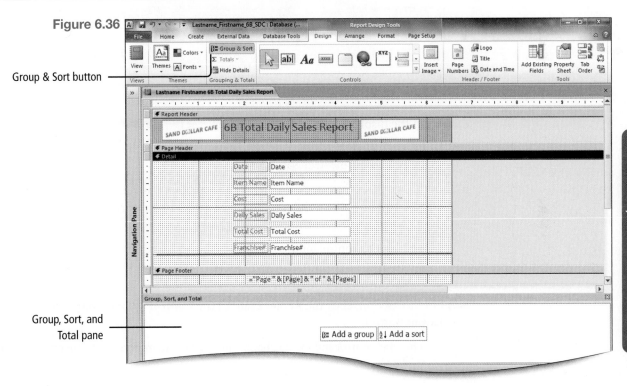

2 In the **Group, Sort, and Total Pane**, click the **Add a group** button. A list of fields that are used in the report displays as shown in Figure 6.37.

Figure 6.37

Fields used in the report

3 From the displayed list, click **Item Name**.

> An empty Item Name Header section is inserted above the Detail section. The report will be grouped by the Item Name, and the Item Names will be sorted in ascending order.

4 In the **Detail** section, click the **Item Name text box control**. Point to the selected text box control until the pointer ⏹ displays. Drag downward until a thin orange line displays below the **Franchise#** controls.

> The text box control for this field will be moved to the Item Name Header section in the report. Recall that moving the controls to the bottom of the stacked layout makes it easier to remove the controls from the stacked layout.

5 On the Ribbon, click the **Arrange tab**. In the **Control Layout group**, click the **Remove Layout** button.

> The label control and the text box control for the Item Name field are removed from the stacked layout.

6 Right-click the selected **Item Name text box control** to display the shortcut menu, and click **Cut**. Click the **Item Name Header** section bar to select it, right click to display the shortcut menu, and click **Paste**.

> The controls for the Item Name are moved from the Detail section to the Item Name Header section. Because the report is being grouped by this field, the controls should be moved out of the Detail section.

7 In the **Item Name Header** section, click the **Item Name label control**, and then press (Del). Click the **Item Name text box control** to select it, and then drag it to the right until the left edge of the control aligns with the **1-inch mark on the horizontal ruler**. Compare your screen with Figure 6.38.

> Because the records are grouped by the data in the Item Name field, the name of the field is unnecessary.

Figure 6.38

Item Name text box
control moved from
Detail section

8 **Save** the report, and then switch to **Report** view. Scroll down, noticing the grouping of records, until the grouping for **Grilled Chicken Skewer** displays. Notice that there are two records, one for Franchise# 12 and another for Franchise# 60. For these two records, notice the dates.

9 Switch back to **Design** view. In the **Group, Sort, and Total Pane**, click the **Add a sort** button, and then click **Date**. Notice that the Date will be sorted from oldest to newest.

10 **Save** the report, and then switch to **Report** view. Scroll down until the **Grilled Chicken Skewer** grouping displays. Within the grouping, the two records are arranged in order by the date with the oldest date listed first.

11 Switch to **Design** view, and then **Close** the **Group, Sort, and Total Pane**. Be sure to click the Close ⊠ button located in the title bar and not the Delete button that is inside the pane.

Activity 6.18 | Adding Calculated Controls to a Report

1 In the **Detail** section, click the **Total Cost text box control**. On the **Design tab**, in the **Grouping & Totals group**, click the **Totals** button, and then compare your screen with Figure 6.39.

A list of *aggregate functions*—functions that group and perform calculations on multiple fields—displays. Before selecting the Totals button, the field that will be used in the aggregate function must be selected. If you wish to perform aggregate functions on multiple fields, you must select each field individually, and then select the aggregate function to apply to the field.

Figure 6.39

Totals button

List of aggregate functions

Field used in aggregate function

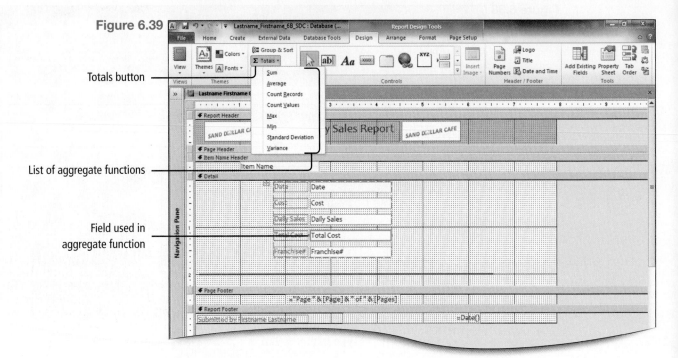

2 In the displayed list of aggregate functions, click **Sum**, and then compare your screen with Figure 6.40.

The Item Name Footer section is added to the report. A calculated control is added to the section that contains the expression that will display the sum of the Total Cost field for each grouping. A calculated control is also added to the Report Footer section that contains the expression that will display the grand total of the Total Cost field for the report. Recall that an expression begins with an equal sign (=). The Sum function adds or totals numeric data. Field names are included in square brackets.

Figure 6.40

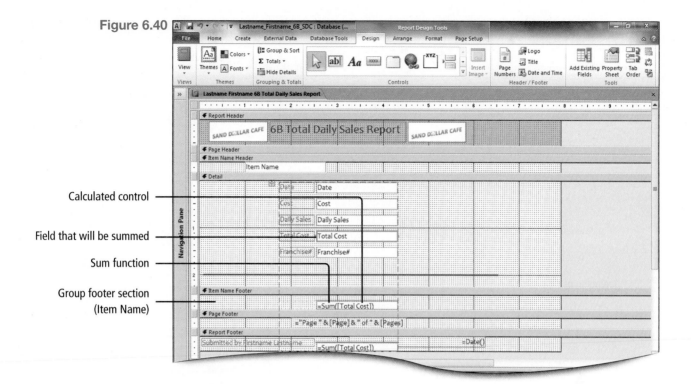

Calculated control

Field that will be summed

Sum function

Group footer section (Item Name)

3 **Save** 🖫 the report, and then switch to **Report** view. Notice that for the first grouping—Berry Smoothie—which only contains one record, the sum of the grouping displays below the horizontal line. Scroll down to the **Grilled Chicken Skewer** grouping, and then notice that the total for the grouping—**$644.40**—displays below the horizontal line for the second record in the grouping.

The placement of the horizontal line is distracting in the report, and there is no label attached to the grouping total.

4 Switch to **Design** view. On the **Design tab**, in the **Controls group**, click the **Text Box** button 🔲. Point to the **Item Name Footer** section until the plus sign (+) of the pointer aligns with the bottom edge of the **Item Name Footer** section bar and with the **0.5-inch mark on the horizontal ruler**. Drag downward to the bottom of the **Item Name Footer** section and to the right to the **2.5-inch mark on the horizontal ruler**.

5 Click inside the text box, and type **=[Item Name] & " Total Cost:"** ensuring that you include a space between the quotation mark and *Total* and that *Item Name* is enclosed in square brackets. Compare your screen with Figure 6.41.

Because a field name is included in the description of the total, a text box control must be used. This binds the control to the Item Name field in the underlying query, which makes this control a bound control. If you wish to insert only string characters as a description—for example, Total Cost—add a label control, which is an unbound control.

Access | Chapter 6

Figure 6.41

Concatenation symbol

Text box control

Beginning of expression

String

6 In the **Item Name Footer** section, click the **label control** that displays to the left of the text box control where you typed the expression. Press Del to delete the text box control's associated label control.

The data in the text box control is descriptive and does not require an additional label control.

7 In the **Item Name Footer** section, click the **text box control** that contains the expression you typed. Point to the left middle sizing handle until the pointer displays. Drag to the left until the left edge of the text box control aligns with the left edge of the design grid. With the text box control selected, hold down Shift. In the **Item Name Footer** section, click the **calculated control** for the sum. On the Ribbon, click the **Arrange tab**. In the **Sizing & Ordering group**, click the **Align** button, and then click **Bottom** to align both controls at the bottom.

8 Point to the top of the **Page Footer** section bar until the pointer ✛ displays. Drag downward to the top of the **Report Footer** section bar to increase the height of the Item Name Footer section so **three dots** display below the **Total Cost** controls.

9 In the **Detail** section, click the **line control**. Point to the line control until the pointer displays. Drag downward into the **Item Name Footer** section under the controls until there are approximately **two dots** between the text box controls and the line control, and then release the mouse button.

The line control is moved from the Detail section to the Item Name Footer section.

10 Point to the top of the **Item Name Footer** section bar until the pointer ✛ displays. Drag upward until approximately **two dots** display between the **Franchise#** controls and the top edge of the **Item Name Footer** section bar. Compare your screen with Figure 6.42.

The height of the Detail section is decreased.

Figure 6.42

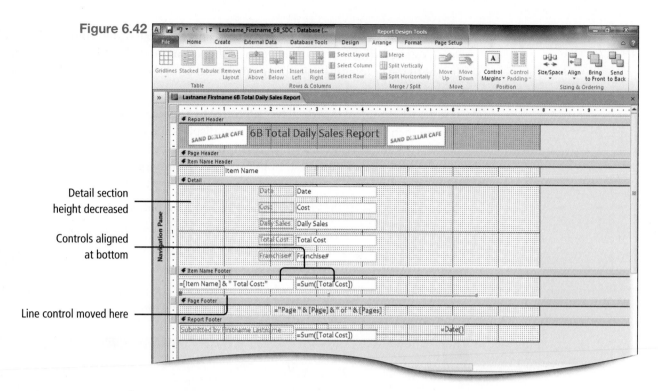

Detail section
height decreased

Controls aligned
at bottom

Line control moved here

11 **Save** 💾 the report, and then switch to **Report** view. Scroll down until the **Grilled Chicken Skewer** grouping displays, and then compare your screen with Figure 6.43.

> The report is easier to read with the horizontal line moved to the grouping footer section and with an explanation of the total for the grouping.

Figure 6.43

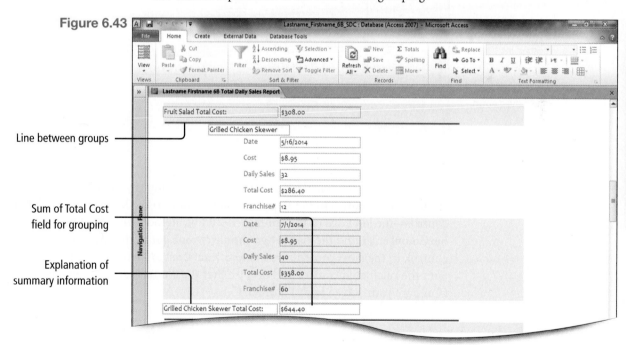

Line between groups

Sum of Total Cost
field for grouping

Explanation of
summary information

12 Hold down Ctrl, and then press End to move to the end of the report. Notice the sum of **$2,661.80**.

> By default, when you insert an aggregate function into a report, a calculated control for the grand total is inserted in the Report Footer section. The control is aligned with the text box control that is being used in the aggregate function. If the Report Footer section is not tall enough and multiple aggregate functions are used, the controls will display on top of one another.

Access | Chapter 6

13 Switch to **Design** view. In the **Report Footer** section, the calculated control displays **=Sum([Total Cost])**. Point to the bottom of the **Report Footer** section—not the section bar—until the pointer displays. Drag downward until the height of the **Report Footer** section is approximately **1 inch**.

14 Click the label control that displays **Submitted by Firstname Lastname**. Hold down Shift, and then click the text box control that displays the **Date** expression. On the Ribbon, click the **Arrange tab**. In the **Sizing & Ordering group**, click the **Size/Space** button, and then click **To Tallest**. In the **Sizing & Ordering group**, click the **Align** button, and then click **Bottom**.

The two controls are the same height and aligned at the bottom edges of the controls.

15 Point to either of the selected controls until the pointer [icon] displays. Drag downward until the bottom edges of the controls align with the bottom edge of the Report Footer section, and then compare your screen with Figure 6.44.

The controls are moved to the bottom of the Report Footer section to increase readability and to make space to insert a label control for the grand total.

Figure 6.44

Calculated control
for grand total

Height of Report Footer
section increased

Controls aligned, resized,
and moved down

16 On the Ribbon, click the **Design tab**. Use the techniques you have practiced previously to add a **label control** in the Report Footer section to the left of the calculated control—the left edge of the control should be aligned with the **0-inch mark on the horizontal ruler** and the right edge should be **one dot** to the left of the calculated control. In the label control, type **Grand Total Cost of All Items:** Align the label control with the calculated control and be sure that the controls are the same height. Compare your screen with Figure 6.45.

Figure 6.45

Label control

Controls aligned
and same height

Alert! | **Does Your Control Display with Two Boxes?**

If your control displays with two boxes—one that displays text and a number; for example Text35, and one that displays Unbound—you selected the Text Box button instead of the Label button. If that happens, click the Undo button, and then begin again.

---

17 **Save** 🖫 the report, and then switch to **Report** view. Hold down Ctrl, and then press End to move to the end of the report. Notice that the grand total is now easier to distinguish because a description of the control has been added and the other controls are moved down.

18 Switch to **Print Preview** view. If necessary, on the **Print Preview tab**, in the **Zoom group**, click the **Two Pages** button. Look at the bottom of Page 1 and the top of Page 2, and notice that the grouping breaks across two pages. In the navigation area, click the **Next Page** button to display Pages 3 and 4. Groupings are split between these pages.

For a more professional-looking report, avoid splitting groupings between pages.

19 In the **Close Preview group**, click the **Close Print Preview** button. Switch to **Design** view. On the **Design tab**, in the **Grouping & Totals group**, click the **Group & Sort** button.

20 In the displayed **Group, Sort, and Total Pane**, on the **Group on Item Name** bar, click **More**. Click the **do not keep group together on one page arrow**, and then click **keep whole group together on one page**. **Close** ☒ the **Group, Sort, and Total Pane**—do not click the Delete button.

21 **Save** 🖫 the report, and then switch to **Print Preview** view. In the navigation area, click the buttons to display pages in the report, and then notice that groupings are no longer split between pages. Also notice that more blank space displays at the bottom of some pages.

22 If you are instructed to submit this result, create a paper or electronic printout. On the **Print Preview tab**, in the **Close Preview group**, click the **Close Print Preview** button. **Close** the report, and then **Open** ⟫ the **Navigation Pane**. **Close** the database, and **Close** Access.

More Knowledge | **Formatting a Report**

You can add a background picture to a report or change the background color of a report using the same techniques you used in forms.

End **You have completed Project 6B** —————————————————

Access | Chapter 6

Content-Based Assessments

Summary

Forms are database objects that are used to interact with the data in tables. In the first project, you created a form in Design view, added sections to the form, and modified the sections. You changed a combo box control to a list box control, and moved controls around on the form. In addition to label controls, you inserted an image control and command button controls. You formatted forms by adding a background color, adding a background picture, and modifying control borders. Finally, you made a form more user friendly by adding a message to the status bar for fields, creating custom ControlTips, and changing the tab order.

Reports are database objects that are used to present data from tables or queries in a professional-looking format. Reports are usually created using queries as the record source. In the second project, you created a report using a wizard and based it on a crosstab query. You also created a report in Design view and modified the sections of the report. You added text box controls to the report that contained expressions. You concatenated strings and field names to build expressions. You also added an image control and a line control to a report. In Design view, you added grouping and sorting levels to the report. You then added calculated controls that used aggregate functions.

Key Terms

Matching

Match each term in the second column with its correct definition in the first column by writing the letter of the term on the blank line in front of the correct definition.

_____ 1. An Access object that provides you with a way to enter, edit, and display data from underlying tables.

_____ 2. Characteristics that determine the appearance, structure, and behavior of an object.

_____ 3. Displays the properties that affect the appearance and behavior of an object.

_____ 4. An object in a form or report in Design view that enables individuals to perform actions or view/enhance data.

_____ 5. Enables an individual to insert an image into any section of a form or report.

_____ 6. Enables an individual to add a command button to a form or report that will perform an action when the button is clicked.

_____ 7. The box where the rulers meet, in the upper left corner of a form in Design view.

A Button control

B Control

C ControlTip

D Focus

E Form

F Form selector

G Image control

H Line control

I Point

J Propagate

K Properties

L Property Sheet

M Property Update Options button

N Tab order

O Themes

Content-Based Assessments

_____ 8. The measurement equal to 1/72 of an inch.

_____ 9. Text that displays when an individual pauses the mouse pointer over a control on a form.

_____ 10. Refers to the order in which the fields are selected when the Tab key is pressed.

_____ 11. To spread, disseminate, or apply.

_____ 12. A button that enables an individual to update the Property Sheet for a field in all objects that use this table as the record source.

_____ 13. Refers to the object that is selected and currently being acted upon.

_____ 14. A design tool that simplifies the process of creating professional-looking objects.

_____ 15. A control that enables an individual to insert a line in a form or a report.

Multiple Choice

Circle the correct answer.

1. What can be used to further enhance every object on a form, including the form itself?
   A. Layout view
   B. Control sheet
   C. Property sheet

2. Which view should be used to create a form, if you want more control over the creation?
   A. Form view
   B. Design view
   C. Layout view

3. Which property enables you to specify the source of the data for a form or a report?
   A. Object source
   B. Record source
   C. Control source

4. An action is applied to a button control using the
   A. Combo Box Wizard
   B. Button Control Wizard
   C. Command Button Wizard

5. Which Form property is modified to apply color to the background of a form?
   A. Background
   B. Back color
   C. Wallpaper

6. What property determines where the background picture for a form displays on the form?
   A. Picture Alignment
   B. Picture Update
   C. Picture Size Mode

7. In the Picture Size Mode property, which setting stretches the image both vertically and horizontally to match the size of the form?
   A. Zoom
   B. Stretch
   C. Clip

8. Which form property enables an individual to add descriptive text that will display in the status bar for a selected control?
   A. Hint Text
   B. Description
   C. Status Bar Text

9. Which section of a report appears at the top of the first printed page?
   A. Report header
   B. Page header
   C. Detail header

10. Functions that group and perform calculations on multiple fields are
    A. aggregate functions
    B. arithmetic functions
    C. logical functions

Apply **6A** skills from these Objectives:

- Create a Form in Design View
- Change and Add Controls
- Format a Form
- Make a Form User Friendly

Skills Review | Project **6C** Party Orders

Marty Kress, Vice President of Marketing for the Sand Dollar Cafe franchise restaurant chain, wants to expand the chain's offerings to include party trays for advance order and delivery. In the following project, you will create a form to use for the data entry of these party order items. Your completed form, if printed, will look similar to Figure 6.46. An electronic version of the form will look slightly different.

Project Files

For Project 6C, you will need the following files:

a06C_Party_Orders
a06C_Logo
a06C_Sand_Dollar

You will save your database as:

Lastname_Firstname_6C_Party_Orders

Project Results

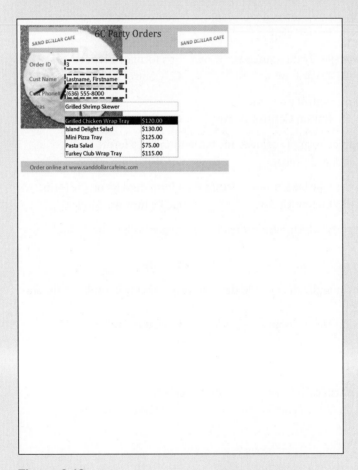

Figure 6.46

(Project 6C Party Orders continues on the next page)

Content-Based Assessments

Skills Review | Project **6C** Party Orders (continued)

1 **Start** Access. Locate and open the **a06C_Party_Orders** file. Save the database in your **Access Chapter 6** folder as **Lastname_Firstname_6C_Party_Orders** If necessary, click **Enable Content**.

2 Double-click **6C Party Orders** to open the table in **Datasheet** view. Take a moment to examine the fields in the table.

a. In any record, click in the **Party Tray** field, and then click the **arrow**. This field is a Lookup field in the *6C Trays* table. In any record, click in the **Extras** field, and then click the **arrow**. This field is a Lookup field in the *6C Menu Items* table.

b. **Close** the table, and then close the **Navigation Pane**.

3 On the Ribbon, click the **Create tab**. In the **Forms** group, click the **Form Design** button.

a. If necessary, on the **Design tab**, in the **Tools group**, click the **Property Sheet** button. On the Property Sheet, click the **Data tab**. Click the **Record Source property setting box arrow**, and then click **6C Party Orders**. Close the **Property Sheet**.

4 On the **Design tab**, in the **Tools group**, click the **Add Existing Fields** button.

a. In the **Field List**, click **Order ID**, hold down Shift, and then click **Extras**. Drag the selected fields onto the design grid until the top of the pointer arrow is aligned at **0.25 inch on the vertical ruler** and **2 inches on the horizontal ruler**, and then release the mouse button. **Close** the **Field List**.

b. With all of the controls still selected, on the **Arrange tab**, in the **Table group**, click the **Stacked** button.

c. Drag the left edge of the selected text box controls to the **0.5-inch mark on the horizontal ruler**. Increase the width of the text boxes by approximately **0.5 inch**. Save the form as **Lastname Firstname 6C Party Order Form**

5 On the **Design tab**, in the **Header/Footer group**, click the **Logo** button.

a. Navigate to the location where the student data files for this textbook are saved. Locate and double-click **a06C_Logo** to insert the logo in the **Form Header**.

b. On the selected logo, point to the right middle sizing handle until the pointer displays. Drag to the right until the right edge of the logo is aligned with the **1.5-inch mark on the horizontal ruler**.

6 In the **Header/Footer group**, click the **Title** button.

a. In the **label control** for the title, replace the text with **6C Party Orders** and then press Enter.

b. Drag the right edge of the title to align it with the **4-inch mark on the horizontal ruler**.

c. With the title selected, on the **Format tab**, in the **Font group**, click the **C**enter button.

7 Scroll down until the **Form Footer** section bar displays. Point to the top of the **Form Footer** section bar until the pointer displays. Drag upward until the top of the Form Footer section bar aligns with the **2.5-inch mark on the vertical ruler**.

a. On the **Design tab**, in the **Controls group**, click the **Label** button. Point to the **Form Footer** section until the plus sign (+) of the pointer aligns with the bottom of the **Form Footer** section bar and the **0.25-inch mark on the horizontal ruler**. Drag downward to the bottom of the **Form Footer** section and to the right to the **3.25-inch mark on the horizontal ruler**.

b. Type **Order online at www.sanddollarcafeinc.com** and then press Enter.

c. With the **label control** in the **Form Footer** section selected, hold down Shift, and then click the **Logo control** and the **Extras label control**. On the Ribbon, click the **Arrange tab**. In the **Sizing & Ordering group**, click the **Align** button, and then click **Left**. **Save** the form.

8 Click and hold the **Party Tray text box control** until the pointer displays. Drag downward until a thin orange line displays on the bottom edges of the **Extras** controls and then release the mouse button.

a. With the **Party Tray text box control** selected, hold down Shift, and then click the **Party Tray label control**, **Extras text box control**, and **Extras label control**.

b. On the **Arrange tab**, in the **Table group**, click the **Remove Layout** button to remove the *Extras* field and the *Party Tray* field from the stacked layout.

c. Click in the **Detail** section to deselect the controls. Right-click the **Party Tray combo box control**. From the shortcut menu, point to **Change To**, and then click **List Box**.

(Project 6C Party Orders continues on the next page)

d. **Save** the form, and then switch to **Form** view. Notice that the **Party Tray list box control** is not wide enough to display all columns and that there are horizontal and vertical scroll bars to indicate there is more data.

e. Click the **Extras combo box arrow** to be sure that none of the menu item names and prices are cut off. Press (Esc).

f. Switch to **Design** view, and click the **Party Tray list box control**. Point to the right edge of the control until the pointer displays. Drag to the right until the right edge of the control aligns with the **4-inch mark on the horizontal ruler**.

g. Switch to **Layout** view. Resize the **Extras combo box control** to be the same size as the **Party Tray list box control**. **Save** the form and switch to **Design** view. Click the **Form Header section bar**.

9 On the **Design tab**, in the **Controls group**, click the **Insert Image** button, and then click **Browse**. In the displayed **Insert Picture** dialog box, navigate to the location where the student data files for this textbook are saved.

a. Locate and double-click **a06C_Logo**.

b. Align the plus sign with the bottom of the **Form Header** section bar and with the **4-inch mark on the horizontal ruler**. Drag downward to the top of the **Detail** section bar and to the right to the **5.25-inch mark on the horizontal ruler**.

c. Click the **image control**—the Sand Dollar Cafe image on the right side in the **Form Header** section. On the **Design tab**, in the **Tools group**, click the **Property Sheet** button. If necessary, on the **Format tab**, change the **Width** property setting to **1.25** and then change the **Height** property setting to **0.625**.

d. In the **Form Header** section, click the **logo control**. On the **Property Sheet**, change the **Width** property setting to **1.25** and change the **Height** property setting to **0.625**.

e. With the logo control selected, hold down (Shift), and then click the **image control**. On the **Arrange tab**, in the **Sizing & Ordering group**, click the **Align** button, and then click **Top**. **Close** the **Property Sheet**.

10 On the Ribbon, click the **Design tab**, and then in the **Controls group**, click the **Button** button.

a. Move the mouse pointer down into the **Detail** section. Align the plus sign (+) of the pointer at **0.25 inches on the vertical ruler** and **3 inches on the horizontal ruler**, and then click.

b. Under **Categories**, click **Record Navigation**. Under **Actions**, click **Find Record**, and then click **Next** two times. In the text box, type **btnFindRecord** and then click Finish.

c. Using the technique you just practiced, add a **button control** right next to the **Find Record button**. Under **Categories**, click **Form Operations**. Under **Actions**, click **Print Current Form**, and then click **Next** two times. Name the button **btnPrtForm** Click **Finish**.

d. With the **Print Current Form button control** selected, hold down (Shift), and then click the **Find Record button control**. On the **Arrange tab**, in the **Sizing & Ordering group**, click the **Align** button, and then click **Top**.

11 Switch to **Layout** view. Click in the **Form Footer** section to the right of the label control.

a. On the **Format tab**, in the **Font group**, click the **Background Color** button. Under **Theme Colors**, in the second row, click the third color—**Tan, Background 2, Darker 10%**.

b. Using the technique you just practiced, change the color of the **Form Header** section to match the **Form Footer** section.

12 Switch to **Design** view, and then double-click the **Form selector** to open the Property Sheet for the form.

a. On the **Property Sheet**, on the **Format tab**, click in the **Picture** property setting box, and then click the **Build** button. Navigate to where the student data files for this textbook are saved. Locate and double-click **a06C_Sand_Dollar** to insert the picture in the form.

b. Click in the **Picture Alignment** property setting box, click the **arrow**, and then click **Form Center**. **Close** the **Property Sheet**, and then **save** the form.

13 Switch to **Layout** view, click the **Order ID text box control**, hold down (Shift), and then click the **Cust Name text box control** and the **Cust Phone# text box control**.

(Project 6C Party Orders continues on the next page)

a. On the **Format tab**, in the **Control Formatting group**, click the **Shape Outline** button. Point to **Line Type**, and click the third line type—**Dashes**.

b. On the **Format tab**, in the **Control Formatting group**, click the **Shape Outline** button. Point to **Line Thickness**, and then click the third line type—**2 pt**.

c. In the **Control Formatting group**, click the **Shape Outline button**. Under **Theme Colors**, in the fifth row, click the third color—**Tan, Background 2, Darker 75%**.

14 Switch to **Form** view, and then click in the **Cust Phone# text box control**. On the left side of the status bar, *Form View* displays—there is no text that helps an individual enter data. **Close** the form, **Save** your changes, and open the **Navigation Pane**.

a. Under **Tables**, right-click **6C Party Orders**; from the shortcut menu, click **Design View**. In the **Cust Phone#** field, click in the **Description** box. Type **Include area code for 10-digit dialing** and then press [Enter].

b. Click the **Property Update Options** button, and then click **Update Status Bar Text everywhere Cust Phone# is used**. In the displayed **Update Properties** dialog box, click **Yes**. **Close** the table, saving changes.

15 Open **6C Party Order Form** in **Design** view. Close the **Navigation Pane**. If necessary, on the **Design** tab, in the **Tools** group, click the **Property Sheet** button.

a. Click the **Print Form** button in the **Detail** section. Notice that the **Property Sheet** is displayed for the button you selected.

b. On the **Other tab**, click in the ControlTip Text property setting box, type **Prints the Current Form** to replace the existing **Print Form** text, and then press [Enter].

c. **Close** the **Property Sheet**, Save the form, and then switch to **Form** view. Point to the **Print Form** button to display the ControlTip.

16 Switch to **Design** view. In the **Detail** section, click the **Order ID text box control**, hold down [Shift], and then click the **Find Record button control** and the **Print Current Form button control**.

a. On the **Design tab**, in the **Tools group**, click the **Property Sheet** button. If necessary, on the **Property Sheet**, click the **Other tab**. On the **Property Sheet**, click in the **Tab Stop** property setting box, click the **arrow**, and then click **No**.

b. Click the **Cust Name text box control**. Click in the **Tab Index** property setting box, and then type **0** **Close** the **Property Sheet**.

17 Switch to **Form** view. With the **Cust Name** control selected, click the **Find Record** button.

a. In the **Find and Replace** dialog box, in the **Find What** box, type **Gonzalez, Ricardo** Click **Find Next**. **Close** the Find and Replace dialog box.

b. In the Cust Name text box, type your **Lastname, Firstname** replacing Ricardo's name. Press [Tab]. In the **Cust Phone#** field, enter your phone number, and then press [Enter]. **Save** the form.

18 If you are instructed to submit this result, click the **Print Current Form** button to create a paper or electronic printout. If you are to submit your work electronically, follow your instructor's directions.

19 **Close** the form, open the **Navigation Pane**, **Close** the database, and then **Exit** Access.

End **You have completed Project 6C**

Content-Based Assessments

- **5** Create a Report
  Based on a Query
  Using a Wizard
- **6** Create a Report in
  Design View
- **7** Add Controls to a
  Report
- **8** Group, Sort, and
  Total Records in
  Design View

Skills Review | Project **6D** Catering

The individual restaurants of Sand Dollar Cafe each maintain a database about the orders that are placed for the catering entity of the business. Reports are run to summarize data in the tables or queries. Creating customized reports will help the managers of each location view the information in the database in a meaningful way. In this project, you will create customized reports. Your completed reports will look similar to Figure 6.47.

Project Files

For Project 6D, you will need the following files:

  a06D_Catering
  a06D_Logo

You will save your database as:

  Lastname_Firstname_6D_Catering

Project Results

Figure 6.47

(Project 6D Catering continues on the next page)

Content-Based Assessments

1 **Start** Access. Locate and open the **a06D_Catering** file. Save the database in your **Access Chapter 6** folder as **Lastname_Firstname_6D_Catering** If necessary, click **Enable Content**.

2 In the Navigation Pane, under **Queries**, double-click **6D Catering _ Crosstab Query**. Take a moment to study the data in the query. **Close** the query, and then close the **Navigation Pane**.

3 On the Ribbon, click the **Create tab**. In the **Reports** group, click the **Report Wizard** button.

  a. Click the **Tables/Queries arrow**, and then click **Query: 6D Catering Crosstab Query**. Under **Available Fields**, click the **All Fields** button to add all of the field names to the **Selected Fields** box. Click **Next** twice.

  b. Click the **arrow** next to the **1** box, and then click **Cust Name**. Leave the sort order as **Ascending**, and then click **Next**.

  c. Under **Layout**, be sure the **Tabular** option button is selected. Under **Orientation**, be sure the **Portrait** option button is selected. Be sure the **Adjust the field width so all fields fit on a page** check box is selected. Click **Next**.

  d. For the title of the report, type **Lastname Firstname 6D Catering by Date** Select **Modify the report's design**, and then click **Finish**.

4 On the Ribbon, click the **Design tab**. In the **Themes** group, click the **Themes** button, and then click the first theme on the sixth row—**Hardcover**.

5 Switch to **Layout** view. If necessary, in the **Cust Phone#** column, point to the right edge of any **text box control**, and then drag to the right until all of the data displays. Click in a blank area of the report to deselect the column. Switch to **Design** view. Drag the right edge of the report to the **7.75-inch mark on the horizontal ruler**.

6 Select all of the controls in the **Page Header** section, by pointing to the top left of the **Page Header** section, holding down your mouse button, and then dragging the mouse across the **Page Header controls** and to the bottom of the **Page Header** section. Release the mouse button.

  a. On the **Format tab**, in the **Font group**, click the **Font color button arrow**. Under **Theme Colors**, on the first row, click the fifth color—**Dark Red, Accent 1**.

7 **Save** the report, and then switch to **Print Preview**. If you are instructed to submit this result, create a paper or electronic printout. **Close Print Preview**. **Close** the report.

8 On the Ribbon, click the **Create tab**. In the **Reports** group, click the **Report Design** button.

  a. On the **Design tab**, in the **Tools group**, click the **Property Sheet** button. On the **Property Sheet**, click the **Data tab**. Click the **Record Source arrow**, click **6D Catering**, and then **Close** the **Property Sheet**.

  b. On the **Design tab**, in the **Tools group**, click the **Add Existing Fields** button. If necessary, click **Show only fields in the current record source** at the bottom of the Field List box.

  c. In the **Field List**, click **Pickup Time**. Hold down Shift, and then click **Price** to select all of the fields. Drag the selected fields into the **Detail** section until the top of the arrow of the pointer is aligned with the **0.25-inch mark on the vertical ruler** and with the **1.5-inch mark on the horizontal ruler**.

  d. With the controls still selected, on the Ribbon, click the **Arrange tab**. In the **Table group**, click the **Stacked** button. **Close** the **Field List**, and then **Save** the report as **Lastname Firstname 6D Catering Report**

9 On the **Design tab**, in the **Header/Footer group**, click the **Logo** button.

  a. Locate and double-click **a06D_Logo** to insert the logo in the Report Header section.

  b. On the selected logo, point to the right middle sizing handle until the pointer displays. Drag to the right until the right edge of the logo is aligned with the **1.5-inch mark on the horizontal ruler**.

10 On the **Design tab**, in the **Header/Footer group**, click the **Title** button. In the **title's label control**, select **Lastname Firstname**, and then press Del.

11 Point to the top edge of the **Page Footer** section bar until the pointer displays. Drag upward until the top of the **Page Footer** section bar aligns with the **2-inch mark on the vertical ruler**.

12 Point to the top edge of the **Detail** section bar until the pointer displays. Drag upward until the top edge of the **Detail** section bar aligns with the bottom edge of the **Page Header** section bar. **Save** the report.

13 On the **Design tab**, in the **Header/Footer group**, click the **Page Numbers** button.

  a. In the displayed **Page Numbers** dialog box, under **Format**, click **Page N**. Under **Position**, click **Bottom of Page [Footer]**, and then click **OK**.

(Project 6D Catering continues on the next page)

b. Resize and move the **Page Number control box** until it fits between the **2-inch and 4-inch marks on the horizontal ruler**.

14 On the **Design tab**, in the **Controls group**, click the **Label** button.

a. Drag the plus sign (+) from the bottom edge of the **Report Footer** section bar at the **0.25-inch mark on the horizontal ruler** to the bottom of the **Report Footer** section at the **3-inch mark on the horizontal ruler**.

b. Using your own first and last names, type **Catering Manager: Firstname Lastname** Press Enter.

15 On the **Design tab**, in the **Header/Footer group**, click the **Date & Time** button. In the **Date and Time** dialog box, under **Include Date**, click the second option button. Under **Include Time**, remove the check mark, and then click **OK**. **Save** the report.

a. Click the **Date text box control**. On the Ribbon, click the **Arrange tab**. In the **Table group**, click the **Remove Layout** button.

b. Right-click the selected control, and click **Cut**. Right-click the **Page Footer** section, and click **Paste**.

c. Move the **Date text box control** until the right edge of the text box control aligns with the **6.25-inch mark on the horizontal ruler**.

d. Click the **Title text box control** to select it, point to the right middle sizing handle until the pointer displays, and then drag to the right until the right edge of the text box control aligns with the **4.75-inch mark on the horizontal ruler**.

16 Drag the right edge of the design grid to the left until it aligns with the **6.5-inch mark on the horizontal ruler**. **Save** the report.

a. Switch to **Layout** view. In the first record, click the **Tray Desc text box control**, and then point to the right edge of the control until the pointer displays. Drag to the right until all of the text displays in the **Tray Desc text box control**—*Grilled Chicken Skewer Tray*.

17 Switch to **Design** view. In the **Report Header** section, right-click the **logo control**. From the displayed shortcut menu, click **Copy**. Right-click anywhere in the **Report Header** section, and then from the shortcut menu, click **Paste**.

a. Point to the selected logo, and then drag to the right until the left edge of the outlined control aligns with the **4.75-inch mark on the horizontal ruler**.

b. With the image control on the right selected, hold down Shift, and then click the **logo control**. On the Ribbon, click the **Arrange tab**. In the **Sizing & Ordering group**, click the **Align** button, and then click **Bottom**.

c. Resize the **Title text box control** so the right edge is **one dot** away from the image on its right. **Center** the title in the control. Drag the **Page Header section bar** up to the **0.5-inch mark on the vertical ruler**.

18 On the **Design tab**, in the **Grouping & Totals group**, click the **Group & Sort** button.

a. In the **Group, Sort, and Total Pane**, click the **Add a group** button. From the displayed list, click **Pickup Time**.

b. Click the **by quarter arrow** that displays after **from oldest to newest**, and then click **by entire value**. Click the **More arrow**, click the **do not keep group together on one page arrow**, and then click **keep whole group together on one page**.

c. In the **Group, Sort, and Total Pane**, click the **Add a sort** button, and then click **Cust Name**. **Close** the **Group, Sort, and Total Pane**.

19 In the **Detail** section, click the **Pickup Time text box control**. Drag downward until a thin orange line displays at the bottom of the **Price** controls, and then release the mouse button.

a. On the Ribbon, click the **Arrange tab**. In the **Table group**, click the **Remove Layout** button.

b. Move the **Pickup Time text box control** into the **Pickup Time Header** section so the left edge of the text box control aligns with the **1.5-inch mark on the horizontal ruler**.

c. In the **Pickup Time Header** section, click the **Pickup Time label control**, and then press Del.

20 In the **Detail** section, click the **Tray Desc text box control**. On the **Design tab**, in the **Grouping & Totals group**, click the **Totals** button. In the displayed list of aggregate functions, click **Count Records**.

21 In the **Pickup Time Footer** section, select the **Count text box control**, and then holding down Shift, in the **Report Footer** select the **Count text box control**.

(Project 6D Catering continues on the next page)

Skills Review | Project **6D** Catering (continued)

a. On the Ribbon, click the **Arrange tab**. In the **Table group**, click the **Remove Layout** button.

b. Align and resize the controls so the left edge of each control is even with the **5.5-inch marker on the horizontal ruler** and the right edge of each control is even with the **6-inch marker on the horizontal ruler**.

c. On the **Design tab**, in the **Controls group**, click the **Text Box** button. Drag the plus sign (+) from the bottom edge of the **Pickup Time Footer** section at the **2.75-inch mark on the horizontal ruler** to the bottom of the **Pickup Time Footer** section and to the right to the **5.5-inch mark on the horizontal ruler**.

d. Type =[Pickup Time] & " # of Orders:" In the **Pickup Time Footer** section, click the **label control** that displays to the left of the text box control, and then press Del .

e. In the **Pickup Time Footer** section, click the **text box control** that contains the expression you typed. Hold down Shift and click the **count calculated control** in the **Pickup Time Footer**. On the Ribbon, click the **Arrange tab**. In the **Sizing & Ordering group**, click **Size/Space**, and then click **To Tallest**. In the **Sizing & Ordering group**, click the **Align** button, and then click **Bottom**.

22 Drag the right edge of the design grid to the left until it aligns with the **6.5-inch mark on the horizontal ruler**. Switch to **Report** view. Hold down Ctrl , and then press End to move to the end of the report.

23 Switch to **Design** view. Point to the bottom of the **Report Footer** section, and then drag downward until it reaches the **0.5-inch mark on the vertical ruler**.

a. Click the **Count text box control** in the **Report Footer** section, and then drag downward until the

bottom edge of the control aligns with the bottom edge of the **Report Footer** section.

b. Use the techniques you have practiced to add a label control in the **Report Footer** section to the left of the calculated control—the left edge of the control should be aligned with the **4-inch mark on the horizontal ruler**. In the **label control**, type Total # of Orders:

c. Align the label control with the calculated control and then be sure that the controls are the same height.

24 On the Ribbon, click the **Design tab**. In the **Controls group**, click the **Line** button. Point to the bottom of the **Pickup Time Footer** section until the middle of the plus sign (+) of the pointer aligns with the top of the **Page Footer** section bar and the **0-inch mark on the horizontal ruler**. Hold down Shift , drag to the right to the **6.5-inch mark on the horizontal ruler**, and then release the mouse button and Shift .

25 On the **Format tab**, in the **Control Formatting group**, click the **Shape Outline** button. Click **Line Thickness**, and then click the fourth line—**3 pt**. In the **Control Formatting group**, click the **Shape Outline** button. Under **Theme Colors**, on the first row, click the fifth color—**Dark Red, Accent 1**. **Save** the report.

26 Switch to **Print Preview**. Adjust the margins or report width as needed. If you are instructed to submit this result, create a paper or electronic printout. **Close Print Preview**.

Close the report, and then open the **Navigation Pane**. **Close** the database, and then **Exit** Access.

End You have completed Project 6D

Content-Based Assessments

Apply **6A** skills from
these Objectives:

1 Create a Form in
Design View

2 Change and Add
Controls

3 Format a Form

4 Make a Form User
Friendly

Mastering Access | Project **6E** Monthly Promotions

In the following project, you will create a form that will be used to enter the data for the monthly promotions that are offered to guests of the Sand Dollar Cafe restaurant franchise. Your task includes designing a form that will be attractive and provide data entry ease for the staff. Your completed form will look similar to Figure 6.48.

Project Files

For Project 6E, you will need the following files:

a06E_Monthly_Promotions
a06E_Logo
a06E_Dollar

You will save your database as:

Lastname_Firstname_6E_Monthly_Promotions

Project Results

Figure 6.48

(Project 6E Monthly Promotions continues on the next page)

Content-Based Assessments

Mastering Access | Project **6E** Monthly Promotions (continued)

1 **Start** Access. Locate and open the **a06E_Monthly_Promotions** file. Save the database in your **Access Chapter 6** folder as **Lastname_Firstname_6E_Monthly_Promotions** If necessary, click **Enable Content**.

2 On the **Create tab**, in the **Forms group**, click the **Form Design** button. Display the **Property Sheet**. On the **Data tab**, click the **Record Source property setting box arrow**, and then click **6E Monthly Results**. **Close** the **Property Sheet**.

3 On the **Design tab**, in the **Tools group**, click **Add Existing Fields**. In the **Field List**, display the fields for the *6E Monthly Results* table, and then select all of the fields. Drag the selected fields onto the design grid until the top of the arrow of the pointer is aligned with the **0.25-inch mark on the vertical ruler** and aligned with the **1-inch mark on the horizontal ruler**. **Close** the **Field List**.

4 With all of the text box controls selected, display the **Property Sheet**, and then click the **Format tab**. In the **Left** property box, type **1.5** and press Enter. Click anywhere in the **Detail** section to deselect the controls. Select the **Franchise text box control**, and then drag the right edge to the **3-inch mark on the horizontal ruler**. Select the **# Redeemed text box control**, and in the **Property Sheet**, on the **Format tab**, click in the **Width** property box, and then type **0.75** and press Enter. **Save** the form as **Lastname Firstname 6E Promo Form** Switch to **Form** view, and then click the **Promo Month** text box control to view the entries. Switch to **Design** view, and **Close** the Property Sheet.

5 On the **Design tab**, in the **Header/Footer group**, click the **Logo** button, and then insert the **a06E_Logo**. Widen the selected logo to the **1.5-inch mark on the horizontal ruler**.

6 In the **Header/Footer group**, add a **Title**, and then, if necessary, resize the **Title label control** so the entire title is visible. With the title selected, select all of the label controls. On the **Format tab**, in the **Font group**, change the font color to **Aqua, Accent 5, Darker 50%**—the ninth color in the sixth row under Theme colors.

7 Scroll down until the **Form Footer** section bar displays. Point to the top of the **Form Footer**; drag up until the top of the Form Footer section bar aligns with the **1.5-inch mark on the vertical ruler**.

8 On the **Design tab**, in the **Controls group**, click the **Label** button. Point to the **Form Footer** section until the plus sign (+) of the pointer aligns with the bottom of the **Form Footer** section bar and with the **0-inch mark on the horizontal ruler**. Drag downward to the bottom of the **Form Footer** section and to the right to the **4-inch mark on the horizontal ruler**. Type **Coupons may be redeemed at any Sand Dollar Cafe location** Press Enter. Use the techniques you have practiced previously to change the font color to **Aqua, Accent 5, Darker 50%**.

9 On the **Design tab**, in the **Controls group**, click the **Image** button. Move the mouse pointer down into the **Form Footer** section. Align the plus sign (+) of the pointer with the top of the **Form Footer** section and with the **4.25-inch mark on the horizontal ruler**.

10 Drag downward to the bottom of the **Form Footer** section and to the right to the **5-inch mark on the horizontal ruler**. Locate and insert the file **a06E_Dollar**. Display the Property Sheet, and change the **Width** and **Height** to **0.35**

11 On the **Design tab**, in the **Controls group**, click the **Button** button. Move the mouse pointer down into the **Detail** section. Align the plus sign (+) of the pointer with the **0.5-inch mark on the vertical ruler** and the **3.5-inch mark on the horizontal ruler**, and then click.

12 Under **Categories**, click **Form Operations**. Under **Actions**, click **Close Form**, and then click **Next**. Select the **Text** radio button, and then click **Next**. In the text box, type **btnCloseForm** and then click **Finish**. With the button selected, click the **Format tab**, and, in the **Font group**, change the **Font Color** to **Aqua, Accent 5, Darker 50%**.

13 With the **Close Form** button selected, click the **Property Sheet** button. Click the **Other tab**, click in the **Tab Stop** property setting box, click the **arrow**, and then click **No**. **Close** the **Property Sheet**.

14 If you are instructed to submit this result, create a paper or electronic printout of **record 8**. If you are to submit your work electronically, follow your instructor's directions.

15 Click the **Close Form** button, saving changes. Open the **Navigation Pane**. **Close** the database, and then **Exit** Access.

End **You have completed Project 6E**

Content-Based Assessments

Mastering Access | Project **6F** Promotional Results

In the following project, you will create a report that will display the promotions that are offered to guests of the Sand Dollar Cafe restaurant franchise. You will also create a crosstab report that will summarize the results of the promotions. Creating customized reports will help the managers of each location view the information in the database in a meaningful way. Your completed reports will look similar to Figure 6.49.

Project Files

For Project 6F, you will need the following files:

a06F_Promotional_Results
a06F_Logo

You will save your database as:

Lastname_Firstname_6F_Promotional_Results

Project Results

Figure 6.49

(Project 6F Promotional Results continues on the next page)

Content-Based Assessments

1 **Start** Access. Locate and open the **a06F_Promotional Results** file. Save the database in your **Access Chapter 6** folder as **Lastname_Firstname_6F_Promotional_Results** If necessary, click **Enable Content**.

2 Under **Queries**, double-click the **6F Coupons Crosstab Query**. Take a moment to study the data in the query. **Close** the query, and then close the **Navigation Pane**.

3 **Create** a report using the **Report Wizard**. From the **Query: 6F Coupons Crosstab Query**, select all of the fields. Under **Do you want to add any grouping or levels?**, select **City**. **Sort** the records within the report by **Franchise#** in **Ascending** order. Under **Layout**, be sure the **Stepped** option button is selected. Under **Orientation**, click the **Landscape** option button. Be sure the **Adjust the field width so all fields fit on a page** check box is selected. For the title of the report, type **Lastname Firstname 6F Coupons Redeemed** Select **Modify the report's design**, and then click **Finish**.

4 Switch to **Layout** view. If any data is cut off, select the label control, and drag to the right to widen the column to display all data. Reduce the width of any columns that display a lot of blank space to allow for the widened columns. On the **Design tab**, click the **Themes** button, and then apply the **Median** theme.

5 Switch to **Design** view. Insert the **a06F_Logo** image so it appears from the **5.5-inch mark on the horizontal ruler** to the **7-inch mark**, and is the height of the Report Header section.

6 Select the three **Date label controls and textbox controls**. Change the width to **0.8** Change the **Font Color** to **Ice Blue, Accent 1, Darker 50%**—the fifth option in the sixth row under **Theme Colors**.

7 Resize and move controls so you can resize the report to **9.5 inches**, and it prints on one landscape page. **Save** the report. If you are instructed to submit this result, create a paper or electronic printout. **Close** the report.

8 Open the **6F Coupons** query. Switch to **Design** view, and then notice the underlying tables that were used in the creation of the query. **Close** the query, and then close the **Navigation Pane**.

9 On the **Create tab**, open a new report in **Report Design**. On the **Design tab**, display the **Property Sheet**. On the **Data tab**, click the **Record Source property setting**

box arrow, and then click **6F Coupons**. **Close** the **Property Sheet**. Display the **Field List**.

10 From the **Field List**, select all fields included in the query. Drag the selected fields into the **Detail** section of the design grid until the top of the pointer is aligned with the **0.25-inch mark on the vertical ruler** and the **1-inch mark on the horizontal ruler**. With the controls selected, on the **Arrange tab**, in the **Table group**, click the **Tabular** button. **Close** the **Field List**. Drag the **Page Footer section bar** up to the **0.5-inch mark on the vertical ruler**.

11 **Save** the report as **Lastname Firstname 6F Promotions** Switch to **Layout** view to be sure all data is visible in the report. If necessary, adjust the width of any columns where data is cut off. Switch to **Design** view.

12 On the **Design tab**, click the **Group & Sort** button. Click the **Add a group** button, and then from the displayed list, click **City**. Apply **Keep whole group together on one page**. Click the **Add a sort** button, and then click **Visit Date**. **Close** the **Group, Sort, and Total Pane**.

13 In the **Page Header** section, click the **City** label control, and then press (Del). In the **Detail** section, right-click the **City text box control** to display the shortcut menu, and click **Cut**. Click the **City Header** section bar to select it, right-click to display the shortcut menu, and click **Paste**

14 In the **Detail** section, click the **#Redeemed text box control**. On the **Design tab**, click the **Totals** button. From the list of aggregate functions, click **Sum**. Point to the top edge of the **Report Footer** section bar, and then drag up to the bottom of the **Page Footer** section bar.

15 On the **Design tab**, in the **Header/Footer group**, click the **Logo** button, and then insert the **a06F_Logo**. On the **Property Sheet**, increase the width to **1.75** inches and the height to **0.75** inches. In the **Header/Footer group**, click **Title**. Delete your Lastname Firstname from the beginning of the title.

16 Add a **label control** to the **Report Footer**. Position the plus sign of the pointer at the bottom of the **Report Footer** section bar and the **3.5-inch mark on the horizontal ruler**. Drag upward to the top of the **Report Footer** section and to the right to the left edge of the Sum control box. Type **Total # Redeemed Coupons**

(Project 6F Promotional Results continues on the next page)

Access | Chapter 6

Mastering Access | Project **6F** Promotional Results (continued)

17 Click the **Date & Time** button. Under **Include Date**, click the second option button. Do not **Include Time**. Remove the **Date text box control** from the **Layout**.

18 Move the control to the left edge of the **Report Footer**. In the **Report Footer** section, click the **Date text box control** two times. Position the insertion point between the equal sign and the *D*. Type **"Prepared by Firstname Lastname on "&** and then Press Enter. Click the **Title label control**, and resize it so the right edge aligns with the **4-inch mark on the horizontal ruler**. Resize the report to **6.5 inches wide**.

19 Select all of the controls in the **Report Footer**. Be sure they are all the same height and aligned at the bottom.

20 Switch to **Layout** view, and then adjust all controls to fit the data without extending beyond the right margin. **Save** the report. If you are instructed to submit this result, create a paper or electronic printout in **Landscape** orientation. **Close** the report.

21 Open the **Navigation Pane**, **Close** the database, and then **Exit** Access.

End **You have completed Project 6F**

Content-Based Assessments

1 Create a Form in Design View

2 Change and Add Controls

3 Format a Form

4 Make a Form User Friendly

5 Create a Report Based on a Query Using a Wizard

Mastering Access | Project **6G** Wireless

Marty Kress, Vice President of Marketing for Sand Dollar Cafe Franchises, keeps a database on the wireless usage per franchise on a monthly basis. The individual restaurants report the number of customers using the wireless connections and the average length of usage per customer. In this project, you will design a form for the data entry of this data and design a report that can be used by Mr. Kress to plan next year's marketing strategies. Your completed work will look similar to Figure 6.50.

Project Files

For Project 6G, you will need the following files:

    a06G_Wireless
    a06G_Logo

You will save your database as:

    Lastname_Firstname_6G_Wireless

Project Results

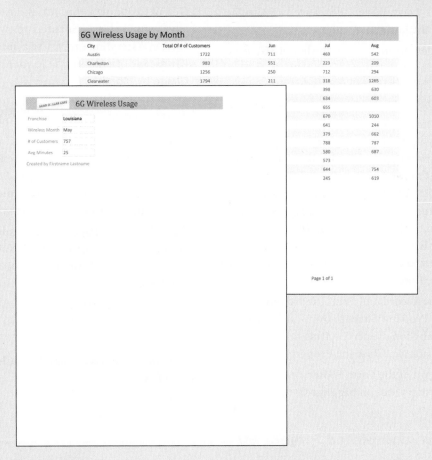

Figure 6.50

(Project 6G Wireless continues on the next page)

Access | Chapter 6

Content-Based Assessments

Mastering Access | Project 6G Wireless (continued)

1 **Start** Access. Locate and open the **a06G_ Wireless** file. Save the database in your **Access Chapter 6** folder as **Lastname_Firstname_6G_Wireless** If necessary, **Enable Content**. Close the **Navigation Pane**.

2 Create a form in **Form Design**. For the **Record Source**, use the **6G Wireless Usage** table. Select all of the fields, and then drag them onto the design grid until the top of the arrow is aligned with the **1-inch mark on the horizontal ruler** and the **0.25-inch mark on the vertical ruler**. **Save** the form as **Lastname Firstname 6G Wireless Usage**

3 With all controls still selected, on the **Arrange tab**, click the **Stacked** button. Add a light blue dashed outline to the text box controls in the **Detail** section.

4 On the **Design tab**, click the **Logo** button. Locate and double-click **a06G_Logo**. Widen the selected logo to the **1.5-inch mark on the horizontal ruler**.

5 Click the **Title** button. Click to the left of **6G**, delete the space and Lastname Firstname, and then press Enter. Double-click the right edge of the title label control to just fit the text.

6 Click the **Button** button. In the **Detail** section, align the plus sign (+) with the **0.5-inch mark on the vertical ruler** and the **2.5-inch mark on the horizontal ruler**, and then click. Under **Categories**, click **Record Operations**. Under **Actions**, click **Add New Record**, and then click **Next**. Next to **Picture**, be sure **Go to New** is selected, and then click **Next**. In the text box, type **btnNewRcrd** and then click **Finish**. Add a button to print the record below the **Add New Record** button. Place a picture on it, and name it **btnPrtRcrd**

7 With the **New Record** and **Print Record** buttons selected, click the **Property Sheet** button. Click the **Other tab**, click in the **Tab Stop** property setting box, click the **arrow**, and then click **No**. **Close** the **Property Sheet**.

8 Point to the top of the **Form Footer**; drag until the top of the Form Footer section bar aligns with the

1.5-inch mark on the vertical ruler. Click the **Label** button. In the **Form Footer** section, align the plus sign (+) pointer with the bottom of the **Form Footer** section bar and the left edge of the form. Click and type **Created by Firstname Lastname** and then press Enter.

9 Switch to **Form** view. Click the **New Record** button. From the list of **Franchises**, select **Louisiana MO**. In the **Wireless Month text box control**, select the date on which this project is due. In the **# of Customers text box control**, type **757** In the **Avg Minutes text box control**, type 25.

10 If you are instructed to submit this result, create a paper or electronic printout of the new, selected record only. **Close** the form and **Save** changes.

11 **Create** a report using the **Report Wizard**. From the **Query: 6G Wireless Crosstab Query**, select the **City, Total Of # of Customers, Jun, Jul**, and **Aug** fields. Do not add any grouping levels. **Sort** records within the report by **City**, in **Ascending** order. Use a **Tabular** layout and a **Landscape** orientation. Title your report as **6G Wireless Usage by Month**

12 Switch to **Layout** view. Adjust control widths to display all field names and data to fit across the page.

13 Switch to **Design** view. Select the **Title** label controls and all of the label controls in the **Page Header** section. Change the font color to **Purple, Accent 4, Darker 50%**. Reduce the width of the **Page # control** so the right edge aligns with the **8-inch mark on the horizontal ruler**.

14 Modify the **Page Footer** by adding **Prepared by Firstname Lastname on** before **Now()**. Widen the control to the **5-inch mark on the horizontal ruler**. Switch to **Print Preview**.

15 If you are instructed to submit this result, create a paper or electronic printout. **Close** the report and **Save** changes.

16 Open the **Navigation Pane**, **Close** the database, and then **Exit** Access.

 You have completed Project 6G

Content-Based Assessments

GO! Fix It | Project 6H Ads

Project Files

For Project 6H, you will need the following files:

a06H_Ads
a06H_Logo

You will save your database as:

Lastname_Firstname_6H_Ads

In the following project, you modify a form that will be used to enter the details of the advertising contracts for the Sand Dollar Cafe franchise restaurant chain. You will also modify a report to group, sort, and total this data.

Make the following modifications to the **6H Costs Form**:

- Apply a Theme. Arrange it in a Stacked Layout.
- The form needs to be identified with the logo and appropriate form title. Be sure to include your first and last names as part of the form title.
- Be sure all field names and data are visible in the form.
- Marty would like to have buttons on the form to add a new record and to print the current record. Use text to identify the buttons, align the buttons, and remove them as tab stops on the form. Change the font color to a Theme color to coordinate with the form.
- Add a solid outline to each of the textboxes on the form and a dotted/dashed outline to the buttons; choose a Theme color to coordinate with the form.
- Add text to appear in the status bar when entering data in the Frequency text box; it should read: *How many times per year?*
- View the form, saving the changes.
- If you are instructed to submit this result, create a paper or electronic printout.

Make the following modifications to the **6H Ad Costs Report**:

- Be sure all field names and data are visible on the report. Remove the colon following each of the Page Header label controls.
- Copy the logo to the right edge of the report. Center the title between the logos. Align the controls.
- Draw a line below the column headings (label boxes). Apply a Theme Color to coordinate with the form.
- Add a control to the left edge of the Report Footer. It should read **Prepared by Firstname Lastname on *date*** (use today's date). Add a text box control aligned at the right edge of the Report Footer. It should calculate the annual cost (Frequency x Cost Per Placement); be sure it displays as currency and includes a descriptive label. Format the font for the label controls to match the line drawn above. Apply a matching outline to the calculated control.
- View the report, saving the changes.
- If you are instructed to submit this result, create a paper or electronic printout.

End **You have completed Project 6H** ——————————————

Content-Based Assessments

GO! Make It | Project **6I** Supply Orders

Project Files

For Project 6I, you will need the following files:

    a06I_Supply_Orders
    a06I_Logo
    a06I_Sand_Dollar

You will save your database as:

    Lastname_Firstname_6I_Supply_Orders

From the student files that accompany this textbook, open the **a06I_Supply_Orders** database file. Save the database in your Access Chapter 6 folder as **Lastname_Firstname_6I_Supply_Orders.** Modify the design of the **6I_Supply_Order** form by modifying and moving controls, modifying the header, and adding a background image. Modify the appearance of the **6I Orders by City** report. Your completed objects, if printed, will look similar to Figure 6.51. An electronic version of the form will look slightly different. Create a paper or electronic printout as directed.

Project Results

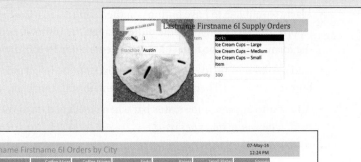

Figure 6.51

End **You have completed Project 6I**

Content-Based Assessments

GO! Solve It | Project **6J** Menu

Project Files

For Project 6J, you will need the following files:

a06J_Menu
a06J_Logo

You will save your database as:

Lastname_Firstname_6J_Menu

Brian Davidson, Executive Chef for the Sand Dollar Cafe restaurant chain, wants to know which menu items are most popular at the individual franchise locations. Open the **a06J_Menu** database and save it as **Lastname_Firstname_6J_Menu** In this project, you will create a form to be used by the managers of the different franchises to enter the most popular menu items. From the *6J Popular Item*s table, use all fields except the ID field. Save the form as **Lastname Firstname 6J Popular Items** In the Detail and Header sections, add a background color and change the font and font color of the label controls. In Design view, resize the Detail section to reduce the blank space. Add **a06J_Logo** and title the form **6J Popular Menu Items** In the Form Footer section, insert a label control aligned with the right edge of the form; it should read **Designed by Firstname Lastname** Adjust the label controls and the text box controls to fit the data. If you are instructed to submit this result, create a paper or electronic printout of only the first record.

Use a wizard to create a report based on the *6J Popular Items Crosstab* query. Select all fields from the query. Sort by Franchise. Title the report **6J Popular Items by Franchise** Center the title across the report, and change the color of the background. In the Report Footer section, modify the date control to include your name. Change the background for the entire Report Footer section to match the Report Header. Adjust all label and text controls to display all data. Resize the report to 8 inches wide.

Modify the *6J Popular Menu Items* report. Add your Lastname Firstname to the title. Add **a06J_Logo** to the Report Header, resize it, and then move the title to the right of the logo. Group the report by Franchise and sort by Sales Month. Be sure the data for each franchise stays on the same page. Select the Sales Month label control and a text box control in the column; center align the column. Change the font color of the label controls for each column. Draw a line below the column headings; change the Outline Color. Add a Report Footer that reads **Report Modified by Firstname Lastname** Save the changes to the report. If you are instructed to submit this result, create a paper or electronic printout.

Performance Level		
Exemplary: You consistently applied the relevant skills.	**Proficient:** You sometimes, but not always, applied the relevant skills.	**Developing:** You rarely or never applied the relevant skills.
Create 6J Popular Items Form — Form created with the correct controls and formatted as directed.	Form created with no more than two missing elements.	Form created with more than two missing elements.
Create 6J Popular Items by Franchise Report — Report created and formatted correctly.	Report created with no more than two missing elements.	Report created with more than two missing elements.
Modify 6J Popular Menu Items Report — Report modified to include the correct controls, grouping, sorting, and formatting.	Report modified with no more than two missing elements.	Report modified with more than two missing elements.

(Performance Element)

End **You have completed Project 6J**

Content-Based Assessments

GO! Solve It | Project **6K** Birthday Coupons

Project Files

For Project 6K, you will need the following files:

> a06K_Birthday_Coupons
> a06K_Sand_Dollar
> a06K_Birthday

You will save your database as:

> Lastname_Firstname_6K_Birthday_Coupons

The Vice President of Marketing, Marty Kress, encourages each of the individual restaurants of the Sand Dollar Cafe franchise to offer birthday coupons to its customers as a promotional venture. Open the **a06K_Birthday_Coupons** database, and then save it as **Lastname_Firstname_6K_Birthday_Coupons** Use the *6K Birthdates* table to create a form to enter the names, birthday months, and e-mail addresses of the customers visiting one of the restaurants. Save the form as **Lastname Firstname 6K Birthday Form** Add a button control to print the current form. Include the Sand Dollar image as the logo and title the form **6K Happy Birthday!** Be sure all data is visible on the form. Add a new record using the form and your own information.

Create a report to display the customers grouped by their birthday month using the months as a section header and sorted by customer name. Save the report as **Lastname Firstname 6K Birthdate Report** Add the **a06K_Birthday** image as the logo resized to 1 inch tall and wide. Add a title. Draw a line above the Birthday Month header control to separate the months; apply a Line Color and Line Style. Save the report as **Lastname Firstname 6K Birthdate Report** Save the report.

Create a report based on the 6K Second Quarter Birthdays query. Include both of the fields arranged in a tabular format. Save the report as **Lastname Firstname 6K Second Quarter Birthdays** Add a title to the report, **Lastname Firstname 6K Second Quarter Birthdays** Add the current date and time to the Report Header section, and then move them to the Report Footer section. Resize the Page Footer section to 0. Apply a dotted outline to the label controls in the Page Header section; choose a Line Color, Line Thickness, and Line Style. Add the **a06K_Birthday** image and place it in the bottom right of the report. Add a count of how many second quarter birthdays there are to the Report Footer; include a descriptive label to the right of the count. Save the report as **Lastname Firstname 6K Second Quarter Birthdays** Adjust the width of the report to fit on a landscape page. Save the changes. If you are instructed to submit the results, create a paper or electronic printout of the objects created.

Performance Level			
	Exemplary: You consistently applied the relevant skills	**Proficient:** You sometimes, but not always, applied the relevant skills.	**Developing:** You rarely or never applied the relevant skills
Create 6K Birthday Form	Form created with the correct fields and formatted as directed.	Form created with no more than two missing elements.	Form created with more than two missing elements.
Create 6K Birthdate Report	Report created with the correct fields and formatted as directed.	Report created with no more than two missing elements.	Report created with more than two missing elements.
Create 6K Second Quarter Birthdays Report	Report created with the correct fields and formatted as directed.	Report created with no more than two missing elements.	Report created with more than two missing elements.

Performance Element (rotated label along left side of table)

End You have completed Project 6K

Outcomes-Based Assessments

Rubric

The following outcomes-based assessments are *open-ended assessments*. That is, there is no specific correct result; your result will depend on your approach to the information provided. Make *Professional Quality* your goal. Use the following scoring rubric to guide you in *how* to approach the problem, and then to evaluate *how well* your approach solves the problem.

The criteria—Software Mastery, Content, Format and Layout, and Process—represent the knowledge and skills you have gained that you can apply to solving the problem. The levels of performance—Professional Quality, Approaching Professional Quality, or Needs Quality Improvements—help you and your instructor evaluate your result.

	Your completed project is of Professional Quality if you:	Your completed project is Approaching Professional Quality if you:	Your completed project Needs Quality Improvements if you:
1-Software Mastery	Choose and apply the most appropriate skills, tools, and features and identify efficient methods to solve the problem.	Choose and apply some appropriate skills, tools, and features, but not in the most efficient manner.	Choose inappropriate skills, tools, or features, or are inefficient in solving the problem.
2-Content	Construct a solution that is clear and well organized, contains content that is accurate, appropriate to the audience and purpose, and is complete. Provide a solution that contains no errors in spelling, grammar, or style.	Construct a solution in which some components are unclear, poorly organized, inconsistent, or incomplete. Misjudge the needs of the audience. Have some errors in spelling, grammar, or style, but the errors do not detract from comprehension.	Construct a solution that is unclear, incomplete, or poorly organized; contains some inaccurate or inappropriate content; and contains many errors in spelling, grammar, or style. Do not solve the problem.
3-Format and Layout	Format and arrange all elements to communicate information and ideas, clarify function, illustrate relationships, and indicate relative importance.	Apply appropriate format and layout features to some elements, but not others. Overuse features, causing minor distraction.	Apply format and layout that does not communicate information or ideas clearly. Do not use format and layout features to clarify function, illustrate relationships, or indicate relative importance. Use available features excessively, causing distraction.
4-Process	Use an organized approach that integrates planning, development, self-assessment, revision, and reflection.	Demonstrate an organized approach in some areas, but not others; or, use an insufficient process of organization throughout.	Do not use an organized approach to solve the problem.

Outcomes-Based Assessments

Apply a combination of the **6A** and **6B** skills.

GO! Think | Project **6L** Vacation Days

Project Files

For Project 6L, you will need the following files:

> a06L_Vacation_Days
> a06L_Logo

You will save your database as:

> Lastname_Firstname_6L_Vacation_Days

In this project, you will create a report to display the information for the employees of the Sand Dollar Cafe related to their vacation days. Open the **a06L_Vacation_Days** database and save it as **Lastname_Firstname_6L_Vacation_Days** From the *6L Vacation Days* table, add the following fields to the report: Employee Name, Allotted Days, and Days Taken. Add a calculated text box control to display the number of vacation days each employee has remaining (Days Allotted-Days Taken) with a label control to describe the field, and format the result as a General Number. In the Report Header section, add the Sand Dollar Cafe logo and a descriptive title. Add a label control to the Report Footer section that reads **Report Designed by Firstname Lastname** Align the left edge with the label controls in the Detail section. Change the background color used in the Report Header and Report Footer sections, and change the font color so they are easy to read. Sort the report on Employee Name. Add a dotted line between employees to make it easier to read. Adjust all label and text controls to display all field names and data. Center page numbers in the report footer. Resize the Detail section to reduce the blank space. Close the space for the Page Header. Adjust the width of the report so it is 6 inches wide. Save the report as **Lastname Firstname 6L Vacation** If you are instructed to submit this result, create a paper or electronic printout.

End You have completed Project 6L ────────────────────────

Apply a combination of the **6A** and **6B** skills.

GO! Think | Project **6M** Seasonal Items

Project Files

For Project 6M, you will need the following files:

> a06M_Seasonal_Items
> a06M_Logo

You will save your database as:

> Lastname_Firstname_6M_Seasonal_Items

The Executive Chef of the Sand Dollar Cafe franchise restaurant chain, Brian Davidson, adds seasonal items to the menu. In this project, you will open the **a06M_Seasonal_Items** database and save it as **Lastname_Firstname_6M_Seasonal_Items** You will create a report using the 6M Seasonal Items table. The report should include all fields grouped by Season, and sorted on the Menu Item. Be sure to keep each group together on a page. Include Season in a section header and total cost in a section footer including descriptive labels. Draw and format a line to separate sections for readability. Apply a theme to the database. Add the Sand Dollar Cafe logo and a report title that includes your Lastname Firstname. Reduce the width of the report to fit on a portrait page with default margins. Reduce the blank space visible in the Page Header and Detail sections of the report. Add page numbering to the right side of the footer. Align all labels and text boxes that you added, and be sure they are the same height. Adjust all label and text controls to display all field names and data. If you are instructed to submit this result, create a paper or electronic printout.

End You have completed Project 6M ────────────────────────

Outcomes-Based Assessments

Apply a combination of the 6A and 6B skills.

You and GO! | Project 6N Club Directory

Project Files

For Project 6N, you will need the following file:

   Lastname_Firstname_5N_Club_Directory (your file from Chapter 5)

You will save your database as:

   Lastname_Firstname_6N_Club_Directory

Create a personal database containing information about a club and its activities, if you do not already have one from Project 5N. Name the new database **Lastname_Firstname_6N_Club_Directory** If you do not have the database from Project 5N, create two related tables, one that lists the activities your organization has planned and the other to serve as the directory of the group. The Activities table should include information about the name (primary key field), date, cost, and location of the activity. The dates must all occur next year; consider attaching directions to the event to the table. The Directory table should include full name, address, phone number, email, and an activity they are planning. If you have the database from Project 5N, save as an Access 2007 Database in your Access Chapter 6 folder.

Use all of the fields in the Directory table in a form. Include a title and applicable image. Be sure all data is visible in the text boxes. Apply a theme to the database. Add a background color to the Report Header and Footer. Select a coordinating font color for the label controls in the Detail section of the form. Add a button to print the current form. Add a form footer that reads **Form created by Firstname Lastname**

Create a report to include all of the fields in the Activities table. Present it in tabular format, sorted by date, in ascending order. In the Report Footer, add a count of how many activities there are, with an appropriate label. Change background, outline, and font colors in the control label boxes to create a well-formatted report. Submit your database as instructed.

You will be using this database in future chapters. Be sure to make corrections to your tables as necessary to prepare for the next chapter.

 You have completed Project 6N ————————————————

Business Running Case

Razvan CHIRNOAGA/Shutterstock

Front Range Action Sports is one of the country's largest retailers of sports gear and outdoor recreation merchandise. The company has large retail stores in Colorado, Washington, Oregon, California, and New Mexico, in addition to a growing online business. Major merchandise categories include fishing, camping, rock climbing, winter sports, action sports, water sports, team sports, racquet sports, fitness, golf, apparel, and footwear.

In this project, you will apply skills you practiced from the Objectives in Access Chapters 4–6. You will update the current database for Frank Osei, the Vice President of Finance, as he manages the company's growth. You will modify existing tables and create a new one to track part-time employee information. In addition, you will create queries to assist Frank as he monitors the company's performance and requests that data be updated. You will also create forms and reports to display information from the current tables and queries. Your printed results will look similar to Figure 2.1.

Project Files

For Project BRC2, you will need the following files:

    aBRC2_Company_Management
    aBRC2_Logo
    aBRC2_Snowboard

You will save your files as:

Lastname_Firstname_aBRC2_Company_
    Management
Lastname_Firstname_aBRC2_Company_
    Management_2014_05_12 (date may differ)

Project Results

Figure 2.1

Business Running Case

Front Range Action Sports

1 **Start** Access. Navigate to the solution file for BRC1. Locate and open the **Lastname_Firstname_aBRC2_ Company_Management** database. If you did not add the **Front Range Action Sports** folder to the **Trust Center**, enable the content.

2 Display **Backstage** view, click **Save & Publish**, and then click **Back Up Database**. Add **Lastname_Firstname** before the default name of the backup file. Click **Save**.

3 **Save** the database as **Lastname_Firstname_aBRC2_ Company_Management** in your **Front Range Action Sports** folder.

4 Open the **Navigation Pane**, if necessary. **Rename** the tables to include your **Lastname Firstname** in front of the table name. Open the **BRC2 Inventory** table in **Design** view. Close the **Navigation Pane**.

a. Add a new field between **Retail Price** and **Category**. The field should be named **Cost** and it should be calculated as **[Retail Price]*0.40** Be sure to set the format as **Currency**.

b. Add a new field at the bottom of the list; name the field **Item Image** and select a data type that will allow an attachment. Switch to **Datasheet** view, saving the changes. Attach **aBRC2_Snowboard** to the first record in the table.

c. If you are instructed to submit this result, create a paper or electronic printout of the first page of the table in **Landscape** orientation. **Close** the table.

5 On the Ribbon, click the **Create** tab. In the **Tables** group, click the **Table Design** button to open a new table in **Design** view. Create the **Lastname Firstname**

BRC2 Employees table using the information in **Table 1** for field design and properties. Determine the appropriate data type based on the field details.

6 Based on the **BRC2_Employees** table, use the **Form Design** tool to create a new form.

a. Add all fields from the table to the form design. Move **Start Date**, **Hourly Wage**, **Max Hours**, and **Part Time** to a second column with about 0.5 inch separating them. Align the **Empl ID** and **Start Date** fields at the top.

b. Add **aBRC2_Logo** to the **Form Header**. Resize the logo so it is **1.5 inches wide** and **0.5 inch tall**. Add a **title** to the **Form Header**; it should read **BRC2 Employees Form**

c. Drag the **Form Footer section bar** upward to the **2-inch mark on the vertical ruler**. Add a label in the form footer that reads **Form Designed by Firstname Lastname**

d. Change the **Theme** to **Apex**. Apply a **Theme color** of your choice to the background of the **Form Header** and **Form Footer**. Use the same color to outline the **label** controls in the **Detail** section of the form. Apply a **line thickness** and **line type** of your choice. In the Detail section, apply a **Theme color** of your choice to the font in the **text box** controls. Do the same in the **Footer** section to the **label** control.

e. Add a command button named **btnPrtForm** to the bottom of the **Form Detail** to print the current form. Use a picture to identify the button. Add a second button to the right of the first named **btnCloseForm**

Table 1

Field Name	Field Details	Field Properties
Empl ID	ID generated for each employee, primary key	
Firstname	Employee's first name	Field size = 18
Lastname	Employee's last name	Field size = 24
Availability	Preferred availability for scheduling	Format to all capital letters. Must be D, E, W, or A (one-character codes stand for day, evening, weekend, any)
Start Date	First day of employment at FRAS	Short date input mask
Hourly Wage	Earnings per hour	Required field
Max Hours	The maximum number of hours the employee wants to work in a week	Must be less than or equal to 40
Part Time	A box to check if the employee works part time	

(Return to Step 5)

(Business Running Case: Front Range Action Sports continues on the next page)

Business Running Case

Front Range Action Sports (continued)

to close the form. Use the **Stop** picture to identify the button. Apply an outline that is the same color, type, and thickness as the label controls in the form. Align the buttons at the top.

f. Remove **btnPrtForm**, **btnCloseForm**, and the **Empl ID** field as tab stops on the form.

g. Save the form as **Lastname Firstname BRC2 Employees Form**

7 Switch to **Form** view. Add the records to the form as shown in **Table 2**.

8 Review the records to be sure all information is visible. Make adjustments to the width of label or text box controls as necessary. If you are instructed to submit this result, create a paper or electronic printout of **record 5**. **Close** the form, saving layout changes.

9 Based on the tables in the database, create the following queries to provide the information requested. Create paper or electronic printouts as directed.

a. Design a query to display the average retail price of the inventory by category. **Run** the query. **Save** the query as **Lastname Firstname BRC2 Average Query** If you are instructed to submit this result, create a paper or electronic printout of the query results. **Close** the query.

b. Design a query to update the **Hourly Wage** for all part-time employees to reflect a 5% increase. The new hourly wage will be 1.05 times the original wage. **Save** the query as **Lastname Firstname BRC2 Update Query** Be careful to **Run** the query only once. **Close** the query. If you are instructed to submit this result, open the **Employees** table, and then create a paper or electronic printout of the table.

c. Design a query to display each employee's **Firstname**, **Lastname**, **Hourly Wage**, **Max Hours**, and **Max Earnings**, which will be calculated by multiplying the hourly wage by the max hours. **Run** the query. **Autofit** all columns. **Save** the query as **Lastname Firstname BRC2 Calculated Query** If you are instructed to submit this result, create a paper or electronic printout of the query results. **Close** the query.

d. Design a query to display the **Company**, **Sport**, and **Retail Price** for all records. **Run** the query. **Save** the query as **Lastname Firstname BRC2 Crosstab Setup Query Close** the query.

e. Create a crosstab query using a **Query Wizard**; select the **BRC2 Crosstab Setup Query** for the basis of the crosstab query. Display **Company** as the row heading, **Sport** as the column heading, and an average of **Retail Price**. Do not display the row sums. **Save** the query as **Lastname Firstname BRC2 Crosstab Query View** the query results, and widen columns as necessary. If you are instructed to submit this result, create a paper or electronic printout of the query results. **Close** the query.

10 Select the **BRC2 Crosstab Query**, and using a **Report Wizard**, create a report.

a. Display all fields in the report. There will be no grouping.

b. Sort the report by **Company**, in ascending order.

c. Use a **tabular** format and **landscape** orientation.

d. Title the report **BRC2 Average Retail Price by Sport and Company**

Table 2

Empl ID	Firstname	Lastname	Availability	Start Date	Hourly Wage	Max Hours	Part Time
1	Chris	Baker	W	02/15/2016	8.00	10	Yes
2	Carol	Labady	D	08/27/2015	8.50	25	Yes
3	Lee	Matthews	A	05/20/2013	8.75	40	No
4	David	Thomas	E	03/23/2015	8.00	20	Yes
5	Elaine	Dietz	W	10/20/2015	8.50	20	Yes

(Return to Step 8)

(Business Running Case: Front Range Action Sports continues on the next page)

e. View the report's design. Adjust the width of the label boxes so the report fits across one page. Adjust the width of the report in Design view.

f. Modify the **Date Page Footer** so it says **Prepared by Firstname Lastname on Current Date** If necessary, adjust the width of the control so all information is visible.

g. Select the **title** and the **Page Footer controls**. Change the font to a **Theme color** of your choice.

h. Add a line below the column headings. Use the same color as you selected for the fonts above.

i. If you are instructed to submit this result, create a paper or electronic printout of the report on one landscape page. **Close** the report, saving changes.

11 Based on the **Inventory** table, create a report in **Design** view.

a. Display the following fields in the report: **Item Name**, **Retail Price**, **Cost**, **Category**, and **Sport** at the **1.5-inch mark on the horizontal ruler**. Save the report as **Lastname Firstname BRC2 Inventory by Sport Report**

b. Reduce the height of the **Detail** section to accommodate the data. Adjust the width of the label controls so all data is visible. Widen the **Item Name** text box until the right edge aligns with the **4-inch mark on the horizontal ruler**. Widen the **Category** text box until the right edge aligns with the **3-inch mark on the horizontal ruler**.

c. Group the report by **Sport**. Delete the **Sport label control**. Move the **Sport textbox control** to the left edge of the **Sport Header** section. Sort the report by **Item Name**, in ascending order.

d. Add the **BRC2_Logo** to the **Report Header**. Resize it to **1.5 inches wide** and **0.5 inch tall**.

e. Add the title **BRC2 Inventory by Sport Report** to the **Report Header**. Reduce the width of the **Title text box control** so the right edge aligns with the **6.5-inch mark on the horizontal ruler**. Center the title in the **label control**.

f. Add a count for the number of items per sport. Use an appropriate text box control to identify the calculation by sport in the **Sport Footer**. Use a label control to identify the calculation in the **Report Footer**. Be sure the label and text box controls are aligned in each section.

g. Add a line at the bottom of the **Sport Footer** to separate each sport section; choose an outline color and line thickness. Apply a **Theme Color** background to the label control and text box control in the **Sport Footer**.

h. Resize the width of the report to **7.5 inches**. In the **Report Footer**, add a label control aligned at the right edge of the report. It should read **Submitted by Firstname Lastname** using your full name.

i. If necessary, reduce the width of the report to fit across a portrait page with default margins.

j. **Save** the report. If you are instructed to submit this result, create a paper or electronic printout of the final page of the report. **Close** the report.

12 **Close** the database, and then **Exit** Access. If you are to submit your work electronically, follow your instructor's directions.

End You have completed Business Running Case 2 ─────────────

Creating Advanced Forms and Reports

OUTCOMES

At the end of this chapter you will be able to:

OBJECTIVES

Mastering these objectives will enable you to:

PROJECT 7A
Create advanced forms.

1. Create a Split Form (p. 467)
2. Create a Form and a Subform (p. 474)
3. Create a Multi-Page Form (p. 486)

PROJECT 7B
Create advanced reports.

4. Create and Modify a Subreport (p. 492)
5. Create a Report Based on a Parameter Query (p. 502)
6. Create an Alphabetic Index (p. 506)

Bill Florence/Shutterstock

In This Chapter

Forms provide a way to enter, edit, and display data; reports display the data in a professional-looking manner. You have created and customized forms and reports. Access 2010 enables you to create a form and also display the data inside the form in Datasheet view or to create forms that contain multiple pages. You have practiced creating relationships between tables and have seen that information from multiple objects can be presented in one object, such as a query that extracts data from multiple tables. If a one-to-many relationship exists between the underlying tables, forms can be used to manipulate data from multiple tables, and reports can display data from multiple tables. You have also practiced creating a parameter query, which, in turn, can be used to create a report based on the criteria entered when the report is opened.

The southwest style of gardening is popular in many areas of the country, not just in the yards and gardens of Arizona and New Mexico. The stylish simplicity and use of indigenous, hardy plants that are traditional in the southwest United States make for beautiful, environmentally friendly gardens in any part of the country. Produced by **JR Desert Productions**, the television show *Southwest Gardens* is broadcast nationwide. The show and its Web site provide tips and tricks for beautiful gardens, highlight new tools and techniques, and present tours of public and private gardens that showcase the southwest style.

Project 7A SWG Episodes

myitlab
Project 7A Training

Project Activities

In Activities 7.01 through 7.07, you will help Ruthann Hansen, president of JR Desert Productions, customize the company's forms. She wants the database forms to display related data. For example, she is interested in displaying the advertisers of the television shows on one form. You will display data in two ways on the same form, display data from multiple tables on one form, and display data on multiple pages on a form. Your completed forms will look similar to Figure 7.1.

Project Files

For Project 7A, you will need the following files:

> a07A_SWG_Episodes
> a07A_SWG_Logo

You will save your files as:

> Lastname_Firstname_7A_SWG_Episodes
> Lastname_Firstname_7A_Tab_Control_Form

Project Results

Figure 7.1
Project 7A SWG Episodes

Objective 1 | Create a Split Form

A *split form* displays data in two views—Form view and Datasheet view—on a single form. The two views display data from the same source and are synchronized with each other at all times. When you select a field in one of the views, the same field displays in the other view. You can add, delete, or edit data in either view. An advantage of displaying data in a split form is the flexibility of finding a record in Datasheet view and then editing the same record in Form view.

Activity 7.01 | Creating a Split Form Using the Split Form Tool

In this activity, you will create a split form from scratch.

1 **Start** Access. Navigate to the location where the student data files for this textbook are saved. Locate and **Open** the **a07A_SWG_Episodes** file. Display Backstage view, and click **Save Database As**. In the **Save As** dialog box, navigate to the drive on which you will be saving your folders and projects for this chapter. Create a new folder named **Access Chapter 7** and Save 🖫 the database as **Lastname_Firstname_7A_SWG_Episodes** in the folder.

2 Enable the content or add the Access Chapter 7 folder to the Trust Center. In the **Navigation Pane**, double-click **7A TV Show Advertisers** to open the table in Datasheet view. In the first record, in the **TV Show #** field, click the **arrow** to the right of *SWG01-01* to display a list of television show codes. In the first record, click in the **Advertiser** field, and then click the **arrow** to the right of *All Woods Lumber Supply* to display a list of advertisers.

> Both of these fields are lookup fields. The TV Show # field looks up data in the *7A TV Shows* table. The Advertiser field looks up data in the *7A Advertiser Info* table. Because these fields look up data in specific tables, you will not change the names of the existing tables and forms in this database. If you did rename the tables, the lookup fields would not be able to locate the related tables.

3 Press (Esc) to close the list. If the small pencil displays in the record selector box, press (Esc) one more time. **Close** ✕ the table.

4 In the **Navigation Pane**, double-click **7A SWG Employees** to open the table in Datasheet view. Take a moment to review the fields in the table. Scroll to the right, if necessary, until the **Attachment** field displays. In the **Attachment** field, double-click any record. In the displayed **Attachments** dialog box, click **Open** to display a photograph of the employee. **Close** the window with the picture, and then **Close** the **Attachments** dialog box. **Close** ✕ the table.

The image shows a sidebar tab reading "Access | Chapter 7"

5 Close ⊲ the **Navigation Pane**. With the **7A SWG Employees** table selected, on the Ribbon, click the **Create tab**. In the **Forms group**, click the **More Forms** button, and then click **Split Form**. Compare your screen with Figure 7.2.

The underlying table or query does not need to be open to create a split form as long as it is selected before clicking the Create tab on the Ribbon.

The split form displays in Layout view. The top section of the split form displays the data in Form view, and the bottom section of the split form displays the data in Datasheet view.

Figure 7.2

Split form in Layout view

Form section

Datasheet section

6 In the datasheet section of the split form, click anywhere in the first record, and then press ↓. Notice that the form section displays the data and photograph for the second record—the two sections are synchronized.

7 Save 🖫 the split form as **Lastname Firstname 7A SWG Employees Split Form**

Activity 7.02 | Formatting a Split Form

In this activity, you will enhance the split form by modifying the fields and form properties.

1 In the datasheet section of the split form, click anywhere in the first record. In the form section of the split form, click the **Photo** for *Andi Shell*, and then compare your screen with Figure 7.3.

A Mini toolbar displays above Andi's photograph. If the Mini toolbar does not display, point to the picture. A *Mini toolbar* is a miniature, semitransparent toolbar that is used to work with objects on the screen. In this case, the Mini toolbar displays a Back button, a Forward button, and a Manage Attachments button. If there were multiple attachments for this record, clicking the Back button would display the next attachment, and clicking the Forward button would display the previous attachment. Clicking the Manage Attachments button would display the Attachments dialog box.

Recall that the Layout Selector is used to select all of the fields in the column. Clicking any field in a column displays the Layout Selector for the column.

Figure 7.3

Layout Selector

Manage Attachments button

Forward button

Back button

Mini toolbar

2 Select the **Photo attachment control** and **Photo label control**, and then on the Ribbon, click the **Arrange tab**. In the **Table group**, click the **Stacked** button. Notice that both controls have been removed from the stacked layout.

The Photo field is moved outside of the form, to the left margin, since it was removed from the stacked layout. A dotted placeholder displays the original position in the stacked layout.

3 Click in the **Photo attachment control**—the box displaying the photograph. On the **Design tab**, in the **Tools group**, click **the Property Sheet** button. Be sure the Property Sheet displays *Selection type: Attachment*. On the **Property Sheet Format tab**, click in the **Picture Alignment** property setting box—it displays *Top Left*—and then click the **arrow** to review the options. Click **Bottom Left**, and then **Close** ⊠ the **Property Sheet**.

Aligning the photograph at the left edge of the attachment control makes it easier to adjust the width of the control. Recall that you must remove a field from the predefined layout to resize only that field.

4 Point to the right edge of the **Photo attachment control** until the pointer ↔ displays. Drag to the left until the border aligns with the right edge of the photograph, and then compare your screen with Figure 7.4.

Figure 7.4

Layout Selector for Photo control

Attachment control resized (width decreased)

5 Press [PgDn] to display the second record. Scroll down, if necessary, and notice that the width of the attachment control is also decreased for this record.

6 **Save** 🖫 the split form. With the **Photo attachment control** selected, right-click and click **Form Properties** to display the form's Property Sheet.

7 Click the **Selection type arrow**. If **Form** is not selected, click **Form** to display the **Form Property Sheet**. On the **Property Sheet Format tab**, scroll down, if necessary, until the properties that relate to split forms display, and then compare your screen with Figure 7.5. Take a moment to study the six properties that directly relate to split forms, as described in the table in Figure 7.6.

Figure 7.5

Property Sheet for form

Split form properties

Split Form Properties

Property	Description	View(s) in Which the Property Can Be Set
Split Form Size	Specify an exact height or width, depending on whether the form is split vertically or horizontally, for the form section of the split form. For example, type *1* to set the form height or width to 1 inch. Type *Auto* to set the size by other means, such as dragging the splitter bar in Layout view. The default is *Auto*.	Design or Layout
Split Form Orientation	Define whether the datasheet displays above, below, to the left, or to the right of the form. The default is *Datasheet on Bottom*.	Design
Split Form Splitter Bar	If set to *Yes*, the form and datasheet can be resized by moving the splitter bar that separates the two sections. If set to *No*, the splitter bar is hidden, and the form and datasheet cannot be resized. The default is *Yes*.	Design
Split Form Datasheet	If set to *Allow Edits* and the form's source can be updated, editing can be done in the datasheet section. If set to *Read Only*, editing cannot be done in the datasheet section. The default is *Allow Edits*.	Design or Layout
Split Form Printing	Define which section of the form is printed. If set to *Form Only*, only the form section is printed. If set to *Datasheet Only*, only the datasheet section is printed. The default is *Datasheet Only*.	Design or Layout
Save Splitter Bar Position	If set to *Yes*, the form opens with the splitter bar in the same position in which it was saved. If set to *No*, the form and datasheet cannot be resized, and the splitter bar is hidden. The default is *Yes*.	Design

Figure 7.6

8 On the **Property Sheet**, click in the property setting box for **Split Form Printing**, click the **arrow**, and then click **Form Only**. Notice that you can print either the Form or the Datasheet, but not both.

9 On the **tab row**, right-click **7A SWG Employees Split Form**, and then click **Design View**. On the **Property Sheet** for the form, click in the **Split Form Orientation** property setting box, and then click the **arrow**. Compare your screen with Figure 7.7. If necessary, increase the width of the Property Sheet to display all four of the property settings.

Figure 7.7

Split Form Orientation property settings

10 Click **Datasheet on Top**, and then **Close** [×] the Property Sheet.

Alert! | Does a Message Display, Prompting You to Change to Design View?

If you try to change a property that can only be changed in Design view, Access displays a message prompting you to change to Design view. If you then try to change a property that can only be changed in Layout view, Access will display the same message. If this happens, switch to Design view and then switch back to Layout view, or change to Design view, and then change the property settings. All split form properties can be changed in Design view.

---

11 Switch to **Layout** view.

The datasheet section displays above the form section of the split form. A splitter bar divides the two sections.

12 Point to the splitter bar until the pointer [↕] displays. Drag upward until the dark horizontal line displays between the records with an **ID#** of **1047** and **1314**.

In the datasheet section, Records 1 through 4 display, and the height of the form section is increased.

13 Switch to **Design** view. On the **Design tab**, in the **Header/Footer group**, click the **Logo** button. Navigate to the location where the student data files are saved, and then double-click **a07A_SWG_Logo**. Click the **Property Sheet** button to display the Property Sheet for the logo. Click in the **Size Mode** setting box—*Clip* is displayed. Click the arrow, and then click **Zoom**. **Close** [×] the **Property Sheet**.

When a logo is inserted in a form or report that includes a logo placeholder, the Size Mode property is set to *Clip*, and the image may be too large to display in the control. By setting the property to *Zoom*, the image is resized to fit the control while maintaining the proportions of the object.

14 Increase the width of the **logo control** to approximately **1.5 inches**. Click in the title's **label control**, and then click at the beginning of the line. Using your own first and last names, type **Lastname Firstname** to add your name before the title of the form and press Enter to accept the changes. Switch to **Form** view, and then compare your screen with Figure 7.8.

Figure 7.8

Datasheet section

Splitter bar

Logo inserted and resized

Form section

15 **Save** 🖫 the form. Press PgDn to display **Record 11**. In the form section, change the **First Name** from *Alan* to **Adam** and then press Tab. Notice that in the datasheet section, the same record—*ID# 6894*—is selected and is in the editing mode. Also notice that the **First Name** field has been updated in the datasheet section.

> Recall that you can only make changes to the data in the fields with the form displayed in Form view.

16 In the form section, on the left side, click the **Record Selector** bar. If you are instructed to submit this result, create a paper or electronic printout of the selected record. **Close** ✕ the form. **Open** » the **Navigation Pane**.

> The form section prints because you set the Split Form Printing property to Form Only.

More Knowledge | Adding or Deleting a Field

To add a field to a split form in Layout view, display the Field List—on the Format tab, in the Controls group, click the Add Existing Fields button. Drag the field from the Field List to the datasheet section or the form section. The field will be added to both sections of the split form.

To delete a field from a split form, you must delete it from the form section. The field will then be removed automatically from the datasheet section.

Activity 7.03 | Converting an Existing Form into a Split Form

In this activity, you will convert *7A TV Shows Form* into a split form.

1 In the **Navigation Pane**, under **Forms**, right-click **7A TV Shows Form**, and then click **Design View**. **Close** « the **Navigation Pane**. On the **Design tab**, in the **Tools** group, click the **Property Sheet** button to display the Property Sheet for the form. If the Property Sheet does not display *Selection type: Form*, click the Selection type arrow, and then click Form.

> To convert an existing form to a split form, the form must be open in Design view.

2 On the **Property Sheet Format tab**, click in the **Default View** property setting box— *Single Form* is displayed. Click the **arrow**, and then click **Split Form**. **Close** ☒ the **Property Sheet**, and then switch to **Layout** view.

> The split form displays with the datasheet section on top; Access applied the same Split Form Orientation to this split form as the previous split form.

3 Switch to **Design** view, and then using the techniques you practiced in Activity 7.2, change the **Split Form Orientation** to display the **Datasheet on Bottom**. **Close** ☒ the **Property Sheet**, display the split form in **Layout** view, and then compare your screen with Figure 7.9.

Figure 7.9

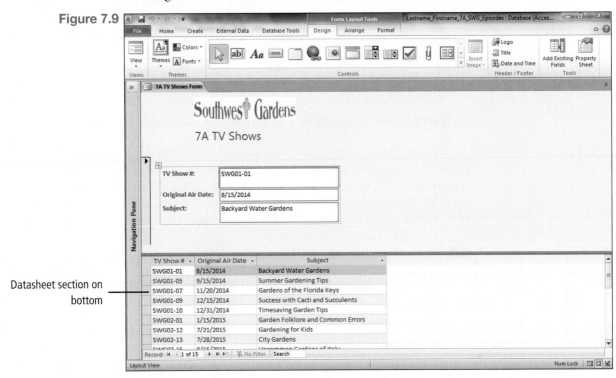

Datasheet section on bottom

4 In the form section, click the **title's label control**, and then click at the beginning of the line. Using your own first and last names, type **Lastname Firstname** and then press [Spacebar].

5 Switch to **Design** view. Hold down [Shift], click the **title's label control**, and then click the **label control** for **TV Show #**. On the Ribbon, click the **Arrange tab**. In the **Sizing & Ordering group**, click the **Align** button, and then click **Left**.

> The left edge of the title's label control is aligned with the left edge of the TV Show # label control.

6 Click in an empty area of the design grid to deselect the controls, and then click the **title's label control**. Point to the right edge of the **title's label control** until the pointer ↔ displays. Drag to the right until the right edge of the label control aligns with the right edges of the text box controls in the Detail section. If your entire name does not display within the title's label control, click the **Home tab**, and in the **Font group**, reduce the font size of the text.

> Even though the entire title displays in Layout view and in Form view, if the title is truncated in Design view, it will be truncated when you print the form.

7 **Save** 🖫 and **Close** ☒ the form. **Open** » the **Navigation Pane**. Under **Forms**, right-click **7A TV Shows Form**, and then click **Rename**. Type **Lastname Firstname 7A TV Shows Split Form** and then press [Enter].

> Recall that an object must be closed before you can rename it.

8 Double-click **7A TV Shows Split Form** to open it in Form view. Be sure that **Record 1** is displayed. In the form section, on the left side, click the **Record Selector** bar. If you are instructed to submit this result, create a paper or electronic printout of the selected record.

9 **Close** ☒ the form, and then **Close** ☒ the **Navigation Pane**.

Objective 2 | Create a Form and a Subform

In the previous activities, you created a split form that displayed the datasheet of the underlying table—the data in the form section was the same data as that displayed in the datasheet section. A *subform* is a form that is embedded within another form—the *main form*—and is used to view, enter, and edit data that is related to data in the main form. A subform is similar to a subdatasheet—the data in the related table is displayed without having to open another table or form.

Activity 7.04 | Creating a Form and a Subform Using the Form Tool

If Access finds a single table that has a one-to-many relationship with the table used to create a form, Access adds the datasheet as a subform to display the related records. In this activity, you will create the main form using the *7A TV Shows* table. Because a one-to-many relationship has been created between this table and the *7A TV Show Advertisers* table, the datasheet for the *7A TV Show Advertisers* table will be inserted as a subform.

1 Click the **Database Tools** tab, and, in the **Relationships group**, click the **Relationships** button. If the tables do not display in the Relationships window, on the **Design tab**, in the **Relationships group**, click the **All Relationships** button. If necessary, expand the table boxes and rearrange them so that it is easier to view the relationships as shown in Figure 7.10. Take a moment to study the established relationships.

This is an example of a ***many-to-many relationship*** between the *7A TV Shows* table and the *7A Advertiser Info* table. *Many* television shows can have *many* advertisers. Conversely, *many* advertisers can advertise on *many* television shows.

To create the *many-to-many relationship* between *7A TV Shows* and *7A Advertiser Info*, the *7A TV Show Advertisers* table was created. This table is known as a ***junction table***. It breaks down the many-to-many relationship into two *one-to-many relationships*. The data from the primary key fields—*TV Show #* and *Advertiser*—from the two tables are added to the junction table, which records each instance of the relationship. The primary key fields from the two tables are connected to the foreign key fields in the junction table.

Figure 7.10

One-to-many relationships

Junction table

Many-to-many relationship

> **Note | Specifying Multiple Primary Key Fields**
>
> A junction table contains data from the primary key fields in two tables. The fields in the junction table are designated as primary key fields. In Design view, to specify multiple fields as primary key fields, hold down the Ctrl key, and then click the row selector boxes for each primary key field. On the Design tab, in the Tools group, click the Primary Key button. A junction table can include fields other than the common fields from the two related tables.

2 **Close** ☒ the Relationships window, saving changes if prompted. **Open** ≫ the **Navigation Pane**. Under **Tables**, click **7A TV Shows**. On the Ribbon, click the **Create tab**, and then in the **Forms group**, click the **Form** button. **Close** ≪ the **Navigation Pane**, and then compare your screen with Figure 7.11.

Figure 7.11

Main form—7A TV Shows table

Subform—7A Advertisers table

Navigation area for subform

Navigation area for main form

3 In the main form, click the **TV Show # text box control**, if necessary, and then press PgDn until record **15** is displayed, observing changes in the subform and in the two record navigators.

> As you scroll through the records in the *7A TV Shows* table, the subform displays the related records for each television show. For example, in record 15, the TV Show # is *SWG03-06*, and three advertisers support this show.

4 In the main form, click the **Subject text box control**. Point to the right edge of the text box control until the pointer ↔ displays, and then drag the right edge of the text box control to the left until there is approximately **1 inch** of space between *Devices* and the right edge of the text box control.

> Because the controls are part of the same stacked layout, the width of all of the text box controls is decreased.

Access | Chapter 7

5 Click anywhere in the subform. Notice that the Layout Selector ⊞ displays above the upper left corner of the subform while the datasheet is selected with border around it. The Layout Selector also displays above the upper left corner of the main form because the forms are stacked. Click the **Arrange tab**, and in the **Table group**, click **Stacked** to remove the subform from the stacked layout. The subform is moved to below its placeholder. Click the original placeholder, and then compare your screen with Figure 7.12.

> Notice that the subform is removed from the stacked layout, but the placeholder remains. You cannot move the subform back to that area of the form without deleting the placeholder first. If you don't delete the placeholder, the subform is placed back in the stacked layout and resized to match the main form.

Figure 7.12

Original placeholder for subform

Subform removed from the Stacked Layout

6 Press Del. Click the subform to select it. Point to the right edge of the subform until the pointer ↔ displays, and then drag the right edge of the subform to the left until it aligns with the right edge of the **Advertiser** control box. Point to the subform **Layout Selector** ⊞ until the pointer ⊹ displays, and then drag upward and to the right until the subform is centered under the text box controls in the main form. **Save** 🖫 the form as **Lastname Firstname 7A TV Shows and Advertisers**

> Be sure to leave some space between the main form and the subform so it is not returned to the Stacked Layout. If it returns to that layout, click Undo, and move the subform again.

7 Switch to **Design** view. On the **Design tab**, in the **Header/Footer group**, click the **Logo** button. Navigate to the location where the student data files for this textbook are saved. Locate and double-click **a07A_SWG_Logo** to insert the logo in the form header. Click the **Property Sheet** button to display the Property Sheet for the logo. Click in the **Size Mode** property box, click the arrow, and then click **Zoom**. Close ☒ the **Property Sheet**. Point to the bottom right edge of the control until the pointer ⬉ displays; drag down until it is at the bottom of the **Detail section bar** and right until it is between the *S* and *h* in *Shows*, and then compare your screen to Figure 7.13.

Figure 7.13

Logo inserted and resized

Subform control is centered

8 Click at the beginning of the title label control, and type **Lastname Firstname** and press Spacebar once. To the right of *Shows*, press Spacebar one time, hold down Shift, and then press Enter. Type **and Advertiser Subform** Press Enter.

The title now displays on two lines in the label control.

9 Point to the right edge of the **title's label control** until the pointer ↔ displays—the right edge may display at the very right side of your screen. Drag to the left until there is approximately **0.25 inch** of space between *Shows* and the right edge of the label control. With the **title's label control** selected, on the **Format tab**, in the **Font group**, click the **Center** button ≡.

10 Resize the width of the form to **7 inches**. Compare your screen with Figure 7.14. Notice that the subform control displays the related table's name—*Table.7A TV Show Advertisers*. Also, notice that the title's label control may not display the entire title. Be sure it is visible before moving on.

Although you can make most adjustments to a form in Layout view, you should adjust the title's control in Design view to ensure the form's title will print as desired. With narrow margins for a form and with Portrait orientation, the right edge of the form should not exceed 7.5 inches on the horizontal ruler; otherwise, pages will print with only the background color in the form header.

Figure 7.14

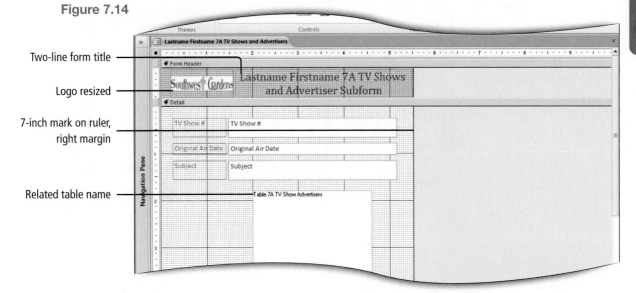

Two-line form title

Logo resized

7-inch mark on ruler, right margin

Related table name

Access | Chapter 7

11 Save 🖫 the form, and then switch to **Form** view. On the left side of the form, click the **Record Selector** bar, and then if you are instructed to submit this result, create a paper or electronic printout of only Record 1—the selected record. Notice that both the main form and the subform print. **Close** ☒ the form.

Activity 7.05 | Creating a Form and a Subform Using the Form Wizard

Use the Form Wizard to create a form and a subform when you want to have more control over the design of the subform, or if the underlying table or query has more than one relationship established. If the underlying table or query that is on the *one* side of the relationship is related to more than one table or query on the *many* side of the relationship, the subform will not automatically be created when the form is created. The same technique can be used to create a split form between two tables that have a many-to-many relationship.

1 On the Ribbon, click the **Create tab**. In the **Forms group**, click the **Form Wizard** button. In the **Form Wizard** dialog box, click the **Tables/Queries arrow**, and then click **Table: 7A TV Shows**, which is on the *one* side of the relationship with the **7A Advertiser Info** using the junction table.

> It does not matter which table you select first; in a later dialog box, you can select the table that displays in the main form and the table that displays in the subform.

2 Under **Available Fields**, click the **All Fields** button to add all of the fields to the **Selected Fields** box. In the same dialog box, click the **Tables/Queries arrow**, and from the displayed list, click **Table: 7A Advertiser Info**, which is on the *many* side of the relationship with the **7A TV Shows** table. Add **All Fields** to the **Selected Fields** box. Click **Next**, and then compare your screen with Figure 7.15.

> The second Form Wizard dialog box displays with a preview of how the data will be arranged. The order in which you select the tables or queries to be included in the main form and subform does not matter because you can change the way the data is displayed in this Form Wizard dialog box. If a relationship between the tables has not been established, this Form Wizard dialog box will not display.

Figure 7.15

Main form—fields from 7A TV Shows table

Subform—fields from 7A Advertiser Info table

3 Under **How do you want to view your data?**, click **by 7A Advertiser Info**, and notice that the form will display with the *7A Advertiser Info* table as the main form and the *7A TV Shows* table as the subform. Under the preview of the form, click **Linked forms**, and notice the preview displays two separate forms with a button on the main form that represents the link between the two forms.

A **linked form** is a related form that is not stored within the main form. To view the data in a linked form, click on the link that is displayed on the main form.

> **Note** | Switching Main Form and Subform Tables
>
> If the tables have a one-to-many relationship, and you switch the view to display the many side as the main form and the one side as the subform, the form will display as a single form instead of a main form with a subform. With a one-to-many relationship, the main form should display the table on the one side of the relationship, and the subform should display the table on the many side of the relationship

4 Click **Form with subform(s)**, and then click **Next** to display the third **Form Wizard** dialog box, where you can select the subform layout. Notice the two layouts are **Tabular** and **Datasheet**, with Datasheet being the default layout.

Both layouts arrange the subform data in rows and columns, but the tabular layout is more customizable. You can add color, graphics, and other elements to a tabular subform. The subform you created in the previous activity used the datasheet layout, which is more compact than the tabular layout.

5 Click **Tabular**, and then click **Next** to display the last **Form Wizard** dialog box. In the **Form** text box, select the existing text, and then type **Lastname Firstname 7A Advertiser Info Form** In the **Subform** text box, select the existing text, type **Lastname Firstname 7A TV Shows Subform** and then click **Finish**.

The form and subform display in Form view. Notice that all of the fields and data are not visible in the subform.

6 Switch to **Design** view. Using the lasso technique practiced in Activity 6.12, select all of the controls in the main form. On the **Arrange tab**, in the **Table** group, click the **Stacked** button.

7 Switch to **Layout** view. In the subform, click the **TV Show # label control**. Hold down Shift, and then click the **TV Show # text box control** to select both controls. Point to the right edge of the **TV Show # text box control** until the pointer ↔ displays. Drag the right edge of the control to the left until there is approximately **0.25 inch** of space between the word *TV Show #* and the right edge of the *TV Show # label control*.

8 Click the **Subject label control**; hold down Shift and click the **Subject text box control**. On the **Design tab**, in the **Tools** group, click the **Property Sheet** button to display the Property Sheet for *Multiple selection*. Select the **Width** property setting on the **Format tab**. Type **3** and press Enter. Hold down Shift and click the **Original Air Date text box** and **label controls**. Drag the controls to the left until the **Original Air Date** appears immediately to the right of **TV Show #**.

The widths of the controls are decreased.

9 Click the **Layout Selector** ⊞ in the upper left corner of the subform; the Selection Type should now read *Subform/Subreport* on the Property Sheet. Select the **Width** property setting, and then type **6** Press Enter, and type **3** in the **Height** property setting. **Close** × the Property Sheet.

The width and height of the subform are adjusted, and the horizontal scrollbar in the subform does not display.

10 Click the main form, and navigate to **Record 9**—*Advertiser* of *Maricopa County Stone and Marble*. In the main form, click the **Advertiser text box control**. Point to the right edge of the text box control until the pointer ↔ displays. Drag to the left until there is approximately **0.5 inch** of space between the data in the **Advertiser** field and the right edge of the text box control. Recall that the controls are grouped together in a stacked layout, so adjusting the size of one control adjusts the sizes of all of the controls.

11 Click the **Phone text box control**; hold down Shift and click the **Phone label control**. Point to the **Phone text box control** until the pointer 🕂 displays. Drag upward until an orange horizontal line displays between the **Contact Person** field and the **City** field. Click the **City text box control**. Hold down Shift, and then click the **City label control**, the **State text box control**, and the **State label control** to select all four controls. On the Ribbon, click the **Arrange tab**. In the **Table group**, click the **Stacked** button to remove the controls from the Stacked Layout. Delete the placeholders from the stacked layout.

> Recall that it is easier to remove fields from a stacked layout when they are at the bottom of the layout, and the placeholders remain once the controls are removed from the stacked layout.

12 Click the **City label control** to display the **Layout Selector** ⊞ for the controls. Point to the **Layout Selector** until the pointer 🕂 displays, and then drag upward and to the right until the **City** field aligns with the **Contact Person** field and there is approximately **0.5 inch** of space between the **Contact Person text box control** and the **City label control**. Click in a blank area of the form to deselect the controls. Click the **City label control**, and then point to the right edge of the **City label control** until the pointer ↔ displays. Drag the right edge of the **City label control** to the left until there is approximately **0.5 inch** of space between the word *City* and the right edge of the **City label control**. **Save** 💾 the form. Compare your screen with Figure 7.16.

> After removing the fields from the stacked layout, they are grouped as a separate layout for ease in making adjustments to the controls. The widths of the City and State label controls are decreased so that the text box controls will not exceed the allowable width when printed.

Figure 7.16

Main form—fields from 7A Advertiser Info table

Widths of label controls decreased

Fields moved from the first column

Subform—fields from 7A TV Shows table

13 Using the techniques you have practiced, remove the **Advertiser textbox control** and the **Advertiser label control** from the stacked layout, and then delete the placeholders from the stacked layout. Move the left column down so the **Contact Person** field aligns with the **City** field. Click the **Advertiser label control**. Hold down Shift, and then click the **Advertiser text box control** to select both controls. Point to one of the selected controls until the pointer displays. Drag upward and to the right until the controls are approximately centered above the controls on the left and the controls on the right.

The Advertiser field is contained in its own stacked layout.

14 Click the **subform** to display the **Layout Selector** [image] for the subform. Point to the **Layout Selector** until the pointer [image] displays. Drag the subform upward until there is approximately **0.5 inch** of space between the **Phone** field and the subform, and the subform aligns with the left edge of the **Phone text box control**. Click the **subform label control**—*7A TV Shows*—and press Del to remove the label from the subform control. Compare your screen with Figure 7.17.

Figure 7.17

Fields moved to new location

Subform control moved to new location

15 **Save** [image] the form, and switch to **Design** view. Using the techniques you have practiced, in the main form, add a **Logo** to the Form Header section using **a07A_SWG_Logo**, and then adjust the size of the logo so it is easily read. Resize the form **title's label control** so it displays to the right of the logo, and place *7A Advertiser Info Form* on the second line of the title. **Center** [image] the text in the form title's label control, and, if necessary, align the right edge of the form title's label control with the right edge of the subform. If necessary, resize the form width to **7.75 inches** so no extraneous pages print when the form is printed.

16 Switch to **Form** view. Press [PgDn] until the record for **Arizona Bank**—*Record 4*—displays. Compare your screen with Figure 7.18. If you are instructed to submit this result, create a paper or electronic printout of only this record.

Figure 7.18

Name displayed on second line of title

Logo inserted in main form header

17 **Close** ☒ the form, saving changes. **Open** ⟩⟩ the **Navigation Pane**. Under **Forms**, **7A Advertiser Info Form** and **7A TV Shows Subform** display. Double-click **7A Advertiser Info Form** to open it in Form view. The subform is embedded in the form. Double-click **7A TV Shows Subform** to open it in Form view. This form displays the fields from the *7A TV Shows* table that are used in the subform of *7A Advertiser Info Form*.

When a subform is created in a main form, a separate form object is created and displays in the Navigation Pane under Forms.

18 **Close** all forms.

> **More Knowledge** | Adding the Table Name to the Subform
>
> To add the name of the table used to create the subform at the top of the subform, add a label control to the Form Header section of the subform. Then type the name of the table. If the table name is added to the Form Header section, the label control with the table name that displays to the left of the subform should be deleted.

Activity 7.06 | Creating a Subform by Dragging a Related Table onto an Existing Form

In this activity, you will create a subform by dragging an existing table—*7A TV Show Advertisers*—on the *many* side of the relationship onto an existing form—*7A TV Shows Main Form*—on the *one* side of the relationship. When a table has more than one relationship with other tables, this method is helpful in adding a subform to a form.

1 In the **Navigation Pane**, under **Forms**, open **7A TV Shows Main Form** in Design view. On the **Design tab**, in the **Controls group**, click the **More** arrow, and be sure that the **Use Control Wizards** option is active.

> The existing form must be open in Design view before dragging a related table onto it. If you try to drag a related table onto a form in Layout view, an error message displays.

2 In the form, point to the top of the **Form Footer section bar** until the pointer ⬍ displays. Drag downward to the **3-inch mark on the vertical ruler** to create more space in the Detail section.

3 In the **Navigation Pane**, under **Tables**, drag **7A TV Show Advertisers** onto *7A TV Shows Main Form* to the **1.75-inch mark on the vertical ruler** and **0.25-inch mark on the horizontal ruler**. The first **SubForm Wizard** dialog box displays. Compare your screen with Figure 7.19.

> Notice at the bottom of the dialog box that Access will display records from the *7A TV Show Advertisers* table for each record in the *7A TV Shows* table using the *TV Show #* field—the common field.

Figure 7.19

SubForm Wizard
dialog box

4 In the **SubForm Wizard** dialog box, click **Define my own**.

The SubForm Wizard dialog box changes to display list boxes in which you can select the fields that link the main form to the subform.

5 Under **Form/report fields**, in the **first list box**, click the **arrow**, and then click **TV Show #**. Under **Subform/subreport fields**, in the **first list box**, click the **arrow**, and then click **TV Show #**. Compare your screen with Figure 7.20.

The same field is used to link the form and the subform as when *Choose from a list* was selected. By default, Access uses the fields that are used to create the join line in the relationship between the tables. You should select *Define my own* when you want to use fields other than the common fields as defined in the relationship.

Figure 7.20

Common field

Subform—7A TV Show Advertisers

Main form—7A TV Shows TV Show #

6 Click **Next**. Under **What name would you like for your subform or subreport?**, type **Lastname Firstname 7A TV Show Advertisers Subform** and then click **Finish**. Compare your screen with Figure 7.21.

The subform displays under the label and text box controls of the main form, and a subform label control displays above the subform.

Figure 7.21

Main form—7A TV Shows

Subform label control

Subform—7A TV Show Advertisers

7 With the subform control selected, point to the **bottom middle sizing handle** of the subform control until the pointer ⬍ displays. If the subform is not selected, point to the bottom edge of the subform control, and then click to display the sizing handles. Drag downward to the **3.5-inch mark on the vertical ruler**. Point to the top of the **Form Footer section bar** until the pointer displays, and then drag upward to the bottom of the subform control. **Save** 🖫 the form, and then **Close** « the **Navigation Pane**.

8 Switch to **Layout** view. If necessary, resize controls so both fields are visible in the subform. Press (PgDn) to display the record for each television show and the related record(s) in the subform. Notice that the **TV Show #** field displays in both the main form and the subform.

9 In the record navigator for the main form, click the **First Record** button. Switch to **Design** view. In the subform control, click the **TV Show # label control**, hold down (Shift) and click the **TV Show # text box control**. Press (Del), and then switch to **Layout** view.

The *TV Show #* field is removed from the subform.

10 Click the **subform control**. Point to the bottom right corner of the **subform control** until the pointer ⬉ displays. Drag upward and to the left until there is approximately **0.25** inch of blank space between the **Advertiser** controls and the bottom and right edges of the subform. Compare your screen with Figure 7.22.

Figure 7.22

Subform height and width adjusted

11 Click the **subform label control**, which displays *Lastname Firstname 7A Show Advertisers Subform*, and then press (Del) to remove the label control from the subform.

12 Click anywhere in the subform, and then point to the displayed **Layout Selector** ⊞ until the pointer 🖑 displays. Drag to the right until the subform is centered under the form data.

13 Switch to **Design** view, saving changes if necessary. Change the title of the form to **Lastname Firstname 7A TV Shows and Advertisers** and then move **7A TV Shows and Advertisers** onto the second line. Adjust the width of the **title's label control** so that the left edge of the label control aligns with the left edge of the field label controls and the right edge of the label control aligns with the right edge of the field text box controls. In the title's label control, **Center** ≡ the text, and then compare your screen with Figure 7.23.

Figure 7.23

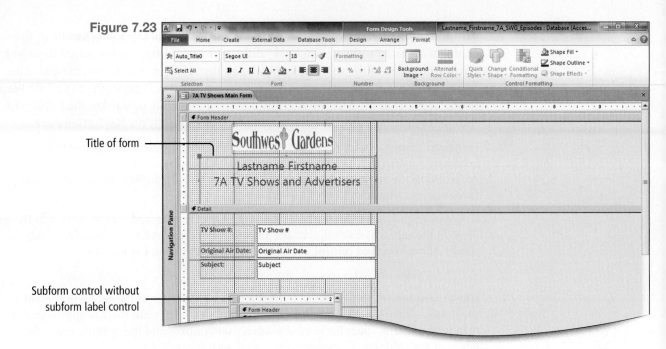

Title of form

Subform control without
subform label control

14 Save 💾 the form, and switch to **Form** view. If you are instructed to submit this result, create a paper or electronic printout of only the last record.

15 Close ☒ the form and open ⟫ the **Navigation Pane**. Under **Forms**, **Rename** *7A TV Shows Main Form* to **Lastname Firstname 7A TV Shows Main Form and Advertisers Subform**

> **More Knowledge | Creating a Form with Two Subforms or Nested Subforms**
>
> A form can contain more than one subform. The main form should have a one-to-many relationship with the first subform. The first subform should have a one-to-many relationship with the second subform. The main form would contain both subform controls. To create a form with two subforms, use the Form Wizard, selecting each table from the Tables/Queries drop-down list and each table's fields.
>
> A form can also contain *nested subforms*. The main form should have a one-to-many relationship with the first subform. The first subform should have a one-to-many relationship with the second subform. Instead of the main form containing both subform controls, the first subform would contain the second subform control. You can have a maximum of seven levels of subforms.

Objective 3 | Create a Multi-Page Form

A *multi-page form* displays the data from the underlying table or query on more than one page. Creating a multi-page form enables you to divide a long form into sections that display on separate pages or to display subforms on different tabs within the main form. A multi-page form enables the user to display only the data that needs to be accessed and displays the form in a more organized format.

Activity 7.07 | Creating a Multi-Page Form Using the Tab Control

In this activity, you will modify a form to create a multi-page form using the *tab control*. A tab control is used to display data on the main form on different tabs, similar to the way database objects, such as forms and tables, display on different tabs.

1 In the **Navigation Pane**, under **Forms**, open **7A SWG Employees TC Form** in Design view, and then close $\boxed{«}$ the **Navigation Pane**. Point to the top of the **Form Footer section bar** until the pointer $\boxed{\updownarrow}$ displays. Drag downward to the **3-inch mark on the vertical ruler** to increase the height of the Detail section.

2 On the **Design tab**, in the **Controls group**, click the **Tab Control** $\boxed{\square}$ button. Move the pointer $\boxed{\square}$ into the **Detail** section until the plus (+) sign of the pointer is aligned approximately with the **0.25-inch mark on the horizontal ruler** and with the **0.25-inch mark on the vertical ruler**. Click one time, and then compare your screen with Figure 7.24.

> A tab control is inserted into the Detail section of the form. There are two tabs on the tab control. Each tab represents a separate page on the form. Do not be concerned if the page numbers on your tabs differ from those displayed in Figure 7.24.

Figure 7.24

Tabs for pages on the form—your page numbers may differ

Tab control

3 In the selected **tab control**, point to the **right middle sizing handle** until the pointer $\boxed{\leftrightarrow}$ displays. Drag to the right until the right edge of the tab control aligns with the **6-inch mark on the horizontal ruler**.

4 On the **Design tab**, in the **Tools group**, click the **Add Existing Fields** button.

> The Field List for the *7A SWG Employees* table displays.

5 In the **Field List**, click **ID#**. Hold down Shift, and then click **Last Name** to select three fields. Hold down Ctrl, click **Hire Date**, and then click **Photo** to select two additional fields. Point to a selected field, and then drag downward and to the left onto the first tab until the top of the arrow of the pointer aligns with the **1.5-inch mark on the horizontal ruler** and with the **0.75-inch mark on the vertical ruler**. Release the mouse button. Compare your screen with Figure 7.25.

> The controls for the fields are arranged in a column on the first tab in the tab control, and Access automatically adjusts the height of the tab control so that all of the controls display. The controls are not grouped together.

Figure 7.25

7A SWG Employees
Field List

Fields dragged to first tab

6 **Close** ✕ the **Field List**. Click in an empty area of the tab control to deselect the controls. Hold down Shift, and then click the **label controls** for the **Hire Date** and **Photo** fields, the **text box control** for **Hire Date**, and the control for the **Photo**. Point to the selected controls until the 🖑 pointer displays. Drag to the right and upward until the *Hire Date* controls align with the *ID#* controls and there is approximately **0.5 inch** of space between the two columns. Do not be concerned if the controls do not exactly align.

7 With the controls selected, on the Ribbon, click the **Arrange tab**. In the **Table group**, click the **Stacked** button to group the controls together. Click the **ID# label control** to deselect the controls in the second column. Using the techniques you have just practiced, select all of the controls in the first column, and then group them together in a **Stacked** layout.

8 Click the **Layout Selector** ⊞ for the first column. Hold down Shift, click the **Hire Date label control**, and then click the **Layout Selector** above the second column to select both columns. On the **Arrange tab**, in the **Sizing & Ordering group**, click the **Align** button, and then click **Top**. Compare your screen with Figure 7.26.

Figure 7.26

Columns aligned
at top edges

9 **Save** 🖫 the form, and then switch to **Layout** view. Press PgDn several times to display the other records in the table, ensuring that all of the data displays in all of the fields.

10 Switch to **Design** view. In the **Detail** section, click the **second tab**, which has no controls added to it. On the **Design tab**, in the **Tools group**, click the **Add Existing Fields** button. In the **Field List**, click **Address**. Hold down Shift, and then click **Phone** to select five fields. Point to the selected fields, and then drag downward and to the left onto the second tab until the top of the arrow of the pointer aligns with the **1.5-inch mark on the horizontal ruler** and with the **0.75-inch mark on the vertical ruler**.

11 Using the techniques you have practiced, move the **Phone label control** and **Phone text box control** upward and to the right until the controls are aligned with the **Address** controls. Arrange the **Phone controls** in a **Stacked** layout. Arrange the eight controls in the first column in a **Stacked** layout. Align the tops of both columns, **Close** ☒ the **Field List**, and then compare your screen with Figure 7.27.

Figure 7.27

Controls added to second tab

12 **Save** 🖫 the form, and then switch to **Layout** view. Click the **second tab** and notice that the data in the **Address** field is truncated. Press PgDn three times to display **Record 4**. Point to the right edge of the **Address text box control** until the pointer ↔ displays, and then drag to the right until the entire address displays in the text box control. Move the **Phone label control** to the right, if necessary.

13 Right-click the **first page** of the form, and then click **Properties**. The Property Sheet should display *Selection type: Page*, and the Selection type box should display the tab's page number. If necessary, change the *Selection type*. Click in the **Caption** property setting box, type **Employee Name and Photo** and then press Enter.

> The first tab displays the text you entered in the Caption property setting box.

14 In the form, click the **second tab** to display the **Property Sheet** for the second tab. Click in the **Caption** property setting box, type **Address and Phone** and then press Enter to change the text on the second tab. **Close** ☒ the **Property Sheet**. In the form, click the **Employee Name and Photo tab** to display the first page of the form.

15 Change the **title** of the form to **Lastname Firstname 7A Employees Tab Control Form** and then place **Tab Control Form** on the second line of the title. Switch to **Form** view.

16 Save ⊟ the form, and, navigate to **Record 6**. Press ⌐Alt⌐ + ⌐PrtScr⌐ to place a copy of the screen into the Clipboard. Open **Microsoft Office Word 2010**. Type your **Firstname Lastname** and press ⌐Enter⌐. Type **Activity 7.07 Step 16** and press ⌐Enter⌐. On the **Home tab**, in the **Clipboard group**, click the **Paste** button to place the screenshot in the Word document window. Press ⌐Ctrl⌐ + ⌐End⌐ to move to the end of the Word document, and press ⌐Ctrl⌐ + ⌐Enter⌐ to move to the next page. **Minimize** the Word window.

> Because it takes a long time for Access to format a form that contains a tab control for printing, you are copying the screens displaying the data on the tabs into Word, and then printing the Word document.

17 In the **Access** window, on the form, click the **Address and Phone tab**. Press ⌐Alt⌐ + ⌐PrtScr⌐ to place a copy of the screen into the Clipboard. On the taskbar, click the **Microsoft Word** button to display the Word document. In the **Word** window, on the **Home tab**, in the **Clipboard group**, click the **Paste** button to place the second page of the form in the Word document window.

18 In the **Word** window, on the **Quick Access Toolbar**, click the **Save** ⊟ button. Navigate to the **Access Chapter 7** folder, and save the file as **Lastname_Firstname_7A_Tab_ Control_Form** If you are instructed to submit this result, create a paper or electronic printout of the document.

> The screen copy of the first tab prints on the first page, and the screen copy of the second tab prints on the second page.

19 Close the **Word** window. If necessary, on the taskbar, click the **Access** button. In **Access**, **Close** ⌐X⌐ the form, and then **Open** ⌐»⌐ the **Navigation Pane**. **Close** the database, and then **Exit** Access.

End You have completed Project 7A ──────────

Project 7B Online Orders

Project 7B Training

Project Activities

In Activities 7.08 through 7.14, you will create advanced reports that will help the president and officers of the production company view the information in a database in a different way. JR Desert Productions maintains a Web site where customers can order gardening supplies that are featured in the *Southwest Gardens* television show. You will create advanced reports that display data from multiple tables and from a parameter query. You will also create an alphabetic index of garden suppliers. Your completed reports will look similar to Figure 7.28.

Project Files

For Project 7B, you will need the following file:

a07B_Online_Orders

You will save your database as:

Lastname_Firstname_7B_Online_Orders

Project Results

Figure 7.28
Project 7B Online Orders

Objective 4 | Create and Modify a Subreport

A *subreport* is a report that is embedded within another report—the *main report*. The main report is either bound or unbound. A *bound report* displays data from an underlying table, query, or SQL statement as specified in the report's Record Source property; an *unbound report* does not. An *SQL (pronounced "sequel") statement* is an instruction using Structured Query Language. An example of an unbound report being used as the main form would be a report that displays a title, logo, and date, similar to a report header. A main report can also contain a subform instead of a subreport. A main report can contain up to seven levels of subforms and subreports.

Activity 7.08 | Using the SubReport Wizard to Create a Subreport

In this activity, you will create a subreport using the SubReport Wizard. The main report will display the online orders, and the subreport will display the products that were ordered. Before creating a subreport using the SubReport Wizard, the underlying tables or queries should have established relationships.

1 **Start Access.** Navigate to the location where the student data files for this textbook are saved. Locate and open the **a07B_Online_Orders** file. Save the database in your **Access Chapter 7** folder as **Lastname_Firstname_7B_Online_Orders**

2 If you did not add the Access Chapter 7 folder to the Trust Center, enable the content. Because some of the fields in the tables are lookup fields, you will not rename any of the tables. **Close** ☒ the **Navigation Pane**.

3 On the Ribbon, click the **Database Tools tab**. In the **Relationships group** click the **Relationships** button. button. Take a moment to review the relationships between the tables.

There is a *one-to-many* relationship between the *7B SWG Suppliers* table and the *7B Online Orders* table. There is a *one-to-many* relationship between the *7B Online Orders* table and the *7B Online Order Detail* table. There is a *one-to-many* relationship between the *7B Online Garden Supplies* table and the *7B Online Order Detail* table. The *7B Online Order Detail* table is a junction table that is used to create a *many-to-many* relationship between the *7B Online Orders* table and the *7B Online Garden Supplies* table.

4 **Close** ☒ the Relationships tab, and then **Open** ☒ the **Navigation Pane**. Under **Reports**, right-click **7B Orders Report**, and then click **Copy**. On the **Home tab**, in the **Clipboard group**, click the **Paste** button. In the **Paste As** dialog box, under **Report Name**, and with the existing text selected, type **Lastname Firstname 7B Orders Main Report** and then click **OK**.

In the Navigation Pane under Reports, the newly named copy of the *7B Orders Report* displays.

5 Open **7B Orders Main Report** in **Design** view, and then **Close** ☒ the **Navigation Pane**. Click the **small box** in the upper left corner of the report, where the top and left margins intersect. Recall that clicking this box selects the report. On the Ribbon, click the **Design tab**. In the **Tools group**, click the **Property Sheet** button.

The Property Sheet should display *Selection type: Report*.

6 Click the **Property Sheet Data tab**. Notice that the **Record Source** property setting is *7B Online Orders*. **Close** ⊠ the **Property Sheet**.

> 7B Orders Main Report is bound to the 7B Online Orders table.

7 In the **Report Header** section, click the **title's label control**, and change *Lastname Firstname* to your own last and first names, and then press Enter. In the report, point to the top of the **Page Footer section bar** until the pointer ⊞ displays. Drag downward to the **1-inch mark on the vertical ruler** to make room in the Detail section for the subreport.

8 On the **Design tab**, in the **Controls group**, click the **More** arrow, and be sure that the **Use Control Wizards** option is active. In the **Controls group**, click the **Subform/ Subreport** 🔲 button. Move the mouse pointer down into the **Detail** section until the top of the plus (+) sign of the pointer aligns with the **1-inch mark on the horizontal ruler** and with the **0.5-inch mark on the vertical ruler**, and then click.

> A subreport control is inserted into the Detail section of the report, and the SubReport Wizard dialog box displays. The control displays *Unbound* because the control has not yet been linked to a record source.

9 In the **SubReport Wizard** dialog box, be sure that **Use Existing Tables and Queries** is selected, and then click **Next**.

> The second SubReport Wizard dialog box enables you to select the table or query and the fields to use in the subreport.

10 Click the **Tables/Queries box arrow**, and from the displayed list, click **Table: 7B Online Order Detail**. Under **Available Fields**, double-click **Product**, and then double-click **Quantity** to move the fields to the **Selected Fields** box. Click **Next**.

> The third SubReport Wizard dialog box enables you to define the fields that link the main form to the subreport. Because there is a one-to-many relationship between the two tables, the default setting is to show the data in the *7B Online Order Detail* table for each record in the *7B Online Orders* table.

11 Click **Next**, name the report **Lastname Firstname 7B Products Ordered Subreport** and then click **Finish**. **Save** 🖫 the main report. Switch to **Report** view, and then compare your screen with Figure 7.29.

> The subreport data displays under each record from the *7B Online Orders* table. For example, for *Order # SWG100*, two 36.5″ Floral Shovels were ordered.

Figure 7.29

Record from 7B Online Orders table

Related records from 7B Online Order Detail table

Activity 7.09 | Modifying a Subreport

Just like the main report, the subreport can be modified. In this activity, you will remove the name of the subreport, apply conditional formatting in the subreport, and change the border color of the subreport. You can modify the subreport in either Layout view or Design view.

1 Switch to **Layout** view. In any subreport control, click the **subreport label control**, which displays *7B Products Ordered Subreport*, and then press Del.

The label control for the subreport no longer displays.

2 In any subreport control, click the **Quantity text box control**. On the **Format tab**, in the **Control Formatting** group, click the **Conditional Formatting** button. The **Conditional Formatting Rules Manager** dialog box displays to show formatting rules for the *Quantity* field. Click the **New Rule** button, and compare your screen with Figure 7.30.

Conditional formatting is a way to apply formatting to specific controls based on a comparison to a rule set in the New Rule dialog box. It is one way to draw attention to an entry that might require additional action.

Figure 7.30

Conditional Formatting—
New Formatting
Rule dialog box

Displays rule used
to check values

Preview area for
formatting applied
based on the condition

3 Click the arrow to the right of the box that displays *between*, and select **greater than or equal to**. Click in the empty text box, and type **3** The rule will format only cells where the *Field Value is greater than or equal to 3*.

The rule has now been set; however, no format options have been set. These settings are applied using the buttons below the rule.

4 Click the **Bold B** button, and then click the **Background color** button arrow. Under **Standard Colors**, on the fifth row, click the last color—**Brown 4**. Click **OK** to close the **New Formatting Rule** dialog box. Click **OK** to close the **Conditional Formatting Rules Manager**.

For any items ordered, if the quantity is 3 or more, the quantity will display bold with a light brown background. This will alert the staff to determine if special shipping options might be necessary.

5 Click anywhere in the subreport, and then click the **Layout Selector** 田. On the **Format tab**, in the **Control Formatting group**, click the **Shape Outline button arrow**. Under **Theme Colors**, on the first row, click the fourth color—**Dark Blue, Text 2**. Again click the **Shape Outline button arrow**, and then point to **Line Thickness**. In the displayed list, click the third line—**2 pt**—and then click anywhere in the main form to display the results of the formatting. Switch to **Report** view. Compare your screen with Figure 7.31.

The subreport displays with a thicker blue border.

Figure 7.31

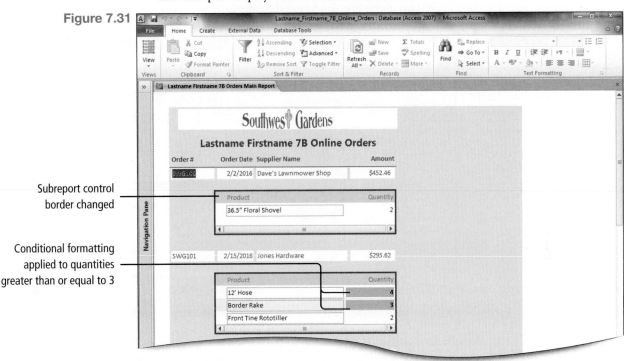

Subreport control border changed

Conditional formatting applied to quantities greater than or equal to 3

> **Note** | Removing a Horizontal Scroll Bar
>
> Adding the thicker border decreased the area where the data displays, and it may cause a horizontal scroll bar to display at the bottom of the subreport. If so, in Layout view, click the subreport control—not a field label control or text box control in the subreport—and then point to the right edge of the subreport control until the pointer displays. Drag the right edge of the subreport control to the right until the horizontal scroll bar no longer displays.

6 **Save** 🖫 the report. If you are instructed to submit this result, view the report in **Print Preview**, be sure the **Margins** are set to **Narrow**, and then create a paper or electronic printout.

7 **Close** the Print Preview window and the report, and then **Open** ⏩ the **Navigation Pane**.

Activity 7.10 | Creating a Subreport by Adding an Object to an Existing Report

In this activity, you will drag the *7B Online Orders* table onto the *7B SWG Suppliers Report* to create a subreport. For the subreport to be linked to the main report, the underlying tables should have an established relationship. You can also create a subreport by dragging an existing form, subform, query, report, or subreport onto a report.

1 In the **Navigation Pane**, under **Reports**, locate **7B SWG Suppliers Report**, and then open the report in **Design** view. In the report, point to the top of the **Page Footer section bar** until the pointer ⬍ displays. Drag downward to the **1.75-inch mark on the vertical ruler** to make room in the Detail section for the subreport.

2 In the **Navigation Pane**, under **Tables**, click **7B Online Orders**, and then drag the table to the right onto the **Detail** section until the top of the pointer aligns with the **1-inch mark on the horizontal ruler** and the **0.75-inch mark on the vertical ruler**. The **SubReport Wizard** dialog box displays, as shown in Figure 7.32.

The SubReport Wizard suggests that the report shows the Online Orders for each record in the Suppliers using Supplier Name. If you were dragging an existing report onto this report that had an established relationship between the underlying tables, the SubReport Wizard dialog box would not display.

Figure 7.32

SubReport Wizard dialog box

3 In the **SubReport Wizard** dialog box, be sure that **Choose from a list** is selected, and then click **Next**. Name the subreport **Lastname Firstname 7B Orders Subreport** and then click **Finish**. **Save** 🖬 the report. In the **Navigation Pane**, notice that the newly created subreport displays under **Reports**.

4 Press `F4` to display the Property Sheet for the subreport, and then **Close** `«` the **Navigation Pane**. If necessary, click the **Property Sheet Data tab**, click in the **Link Master Fields** property setting box, and then click the **Build** button.

The Subreport Field Linker dialog box displays. The fields that are used to link the two underlying record sources together are displayed; the Master Fields property setting box displays the linked field in the main report, and the Child Fields property setting box displays the linked field in the subreport. Use the Subreport Field Linker dialog box to change the linked fields if the subreport does not display the data in the manner you intended. If you are unsure of which fields to link, click the Suggest button.

5 In the **Subreport Field Linker** dialog box, click **OK**. **Close** ⊠ the **Property Sheet**, and then switch to **Layout** view. Notice that **Record 1** displays no data in the subreport; no orders have been placed with A&S Garden Supply.

6 In the main report, locate Record 2—**Martinez Nurseries**. Notice that Record 2 displays one order in the subreport and displays the name of the supplier in the third field. In the **subreport control** for **Record 2**, click **Martinez Nurseries**, press `Shift`, and click the **Supplier Name label control**. Press `Del` to remove the label and text box controls and the redundant data. Resize the other three controls so they are wide enough to just view the data. Move the controls to close large gaps between fields.

7 Click the **subreport's Layout Selector** ⊞, and then press (F4) to display the Property Sheet for the subreport. Click the **Property Sheet Format tab**, select the text in the **Width** property setting box, type **3.5** and then press (Enter) to change the width of the subreport control. **Close** ⊠ the **Property Sheet**.

8 Click the **subreport label control**—*Lastname Firstname 7B Orders Subreport*. Change the **Font Color** of the text in the selected label control to **Dark Blue, Text 2**, and then add **Bold** formatting to the text. Point to the selected label control until the ⊹ pointer displays, and then drag the control to the right until it is approximately centered between the margins of the subreport control.

> The subreport has been modified, and the redundant field has been removed. A horizontal scroll bar displays in the subreport.

9 Switch to **Design** view, saving changes to the main report and subreport. Select the **Subreport Header**, and change the background color to **Brown 4**. Click the **Order #** **label control**, hold down (Shift), click the **Order Date label control**, and then click the **Amount label control** to select all three label controls, scrolling to the right as necessary. Change the **Font Color** to **Dark Blue, Text 2**. Switch to **Layout** view. If necessary, adjust the width of the phone number text box control to keep the number on one line, and then compare your screen with Figure 7.33.

Figure 7.33

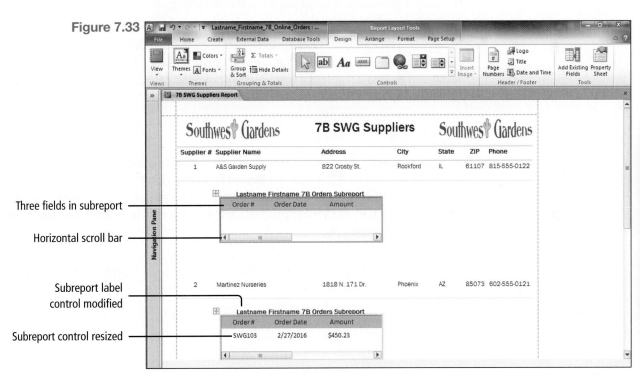

Three fields in subreport

Horizontal scroll bar

Subreport label
control modified

Subreport control resized

10 **Save** 🖫 the report, and then switch to **Design** view.

Activity 7.11 | Displaying a Total from a Subreport on the Main Report

1 Click the subreport to select it. On the **Design tab**, in the **Tools** group, click the **Subreport in New Window** button ▦.

The subreport displays on its own tab, and all of the controls are displayed, which makes it easier to edit.

2 On the **Design tab**, in the **Tools group**, click the **Property Sheet** button. Be sure that the Property Sheet displays *Selection type: Report*. On the **Property Sheet Format tab**, change the **Width** property setting to **3.5** and then **Close** ☒ the **Property Sheet**.

Recall that the subreport control displayed a horizontal scroll bar—this is because the actual subreport's width was wider than the size of the control. By making the width of the report the same as the width of the subreport control, the scroll bar will no longer display in the *7B SWG Suppliers Report since it is not really necessary to view data.*

3 In the **Detail** section, click the **Amount text box control**. On the **Design tab**, in the **Grouping & Totals group**, click the **Totals** button, and then click **Sum** to insert a calculated control into the Report Footer section.

4 **Save** ▤ the subreport, and then **Close** *7B Orders Subreport.*

To view the results of the changes made to the subreport in the main report, you first must close the subreport.

5 Switch *7B SWG Suppliers Report* to **Report** view. Notice that the horizontal scroll bar no longer displays, and in the subreport controls, **Record 1** displays a total Amount of **$0.00** and **Record 2** displays a total Amount of **$450.23**. Scroll down to display **Record 7**, which displays a total Amount of **$428.49**.

Adding a sum to a field in the subreport causes the sum to display in the subreport control on the main form.

6 Switch to **Design** view. On the **Design tab**, in the **Tools group**, click the **Subreport in New Window** button ▦. Click the **Report Footer section bar**, and then press F4 to display the Property Sheet for the Report Footer section. On the **Property Sheet Format tab**, click in the **Visible** property setting box, which displays **Yes**. Click the **arrow**, and then click **No**.

The data in the Report Footer section will not display when the report is displayed in any view other than Design view. You will be displaying the calculated field in the main form, so it is being hidden from view.

7 In the **Report Footer** section, click the **calculated control**. The **Property Sheet** displays *Selection type: Text Box*, and the **Selection type** box displays *AccessTotalsAmount*. Click the **Property Sheet Other tab**, and then click in the **Name** property setting box. Select **AccessTotalsAmount**, type **Total Amount** and then press (Enter). Compare your screen with Figure 7.34.

> The Selection type box displays Total Amount, which is the new name of the text box control that displays the sum of the amount field. Rename controls to easily remember the name, especially if the control name is used somewhere else in the form. You will be using this control name to display the total of the amount field in the main form.

Figure 7.34

Name given to text box control

8 **Close** ☒ the **Property Sheet**, **Save** 💾 the report, and then **Close** *7B Orders Subreport*. Switch *7B SWG Suppliers Report* to **Report** view, and notice that the sum of the Amount field no longer displays in the subreport control.

9 Switch to **Design** view. On the **Design tab**, in the **Controls group**, click the **Text Box** ⓐⓑ button. Move the mouse pointer down to the **Detail** section until the top of the plus (+) sign aligns with the **6-inch mark on the horizontal ruler** and with the **1-inch mark on the vertical ruler**, and then click. Compare your screen with Figure 7.35.

> A text box control with an associated label control displays in the Detail section. The text box control displays Unbound because the control is not linked to a field.

Figure 7.35

Unbound text box control

Label control—name may differ

10 In the **Detail** section, click the **label control** that is associated with the unbound text box control, and then press F4 to display the Property Sheet for the label control. Click the **Property Sheet Format tab**, select the text in the **Caption** property setting box, and then type **Total Amt:** Select the text in the **Width** property setting box, type **.75** and then press Enter to increase the width of the label control.

> The Caption property setting controls the text that is displayed in the label control associated with the unbound text box control.

11 In the **Detail** section, click the **unbound text box control**. If the control is hidden behind the Property Sheet, decrease the width of the Property Sheet by dragging the left edge of the Property Sheet to the right. Click the **Property Sheet Data tab**, and then click in the **Control Source** property setting box. Click the **Build** button.

> The Expression Builder dialog box displays. Although you can type the expression directly in the Control Source property setting box, the Expression Builder dialog box is similar to the Zoom dialog box, where you can see the entire typed expression. The Control Source property setting is used to link the text box control to a field.

--▶ **12** In the **Expression Builder** dialog box, using your own first and last names and double-clicking the correct objects as they appear in the drop-down list, type **=IIf(IsError ([Lastname Firstname 7B Orders Subreport].[Report]![Total Amount]),0,[Lastname Firstname 7B Orders Subreport].[Report]![Total Amount])** and then compare your screen with Figure 7.36.

> The expression starts with an equal (=) sign and is followed by the IsError function within the IIf function. The IIf function checks for the #Error message in the Total Amount field of 7B Orders Subreport. If #Error is found, 0 is displayed in the field; otherwise, the data in the Total Amount field is displayed. A period separates the report name with the object name, which is also enclosed in brackets. The object name, in this case [Report], is only necessary if the name of the report is the same as the underlying record source. The exclamation (!) mark is called the ***bang operator***. The bang operator tells Access that what follows it is an object that belongs to the object that precedes it in the expression. In this expression, Total Amount is an object in the 7B Orders Subreport Report.

Another Way

If the subreport contains data for each control on the main report, you could have typed a more simple expression of =[7B Orders Subreport Firstname Lastname].[Report]! [Total Amount]. The expression starts with an equal (=) sign and is followed by the name of the report enclosed in brackets. A period separates the report name with the object name—Report—which is also enclosed in brackets. The bang operator is used to identify Total Amount as an object in the 7B Orders Subreport report. If the subreport does not contain any data for any control on the main report, the control on the main report displays #Error when printed using the simplified expression.

Figure 7.36

Source field name
Source report name
Source object type
Bang operator

13 In the **Expression Builder** dialog box, click **OK**, and then press ↓.

> The expression displays in the Control Source property setting box.

14 Click the **Property Sheet Format tab**. Click in the **Format** property setting box, click the displayed **arrow**, and then click **Currency**. **Close** ☒ the **Property Sheet**.

> The data that was typed in the Control Source property setting box displays in the text box control.

15 With the **text box control selected**, point to the small gray box that displays in the upper left corner of the text box control until the pointer displays. Drag to the left until the left edge of the text box control aligns with the right edge of the label control that displays *Total Amt:*.

> Dragging the small box that displays in the upper left corner of a control enables you to move only that control. If you point to any other part of the control before dragging, the control and its associated controls are moved.

16 **Save** 🖫 the report, and then switch to **Report** view. Scroll down to display **Records 6 and 7**, and then compare your screen with Figure 7.37.

> The sum of the Amount field in the subreport is displayed in the main report and is formatted as Currency.

Figure 7.37

Sum of Amount field in subreport

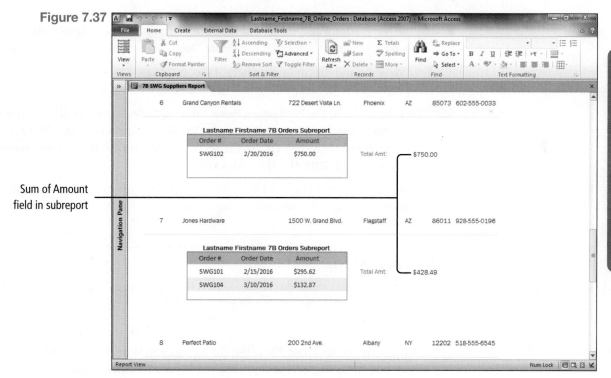

17 If you are instructed to submit this result, view the report in **Print Preview**, be sure the **Margins** are set to **Narrow**, and then create a paper or electronic printout.

18 **Close** the Print Preview window and the report, and then **Open** ⟩⟩ the **Navigation Pane**.

Objective 5 | Create a Report Based on a Parameter Query

Recall that a **parameter query** prompts you for criteria before running the query. Using a parameter query as the record source for a report enables the user to set the criteria for the report when the report is opened. Recall that when a report is opened, the underlying table or query in the report is read to ensure that the report displays the most current data. JR Desert Productions maintains a table to keep track of the Web site orders. A parameter query was created to display the orders between a range of dates.

Activity 7.12 | Creating a Report Based on a Parameter Query

In this activity, you will view the design of the *7B Orders - Parameter Query*, and then create a report based on the parameter query.

1 In the **Navigation Pane**, under **Tables**, double-click **7B Online Orders** to open the table in **Datasheet** view. Notice that the **Order Date** data ranges from 2/2/2016 to 3/10/2016.

When you run the parameter query, if you enter a range for which there is no data or if you enter the data incorrectly, the resulting fields will be empty.

2 **Close** the table. In the **Navigation Pane**, under **Queries**, double-click **7B Orders - Parameter Query**. In the **Enter Parameter Value** message box, under **Enter first date**, type **2/1/16** and then click **OK**. In the second message box, under **Enter second date**, type **February 15, 2016** and then click **OK**.

Because the Order Date field has a data type of Date, you can enter the date in several formats. The query is run and displays orders between February 1, 2016, and February 15, 2016.

3 **Close** the query, and then **Close** ⟨⟨ the **Navigation Pane**. On the Ribbon, click the **Create tab**. In the **Reports group**, click the **Report Wizard** button.

Because the query was selected in the Navigation Pane, the *7B Orders - Parameter Query* displays in the Tables/Queries box.

4 In the **Report Wizard** dialog box, click the **All Fields** button to move all of the fields from the Available Fields box to the **Selected Fields** box, and then click **Next**.

5 In the second **Report Wizard** dialog box, under **How do you want to view your data?**, click **by 7B Online Garden Supplies**, and then click **Next** two times. In the fourth **Report Wizard** dialog box, **sort** the records by **Order Date** in **Ascending** order, and then click **Next** two times.

6 In the last **Report Wizard** dialog box, name the report **Lastname Firstname 7B Items Ordered by Date Range Report** and then click **Finish**.

> An Enter Parameter Value message box displays. Because the report is based on a parameter query, you must enter the parameter values.

7 For the first date, type **2/1/16** and for the second date, type **2/15/16** Click **OK**, and then compare your screen with Figure 7.38.

> Four records are extracted from the underlying tables based on the parameter values entered. Four fields are included in the report, but all data may not be visible on this page. In that case, adjustments will need to be made to controls so all data is visible and the report prints on one page.

Figure 7.38

Four items ordered between 2/1/2016 and 2/15/2016

Access | Chapter 7

8 On the **tab row**, right-click the **7B Orders by Date Range Report tab**, and then click **Layout View**. Resize the text box controls and label controls for the **Item** and **Supplier Name** so that there is approximately **0.25** inch of blank space following the longest item in each column. Resize the **Order Date** field to fully display the data, and then resize the **Quantity** field to fit the label control. Adjust the field placement so all fields display on the page.

9 Switch to **Design** view. Resize the width of the report to **7.5 inches**. In the **Page Footer** section, click to select the **Page Numbering** text box. Point to the small gray box that displays in the upper left corner of the text box control until the pointer displays. Drag to the left until the right edge of the text box control aligns with the right edge of the **Quantity** controls. **Save** 🖫 the report.

Activity 7.13 | Printing the Parameters in the Report

The parameters used in the creation of the report can be printed as a part of the report by adding a text box control to a section. In this activity, you will add a text box control to the Report Header section to display the parameter values as a subtitle.

1 Point to the top of the **Page Header section bar** until the pointer 🛨 displays. Drag downward to the top of the **Item Header** section bar to increase the size of the **Report Header**.

2 On the **Design tab**, in the **Controls group**, click the **Text Box** ⌷ᵃᵇ⌷ button. In the **Report Header** section, align the top of the plus (+) sign of the pointer with the **1-inch mark on the horizontal ruler** and **three dots** below the label control for the report title, and then click.

> Recall that adding a text box control to the design also adds an associated label control that can be used to describe the data in the text box control.

3 Click the **label control** that is associated with the newly added text box control, and then press [Del].

4 Click the unbound **text box control**, and then press [F4] to display the Property Sheet for the control. Click the **Property Sheet Data tab**, click in the **Control Source** property setting box, and then click the **Build** button. In the displayed **Expression Builder** dialog box, type **="Between "&[Enter first date]&" and "&[Enter second date]** and then compare your screen with Figure 7.39.

> Recall that an expression must begin with an equal sign (=). The word *Between* and a space will print. The & symbol concatenates the string with the next part of the expression. *Enter first date* is enclosed in square brackets because it is part of the criteria that is retrieved from the parameter query. You must type the criteria exactly as it displays in the criteria of the parameter query. The criteria will be concatenated with the space, the word *and*, and another space. This is concatenated with the second criteria.

Figure 7.39

Spaces should occur after
Between and before
and after *and*

String expression

Criteria must be entered
exactly as it displays
in parameter query

5 In the **Expression Builder** dialog box, click **OK**, and then press ↓ to save the property setting.

Alert! | Did a Message Box Display?

If a message box displays stating that the expression you entered contains invalid syntax, click OK. Click the Control Source Build button, and then view Figure 7.39 to be sure that you typed the expression correctly. Common errors include not typing the equal sign, using parentheses instead of square brackets, leaving out the beginning or ending quotation marks, or leaving out one of the & symbols.

---

6 **Close** the **Property Sheet**. On the **Format tab**, in the **Font group**, click the **Font Color button arrow** A ·. Under **Theme Colors**, on the first row, click the fourth color—**Dark Blue, Text 2**.

7 With the text box control selected, in the **Font group**, click the **Center** button ▤. In the **Font group**, click the **Font Size button arrow**, and from the displayed list, click **14**. Increase the width of the text box control until the entire expression displays.

8 On the Ribbon, click the **Arrange tab**. In the **Sizing & Ordering group**, click the **Size/Space** button, and then click **To Fit**.

The height of the text box control is increased to fit the size of the text, and the width of the text box control will adjust to fit the title that displays in Layout view, Report view, and Print Preview view.

Access | Chapter 7

9 Save 🖫 the report, and switch to **Report** view. For the first date, enter **2/1/16** and for the second date, enter **2/15/16**

The report displays with a subtitle of *Between 2/1/16 and 2/15/16*. When the criteria is displayed in the report, be sure to enter the criteria in a consistent manner. For example, do not enter 2/1/16 for the first date and February 15, 2016, for the second date. If you do, the subtitle will display as *Between 2/1/16 and February 15, 2016*.

Alert! | **Did Another Message Box Display?**

If an unexpected Enter Parameter Value message box displays when you try to print or preview a report, you may have misspelled one of the criteria or a field name in the expression. The parameter criteria in this report must match exactly to the parameter criteria used in the query. If this happens, click Cancel to return to Design view and correct the error.

---

10 Switch to **Print Preview** view. If you are instructed to submit this result, create a paper or electronic printout. **Close** the Print Preview window and the report, and then **Open** 》 the **Navigation Pane**.

Objective 6 | Create an Alphabetic Index

A report can display an *alphabetic index*, similar to the grouping of addresses in an address book. An alphabetic index groups items by a common first character. For example, all of your contacts can be sorted by last name in ascending order. All of the last names beginning with the letter *A* are grouped together under the letter *A*. All of the last names beginning with the letter *B* are grouped together under the letter *B*, and so on.

Activity 7.14 | Creating an Alphabetic Index

In this activity, you will create an alphabetic index of the suppliers' names from the *7B SWG Suppliers* table, using the *7B SWG Supplier Names Query*.

1 In the **Navigation Pane**, under **Queries**, double-click **7B SWG Supplier Names Query**. Take a moment to review the data in the query, and then switch to **Design** view.

The query displays the Supplier Name field in ascending order from the *7B SWG Suppliers* table.

2 Close ✕ the query, and then Close 《 the **Navigation Pane**.

3 On the Ribbon, click the **Create tab**. In the **Reports group**, click the **Report Wizard** button.

4 Because the query was selected in the Navigation Pane, in the **Report Wizard** dialog box, in the **Tables/Queries** box, **Query: 7B SWG Supplier Names Query** displays. If it does not display, click the **Tables/Queries arrow**, and then click **Query: 7B SWG Supplier Names Query**.

5 Under **Available Fields**, double-click **Supplier Name** to add the field name to the **Selected Fields** box, and then click **Next**.

Because the query sorts the Supplier Name in ascending order, the field will automatically be sorted in the same manner in the report.

6 Click **Next**. Under **Layout**, be sure that the **Tabular** option button is selected. Under **Orientation**, be sure that the **Portrait** option button is selected, and then click **Next**.

7 For the title of the report, type **Lastname Firstname 7B Supplier Alphabetic Index** and then click **Finish**. Compare your screen with Figure 7.40.

The report displays in Print Preview. Because the column heading is difficult to see and some of the supplier names are truncated, the report needs some modifications.

Figure 7.40

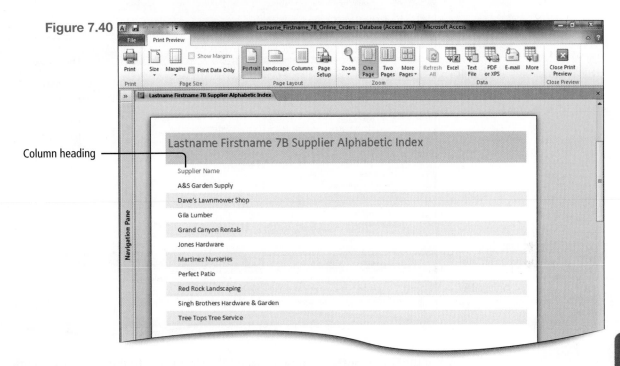

Column heading

8 On the **Print Preview tab**, in the **Close Preview group**, click the **Close Print Preview** button. In **Design** view, click anywhere in an empty area of the design grid to deselect the controls, and then click the **Supplier Name label control**. Be sure that the orange border only displays around the Supplier Name label control. Press Del to remove the Supplier Name label control from the report.

9 Save 🖫 the report, and then switch to **Layout** view. If necessary, expand the width of the **Supplier Name text box control** so that all of the data displays for every record.

10 On the **Design tab**, in the **Grouping & Totals group**, click the **Group & Sort** button. In the **Group, Sort, and Total pane**, click **Add a group**. From the displayed list, click **Supplier Name**.

The report must be grouped by Supplier Name to create an alphabetic index of the names.

Access | Chapter 7

11 In the **Group, Sort, and Total pane**, on the **Group bar**, click the **More arrow**. Click the **by entire value arrow**, and from the displayed list, click the **by first character** option button. Click in an empty area of the report, and then compare your screen with Figure 7.41.

The first letter of the Supplier Name displays above the supplier names along with a label control that displays Supplier Name. You can select more than one character for the index.

Figure 7.41

Letter displays in header section

Displays first character as grouping level

Grouped by Supplier Name

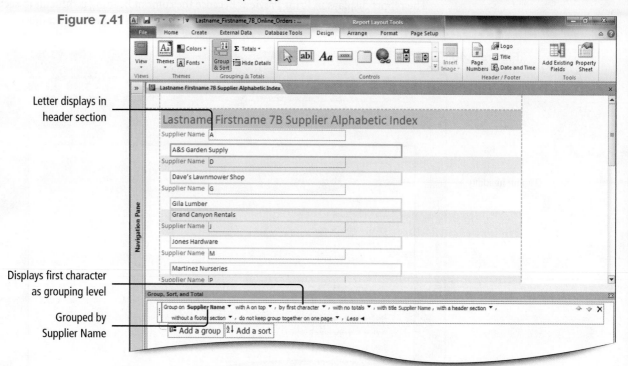

12 In the **Group, Sort, and Total pane**, on the **Group bar**, to the right of **with title**, click the **Supplier Name** link. With *Supplier Name* selected, in the displayed **Zoom** dialog box, press ⎡Del⎤, and then click **OK**. Delete the placeholder from the **Supplier Name control**. **Close** ⊠ the **Group, Sort, and Total pane**—do *not* click the Delete button.

13 Click the **Supplier text box control** for the first record—*A&S Garden Supply*. Point to the control until the pointer ⇱ displays. Drag to the right until the left edge of the text box control is approximately **0.5 inch** to the right of the letter *A* in the **Supplier Name header**. Change the **Font Size** to **12**, and then compare your screen with Figure 7.42.

Figure 7.42

Font size changed to 12

Text box controls moved to the right

14 Click the **text box control** that displays the letter *A*, and change the **Font Size** to **16**. Change the **Font Color** to **Dark Blue**, **Text 2**, and then add **Bold** formatting to the text.

15 **Save** 🖫 the report, and then switch to **Report** view. Compare your screen with Figure 7.43.

Figure 7.43

Formatting changed ⎯⎯⎯

16 Switch to **Print Preview** view. If you are instructed to submit this result, create a paper or electronic printout. On the **Print Preview tab**, in the **Close Preview group**, click the **Close Print Preview** button.

17 **Close** ✕ the report, and then **Open** ≫ the **Navigation Pane**. **Close** the database, and **Exit** Access.

End **You have completed Project 7B** ⎯⎯⎯⎯⎯⎯⎯⎯⎯⎯⎯⎯⎯⎯⎯

Content-Based Assessments

Summary

Forms can be simple or complex. In this chapter, you created advanced forms that display data from one or more record sources. You created split forms that display data from one table in two different ways in the same form. You then created subforms using the Form Tool and the Form Wizard and by dragging a related table onto an existing form. Subforms display data from related tables on one form. Forms can be displayed on multiple pages by using the Tab control.

Reports can also be simple or complex. You created advanced reports using some of the same techniques in creating advanced forms. You created subreports by using the SubReport Wizard and by dragging a related table onto an existing report. You then modified the reports to display the data in a professional-looking format. You created a report based on a parameter query and displayed the criteria as a subtitle in the report. Finally, you created a report that displayed an alphabetic index of supplier names.

Key Terms

Matching

Match each term in the second column with its correct definition in the first column by writing the letter of the term on the blank line in front of the correct definition.

_____ 1. A form that displays data in two views—Form view and Datasheet view—on a single form.

_____ 2. A miniature, semitransparent toolbar that is used to work with objects on the screen.

_____ 3. A form that is embedded within another form and is used to view, enter, and edit data that is related to data in the main form.

_____ 4. A table that breaks down the many-to-many relationship into two one-to-many relationships.

_____ 5. A related form that is not stored within the main form.

_____ 6. A form that displays the data from the underlying table or query on more than one page.

_____ 7. A report that is embedded within another report—the main report.

_____ 8. A report that contains a subreport.

_____ 9. A report that does not display data from an underlying table, query, or SQL statement and has an empty Record Source property.

_____ 10. An instruction using Structured Query Language.

_____ 11. The exclamation point (!).

A Alphabetic index

B Bang operator

C Junction table

D Linked form

E Main report

F Mini toolbar

G Multi-page form

H Nested subform

I Parameter query

J Split form

K SQL statement

L Subform

M Subreport

N Syntax

O Unbound report

_____ 12. The set of rules by which words and symbols in an expression are combined.

_____ 13. A query that prompts the user for criteria.

_____ 14. A grouping of items by a common first character.

_____ 15. A subform that is embedded within another subform.

Multiple Choice

Circle the correct answer.

1. Which property defines whether the datasheet displays above, below, to the left, or to the right of the form in a split form?
   - **A.** Split Form Splitter
   - **B.** Split Form Data
   - **C.** Split Form Orientation

2. Which view must be used to convert an existing form into a split form?
   - **A.** Layout view
   - **B.** Design view
   - **C.** Form view

3. Which type of relationship is created using a junction table when one record in one table has many matching records in a second table, and a single record in the second table has many matching records in the first table?
   - **A.** Many-to-many
   - **B.** One-to-one
   - **C.** One-to-many

4. What type of form enables you to divide a long form into sections that display on separate pages or to display subforms on different tabs within the main form?
   - **A.** Nested form
   - **B.** Subform
   - **C.** Multi-page form

5. What object is inserted into a main form so that it displays data on different tabs?
   - **A.** Subform/subreport
   - **B.** Control wizard
   - **C.** Tab control

6. If the underlying table or query has more than one relationship established, the form/subform would best be created using
   - **A.** Form wizard
   - **B.** Design view
   - **C.** Layout view

7. What type of report displays data from an underlying table, query, or SQL statement as specified in the report's Record Source property?
   - **A.** Unbound report
   - **B.** Bound report
   - **C.** Parameter report

8. What operator tells Access that what follows it is an object that belongs to the object that precedes it in the expression?
   - **A.** Expression operator
   - **B.** Bang operator
   - **C.** Bound operator

9. What type of record source should be used to enable a user to set the criteria for a report when the report is opened?
   - **A.** SQL statement
   - **B.** Alphabetic index
   - **C.** Parameter query

10. Which option in a report can display a grouping similar to that of addresses in an address book?
    - **A.** Alphabetic index
    - **B.** File group
    - **C.** A to Z Sort

Apply **7A** skills from these Objectives:

1. Create a Split Form
2. Create a Form and a Subform
3. Create a Multi-Page Form

Skills Review | Project **7C** Historical Gardens

Matthew Lee, coordinator for cultural and historical events of JR Desert Productions, wants the database forms to display related data. For example, he is interested in displaying the contacts for the historical gardens on one form. In this project, you will customize the company's forms to display data in two ways on the same form, to display data from multiple tables on one form, and to display data on multiple pages on a form. Your completed work will look similar to Figure 7.44.

Project Files

For Project 7C, you will need the following files:

> a07C_Historical_Gardens
> a07C_SWG_Logo
> A new blank Word document

You will save your files as:

> Lastname_Firstname_7C_Historical_Gardens
> Lastname_Firstname_7C_Tab_Control_Form

Project Results

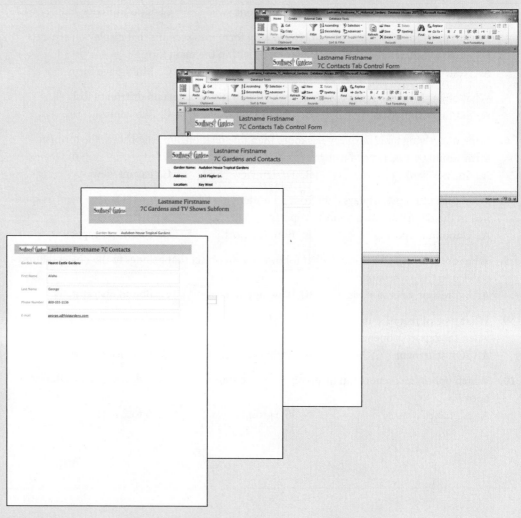

Figure 7.44

(Project 7C Historical Gardens continues on the next page)

Skills Review | Project 7C Historical Gardens (continued)

1 **Start Access**. Open the **a07C_Historical_Gardens** file. Save the database in your **Access Chapter 7** folder as **Lastname_Firstname_7C_Historical_Gardens** If necessary, enable the content.

2 In the **Navigation Pane**, click **7C Contacts** to select the table. **Close** the **Navigation Pane**.

a. On the Ribbon, click the **Create tab**. In the **Forms group**, click the **More Forms** button, and then click **Split Form**. **Save** the split form as **Lastname Firstname 7C Contacts Split Form**

b. On the **Design tab**, in the **Tools group**, click the **Property Sheet** button. Click the **Selection type arrow**. Scroll down and then click **Form**.

c. Click the **Form Property Sheet Format tab**. In the property setting box for **Split Form Printing**, click the **arrow**, and then click **Form Only**.

d. Switch to **Design** view. Click in the **Split Form Orientation** property setting box, and then click the **arrow**. Click **Datasheet on Top**, and then **Close** the **Property Sheet**.

e. Switch to **Layout** view. Point to the splitter bar until the pointer displays. Drag upward until the dark line displays between the fourth and fifth records.

f. On the **Design tab**, in the **Header/Footer group**, click the **Logo** button. Navigate to the student data files, and then double-click **a07C_SWG_Logo**. Display the **Property Sheet**. Click in the **Size Mode** property box, click the arrow, and then click **Zoom**. Close the **Property Sheet**. Increase the width of the **logo control** approximately **1 inch**.

g. Click the **title's label control**. Click at the beginning of the title, and then type your **Lastname Firstname**

h. **Save** the form, and then switch to **Form** view. Press PgDn until **Record 4** displays. In the form section, change the **Phone Number** for *Hearst Castle Gardens* to **800-555-1136**

i. On the left side of the form, click the **Record Selector** bar, and then if you are instructed to submit this result, create a paper or electronic printout of only Record 4—the selected record. **Close** the form. **Open** the **Navigation Pane**.

3 Under **Tables**, click **7C Gardens**. On the Ribbon, click the **Create tab**, and then in the **Forms group**, click the **Form** button. **Close** the **Navigation Pane**.

a. Switch to **Design** view. In the **Detail** section, click on the **Layout Selector** to select the controls in the main form and subform. On the Ribbon, click the **Arrange tab**. In the **Table group**, click the **Remove Layout** button. Click an empty area of the design grid to deselect the controls.

b. Switch to **Layout** view. In the main form, click the **Garden Name text box control**. Press Shift and then click each of the text boxes in the main form. Point to the right edge of one of the text box controls until the pointer displays, and then drag to the left until there is **1 inch** of space between *Gardens* and the right edge of the text box control. Point to the right edge of the **subform control** until the pointer displays. Drag to the left until there is approximately **0.25 inch** of space after the **Subject control** in the subform.

c. Switch to **Design** view. Change the form title to **Lastname Firstname 7C Gardens and TV Shows Subform** Click to the right of **Gardens**. Hold down Shift, and then press Enter. **Save** the form as **Lastname Firstname 7C Gardens and TV Shows Subform**

d. Using the techniques you have practiced, insert **a07C_SWG_Logo** in the Form Header section, and change the **Picture Size Mode** property to **Zoom**.

e. Point to the bottom right corner of the **logo control** until the pointer displays. Drag downward to the top of the **Garden Name label control** and to the right between *TV* and *Shows*.

f. Click in an empty area of the design grid, and then click the **title's label control**. Point to the right edge of the **title's label control** until the pointer displays. Drag to the left until the right edge of the label control aligns with the **6.5-inch mark on the horizontal ruler**. With the **title's label control** selected, on the **Format tab**, in the **Font group**, click the **Center** button.

g. Point to the right edge of the main form until the pointer displays. Drag to the left until the edge aligns with the **7-inch mark on the horizontal ruler**.

h. **Save** the form, and then switch to **Form** view. If you are instructed to submit this result, create a paper or electronic printout of only Record 1—the selected record. **Close** the form.

(Project 7C Historical Gardens continues on the next page)

Content-Based Assessments

4 **Open** the **Navigation Pane**. Under **Forms**, open **7C Gardens Main Form** in **Design** view.

a. On the **Design tab**, in the **Controls group**, be sure that the **Use Control Wizards** button is active. In the form, point to the top of the **Form Footer section bar** until the pointer displays. Drag downward to the **2-inch mark on the vertical ruler**.

b. In the **Navigation Pane**, under **Tables**, drag **7C Contacts** onto **7C Gardens Main Form** to the **1.75-inch mark on the vertical ruler** and even with the left edge of the form.

c. In the **SubForm Wizard** dialog box, click **Define my own**. Under **Form/report fields**, in the **first list box**, click the **arrow**, and then click **Garden Name**. Under **Subform/subreport fields**, in the **first list box**, click the **arrow**, and then click **Garden Name**. Click **Next**. Under **What name would you like for your subform or subreport?**, type **Lastname Firstname 7C Gardens Contact Subform** and then click **Finish**.

d. **Save** the form. Select the subform, and on the **Design tab**, click **Property Sheet**. Change the **Default View** property to **Single Form**. **Close** the **Property Sheet**.

e. In the subform, click the **Garden Name label control**, press Shift, click the **Garden Name text box control**, and then press Del. Switch to **Layout** view.

f. Reduce the size of the **First Name**, **Last Name**, and **Phone Number** controls so there is approximately **0.5 inch** of blank space to the right of the data. Point to the right edge of the **subform control** until the pointer displays. Drag to the left until the **right edge of the subform control** aligns with the **right edge of the text box controls**.

g. Delete the **subform label control**, which displays *Lastname Firstname 7C Gardens Contact Subform*.

h. Change the title of the form to **Lastname Firstname 7C Gardens and Contacts** and then place *7C Gardens and Contacts* on the second line. Adjust the width of the **title's label control** so that the **right edge of the title's label control** aligns with the **right edge of the main form field's text box controls**.

i. **Save** the form. If you are instructed to submit this result, create a paper or electronic printout of only the first record. **Close** the form. In the **Navigation Pane**, under **Forms**, Rename *7C Gardens Main Form* to **Lastname Firstname 7C Gardens and Contacts Form**

5 In the **Navigation Pane**, under **Forms**, open **7C Contacts TC Form** in **Design** view, and then **Close** the **Navigation Pane**.

a. Point to the top of the **Form Footer section bar**, and drag downward to the **3-inch mark on the vertical ruler**. On the **Design tab** in the **Controls group**, click the **Tab Control** button. Move the pointer into the **Detail** section until the plus (+) sign of the pointer is aligned approximately with the **0.25-inch mark on the horizontal and vertical rulers**, and then click.

b. In the selected **tab control**, point to the **right middle sizing handle** until the pointer displays. Drag to the right until the right edge of the tab control aligns with the **6-inch mark on the horizontal ruler**.

c. On the **Design tab**, in the **Tools group**, click the **Add Existing Fields** button. In the **Field List**, click **Garden Name**. Hold down Shift, and then click **Last Name**. Point to a selected field, and then drag onto the first tab until the top of the arrow of the pointer aligns with the **1.5-inch mark on the horizontal ruler** and with the **0.75-inch mark on the vertical ruler**. **Close** the **Field List**.

d. Click anywhere in the report to deselect the controls. Click the **Garden Name text box control**, and point to the **right edge** of the control until the pointer displays. Drag to the right until the right edge aligns with the **5-inch mark on the horizontal ruler**.

e. Click to select the **Last Name label control**, press Shift, and click to select the **Last Name text box control**. Drag the controls to the right and upward until they align with the **First Name controls** and there is approximately **0.5 inch** of space between the two text box controls.

f. In the **Detail** section, click the **second tab**, which has no controls. On the **Design tab**, in the **Tools group**, click the **Add Existing Fields** button. In the **Field List**, click **Phone Number**. Hold down Shift, and then click **E-mail**. Point to the selected fields, and then drag onto the second tab until the top of the pointer arrow aligns with the **1.5-inch mark on the horizontal ruler** and the **0.75-inch mark on the vertical ruler**. **Close** the **Field List**. **Save** the form.

g. Right-click the **first page**, and then click **Properties**. The Property Sheet displays *Selection type: Page*. Click in the **Caption** property setting box, type **Contact Name** and then press Enter.

(Project 7C Historical Gardens continues on the next page)

Content-Based Assessments

h. Click the **second tab** to display its **Property Sheet**. Click in the **Caption** property setting box, type **Contact Info** and then press Enter. **Close** the **Property Sheet**.

i. In the form, click the **Contact Name** to display the first page of the form. Change the form's **title** to **Lastname Firstname 7C Contacts Tab Control Form** and then place *7C Contacts Tab Control Form* on the second line. Align the right edge of the title's label control with the right edge of the tab control, and then switch to **Form** view.

j. **Save** the form, and navigate to **Record 4**. Press Alt + PrtScr to place a copy of the form into the Office Clipboard. Open **Microsoft Office Word 2010**. Type your **Firstname Lastname** and then press Enter. Type **Project 7C Step 5J** and then press Enter. On the **Home tab**, in the **Clipboard group**, click the **Paste**

button. Press Ctrl + End to move to the end of the Word document, and then press Ctrl + Enter to insert a page break. **Minimize** the Word window.

k. In the **Access** window, on the form, click the **Contact Info tab**. Press Alt + PrtScr. On the taskbar, click the **Microsoft Word** button to display the Word document. **Paste** the screen in the Word document. On the **Quick Access Toolbar**, click the **Save** button, and save the file as **Lastname_Firstname_7C_Tab_Control_Form** in your **Access Chapter 7** folder. If you are instructed to submit this result, create a paper or electronic printout of the document. **Close** the **Word** window.

6 If necessary, on the taskbar, click the Access button. In the **Access** window, **Close** the form, and then **Open** the **Navigation Pane**. **Close** the database, and then **Exit** Access. Submit your work as directed.

End **You have completed Project 7C** ————————————————

Apply **7B** skills from these Objectives:

- 4 Create and Modify a Subreport
- 5 Create a Report Based on a Parameter Query
- 6 Create an Alphabetic Index

Skills Review | Project **7D** Featured Gardens

JR Desert Productions maintains a database of the historic gardens that are featured in the *Southwest Gardens* television show. Creating advanced reports will help the president and officers of the production company view the information in the database in a different way. In this project, you will create advanced reports that display data from multiple tables and from a parameter query. You will also create an alphabetic index of historic gardens. Your completed reports will look similar to Figure 7.45.

Project Files

For Project 7D, you will need the following file:

a07D_Featured_Gardens

You will save your database as:

Lastname_Firstname_7D_Featured_Gardens

Project Results

Figure 7.45

(Project 7D Featured Gardens continues on the next page)

Content-Based Assessments

1 **Start Access**. Open the **a07D_Featured_Gardens** file. Save the database in your **Access Chapter 7** folder as **Lastname_Firstname_7D_Featured_Gardens** If necessary, enable the content.

2 Make a copy of the *7D Gardens Report*, name it **Lastname Firstname 7D Gardens Main Report** and then open in **Design** view.

a. In the **Report Header** section, click the **title label control**. Add your **Lastname Firstname** before the title.

b. In the report, point to the top of the **Page Footer section bar**, and then drag it downward to the **1.75-inch mark on the vertical ruler**.

c. On the **Design tab**, in the **Controls group**, be sure the **Use Controls Wizard** button is active. In the **Controls group**, click the **Subform/Subreport** button. Point to the **Detail** section so the plus sign (+) aligns with the **0.25-inch mark on the horizontal ruler** and the **0.5-inch mark on the vertical ruler**, and then click.

d. In the dialog box, **Use existing Tables and Queries** should be selected, and then click **Next**. Select **Table: 7D TV Shows**. Under **Available Fields**, double-click **TV Show #**, **Original Air Date**, and **Subject**. Click **Next** two times. Name the report **Lastname Firstname 7D TV Shows Subreport** Click **Finish**.

e. Delete the **subreport label control**. Right-click the **Report Header** in the subreport and point to the **Fill/Back Color arrow**. On the sixth row, click the last color—**Brown 5**. Select the label controls in the subreport, and then, on the **Format tab**, in the **Font group**, click the **Font Color button arrow**. Under **Theme Colors**, on the first row, click the first color—**White, Background 1. Save** the report.

f. Switch to **Layout** view. Click the **Original Air Date** text box control. On the **Format tab**, in the **Control Formatting group**, click the **Conditional Formatting** button. In the dialog box, click the **New Rule** button. Click the arrow to the right of the box that displays *between*, and select **less than**. Click inside the empty text box, and type **1/1/15**

g. Click the **Bold** button, and then click the **Font color** button arrow. Under **Standard Colors**, on the sixth row, click the last color—**Brown 5**. Click **OK** two times.

h. Scroll down to the subreport for *Missouri Botanical Gardens*, and click the **TV Show # label** and **text box controls**. Resize them so they are just wide enough to display the data. Click the **Subject label** and **text box controls**, and then drag to the left until there is approximately **0.25 inch** after *Errors*. Move the controls to the left to close the blank space. Resize the subreport control so it is just wide enough to display the data.

i. Switch to **Design** view. Select the subreport control. On the **Format tab**, in the **Control Formatting group**, click the **Shape Outline button**. Under **Theme Colors**, on the first row, click the fifth color—**Orange, Accent 1**. Add an **Orange, Accent 1, 1 pt** border to the **logo control** in the Report Header, and then **Save** the form.

j. Click any **subreport control**, and then on the **Design tab**, in the **Tools group**, click the **Subreport in New Window** button. Resize the subreport to **4.75 inches wide**. In the **Detail** section, click the **TV Show # text box control**. On the **Design tab**, in the **Grouping & Totals group**, click the **Totals** button, and then click **Count Records** to insert a calculated control.

k. Click the **Report Footer section bar**, and then press **F4**. On the **Property Sheet Format tab**, click in the **Visible** property setting box. Set it to **No**.

l. Click the **Count calculated control**, and then click the **Property Sheet Other tab**. In the **Name** property setting box, type **Count of Shows Close** the **Property Sheet. Save** and **Close** the subreport.

m. On the **Design tab**, in the **Controls group**, click the **Text Box** button. Move the mouse pointer to the **Detail** section until it aligns with the **6.25-inch mark on the horizontal ruler** and the **1.5-inch mark on the vertical ruler**, and then click.

n. Click the associated **label control**, and then press **F4**. Click the **Property Sheet Format tab**, in the **Caption** property setting box, type **# of TV Shows:** In the **Width** property setting box, type **1** and then press **Enter**. Drag the **# of TV Shows label control** until it aligns with the left edge of the unbound control.

o. Scroll to the right, and click the **unbound text box control**. Click the **Property Sheet Data tab**, and then click in the **Control Source** property setting box. Click the **Build** button. In the dialog box, using your own first and last names and double-clicking objects from the drop-down list, type **=IIf(IsError([Lastname Firstname 7D TV Shows Subreport].[Report]! [CountofShows]),0,[Lastname Firstname 7D TV Shows Subreport].[Report]![CountofShows])** In the **Expression Builder** dialog box, click **OK. Close** the

(Project 7D Featured Gardens continues on the next page)

Property Sheet. Resize the textbox control so the right edge aligns with the **7-inch mark on the horizontal ruler**. Resize the report to **7.25 inches wide**.

p. **Save** the report. If you are instructed to submit this result, view the report in **Print Preview**, and then create a paper or electronic printout of the first page. **Close** the Print Preview window and the report.

3 **Open** the **Navigation Pane**. Make a copy of **7D Gardens Report**, name it **Lastname Firstname 7D Featured Gardens Report** and then open in **Design** view.

a. In the **Report Header** section, click the **title label control**. Select the text, type **Lastname Firstname 7D Garden Contacts** and then press Enter.

b. Point to the top of the **Page Footer** section bar, and drag downward to the **1.5-inch mark on the vertical ruler**.

c. In the **Navigation Pane**, under **Tables**, click **7D Contacts**, and then drag the table onto the **Detail** section until the pointer aligns with the **0.5-inch mark on the horizontal and vertical rulers**. In the **SubReport Wizard** dialog box, be sure that **Choose from a list** is selected. **Show 7D Contacts for each record in 7D Gardens using Garden Name** is selected, and then click **Next**. Name the subreport **Lastname Firstname 7D Contacts Subreport** and then click **Finish**.

d. If necessary, select the subreport, press F4, and then **Close** the **Navigation Pane**. Click the **Property Sheet Data tab**, click in the **Link Master Fields** property setting box, and then click the **Build** button. In the **Subreport Field Linker** dialog box, click **OK**. Click the **Format tab**, and in the **Width** property setting box, type **8.5 Close** the **Property Sheet**.

e. Switch to **Layout** view. In the subreport, delete the controls for **Garden Name**. Adjust the widths and positions of the remaining controls to fit data without gaps of blank space between fields.

f. Switch to **Design** view, saving changes. Resize the **subreport control** to **5 inches wide**. Select the **subreport label control**, and drag to the right until it is approximately centered across the subreport control.

g. Change the **Font Color** of the text in the selected label control to **Orange, Accent 1**, and then **Bold** the text.

h. In the subreport, apply a **Background Color** of **Orange, Accent 1, Darker 50%** to the **Subreport**

Header. Select the **label controls** in the **Subreport Header**, and change the **Font Color** to **White**.

i. Adjust the width of the report to **7 inches wide**. **Save** the report, and then switch to **Report** view.

j. If you are instructed to submit this result, view the report in **Print Preview**, and then create a paper or electronic printout of the first page. **Close** the Print Preview window and the report.

4 In the Ribbon, click the **Create tab**. In the **Reports group**, click the **Report Wizard** button.

a. In the **Report Wizard** dialog box, **Select** the **Query: 7D TV Shows Parameter Query**. Move all of the fields to the **Selected Fields** box, and then click **Next** two times. Sort the records by **Original Air Date** in **Ascending** order, and then click **Next** two times. Name the report **Lastname Firstname 7D 2016 TV Shows Report** and then click **Finish**. For the first date, type **1/1/16** and for the second date, type **12/31/16**

b. Switch to **Layout View**. Resize all label and text box controls to fit the data within the page constraints. **Save** the report, and then switch to **Design** view.

c. Point to the top of the **Page Header section bar**, and drag downward to the top of the **Featured Garden Header section bar**.

d. On the **Design tab**, in the **Controls group**, click the **Text Box** button. In the **Report Header** section, align the top of the plus (+) sign of the pointer with the **1-inch mark on the horizontal ruler** and the **0.5-inch mark on the vertical ruler**, and then click. Click the associated **label control**, and then press Del.

e. Click the **unbound text box control**, and then press F4. Click the **Property Sheet Data tab**, click in the **Control Source** property setting box, and then click the **Build** button. In the displayed **Expression Builder** dialog box, type **="Original Air Date Between "&[Enter first date]&" and "&[Enter second date]** Click **OK**. **Close** the Property Sheet.

f. With the text box control selected, on the **Format tab**, in the **Font group**, click the **Center** button. In the **Font group**, click the **Font Size button arrow**, and click **14**. Increase the size of the text box control until it is the same size and aligns with the Report title.

g. **Save** the report, and switch to **Report** view. For the first date, enter **1/1/16** and for the second date, enter **12/31/16** Switch to **Print Preview** view. If you are

(Project 7D Featured Gardens continues on the next page)

instructed to submit this result, create a paper or electronic printout. **Close** the Print Preview window and the report, and then **Open** the **Navigation Pane**.

5 In the **Navigation Pane**, under **Queries**, click **7D Garden Contacts Query**, and then **Close** the **Navigation Pane**. On the Ribbon, click the **Create tab**. In the **Reports group**, click the **Report Wizard** button.

a. In the **Report Wizard** dialog box, **Query: 7D Garden Contacts Query** should display. Move all of the fields to the **Selected Fields** box, and then click **Next**. Click the **Remove Field** button to remove the grouping. Click **Next** three times. For the title of the report, type **Lastname Firstname 7D Contacts Alphabetic Index** and then click **Finish**. **Close** Print Preview.

b. **Save** the report, and then switch to **Layout** view. Adjust the width of all controls so that all of the data displays for every record.

c. On the **Design tab**, in the **Grouping & Totals group**, click the **Group & Sort** button. In the **Group, Sort, and Total pane**, click **Add a group**. From the displayed list, click **Last Name**. On the **Group bar**, click the **More arrow**. Click the **by entire value arrow**, and click the **by first character** option button. Click in an empty area of the report.

d. In the **Group, Sort, and Total pane**, on the **Group bar**, to the right of **with title**, click the **Last Name** link. With *Last Name* selected, in the displayed **Zoom** dialog box, press [Del], and then click **OK**. Delete the empty label control box placeholder. **Close** the **Group, Sort, and Total pane**.

e. Switch to **Layout** view. Click the **text box control** that displays the letter *B*. If necessary, drag to the left edge of the report. On the **Format tab**, in the **Font group**, change the **Font Size** to **16**.

f. **Save** the report, and then switch to **Report** view. If you are instructed to submit this result, switch to **Print Preview** view, and then create a paper or electronic printout of the report. **Close** Print Preview.

g. **Close** the report, and then **Open** the **Navigation Pane**. **Close** the database, and **Exit** Access. Submit your work as directed.

End **You have completed Project 7D** ————————————————

Content-Based Assessments

1 Create a Split Form

2 Create a Form and a
   Subform

3 Create a Multi-Page
   Form

Mastering Access | Project **7E** Phone Orders

JR Desert Productions maintains a database where customers can place telephone orders for the gardening supplies that are featured in the *Southwest Gardens* television show. Ruthann Hansen, president of JR Desert Productions, wants the database forms to display related data. For example, she is interested in displaying the orders on one form. She also wants to display the CSR (customer service representative) information in a tab control form. In the following project, you will customize the company's forms to display data in two ways on the same form, to display data from multiple tables on one form, and to display data on multiple pages on a form. Your completed forms will look similar to Figure 7.46.

Project Files

For Project 7E, you will need the following files:

> a07E_Phone_Orders
> a07E_SWG_Logo
> A new blank Word document

You will save your files as:

> Lastname_Firstname_7E_Phone_Orders
> Lastname_Firstname_7E_Tab_Control_Form

Project Results

Figure 7.46

(Project 7E Phone Orders continues on the next page)

1 Start Access. Locate and open the **a07E_Phone_Orders** file. Save the database in your **Access Chapter 7** folder as **Lastname_Firstname_7E_Phone_Orders** If necessary, enable the content.

2 In the Navigation Pane, click **7E SWG CSRs** and then **Close** the **Navigation Pane**. Create a split form, and **Save** it as **Lastname Firstname 7E SWG CSRs Split Form**

3 Switch to **Design** view. In the **Property Sheet**, click the **Selection type arrow**. Click **Form** to display the Form Property Sheet. Click the **Split Form Printing** property setting box arrow, and then click **Form Only**. Click the **Split Form Orientation** property setting box arrow, and then click **Datasheet on Top**. Close the **Property Sheet**.

4 Switch to **Layout** view. Move the **Split Form Splitter Bar** between records 4 and 5. Select the Photo controls for *Andi Shell*. On the **Arrange tab**, click **Tabular** to remove the Photo field from the layout. Delete the **Photo label control**. Click the **Photo control**. In the **Property Sheet**, click **Picture Alignment** property setting box arrow, and then click **Top Right**. Close the **Property Sheet**. Align the left edge of the **Photo control** with the left edge of the photograph. **Save** the form.

5 Add the **a07E_SWG_Logo** to the form, and change the **Picture Size Mode** property to **Zoom**. Increase the width of the logo control to approximately **2 inches**. Click the **title's label control**, and then type your **Lastname Firstname** at the beginning. Resize the **label control** to fit the title. **Save** the form.

6 Switch to **Form** view, and then navigate to the last record. In the form section, change the **First Name** from *Susan* to **Evelyn Save** the form. If you are instructed to submit this result, create a paper or electronic printout of only Record 15. **Close** the form. **Open** the **Navigation Pane**.

7 Click the **7E Orders** table. Click the **Create tab**, and then click the **Form** button. **Close** the **Navigation Pane**. In the main form, click the **Supplier Name combo box control**. Point to the right edge of the **text box control** until the pointer displays, and then drag the right edge of the control to the left until there is approximately **1 inch** of space between *Shop* and the right edge of the text box control.

8 Remove the subform from the stacked layout and delete the original subform placeholder. Switch to **Design** view. Drag the right edge of the subform to the left until it aligns with the **2.75-inch mark on the horizontal ruler**. Move the subform under and to the center of the bottom of the main form. Drag the bottom edge upward until it aligns with the **3-inch mark on the vertical ruler**.

9 **Save** the form as **Lastname Firstname 7E Orders** Add the **a07E_SWG_Logo** to the form, and change the **Picture Size Mode** property to **Zoom**. Drag the right bottom corner of the control downward to the bottom of the **Detail** section bar and to the right until it aligns with the **2-inch mark on the horizontal ruler**.

10 Select the **Title label control** box and resize the placeholder so the right edge aligns with the **6-inch mark on the horizontal ruler**. Edit the **title** to be **Lastname Firstname 7E Orders and Details Subform** with your name on the first line. **Center** the title text.

11 Point to the right edge of the form. Drag to the left until the right edge of the form aligns with the **6-inch mark on the horizontal ruler.**

12 **Save** the form, and then switch to **Form** view. If you are instructed to submit this result, create a paper or electronic printout of only **Record 1. Close** the form. **Open** the **Navigation Pane**.

13 Open **7E SWG CSRs TC Form** in **Design** view. Drag the **Form footer section bar** downward to the **3-inch mark on the vertical ruler**. Insert a tab control at the **0.5-inch mark on the horizontal ruler** and the **0.25-inch mark on the vertical ruler**. Increase the size of the tab control by dragging to the right until the right edge aligns with the **4-inch mark on the horizontal ruler**.

14 To the **first page** of the **tab control**, at the **1-inch mark on the horizontal ruler** and the **top edge of the tab sheet**, add the following fields: **ID#, First Name, Last Name, Hire Date**, and **Photo**. Expand the width of the **First Name** and **Last Name text box controls** to the **2.5-inch mark on the horizontal ruler**. Delete the **Photo label control**, and then position the left edge of the **Photo control** at the **3-inch mark on the horizontal ruler** and the top edge of the photo aligned with the top edge of the **ID# text box control**. In the first page of the tab control **Caption** property, type **Badge**

15 To the **second page** of the **tab control**, at the **1-inch mark on the horizontal ruler** and the **top edge of the tab sheet**, add the following fields: **Address, City, State, Postal Code**, and **Phone**. Expand the widths of all text box controls to the **3-inch mark on the horizontal ruler**. Edit the **Caption** property to display **Contact Info**

16 Change the **title** of the form to **Lastname Firstname 7E CSRs Tab Control Form** placing *Tab Control Form* on a

(Project 7E Phone Orders continues on the next page)

Mastering Access | Project **7E** Phone Orders (continued)

second line. Align the right edge of the title's label control with the **5-inch mark on the horizontal ruler**. **Center** the text of the title. Resize the form to **5 inches** wide. Switch to **Form** view.

17 **Save** the form and navigate to **Record 7**. Using the Office Clipboard, **Copy** and **Paste** the first and second tabs into a Word document. **Save** this document as

Lastname_Firstname_7E_Tab_Control_Form If you are instructed to submit this result, create a paper or electronic printout of the **Word** document.

18 **Close** the **Word** window. In the **Access** window, **Close** the form, and then **Open** the **Navigation Pane**. **Close** the database, and then **Exit** Access. Submit your work as directed.

End **You have completed Project 7E** ——————————————————

Content-Based Assessments

Apply **7B** skills from these Objectives:

- 4 Create and Modify a Subreport
- 5 Create a Report Based on a Parameter Query
- 6 Create an Alphabetic Index

Mastering Access | Project **7F** Customer Service

JR Desert Productions maintains a customer service order phone line where viewers can order gardening supplies that are featured in the *Southwest Gardens* television show. Creating advanced reports will help the president and officers of the production company study the information in the database in a different way. In the following project, you will create advanced reports that display data from multiple tables and from a parameter query. You will also create an alphabetic index of the last names of the customer service representatives. Your completed reports will look similar to Figure 7.47.

Project Files

For Project 7F, you will need the following files:

a07F_Customer_Service
a07F_SWG_Logo

You will save your database as:

Lastname_Firstname_7F_Customer_Service

Project Results

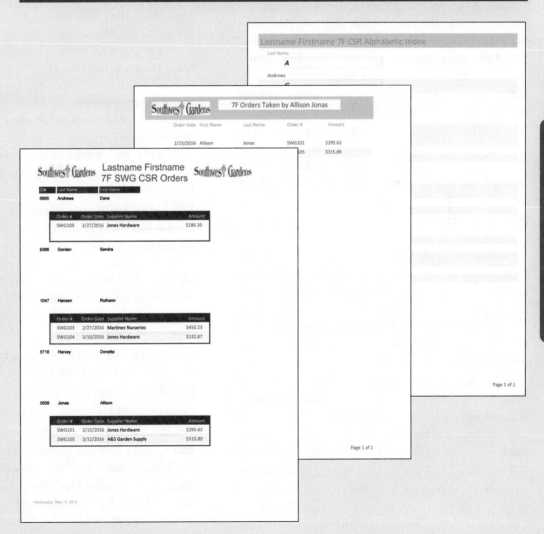

Figure 7.47

(Project 7F Customer Service continues on the next page)

1 **Start Access**. Open the **a07F_Customer_Service** file. Save the database in your **Access Chapter 7** folder as **Lastname_Firstname_7F_Customer_Service** If necessary, enable the content.

2 Make a copy of the **7F CSRs Report** and save it as **Lastname Firstname 7F CSR Orders Report** Open the report in **Design** view. **Close** the **Navigation Pane**.

3 Edit the **Title** of the report by changing *Lastname Firstname* to your first and last names. **Center** the text in the control.

4 Drag the **Page Footer Section bar** down to the **1.5-inch mark on the vertical ruler**. Insert a **Subform/Subreport** control at the **0.5-inch mark on the horizontal and vertical rulers**.

5 Using the **SubReport Wizard**, select **Use existing Tables and Queries**. From the **7F Orders** table, select the following fields in this order: **Order #**, **Order Date**, **Supplier Name**, and **Amount**. **Show 7F Orders for each record in 7F SWG CSRs using ID#**. Add your **Lastname Firstname** to the beginning of the subreport's default name.

6 Switch to **Layout** view. Delete the **subreport label control**. Scroll down to see the subreport for *Singh Brothers Hardware and Garden*. Resize the label and text box controls to just fit the data. Move the controls to close blank space between fields. Add a border of **Line Color Brown 5** and **2 pt Thickness** to the subreport. **Save** the report.

7 Select the subreport, and open it in its own window. Resize the subreport control to **5 inches wide**. Change the **Back Color** report header in the subreport to **Brown 5**. Select the label controls, and then change the **Font Color** to **White, Background 1**. **Save** and close the subreport. Resize the **subreport control** until the right edge aligns with the **5-inch mark on the horizontal ruler**. If necessary, drag the **Page Footer section bar** back up to the **1.5-inch mark on the horizontal ruler**.

8 Switch to **Layout** view. In any subreport control, click the **Amount** text box control. Display the **Conditional Formatting** dialog box, and create a **New Rule** to format the font for any **Amount** greater than **500** as **Brown 5**, **Bold**. Resize the report to **7.5 inches** wide. **Save** the report.

9 If you are instructed to submit this result, view the report in **Print Preview**, and then create a paper or electronic printout of only the first page of the report. **Close** the report, and then **Open** the **Navigation Pane**.

10 Click to select the **7F CSR Parameter Query**. Using the **Report Wizard**, add all **Available Fields** to the **Selected Fields** list. View the data by **7F Orders**. **Group** on the **ID#** field. **Sort Ascending** by **Order Date**. Use **Stepped** layout and **Portrait** orientation. Title the report **Lastname Firstname 7F Orders by CSR** Select **Modify the report's design**, and then click **Finish**. **Close** the **Navigation Pane**. Save the report.

11 Delete the label and textbox controls for the **ID** field. Resize the **First Name** and **Last Name controls** to **1.25 inches** each. Move the fields to remove the blank space between them.

12 Delete the report title's control box. To the **Report Header section**, add the **a07F_SWG_Logo**. Expand the width of the logo to the **2-inch mark on the horizontal ruler** and to the bottom of the **Report Header section**. Delete the **Title** placeholder. Add a **text box control** to the right of the logo. Delete the **text box label control**. Click the unbound text box control. Click the **Property Sheet Data tab**, and then click in the **Control Source** property setting box. Open the **Expression Builder** dialog box. Type the following concatenated string in the text control box: =**"7F Orders Taken by "&[First Name]&"** **"&[Last Name]** Align and resize the title between the **2.25-** and **6-inch marks on the horizontal ruler**. **Center** the text in the control. Change the font size to **16**. Size the textbox **To Fit**.

13 In the **Page Footer section**, click in the **Now()** **control box** to the right of the equal sign. Type **"Report prepared by Firstname Lastname on "&** Widen the control so the right edge aligns with the **4.5-inch mark on the horizontal ruler**. Resize the **Page number control** so the right edge aligns with the **7-inch mark on the horizontal ruler**. Resize the report to **7 inches wide**. **Save** the report.

14 Switch to **Report** view. In the **Enter Parameter Value** message box, under **Enter CSR#**, type **0559**

15 If you are instructed to submit this result, create a paper or electronic printout. **Close** the report, saving changes. **Open** the **Navigation Pane**.

16 Click **7F CSR Last Names Query**. Create a report using the **Report Wizard**. From the **Available fields** list, add **Last Name** to the **Selected Fields list**. No sorting is required. Use **Tabular** layout and **Portrait** orientation. Title the report **Lastname Firstname 7F CSR Alphabetic Index**

(Project 7F Customer Service continues on the next page)

17 Close Print Preview. Switch to **Layout** view. In the **Group, Sort, and Total** pane, click **Add a group**, and then click **Last Name**. On the **Group bar**, click the **More arrow**. Click the **by entire value** arrow, and click the **by first character** option button. Click in an empty area of the report. Click **do not keep group together on one page**, and from the displayed list, click **keep whole group together on one page**. Remove the **Lastname** title. **Save** the report.

18 Click the **text box control** that displays the letter *A*, and change the **Font Size** to **16**. Click the **Font Color**

button arrow. Under **Theme Colors**, on the first line, click the fourth color—**Dark Blue, Text 2**—and then apply **Bold** and **Italic**.

19 **Save** the report, and then switch to **Print Preview**. If you are instructed to submit this result, create a paper or electronic printout of the first page of the report.

20 **Close** the report, and then **Open** the **Navigation Pane**. **Close** the database, and then **Exit** Access. Submit your work as directed.

End You have completed Project 7F

Content-Based Assessments

Apply **7A** and **7B** skills
from these Objectives:

 ▣ Create a Multi-Page
    Form
 ▣ Create a Report
    Based on a
    Parameter Query

Mastering Access | Project **7G** Garden Tours

JR Desert Productions produces the television show *Southwest Gardens*. The show's hosts present tours of public and private gardens that showcase the southwest style. Matthew Lee maintains an updated database about the tours of the featured historic gardens. In this project, you will design a multi-page form for the gardens and tour information that will be used to update this part of the production. You will also create a report based on a parameter query using the name of the garden. Your completed work will look similar to Figure 7.48.

Project Files

For Project 7G, you will need the following files:

> a07G_Garden_Tours
> a07G_SWG_Logo
> **A new blank Word document**

You will save your files as:

> Lastname_Firstname_7G_Garden_Tours
> Lastname_Firstname_7G_Garden_Tours_Tabs

Project Results

Figure 7.48

(Project 7G Garden Tours continues on the next page)

Content-Based Assessments

Mastering Access | Project **7G** Garden Tours (continued)

1 **Start Access.** Open the **a07G_Garden_Tours** file. Save the database in your **Access Chapter 7** folder as **Lastname_ Firstname_7G_Garden_Tours** If necessary, enable the content.

2 Open **7G Featured Gardens and Tours Form** in **Design** view, and then **Close** the **Navigation Pane.** Drag the top of the **Form footer** section bar down to the **3-inch mark on the vertical ruler.** In the Detail section, add a **tab control** at the **0.25-inch mark on the vertical and horizontal rulers.**

3 Extend the right edge of the **tab control** to the **5-inch mark on the horizontal ruler.** To the first page of the **tab control**, on the **Property Sheet**, add a caption of **Garden** From the Field List, add the **Garden Name**, **City**, and **State/Country** field at the **1.5-inch mark on the horizontal ruler** and the **0.75-inch mark on the vertical ruler.** Extend the **text box controls** to the **4.5-inch mark on the horizontal ruler.** To the second page of the **tab control**, add a caption of **Tours** Add the **Times**, **Cost**, and **Reservations** fields to the same position as the first page.

4 Add your **Lastname Firstname** before the **title** of the form, and then press Shift + Enter . **Center** the title. **Save** the form. Use the Office Clipboard and Microsoft Word to display both tab controls of **Record 6**. Save this document as **Lastname_Firstname_7G_Garden_Tours_Tabs**

5 If you are instructed to submit this result, create a paper or electronic printout of the document. Close the **Word** window. Return to the **Access** window, **Close** the form, and then **Open** the **Navigation Pane**

6 Click the **7G Garden Tours Query. Close** the **Navigation Pane.** Create a report using the **Report Wizard.** Use all of the fields. View your data by *7G Historical Gardens.* Do not add any grouping levels. **Sort** by **Subject** in **Ascending** order. Use **Block** layout and **Landscape** orientation. Title it **Lastname Firstname 7G Featured Garden Tours** Modify the report's design.

7 Select the **title control.** Change the **Font Color** to **Red, Accent 2** and the font size to **24.** Resize the control to fit the title. Resize the controls so the report width can be adjusted to **10 inches** wide.

8 Switch to **Layout** view. In the **Enter Parameter Value message** box, type **Biltmore Estate Save** the report.

9 If you are instructed to submit this result, create a paper or electronic printout.

10 Close the **Print Preview** window and the report, and then **Open** the **Navigation Pane. Close** the database, and then **Exit Access.** Submit your work as directed.

End **You have completed Project 7G** ——————————

Content-Based Assessments

GO! Fix It | Project **7H** Contests

Project Files

For Project 7H, you will need the following files:

> a07H_SWG_Contests
> a07H_SWG_Logo

You will save your database as:

> Lastname_Firstname_7H_SWG_Contests

Southwest Gardens offers three yearly sweepstakes to program viewers who subscribe to the show's newsletter online. In the following project, you will modify a form and a subform to enter the data for the sweepstakes participants. You will also modify a subreport based on the entries. Make the following modifications to the **7H Contest Entries Form**:

- Be sure all field names and data are visible in the form. In the main form, drag the right edge of the textbox controls to the 5-inch mark on the horizontal ruler. Align the right edge of the subform with the 4.5-inch mark on the horizontal ruler. Resize the form's width to 6 inches.

- Resize the subform so you can view all nine records and the new record row in Form 1. Add a 2 pt border around the subform in a theme color.

- Move the subform down to allow 1 inch of space between the form and subform. Edit the subform title control to read **Contest Entries Posted by Firstname Lastname** Increase the font size of the title to 14; change the color to match the subform border, and make it bold. Resize the control as necessary. Center the label across the main form area placed right above the subform. Center the subform below the subform's title control.

- If you are instructed to submit this result, create a paper or electronic printout of Record 1.

Make the following modifications to the **7H Contestant Report**:

- In the main report, increase the font for all controls to 10 point; size the controls to fit the data. Resize the Description textbox control until it reaches the 5-inch mark on the horizontal ruler. Bold the description.

- In the subreport, delete the Contest label control and text box control. Delete the subreport label control. Resize the subreport to 2.25 inches wide and 3.25 inches high.

- Select the E-mail textbox control, and click the Totals button on the Design tab. Count the contestants; be sure to include a descriptive label.

- Edit the Page footer to include your name before the date by typing "**Prepared by Firstname Lastname on **"& to the right of the =.

- Copy and paste the logo to the right of the title so the left edge aligns with the 5.5-inch mark on the horizontal ruler. Center the title between the logos.

- Draw a line below the column headings (label controls) to the right edge of the Description text box control. Apply a color to coordinate with the form.

- Adjust the width of the report so it displays on one portrait page.

- If you are instructed to submit this result, create a paper or electronic printout.

End You have completed Project 7H ————————————

Content-Based Assessments

GO! Make It | Project 7I Advertising

Project Files

For Project 7I, you will need the following files:

a07I_Advertising
a07I_SWG_Logo
A new blank Word document

You will save your files as:

Lastname_Firstname_7I_Advertising
Lastname_Firstname_7I_Tab_Control_Form

From the student files that accompany this textbook, open the **a07I_Advertising** database file. Save the database in your Access Chapter 7 folder as **Lastname_Firstname_7I_Advertisers** Modify the design of the tab control form to display the appropriate fields and caption on each tab. Modify the design of the report so it displays the 7I TV Shows information in a subreport, removing the repeated field from the subreport. Your form and report should display as shown in Figure 7.49. Create a paper or electronic printout as directed.

Project Results

Figure 7.49

End **You have completed Project 7I**

Content-Based Assessments

GO! Solve It | Project **7J** Host Travel

Project Files

For Project 7J, you will need the following files:

> a07J_Host_Travel
> a07J_SWG_Logo

You will save your database as:

> Lastname_Firstname_7J_Host_Travel

Andi Shell and Lynda Kay are co-hosts of the television show *Southwest Gardens*. The show includes some broadcasts from beautiful historic gardens around the world. The travel itineraries for the hosts have to be planned a year or more in advance. In this project, you will open the **a07J_Host_Travel** database and save it as **Lastname_Firstname_7J_Host_Travel**

Create a split form based on the **7J Historical Gardens** table. Set the form so it is printed, and place the datasheet on top. Move the splitter bar between records **6** and **7**. Add your **Lastname Firstname** before the form title. Save the form as **Lastname Firstname 7J Historical Gardens Split Form** Create a paper or electronic printout of Record 3.

Make a copy of **7J SWG Employees Form**. Name the copy **7J SWG Employees Main Form** Using the copy as the main form, create a subform from the **7J Itinerary** table. Change the subform's default view property to single form. Save the subform using the default name. Resize the subform so no scroll bars display. Remove the Host text box control and label control from the subform. Delete the subform label control. Adjust all label and text box controls to display all data. Add your first and last names to the form title, and place *7J SWG Employees* on a second line. Save the form. Create a paper or electronic printout of the first record of the form.

Using the **7J Itinerary Parameter Query**, create a report. Display the records by **7J Itinerary**, do not apply any grouping, and sort by **Arrive**. Display the report in Landscape orientation, and name the report **Lastname Firstname 7J Itinerary**. Add the **a07J_SWG_Logo**. Add an appropriate subtitle identifying the report and host by using the parameter in a report header text box control. Remove First Name from the report detail. Apply color in backgrounds, outlines, and fonts to create a well-formatted report. Resize the controls so all data displays on one page. Create an itinerary for each host—Andi and Lynda. If you are instructed to submit this result, create a paper or electronic printout of the reports for Andi and Lynda. Create a paper or electronic printout of the itinerary reports for each host.

Performance Criteria		Performance Element		
		Exemplary: You consistently applied the relevant skills	**Proficient:** You sometimes, but not always, applied the relevant skills	**Developing:** You rarely or never applied the relevant skills
	Create 7J Historical Gardens Split Form	Split Form created with correct fields and formatted as directed.	Split Form created with no more than two missing elements.	Split Form created with more than two missing elements.
	Create 7J SWG Employees Main Form/Host Itinerary Subform	Form created with correct fields and formatted as directed.	Form created with no more than two missing elements.	Form created with more than two missing elements.
	Create 7J Itinerary	Parameter report created and formatted correctly.	Parameter report created with no more than two missing elements.	Parameter report created with more than two missing elements.

End You have completed Project 7J

Content-Based Assessments

GO! Solve It | Project 7K Special Programming

Project Files

For Project 7K, you will need the following files:

a07K_Special_Programming
a07K_SWG_Logo
A new blank Word document

You will save your files as:

Lastname_Firstname_7K_Special_Programming
Lastname_Firstname_7K_Special_Programming_Tabs

Ruthann Hansen, president of JR Desert Productions, has scheduled special programming segments for the *Southwest Gardens* television show. These segments will focus on holiday and seasonal topics.

Open the **a07K_Special_Programming** database and save it as **Lastname_Firstname_7K_ Special_Programming** In this project, you will use the **7K TV Shows Form** to create a multi-page form. To the first tab, add the **TV Show #** and the **Original Air Date** fields with a caption of **Show** To the second tab, add the **Program**, **Subject**, and **Featured Garden** fields with a caption of **Programming** Adjust all controls to display all data. In the title, replace Lastname Firstname with your first and last names. Create a Microsoft Word document to show the contents of both tabs for **Record 15**. Save this document as **Lastname_Firstname_7K_Special_Programming_Tabs** If you are instructed to submit this result, create a paper or electronic printout of this document.

Open the **7K Special Programs** report in Design view. Add the **7K TV Show Advertisers** table as a subreport. Link the forms using the TV Show # field. Accept the default name for the subreport. Remove the TV Show # controls from the subreport and reduce the width to 3 inches. Delete the subreport label control. Add a logo and title to the report. Add your name in the Report Footer. Apply color in backgrounds, outlines, and fonts to create a well-formatted report. Save the report. If you are instructed to submit this result, create a paper or electronic printout of the report.

Create an alphabetical index on **7K Special Programs** using the Program field sorted in Ascending order. Format the text box controls containing the letters. Arrange and adjust label and text box controls to display all data. Save as **Lastname Firstname 7K Special Programming Index** If you are instructed to submit this result, create a paper or electronic printout of the report.

		Performance Element		
		Exemplary: You consistently applied the relevant skills	**Proficient:** You sometimes, but not always, applied the relevant skills	**Developing:** You rarely or never applied the relevant skills
Performance Criteria	Create 7K Special Programming Form	Form created with correct fields and formatted as directed.	Form created with no more than two missing elements.	Form created with more than two missing elements.
	Create 7K Special Programs Report	Report/subreport created and formatted correctly.	Report/subreport created with no more than two missing elements.	Report/subreport created with more than two missing elements.
	Create 7K Special Programming Index	Index created and formatted correctly.	Index created with no more than two missing elements.	Index created with more than two missing elements.

End You have completed Project 7K

Outcomes-Based Assessments

Rubric

The following outcomes-based assessments are *open-ended assessments*. That is, there is no specific correct result; your result will depend on your approach to the information provided. Make *Professional Quality* your goal. Use the following scoring rubric to guide you in *how* to approach the problem and then to evaluate *how well* your approach solves the problem.

The *criteria*—Software Mastery, Content, Format and Layout, and Process—represent the knowledge and skills you have gained that you can apply to solving the problem. The *levels of performance*—Professional Quality, Approaching Professional Quality, or Needs Quality Improvements—help you and your instructor evaluate your result.

	Your completed project is of Professional Quality if you:	Your completed project is Approaching Professional Quality if you:	Your completed project Needs Quality Improvements if you:
1-Software Mastery	Choose and apply the most appropriate skills, tools, and features and identify efficient methods to solve the problem.	Choose and apply some appropriate skills, tools, and features, but not in the most efficient manner.	Choose inappropriate skills, tools, or features, or are inefficient in solving the problem.
2-Content	Construct a solution that is clear and well organized, contains content that is accurate, appropriate to the audience and purpose, and is complete. Provide a solution that contains no errors in spelling, grammar, or style.	Construct a solution in which some components are unclear, poorly organized, inconsistent, or incomplete. Misjudge the needs of the audience. Have some errors in spelling, grammar, or style, but the errors do not detract from comprehension.	Construct a solution that is unclear, incomplete, or poorly organized; contains some inaccurate or inappropriate content; and contains many errors in spelling, grammar, or style. Do not solve the problem.
3-Format and Layout	Format and arrange all elements to communicate information and ideas, clarify function, illustrate relationships, and indicate relative importance.	Apply appropriate format and layout features to some elements, but not others. Overuse features, causing minor distraction.	Apply format and layout that does not communicate information or ideas clearly. Do not use format and layout features to clarify function, illustrate relationships, or indicate relative importance. Use available features excessively, causing distraction.
4-Process	Use an organized approach that integrates planning, development, self-assessment, revision, and reflection.	Demonstrate an organized approach in some areas, but not others; or, use an insufficient process of organization throughout.	Do not use an organized approach to solve the problem.

Outcomes-Based Assessments

GO! Think | Project **7L** Plants

Project Files

For Project 7L, you will need the following files:

a07L_Plants
a07L_SWG_Logo

You will save your database as:

Lastname_Firstname_7L_Plants

As a promotion for the *Southwest Gardens* television show, Ruthann Hansen, president of JR Desert Productions, is always looking for ways to increase the attendance of the live studio audience. She has decided to offer a featured plant to the guests in the audience.

Open the **a07L_Plants** database and save it as **Lastname_Firstname_7L_Plants** In this project, you will create a split form based on the **7L Flower/Plant** table. In the form, adjust label and text box controls to display all data. Delete the **Photo label control** and arrange the label and text box controls so that the first column contains the ID#, Photo, Common Name, and Scientific Name fields. The photo should align with the left edge of the text boxes in the first column. The second column should display the other four fields. Add the **a07L_SWG_Logo** to the form header. Edit the form title to include your first and last names. Select the option to print the form only. Save the form as **Lastname Firstname 7L Flower/Plant Split Form** If you are instructed to submit this result, create a paper or electronic printout of the form of record 1 only.

Open the **7L TV Shows Form** in Design view. Drag the **7L Historical Gardens** table to the design grid. Link Featured Garden to Garden Name. Drag the **7L Flower/Plant** table to the design grid to the right of the Historical Gardens subform. Link Featured Plant to ID#. Rename the form as **7L Shows and Flower/Plants Form** Open each of the subforms and change the Default View property to Single Form. Modify each of the subform label controls to be a descriptive title. Size the subforms to display all controls and eliminate any scroll bars. If you are instructed to submit this result, select record 1 of the main form. Create a paper or electronic printout of record 4 only.

End **You have completed Project 7L**

Outcomes-Based Assessments

GO! Think | Project **7M** Seminars

Project Files

For Project 7M, you will need the following files:

a07M_Seminars
a07M_SWG_Logo
A new blank Word document

You will save your files as:

Lastname_Firstname_7M_Seminars
Lastname_Firstname_7M_Tab_Control_Form

Ruthann Hansen, president of JR Desert Productions, has tasked three of her employees with the responsibility of researching and lecturing on various seminar topics. These seminars are held at the television studio from which the *Southwest Gardens* show is broadcasted.

In this project you will open the **a07M_Seminars** database and save it as **Lastname_Firstname_7M_Seminars** Using **7M Seminar and Lecturer**, you will create a multi-page form using fields from the **7M SWG Seminars** table and the **7M SWG Lecturer** table. Display the seminar information on the first tab (date and topic) and lecturer information on the second tab (full name and photo). Add appropriate captions to the tabs. Resize the tab control as necessary. Adjust all label and text box controls to display all data. Add the **a07M_SWG_Logo** and size the width to approximately 2 inches. Add a title that includes your first and last names. Save the form. Select the fifth record. Use the Office Clipboard and Microsoft Word to save a copy of both tabs of the form. Save this document as **Lastname_Firstname_7M_Tab_Control_Form** If you are instructed to submit this result, create a paper or electronic printout of the document.

Open the **7M SWG Lecturer** report. Drag the **7M Seminars** table into the Detail area. Remove the Lecturer controls, and resize the subreport to 4 inches wide. Delete the subreport label control. In the report title, replace Lastname Firstname with your name. In the subreport's Report Header, change the font color for the text boxes. Change the color of the outline to match. Save the report. Resize the report to 6.5 inches wide. If you are instructed to submit this result, create a paper or electronic printout of the report.

 You have completed Project 7M ——————————————

Outcomes-Based Assessments

You and GO! | Project **7N** Club Directory

Project Files

For Project 7N, you will need the following file:

Lastname_Firstname_6N_Club_Directory (your file from Chapter 6)

You will save your database as:

Lastname_Firstname_7N_Club_Directory

Create a personal database containing information about a club and its activities if you do not already have one from Project 4N. Name the new database **Lastname_Firstname_7N_Club_Directory** If you do not have the database from Project 6N, create two related tables, one that lists the activities your organization has planned and the other to serve as the directory of the group. The **Activities** table should include information about the name (primary key field), date, cost, and location of the activity. The dates must all occur next year, and consider attaching directions to the event to the table. The **Directory** table should include full name, address, phone number, email, and an activity they are planning. If you have the database from Project 6N, save as an Access 2007 Database in your Access Chapter 7 folder.

Create a split form from the **Directory** table. Be sure the datasheet displays on top and the Split Form Printing property is set to Form Only. Edit the title so it reads **Lastname Firstname Club Membership** and your Club Membership displays on a second line. Be sure all data is visible on the form; move the Split Form Splitter Bar as necessary. Apply a 2-pt outline to the label controls. Save the form as **Lastname Firstname 7N Membership Split Form** If you are instructed to submit this result, create a paper or electronic printout of the form for Record 3 only.

Create a report that includes all of the fields in the **Activity** table. Add the **Directory** table as a subreport below the main report. The title of the report should be **Membership Activity Report** Edit the date footer to include **Prepared by Firstname Lastname on** before the date. Be sure all data is visible in the report, and apply formatting as desired. Save the report as **Lastname Firstname 7N Membership Activity Report** If you are instructed to submit this result, create a paper or electronic printout of the report.

You will be using this database in future chapters. Be sure to make corrections to your tables as necessary to prepare for the next chapter.

End **You have completed Project 7N** ———————————————————

Creating Macros, PivotTables, and PivotCharts

OUTCOMES

At the end of this chapter you will be able to:

OBJECTIVES

Mastering these objectives will enable you to:

PROJECT 8A
Create and modify macros.

1. Create a Standalone Macro with One Action (p. 539)
2. Add Multiple Actions to a Standalone Macro (p. 546)
3. Create a Macro Group (p. 550)
4. Associate a Macro with an Event (p. 559)
5. Create an Embedded Macro (p. 562)
6. Print Macro Details (p. 564)

PROJECT 8B
Create and modify PivotTables and PivotCharts.

7. Create a PivotTable from a Query (p. 568)
8. Create a PivotChart from a PivotTable (p. 572)

Lorelyn Medina/Shutterstock

In This Chapter

Macros provide a way to automate tasks that you may need to perform repeatedly. For example, you may create a report or query that you open and print on a weekly basis. You can create a macro that prints the report when the user clicks a command button.

Data in tables, queries, or forms can be displayed as a PivotTable or PivotChart to provide a more analytical view of the data, like in Microsoft Excel. A PivotTable is used to organize, arrange, analyze, and summarize data in a meaningful way. A PivotChart is a graphical view of the data in a PivotTable. In both PivotTables and PivotCharts, you can rearrange the data to display it with different row and column headings to perform a different analysis of the data.

Providence and Warwick Hospital serves the metropolitan area of Providence, Rhode Island, and the surrounding cities of Warwick, Rhode Island, and Fall River, Massachusetts. It is a world-class medical facility providing care to adults and children through the hospital as well as a number of social service and multidisciplinary facilities, such as the Asthma Center and Adult Metabolism Clinic. Scientists at the hospital conduct research and clinical trials of new drugs. The hospital's medical staff focuses on innovation and new technologies to provide quality patient care to patients at every stage of life.

Project 8A Benefit Sessions

Project Activities

In Activities 8.01 through 8.10, you will help Margo Dalton, Vice President of Operations for Providence and Warwick Hospital, customize the database to display a form when the database is opened. She also wants to add buttons on the form to automate some of the most common tasks, such as displaying room information for an event or finding an event. You will create macros to automatically display a form and message box when an individual opens the database. You will associate command buttons with a macro, group macros, and embed macros within a form, in addition to creating conditions that control whether a macro runs. Finally, you will display and print a report that documents the details of the macros you created. When completed, your results will look similar to Figure 8.1.

Project Files

For Project 8A, you will need the following file:

a08A_Benefit_Sessions

You will save your database as:

Lastname_Firstname_8A_Benefit_Sessions

Project Results

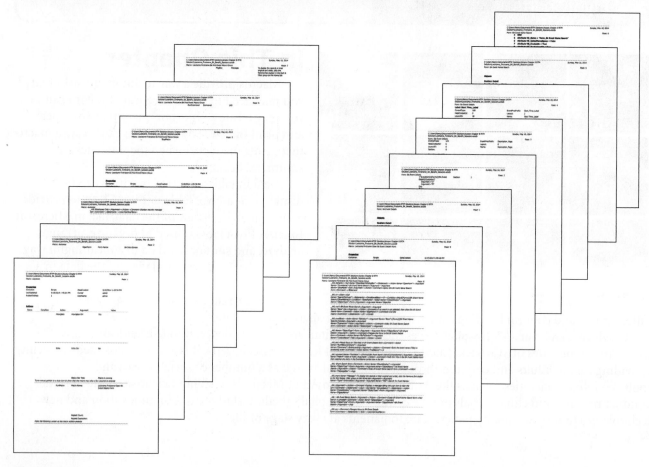

Figure 8.1
Project 8A Benefit Sessions

Objective 1 | Create a Standalone Macro with One Action

A *macro* is a series of actions grouped as a single command to accomplish a task or multiple tasks automatically. A *standalone macro* is an object displayed under Macros in the Navigation Pane. Some of the more commonly used actions are to open a report, find a record, or apply a filter to an object. An *action* is a self-contained instruction that can be combined with other actions to automate tasks.

Before creating a macro, you should list the actions you want to occur and in what order. You should determine if an argument applies to the action. An *argument* is a value that provides information to the action, such as the words to display in a message box. You should also determine if any conditions should be specified. A *condition* specifies that certain criteria must be met before the macro executes.

Activity 8.01 | Creating a Standalone Macro

In this activity, you will create a standalone macro that will display the *8A Event Details* form when the macro is run.

1 **Start** Access. Navigate to the location where the student data files for this textbook are saved. Locate and open the **a08A_Benefit_Sessions** file. Display **Backstage** view, and click **Save Database As**. In the **Save As** dialog box, navigate to the drive on which you will be saving your folders and projects for this chapter. Create a new folder named **Access Chapter 8** and save the database as **Lastname_Firstname_8A_Benefit_Sessions** in the folder.

2 If necessary, add the Access Chapter 8 folder to the Trust Center. In the Navigation Pane, under **Forms**, click **8A Event Details** to select the form.

> For this chapter, you must add the Access Chapter 8 folder to the Trust Center—you cannot just enable the content, because some of the macros need to be trusted and will not execute properly if the database is not trusted.

3 **Close** « the **Navigation Pane**.

4 On the Ribbon, click the **Create tab**. In the **Macros & Code group**, click the **Macro** button, and then compare your screen with Figure 8.2.

> The Macro Designer displays, which allows you to build the list of actions to be carried out when the macro runs. The Add New Action bar displays in the Macro Designer window, and the Action Catalog task pane displays on the right side of the screen. The buttons on the Macro Tools Design tab are used to run, test, or modify a macro; to expand or collapse actions; and to display panes in the Macro Designer or to display more actions.

Figure 8.2

Macro Tools Design tab ⎯

Action Catalog Pane ⎯

Add New Action bar ⎯

Macro Designer ⎯

5 In the **Macro Designer**, in the **Add New Action bar,** click the displayed **arrow**, and then compare your screen with Figure 8.3.

Because the Show All Actions button is not active, a shorter list of macro actions displays. These macro actions can be used in a database that is not trusted. You can click the Show All Actions button to display a longer list of macro actions; however, if the database is not trusted and you select a macro action that requires the database to be trusted, the macro will not execute, and a message box will display.

Figure 8.3

Button not active ⎯

List of trusted macro actions ⎯

6 Scroll down the displayed list, and then click **OpenForm** to display the **OpenForm Action Block**. Compare your screen with Figure 8.4.

Figure 8.4

OpenForm Action Block

Opens in Form view

Uses form properties

7 In the **Form Name** box, click the displayed **arrow**, and then click **8A Event Details**.

This is a required argument.

8 In the **View** box, click the **arrow**. Notice that you can open the form in Form view, Design view, Print Preview, Datasheet view, PivotTable view, PivotChart view, or Layout view. Be sure that **Form** is selected.

The OpenForm action opens a form in Form view by default.

9 Point to the **Filter Name** box until the ScreenTip appears; read the description. Repeat the process in the **Where Condition** box and the **Data Mode** box. Be sure that these arguments are left blank.

The Data Mode argument is used for forms that open in either Form view or Datasheet view. If left blank, Access opens the form in the data entry mode set in the form's Allow Edits, Allow Deletions, Allow Additions, and Data Entry property settings

10 Point to the **Window Mode** box, and then read the description. Click the arrow, and notice the options for displaying the form. Be sure that Window Mode setting is **Normal**.

Access | Chapter 8

11 In the **Action Catalog pane**, under **Program Flow**, double-click **Comment**. In the **Comment text box** that displays below the **OpenForm Action Block**, type **Displays the 8A Event Details form when the macro is run** Compare your screen with Figure 8.5.

You should always enter a description of a macro so that you and others can determine easily the actions that will occur when the macro runs. A green arrow displays to the right of the Comments dialog box. Click it to move the comment above the action arguments.

Figure 8.5

Arguments left blank in Action Block

Comment

12 On the **Design** tab, in the **Tools** group, click the **Run** button.

A message displays stating that you must save the macro before you run it.

13 In the displayed message box, click **Yes** to save the macro. In the **Save As** dialog box, type **Lastname Firstname Open 8A Event Details Form** and then click **OK**.

The macro is saved and runs. When the macro runs, it displays the *8A Event Details* form.

14 **Close** ☒ the **8A Event Details** form, and then **Close** ☒ the Macro Designer. **Open** ⟫ the **Navigation Pane**, and then compare your screen with Figure 8.6.

In the Navigation Pane, a new group—Macros—displays, and the newly created macro object displays under the group name.

Figure 8.6

Macro group

Macro object

15 In the **Navigation Pane**, under **Macros**, double-click **Open 8A Event Details Form**.

Double-clicking a macro object causes the macro to run.

16 Close ☒ the form.

Activity 8.02 │ Opening a Form in Its Own Window

In this activity, you will modify the properties of a form to create a pop-up, modal window. A **pop-up window** displays (pops up), usually contains a menu of commands, and stays on the screen until the user selects one of the commands. A **modal window** is a child (secondary window) to a parent window—the original window that opened the modal window—that takes over control of the parent window. A user cannot press any controls or enter any information in the parent window until the modal window is closed. Both pop-up and modal windows are commonly used when the database designer wants to direct a user's focus to the information in the window.

1 In the **Navigation Pane**, under **Forms**, double-click **8A Intro Screen** to open the form in **Form** view.

Like most of the objects you have opened, the form displays with its own tab.

2 Switch to **Design** view. On the **Design tab**, in the **Tools group**, click the **Property Sheet** button. If the Property Sheet does not display *Selection type: Form*, click the Selection type arrow, and then click Form.

3 On the **Property Sheet**, click the **Other tab**. Click the **Pop Up property setting arrow**, and then click **Yes**. Click in the **Modal property setting box**, click the **arrow**, and then click **Yes**. Compare your screen with Figure 8.7.

The Pop Up property setting of Yes displays the object in its own window on top of all other opened objects. A setting of No displays the object as a tabbed object. Changing the Pop Up setting to Yes is most common for objects that you want to get the attention of the individual using the database. The Modal property setting is used to keep the focus on the opened form, since you cannot change the focus to another database object until the form is closed.

Figure 8.7

Pop Up property setting changed

Property sheet for form

Modal property setting changed

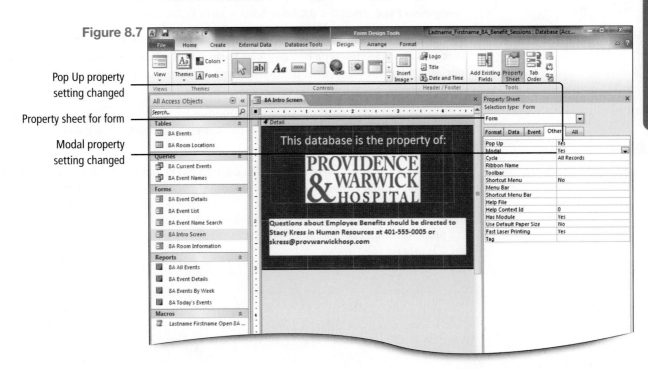

4 **Close** the **Property Sheet**, and then **Close** the form, saving changes when prompted. In the **Navigation Pane**, under **Macros**, double-click **Open 8A Event Details Form**, and then under **Forms**, double-click **8A Intro Screen** to open both forms in Form view. Notice the text in the title bar of the pop-up window. In the **Navigation Pane**, under **Forms**, double-click **8A Room Information**, and notice that the form does not open. Compare your screen with Figure 8.8.

8A Event Details opens as a tabbed object, and *8A Intro Screen* opens in its own pop-up window. The pop-up window can be moved or closed. Until it is closed, the focus cannot be changed to another database object; that is why you cannot open the *8A Room Information* form. The *8A Intro Screen* form does not display Minimize or Maximize buttons, only a Close button because the Modal property setting is Yes. A Modal property setting of No can display the Minimize and Maximize buttons.

Figure 8.8

Focus on 8A Intro Screen form

Close button

Pop-up window

5 **Close** the **8A Intro Screen form**, and then **Close** the **8A Event Details form**. In the **Navigation Pane**, open the **8A Intro Screen** form in **Design** view.

6 On the **Design** tab, in the **Tools** group, click the **Property Sheet** button, if necessary. Be sure that the **Selection type** box displays **Form**. On the **Property Sheet**, click the **Format** tab, and then take a moment to review some of the property settings for this form while comparing your screen with Figure 8.9.

The text entered in the Caption property displays on the title bar of the form when in Form view. The Allow Form View property setting is Yes, while all of the other views are disabled.

The Border Style property setting is Dialog, which is a thick border that can include a title bar with a Close button. The form cannot be resized, maximized, or minimized with this border style. Because this is a custom form that does not display any records from an underlying table or query, the Record Selectors, Navigation Buttons, and Scroll Bars property settings have been set to No.

Figure 8.9

Text displayed in title bar of form

Will only display in Form view

Border style

No record selector box, navigation buttons, or scroll bars

7 **Close** the **Property Sheet**, **Close** the form, and then **Close** « the **Navigation Pane**.

Activity 8.03 | Creating a Second Standalone Macro that Executes Automatically

In this activity, you will create another standalone macro that will open the *8A Intro Screen* form when the database is opened.

1 On the Ribbon, click the **Create tab**. In the **Macros & Code group**, click the **Macro button** to display the **Macro Designer**.

2 In the **Macro Designer**, in the **Add New Action bar**, click the **arrow**, scroll down, and then click **OpenForm**. In the **OpenForm Action Block**, click the **Form Name arrow**, and then click **8A Intro Screen**.

3 If necessary, on the **Design tab**, in the **Show/Hide group**, click the **Action Catalog** button to display the **Action Catalog pane**. In the **Action Catalog pane**, double-click **Comment**, and then type **Opens the 8A Intro Screen form** Compare your screen with Figure 8.10.

Figure 8.10

Action

Form that will be opened when macro runs

Description of the macro (Comment)

Access | Chapter 8

4 On the **Quick Access Toolbar**, click the **Save** 🔲 button. In the **Save As** dialog box, type **Autoexec** and then click **OK**.

> When a macro is named *Autoexec*, Access automatically runs or executes the macro each time the database is opened. There can be only one macro in a database named *Autoexec*.

5 **Close** the Macro Designer, and then **Open** 〉〉 the **Navigation Pane**. Notice that in the Navigation Pane, under **Macros**, **Autoexec** displays. Double-click **Autoexec** to run the macro.

> The *8A Intro Screen* form displays in its own pop-up, modal window.

6 **Close** the form. Display **Backstage** view, and then click **Close Database**. In **Backstage** view, click **Recent**, and then click **8A_Benefit_Sessions**.

> The macro automatically executes or runs when the *8A_Benefit_Sessions* database opens, and it displays the pop-up, modal *8A Intro Screen* form. Because this is a trusted macro action, the macro will execute even if the database has not been trusted or the content enabled.

7 **Close** the form.

Objective 2 | Add Multiple Actions to a Standalone Macro

In the previous activities, you created two macros that each contained only one action—opening a form. A macro can contain multiple actions that are executed in a specified order. For example, you can display a busy icon as the macro executes, which is especially useful for macros with multiple actions, to let the user know that Access is working on a process. This can be followed by an action that runs another standalone macro—for example, opening a form. And then you can select the title bar on the form, maximize the form, and then turn off the busy icon.

Activity 8.04 | Adding Multiple Actions to an Existing Standalone Macro

In this activity, you will modify the *Autoexec* macro and add more actions to the macro.

1 In the **Navigation Pane**, under **Macros**, right-click **Autoexec**, and then click **Design View**. **Close** 〈〈 the **Navigation Pane**.

2 In the **Action Catalog pane**, click in the **Search box**, and then type **dis** Under **System Commands**, double-click **DisplayHourglassPointer** to display the **DisplayHourglassPointer Action Block**. Notice that the default argument is *Yes*.

> When you search for an action using the Action Catalog pane, a description of the macro selected appears at the bottom of the pane. The Hourglass action changes the normal pointer to a busy icon to inform the user that some action is taking place. On a slower computer, the icon will keep the user from thinking that something is wrong with the database. If the computer is fast, the busy icon may not display. When the macro finishes running, the normal mouse pointer displays.

3 Click inside the **Add New Action bar**, type **'Turns mouse pointer to a busy icon to show that the macro may take a few seconds to execute** and then press Enter.

> Typing a single quote before the comment identifies the text that follows as a comment. The Comment block displays after you press Enter.

4 On the **Design** tab, in the **Show/Hide** group, click the **Show All Actions** button.

Recall that the default list of macros displays only trusted macro actions. The next macro action that you will add to the macro is not a trusted macro action. For the macro to execute properly, you must add the location of the database to Trusted Locations or enable the content. Because this macro is used to open a pop-up, modal window, the database location must be trusted. The modal form will open automatically when the database is opened, and you cannot enable the content until the form is closed.

5 In the **Action Catalog pane**, click in the **Search box**, and then replace any existing text with **ech** Under **Macro Commands**, double-click **Echo**. In the **Echo Action Block**, click **arrow** in the **Echo On** box, and then click **No**. Click in the **Status Bar Text** box, and type **Macro is running** Click inside the **Add New Action bar** and type **'Hides the flickering screen as the macro actions execute** and then press Enter. Compare your screen with Figure 8.11.

The Echo macro action hides or displays the results of the macro while it runs. Changing the Echo On argument to *No* hides the results. The Status Bar Text argument displays text on the status bar while the macro is running with Echo On set to No. The icon that displays in the Action Argument box indicates that the macro action is not safe.

Figure 8.11

Macro action is not trusted

Does not display results of macro while it runs

Text that displays in status bar while macro is running

6 In the **Action Catalog pane**, click in the **Search box**, and then replace any existing text with **Run** Under **Macro Commands**, double-click **RunMacro**.

The RunMacro action is used to run a macro from within another macro.

7 In the **RunMacro Action Arguments block**, click the **Macro Name box arrow**, and then click **Open 8A Event Details Form**. Point to the **Repeat Count** box, and then read the description. Point to the **Repeat Expression** box, and then read the description.

The Repeat Count and Repeat Expression action arguments are used when the macro should be run more than one time. Left blank, the macro will run only one time.

8 Click inside the **Add New Action bar**, type **'Opens the 8A Event Details form** and then press Enter.

9 In the **Action Catalog pane**, click in the **Search box**, and then replace any existing text with **mes** Under **User Interface Commands**, double-click **MessageBox**.

The MessageBox macro action is a trusted action that displays a message box that contains a warning or informational message.

10 In the **Action Arguments** box, click in the **Message** box, and then type **Only employees of Providence & Warwick Hospital are authorized to access this database. Unauthorized use will result in legal action.**

11 Point to the **Beep** box, and read the description of the Beep argument. Be sure that the Beep argument is **Yes**. Click the **Type arrow**, and then click **Warning!** Read the description of the **Type** argument and the different settings. Click in the **Title** box, read the description of the argument, and then type **For Use by Providence & Warwick Hospital Employees Only!**

> The MessageBox macro action can contain up to four arguments.

12 Click inside the **Add New Action bar**, type **'Displays a security message box** and press Enter.

13 Scroll to the top of the **Designer window**. Click the **OpenForm** action to make it active. Click the green down-pointing arrow at the right of the title two times to move the action below the **DisplayHourglassPointer** action. (Be sure to click twice, not double-click.) Click the green down-pointing arrow in the **OpenForm** action box five more times or until it appears below the comment *Opens the 8A Event Details Form*. Alternatively, you can point to the edge of the Action or Comment blocks and drag them to a new position. Compare your screen with Figure 8.12.

> When you point to the top edge of an Action or Comment block to move it, the mouse pointer does not change in appearance. As you drag the box, an orange line will appear at positions where the box can be dropped.

Figure 8.12

OpenForm macro moved below *Opens 8A Event Details form* comment

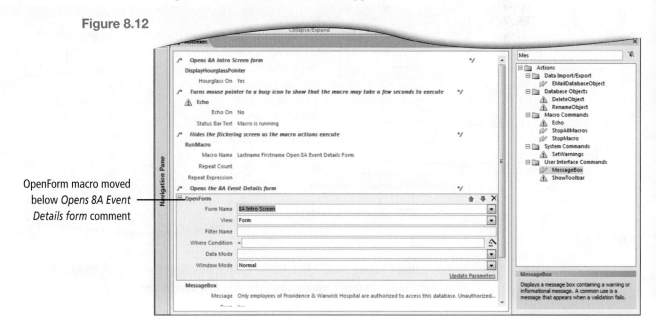

14 Click the green down-pointing arrow to the right of the **OpenForm macro comment** until you move it below the **OpenForm macro action**.

15 In the **Action Catalog pane**, click in the **Search box**, and then replace any existing text with **Dis** Under **System Commands**, double-click **DisplayHourglassPointer**. In the **Action Arguments box**, click the **Hourglass On arrow**, and then click **No**. Click inside the **Add New Action bar**, type **'Restores the normal mouse pointer** and then press Enter.

> The normal mouse pointer will be displayed to let the user know that the macro is finished executing.

16 In the **Action Catalog pane**, click in the **Search box**, and then replace any existing text with **Ech** Under **Macro Commands**, double-click **Echo**. Notice that in the **Action Block**, in the **Echo On** box, the setting is **Yes**. Click inside the **Add New Action bar**, type **'Displays screen results** and then press Enter.

Screen actions will no longer be hidden from the individual using the database.

> **Note** | Turning Off Macro Actions
>
> Access automatically restores Hourglass and Echo to the default settings after a macro has finished running to protect inexperienced macro programmers from causing the system to continue displaying the hourglass icon, which might lead the user to think that the database is operating incorrectly or is frozen. Even though Access restores these settings, it is good practice to always restore what you turn off. This will lead to better coding if you write Visual Basic code to execute commands.

17 On the **Quick Access Toolbar**, click the **Save** 🖫 button. On the **Design tab**, in the **Tools group**, click the **Run** button. Point to the Access window title bar, and then compare your screen with Figure 8.13.

Access does not always wait for one action to complete before going on to the next action. Notice that the *8A Event Details* form is not yet open; however, the *8A Intro Screen* is open with a message box displayed on top of it. A beep sounded when the message box displayed. The hourglass displays, and the status bar displays *Macro is running*.

Figure 8.13

8A Intro Screen form

Macro Designer

Busy (Display Hourglass action)

Message box

Status bar message

> **Alert!** | Did a Message Box Display?
>
> If a message box displays stating that *The 'Echo' macro action cannot be run in disabled mode*, you did not add the Access Chapter 8 folder to Trust Center. The Echo macro action is not trusted by default. To correct this, click OK, click Stop All Macros, and then add the Access Chapter 8 folder to the Trust Center.

18 In the displayed message box, click **OK**. The **8A Event Details** form displays underneath the **8A Intro Screen** form. **Close** the **8A Intro Screen** form. On the **tab row**, right-click any tab, and then click **Close All**.

19 Display **Backstage** view, and then click **Close Database**. Click **Recent**, and then click **8A_Benefit_Sessions**.

> The Autoexec macro automatically executes or runs when the *8A_Benefit_Sessions* database opens, and it displays the pop-up, modal *8A Intro Screen* form with the message box on top of it.

20 In the displayed message box, click **OK**. **Close** the **8A Intro Screen form**, and then **Close** the **8A Event Details form**. Open ⟩⟩ the **Navigation Pane**.

More Knowledge | Debugging a Macro

Debugging is using a logical process to find and reduce the number of errors in a program. To debug a macro, you can use *single stepping*, which executes one action at a time. Single stepping allows you to observe the results of each macro action to isolate an action that may be causing an error or producing unwanted results.

To single step through a macro, open the macro in Design view. On the Design tab, in the Tools group, click the Single Step button. In the Tools group, click the Run button. The Macro Single Step dialog box displays information about the macro, including the macro name, the condition, the action name, the arguments, and an error number. An error number of 0 indicates that no error has occurred. In this dialog box, you can carry out the macro action by clicking Step. You can stop the macro and close the dialog box by clicking Stop All Macros, or you can turn off single stepping and run the rest of the macro by clicking Continue.

When the macro has fully executed, be sure to turn off single stepping on the Design tab in the Tools group by clicking the Single Step button.

Objective 3 | Create a Macro Group

In the previous activities, you created a standalone macro with one action and another standalone macro with multiple actions. As you continue to create more macros, you may want to group related macros by creating a *macro group*. A macro group is a set of submacros grouped by a common name that displays as one macro object in the Navigation Pane. For example, you might want to create a macro group that opens several forms or reports in a database.

Activity 8.05 | Creating the First Macro in a Macro Group

In this activity, you will create the first macro in the macro group that will open the *8A Event Name Search Dialog Box* form.

1 In the **Navigation Pane**, under **Forms**, double-click **8A Event Details**, and then double-click **8A Event Name Search Dialog Box** to open the forms in **Form** view. Point to the title bar of the **Event Name Search Dialog Box**, and then drag the pop-up form downward and to the right until, on the **8A Event Details** form, the buttons under the title display. Compare your screen with Figure 8.14.

> In this activity, you will create a macro group that executes and opens the *8A Event Name Search Dialog Box* form when a user clicks on the Find Event button on the *8A Event Details* form.

Figure 8.14

Button to open the Event Name Search box

8A Event Name Search Dialog Box

2 **Close** the **Event Name Search dialog box**, and then **Close** the **8A Event Details form**. **Close** ⟪ the **Navigation Pane**.

3 On the Ribbon, click the **Create tab**. In the **Macros & Code group**, click the **Macro button**. On the **Design tab**, in the **Show/Hide group**, click the **Show All Actions** button.

Recall that the Show All Actions button displays trusted and untrusted macro actions

4 If necessary, in the **Action Catalog**, click the **Clear Filter** button to the right of the Search box to delete the entry. Double-click **Group** in the **Action Catalog pane**. In the **Macro Designer**, in the **Group** box, type **8A Find Event Macro Group** to identify the group. Using one of the techniques you have learned, add the following comment: **Purpose: To enable the user to search for a specific event in the 8A Event Details form**

It is a good practice to start a macro group with a name and a description of the macro group's purpose.

5 In the **Action Catalog pane**, double-click **Submacro** and type **OpenSearchDialogBox**

In macro groups, submacro names are needed to distinguish the individual macros from one another. Within a macro group, the submacro name is entered before the macro actions in each submacro. The macro ends when *end submacro* is encountered. Macro names are limited to 64 characters. Because macros perform an action or actions, it is good practice to start the name of the macro with a verb—in this case, Open.

6 In the **Submacro**, using one of the techniques you have learned, add an **OpenForm** action. In the **OpenForm Action Block**, click the **Form Name arrow**, and then click **8A Event Name Search Dialog Box**. Click the **Data Mode arrow**, and then click **Edit**. Add the following comment: **Opens the 8A Event Name Search Dialog Box form** Compare your screen with Figure 8.15.

Editing is enabled so that the user can enter an event name in the combo box on the *8A Event Name Search Dialog Box* form. Because the form property has been set to open as a pop-up window, the Window Mode setting of Normal is appropriate.

Figure 8.15

Description of macro group

First macro

Form opened by macro action

Editing enabled on the form

7 Save 💾 the macro group as **Lastname Firstname 8A Find Event Macro Group**

8 On the **Database Tools tab**, in the **Macro group**, click the **Run Macro** button, and then, in the **Macro Name** list, click **8A Find Event Macro Group.OpenSearchDialogBox**. In the **RunMacro** dialog box, click **OK**. **Close** the form.

> Because the macro is associated with a Macro group, it must be run using the Run Macro button on the Database Tools tab. Keep in mind that some macro actions are dependent upon other macro actions that have previously executed, and independently, a macro action may not execute properly if run out of order.

Activity 8.06 | Creating a Second Macro in a Macro Group

In this activity, you will create a second macro in the macro group that will check to see if a value is entered for the event name in the *8A Event Name Search Dialog Box*, hide the *8A Event Name Search Dialog Box* form, change the focus to the *8A Event Details* form, select the title of the event on the *8A Event Details* form, sort the records by the event name, find the requested event, close the *8A Event Name Search Dialog Box* form, and display a message to the user with a reminder to display all of the records.

1 In the **Macro Designer**, double-click **Submacro** in the **Action Catalog pane**, and type **SearchForEvent** In the **Action Catalog pane**, double-click **If**.

> The If Action Argument pane displays in the SearchForEvent submacro to control the program flow. In some macros, an action should execute only if a condition is true. For example, if the user does not select a value in the combo box on the *8A Event Name Search Dialog Box* form, the macro should not execute.

2 In the **Submacro**, to the right of the **If** textbox, click the **Build** 📐 button. In the **Expression Builder** dialog box, type **IsNull([Forms]![8A Event Name Search]![EventName])** selecting items as they appear in the list to reduce errors. Compare your screen with Figure 8.16.

> The expression used for the condition checks the EventName combo box in the *8A Event Name Search Dialog Box* form to determine if the combo box is blank—IsNull. Recall that the exclamation (!) mark is the bang operator that separates the object type from the object name.

Figure 8.16

Expression used for condition

Bang operator

Macro name

Conditional action

---

3 In the **Expression Builder** dialog box, click **OK**. In the **If Arguments block**, add the **CloseWindow** action using one of the techniques you have learned. In the **Close Window Action Block**, click the **Object Type arrow**, and then click **Form**. Click the **Object Name arrow**, and then click **8A Event Name Search Dialog Box**. Click the **Save arrow**, and then click **No**. Add the following comment: **If an event is not selected, then close the 8A Event Name Search Dialog Box form**

> If Access finds that the EventName combo box is blank, it will close the *8A Event Name Search Dialog Box* form without saving changes made to the form. Recall that the warning symbol in the row selector box indicates that this Macro Action is not trusted.

4 In the **If Arguments block**, add the **StopMacro** action. Notice that there are no action arguments for the StopMacro action. Add the following comment: **Exit the macro**

> If the EventName combo box is blank, and the form closes, the macro stops executing.

5 In the **Macro Designer**, click the **Submacro:SearchForEvent** textbox to activate the **Add New Action bar** below the **End If** label. If necessary, click the **Show All Actions** button in the **Show/Hide** group on the **Design tab**. Add the **SetValue** action. In the **Set Value Action Block**, to the right of the **Item** textbox, click the **Build** button to open the **Expression Builder**. Compare your screen with Figure 8.17.

> The SetValue macro action is an untrusted action used to set the value of a field, control, or property on a form, a form datasheet, or a report. The item is the name of the field, control, or property whose value you want to set. You must use the full *syntax* to refer to the item—do not just type the field, control, or property name. Syntax refers to the spelling, grammar, and sequence of characters of a programming language.

> The operator buttons and list boxes in the Expression Builder can help you build the expression using correct syntax. As you select an object in the first list box, the second and third list boxes will populate. In the first list box, the plus sign (+) next to an object indicates that more items display under the object; click the plus sign (+) or double-click the object name to expand the list. The minus sign (–) indicates that the list under the object is fully expanded. Click the minus sign (–) or double-click the object name to collapse the list.

Figure 8.17

Expression Builder

Click to display subitems

First list box

Second list box

Third list box

Alert! | **Did the SetValue Action Appear Before the End If Label?**

If the SetValue action appears before the End If label, you didn't click the Submacro SearchForEvent Action block before adding the new action. To correct this, move the SetValue action below the End If label using either technique practiced in the chapter.

6 In the **Expression Builder** dialog box, in the **Expression Elements** list box, click the plus sign to the left of **Lastname_Firstname_8A_Benefit_Sessions.accdb** to display the list of objects in the database—use the horizontal scroll bar to display the entire name of the database. Double-click **Forms** to expand the list, and double-click **All Forms**. Scroll down, and then click **8A Event Name Search Dialog Box**—use the horizontal scroll bar to display the entire name of the form.

The Expression Categories list box displays controls on the form. The Expression Values list box displays property settings and events that can be associated with the form or the controls on the form. An *event* is any action that can be detected by a program or computer system, such as clicking a button or closing an object. Selecting an object in the Expression Categories list box causes the values or events in the Expression Values list box to change, because different objects have different property settings or events associated with them.

7 In the **Expression Categories** list box, be sure that <**Form**> is selected. In the **Expression Values** list box, scroll down, double-click **Visible**, and then compare your screen with Figure 8.18.

The Expression Builder displays the correct syntax for the Visible property of the *8A Event Name Search Dialog Box*, which is a form. Instead of using the Expression Builder, you can type the expression in the Item box in the Action Block. An advantage of using the Expression Builder is that Access will insert square brackets and parentheses where they are required.

Figure 8.18

Square brackets required because of spaces in form name

Type of object

Object name

Property of object

8 In the **Expression Builder**, click **OK**. In the **Set Value Action Block**, click in the **Expression box**, and then type **False**

This macro action sets the Visible property setting of the *8A Event Name Search Dialog Box* form to false; in other words, it will hide the *8A Event Name Search Dialog Box* form.

9 Add the following comment: **Hides 8A Event Name Search Dialog Box form** Compare your screen with Figure 8.19.

Figure 8.19

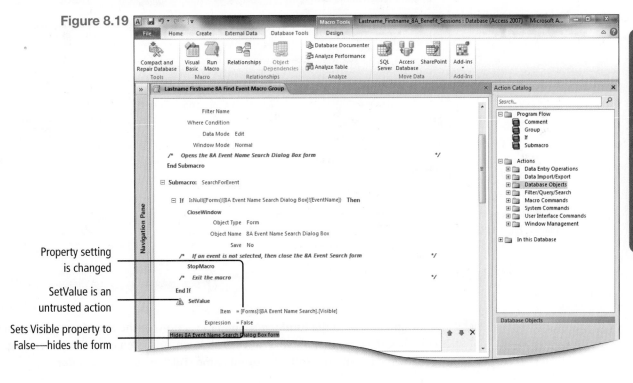

Property setting is changed

SetValue is an untrusted action

Sets Visible property to False—hides the form

Access | Chapter 8

10 In the **Submacro**, add the **SelectObject** action. In the **SelectObject Action Block**, click the **Object Type arrow**, and then click **Form**. Click the **Object Name arrow**, and then click **8A Event Details**. Be sure that the **In Database Window** box displays **No**. Add the following comment: **Changes the focus to the 8A Event Details form**

> The SelectObject action is used to put the focus on a specified database object so that an action can be applied to that object. Recall that the *8A Event Details* form is automatically opened when the database is opened. Therefore, the In Database Window setting should be set to No. If the form is not open, Access needs to open it from the Navigation Pane, and the In Database Window setting should be set to Yes.

> So far, the macro group will open the *8A Event Name Search Dialog Box* form and then check to see if the EventName field displays data. If not, the macro stops executing. If data is displayed in the EventName field, the *8A Event Name Search Dialog Box* form will be hidden, and the focus will shift to the *8A Event Details* form.

11 In the **Submacro**, add the **GoToControl** action. In the **GoToControl Action Block**, in the **Control Name** box, type **Title** Add the following comment: **Places focus on Title field on 8A Event Details form** Compare your screen with Figure 8.20.

> In the previous action, the focus was changed to the *8A Event Details* form. With this action, the focus is placed on a specific text box control named *Title* on that form.

Figure 8.20

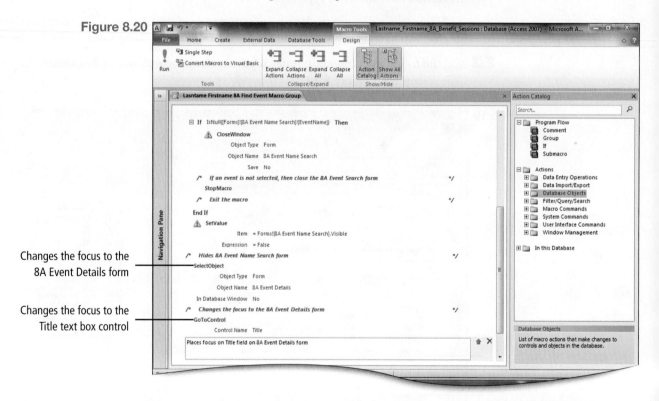

Changes the focus to the 8A Event Details form

Changes the focus to the Title text box control

12 In the **Submacro**, add the **RunMenuCommand** action. In the **RunMenuCommand Action Block**, click the **Command** box **arrow**, scroll down, and then click **SortAscending**. Add the following comment: **Sorts the event name (Title) in ascending order**

> The RunCommand action is used to execute an Access command, such as Sort Ascending or Save a Record.

13 In the **Submacro**, add the **FindRecord** action. In the **FindWhat** box, type **=[Forms]![8A Event Name Search Dialog Box]![EventName]** selecting items as they appear in the list to reduce errors Be sure that you have entered the expression correctly. Click the **Match box arrow**, and then click **Start of Field**. Point to each of the other Action Arguments boxes, reading the description of each argument and being sure not to change any of the settings. Add the following comment: **Finds the Title in the 8A Event Details form that matches the entry in the EventName combo box in the 8A Event Name Search Dialog Box form** and then compare your screen with Figure 8.21.

The FindRecord action locates the first or next record that meets the specified search criteria; in this case, the data in the EventName field of the *8A Event Name Search Dialog Box* form must match the data in the Title field of the *8A Event Details* form. This macro action is similar to using the Find button on the Home tab.

Figure 8.21

FindRecord macro action

Search criteria

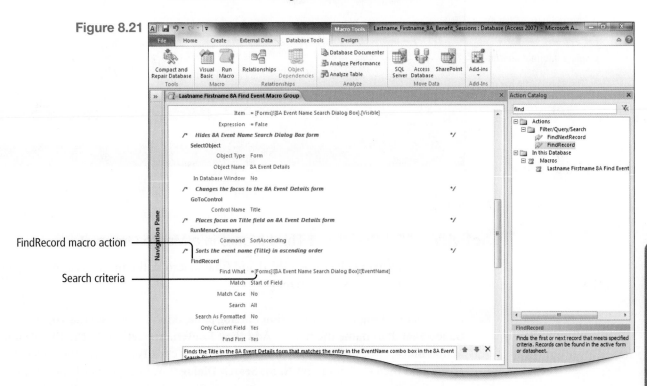

14 In the **Submacro**, add the **CloseWindow** action. In the **CloseWindow Action Block**, click the **Object Type arrow**, and then click **Form**. Click the **Object Name arrow**, and then click **8A Event Name Search Dialog Box**. Be sure **Prompt** appears in the **Save** box. Add the following comment: **Closes 8A Event Name Search form**

The Close action closes a specified object. If no object is specified in the Object Name box, the active object is closed.

15 In the **Submacro**, add the **MessageBox** action. In the **MessageBox Action Block**, click in the **Message** box, and then type **To display the records in their original sort order, on the Home tab, in the Sort & Filter group, click the Remove Sort button** Click the **Type** box arrow, and then click **Information**. Click in the **Title** box, and then type **Search for Event Name** Add the following comment: **Displays a message telling the user how to clear the sort** Compare your screen with Figure 8.22.

Recall that if an individual filters or sorts records and closes the database, when the database is reopened, the filter or sort is still applied to the object.

Access | Chapter 8

Figure 8.22

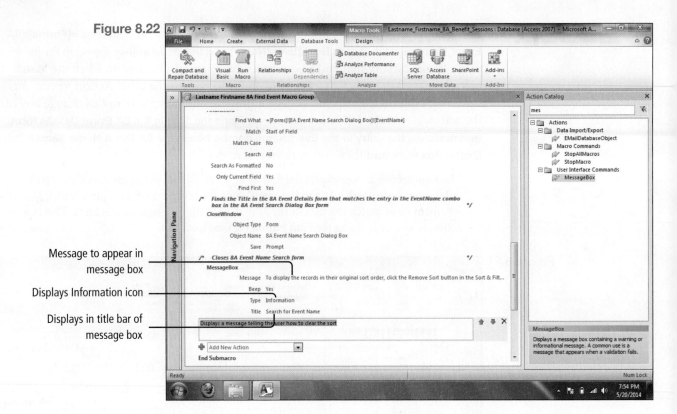

Message to appear in message box

Displays Information icon

Displays in title bar of message box

16 Save 🖫 the macro group.

Activity 8.07 │ Creating a Third Macro in a Macro Group

In this activity, you will create a third and final macro in the macro group that will close the *8A Event Name Search* form.

1 In the **Macro Designer**, in the **Action Catalog pane**, double-click **Submacro**, and type **CancelSearch** to name the macro. Add the **CloseWindow** action. In the **CloseWindow Action Block**, click the **Object Type arrow**, and then click **Form**. Click the **Object Name arrow**, and then click **8A Event Name Search Dialog Box**. Be sure that **Prompt** appears in the **Save** box. Add the following comment: **Closes 8A Event Name Search Dialog Box form when search is canceled**

> This macro will be used to close the *8A Event Name Search Dialog Box* form when the Cancel button on the form is clicked.

2 In the **Submacro**, add the **SelectObject** action. In the **SelectObject Action Block**, click the **Object Type arrow**, and then click **Form**. Click the **Object Name arrow**, and then click **8A Event Details**. Be sure that the **In Database Window** box displays **No**. Add the following comment: **Changes the focus to 8A Event Details form** Compare your screen with Figure 8.23.

> After the *8A Event Name Search Dialog Box* form is closed, the focus is placed on the *8A Event Details* form.

Figure 8.23

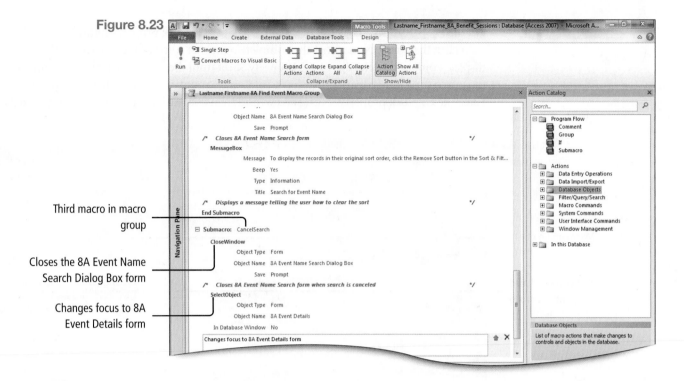

Third macro in macro group

Closes the 8A Event Name Search Dialog Box form

Changes focus to 8A Event Details form

3 **Save** 💾 the macro group. **Close** the Macro Designer, **Open** » the **Navigation Pane**, and notice that under **Macros**, the macro group displays as one macro object.

Double-clicking the macro does not cause this macro to execute because the macro has not been associated with the buttons on the *8A Event Details* form or the *8A Event Name Search Dialog Box* form.

Objective 4 | Associate a Macro with an Event

Recall that an event is any action that can be detected by a program or computer system, such as clicking a button or closing an object. For example, clicking the Find Event button on the *8A Event Details* form causes a system event, upon which Access can execute a macro.

Activity 8.08 | Associating a Command Button with a Macro

In this activity, you will associate clicking the Find Event button on the *8A Event Details* form with a macro—the *8A Find Event Macro Group* macro. Clicking the Find Event button will cause the macro to execute.

1 In the **Navigation Pane**, under **Forms**, double-click **8A Event Details** to display the form in **Form** view. On the form, click the **Find Event** button, and notice that nothing happens because the button is not associated with any event.

2 **Close** « the **Navigation Pane**, and then switch the form to **Design** view. In the **Form Header section**, right-click the **Find Event** button, and then click **Properties**. Be sure that the **Property Sheet** displays *Selection type: Command button* and that the **Selection type** box displays *cmdFindEvent*.

3 On the **Property Sheet**, click the **Event tab**. Click the **On Click** property setting box, and then click the **arrow**. Notice that the complete names of some of the macros do not display. Point to the **left edge** of the **Property Sheet** until the ⟷ pointer displays. Drag to the left to the **4.5-inch mark on the horizontal ruler** or until the complete names display. Click the **On Click** property setting **arrow**, and then compare your screen with Figure 8.24.

All of the macros that have been created display in the list.

Figure 8.24

Property sheet widened

Macro group object

Macros included
in Macro group

4 In the displayed list, click **8A Find Event Macro Group.OpenSearchDialogBox**.

When you click on the Find Event button in the *8A Event Details* form, the OpenSearchDialogBox macro in the *8A Find Event Macro Group* will execute.

5 On the **Property Sheet**, click the **Format tab**. In the **Caption** property setting box, click to the left of **Find Event**, and then type **&**

The ampersand (&) causes the letter that follows it to be underlined on the button, which will enable the user to use a shortcut key combination to access the button instead of clicking on the button. The user presses [Alt] + the letter to activate the button. For this button, the shortcut is [Alt] + [F].

6 Close the **Property Sheet**, **Save** 🖫 the form, and then switch to **Form** view. Notice that on the **Find Event** button, the letter **F** is underscored, which indicates that pressing [Alt] + [F] is the same action as clicking on the button.

7 Click the **Find Event** button, and then compare your screen with Figure 8.25.

The Event Name Search dialog box displays, which is the *8A Event Name Search Dialog Box* form.

Figure 8.25

Shortcut key indicator

8A Event Name Search
Dialog Box

8 **Close** the **Event Name Search** dialog box. Press ⎇Alt + ⓕF. Notice that the **Event Name Search** box displays.

9 **Close** the **Event Name Search** dialog box. Do not close the **8A Event Details** form. **Open** ⑊» the **Navigation Pane**. Under **Forms**, right-click **8A Event Name Search Dialog Box** and then click **Design View**. **Close** ⑊« the **Navigation Pane**.

10 Right-click the **OK** button, and then click **Properties**. On the **Property Sheet**, click the **Event tab**. Click the **On Click** property setting **arrow**, and then click **8A Find Event Macro Group.SearchForEvent**. On the **Property Sheet**, click the **Format tab**. In the **Caption** box, click to the left of **OK**, and then type **& Close** the **Property Sheet**. **Save** 🖫 the form, and then switch the form to **Form** view.

When the OK button is clicked or the user presses ⎇Alt + Ⓞ, the second macro in the *8A Find Event Macro Group* executes.

11 In the **Enter an Event Name combo box**, click the **arrow**, and then click **Life Insurance Plan**. Click **OK**, and then compare your screen with Figure 8.26.

The macro executes, the *8A Event Details* form displays the first record—Record 7—with an event name (Title) of Life Insurance Plan, and a message box displays, telling you to click the Remove Sort button to display the records in the original sort order.

Figure 8.26

Message box created in macro

Life Insurance Plan event found

Record 7

12 In the displayed message box, click **OK**. Press ⎇Alt + ⓕF to display the Event Name Search box. In the **Event Name Search** box, in the **Enter an Event Name combo box**, type **ey** and notice that Access displays *Eye Care Plan*. Press ⎇Alt + Ⓞ. In the displayed message box, click **OK**.

Instead of selecting an item from the list, you can type the first few letters of the event name. If Access finds the event name in the list, it displays in the combo box. Record 7 is displayed.

13 On the **Home tab**, in the **Sort & Filter** group, click the **Remove Sort** button.

14 Open [>>] the **Navigation Pane**. Under **Forms**, open the **8A Event Name Search Dialog Box** form in **Design** view, and then **Close** [<<] the **Navigation Pane**.

15 Right-click the **Cancel** button, and then click **Properties**. On the **Property Sheet**, click the **Event tab**, click the **On Click** property setting **arrow**, and then click **8A Find Event Macro Group.CancelSearch**. Click the **Property Sheet Format tab**. In the **Caption** property setting box, click to the left of **Cancel**, type **&** and then **Close** the **Property Sheet**. **Save** [💾] the form, and then switch the form to **Form** view.

> Clicking the Cancel button on the *8A Event Name Search Dialog Box* form causes the third macro in the macro group to execute.

16 In the **Event Name Search** box, click the **Cancel** button. Alternatively, press [Alt] + [C]. Click **No** to close the form without saving.

> The form closes, and the focus is placed on the *8A Event Details* form.

Objective 5 | Create an Embedded Macro

An *embedded macro* is a macro that is stored in the event properties of forms, reports, or controls. They are not displayed in the Navigation Pane under Macros. Embedded macros are easier to manage because you do not have to keep track of the separate macro objects. Unlike standalone macros, when objects containing embedded macros are copied, imported, or exported, the macros are also copied, imported, or exported. Any standalone macro can be created as an embedded macro.

Activity 8.09 | Creating an Embedded Macro

In this activity, you will create an embedded macro that will execute when the *Room Info* button is clicked on the *8A Event Details* form.

1 Switch the **8A Event Details** form to **Design** view. Right-click the **Room Info** button, and then click **Properties**. Be sure that the **Property Sheet** displays *Selection type: Command button* and the **Selection type** box displays *cmdRoomInfo*. Drag the left edge of the **Property Sheet** to the right to decrease the width of the Property Sheet.

2 On the **Property Sheet**, click the **Event tab**. In the **On Click** property setting box, click the **Build** button, and then compare your screen with Figure 8.27.

> The Choose Builder dialog box displays for you to select the Macro Builder, the Expression Builder, or the Code Builder. You have previously used the Macro Builder and the Expression Builder. The Code Builder is used for programming in Microsoft Visual Basic.

Figure 8.27

Click to create macros

Click to create expressions

Click to create Microsoft Visual Basic programming code

3 In the **Choose Builder** dialog box, click **Macro Builder**, and then click **OK** to display the Macro Designer.

4 In the **Macro Designer**, add the **OpenForm** action using one of the techniques you have learned. In the **OpenForm Action Block**, click the **Form Name arrow**, and then click **8A Room Information**. Click in the **Where Condition** box, type **[Location]=[Forms]! [8A Event Details]![Location]** selecting items as they appear in the list to reduce errors and then compare your screen with Figure 8.28.

The Where Condition property selects the records from the *8A Room Information* form for the room Location displayed on the *8A Event Details* form.

Figure 8.28

Where Condition property

5 In the **OpenFormAction Block**, click the **Data Mode arrow**, and then click **Read Only** to enable the user to only view the data in the *8A Room Information* form. Add the following comment: **Opens 8A Room Information form for room indicated on 8A Event Details form**

6 **Close** the **Macro Designer**. In the displayed message box, click **Yes** to save the changes made to the macro and to update the **On Click** property. Compare your screen with Figure 8.29.

In the Property Sheet, the On Click property displays *[Embedded Macro]*. To display the macro, click the Build button.

Figure 8.29

On Click property

Indicates a macro is embedded for this event

Click to display actions of embedded macro

Access | Chapter 8

7 On the **Property Sheet**, click the **Format tab**. In the **Caption** box, click to the left of **Room Info**, and then type **&** to create a shortcut key using the letter *R*. **Close** the **Property Sheet**, **Save** the form, and then switch the *8A Event Details* form to **Form** view.

8 On the **8A Event Details** form, click the **Find Event** button. In the **Enter an Event Name** combo box, click the **arrow**, click **Dental Plan**, and then click **OK**. In the displayed message box, click **OK**. On the **8A Event Details** form, click the **Room Info** button. Alternatively, press Alt + R.

> The *8A Room Information* form displays as a pop-up window and provides information about the Blue Bird Room, the Location listed on the *8A Event Details* form.

9 **Close** the *8A Room Information* form. In the **8A Event Details** form, in the record navigator, click the **Last Record** button. In the **8A Event Details** form, click the **Room Info** button, and then compare your screen with Figure 8.30.

> The pop-up window displays room information for the Lone Star Room, the same room location displayed on the *8A Event Details* form as indicated by the Filtered button to the right of the record navigator in the *8A Room Information* form.

Figure 8.30

Location matches

Filtered by location

10 **Close** the *8A Room Information* form, and then **Close** the *8A Event Details* form, saving changes, if necessary. **Open** [»] the **Navigation Pane**. Notice that under **Macros**, the macro you created to display the *8A Room Information* form does not display— embedded macros do not display in the Navigation Pane.

Objective 6 | Print Macro Details

Use the **Database Documenter** to create a report that contains detailed information about the objects in a database, including macros, and to create a paper record.

Activity 8.10 | Printing Macro Details

In this activity, you will use the Database Documenter to print out the details of the macros that you have created in this project.

1 **Close** [«] the **Navigation Pane**. From the **Database Tools tab**, in the **Analyze group**, click the **Database Documenter** button. In the displayed **Documenter** dialog box, click the **Macros tab**, and then compare your screen with Figure 8.31.

> The Documenter dialog box displays tabs for each object type and a tab for the current database. Only standalone macros display on the Macros tab. Macros that are run are embedded with an object and will display as a property of the object.

Figure 8.31

Documenter dialog box ──

Macros tab ──

2 In the **Documenter** dialog box, click the **Options** button, and then compare your screen with Figure 8.32.

The Print Macro Definition dialog box displays. Properties, actions, arguments, and permissions by user and group can be displayed in the printed report.

Figure 8.32

Print Macro Definition dialog box ──

Options button ──

3 If necessary, click the **Permissions by User and Group** check box to clear it, and then click **OK**. In the **Documenter** dialog box, click **Select All**, and then click **OK**. Click in the middle of the document to zoom in, scroll up to display the top of the report, and then compare your screen with Figure 8.33.

The Object Definition opens in Print Preview, and displays the first page of information about the macro named *Autoexec*, including actions, arguments, conditions, and comments.

Figure 8.33

Database name ──

Macro name ──

Action ──

Action arguments ──

4 Click the **Next Page** button **three** times to display the details of the **8A Find Event Macro group** macro.

5 If you are instructed to submit this result, create a paper or electronic printout. Include the project, activity, and step number in the file name if you create an electronic printout. On the **Print Preview tab**, in the **Close Preview group**, click the **Close Print Preview** button.

6 From the **Database Tools tab**, in the **Analyze group**, click the **Database Documenter** button. In the **Documenter** dialog box, click the **Forms tab**. Click the **Options** button. In the **Print Form Definition** dialog box, if necessary, clear the check boxes for **Properties** and **Permissions by User and Group**, and then click **OK**.

7 In the **Documenter** dialog box, click the **8A Event Details** and **8A Event Name Search Dialog Box** forms.

These forms have macros associated with command buttons and an embedded macro.

8 In the **Documenter** dialog box, click **OK**. In the **Object Definition** print preview, zoom in, and then scroll up to display the top of the first page, noticing that the report displays properties of the **8A Event Details** form. Scroll down to display the bottom of the page. Compare your screen with Figure 8.34.

The properties of the Find Event button—Command Button: cmdFindEvent—and the beginning of the properties of the Room Info button–cmdRoomInfo–display.

Figure 8.34

Embedded macro details

9 If you are instructed to submit this result, create a paper or electronic printout.

10 On the **Print Preview tab**, in the **Close Preview group**, click the **Close Print Preview** button. Open the **Navigation Pane**. **Close** the database, and then **Exit** Access.

End **You have completed Project 8A**

Project 8B Nursing Salaries

myitlab
Project 8B Training

Project Activities

In Activities 8.11 through 8.14, you will help Margo Dalton, Vice President of Operations, compare nursing salaries, including regular pay and overtime pay by department. You will create a PivotTable and a PivotChart to analyze the nursing salaries by department and by quarter. Your completed PivotTable and PivotChart will look similar to Figure 8.35.

Project Files

For Project 8B, you will need the following file:

  a08B_Nursing_Salaries

You will save your database as:

  Lastname_Firstname_8B_Nursing_Salaries

Project Results

Figure 8.35
Project 8B Nursing Salaries

Objective 7 | Create a PivotTable from a Query

A **PivotTable** is used to organize, arrange, analyze, and summarize data in a meaningful way. A PivotTable displays trends and patterns at a glance for large amounts of data. In a PivotTable, rows can be categorized by different values, just as you did in the creation of a crosstab query, but you can also include multiple column categories and multiple calculated values. You can **pivot**, or rotate, the table to swap row headings with column headings to display the data in a different way. A **PivotChart** is a graphical view of the data in a PivotTable.

Activity 8.11 | Creating a PivotTable from a Query

In this activity, you will create a PivotTable to summarize nursing salaries per department by quarter.

1 **Start** Access. Navigate to the location where the student data files for this textbook are saved. Locate and open the **a08B_Nursing_Salaries** file. Save the database in your **Access Chapter 8** folder as **Lastname_Firstname_8B_Nursing_Salaries**

2 In the **Navigation Pane**, rename the two tables and the query by adding **Lastname Firstname** to the beginning of the object names. Under **Queries**, double-click **8B Nursing Salaries Query** to run the query.

The query displays department names, the quarter of the year, regular pay, overtime pay, and a calculated field for the total pay—regular pay plus overtime pay—for all of the nursing staff in each department. This query will be used in the creation of the PivotTable.

3 **Close** « the **Navigation Pane**. On the **tab row**, right-click **8B Nursing Salaries Query**, and then click **PivotTable View**. Compare your screen with Figure 8.36.

You can change to PivotTable view from either Datasheet view or Design view. A blank PivotTable design area displays, along with a PivotTable Field List that displays the field names in the *8B Nursing Salaries Query*. If the PivotTable Field List does not display, on the Design tab, in the Show/Hide group, click the Field List button.

The design area has several **drop zones** to which fields are dragged. The drop zones are outlined regions you see when you finish the steps of the PivotTable and PivotChart wizard. To arrange a PivotTable report, you drag fields from the Field List window and drop them onto the drop zones. Generally, the Column Fields drop zone should have the fewest values to avoid having the user scroll horizontally through the values.

Figure 8.36

Field List button

PivotTable Tools Design tab

Drop Zones

PivotTable Field List

4 In the **PivotTable Field List**, drag the **Quarter** field to the **Drop Row Fields Here** area. Drag the **Dept Name** field to the **Drop Column Fields Here** area, and then compare your screen with Figure 8.37.

The four quarters display as row headings. In the PivotTable Field List, Quarter is bolded, indicating that the field is used in the PivotTable. A Grand Total row and column display. Each row heading displays drill buttons, which are similar to expand and collapse buttons. Clicking the plus sign (+) expands or drills down to display more data. Clicking the minus sign (−) collapses or drills up to display less data. The department names display as column headings, with each department displaying drill buttons.

Figure 8.37

Column headings
Bold formatting—fields used in PivotTable
Row headings
Grand Total row
Drill buttons

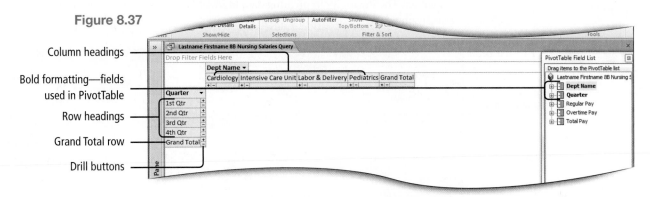

5 In the **PivotTable Field List**, drag the **Regular Pay** field to the **Drop Totals or Detail Fields Here** area, and then compare your screen with Figure 8.38.

The Regular Pay field for each quarter by department displays, enabling you to analyze the differences in nursing salaries for each department or within the same department by quarters.

Figure 8.38

Regular Pay per quarter by department

> **More Knowledge | Filtering a PivotTable**
>
> If this query contained a field with different hospitals, you could add the Hospital field to the Filter Fields drop zone. You could display all of the nursing salaries for each department by quarter for all of the hospitals, or you could select one or more hospitals to compare nursing salaries among the departments of those selected hospitals.

Activity 8.12 | Pivoting the Data and Adding Totals

In this activity, you will pivot the table to swap row headings with column headings to display the data in a different way, and then you will sum the columns and rows.

Another Way

To move the row heading to the column heading area, in the PivotTable Field List, drag the field name to the column heading area. Because a field name can only display in one area, it will be removed from the row heading area.

1 In the **PivotTable design area**, point to **Quarter** until the pointer displays. Click and drag upward and to the right and point to **Dept Name** until a dark blue line displays to the left of Dept Name, and then release the mouse button.

Quarter is moved to a column heading, and the data displays in a different manner.

2 In the **PivotTable design area**, point to **Dept Name** until the pointer displays. Click and drag downward and to the left to the **Drop Row Fields Here** area, and then compare your screen with Figure 8.39.

The departments are changed to row headings, and the data is displayed in a different manner. The flexibility in pivoting data in PivotTables makes this view a valuable tool for analyzing data.

Figure 8.39

Quarter as column headings

Dept Name as row headings

3 In the **PivotTable design area**, click any of the boxes that display **Regular Pay**. On the **Design tab**, in the **Tools group**, click the **AutoCalc** button. From the displayed list, click **Sum**, and then compare your screen with Figure 8.40.

Every row and every column is summed, including the individual Dept Name rows, and a Sum function is added to the PivotTable Field List.

Figure 8.40

Sum of Cardiology Department Regular Pay for all four quarters

Sum of Cardiology Department Regular Pay for 1st Quarter

Sum of 1st Quarter Regular Pay for all departments

Sum function added to PivotTable Field List

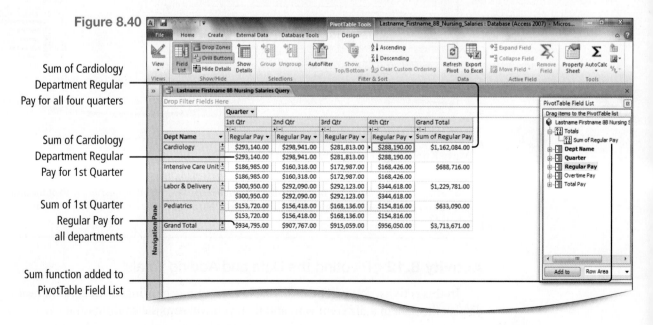

4 In the **PivotTable design area**, under **Dept Name** and to the right of **Cardiology**, click the **Drill Up** button (−) to collapse the total row for Cardiology. Repeat the procedure for the **Intensive Care Unit** row, the **Labor & Delivery** row, and the **Pediatrics** row.

> The PivotTable now displays the data in a more readable format.

5 **Close** the **PivotTable Field List**. To the right of **Quarter**, click the **arrow**. From the displayed list, click **3rd Qtr** and then click **4th Qtr** to clear the check boxes for these two quarters. Click **OK**. Notice that only data for the first two quarters displays, and the grand totals only sum the amounts for the two quarters. Also notice on the **Design tab**, in the **Filter & Sort group**, that the **AutoFilter** button is active, indicating that you are not viewing all of the data in the PivotTable.

6 On the **Design tab**, in the **Filter & Sort group**, click the active **AutoFilter** button.

> The Filter—displaying only 1st and 2nd Qtr data—is removed, and all of the data is visible.

7 On the **Design** tab, in the **Filter & Sort** group, click the **AutoFilter** button.

> The most recent filter is applied to the PivotTable, and only the 1st and 2nd quarter data displays.

8 To the right of **Dept Name**, click the **arrow**. From the displayed list, click **Intensive Care Unit**, and then click **Pediatrics** to clear the check boxes for these two departments. Click **OK**, and then compare your screen with Figure 8.41.

> Only data for the Cardiology and Labor & Delivery departments for the first two quarters displays. PivotTables enable you to display only the data you want to see when you are analyzing and comparing data.

Figure 8.41

AutoFilter button

Quarter filtered

Dept Name filtered

9 Using the technique you practiced, remove all filters. Collapse (−) the **Intensive Care Unit** row, and then collapse the **Pediatrics** row.

Activity 8.13 | Removing Fields from and Adding Fields to the PivotTable

In this activity, you will remove fields from and add fields to the PivotTable to display the data in a different way, and then you will sum the columns and rows.

1 On the **Design tab**, in the **Show/Hide group**, click the **Field List** button to display the PivotTable Field List.

2 In the **PivotTable Field List**, right-click **Sum of Regular Pay**, and then click **Delete**. In the **PivotTable design area**, expand (+) the **1st Qtr**, **2nd Qtr**, **3rd Qtr**, and **4th Qtr** columns to display the Regular Pay data for each department.

3 In the **PivotTable design area**, click any box that displays **Regular Pay**. On the **Design tab**, in the **Active Field group**, click the **Remove Field** button.

Only row headings and column headings display.

4 In the **PivotTable Field List**, drag **Total Pay** to the **Drop Totals or Detail Fields Here** area.

Total Pay is calculated by adding Regular Pay and Overtime Pay.

5 In the **PivotTable design area**, click any box that displays **Total Pay**. On the **Design tab**, in the **Tools group**, click the **AutoCalc** button, and then click **Sum**. Collapse (–) each of the **Dept Name row headings** so that the total for each department does not display, and then compare your screen with Figure 8.42.

Instead of just looking at Regular Pay statistics, you are now viewing the total pay, including overtime, for each department by quarter.

Figure 8.42

Total Pay summed

Regular Pay not bold—
removed from PivotTable

Total Pay field added
to PivotTable

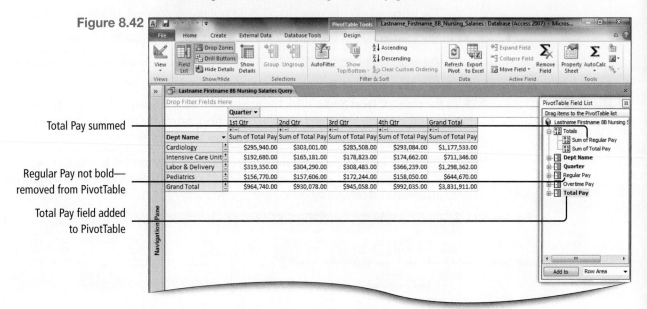

6 On the **Design tab**, in the **Show/Hide group**, click the active **Drop Zones** button.

The Drop Filter Fields Here area no longer displays.

7 **Close** the **PivotTable Field List**, and then **Save** the PivotTable. View the PivotTable in **Print Preview**, and then change the **Margins** to **Normal**. If you are instructed to submit this result, create a paper or electronic printout of the PivotTable. On the **Print Preview tab**, in the **Close Preview group**, click the **Close Print Preview** button.

Objective 8 | Create a PivotChart from a PivotTable

A PivotChart is a graphical view of the data included in the PivotTable, although you can create a PivotChart without first defining a PivotTable. If you design a PivotChart, a PivotTable will automatically be created. To create a PivotChart from a PivotTable, the PivotTable must contain a calculated field.

Activity 8.14 | Creating a PivotChart from a PivotTable

In this activity, you will create a PivotChart from the PivotTable you created in the previous activities.

1 On the **tab row**, right-click **8B Nursing Salaries Query**, and then click **PivotChart View**. **Close** the **Chart Field List**, and then compare your screen with Figure 8.43.

Because the PivotTable was already created, Access converts the data into a graphical representation of the data in the PivotTable. At the top of the PivotChart is the name of the field—Total Pay—that has been summed. The row headings—Dept Names—display at the bottom of the PivotChart, and the data displays within the PivotChart. Both Quarter and Dept Name display filter arrows to limit the chart to displaying only the data you want to analyze.

Figure 8.43

Data per quarter

Total Pay field summed

Filter arrow for Quarter

Department names

Filter arrow for Dept Name

More Knowledge | Creating a PivotChart

In the Navigation Pane, select the underlying object, and then close the Navigation Pane. On the Ribbon, click the Create tab. In the Forms group, click the More Forms button, and then click the PivotChart button. If the Chart Field List does not display, on the Design tab, in the Show/Hide group, click the Field List. Drag the fields onto the PivotChart design area, much like you dragged the fields onto the PivotTable design area.

---

2 On the right side of the **PivotChart design area**, click the **Quarter arrow**—scroll to the right, if necessary. Click **1st Qtr** and **2nd Qt**r to clear the check boxes, and then click **OK**.

Just as you did in the PivotTable view, you can filter the quarters or department names, making this a flexible tool for analyzing data.

3 Using the technique you just practiced, display the data for all four quarters. On the left side of the **PivotChart design area**, click **Axis Title**. On the **Design tab**, in the **Tools group**, click the **Property Sheet** button. In the **Properties** dialog box, click the **Format tab**. In the **Caption** box, select **Axis Title**, and then type **Total Pay Per Quarter**

4 At the bottom of the **PivotChart design area**, click **Axis Title** to display the **Properties** dialog box for this object. In the **Caption** box, select **Axis Title**, and then type **Department Name** Next, **Close** the **Properties** dialog box, and then compare your screen with Figure 8.44.

The axis titles have been changed to display a description of the data on the PivotChart.

Figure 8.44

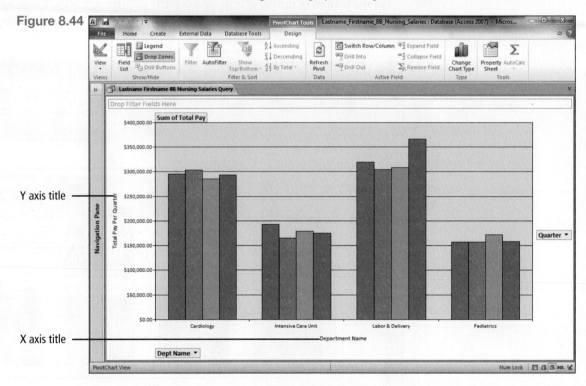

Y axis title

X axis title

5 On the **Design tab**, in the **Show/Hide group**, click the **Legend** button.

A legend displays under Quarter. A *legend* is text that describes the meaning of colors and patterns used in a chart.

6 Click in an empty area of the chart to deselect the axis title. On the **Design tab**, in the **Type group**, click the **Change Chart Type** button. In the displayed **Properties** dialog box, on the **Type tab**, notice that the chart type is a **Clustered Column** chart. On the left side of the dialog box, click **Bar**, and then click the first chart type, which changes the chart to a **Clustered Bar** chart type.

Column charts and bar charts are ideal for displaying varying values for different categories. Line charts are ideal for displaying changes in data over time, and pie charts are ideal for showing the percentages of a total amount.

7 Close the **Properties** dialog box. On the **Design** tab, in the **Active Field** group, click the **Switch Row/Column** button.

The row and column headings are pivoted to display the data in a different manner. The legend displays department names instead of quarters.

8 Using the techniques you have practiced, change the left axis title to **Quarter** On the bottom of the PivotChart, click any of the numbers representing the Total Pay Per Quarter. In the **Tools group**, click the **Property Sheet** button. In the displayed **Properties** dialog box, click the **Format tab**. Click the **Number arrow** to familiarize yourself with the options, and then click **Currency**.

The figures representing the Total Pay Per Quarter display with the Currency format with two decimal places.

9 On the **Design tab**, in the **Show/Hide group**, click the **Drop Zones** button, and then click in an empty area of the chart to deselect the dollar amounts.

> After you have decided which departments and quarters to include, you can exclude the column and row heading filter arrows from the PivotChart.

10 On the **Design tab**, in the **Tools group**, click the **Property Sheet** button. In the **Properties** dialog box, on the **General tab**, under **Add**, click the **Add Title** 📊 button.

11 At the top of the **PivotChart design area**, click **Chart Workspace Title**. In the **Properties** dialog box, click the **Format tab**. In the **Caption** box, select the text, type **Lastname Firstname 8B Nursing Salaries by Department** and then press Enter. **Close** the **Properties** dialog box, and then compare your screen with Figure 8.45.

Figure 8.45

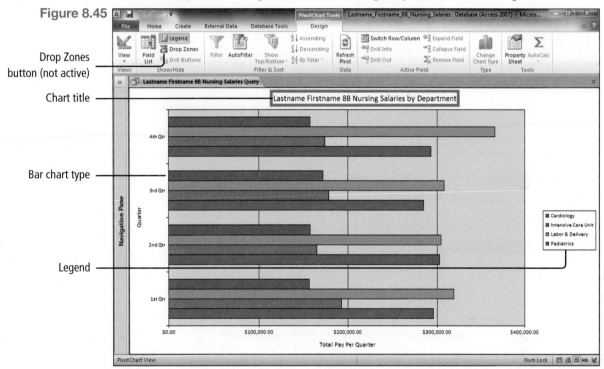

Drop Zones button (not active)

Chart title

Bar chart type

Legend

12 **Save** the PivotChart, and then view the PivotChart in **Print Preview**. If you are instructed to submit this result, create a paper or electronic printout of the PivotChart in **Landscape** orientation. Add the word *Chart* to the file name if you create an electronic printout. On the **Print Preview tab**, in the **Close Preview group**, click the **Close Print Preview** button, and then **Close** the PivotChart.

13 **Open** ⏵ the **Navigation Pane**. Under **Queries**, double-click **8B Nursing Salaries Query** to run the query. **Close** ⏴ the **Navigation Pane**. On the **tab row**, right-click **8B Nursing Salaries Query**, and then click **PivotTable View**.

> The PivotTable displays as it was saved.

14 On the tab row, right-click **8B Nursing Salaries Query**, and then click **PivotChart View**.

> The PivotChart displays as it was saved. To view a PivotTable or PivotChart, the underlying object must be open in either Datasheet view or Design view. You cannot display the PivotTable or PivotChart by right-clicking the underlying object in the Navigation Pane.

15 **Close** the PivotChart, and then **Open** ⏵ the **Navigation Pane**. **Close** the database, and then **Exit** Access.

End **You have completed Project 8B** ———————————————

Access | Chapter 8

Summary

Macros are created to automate database tasks. In this chapter, you created standalone macros with one or more actions and action arguments. You created a macro group and added conditions to macro actions. You associated a macro with the clicking of a button and created an embedded macro. You printed documentation of the macro details using the Database Documenter.

PivotTables and PivotCharts display data in a different manner that is helpful when analyzing data. You created a PivotTable that summarized data by department and quarter and then pivoted the data to display it by quarter and then department. You created a PivotChart to display the same data in a graphical representation.

Key Terms

Matching

Match each term in the second column with its correct definition in the first column by writing the letter of the term on the blank line in front of the correct definition.

_____ 1. A series of actions grouped as a single command to accomplish a task or multiple tasks automatically.

_____ 2. A self-contained instruction.

_____ 3. A view of data that is used to organize, arrange, analyze, and summarize data in a meaningful way.

_____ 4. A graphical view of the data in a PivotTable.

_____ 5. A macro contained in a macro object that displays under Macros in the Navigation Pane.

_____ 6. A value that provides information to the macro action, such as the words to display in a message box or the control upon which to operate.

_____ 7. A specification that certain criteria must be met before the macro action executes.

_____ 8. A window that displays, usually contains a menu of commands, and stays on the screen only until a user selects one of the commands.

_____ 9. A child (secondary window) to a parent window that takes over control of the parent window.

_____ 10. The action of using a logical process to find and reduce the number of errors in a program.

_____ 11. A debugging tool that executes one macro action at a time, enabling you to observe the results of each macro action and isolate any action that may be causing an error or that produces unwanted results.

A Action

B Argument

C Condition

D Debugging

E Drop zone

F Macro

G Macro group

H Modal window

I Pivot

J PivotChart

K PivotTable

L Pop-up window

M Single stepping

N Standalone macro

O Syntax

____ 12. A set of macros grouped by a common name that displays as one macro object in the Navigation Pane.

____ 13. A reference to the spelling, grammar, and sequence of characters of a programming language.

____ 14. To rotate data in a PivotTable or PivotChart by changing row headings to column headings, and vice versa.

____ 15. Outlined regions to which fields are dragged on a PivotTable or PivotChart.

Multiple Choice

Circle the correct answer.

1. When designing a macro, list the actions to occur and
   - **A.** the tab they are under
   - **B.** the order in which they occur
   - **C.** the action arguments

2. Which window takes control over a parent window and must be closed before entering information in the parent window?
   - **A.** Pop-up window
   - **B.** Modal window
   - **C.** Macro window

3. What name is given to a macro that automatically runs each time the database is opened?
   - **A.** Autoexec
   - **B.** Startup
   - **C.** Autorun

4. Which debugging tool enables you to isolate any action that may be causing an error or produces unwanted results?
   - **A.** Macro Editor
   - **B.** Macro Designer
   - **C.** Single-Stepping

5. A set of macros grouped by a common name that displays as one macro object in the Navigation Pane is called a macro
   - **A.** collection
   - **B.** cluster
   - **C.** group

6. Which symbol on a caption allows the user to use a key combination to access the button instead of clicking on the button?
   - **A.** at symbol (@)
   - **B.** number sign (#)
   - **C.** ampersand (&)

7. What type of macro is stored in the event properties of forms, reports, or controls?
   - **A.** Embedded
   - **B.** Attached
   - **C.** Stand alone

8. What view is used to display trends and patterns for large amounts of data at a glance?
   - **A.** PivotTable
   - **B.** PivotQuery
   - **C.** PivotChart

9. When you are not viewing all of the data in the PivotTable, which button is active on the Design tab?
   - **A.** AutoFilter
   - **B.** AutoCalc
   - **C.** Field List

10. What is the name for the text that describes the meaning of colors and patterns used in a chart?
    - **A.** Chart type
    - **B.** Axis
    - **C.** Legend

Content-Based Assessments

Apply **8A** skills from these Objectives:

1. Create a Standalone Macro with One Action
2. Add Multiple Actions to a Standalone Macro
3. Create a Macro Group
4. Associate a Macro with an Event
5. Create an Embedded Macro
6. Print Macro Details

Skills Review | Project **8C** Hospital Departments

Margo Dalton, Vice President of Operations for Providence and Warwick Hospital, wants to customize her database of department information to display a form when the database is opened. She also wants to add buttons to the form to automate some of the most common tasks, such as adding a new department and printing a record. In this project, you will create macros to automatically display a form and message box when the database is opened. You will associate command buttons with a macro, group macros, and embed macros within a form. Finally, you will display and print a report that documents the details of the macros you created. Your completed work will look similar to Figure 8.46.

Project Files

For Project 8C, you will need the following file:

a08C_Hospital_Departments

You will save your database as:

Lastname_Firstname_8C_Hospital_Departments

Project Results

Figure 8.46

(Project 8C Hospital Departments continues on the next page)

Content-Based Assessments

1 **Start** Access. Locate and open the **a08C_Hospital_ Departments** file. Save the database in your **Access Chapter 8** folder as **Lastname_Firstname_8C_Hospital_ Departments** and then **Close** the **Navigation Pane**.

2 On the Ribbon, click the **Create tab**. In the **Macros & Code group**, click the **Macro button**.

a. In the **Macro Designer**, in the **Add New Action bar,** click the **arrow**, and then click **OpenReport**. In the **Open Report Action Block**, in the **Report Name** box, click the **arrow**, and then click **8C Supervisors**. In the **View** box, be sure that **Report** is selected. The **Filter Name** and **Where Condition** boxes should be blank. In the **Window Mode** box, be sure that the setting is **Normal**.

b. In the **Action Catalog pane**, double-click **Comment**, and type **Opens 8C Supervisors report in Report view**

c. On the **Design tab**, in the **Tools group**, click the **Run** button. In the displayed message box, click **Yes** to save the macro. In the **Save As** dialog box, type **Lastname Firstname 8C Open Supervisors Report** and then click **OK**. **Close** the **8C Supervisors** report, and then **Close** the Macro Designer.

3 **Open** the **Navigation Pane**. Under **Forms**, right-click **8C Intro Screen**, and then click **Design View**. On the **Design tab**, in the **Tools group**, click the **Property Sheet** button. On the **Property Sheet Other tab**, click the **Pop Up property setting arrow**, and then click **Yes**. Click in the **Modal** property setting box, click the **arrow**, and then click **Yes**. **Close** the **Property Sheet**, and then **Close** the form, saving changes when prompted. **Close** the **Navigation Pane**.

4 On the Ribbon, click the **Create tab**. In the **Macros & Code group**, click the **Macro button**.

a. In the **Macro Designer**, add the **OpenForm** action. In the **OpenForm Action Block**, click the **Form Name arrow**, and then click **8C Intro Screen**. Add the following comment: **Opens 8C Intro Screen form**

b. On the **Quick Access Toolbar**, click the **Save** button. In the **Save As** dialog box, type **Autoexec** and then click **OK**. **Close** the Macro Designer, and then **Open** the **Navigation Pane**. In the **Navigation Pane**, under **Macros**, double-click **Autoexec** to run the macro. **Close** the form.

5 In the **Navigation Pane**, under **Macros**, right-click **Autoexec**, and then click **Design View**. **Close** the **Navigation Pane**.

a. Add the **DisplayHourglassPointer** action. Notice that the default argument is *Yes*. Add the following comment: **Turns mouse pointer into a Busy icon.**

b. On the **Design tab**, in the **Show/Hide group**, click the **Show All Actions** button. In the **Macro Designer**, add the **Echo** action. In the **Echo Action Block**, click the **Echo On arrow**, and then click **No**. Click in the **Status Bar Text** box, and type **Macro is running** Add the following comment: **Hides the flickering screen as the macro runs**

c. Add the **RunMacro** action. In the **RunMacro Action Block**, click the **Macro Name arrow**, and then click **8C Open Supervisors Report**. The **Repeat Count** box and the **Repeat Expression** box should be blank. Add the following comment: **Runs 8C Open Supervisors Report macro**

d. Add the **MessageBox** action. In the **MessageBox Action Block**, click in the **Message** box, and then type **Only supervisors at Providence & Warwick Hospital are authorized to access this database.** In the **Beep** box, be sure that the Beep argument is **Yes**. Click the **Type** box **arrow**, and then click **Warning!**. Click in the **Title** box, and then type **For Use by Providence & Warwick Hospital Supervisors Only!** Add the following comment: **Displays a warning message box**

e. In the **Macro Designer**, add the **DisplayHourglass Pointer** action. In the **DisplayHourglassPointer Action Block**, click the **Hourglass On arrow**, and then click **No**. Add the following comment: **Restores the mouse pointer**

f. Add the **Echo** action. Add the following comment: **Displays screen results**

g. Scroll to the top of the **Action Argument** box. Click the **OpenForm** action to make it active, and then move the action below the comment **Runs 8C Open Supervisors Report**

h. Move the **OpenForm macro comment** below the **OpenForm action**.

i. **Save** the macro. On the **Design tab**, in the **Tools group**, click the **Run** button. In the displayed

(Project 8C Hospital Departments continues on the next page)

message box, click **OK. Close** the **8C Intro Screen** form. On the **tab row**, right-click any tab, and then click **Close All.**

6 On the Ribbon, click the **Create tab**. In the **Macros & Code group**, click the **Macro button**. On the **Design tab**, in the **Show/Hide group**, click the **Show All Actions** button.

a. In the **Action Catalog pane**, double-click **Group**. Click in the **Group** box, and type **8C Add Dept Macro Group** Add the following comment: **Purpose: To enable a user to add a department to the 8C Dept Directors form** On the **tab row**, right-click **Macro1**, click **Save**, and then type **Lastname Firstname 8C Add Dept Macro Group**

b. In the **Action Catalog pane**, double-click **Submacro**, and type **GoToNewRecord** In the **Submacro**, add the **GoToRecord** action. In the **GoToRecord Action Block**, click the **Object Type arrow**, and then click **Form**. Click the **Object Name arrow**, and then click **8C Dept Directors**. Be sure that **New** appears in the **Record** box. Add the following comment: **Goes to new record**

c. In the submacro, add the **GoToControl** action. In the **GoToControl Action Block**, click in the **Control Name box**, and then type **Department ID** Add the following comment: **Moves focus from button to Department ID field**

d. In the submacro, add the **SetValue** action. In the **SetValue Action Block**, click in the **Item** box, and type **[Forms]![8C Dept Directors]![cmdAddNew] .[Visible]** Click in the Expression box, and type **No** Add the following comment: **Hides the Add Dept button**

e. In the submacro, add the **SetValue** action. In the **SetValue Action Block**, click in the **Item** box, and type **[Forms]![8C Dept Directors]! [cmdShowAll].[Visible]** Click in the **Expression** box and type **Yes** Add the following comment: **Displays the Show All button**

f. In the **Action Catalog pane**, double-click **Submacro**, and type **ShowAll** In the **ShowAll Submacro**, under **Add New Action**, click the arrow, and then click **ShowAllRecords**. Add the following comment: **Shows all records and exits data entry**

g. In the submacro, add the **GoToControl** action. In the **GoToControl Action Block**, click in the **Control Name** box, and type **Department ID** Add the following comment: **Moves focus from button to Department ID field**

h. In the submacro, add the **SetValue** action. In the **SetValue Action Block**, to the right of the **Item** box, click the **Build** button. In the **Expression Builder**, type **[Forms]![8C Dept Directors]![cmdAddNew] .[Visible]**and then click **OK**. Click in the **Expression** box, and type **Yes** Add the following comment: **Shows the Add Dept button**

i. In the submacro, add the **SetValue** action. In the **SetValue Action Block**, click in the **Item** box, and type **[Forms]![8C Dept Directors]! [cmdShowAll] .[Visible]** Click in the **Expression** box, and then type **No** Add the following comment: **Hides the Show All button**

j. **Save** the macro group. **Close** the **Macro Designer**, and then **Open** the **Navigation Pane**.

7 In the **Navigation Pane**, **Open** the **8C Dept Directors** form in **Design** view. **Close** the **Navigation Pane**

a. In the **Form Header section**, right-click the **Add Dept** button, and then click **Properties**. Be sure that the **Property Sheet** displays *Selection type: Command button* and that the **Selection type** box displays *cmdAddNew*.

b. Point to the **left edge** of the **Property Sheet** until the pointer displays. Drag to the left to the **4.5 inch mark on the horizontal ruler**.

c. On the **Property Sheet**, click the **Event tab**. Click the **On Click** property setting **arrow**. In the displayed list, click **Lastname Firstname 8C Add DeptMacro Group.GoToNew Record**. On the **Property Sheet**, click the **Format tab**. In the **Caption** property setting box, click to the left of **Add Dept**, and then type **&**

d. On the **Property Sheet** in the **Selection type** box click **cmdShowAll**. On the **Property Sheet**, click the **Event tab**. Click the **On Click** property setting **arrow**. In the displayed list, click **Lastname Firstname 8C Add DeptMacro Group.ShowAll**. On the **Property Sheet**, click the **Format tab**. In the **Caption** property setting box, click to the left of **Show All**, and then type **& Close** the **Property Sheet**.

e. Switch to **Form** view. Click the **Add Dept** button. In the **Department ID** field type **1236-D** Press Tab, and type **Nutrition Services** Enter your information for all of the remaining fields except Supervisor ID. In the **Supervisor ID** field, type **417-Sup** and then press Enter. Switch to **Design** view.

(Project 8C Hospital Departments continues on the next page)

f. In the **Form Header section**, right-click the **Print** button, and then click **Properties**. Be sure that the **Property Sheet** displays *Selection type: Command button* and that the **Selection type** box displays *cmdPrintRec*. On the **Property Sheet**, click the **Event tab**. In the **On Click** property setting box, click the **Build** button. In the **Choose Builder** dialog box, be sure **Macro Builder** is selected and click **OK**.

g. In the **Macro Designer**, under **Add New Action**, add the **RunMenuCommand** action. In the **RunMenuCommand Action Block**, click the **Command** box **arrow**, and click **SelectRecord**. Add the following comment: **Selects the current record**

h. Add the **RunMenuCommand** action. In the **RunMenu Command Action Block**, click the **Command** box **arrow**, and then click **PrintSelection**. Add the following comment: **Prints the current record**

i. **Close** the Macro Designer. In the displayed message box, click **Yes**. Make sure the **Print** button is selected. On the **Property Sheet**, click the **Format tab**. In the **Caption** box, click to the left of **Print**, and then type **&**.

Close the **Property Sheet**, and then switch the **8C Dept Directors** form to **Form** view.

j. If you are instructed to submit this result, press PgDn until you display the record that contains your first and last names in the Director fields. Click in the **Department ID** field. Click the **Print** button to create a paper printout, or create an electronic printout. **Close** the **8C Dept Directors** form.

8 On the **Database Tools tab**, in the **Analyze group**, click the **Database Documenter** button.

a. In the **Documenter** dialog box, click the **Macros tab**, and then click the **Options** button. If necessary, click the check box to deselect **Permissions by User and Group**, and then click **OK**. In the **Documenter** dialog box, click **Select All**, and then click **OK**. If you are instructed to submit this result, create a paper or electronic printout. On the **Print Preview tab**, in the **Close Preview group**, click the **Close Print Preview** button.

9 **Open** the **Navigation Pane**. **Close** the database, and then **Exit** Access.

End You have completed Project 8C ————————————

Content-Based Assessments

Skills Review | Project **8D** Gift Shop

Margo Dalton, Vice President of Operations, wants to compare the prices of the items available in the hospital gift shop. In this project, you will create a PivotTable and a PivotChart to analyze the value of the inventory based on the quantity in stock and the selling price of the items. Your completed PivotTable and PivotChart will look similar to Figure 8.47.

Project Files

For Project 8D, you will need the following file:

a08D_Gift_Shop

You will save your database as:

Lastname_Firstname_8D_Gift_Shop

Project Results

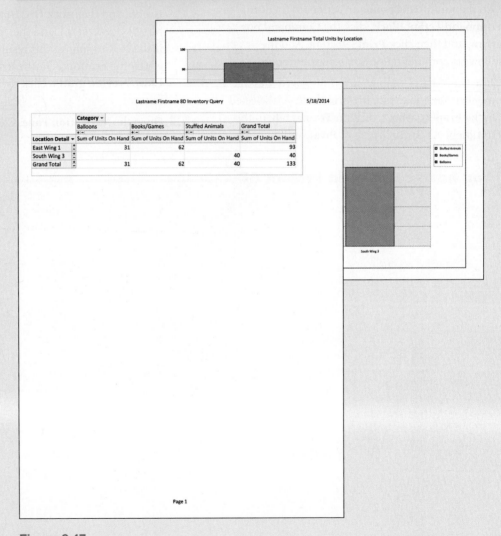

Figure 8.47

(Project 8D Gift Shop continues on the next page)

Content-Based Assessments

1 **Start** Access. Locate and open the **a08D_Gift_Shop** file. Save the database in your **Access Chapter 8** folder as **Lastname_Firstname_8D_Gift_Shop**

2 In the **Navigation Pane**, **rename** the two tables, the query, and the report by adding your **Lastname Firstname** to the beginning of the object names. Under **Queries**, double-click **8D Inventory Query** to run the query.

a. **Close** the **Navigation Pane**. On the **tab row**, right-click **8D Inventory Query**, and then click **PivotTable View**. If necessary, on the **Design** tab, in the **Show/Hide** group, click the **Field List** button. From the **PivotTable Field List**, drag the **Category** field to the **Drop Row Fields Here** area. Drag the **Location Detail** field to the **Drop Column Fields Here** area, and then drag the **Value** field to the **Drop Totals or Detail Fields Here** area.

b. In the **PivotTable design area**, point to **Category** until the pointer displays. Click and drag upward and to the right until a dark blue line displays to the left of **Location Detail**, and then release the mouse button. In the **PivotTable design area**, point to **Location Detail** until the pointer displays. Click and drag downward and to the left to the **Drop Row Fields Here** area.

c. In the **PivotTable design area**, click any one of the **Value** boxes. On the **Design tab**, in the **Tools group**, click the **AutoCalc** button. From the displayed list, click **Sum**.

d. In the **PivotTable design area**, under **Location Detail** and to the right of **Cooler A, Basement**, click the **Drill Up** button (−) to collapse the total row for Cooler A. Repeat the procedure for the **East Wing1**, **North Wing2**, and **South Wing3** rows.

e. **Close** the **PivotTable Field List**. Click the **Category arrow**. From the displayed list, click **Candy**, and then click **Flowers and Plants** to deselect these two categories, and then click **OK**. Notice that only data for Balloons, Stuffed Animals, and Books/Games display, and the grand totals only sum the amounts for these three categories.

f. Collapse each of the **Location Detail row headings** so that the detail for each Location Detail does not display.

g. On the **Design tab**, in the **Show/Hide group**, click the **Field List** button to display the **PivotTable Field List**. In the **PivotTable Field List**, right-click **Sum of Value**, and then click **Delete**. In the **PivotTable design area**,

if necessary, expand the **Category** columns to display the **Value** data for each category.

h. Right-click one of the **Value** boxes, and from the shortcut menu, click **Remove**. In the **PivotTable Field List**, drag **Units on Hand** to the **Drop Totals or Detail Fields Here** area. In the **PivotTable design area**, click any **Units on Hand** box. On the **Design tab**, in the **Tools group**, click the **AutoCalc** button, and then click **Sum**. If necessary, collapse each of the **Location Detail row headings** so that the detail for each Location Detail does not display.

i. On the **Design tab**, in the **Show/Hide group**, click the active **Drop Zones** button. **Close** the **PivotTable Field List**, and then **Save** the PivotTable. View the PivotTable in **Print Preview**, and then change the **Margins** to **Normal**. If you are instructed to submit this result, create a paper or electronic printout of the PivotTable. On the **Print Preview tab**, in the **Close Preview group**, click the **Close Print Preview** button, leaving the PivotTable open for the next step.

3 On the **tab row**, right-click **8D Inventory Query**, and then click **PivotChart View**.

a. **Close** the **Chart Field List**. On the left side of the **PivotChart design area**, click **Axis Title**. On the **Design tab**, in the **Tools group**, click the **Property Sheet** button. In the **Properties** dialog box, click the **Format tab**. In the **Caption** box, select **Axis Title**, and then type **Total Units on Hand.**

b. At the bottom of the **PivotChart design area**, click **Axis Title** to display the **Properties** dialog box for this object. In the **Caption** box, select **Axis Title**, and then type **Location Detail** Click in an open area of the chart.

c. On the **Property Sheet General tab**, click the **Add Title** button. Click **Chart Workspace Title** to display the **Properties** dialog box for this object, and click the **Format tab**. In the **Caption** box, select **Chart Workspace Title**, and type **Lastname Firstname Total Units by Location Close** the **Properties** dialog box.

d. On the **Design tab**, in the **Show/Hide group**, click the **Legend** button. In the **Type group**, click the **Change Chart Type** button. In the displayed **Properties** dialog box, on the **Type tab**, notice that the chart type is a **Clustered Column** chart. Click the second chart type, which changes the chart to a **Stacked Column** chart type.

(Project 8D Gift Shop continues on the next page)

Content-Based Assessments

e. On the left side of the PivotChart, click any of the numbers representing the **Total Units on Hand**. In the displayed **Properties** dialog box, click the **Format tab**. Under Text format, click the **Bold** button to add bold to the values. **Close** the **Properties** dialog box.

f. On the **Design tab**, in the **Show/Hide group**, click the **Drop Zones** button.

g. **Save** the PivotChart, and then view the PivotChart in **Print Preview**. Click the **Landscape** button. If you are instructed to submit this result, create a paper or electronic printout. Add the word **Chart** to the file name if you create an electronic printout. On the **Print Preview tab**, in the **Close Preview group**, click the **Close Print Preview** button.

4 **Close** the PivotChart, and then **Open** the **Navigation Pane**. **Close** the database, and then **Exit** Access.

End **You have completed Project 8D** ⎯⎯⎯⎯⎯⎯⎯⎯⎯⎯⎯⎯⎯⎯⎯

Content-Based Assessments

Apply **8A** skills from these Objectives:

- 1 Create a Standalone Macro with One Action
- 2 Add Multiple Actions to a Standalone Macro
- 3 Create a Macro Group
- 4 Associate a Macro with an Event
- 5 Create an Embedded Macro
- 6 Print Macro Details

Mastering Access | Project **8E** Orthopedic Supplies

Margo Dalton, Vice President of Operations for Providence and Warwick Hospital, wants to customize the orthopedic supplies database to display a form when the database is opened. She also wants to add buttons on the form to automate some of the most common tasks, such as adding a new department and printing a record. In this project, you will create macros to automatically display a form and message box when the user opens the database. You will associate command buttons with a macro, group macros, and embed macros within a form. Finally, you will display and print a report that documents the details of the macros you created. Your completed work will look similar to Figure 8.48.

Project Files

For Project 8E, you will need the following file:

a08E_Orthopedic_Supplies

You will save your database as:

Lastname_Firstname_8E_Orthopedic_Supplies

Project Results

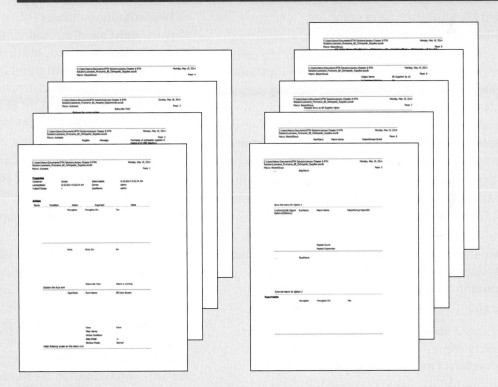

Figure 8.48

(Project 8E Orthopedic Supplies continues on the next page)

Access | Chapter 8

Content-Based Assessments

1 Start Access. Locate and open the **a08E_Orthopedic_Supplies** file. Save the database in your **Access Chapter 8** folder as **Lastname_Firstname_8E_Orthopedic_Supplies Close** the **Navigation Pane**.

2 On the **Create tab**, click the **Macro button**. On the **Design tab**, in the **Show/Hide group**, click the **Show All Actions** button. Create a macro to open the **8E Intro Screen** form. In the **Macro Designer**, under **Add New Action**, click **OpenForm**. For **Form Name**, click **8E Intro Screen**. Add the following comment: **Displays 8E Intro Screen** Then **Run** the macro and **Save** it as **Autoexec**

3 Modify the **Autoexec** macro. Add the action **DisplayHourglassPointer** with the **Comment Displays the busy icon** Add the **Echo** action with the **Comment Hides the flickering screen as the macro runs** In the **Echo Action Block**, change the **Echo On** box to **No**. Click in the **Status Bar Text** box, and then type **Macro is running** Move the **OpenForm** action and comment below the **Echo** macro comment.

4 In the **Macro Designer**, at the bottom of the current list of actions, add a **MessageBox** action. Type a **Message** that displays **Purchases of orthopedic supplies in excess of $1,000 require a signature from Joy Roberts** Add a **Beep**, and change the **Type** box to **Information**. Title the **Message** box **For Purchases over $1,000** Add a **Comment** that reads **Displays purchasing information**

5 In the **Macro Designer**, add an **Echo** action. In the **Echo Action Block**, be sure the **Echo On** box is set to **Yes**. Add a **Comment** that says **Displays screen results**

6 In the **Macro Designer**, add a **DisplayHourglass Pointer** action. In the **DisplayHourglassPointer Action Block**, change the **Hourglass On** box to **No**. Add a **Comment** that says **Restores the mouse pointer**

7 **Close** the Macro Designer, and **Save** the macro.

8 Create a **Macro Group** to print the reports. Name this macro group **ReportGroup** with a **Comment: Purpose: Select report printing options**

9 Create a **Submacro** named **Options** with the action **OpenForm** opening the **8E Report Options** form in Form view and Edit mode. Add the **Comment: Opens 8E Report Options form**

10 Create a **Submacro** named **PrintReport** Add an **IF** condition **1=[Forms]![8E Report Options]![Options]** and the **RunMacro** action for the **ReportGroup.ReportAlpha** macro. Add the **Comment: Runs the macro for option 1**

and then add the **StopMacro** action below the RunMacro action. In the submacro, below the first end if, add another **IF** condition **2=[Forms]![8E Report Options]![Options]** and the **RunMacro** action for the **ReportGroup.ReportID** macro. Add the **Comment: Runs the macro for option 2** and then add the **StopMacro** action.

11 Create a **Submacro** named **ReportAlpha** Add an action to **DisplayHourglassPointer**. Add the **RunMacro** for **ReportGroup.Cancel**, and add the **Comment: Closes 8E Report Options form** Add the **OpenReport** action to open **8E Suppliers Alpha** report in Print Preview. Add the **Comment: Opens report in print preview** Add the **SelectObject** action to select the **8E Suppliers Alpha** report, and add the **Comment: Changes focus to 8E Suppliers Alpha** Finally, add a macro action to turn off the hourglass.

12 Create a **Submacro** named **ReportID** Add an action to **DisplayHourglassPointer**. Add the **RunMacro** for **ReportGroup.Cancel**, and add the **Comment: Closes 8E Report Options form** Next, add the **OpenReport** action to open **8E Suppliers by ID** report in Print Preview. Add the **Comment: Opens report in print preview** Add the **SelectObject** action to select the **8E Suppliers by ID** report, and add the **Comment: Changes focus to 8E Suppliers by ID** Finally, add a macro to turn off the hourglass.

13 Create a **Submacro** named **Cancel**. Add the **CloseWindow** action to close the **8E Report Options** form; add the **Comment: Closes 8E Report Options form**

14 **Close** the **Macro Designer**, saving the group as **ReportGroup**

15 Open the **8E Report Options** form in **Design** view. Right-click the **Print Report** button, and then click **Properties**. Click the **Event tab**. Click the **On Click** property setting box **arrow**, and click **ReportGroup. PrintReport**. On the **Format tab**, click in the **Caption** property setting and type **&** before *Print Report*. Click the **Cancel** button. In the **On Click** property setting select **ReportGroup.Cancel**. On the **Format tab**, click in the **Caption** property setting and type **&** before *Cancel*. **Close** the Property Sheet and **Close** the form, saving changes.

16 Open the **8E Suppliers** form in **Design** view. Right-click the **Print Report** button, and then click **Properties**. Click the **Event tab**. Click in the **On Click** property setting box, and then click the **Build** button. In the

(Project 8E Orthopedic Supplies continues on the next page)

Content-Based Assessments

Macro Designer, add the **OpenForm** action to open the **8E Report Options** form in Form view and Edit mode. Add a **Comment Opens 8E Report Options form Close** the Macro Designer, saving the changes. **Close** the **Property Sheet**.

17 Switch to **Form** view, saving changes. Click the **Print Report** button. Test each report option and **Close Print Preview**. **Close** the **8E Suppliers** form.

18 Open the **Database Documenter**. In the displayed **Documenter** dialog box, click the **Macros tab**, and then click the **Options** button. If necessary, clear the **Permissions by User and Group** check box, and then click **OK**. In the **Documenter** dialog box, click **Select All**, and then click **OK**. If you are instructed to submit this result, create a paper or electronic printout. **Close Print Preview**.

19 **Close** the database, and then **Exit** Access.

End **You have completed Project 8E** ———————————————————

Apply **8B** skills from these Objectives:

7 Create a PivotTable from a Query

8 Create a PivotChart from a PivotTable

Mastering Access | Project **8F** Annual Purchases

Perry Sanders, Community Relations Director, wants to compare the orthopedic supply orders over the past three years. In this project, you will create a PivotTable and a PivotChart to analyze the orders. Your completed PivotTable and PivotChart will look similar to Figure 8.49.

Project Files

For Project 8F, you will need the following file:

    a08F_Annual_Purchases

You will save your database as:

    Lastname_Firstname_8F_Annual_Purchases

Project Results

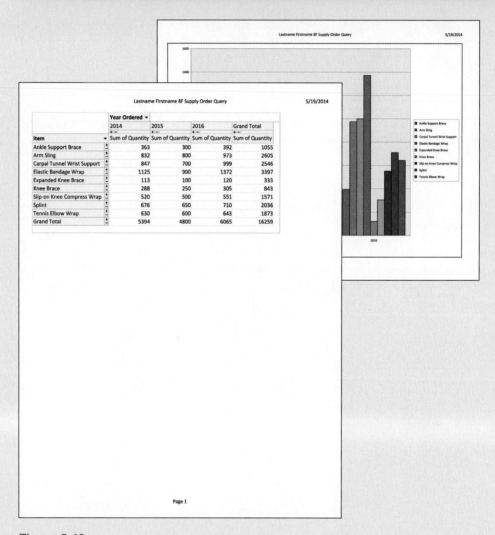

Figure 8.49

(Project 8F Annual Purchases continues on the next page)

Mastering Access | Project **8F** Annual Purchases (continued)

1 Start Access. Locate and open the **a08F_Annual_Purchases** file. Save the database in your **Access Chapter 8** folder as **Lastname_Firstname_8F_Annual_Purchases**

2 In the **Navigation Pane**, **Rename** the two tables and the query by adding your **Lastname Firstname** to the beginning of the object names. Under **Queries**, double-click **8F Supply Order Query** to run the query.

3 **Close** the **Navigation Pane**. On the **tab row**, right-click **8F Supplies Query**, and then click **PivotTable View**. If the **Field List** is not displayed, on the **Design** tab, in the **Show/Hide** group, click the **Field List** button.

4 In the **PivotTable Field List**, drag the **Item** field to the **Drop Row Fields Here** area. Drag the **Year Ordered** field to the **Drop Column Fields Here** area. Drag the **Quantity** field to the **Drop Totals or Detail Fields Here** area.

5 In the **PivotTable design area**, click any one of the **Quantity** boxes. On the **Design tab**, in the **Tools group**, click the **AutoCalc** button, and then click **Sum**. Hide the **Drop Zones** and collapse the **Drill buttons**.

6 **Close** the **PivotTable Field List**, and then **Save** the PivotTable. View the PivotTable in **Print Preview**. If you are instructed to submit this result, create a paper or electronic printout of the PivotTable. **Close** the **Print Preview**.

7 On the **tab row**, right-click **8F Supplies Query**, and then click **PivotChart View**. **Close** the **Chart Field List**. In the **Active Field group**, click the **Switch Row/Column** button. On the left side of the **PivotChart design area**, edit the **Axis Title** to display **Quantity Ordered** At the bottom of the **PivotChart design area**, edit the **Axis Title** to display **Year** Then **Close** the Properties dialog box. Add the **Legend** to the chart, and then click the **Drop Zones** button.

8 **Save** the PivotChart, and then view the PivotChart in **Print Preview**. If you are instructed to submit this result, create a paper or electronic printout of the PivotChart in **Landscape** orientation. Add the word **Chart** to the file name if you create an electronic printout. **Close Print Preview**, and then **Close** the PivotChart.

9 **Open** the **Navigation Pane**. **Close** the database, and then **Exit** Access.

End **You have completed Project 8F**

Access | Chapter 8

Content-Based Assessments

Mastering Access | Project **8G** Hospital Expansion

Paul Sandheinrich, CEO of the Providence and Warwick Hospital in Providence, Rhode Island, has proposed expanding one of the hospital's facilities. In this project, you will create a PivotTable to summarize the budgeted amounts for this expansion project. You will then build a macro embedded in a button on the 8G Projects form to open the PivotTable in Print Preview. Your completed PivotTable and Document Analyzer Form report will look similar to Figure 8.50.

Project Files

For Project 8G, you will need the following file:

    a08G_Hospital_Expansion

You will save your database as:

    Lastname_Firstname_8G_Hospital_Expansion

Project Results

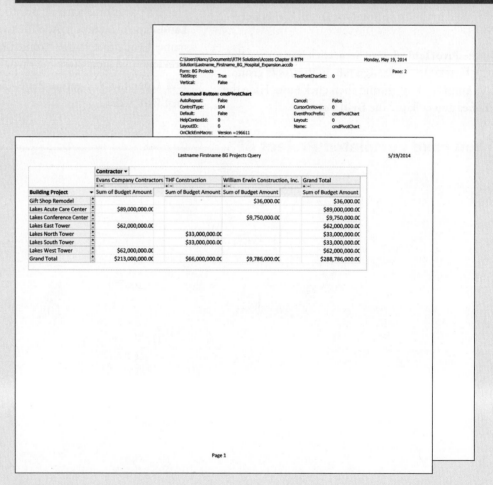

Figure 8.50

(Project 8G Hospital Expansion continues on the next page)

Content-Based Assessments

Mastering Access | Project **8G** Hospital Expansion (continued)

1 **Start** Access. Locate and open the **a08G_Hospital_Expansion** file. Save the database in your **Access Chapter 8** folder as **Lastname_Firstname_8G_Hospital_Expansion** Rename the **8G Projects Query** by adding your **Lastname Firstname** to the beginning of the query name.

2 Open the **8G Projects Query** and switch to **PivotTable** view. From the **Field List**, drag the **Building Project** field to the **Drop Row Fields Here** area. Drag the **Contractor** field to the **Drop Column Fields Here** area. Drag the **Budget Amount** field to the **Drop Totals or Detail Fields Here** area. Auto calculate the **Sum** for the **Budget Amount**. Hide **Details** and **Drop Zones**. **Close** the **PivotTable**, saving changes.

3 Open the **8G Projects** form in **Design** view. Click the **Summary** button and open the **Property Sheet**. On the **Event** tab, click the **On Click Build** button, and then open the **Macro Designer**. In the **Add New Action bar**, select **OpenQuery**. Open the **8G Projects Query** in **PivotTable** view. Set the **Data Mode** to **Read Only**. Add a **Comment Opens the PivotTable for the 8G Projects query** In a

second **Action** box, add a **RunMenuCommand** with a **Command** of **PrintPreview**, and a **Comment Switches to Print Preview Close** the Macro Designer, saving changes.

4 Switch the **8G Projects** form to **Form** view. Click the **Summary** button. Click the **Landscape** button. Set **Margins** to **Normal**. If you are instructed to submit this result, create a paper or electronic printout. Close Print Preview.

5 **Close** the query and the form. Run the **Database Documenter**. Select the **Forms** tab, and click **8G Projects**. Click the **Options** button and under **Include for Form**, select the **Code** check box only. Click the **Properties** button. Under **Print Categories**, be sure only **Other Properties** is selected. Click **OK** three times. If you are instructed to submit this result, create a paper or electronic printout of only page 2 of the report. Include the project number, 8G, in the file name if you create an electronic printout. **Close PrintPreview**.

6 **Open** the **Navigation Pane**. **Close** the database, and then **Exit** Access.

End **You have completed Project 8G**

Content-Based Assessments

GO! Fix It | Project **8H** Medical Transcription

Project Files

For Project 8H, you will need the following file:

a08H_Medical_Transcription

You will save your database as:

Lastname_Firstname_8H_Medical_Transcription

In this project, you will create an Autoexec macro that will open both forms in the database. You will create a macro group that will search for a specific transcriptionist and associate macros of this group with an event and embed a macro in the *8H Transcriptionists* form. Finally, you will view a PivotTable to display the number of lines each transcriptionist completes by document type.

- Create an Autoexec macro to open the **8H Search** form and then the **8H Transcriptionists** form, both in Form view and Normal Window Mode. Add a descriptive comment to each action.

- Create a macro to locate a transcriptionist in the **8H Transcriptionists** form. Show all actions, and include comments. Save the macro as **Lastname Firstname 8H Search**

  - Add an **IF** condition based on the condition **IsNull([Forms]![8H Search]![LastName])** It should close the **8H Search** form without saving, and stop the macro.

  - Add a **SetValue** action with an item **[Forms]![8H Search].[Visible]** set to **False**.

  - Add a **SelectObject** action to select the **8H Transcriptionist** form, and then a **GoToControl** action to go to the **Last Name** field in the form. Add an action to **RunMenuCommand: Sort Ascending**.

  - Add a **FindRecord** action to find **=[Forms]![8H Search]![LastName]** matching the whole field in the current form, finding the first occurrence. Then close the **8H Search** form without saving.

  - Add a **MessageBox** action titled **Search for Transcriptionist** to provide the following information: **Click the Remove Sort button to restore original order**

- Associate the **OK** button in the **8H Search** form with an **OnClick** action running the **8H Search** macro

- On the **8H Transcriptionists** form, embed a macro in the **Print** button to print the current record.

- Run the **Database Documenter** for all macros and the **8H Transcriptionist** form. Include **Properties** and **Actions and Arguments**. If you are instructed to submit this result, create a paper or electronic printout.

- Rename the query by adding your **Lastname Firstname** to the beginning of the query name. Open the query, and then switch to **PivotTable** view.

  - Display **Doc Type** as the row headings, **Last Name** as the column headings, and **# of Lines** as the detail section. Add an **Auto Calculation** for the **Average # of Lines** by **Doc Type**.

  - Remove the **Drop Zones** from the table and collapse the details. If you are instructed to submit this result, create a paper or electronic printout.

End You have completed Project 8H ————————————————

Content-Based Assessments

GO! Make It | Project **8I** Recruiting Events

Project Files

For Project 8I, you will need the following file:

a08I_Recruiting_Events

You will save your database as:

Lastname_Firstname_8I_Recruiting_Events

From the student files that accompany this textbook, open the **a08I_Recruiting_Events** database file. Save the database in your Access Chapter 8 folder as **Lastname_Firstname_8I_ Recruiting_Events** Create an autoexec macro to display the 8I Intro Screen form when the database opens. Add your **Lastname Firstname** to the beginning of the 8I Events Query, and open it. Switch to PivotTable view to display the number of candidates by Specialty (row headings) and Semester (column headings). View the query in PivotChart view with appropriate axis titles and a legend. Compare your macro, PivotTable, and PivotChart to those shown in Figure 8.51. Create a paper or electronic printout as directed.

Project Results

Figure 8.51

End You have completed Project 8I ——————————

Content-Based Assessments

GO! Solve It | Project **8J** Dictation Department

Project Files

For Project 8J, you will need the following file:

a08J_Dictation_Department

You will save your database as:

Lastname_Firstname_8J_Dictation_Department

Margo Dalton, Vice President of Operations, coordinates the dictation jobs from the physicians with the transcription jobs for the hospital. She needs to consider the number of lines per document and the length of the dictation. Open the **a08J_Dictation_Department** database and save it as **Lastname_Firstname_8J_Dictation_Department** In this project, you will create an Autoexec macro to open the **8J Providers** form in Form view. You will then create a macro group to locate a particular provider by last name or cancel the search if nothing is selected. Name the macro group **Lastname Firstname 8J Find Provider Group** Associate sub macros from the group with the OK and Cancel buttons on the **8J Search** form. If you are instructed to submit this result, create a paper or electronic printout of the details of the macros.

Add your **Lastname Firstname** to the beginning of the **8J Dictated Minutes** query name. Create a PivotTable using the data from the query. Use the First Name for the column headings and the Doc Type for the row headings. The Length of the dictation should be placed in the detail area, and then display the average lengths of dictation. Collapse the details, and remove the drop zones. Create a PivotChart from the **8J Dictated Minutes** query. Switch row/column data. Add a legend, appropriate axis titles, and a chart title. Save the PivotTable and the PivotChart. If you are instructed to submit this result, create a paper or electronic printout of both the table and chart in landscape orientation.

	Performance Level		
Performance Element	**Exemplary:** You consistently applied the relevant skills	**Proficient:** You sometimes, but not always, applied the relevant skills	**Developing:** You rarely or never applied the relevant skills
Create Autoexec macro	Autoexec created with correct actions, arguments, and comments.	Autoexec created with no more than two missing actions, arguments, or comments.	Autoexec created with more than two missing actions, arguments, or comments.
Create 8J FindProviderGroup macro group	FindProviderGroup created with correct actions, arguments, and comments.	FindProviderGroup created with no more than two missing actions, arguments, or comments.	FindProviderGroup created with more than two missing actions, arguments, or comments.
Create PivotTable from 8J Dictated Minutes query	PivotTable created and formatted correctly.	PivotTable created with no more than two missing elements.	PivotTable created with more than two missing elements.
Create PivotChart from 8J Dictated Minutes query	PivotChart created and formatted correctly.	PivotChart created with no more than two missing elements.	PivotChart created with more than two missing elements.

End **You have completed Project 8J** ————————————————

Content-Based Assessments

GO! Solve It | Project 8K Stay Length

Project Files

For Project 8K, you will need the following file:

a08K_Stay_Length

You will save your database as:

Lastname_Firstname_8K_Stay_Length

The Vice President for Operations at the Providence Warwick Hospital, Margo Dalton, must prepare a report on the length of patient hospital stays. She needs your help to present this data in a meaningful way. You have suggested creating a PivotTable and PivotChart. Open the **a08K_Length_ of_Stay** database and save it as **Lastname_Firstname_8K_Stay_Length** Create an Autoexec standalone macro to display the **8K Intro Screen** form.

Add your **Lastname Firstname** to the beginning of the **8K Stay Length** query. Using this query, create a PivotTable to display the analysis of the average Stay Length in a particular facility. Display only In-Patients and Out-Patients in all facilities. Create a PivotChart in Clustered Column chart type, switching the rows and columns as necessary. Filter the chart to display only **P & W Eastside Health Center**, **P & W Southside Medical Center**, and **Providence & Warwick Hospital**. Add a legend and title to the chart, and remove the drop zones.

If you are instructed to submit this result, create a paper or electronic printout of the PivotTable and PivotChart with Normal margins. If you are instructed to submit the macro details, create a paper or electronic printout.

		Performance Level	
	Exemplary: You consistently applied the relevant skills	**Proficient:** You sometimes, but not always, applied the relevant skills	**Developing:** You rarely or never applied the relevant skills
Create Autoexec	Autoexec created with correct actions, arguments, and comments.	Autoexec created with no more than two missing actions, arguments, or comments.	Autoexec created with more than two missing actions, arguments, or comments.
Create PivotTable from 8K Stay Length query	PivotTable created and formatted correctly.	PivotTable created with no more than two missing elements.	PivotTable created with more than two missing elements.
Create PivotChart from 8K Stay Length query	PivotChart created and formatted correctly.	PivotChart created with no more than two missing elements.	PivotChart created with more than two missing elements.

Performance Element (vertical label)

End You have completed Project 8K ———————————

Outcomes-Based Assessments

Rubric

The following outcomes-based assessments are *open-ended assessments*. That is, there is no specific correct result; your result will depend on your approach to the information provided. Make *Professional Quality* your goal. Use the following scoring rubric to guide you in *how* to approach the problem and then to evaluate *how well* your approach solves the problem.

The *criteria*—Software Mastery, Content, Format and Layout, and Process—represent the knowledge and skills you have gained that you can apply to solving the problem. The *levels of performance*—Professional Quality, Approaching Professional Quality, or Needs Quality Improvements—help you and your instructor evaluate your result.

	Your completed project is of Professional Quality if you:	Your completed project is Approaching Professional Quality if you:	Your completed project Needs Quality Improvements if you:
1-Software Mastery	Choose and apply the most appropriate skills, tools, and features and identify efficient methods to solve the problem.	Choose and apply some appropriate skills, tools, and features, but not in the most efficient manner.	Choose inappropriate skills, tools, or features, or are inefficient in solving the problem.
2-Content	Construct a solution that is clear and well organized, contains content that is accurate, appropriate to the audience and purpose, and is complete. Provide a solution that contains no errors in spelling, grammar, or style.	Construct a solution in which some components are unclear, poorly organized, inconsistent, or incomplete. Misjudge the needs of the audience. Have some errors in spelling, grammar, or style, but the errors do not detract from comprehension.	Construct a solution that is unclear, incomplete, or poorly organized; contains some inaccurate or inappropriate content; and contains many errors in spelling, grammar, or style. Do not solve the problem.
3-Format and Layout	Format and arrange all elements to communicate information and ideas, clarify function, illustrate relationships, and indicate relative importance.	Apply appropriate format and layout features to some elements, but not others. Overuse features, causing minor distraction.	Apply format and layout that does not communicate information or ideas clearly. Do not use format and layout features to clarify function, illustrate relationships, or indicate relative importance. Use available features excessively, causing distraction.
4-Process	Use an organized approach that integrates planning, development, self-assessment, revision, and reflection.	Demonstrate an organized approach in some areas, but not others; or, use an insufficient process of organization throughout.	Do not use an organized approach to solve the problem.

Outcomes-Based Assessments

GO! Think | Project **8L** Patient Charges

Project Files

For Project 8L, you will need the following file:

a08L_Patient_Charges

You will save your database as:

Lastname_Firstname_8L_Patient_Charges

Paul Sandheinrich, CEO for Providence and Warwick Hospital, wants to study the patient charges accrued over the past few months at each of the facilities. Open the **a08L_Patient_Charges** database, close the Intro Screen, and save the database as **Lastname_Firstname_8L_Patient_Charges** Create a standalone macro to open the **8L Patient Charges** report in Report view for the user to enter a facility name. Save this macro as **Lastname Firstname Charge Report** Use P&W Asthma Center as the facility from which to generate the report. Open the **8L Patient Charges** report in Design view, close the Intro screen again, and embed macros in both buttons in the Report Header. In the Display another facility button, embed a macro to close the current report without saving and open the **8L Patient Charges** report to allow selection of a different facility. In the Close Database button, embed a macro to close the report without saving and close the database.

If you are instructed to submit this result, create a paper or electronic printout of the report and macro details.

 You have completed Project 8L ————————————

GO! Think | Project **8M** Clinical Trials

Project Files

For Project 8M, you will need the following file:

a08M_Clinical_Trials

You will save your database as:

Lastname_Firstname_8M_Clinical_Trials

Perry Sanders, Community Relations Director, is very concerned about the health problems of the people living in the metropolitan area of Providence and the surrounding cities of Warwick and Fall River. She has requested the services of two of the doctors on the hospital staff to coordinate studies of these major health problems. In this project, you will open the **08M_Clinical_Trials** database and save it as **Lastname_Firstname_8M_Clinical_Trials**

Create an Autoexec macro to open the 8M Intro Screen and Beep when the database is opened. Create a PivotTable from the **8M Trials by Physician** query. Use the Medical Record # as the field to count the number of patients in each study. Display these counts by study and physician's last name. Create and format a PivotChart to display the number of patients by physician's last name. Display a Stacked Column chart with a descriptive Chart Title. Next, create a standalone macro to open the **8M Trials by Physician** query in PivotTable view. Name this macro **Lastname Firstname 8M PivotTable** Create a second standalone macro to open the **8M Trials by Physician** query in PivotChart view. Name this macro **Lastname Firstname 8M PivotChart**

If you are instructed to submit this result, create a paper or electronic printout of the macro details, the PivotTable, and the PivotChart.

 You have completed Project 8M ————————————

Outcomes-Based Assessments

You and GO! | Project **8N** Club Directory

Project Files

For Project 8N, you will need the following file:

> Lastname_Firstname_7N_Club_Directory

You will save your document as:

> Lastname_Firstname_8N_Club_Directory

Create a personal database containing information about a club and its activities if you do not already have one from Project 7N. Name the new database **Lastname_Firstname_8N_Club_Directory** If you do not have the database from Project 7N, create two related tables, one that lists the activities your organization has planned and the other to service as the directory of the group. The **Activities** table should include information about the name (primary key field), date, cost, and location of the activity. The dates must all occur next year, and consider attaching directions to the event to the table. The **Directory** table should include full name, address, phone number, e-mail, and an activity they are planning. Also, use all of the fields in the directory table in a form. Include a title and applicable image. Be sure all data is visible in the text boxes. Add a background color to the report header and footer. Select a coordinating font color for the label controls in the Detail section of the form. Add a button to print the current form. If you have the database from Project 7N, save as an Access Database in your Access Chapter 8 folder.

Open the **Directory** form in Design view. Add a button labeled **Print Record**, and then embed a macro to run when the Print Record button is clicked. The macro should print the selected record only.

Open the query that displays a list of events, along with the location and price. View the query in PivotTable view to display the price by event and location. The events should display as row headings and the locations as column headings.

If you are instructed to submit this result, create a paper or electronic printout of the macro details and the PivotTable.

You will be using this database in future chapters. Be sure to make corrections to your tables as necessary to prepare for the next chapter.

End **You have completed Project 8N** ————————————————————

Integrating Access with Other Applications

OUTCOMES

At the end of this chapter you will be able to:

PROJECT 9A
Import data from and link to data in other Office applications.

PROJECT 9B
Export data to Office applications, to HTML, and to XML files; create memos using mail merge.

OBJECTIVES

Mastering these objectives will enable you to:

1. Import Data from a Word Table (p. 601)
2. Import Data from an Excel Workbook (p. 610)
3. Insert an Excel Chart into a Report (p. 613)
4. Import from and Link to Another Access Database (p. 617)

5. Export Data to Word (p. 622)
6. Use Mail Merge to Integrate Access and Word (p. 627)
7. Export Data to Excel (p. 632)
8. Export Data to an HTML File and an XML File (p. 637)

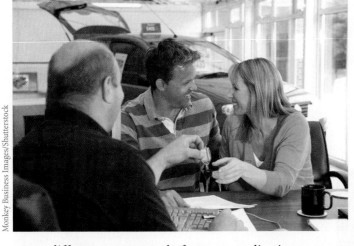

Monkey Business Images/Shutterstock

In This Chapter

Although you can create tables by entering all of the data into the tables, the data may already exist in other files, such as a Word table, an Excel worksheet, another Access database, or another database application. You can either import data from another source or link to the data in an external source.

You can also export data from an Access database into a variety of different applications, such as Word, Excel, another Access database, or another database application. You can also use the data in an Access object to create individualized memos or letters. To share database information across different computer platforms or applications, you can export your tables, forms, queries, or reports using XML, a markup language similar to HTML, the markup language used to create Web pages.

Liberty Motors has one of eastern Missouri's largest inventories of popular new car brands, sport utility vehicles, hybrid cars, and motorcycles. Their sales, service, and finance staff are all highly trained and knowledgeable about their products, and the company takes pride in its consistently high customer satisfaction ratings. Liberty also offers extensive customization options for all types of vehicles through its accessories division. Custom wheels, bike and ski racks, car covers, and chrome accessories are just a few of the ways Liberty customers customize their cars.

Project 9A Liberty Motors

Project Activities

In Activities 9.01 through 9.08, you will assist Phillip Garrett, President of Liberty Motors, and Jeanine Thomas, Finance Manager, in bringing data from Word, Excel, and other Access databases into a new Access database to create queries and reports. They need to import data from Microsoft Word and Excel as well as link information from another Access database. Your results will look similar to Figure 9.1.

Project Files

For Project 9A, you will need the following files:

> New blank Access database
> a09A_Employees.docx
> a09A_Used_Auto_Inventory.xlsx
> a09A_Logo.jpg
> a09A_Used_Auto_Chart.xlsx
> a09A_SUVs_and_Motorcycles.accdb

You will save your files as:

> Lastname_Firstname_9A_Liberty_Motors.accdb
> Lastname_Firstname_9A_Employees_Table.txt

Project Results

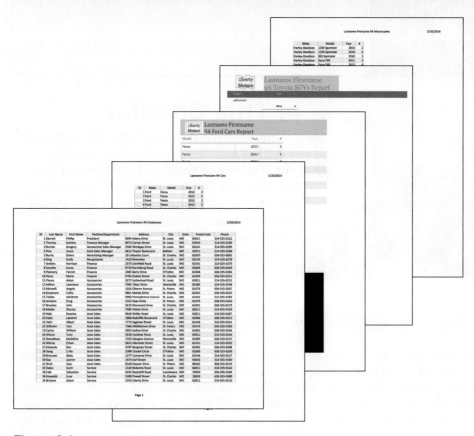

Figure 9.1
Project 9A Liberty Motors

Objective 1 | Import Data from a Word Table

When you create a database, you can type the records directly into a table. You can also *import* data from a variety of sources. Importing is the process used to bring *in* a copy of data from one source or application to another application. For example, you can import data from a Word table or Excel spreadsheet into an Access database.

As you import data from the various applications, be sure to read what may happen to the data. Sometimes an existing table will be overwritten, and sometimes data will be appended to the imported object if an object with the same name exists in the database. Sometimes you can change the data in the database, and the change will be updated in the source document and vice versa; sometimes the data will not be synchronized between the imported object and the source object.

Activity 9.01 | Preparing a Word Table for Importing

In this activity, you will create an empty database to store an imported Word table and then prepare the Word table for the import process.

1 **Start** Access. On the right side of the screen, under **File Name**, select the text, and then type **Lastname_Firstname_9A_Liberty_Motors** Click the **Browse** button. Navigate to the drive on which you will be saving your folders and projects for this chapter, create a new folder named **Access Chapter 9**, and then click **OK**. Click the **Create** button to create the database, and then **Close** ☒ the displayed table.

> You have created an empty database to store the table that you will import from Word.

2 **Close** the database, and then **Exit** Access.

3 **Start** Word. Display **Backstage** view, and then click **Open**. Navigate to the location where the student data files for this textbook are saved. Locate and open the **a09A_Employees** file. Notice that employee data is saved in a table in this Word document.

4 On the Ribbon, click the **Table Tools Layout tab**. In the **Data group**, click the **Convert to Text** button, and then compare your screen with Figure 9.2.

> To import data from a Word table into an Access table, the data must be *converted* or changed to a *delimited file*—a file where each record displays on a separate line and the fields within the record are separated by a single character called a *delimiter*. A delimiter can be a paragraph mark, a tab, a comma, or another character.

Figure 9.2

Convert to Text button

Word table

Convert Table to Text dialog box

Text delimiters

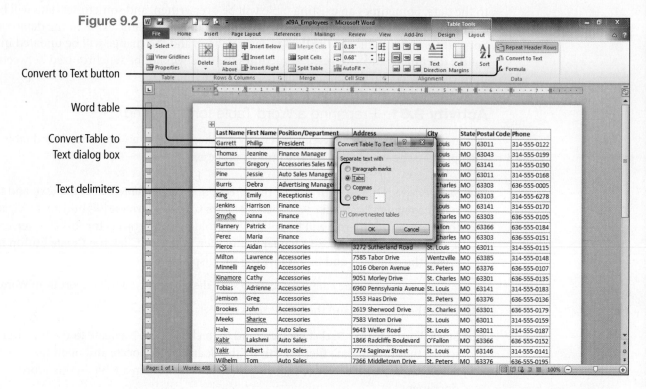

5 In the displayed **Convert Table to Text** dialog box, be sure that the **Tabs** option button is selected—this is the delimiter character you will use to separate the data into fields—and then click **OK**.

6 On the **Home tab**, in the **Paragraph group**, click the **Show/Hide** ¶ button to display formatting marks if they are not already displayed. Click anywhere in the document to deselect the text, and then compare your screen with Figure 9.3.

> Clicking the Show/Hide button enables you to see the tabs between the fields and the paragraph marks at the end of each line. Word also flags some proper names as spelling errors because they are not listed in the Word dictionary.

Figure 9.3

Show/Hide button

Word flags unrecognized proper names

Tab character separates fields

Paragraph mark at end of lines

7 Display **Backstage** view, click **Save As**, and then navigate to the **Access Chapter 9** folder. In the **Save As** dialog box, in the **File name** box, select the existing text, and then type **Lastname_Firstname_9A_Employees_Table** Click the **Save as type arrow**, and from the displayed list, scroll down, and then click **Plain Text**. In the **Save As** dialog box, click **Save**, and then compare your screen with Figure 9.4.

> A Word table must be converted to a delimited text file and then saved as either *Plain Text* or Rich Text. Data stored in Plain Text format contains no formatting, such as bold or italics. Plain Text stores the data using the *ASCII*—American Standard Code for Information Interchange—character set. The File Conversion dialog box displays for you to confirm the conversion to a text file.

Figure 9.4

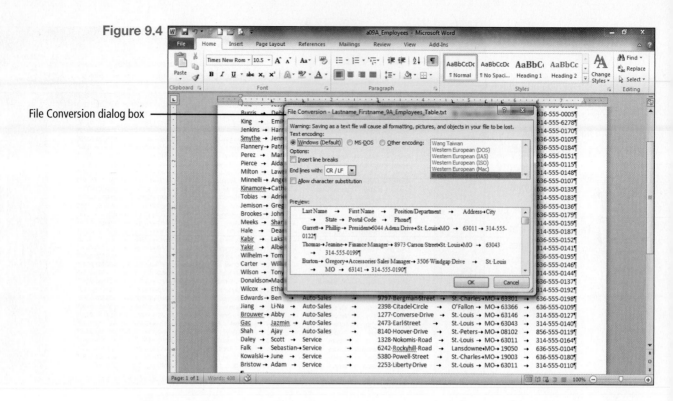

File Conversion dialog box

8 In the displayed **File Conversion** dialog box, accept the default settings, and then click **OK**. **Close** the document, and **Exit** Word.

Activity 9.02 | Importing Data from a Word Table

In this activity, you will import the Word table data that is stored in a delimited text file into your 9A_Liberty_Motors database.

1 **Start** Access. On the left side of the opening screen, click **Recent**, and click **9A_Liberty_ Motors** to open the empty database. Enable the content or add the Access Chapter 9 folder to the Trust Center. Notice that in the Navigation Pane, there are no tables in the database.

2 On the **External Data tab**, in the **Import & Link group**, click the **Text File** button. In the displayed **Get External Data - Text File** dialog box, to the right of the **File name** box, click **Browse**. Navigate to the **Access Chapter 9** folder. In the **File Open** dialog box, double-click **9A_Employees_Table**, and then compare your screen with Figure 9.5.

The source file—the one being imported—is listed in the File name box. When importing, if a table with the same name as the imported table does not exist, Access creates the object. If a table with the same name exists in the database, Access may overwrite its contents with the imported data. If you modify data in the original text file, the data will not be updated in the Access database.

A **link** is a connection to data in another file. When linking, Access creates a table that maintains a link to the source data. You cannot change or delete data in a linked Access table; however, you can add new records.

Figure 9.5

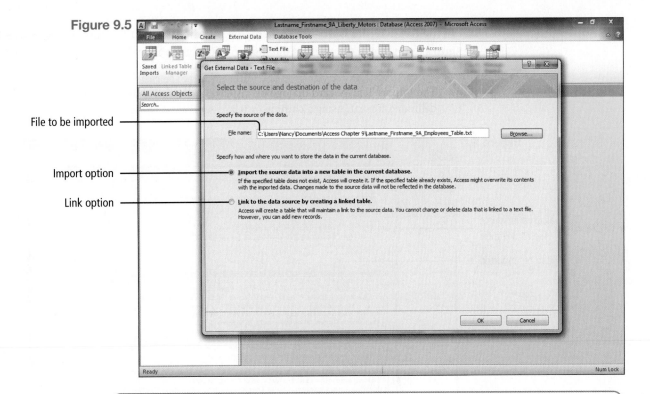

File to be imported

Import option

Link option

Note | Importing Versus Linking Database Files

Import when any of the following is true:

• The source file size is small and is changed infrequently.

• Data does not need to be shared with individuals using other database applications.

• You are replacing an old database application, and the data is no longer needed in the older format.

• You need to load data from another source to begin populating tables.

• You need the performance of Access 2010 while working with data from other database formats.

Link to a source when any of the following is true:

• The file is larger than the maximum capacity of a local Access database (2 gigabytes).

• The file is changed frequently.

• Data must be shared on a network with individuals using other database applications.

• The application is distributed to several individuals, and you need to make changes to the queries, forms, reports, and modules without changing the data already entered into the underlying tables.

3 In the **Get External Data - Text File** dialog box, be sure that the **Import the source data into a new table in the current database** option button is selected, and then click **OK**. Compare your screen with Figure 9.6.

The Import Text Wizard dialog box displays, indicating that the data seems to be in a delimited format, using a comma or tab to separate each field.

Figure 9.6

Tab was used in source file as delimiter

File to be imported

4 In the **Import Text Wizard** dialog box, be sure that the **Delimited** option button is selected and click **Next**.

In this Import Text Wizard dialog box, you select the delimiter that you used when you created the text file.

5 Click each delimiter option button, and then notice how the text is affected in the preview window. When you are finished, be sure that the **Tab** option button is selected. Select the **First Row Contains Field Names** check box to convert the field names to column headings instead of first record data. Click the **Text Qualifier arrow**, and notice that a single quotation mark and a double quotation mark display. If you are working with a file that includes text in quotation marks, you would indicate this by selecting either the single quotation mark or the double quotation mark. Be sure that {**none**} is selected, and then compare your screen with Figure 9.7.

Figure 9.7

Click if text is surrounded
by single or double
quotation marks

Tab was used in source
file as delimiter

Select if first row
contains field name

6 Click **Next**, and then compare your screen with Figure 9.8.

In this Import Text Wizard dialog box, under Field Options, you can change the field
name, set the data type, index the field, or skip the importing of the field.

Figure 9.8

Field options for
selected field

Select to not import
the selected field

Scroll to display
more fields

Scroll to display
more records

Access | Chapter 9

> **Note** | Saving Data as a New Table or Appending Data
>
> If there is an existing table in the database, another Import Text Wizard dialog box displays before the one enabling you to change field options. This dialog box enables you to save the imported table as a new table or in an existing table. If you select the existing table, the data will be **appended**—added—to the end of the existing table.

7 The Field Options for the **Last Name** field are correct. Use the horizontal scroll bar to display the fields on the right. Click in the **Postal Code** field to select the field. Under **Field Options**, click the **Data Type arrow**, and then click **Text**.

> Because Access determined that the Postal Code field contained all numbers, it assigned a data type of Long Integer. Recall that fields containing numbers that are not used in calculations should have a data type of Text.

8 Click **Next** to display primary key options, and then compare your screen with Figure 9.9.

Figure 9.9

Primary key options

Access adds ID field as primary key

9 Be sure that the **Let Access add primary key** option button is selected, and then click **Next**. Import to the new table named **Lastname Firstname 9A Employees**

> In this dialog box, you can accept the default name of the table or type a new name.

10 Click **Finish**. Because there are no errors in the imported file, the **Get External Data - Text File** dialog box displays, which enables you to save the import steps for future use.

> When you import or export data in Access, you can save the settings you used so that you can repeat the process at any time without using the wizard. The name of the source file, the name of the destination database, primary key fields, field names, and all the other specifications you set are saved. You cannot save the specifications for linking or exporting only a portion of a table. Even though all of the specifications are saved, you can still change the name of the source file or destination file before running the import or export specification again.

> **Alert!** | Did an Error Message Box Display After Clicking Finish?
>
> If a message box displays, there may be extra blank lines at the end of the text file, which cause blank records to be inserted into the database. If this occurs, click OK two times. Open the new table, delete any empty records, display the table in Design view, and then set the appropriate field as the primary key.

11 Select the **Save import steps** check box to display additional options. Click in the **Description** box, and then type **Imports a tab-delimited file that was a Word table** Notice that if you are using Outlook, you can create an Outlook Task to remind you when to repeat the import operation. Click **Save Import**, and notice that in the **Navigation Pane**, the **9A Employees Table** displays.

> Access creates and saves the import specification in the current database. You cannot move or copy the specification to another database.

12 On the **External Data tab**, in the **Import & Link group**, click the **Saved Imports** button, and then compare your screen with Figure 9.10.

> The Manage Data Tasks dialog box displays with two tabs—one for Saved Imports, and one for Saved Exports. Clicking the Run button performs the operation using the selected specification. You can schedule execution by clicking the Create Outlook Task button or delete a specification by clicking the Delete button. You can change the name or description of a specification, change the source file in an import operation, or change the destination file in an export operation by clicking the appropriate section in the specification.

Figure 9.10

The destination

The source file

The description
of the import

13 In the **Manage Data Tasks** dialog box, click **Close**.

Access | Chapter 9

14 Double-click **9A Employees** to open the table in **Datasheet** view, and then **Close** ⟪ the **Navigation Pane**. Adjust the widths of all of the fields to display all of the data and the entire field name for each field.

> All of the data from the Word table, which was converted to a delimited file, has been imported successfully into a table within the database, saving you from typing the data.

More Knowledge | Importing from Other Applications

If you have data in other applications that you would like to import or link to your Access database, explore the options on the External Data tab, in the Import & Link group, by clicking the More button. A SharePoint List is a list of documents maintained on a server running Microsoft Office SharePoint Server. A SharePoint Server enables you to share documents with others in your organization. XML, which stands for eXtensible Markup Language, is the standard language for defining and storing data on the Web. You also can import data from other database applications, such as dBASE and ODBC databases. ODBC stands for Open Database Connectivity, a standard that enables databases using SQL statements to interface with one another. You can also import or link to an Outlook folder. Data can also be imported or linked to an HTML—HyperText Markup Language—document or Web document. HTML is a language used to display Web pages.

---

15 If you are instructed to submit this result, create a paper or electronic printout of the **first page** of the table in **Landscape** orientation, changing **Margins**, if necessary, to print all of the fields, and ensuring that the table name displays in the header. **Save** 🖫 the table, and then **Close** ✕ the table.

Objective 2 | Import Data from an Excel Workbook

Jessie Pine, the Auto Sales Manager, keeps an inventory of used cars, SUVs, and motorcycles in an Excel *workbook*. A workbook is an Excel file that contains one or more *worksheets*. A worksheet is the primary document used in Excel to save and work with data that is arranged in columns and rows. You can import the data from an Excel workbook into Access by copying the data from an open worksheet and pasting it into an Access datasheet, by importing a worksheet into a new or existing Access table, or by creating a link to a worksheet from an Access database. There is no way to save the workbook as an Access database within Excel; the individual worksheets within a workbook must be imported into an Access database.

Activity 9.03 | Importing Data from an Excel Worksheet

In this activity, you will import an Excel worksheet containing the used car inventory, creating a new table in your database.

1 If necessary, on the Ribbon, click the **External Data tab**. In the **Import & Link group**, click the **Excel** button.

> The Get External Data - Excel Spreadsheet dialog box displays, indicating that you can import the source data into a new table, append a copy of the records to an existing table, or link to the Excel worksheet.

2 In the **Get External Data - Excel Spreadsheet** dialog box, to the right of the **File name** box, click the **Browse** button. Navigate to the location where the student data files for this textbook are saved. Locate the **a09A_Used_Auto_Inventory** file, and then notice the icon to the left of the file name; it indicates the file is an Excel 2010 file. **Open** the file.

3 In the **Get External Data - Excel Spreadsheet** dialog box, click **OK**, and then compare your screen with Figure 9.11.

> The first Import Spreadsheet Wizard dialog box displays. A ***spreadsheet*** is another name for a worksheet. On this page you can select one worksheet—you can import only one worksheet at a time during an import operation. If you want to import several worksheets, save the import specification, and then change the source data. The first row displays column headings.

Figure 9.11

Import Spreadsheet Wizard dialog box

Display named ranges

First row displays column headings

Data in Ford Cars worksheet

Worksheets in a09A_ Used_Auto_Inventory workbook

4 In the **Import Spreadsheet Wizard** dialog box, click the **Show Named Ranges** option button, and then in the box, click **Ford**.

> This is the same data that displays in the *Ford Cars* worksheet, but without the column headings. If the Excel worksheet contains named ranges, you can select the Show Named Ranges option button. A ***range*** includes two or more selected cells on a worksheet that can be treated as a single unit. A ***named range*** is a range that has been given a name, making it easier to use the cells in calculations or modifications. A ***cell*** is the small box formed by the intersection of a column and a row.

5 Click **Show Worksheets**, and be sure that **Ford Cars** is selected. Click **Next** to display the second Import Spreadsheet Wizard dialog box. Notice that the wizard assumes that the first row contains column headings, and that Access uses the column headings as field names.

6 Click **Next** to display the third **Import Spreadsheet Wizard** dialog box.

> Just as you did when importing a text file, you can change the field name, index the field, set the data type, or remove the field from the import operation.

Access | Chapter 9

7 Click **Next**. In the fourth **Import Spreadsheet Wizard** dialog box, be sure that **Let Access add primary key** is selected, and then click **Next**.

8 In the final **Import Spreadsheet Wizard** dialog box, in the **Import to Table** box, type **Lastname Firstname 9A Cars** and then click **Finish**. Because you do not want to save the import steps, in the **Get External Data - Excel Spreadsheet** dialog box, click **Close. Open** [»] the **Navigation Pane**, and then notice that the table displays in the Navigation Pane.

9 In the **Navigation Pane**, double-click **9A Cars** to open the table in **Datasheet** view. **Close** [«] the **Navigation Pane**, and then compare your screen with Figure 9.12.

The data from the *Ford Cars* worksheet in the *a09A_Used_Auto_ Inventory* Excel workbook has been imported into this new table.

Figure 9.12

New table created

Imported data from Excel worksheet

10 Close [×] the table.

More Knowledge | Importing from a Workbook That Contains a Chart

If a workbook contains a chart on a separate worksheet, when you try to import any worksheet into Access, a message box displays stating that the wizard cannot access the information in the file and that you should check the file you want to import to see if it exists and if it is in the correct format. You should make a copy of the workbook, open the copied workbook, and then delete the worksheet containing the chart or move the chart to the sheet with the related data. Save the workbook, close it, and then import the data from any of the worksheets.

Activity 9.04 | Appending Data from Excel to a Table

In this activity, you will append data from an Excel worksheet to the *9A Cars* table. To append data, the table must already be created.

1 If necessary, on the Ribbon, click the **External Data tab**. In the **Import & Link group**, click the **Excel** button. In the **Get External Data - Excel Spreadsheet** dialog box, click **Browse**. Navigate to the location where the student data files for this textbook are saved. Locate and **Open** the **a09A_Used_Auto_Inventory** file.

2 Under **Specify how and where you want to store the data in the current database**, click **Append a copy of the records to the table**. Click the **table name box arrow** to display the names of the two tables that are saved in the database. Be sure that **9A Cars** is selected, and then click **OK**.

3 In the first **Import Spreadsheet Wizard** dialog box, click the **Chevrolet Cars** worksheet, and then click **Next**. In the second **Import Spreadsheet Wizard** dialog box, notice that Access has determined that the first row matches the field names contained in the existing table and that you cannot clear the check box. Click **Next**.

4 In the **Import Spreadsheet Wizard** dialog box, click **Finish** to import the data to the **9A Cars** table in the current database.

5 In the **Get External Data - Excel Spreadsheet** dialog box, click **Close**, and then **Open** ⨠ the **Navigation Pane**. Double-click **9A Cars** to display the table in **Datasheet** view. **Close** ⨞ the **Navigation Pane**, and then compare your screen with Figure 9.13.

The data from the *Chevrolet Cars* worksheet in the *a09A_Used_Auto_Inventory* workbook is appended to the *9A Cars* table in your database.

Figure 9.13

Data imported and appended

6 If you are instructed to submit this result, create a paper or electronic printout of the table. **Close** ☒ the table.

Objective 3 | Insert an Excel Chart into a Report

A *chart* is a graphic representation of data. Data presented in a chart is easier to understand than a table of numbers. *Column charts* display comparisons among related numbers, *pie charts* display the contributions of parts to a whole amount, and *line charts* display trends over time. Excel is the best tool for creating a chart because there are a wide variety of chart types and formatting options.

Access | Chapter 9

Activity 9.05 | Creating a Query and a Report

In this activity, you will create a query. Using the query, you will create a report that will be used in the next activity.

1 On the Ribbon, click the **Create tab**. In the **Queries group**, click the **Query Design** button. In the **Show Table** dialog box, double-click **9A Cars** to add the table to the Query Design workspace, and then **Close** the **Show Table** dialog box.

2 Expand the field list to display the entire table name. In the field list, click **Make**. Hold down [Shift], and then click **#** to select all four fields. Drag the selected fields down into the first column of the design grid, and then compare your screen with Figure 9.14.

Figure 9.14

Field list expanded

Four fields added to design grid

3 In the design grid, under **Make**, click in the **Criteria** box, and then type **Ford**

4 On the **Design tab**, in the **Results group**, click the **Run** button to display only the Ford cars.

5 Switch the query to **Design** view. In the design grid, under **Make**, on the **Show** row, clear the check box, and then **Run** the query.

> Recall that clearing the Show check box hides the field from the query. Because this query only displays Ford cars, hiding this field is appropriate.

6 Save 🖫 the query as **Lastname Firstname 9A Ford Cars Query** and then **Close** ✕ the query. **Open** » the **Navigation Pane**, and then notice that the query displays in the Navigation Pane.

7 In the **Navigation Pane**, under **Queries**, click **9A Ford Cars Query** to select the query, and then **Close** « the **Navigation Pane**.

8 On the Ribbon, click the **Create tab**. In the **Reports group**, click the **Report** button. Switch to **Design** view.

9 In the **Report Header** section, delete the **Date** and **Time text box controls**. Click anywhere in the **title**, double-click **Query** to select the word, and then type **Report** Delete the space before **9A**, and then press [Shift] + [Enter]. Press [Enter].

10 Click the image to the left of the title to select it. On the **Design tab**, in the **Header/Footer group**, click the **Logo** button. Navigate to the location where the data files for this chapter are saved, and then double-click **a09A_Logo** to insert the logo. In the **Tools group**, click the **Property Sheet** button. Display the **Property Sheet Format tab**. Click in the **Size Mode** property box, and select **Zoom**. Resize the image so the right edge aligns with the **1-inch mark on the horizontal ruler**. **Close** [X] the **Property Sheet**.

11 In the **Page Footer** section, delete the **Page number text box control**. Resize the report to 6.5 inches wide. Compare your screen with Figure 9.15.

Figure 9.15

Date/time controls removed form Report Header

Right margin at 6.5 inches

Page number textbox control removed from Page Footer

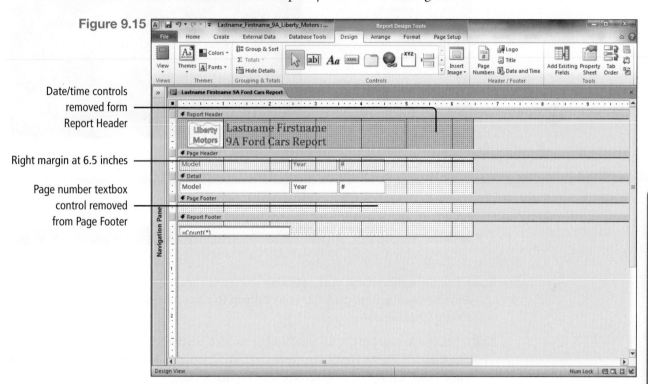

12 Save [💾] the report as **Lastname Firstname 9A Ford Cars Report**

Activity 9.06 | Inserting an Excel Chart into a Report

In this activity, you will insert an Excel chart into *9A Ford Cars Report*.

1 In the report, in **Design** view, point to the top of the **Report Footer section bar** until the pointer [↕] displays. Drag the section down to the **4-inch mark on the vertical ruler** to increase the size of the Page Footer section.

2 **Start** Excel. If necessary, maximize the Excel window. Display **Backstage** view, and then click **Open**. Navigate to the location where the data files for this chapter are saved, and then double-click **a09A_Used_Auto_Chart** to open the workbook. Compare your screen with Figure 9.16.

The workbook opens with the *Cars* worksheet displaying. A pie chart has been saved in the worksheet and displays the number of cars for each model of Ford vehicles.

Figure 9.16

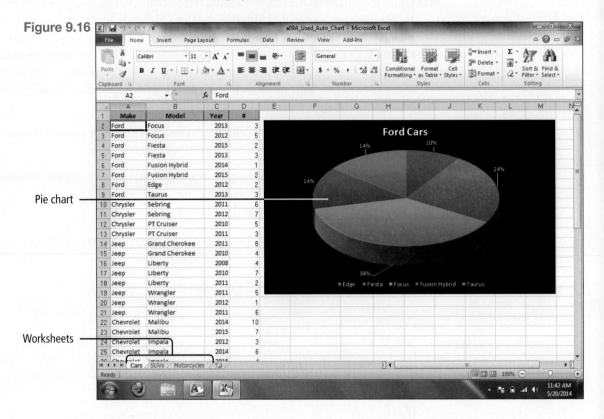

3 Click the outside edge of the **pie chart** to select the entire chart. On the **Home tab**, in the **Clipboard group**, click the **Copy** button to place a copy of the pie chart in the Office Clipboard.

4 Click the Access button on the Taskbar to activate the 9A Ford Cars Report in the database. In the **9A Ford Cars Report**, right-click the **Page Footer section bar**, and then click **Paste**. Compare your screen with Figure 9.17.

The pie chart is pasted into the Page Footer section of the report.

Figure 9.17

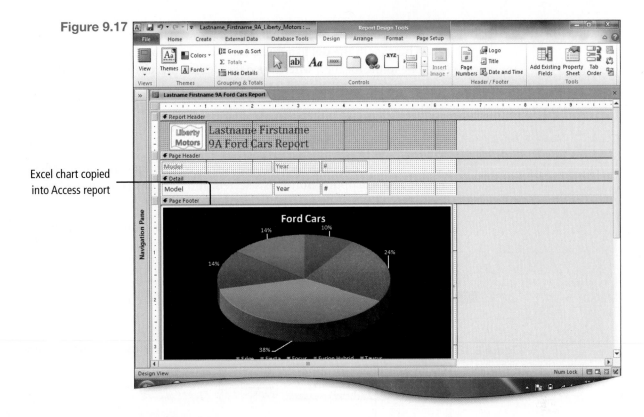

Excel chart copied into Access report

5 **Save** 💾 the report, and then switch to **Report** view. If you are instructed to submit this result, create a paper or electronic printout. **Close** ☒ the report. **Close** Excel.

Objective 4 | Import from and Link to Another Access Database

When you import data from another Access database, Access creates a copy of the source data without altering the source data. All of the objects in a database can be imported or copied to another Access database in a single operation. Import data from another Access database when you need to create similar tables or when you want to use the structure of the source database tables. Link to data in another Access database when the data is shared among multiple databases or if someone else needs to have the ability to add records and use the data, but not change the structure of the table.

Activity 9.07 | Importing Data from Another Access Database

In this activity, you will import the data contained in another Access database.

Access | Chapter 9

1 On the Ribbon, click the **External Data tab**. In the **Import & Link group**, click the **Access** button. In the **Get External Data - Access Database** dialog box, click **Browse**. Navigate to the location where the data files for this chapter are saved, and then double-click **a09A_SUVs_and_Motorcycles**.

> The source database must be closed before you can import data from it. The destination database must be open. To import the data into a new database, you must create a blank database that does not contain any objects before starting the import operation.

2 Be sure that the **Import tables, queries, forms, reports, macros, and modules into the current database** option button is selected, and then click **OK**. In the **Import Objects** dialog box, click the **Tables** tab.

> The Import Objects dialog box displays the two tables contained in the a09A_SUVs_and_ Motorcycles database. To choose multiple types of objects, first select one object, click the relevant tab, and then click the desired object on that tab. To cancel a selected object, click the object again.

3 In the **Import Objects** dialog box, click **9A SUVs**, and then compare your screen with Figure 9.18.

Figure 9.18
Import Objects dialog box
Tables in source database
Tabs for object types

Note | Importing Queries, Forms, and Reports

You can import table relationships, custom menus and toolbars, saved import/export specifications, and custom Navigation Pane groups. For tables, you can import the table definition and data or only the table definition. The *definition* is the structure of the database—the field names, data types, and field properties. You can import queries as queries or as tables. If you import a query as a query, you must also import the underlying table or tables used to create the query.

   Importing a query, form, report, subform, or subreport does not automatically import the underlying record sources. If you create one of these objects using the data in two related tables, you must also import those two tables; otherwise, these objects will not open properly.

4 In the **Import Objects** dialog box, click the **Queries tab**, and then click **9A Toyota SUVs Query**. Click the **Forms tab**, and then click **9A SUVs Form**. Click the **Reports tab**, click **9A Toyota SUVs Report**, and then click **OK**.

The Get External Data - Access Database dialog box displays, enabling you to save the import steps. If Access encounters any errors in the import operation, messages will display. To cancel the import operation during the importing process, press Ctrl + Break.

5 In the **Get External Data - Access Database** dialog box, click **Close**.

6 **Open** » the **Navigation Pane**, and then compare your screen with Figure 9.19.

A table, query, form, and report have been imported to the open database.

Figure 9.19

Imported table

Imported query

Imported form

Imported report

Alert! | Were All Four Objects Not Imported?

If all four objects were not imported, you may not have clicked the object in the Import Objects dialog box. To correct this, run the import operation again, and select the missing object or objects. Do not select objects that were imported correctly. For example, if you correctly imported the *9A SUVs* table, and then you import it again, a second *9A SUVs* table will be imported and will be named *9A SUVs1*.

---

7 In the **Navigation Pane**, under **Reports**, right-click **9A Toyota SUVs Report**, and then click **Layout View**. Click the title one time to select the title. Click to the left of **9A** to enter into editing mode, type your **Lastname Firstname** and then press Shift + Enter. Press Enter. On the **Format tab**, in the **Font group**, click the **Background Color arrow**, and then, under **Theme Colors**, select the fourth color in the second row—**Dark Blue, Text 2, Lighter 80%**.

8 Switch to **Report** view. **Save** 🖫 the report. If you are instructed to submit this result, create a paper or electronic printout.

9 **Close** ✕ the report, and then **Close** « the **Navigation Pane**.

Activity 9.08 | Linking to a Table in Another Access Database

In this activity, you will link to the data in the *9A Motorcycles* table in the *a09A_SUVs_ and_Motorcycles* database. You can link only to tables in another Access database; you cannot link to queries, forms, reports, macros, or modules.

1 On the Ribbon, click the **External Data tab**. In the **Import & Link group**, click the **Access** button. In the **Get External Data - Access Database** dialog box, **Browse** to the location where the data files for this chapter are saved, and then double-click **a09A_SUVs_and_Motorcycles**.

2 In the **Get External Data - Access Database** dialog box, click the **Link to the data source by creating a linked table** option button, and then click **OK**.

Changes made to the data in Access will be propagated to the source data and vice versa. If the source database requires a password, that password is saved with the linked table. You cannot make changes to the structure of the table in the linked table.

3 In the **Link Tables** dialog box, on the **Tables tab**, click **9A Motorcycles**, and then click **OK**.

4 **Open** [»] the **Navigation Pane**, if necessary, and then compare your screen with Figure 9.20.

The 9A Motorcycles linked table displays in the Navigation Pane under Tables. The arrow that displays to the left of the icon indicates that this is a linked object.

Figure 9.20

Linked Access table

5 In the **Navigation Pane**, under **Tables**, right-click **9A Motorcycles**, and then click **Rename**. Click at the beginning of the line, type your **Lastname Firstname** press [Spacebar] and then press [Enter].

6 In the **Navigation Pane**, under **Tables**, double-click **9A Motorcycles** to display the table in **Datasheet** view. Adjust the widths of the columns as necessary.

7 If you are instructed to submit this result, create a paper or electronic printout. If you submit this database electronically, also submit **a09A_SUVs_and_Motorcycles.accdb** in order to view the linked objects properly. **Close** [×] the table, saving changes when prompted. **Close** the database, and then **Exit** Access.

End **You have completed Project 9A**

Project 9B Used Car Inventory

myitlab
Project 9B Training

Project Activities

In Activities 9.09 to 9.15, you will help some of the sales staff at Liberty Motors who are using information from Access databases in other applications. In addition, you need to help the Webmaster include data on the company's Web site. Access enables you to export data from an Access database into other applications, such as Word, Excel, or another Access database, and merge data from an Access database with a Word document. You can also export data to be used on a Web page. Your completed files will look similar to Figure 9.21.

Project Files

For Project 9B, you will need the following files:

a09B_Used_Car_Inventory.accdb
a09B_Memo.docx

You will save your files as:

Lastname_Firstname_9B_Used_Car_Inventory.accdb
Lastname_Firstname_9B_Exported_Jeeps_Query.rtf
Lastname_Firstname_9B_Jeeps.docx
Lastname_Firstname_9B_Custom_Memo.docx
Lastname_Firstname_9B_Memo_Main
Lastname_Firstname_9B_Used_Vehicles.xlsx
Lastname_Firstname_9B_Used_Vehicles.pdf
Lastname_Firstname_9B_Jeeps_in_Stock.html
Lastname_Firstname_9B_Jeeps_in_Stock.rtf
Lastname_Firstname_9B_Jeeps_XML_File.htm
Lastname_Firstname_9B_Jeeps_XML_File.xml
Lastname_Firstname_9B_Jeeps_XML_File.xsl

Project Results

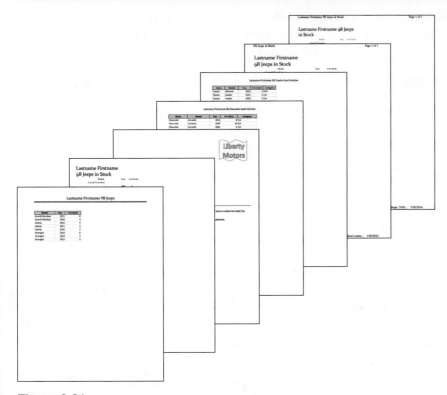

Figure 9.21
Project 9B Used Car Inventory

Access | Chapter 9

Objective 5 | Export Data to Word

You can *export* a table, query, form, or report to Word 2010. Exporting is the process used to send *out* a copy of data from one source or application to another application. You can then e-mail the Word document rather than the entire database. Exporting to Word is also helpful if you have a table that you want to format more than you can in an Access table. When you export an Access object, the Export Wizard creates a copy of the object's data in a Microsoft Word Rich Text Format file; an extension of .rtf is used. Hidden fields are not exported with tables, queries, and forms; visible fields and records display as a table in the Word document. When you export a report, the Export Wizard copies the report data and the design layout, making the Word document resemble the report as closely as possible.

Activity 9.09 | Exporting an Access Query to Word

In this activity, you will export a query to Word 2010. The database must be open in Access to perform the export operation because there is no Access import feature in Word.

1 **Start** Access. Navigate to the location where the student data files for this textbook are saved. Locate and open the **a09B_Used_Car_Inventory** file. Save the database in the **Access 2010 Database** format in your **Access Chapter 9** folder as **Lastname_Firstname_ 9B_Used_Car_Inventory** Enable the content, or add the Access Chapter 9 folder to the Trust Center.

2 In the **Navigation Pane**, **Rename** the two queries and one report by adding your **Lastname Firstname** to the beginning of the object names. Under **Queries**, double-click **9B Jeeps** to run and display the query results.

The query displays the model name, the year of the vehicle, and the number of Jeeps in stock.

3 Switch the query to **Design** view, expand the field lists so all data displays fully, and then compare your screen with Figure 9.22.

The underlying source of this query is the *9B Used Vehicles* query. In the design grid, in the last column, the criteria is *Jeep*, which extracts records with this criteria in the Make field. The field is hidden from the results because the data is redundant.

Figure 9.22

Underlying source of data

Hidden field

Criteria—only Jeep
Make extracted

4 **Close** ☒ the query. In the **Navigation Pane**, under **Queries**, right-click **9B Jeeps**, point to **Export**, and then click **Word RTF File**. Alternatively, on the Ribbon, click the **External Data** tab, and then in the **Export** group, click the **More** button, and then click **Word**. Compare your screen with Figure 9.23.

> The Export - RTF File dialog box displays, which enables you to select the destination for the data you want to export. Because the Export Wizard always exports formatted data, this option is selected and inactive. To display the Word document after the export operation is complete, select the check box for *Open the destination file after the export operation is complete*. The last selection—*Export only the selected records*—is inactive. If you want to export some of the records, before you begin the export operation, open the object and select the records.

Figure 9.23

Export - RTF File dialog box

Default storage location; yours will differ

Exported data will be formatted

Exports selected records in open database object

5 In the **Export - RTF File** dialog box, click **Browse**. Navigate to the **Access Chapter 9** folder. In the **File name** box, select the existing file name, type **Lastname_Firstname_9B_Exported_Jeeps_Query** and then click **Save**.

> **Note** | Exporting Data into an Existing Word Document
>
> When you export from Access to Word, the data is always exported into a new Word document. If you select an existing document, the Export Wizard overwrites the Word document with the new data. To insert the data into an existing Word document, export the data from Access into a new Word document, and then copy the data from the new Word document and paste it into the existing Word document. Alternatively, copy rows directly from an Access table, query, form, or report, and then paste them into the existing Word document.

6 In the **Export - RTF File** dialog box, under **Specify export options**, select the **Open the destination file after the export operation is complete** check box, and then click **OK**. If the Word document window does not fill the entire screen, click the Maximize button. Compare your screen with Figure 9.24. Do not be concerned if the paragraph symbols do not display.

The query data is exported to a Word document. Because the Word document did not exist, a new document was created. The data is displayed as a table in Word with the field names as column headings. The hidden field—Make—does not display. In the title bar of the Word document, *[Compatibility Mode]* displays because this document has an .rtf extension instead of the standard .docx extension.

Figure 9.24

Word document name

Compatibility Mode

Records

Field names

Table

7 In Word, on the Ribbon, click the **Insert tab**. In the **Header & Footer group**, click the **Header** button. In the **Built-In** gallery, click **Alphabet**, and then type **Lastname Firstname 9B Jeeps** In the **Close group**, click the **Close Header and Footer** button.

8 On the **Quick Access Toolbar**, click the **Save** button, and then compare your screen with Figure 9.25.

A message displays stating that a feature in the document is not supported by earlier versions of Word, meaning that a document with an .rtf extension cannot display the data in the same manner as Word. Although the summary is cryptic, in this case, an .rtf document cannot display content controls. If you click Continue, Word converts the header data to static text.

Figure 9.25

Compatibility issue with .rtf document

Click to display content control as static text

9 In the message box, click **Cancel**. Display **Backstage** view, and click **Save As**. If necessary, navigate to the **Access Chapter 9** folder. Click in the **Save as type** box, and select **Word Document (*.docx)**. Change the file name to **Lastname_Firstname_ 9B_Jeeps** In the **Save As** dialog box, click **Save**.

> A message box displays stating that you are about to save your document to one of the new file formats and that changes may be made in the layout of the document.

10 In the displayed message box, click **OK**. If you are instructed to submit this result, create a paper or electronic printout.

11 Close [X] the Word window. In the **Export-RTF File** dialog box, click **Close**.

Activity 9.10 | Exporting an Access Report to Word

In this activity, you will export the *9B Jeeps in Stock* report to a Word document.

1 In the **Navigation Pane**, under **Reports**, double-click **9B Jeeps in Stock** to open the report. Switch to **Layout** view. Click the title—**9B Jeeps in Stock**—two times to enter into editing mode. Click to the left of **9B**, type **Lastname Firstname** using your own first and last names, and then press [Shift] + [Enter]. Press [Enter], and then **Save** [icon] the report.

> The report displays Jeep models, the year, and the number of vehicles in stock for each year of the model. Each model is summed, and at the bottom of the report, the total number of Jeeps displays.

2 Close [X] the report. In the **Navigation Pane**, under **Reports**, right-click **9B Jeeps in Stock**, point to **Export**, and then click **Word RTF File**. Be sure that the **File name** box displays the correct path to your **Access Chapter 9** folder. In the **File name** box, select the existing file name, and type **Lastname_Firstname_9B_Jeeps_in_Stock** Under **Specify export options**, click the **Open the destination file after the export operation is complete** check box, and then click **OK**. Compare your screen with Figure 9.26.

> A message box displays, and then the document opens in Word. Although all of the data is exported, it is not aligned as nicely as it was in the Access report. You would probably want to do some further formatting in Word. All of the data is separated by tabs.

Figure 9.26

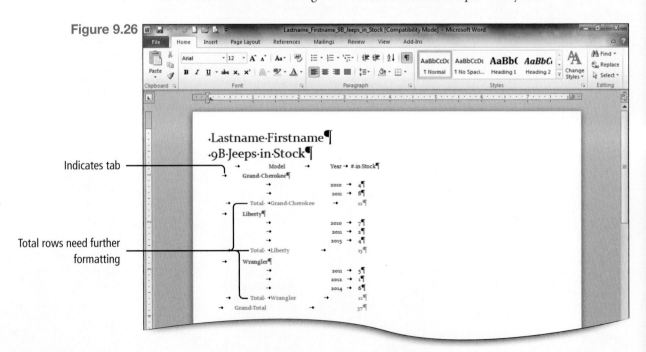

Indicates tab

Total rows need further formatting

3 If you are instructed to submit this result, create a paper or electronic printout. **Close** ![X] the Word window. In the **Export - RTF File** dialog box, click **Close**.

Objective 6 | Use Mail Merge to Integrate Access and Word

Using Word's *mail merge* feature, letters or memos are created by combining, or *merging*, two documents—a *main document* and a *data source*. The main document contains the text of a letter or memo. The data source—an Access table or query—contains the names and addresses of the individuals to whom the letter, memo, or other document is being sent. Use the Mail Merge Wizard within Access to create a direct link between the table or query and the Word document.

Activity 9.11 | Merging an Access Table with a Word Document

In this activity, you will create individual memos to the employees of Liberty Motors to inform them of an upcoming staff meeting. You will create the memos by merging the individual names and position or department in the 9B Employees Table with a memo created in Microsoft Word.

1 **Open** ![»] the **Navigation Pane**, if necessary, Click **9B Employees Table** to select the table. On the Ribbon, click the **External Data tab**. In the **Export group**, click the **Word Merge** button.

The Microsoft Word Mail Merge Wizard starts. In this first dialog box, you can link the data in the table to an existing Word document or create a new Word document and then link the data in the table to the new document.

2 Be sure that **Link your data to an existing Microsoft Word document** is selected, and then click **OK**. In the **Select Microsoft Word Document** dialog box, navigate to the location where the student data files for this textbook are saved. Locate and open the **a09B_Memo** file; click the **Microsoft Word** button on the taskbar to view the memo, and then compare your screen with Figure 9.27.

Microsoft Word opens with the memo on the left and the Mail Merge task pane on the right.

Figure 9.27

Microsoft Word window ⎯⎯

Mail Merge task pane ⎯⎯

Maximize button ⎯⎯

a09A_Memo document ⎯⎯

3 On the **Microsoft Word** title bar, click the **Maximize** ⬚ button. At the bottom of the **Mail Merge** task pane, notice that the wizard is on **Step 3 of 6**.

Because you are using an existing Word document, the first two steps are already defined.

4 In the **Mail Merge** task pane, under **Select recipients**, be sure that **Use an existing list** is selected. Under **Use an existing list**, click **Edit recipient list**, and then compare your screen with Figure 9.28.

The Mail Merge Recipients dialog box displays, enabling you to sort the list, filter the list, find duplicate entries, find a particular recipient or group of recipients, validate addresses, add recipients to the list, or remove recipients from the list.

Figure 9.28

Mail Merge Recipients
dialog box

Click to deselect recipient;
remove from the list

List options

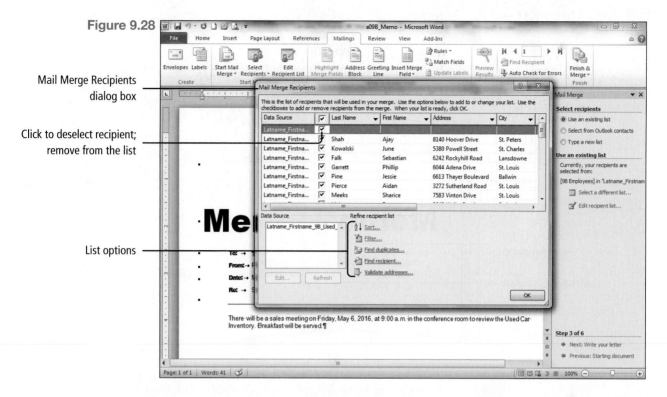

5 In the **Mail Merge Recipients** dialog box, on the row for **Phillip Garrett**, clear the **check box** to the left of **Garrett** to remove this record from the list of recipients. Click the **Last Name arrow**, and then click **Sort Ascending**. Notice that the first record is empty. In this **empty record**, clear the **check box** to the left of where the last name would display, and then click **OK**.

> Because the memo is from Phillip Garrett, a memo should not be addressed to him. Sorting enables you to display any blank records at the beginning of the list.

6 In the **Mail Merge** task pane, under **Step 3 of 6**, click **Next: Write your letter**. Take a moment to read the information in the **Mail Merge** task pane. If necessary, on the **Home tab**, in the **Paragraph group**, click the **Show/Hide** button to display the paragraph marks. On the left side of the screen in the memo, click to the right of **To:** and to the left of the paragraph symbol, above the letter **P** in *Phillip*. In the **Mail Merge** task pane, under **Write your letter**, click **More items**, and then compare your screen with Figure 9.29.

> The Insert Merge Field dialog box displays, which enables you to select a field from the database to insert into the memo. The Match Fields button enables you to map the fields in the table to the mail merge fields that are built into Word. For example, this table contains a field named Position/Department that could be mapped to the Word mail merge field entitled Job Title.

Figure 9.29

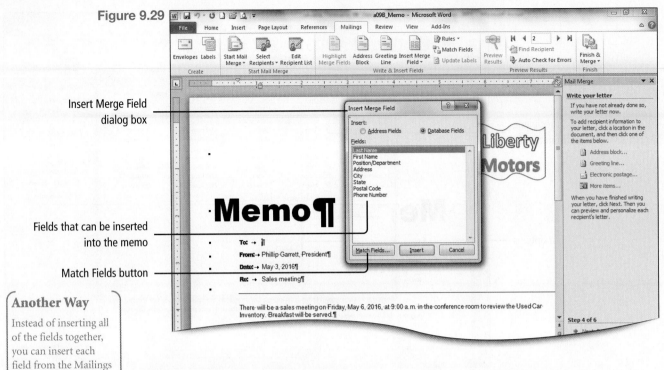

Insert Merge Field dialog box

Fields that can be inserted into the memo

Match Fields button

7 In the **Insert Merge Field** dialog box under **Fields**, click **First Name**, and then click **Insert**. Alternatively, double-click the field. Click **Last Name**, and then click **Insert**. Click **Position/Department**, and then click **Insert**. Click **Close**, and then compare your screen with Figure 9.30.

Word inserts each field name surrounded with the characters << and >>. There are no spaces between the field names.

Figure 9.30

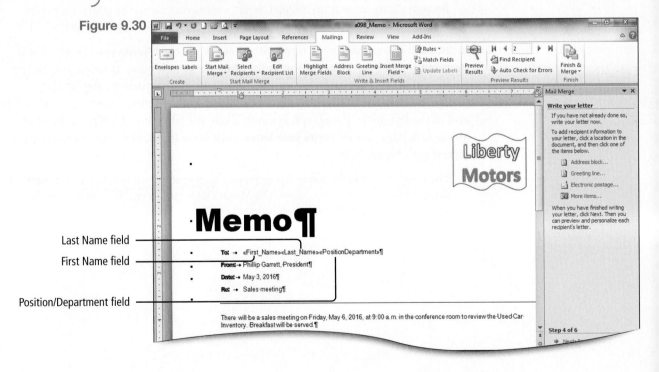

Last Name field

First Name field

Position/Department field

8 In the **memo**, click to the left of <<**Last_Name**>>, and then press [Spacebar] to insert a space between the First_Name and Last_Name fields. Click to the left of <<**PositionDepartment**>>, hold down [Shift], and then press [Enter] to move the field to the next line. Compare your screen with Figure 9.31.

Because the memo has built-in formatting, you must press [Shift] + [Enter] to insert a line break to align the Position/Department field directly under the First Name field. If you press [Enter] to insert a paragraph break, the Position/Department field will align at the left margin and a blank line will display above it.

Figure 9.31

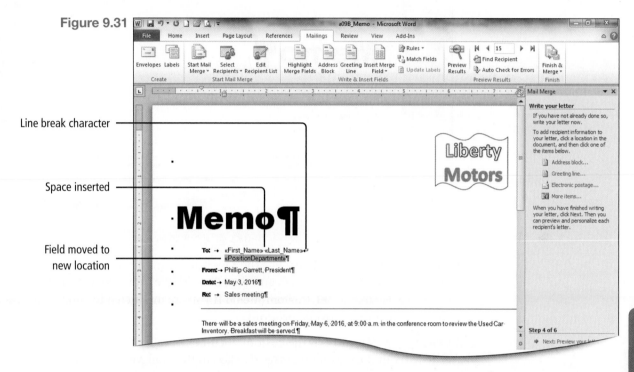

Line break character

Space inserted

Field moved to new location

9 In the **Mail Merge** task pane, under **Step 4 of 6**, click **Next: Preview your letters**. Notice that the first memo displays with a recipient name of **Adam Bristow**. In the **Mail Merge** task pane, under **Preview your letters**, click the **Next record** button to display the memo for the next recipient. Continue clicking the **Next record** button until the letter addressed to *Deanna Hale*(Recipient 15) displays.

10 In the **Mail Merge** task pane, under **Step 5 of 6**, click **Next: Complete the merge**, and notice that in this step, you can either print the memos or personalize the memos. In the **Mail Merge** task pane, under **Merge**, click **Edit individual letters**.

By clicking *Edit individual letters*, you can customize one or more of the merged memos.

11 In the displayed **Merge to New Document** dialog box, click **Current record**, and then click **OK**.

The memo addressed to Deanna Hale displays. At the end of the memo, a section break displays to demonstrate the end of the merged information for that record.

12 Press [Ctrl] + [End] to move to the end of the memo after the section break. Using your own first and last names, type **Please bring your PowerPoint presentation to the meeting, and give it to Firstname Lastname.** and then compare your screen with Figure 9.32.

Figure 9.32

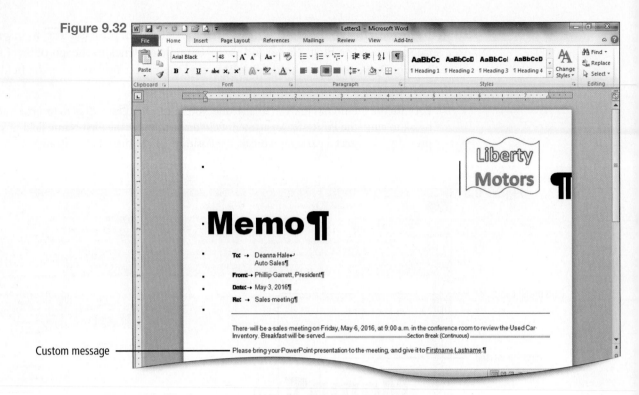

Custom message

13 On the **Quick Access Toolbar**, click the **Save** button. In the **Save As** dialog box, navigate to your **Access Chapter 9** folder, and then **Save** 🔲 the Word document as **Lastname_Firstname_9B_Custom_Memo** If you are instructed to submit this result, create a paper or electronic printout.

14 **Close** [X] Word to exit the custom document. Notice that the memo to Deanna Hale without the custom message displays in the Mail Merge wizard.

15 From the **Backstage** view, click **Save As**. In the **Save As** dialog box, save the Word document as **Lastname_Firstname_9B_Memo_Main** and then **Close** [X] Word. If the database is not displayed, on the status bar, click the **Microsoft Access** button to restore the Access window to the screen.

Objective 7 | Export Data to Excel

You can copy data from an Access database into a worksheet by exporting a table, form, or query to an Excel workbook; however, you cannot export reports, macros, or modules to Excel. When you export a table or form that contains subdatasheets or subforms, only the main datasheet or main form is exported. You can export only one database object in a single export operation; however, you can merge the data in multiple worksheets in Excel after completing the individual export operations.

Export data to Excel if users share the data and some work with Access while others work with Excel. You can store the data in Access and then export it to Excel to analyze the data.

Activity 9.12 | Exporting Selected Records to Excel

In this activity, you will export selected records—Chevrolet vehicle data—from an Access query to an Excel workbook.

1 In the **Navigation Pane**, under **Queries**, double-click **9B Used Vehicles** to run the query and to display the results. **Close** [«] the **Navigation Pane**.

2 Click the arrow to the right of **Make** in the title row of the query results. Click the **Select All** check box to remove the checkmark displaying all makes. Click the check box next to **Chevrolet** to filter the table to display only that make of vehicle. Click **OK**. Select those records, and then compare your screen with Figure 9.33.

Figure 9.33

Selected Chevrolet records

3 On the Ribbon, click the **External Data tab**, and in the **Export group**, click **Excel**.

4 In the displayed **Export - Excel Spreadsheet** dialog box, in the **File name** box, be sure that the path to your **Access Chapter 9** folder is correct. In the **File name** box, select the existing file name, and type **Lastname_Firstname_9B_Used_Vehicles** Notice that in the **File format** box, the file will be saved as an Excel Workbook with an extension of .xlsx, which is the extension used for Excel 2010.

5 In the **Export - Excel Spreadsheet** dialog box, under **Specify export options**, select the **Export data with formatting and layout** check box. Select the **Open the destination file after the export operation is complete** check box, and then select the **Export only the selected records** check box.

Because you selected records in the query, the *Export only the selected records* option is active.

6 In the **Export - Excel Spreadsheet** dialog box, click **OK**, and then compare your screen with Figure 9.34.

Excel opens and displays the exported data in a worksheet within the workbook. The worksheet name is the same as the query from which the data was exported. The workbook name displays in the Excel window title bar.

Figure 9.34
Workbook name
Field names
Records
Worksheet name

7 At the bottom of the worksheet, right-click the **Worksheet tab**, and then click **Rename**. Type **9B Chevrolet** and then press (Enter). **Save** the workbook, and then **Minimize** the Excel workbook.

8 If necessary, click the **Microsoft Access** button on the taskbar to restore the Access window and display the query.

Activity 9.13 | Copying Selected Records to an Existing Excel Workbook

In this activity, you will export selected records—Toyota vehicle data—from an Access query to an Excel workbook by copying and pasting the records.

1 In the datasheet, using the techniques you practiced in the previous activity, filter the table and select all of the records displaying a **Make** of **Toyota**.

2 On the Ribbon, click the **Home tab**. In the **Clipboard group**, click the **Copy** button. Alternatively, right-click in a blank area of the datasheet, and then click **Copy**; or press Ctrl + C.

3 On the taskbar, click the **Microsoft Excel** button to make the Excel window active.

4 At the bottom of the worksheet, to the right of the **9B Chevrolet tab**, click the **Insert Worksheet tab**. Compare your screen with Figure 9.35.

A blank worksheet is inserted to the right of the *Chevrolet* worksheet. A dark border displays around cell A1.

Figure 9.35

Cell A1

Insert Worksheet tab

New worksheet

5 With cell **A1** selected, on the **Home tab**, in the **Clipboard group**, click the **Paste** button. Alternatively, press Ctrl + V.

The selected records are pasted into the *9B_Used_Vehicles* workbook on a separate worksheet.

> **Note** | Exporting Data into an Existing Workbook
>
> If you use the Export Wizard to export selected records into an existing workbook, the original data in the Excel workbook is overwritten.

6 Point to the column border between **B** and **C** until the pointer displays. Drag to the right until all of the data in cell **B9**—*Highlander*—displays on one line.

7 Using the techniques you practiced in the previous activity, **Rename** the worksheet as **9B Toyota** and then compare your screen with Figure 9.36.

There are now two worksheets in the *9B_Used_Vehicles* workbook— *9B Chevrolet* and *9B Toyota*. The *9B Toyota* worksheet is active.

Figure 9.36

Column with width increased

9B Toyota worksheet

9B Chevrolet worksheet

8 **Save** the workbook. On the Ribbon, click the **Insert tab**. In the **Text group**, click the **Header & Footer** button. In the header box, type **Lastname Firstname 9B Toyota Used Vehicles** Click anywhere in the worksheet to move the insertion point out of the header box.

9 At the bottom of the workbook, click the **9B Chevrolet tab**. Insert a **Header** of **Lastname Firstname 9B Chevrolet Used Vehicles** and then click anywhere in the worksheet to move the insertion point out of the header box.

10 Save the workbook. Unless you are required to submit your files electronically, display **Backstage** view, and then click **Print**. In the **Print** dialog box, under **Print what**, click **Entire workbook**, and then click **OK**. If you are directed to submit an electronic printout of this workbook, display **Backstage view**, and then click **Save & Send**. Click **Create PDF/XPS Document**, and then click the **Create a PDF/XPS** button. In the **Publish a PDF or XPS** dialog box, click the **Options** button, and then select **Entire workbook**. Click **OK**, and then click **Publish**.

Both worksheets print with the header information at the top of the page.

11 Close the **Excel** workbook. In the **Access** window, **Close** ⊠ the **9B Used Vehicles** query without saving, and then **Open** ⊠ the **Navigation Pane**.

Objective 8 | Export Data to an HTML File and an XML File

If you need to display an Access object on a Web page, you can export the object to an **HTML** format, **HyperText Markup Language**—the language used to display Web pages. Web pages are text files that contain text and codes—known as **tags**—that the Web browser interprets as the page is loaded. A tag begins with the < character and ends with the > character; for example, to apply bold formatting to the word *Access*, you would add a beginning and an ending tag to the word—<b>Access</b>. The <b> tag identifies where the bold formatting begins. The </b> tag identifies where the bold formatting ends.

XML, **eXtensible Markup Language**, is the standard language for describing and delivering data on the Web. Similar to HTML, XML uses tags to organize and present data. Unlike HTML, which uses standard tags, XML enables you to create your own set of tags. With an XML document, the data can be displayed on a Web page, included in a Word document, analyzed in Excel, imported into a different database, or imported into many other programs that recognize XML files.

Activity 9.14 | Exporting a Report to an HTML File

In this activity, you will export the *9B Jeeps in Stock* report to an HTML file.

1 In the **Navigation Pane**, under **Reports**, right-click **9B Jeeps in Stock**, point to **Export**, and then click **HTML Document**.

2 In the displayed **Export - HTML Document** dialog box, in the **File name** box, be sure that the file will be saved in the **Access Chapter 9** folder. In the **File name** box, select the existing file name, and type **Lastname_Firstname_9B_Jeeps_in_Stock.html** Under **Specify export options**, select the **Open the destination file after the export operation is complete** check box, and then click **OK**.

3 In the displayed **HTML Output Options** dialog box, click **OK**, and then compare your screen with Figure 9.37.

The document displays in Microsoft Internet Explorer or in your default Web browser.

Figure 9.37

Microsoft Internet
Explorer; your Web
browser may be different

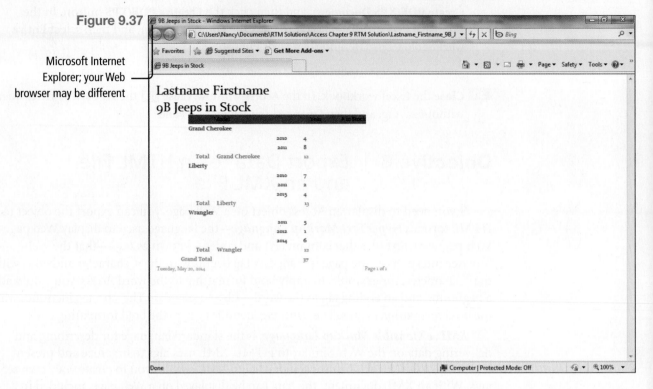

4 Right-click in an empty area of the Web page, and then click **View Source**. Compare your screen with Figure 9.38.

The HTML code displays in a new window. This is the actual document that was exported. The Web browser interprets the HTML tags and displays the text as a readable document. If you know HTML coding, you can format this document so that the column headings are more readable.

Figure 9.38

HTML code

Tags

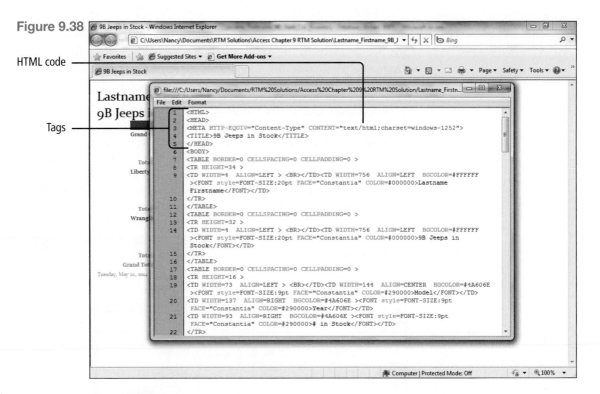

5 **Close** [X] the window displaying the source code. If you are instructed to submit this result, create a paper or electronic printout of the Web page.

6 **Close** the Web browser window. In the **Export - HTML Document** dialog box, click the **Close** button.

Activity 9.15 | Exporting a Report to an XML File

In this activity, you will export the *9B Jeeps in Stock* report to an XML file.

1 In the **Navigation Pane**, under **Reports**, right-click **9B Jeeps in Stock**, point to **Export**, and then click **XML File**.

Access | Chapter 9

2 In the displayed **Export - XML File** dialog box, in the **File name** box, be sure that the file will be saved in the **Access Chapter 9** folder. Select the file name, and then type **Lastname_Firstname_9B_Jeeps_XML_File.xml** Click **OK**, and then compare your screen with Figure 9.39.

> The Export XML dialog box displays. When you export data to XML, multiple files can be created. An *XML schema* is a document with an .xsd extension that defines the elements, entities, and content allowed in the document. It defines the tag names and defines the order, relationships, and data type you use with each tag. The schema is essential to ensure that all of the table relationships and data types are preserved when the data is imported into another database. An XML file cannot be viewed directly in a Web browser. *XML presentation files* can be created so that the data can be viewed in a Web browser.

Figure 9.39

Data in XML format

Export schema check box

Create presentation files check box

3 In the **Export XML** dialog box, be sure that the **Data (XML)** check box is selected, and then select the **Presentation of your data (XSL)** check box. Click **OK**. In the **Export - XML File** dialog box, click **Close**.

> Because XML files are typically imported into other applications, there is no option to view the file after the export operation.

4 On the taskbar, click the **Start** button, and then click **Computer**. Navigate to the location where the **Access Chapter 9** folder is saved, and open the folder. Compare your screen with Figure 9.40.

> In Details view, the name, size, and type of each file is displayed, in addition to the Date and Time the file was modified. Your dates and times will differ. The Type column shows two HTML documents—*9B_Jeeps_in_Stock* and *9B_Jeeps_XML_File*. *9B_Jeeps_in_Stock* is the HTML file that you created when you exported to an HTML file. *9B_Jeeps_XML_File* is an HTML presentation file that was created when you selected the *Presentation of your data (XSL)* check box while exporting to an XML file.

> There is also an *XSL Stylesheet* file named *9B_Jeeps_XML_ File*. This is the second presentation file that is used to create the HTML file. Finally, there is an XML document that stores the data that was exported.

Figure 9.40

HTML file

Presentation HTML
file for XML file

XSL stylesheet file

XML document

---

5 Locate the **9B_Jeeps_XML_File** that displays a **Type** of **HTML Document**, and then double-click it.

> Because you created the two presentation files when you exported the report to an XML file, the report displays in your Web browser. If it does not, read the Alert that follows.

Alert! | Did an Information Bar Message Box Display?

If an Information Bar message box displays, your Web browser is blocking content from displaying. In the dialog box, click OK. Click the Information bar, and then click Allow Blocked Content. In the Security Warning message box, click Yes. The procedure may differ depending upon your Web browser.

---

6 If you are instructed to submit this result, create a paper printout of the Web page, or submit your files electronically as directed.

7 **Close** the Web browser window, and then **Close** the Access Chapter 9 window. **Close** the database, and then **Exit** Access.

More Knowledge | Exporting Data to Another Access Database

You can copy data from one Access database into another Access database. Copying and pasting is easiest, but exporting offers you more options. You can export all of the database objects into another database. However, to export selected records, you must copy and paste the records.

Exporting an object to another database is similar to importing the object from the first database, although you cannot export multiple objects in a single operation. If you want to export multiple objects, it is easier to open the destination database and perform an import operation. You cannot export table relationships, import and export specifications, custom menu bars, custom toolbars, or a query as a table.

Export database objects when you want to copy the table structure to another database as a shortcut for creating a new table, when you want to copy the layout and design of a form or report as a shortcut for creating a new form or report, or when you want to copy the latest version of a table or form to another database at regular intervals using the export specification.

End **You have completed Project 9B**

Summary

Importing is the process of copying *in* data from another application. Linking is the process of connecting to data in another application, and exporting is the process of copying *out* data to another application. In this chapter, you imported data from a Word table after converting the table to a text file. You saved the import specifications so that you could use the steps in another import operation. You imported data from an Excel worksheet to a table in Access and then used the import feature to append data from Excel to the same table. You copied an Excel chart to an Access report, imported data from another Access database, and linked to data in another Access database. You reversed the process by exporting a query and report to Word. You exported selected records to Excel, and copied and pasted records from Access to Excel. You created individual memos for the employees by using the Mail Merge feature within Access. Finally, you exported an Access report to an HTML file and to an XML file, viewing both in a Web browser.

Key Terms

appended 608	**eXtensible Markup Language** 637	**pie chart** 613
ASCII 603	**HTML** 637	**Plain Text** 603
cell 611	**HyperText Markup Language** 637	**range** 611
chart................................613	**import** 601	**spreadsheet** 611
column chart...................613	**line chart** 613	**tags** 637
convert 602	**link** 604	**workbook** 610
data source 627	**mail merge** 627	**worksheet** 610
definition 618	**main document**...............627	**XML** 637
delimited file 602	**named range**.................611	**XML presentation files** ..640
delimiter 602		**XML schema** 640
export 622		

Matching

Match each term in the second column with its correct definition in the first column by writing the letter of the term on the blank line in front of the correct definition.

_____ 1.   To bring in a copy of data from one source or application to another application.

_____ 2.   The character set for data stored as Plain Text, without any formatting.

_____ 3.   A connection to data in another file.

_____ 4.   The acronym for the standard language for describing and delivering data on the Web.

_____ 5.   A naming tool that makes it easier to use the cells in calculations or modifications.

_____ 6.   The acronym for a language used to display Web pages.

_____ 7.   To combine a main document created in Microsoft Word with a data source created in Access.

_____ 8.   The primary document used in Excel to save and work with data that is arranged in columns and rows.

_____ 9.   An Excel file that contains one or more worksheets.

A ASCII
B Cell
C Chart
D Export
E HTML
F Import
G Link
H Mail merge
I Named range
J Range
K Tags
L Workbook
M Worksheet
N XML
O XML schema

Content-Based Assessments

_____ 10. The small box formed by the intersection of a column and a row in an Excel worksheet.

_____ 11. Includes two or more selected cells on a worksheet that can be treated as a single unit.

_____ 12. A graphic representation of data.

_____ 13. The process used to copy out data from one source or application to another application.

_____ 14. Codes that a Web browser interprets when a Web page is loaded.

_____ 15. A document that defines the elements, entities, and content allowed when data is exported.

Multiple Choice

Circle the correct answer.

1. What type of file uses commas or tabs to separate fields?
   A. Converted   B. Delimited   C. Linear

2. Which of the following tasks can be completed in a destination Access table that is linked to another file?
   A. Change data   B. Add records   C. Delete data

3. In a mail merge operation, which Word document contains the text of the letter or memo to be merged?
   A. Main document   B. Data source   C. Merged document

4. What term describes data that is added to the end of an existing table?
   A. Linked   B. Expended   C. Appended

5. Which type of chart displays the contributions of parts to a whole amount?
   A. Pie chart   B. Line chart   C. Column chart

6. Which type of chart displays trends over time?
   A. Pie chart   B. Line chart   C. Column chart

7. The table structure—field names, data types, and field properties—is the table
   A. definition.   B. outline.   C. description.

8. Which of the following Access objects can be exported to Excel?
   A. Query   B. Report   C. Macro

9. What is the name for code used in HTML to format text?
   A. Marker   B. Tag   C. Range

10. What term describes the two XML files created when an Access object is exported to XML so that the data can be viewed in a Web browser?
    A. XML data   B. XML schema   C. XML presentation files

Content-Based Assessments

Apply **9A** skills from these Objectives:

1. Import Data from a Word Table
2. Import Data from an Excel Workbook
3. Insert an Excel Chart into a Report
4. Import from and Link to Another Access Database

Skills Review | Project **9C** Cars and Motorcycles

Liberty Motors maintains many of its records in Word, Excel, and Access files. Phillip Garrett, President, and Jeanine Thomas, Finance Manager, want to bring the data from these files into an Access database to create queries and reports. In this project, you will import data from Word, Excel, and another Access database and create a link to data in another application. Your completed files will look similar to Figure 9.41.

Project Files

For Project 9C, you will need the following files:

New blank Access database
a09C_Domestic_Chart.xlsx
a09C_Customers.docx
a09C_Sports_Car_Sales.xlsx

a09C_Used_Cars_Inventory.accdb
a09C_Logo.jpg
a09C_Motorcycles.accdb

You will save your files as:

Lastname_Firstname_9C_Cars_and_Motorcycles.accdb
Lastname_Firstname_9C_Customers_Table.txt

Project Results

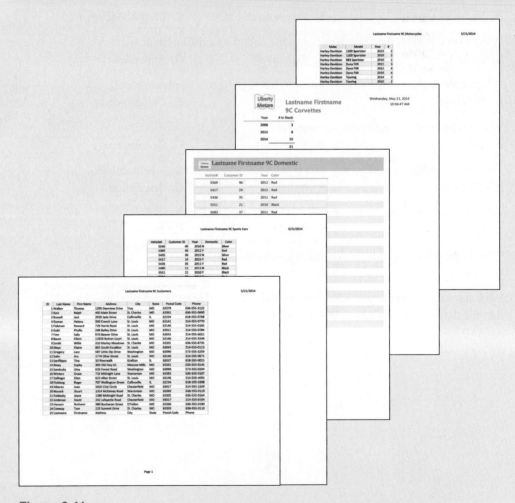

Figure 9.41

(Project 9C Cars and Motorcycles continues on the next page)

Skills Review | Project 9C Cars and Motorcycles (continued)

1 **Start** Access. On the right side of the screen, under **File Name**, select the text, and then type **Lastname_Firstname_9C_Cars_and_Motorcycles** Click the **Browse** button, navigate to the **Access Chapter 9** folder, and then click **OK**. Click the **Create** button. **Close** the displayed table.

2 **Start** Word. Display **Backstage view**, and then click **Open**. Navigate to the location where the student data files for this textbook are saved. Locate and open the **a09C_Customers** file.

  a. On the Ribbon, click the **Table Tools Layout tab**. In the **Data group**, click the **Convert to Text** button. In the dialog box, be sure that the **Tabs** option button is selected, and then click **OK**. Click anywhere to deselect the text.

  b. Display **Backstage view**, click **Save As**, and then navigate to the **Access Chapter 9** folder. Save the file as **Lastname_Firstname_9C_Customers_Table** Click the **Save as type arrow**, and from the displayed list, scroll down, and then click **Plain Text**. Click **Save**, and then click **OK**. **Exit** Word.

3 **Return** to Access. On the Ribbon, click the **External Data tab**, and then in the **Import & Link group**, click the **Text File** button. In the dialog box, to the right of the **File name** box, click **Browse**. Locate **9C Customers Table**, and double-click.

  a. Be sure that the **Import the source data into a new table in the current database** option button is selected, and then click **OK**. In the **Import Text Wizard** dialog box, be sure that the **Delimited** option button is selected. Click **Next**. Be sure that the **Tab** option button is selected, and select the **First Row Contains Field Names** check box. In the **Text Qualifier** box, be sure that **{none}** is selected, and click **Next**.

  b. Click in the **Postal Code** field to select the field. Under **Field Options**, click the **Data Type arrow**, and then click **Text**. Click in the **Phone** field to select the field. Under **Field Options**, click the **Data Type arrow**, and then click **Text**. Click **Next**. Be sure that the **Let Access add primary key** option button is selected, and then click **Next**. Change the name to **Lastname Firstname 9C Customers** Click **Finish**.

  c. Select the **Save import steps** check box. Click in the **Description** box, and then type **Imports a tab-delimited text file that was a Word table** Click **Save Import**. On the **External Data tab**, in the **Import &**

Link group, click the **Saved Imports** button, and confirm that your import file is there. **Close** the dialog box.

4 In the **Navigation pane**, double-click **9C Customers** to open it, and then **Close** the **Navigation Pane**.

  a. To **record 25**, add yourself as a customer. Adjust the widths of all of the fields to display all of the data and the entire field name for each field.

  b. If you are instructed to submit this result, create a paper or electronic printout of the table in **Landscape** orientation, changing **Margins**, if necessary, to print all of the fields. **Save**, and then **Close** the table.

5 On the **External Data tab**, in the **Import & Link group**, click the **Excel** button. In the dialog box, click the **Browse** button. Locate and open the **a09C_Sports_Car_Sales** file. Be certain **Import the source data into a new table in the current database** is selected, and then click **OK**.

  a. In the **Import Spreadsheet Wizard** dialog box, be certain that **Show Worksheets** is selected and **In Stock** is highlighted. Click **Next**.

  b. Be certain that the **First Row Contains Column Headings** check box is selected. Click **Next** two times.

  c. Select **Choose my own primary key**. If necessary, click the **table name** box **arrow**, click **Vehicle#**, and then click **Next**. In the **Import to Table** box, type **Lastname Firstname 9C Sports Cars** and then click **Finish**. In the **Get External Data - Excel Spreadsheet** dialog box, click **Close**.

6 On the **External Data tab**, in the **Import & Link group**, click the **Excel** button. Locate and **Open** the **a09C_Sports_Car_Sales** file.

  a. Click **Append a copy of the records to the table**. If necessary, click the **table name box arrow** and select **9C Sports Cars**. Click **OK**. In the **Import Spreadsheet Wizard** dialog box, be certain that **Show Worksheets** is selected. Click **Special Order**, and then click **Next** two times. Click **Finish**.

  b. In the **Get External Data-Excel Spreadsheet** dialog box, click **Close**, and then **Open** the **Navigation Pane**. Double-click **9C Sport Cars** to open the table. If you are instructed to submit this result, create a paper or electronic printout of the table. **Close** the table, and then **Close** the **Navigation Pane**.

(Project 9C Cars and Motorcycles continues on the next page)

7 On the **Create tab**, in the **Queries group**, click the **Query Design** button. In the **Show Table** dialog box, double-click **9C Sports Cars**, and then click **Close**. In the field list, click **Vehicle#**. Hold down Shift, and then click **Color**. Drag the fields down into the first column of the design grid. In the design grid, under **Domestic**, click in the **Criteria** box, type **Y** and then on the **Show** row, clear the check box. On the **Design tab**, in the **Results group**, click the **Run** button. **Save** the query as **Lastname Firstname 9C Domestic** and then **Close** the query.

8 **Open** the **Navigation Pane**. Under **Queries**, click **9C Domestic** to select the query, and then **Close** the **Navigation Pane**. On the **Create tab**, in the **Reports group**, click the **Report** button.

a. Switch to **Design** view. Click the image to the left of the title. On the **Design tab**, in the **Header/Footer group**, click the **Logo** button. Locate **a09C_Logo**, and then double-click. In the **Tools group**, click the **Property Sheet** button. On the **Property Sheet Format tab**, change the **Size Mode** property to **Zoom**. **Close** the **Property Sheet**. In the **Report Header** section, delete the **Date** and **Time text box controls**. In the **Page Footer** section, delete the **Page number text box control**. In the **Report Footer** section, delete the **Count calculated control**.

b. **Save** the report as **Lastname Firstname 9C Domestic Report** Point to the top of the **Report Footer section bar** until the pointer displays. Drag the section down to the **3-inch mark on the vertical ruler**.

c. **Start** Excel. If necessary, maximize the Excel window. Display **Backstage view**, and then click **Open**. Locate and open **a09C_Domestic_Chart**. Click the outside edge of the **column chart** to select the entire chart. Right-click the chart, and then click **Copy**. In the **9C Domestic Report**, right-click the **Page Footer section bar**, and then click **Paste**. Remove any blank space in the Report Footer section. **Save** the report, and then switch to **Report** view. If you are instructed to submit this result, create a paper or electronic printout. **Close** the report. **Close** the workbook and **Exit** Excel.

9 On the **External Data tab**, in the **Import & Link group**, click the **Access** button. In the **Get External Data - Access Database** dialog box, click **Browse**. Locate and then double-click **a09C_Used_Cars_Inventory**. Be sure that the **Import tables, queries, forms, reports, macros, and modules into the current database** option button is selected, and then click **OK**.

a. In the **Import Objects** dialog box, click the **Tables tab**, and then click **9C Used Vehicles**. Click the **Queries tab**, and then click **9C Corvettes**. Click the **Reports tab**, click **9C Corvettes in Stock**, and then click **OK**.

b. In the dialog box, click **Close**. **Open** the **Navigation Pane**.

10 In the **Navigation Pane**, under **Reports**, right-click **9C Corvettes in Stock**, and then click **Layout View**. Click the title *9C Corvettes* one time to select the title. Click to the left of **9C**, type **Lastname Firstname** and then press Shift + Enter. Press Enter, and **Save** the report. If you are instructed to submit this result, create a paper or electronic printout of the report. **Close** the report.

11 On the **External Data tab**, in the **Import & Link group**, click the **Access** button. In the **Get External Data - Access Database** dialog box, **Browse** to locate and then double-click **a09C_Motorcycles**. Click the **Link to the data source by creating a linked table** option button, and then click **OK**.

a. In the **Link Tables** dialog box, click **9C Motorcycles**, and then click **OK**.

b. In the **Navigation Pane**, under **Tables**, right-click **9C Motorcycles**, and then click **Rename**. Click to the left of **9C**, type **Lastname Firstname**, and then press Spacebar. Press Enter.

c. Double-click **9C Motorcycles** to display the table. Adjust the widths of all of the columns. Unless you are required to submit your database electronically, **Print** the table. If you submit this database electronically, also submit **a09C_Motorcycles** to view the linked objects properly. **Close** the table, saving changes when prompted.

12 **Close** the database, and then **Exit** Access.

End **You have completed Project 9C**

Content-Based Assessments

- **5** Export Data to Word
- **6** Use Mail Merge to Integrate Access and Word
- **7** Export Data to Excel
- **8** Export Data to an HTML File and an XML File

Skills Review | Project **9D** Sport Vehicles

The employees at Liberty Motors would like to be able to analyze their sports car inventory data in other applications in addition to Access. Access enables you to export data from an Access database into applications like Word and Excel, including merging Access data with a Word document. You can also export data to be displayed on a Web page. In this project, you will export data to several types of applications. Your completed files will look similar to Figure 9.42.

Project Files

For Project 9D, you will need the following files:

a09D_Sport_Vehicles.accdb
a09D_SC_Letter.docx

You will save your files as:

Lastname_Firstname_9D_Sport_Vehicles.accdb
Lastname_Firstname_9D_Imports_Query.rtf
Lastname_Firstname_9D_Letter.docx
Lastname_Firstname_9D_Letter_Main.docx
Lastname_Firstname_9D_Imports.docx
Lastname_Firstname_9D_Imports_RTF.rtf
Lastname_Firstname_9D_13-14_Models.xlsx
Lastname_Firstname_9D_13-14_Models.pdf
Lastname_Firstname_9D_Corvettes_in_Stock.html
Lastname_Firstname_9D_Corvettes_XML_File.htm
Lastname_Firstname_9D_Corvettes_XML_File.xml
Lastname_Firstname_9D_Corvettes_XML_File.xsl

Project Results

Figure 9.42

(Project 9D Sport Vehicles continues on the next page)

1 **Start** Access. Navigate to the location where the student data files for this textbook are saved. Locate and open the **a09D_Sport_Vehicles** file. Save the database in the **Access 2010 Database** format in your **Access Chapter 9** folder as **Lastname_Firstname_9D_Sport_Vehicles** Enable the content or add the Access Chapter 9 folder to the Trust Center.

2 In the **Navigation Pane**, under **Queries**, right-click **9D Imports**, point to **Export**, and then click **Word RTF File**. In the **Export - RTF File** dialog box, click **Browse**. Navigate to the **Access Chapter 9** folder. In the **File name** box, select the existing file name, type **Lastname_Firstname_9D_Imports_Query** and then click **Save**. In the **Export - RTF File** dialog box, under **Specify export options**, select the **Open the destination file after the export operation is complete** check box, and then click **OK**.

   a. On the Word Ribbon, click the **Insert tab**. In the **Header & Footer group**, click the **Header** button. In the **Built-In** gallery, scroll down and click **Conservative**, and then type **Lastname Firstname 9D Imported Sports Cars** Click **Pick the Date** down **arrow**, and click **Today**. In the **Close group**, click the **Close Header and Footer** button.

   b. Display **Backstage view**, and click **Save As**. If necessary, navigate to the **Access Chapter 9** folder. Change the file name to **Lastname_Firstname_9D_Imports** Be sure that the **Save as type** box displays **Word Document**, which means the file will be given a .docx extension. In the **Save As** dialog box, click **Save**. In the displayed message box, click **OK**. If you are instructed to submit this result, create a paper or electronic printout. **Close** the Word window. In the **Export - RTF File** dialog box, click **Close**.

3 Click the **9D Customers** table to select it. On the Ribbon, click the **External Data tab**. In the **Export group**, click the **Word Merge** button. Be sure that **Link your data to an existing Microsoft Word document** is selected, and then click **OK**. In the **Select Microsoft Word Document** dialog box, locate and **Open** the **a09D_SC_Letter** file. Click the Microsoft Word button on the taskbar, and **Maximize** the Word window.

   a. In the **Mail Merge** task pane, under **Select recipients**, be sure that **Use an existing list** is selected. Under **Step 3 of 6**, click **Next: Write your letter**. Click to the

right of **Dear**, and then press Spacebar. In the **Mail Merge** task pane, under **Write your letter**, click **More items**. In the **Insert Merge Field** dialog box under **Fields**, double-click **First Name**. Double-click **Last Name**, and then click **Close**. In the letter, click to the left of <<**Last_Name**>>, and then press Spacebar. Type a **colon** after the <<**Last Name**>> field.

   b. In the **Mail Merge** task pane, click **Next: Preview your letters**, and the first letter displays with a recipient name of **Thomas Walker**. Under **Make changes** in the **Mail Merge** task pane, click the **Exclude this recipient** button.

   c. In the **Mail Merge** task pane, click **Next: Complete the merge**. In the **Mail Merge** task pane under **Merge**, click **Edit individual letters**. In the displayed **Merge to New Document** dialog box, click **From** and type **29** Under **To**, also type **29** Click **OK**. In the letter, click at the end of the paragraph that begins *Liberty Motors*, and then press Enter two times. Type **You will look great in that red Corvette!**

   d. On the **Quick Access Toolbar**, click the **Save** button. In the **Save As** dialog box, **Save** the Word document as **Lastname_Firstname_9D_Letter** If you are instructed to submit this result, create a paper or electronic printout of the **current page**, and then click **OK**.

   e. **Close** Word. Save the main document as **Lastname_Firstname_9D_Letter_Main. Close** Word again. If necessary, on the status bar, click the Microsoft Access button to restore the Access window to the screen.

4 In the **Navigation Pane**, under **Reports**, double-click **9D Imports** to open the report. Switch to **Layout** view. Click the title—**9D Imports**—**two** times to enter into editing mode. Click to the left of **9D**, type **Lastname Firstname** using your own first and last names, and then press Shift + Enter. Press Enter, and then **Save** the report.

   a. **Close** the report. In the **Navigation Pane**, under **Reports**, right-click **9D Imports**, point to **Export**, and then click **Word RTF File**. Be sure that the **File name** box displays the correct path to your **Access Chapter 9** folder. Rename the file **Lastname_Firstname_9D_Imports_RTF** Under **Specify export options**, select the **Open the destination file after the export operation is complete** check box, and then click **OK**.

(Project 9D Sport Vehicles continues on the next page)

b. If you are instructed to submit this result, create a paper or electronic printout. **Close** the Word window. In the **Export - RTF File** dialog box, click **Close**.

5 In the **Navigation Pane**, under **Queries**, double-click **9D 12-14 Models** to open the query in Datasheet view. **Close** the **Navigation Pane**. In the title row of the query results, click the arrow to the right of **Year**. Click the **Select All** check box and then click **2013** to filter the data to view only 2013 models. Click **OK**. Select all of the records displayed in the filtered query. Click the **External Data tab**, and in the **Export group**, click **Excel**.

a. In the **Export - Excel Spreadsheet** dialog box, in the **File name** box, be sure that the path to your **Access Chapter 9** folder is correct. In the **File name** box, select the existing file name, and type **Lastname_Firstname_9D_13-14_Models**. Notice that in the **File format** box, the file will be saved as an Excel 2010 Workbook with an extension of .xlsx. Under **Specify export options**, select all three check boxes. Click **OK**.

b. At the bottom of the worksheet, right-click the **Worksheet tab**, and then click **Rename**. Type **9D 2013** and then press Enter. **Save** the workbook, and then **Minimize** Excel.

c. If necessary, on the taskbar, click the **Microsoft Access** button to restore the Access window. Filter the query to display only the 2014 models. Select all of the displayed records. Right-click in the selected area of the datasheet, and then click **Copy**. On the taskbar, click the **Microsoft Excel** button to make the Excel window active. At the bottom of the worksheet, to the right of the **9D 2013**, click the **Insert Worksheet tab**.

d. With **Cell A1** selected, on the **Home tab**, in the **Clipboard group**, click the **Paste** button. Point to the column border between **B** and **C** until the pointer displays. Drag to the right until all of the data in **Cell B1**—*Customer ID*—displays. Using the techniques you have practiced, **Rename** the worksheet as **9D 2014 Save** the workbook.

e. On the Ribbon, click the **Insert tab**. In the **Text group**, click the **Header & Footer** button. In the header box, type **Lastname Firstname 2014 Models** Click anywhere in the worksheet to move the insertion point out of the header box.

f. At the bottom of the workbook, click the **9D 2013 tab**. Insert a **Header** of **Lastname Firstname 2013 Models** and then click anywhere in the worksheet to move the insertion point out of the header box.

g. **Save** the workbook. Unless you are required to submit your files electronically, click the **Office** button, and then click **Print**. In the **Print** dialog box, under **Print what**, click **Entire workbook**, and then click **OK**. If you are directed to submit an electronic printout of this workbook, display **Backstage view**, and click **Save & Send**. Click **Create PDF/XPS Document**, and then click the **Create a PDF/XPS** button. In the **Publish as PDF or XPS** dialog box, click the **Options** button, and then select **Entire workbook**. Click **OK**, and then click **Publish**. **Close** the **Excel** workbook and **Close** Excel.

h. In the **Access** window, Click the arrow to the right of **Year** in the title row of the query results. Click the **Select All** check box to remove the filter. **Close** the **9D 21-14 Models** query without saving, and then **Open** the **Navigation Pane**.

6 In the **Navigation Pane**, under **Reports**, right-click **9D Corvettes in Stock**, and open the report in **Design** view. Add your **Lastname Firstname** to the beginning of the report title, and press Shift + Enter to move **9D Corvettes** to the second line of the title. **Save** and **Close** the report. Right-click **9D Corvettes in Stock**, point to **Export**, and then click **HTML Document**.

a. In the **Export - HTML Document** dialog box, in the **File name** box, be sure that the file will be saved in the **Access Chapter 9** folder. In the **File name** box, select the existing file name, and type **Lastname_Firstname_9D_Corvettes_in_Stock.html** Under **Specify export options**, select the **Open the destination file after the export operation is complete** check box, and then click **OK**. In the **HTML Output Options** dialog box, click **OK**.

b. If you are instructed to submit this result, create a paper or electronic printout of the Web page. **Close** the Web browser window. In the **Export - HTML Document** dialog box, click the **Close** button.

7 In the **Navigation Pane**, under **Reports**, right-click **9D Corvettes in Stock**, point to **Export**, and then click **XML File**. In the **Export - XML File** dialog box, in the **File name** box, be sure that the file will be saved in the **Access Chapter 9** folder. Select only the file name, and then type

(Project 9D Sport Vehicles continues on the next page)

Access | Chapter 9

Content-Based Assessments

Skills Review | Project **9D** Sport Vehicles (continued)

Lastname_Firstname_9D_Corvettes_XML_File.xml Click **OK**. In the **Export XML** dialog box, be sure that the **Data (XML)** check box is selected, and then click the **Presentation of your data (XSL)** check box. Click **OK**. In the **Export - XML File** dialog box, click **Close**.

8 On the taskbar, click the **Start** button, and then click **Computer**. Navigate to the location where the **Access Chapter 9** folder is saved, and open the folder. If necessary, click the **Views** button, and then click **Details**. **Maximize** the window.

a. Locate the **9D_Corvettes_XML_File** that displays a **Type** of **HTML Documen**t and double-click it. If an

Information Bar message box displays, click the Information bar, and then click **Allow Blocked Content**. In the Security Warning message box, click **Yes**.

b. If you are instructed to submit this result, create a paper or electronic printout of the Web page. **Close** the Web browser window, and then **Close** the Access Chapter 9 window.

9 **Close** the database, and then **Exit** Access.

End **You have completed Project 9D** ———————————

Content-Based Assessments

Apply **9A** skills from these Objectives:

1. Import Data from a Word Table
2. Import Data from an Excel Workbook
3. Insert an Excel Chart into a Report
4. Import from and Link to Another Access Database

Mastering Access | Project **9E** Customized Cars

Liberty Motors offers extensive customization options for all types of vehicles through its accessories division. In this project, you will import a Word table as a plain text file. You will import data from an Excel worksheet and create a report with an imported Excel chart. Your completed work will look similar to Figure 9.43.

Project Files

For Project 9E, you will need the following files:

New blank Access database
a09E_Custom_Features.docx
a09E_Package_Sales.xlsx
a09E_Employees.accdb
a09E_Logo.jpg

You will save your files as:

Lastname_Firstname_9E_Customized_Cars.accdb
Lastname_Firstname_9E_Custom_Features.txt

Project Results

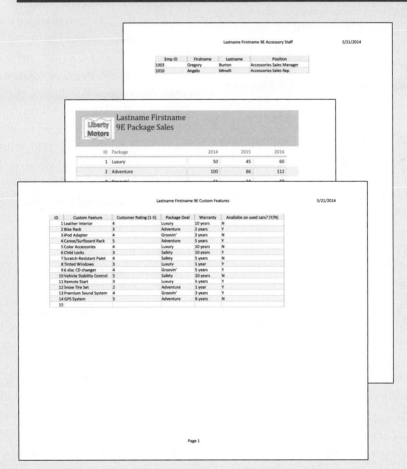

Figure 9.43

(Project 9E Customized Cars continues on the next page)

1 **Start** Access. Create a new blank database called **Lastname_Firstname_9E_Customized_Cars** and save it in your **Access Chapter 9** folder. **Close** the displayed table.

2 **Start** Word. Locate and open the **a09E_Custom_Features** document. On the **Layout tab**, in the **Data group**, click the **Convert to Text** button. Separate the text with **Tabs**, and then click **OK**.

3 Display **Backstage** view, and click **Save As**. Navigate to the **Access Chapter 9** folder. Change the name of the file to **Lastname_Firstname_9E_Custom_Features** Save the file as **Plain Text**. In the displayed **File Conversion** dialog box, accept the default settings, and then **Exit** Word.

4 **Return** to the Access **Lastname_Firstname_9E_Customized_Cars** empty database. On the **External Data tab**, in the **Import & Link group**, click the **Text File** button. **Browse** to the **Access Chapter 9** folder, and then open **9E_Custom_Features**. Be sure that the **Import the source data into a new table in the current database** option button is selected, and then click **OK**.

5 In the **Import Text Wizard** dialog box, be sure that the **Delimited** option button is selected, and click **Next**. Be sure that the **Tab** option button is selected. Select the **First Row Contains Field Names** check box. In the **Text Qualifier** box, be sure that {**none**} is selected, and then click **Next**.

6 Change the **Data Type** in the **Customer Rating (1-5)** field to **Text**. Click **Next**. Be sure that the **Let Access add primary key** option button is selected, and then click **Next**. Edit the table name by replacing the underscores with spaces. Click **Finish**.

7 Select the **Save import steps** check box to display additional options. Click in the **Description** box, type **Imports a tab delimited text file that was a Word table** and then click **Save Import**.

8 Open the **9E Custom Features** table in **Datasheet** view, and adjust the widths of all of the fields to display all of the data and the entire field name for each field.

9 If you are instructed to submit this result, create a paper or electronic printout of the table in **Landscape** orientation. **Save**, and then **Close** the table.

10 In the **Import & Link group**, click the **Excel** button. Locate and open the **a09E_Package_Sales** file. Be certain **Import the source data into a new table in the current database** is selected, and then click **OK**. In the **Import Spreadsheet Wizard** dialog box, be certain that **Show**

Worksheets is selected and **Packages** is highlighted. Click **Next**. Select the **First Row Contains Column Headings** check box. Click **Next** two times. Make sure **Let Access add primary key** is selected, and then click **Next**. Name the table **Lastname Firstname 9E Package Sales** and then click **Finish**. In the **Get External Data - Excel Spreadsheet** dialog box, click **Close**.

11 Select the **9E Package Sales** table and create a new **Report**. Switch to **Design** view. Select the image placeholder to the left of the title and replace with the **a09E_Logo** into the header section of the report with a **Size Mode** property of **Zoom**. In the **Report Header** section, delete the **Date** and **Time text box controls**. Move **9E Package Sales** to the second line of the title. Resize the logo to approximately **1-inch** tall by **1-inch** wide. In the **Page Footer** section, delete the **Page number text box control**. In the **Report Footer** section, delete the **Count calculated control**. Increase the size of the **Page Footer** section to the **2.75-inch mark on the horizontal ruler**. **Save** the report as **Lastname Firstname 9E Package Sales**

12 **Start** Excel. **Open** the **a09E_Package_Sales** workbook. In the **Package Totals** worksheet, select the entire chart. **Copy** the chart to the Office Clipboard. In the Access **9E Package Sales** report, **Paste** the chart in the **Report Footer**. Resize the report to **7 inches wide**. **Save** the report, and then switch to **Report** view. If you are instructed to submit this result, create a paper or electronic printout. **Close** the report. **Exit** Excel.

13 On the **External Data tab**, in the **Import & Link group**, click the **Access** button. Locate and open the **a09E_Employees** database. Click the **Link to the data source by creating a linked table** option button, and then click **OK**. In the **Link Tables** dialog box, click **9E Employees**, and then click **OK**.

14 In the **Import & Link group**, click the **Access** button. Locate and open **a09E_Employees**. Be sure that the **Import tables, queries, forms, reports, macros, and modules into the current database** option button is selected, and then click **OK**. In the **Import Objects** dialog box, click the **Queries tab**, click **9E Accessory Staff**, and then click **OK**. Click **Close**. **Rename 9E Accessory Staff** by adding your **Lastname Firstname** to the beginning of the query name.

15 Double-click **9E Accessory Staff**. If you are instructed to submit this result, create a paper or electronic printout. **Close** the query, and then **Exit** Access.

End **You have completed Project 9E** ⎯⎯⎯⎯⎯⎯⎯⎯⎯⎯⎯

Content-Based Assessments

- **5** Export Data to Word
- **6** Use Mail Merge to Integrate Access and Word
- **7** Export Data to Excel
- **8** Export Data to an HTML File and an XML File

Mastering Access | Project **9F** Custom Packages

The accessories staff would like to be able to analyze data related to luxury features and package sales using Word and Excel. They would also like to be able to display data on the Web. Access enables you to export data from an Access database into these applications and on a Web page. In this project, you will export data to several types of applications, including merging Access data with a flyer created in Word. Your completed files will look similar to Figure 9.44.

Project Files

For Project 9F, you will need the following files:

    a09F_Custom_Packages.accdb
    a09F_Flyer.docx

You will save your files as:

    Lastname_Firstname_9F_Custom_Packages.accdb
    Lastname_Firstname_9F_Accessory_Staff.rtf
    Lastname_Firstname_9F_Accessory_Staff.docx
    Lastname_Firstname_9F_Flyers.docx
    Lastname_Firstname_9F_Flyer_Main.docx
    Lastname_Firstname_9F_Luxury_Features.xlsx
    Lastname_Firstname_9F_Package_Sales.html
    Lastname_Firstname_9F_Package_Sales_XML_File.xml
    Lastname_Firstname_9F_Package_Sales_XML_File.htm
    Lastname_Firstname_9F_Package_Sales_XML_File.xsl

Project Results

Figure 9.44

(Project 9F Custom Packages continues on the next page)

Access | Chapter 9

Content-Based Assessments

Mastering Access | Project **9F** Custom Packages (continued)

1 **Start** Access. Locate and open the **a09F_Custom_Packages** file. Save the database in the **Access 2010 Database** format in your **Access Chapter 9** folder as **Lastname_Firstname_9F_Custom_Packages**

2 In the **Navigation Pane**, under **Queries**, right-click **9F Accessory Staff**, point to **Export**, and then click **Word RTF File**. Navigate to the **Access Chapter 9** folder, and name the file **Lastname_Firstname_9F_Accessory_Staff**

3 Under **Specify export options**, select the **Open the destination file after the export operation is complete** check box, and then click **OK**. On the Word Ribbon, click the **Insert tab**. In the **Header & Footer group**, click the **Header** button. In the **Built-In** gallery, click **Blank**, and then in the **Type text box**, type **Lastname Firstname 9F Accessory Staff** Click the **Close Header and Footer** button. Using the default file name, save the document as a **Word Document** in the **Access Chapter 9** folder. In the displayed message box, click **OK**. If you are instructed to submit this result, create a paper or electronic printout. **Close** the Word window. In the **Export - RTF File** dialog box, click **Close**.

4 Open the **9F Custom Features** table. On the **External Data tab**, in the **Export group**, click the **Word Merge** button. Be sure that **Link your data to an existing Microsoft Word document** is selected, and then click **OK**. Locate and open the **a09F_Flyer** file. Click the Microsoft Word button on the task bar, and maximize the Word window.

5 In the Word **Mail Merge** task pane, under **Select recipients**, be sure that **Use an existing list** is selected, and then click **Next: Write your letter**. One at a time, click to the right of **Package Deal**, **Custom Feature**, and **Warranty**, inserting the appropriate field names. At the bottom of the flyer, replace **Firstname Lastname** with your first and last names. Click **Next: Preview your letters**, and then click **Next: Complete the merge**. Click **Edit Individual Letters**, and then merge records **5-6** only. Save your document in the **Access Chapter 9** folder as **Lastname_Firstname_9F_Flyers** Unless you are required to submit your files electronically, **Print** the document.

6 **Close** Word to exit the merged document. **Save** the document as **Lastname_Firstname_9F_Flyer_Main** and **Close** Word. Restore the Access window to the screen.

7 In the **9F Custom Features** table, **Filter** the results to display only the *Luxury Package Deal* records; select the records. On the **External Data tab**, in the **Export group**, click **Excel**.

8 **Save** the file in your **Access Chapter 9** folder as **Lastname_Firstname_9F_Luxury_Features** Under **Specify export options**, select all three check boxes, and then click **OK**. **Rename** the worksheet **9F Luxury** Insert a **Header**, and type **Luxury Package Sales Rep: Firstname Lastname** **Save** the workbook. If you are instructed to submit this result, create a paper or electronic printout. **Close** the Excel workbook and Excel. In the **Access** window, **Close** the **9F Custom Features** table, but do not save the changes.

9 In the **Navigation Pane**, under **Reports**, open the **9F Package Sales** report in **Design** view. Add your **Lastname Firstname** to the beginning of the title. **Save** and **Close** the report. Right-click the **9F Package Sales** report, point to **Export**, and then click **HTML Document**. Navigate to the **Access Chapter 9** folder, and name the file **Lastname_Firstname_9F_Package_Sales.html** Under **Specify export options**, select the **Open the destination file after the export operation is complete** check box, and then click **OK**. In the **HTML Output Options** dialog box, click **OK**. Click **OK** if you are prompted about the section width.

10 If you are instructed to submit this result, create a paper or electronic printout of the Web page. **Close** the Web browser window. In the **Export - HTML Document** dialog box, click the **Close** button.

11 In the **Navigation Pane**, under **Reports**, right-click **9F Package Sales**, point to **Export**, and then click **XML File**. Save the file in the **Access Chapter 9** folder as **Lastname_Firstname_9F_Package_Sales_XML_File.xml** and then click **OK**. In the **Export XML** dialog box, be sure that the **Data (XML)** check box is selected, and then select the **Presentation of your data (XSL)** check box. Click **OK**. In the **Export - XML File** dialog box, click **Close**.

12 Locate the **9F_Package_Sales_XML_File** that displays a **Type** of **HTML Document** and double-click it. If you are instructed to submit this result, create a paper or electronic printout of the Web page. **Close** the Web browser window, and then **Close** the Access Chapter 9 window.

13 **Exit** Access.

End **You have completed Project 9F**

Apply **9A** and **9B** skills
from these Objectives:

1 Import Data from a
   Word Table

2 Import Data from an
   Excel Workbook

6 Use Mail Merge to
   Integrate Access
   and Word

8 Export Data to an
   HTML File and an
   XML File

Mastering Access | Project **9G** Monthly Promotions

Gregory Burton, Accessories Sales Manager, and Jessie Pine, Auto Sales Manager, at Liberty Motors
have teamed up to offer special monthly promotions to encourage customers to revisit the
showroom. In this project, you will import an Excel worksheet that contains the customer list and a
Word table that contains the promotion details. You will use mail merge to inform the customers
about the promotions. You will export a form created from the promotions table to an HTML file
so it can be viewed as a Web page. Your completed files will look similar to Figure 9.45.

Project Files

For Project 9G, you will need the following files:

New blank Access database
a09G_Promotions_Letter.docx
a09G_Customers.xlsx
a09G_Monthly_Promotions.txt
a09G_Logo.jpg

You will save your files as:

Lastname_Firstname_9G_Monthly_Promotions.accdb
Lastname_Firstname_9G_Promotions_Letter.docx
Lastname_Firstname_9G_Letter_Main.docx
Lastname_Firstname_9G_Monthly_Promotions_HTML.html

Project Results

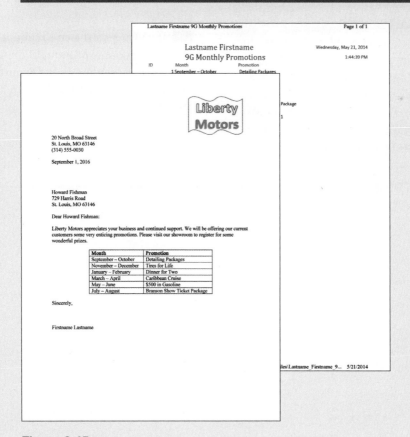

Figure 9.45

(Project 9G Monthly Promotions continues on the next page)

Access | Chapter 9

Content-Based Assessments

Mastering Access | Project **9G** Monthly Promotions (continued)

1 **Start** Access. **Create** a new blank database and save it in the **Access Chapter 9** folder as **Lastname_Firstname_ 9G_Monthly_Promotions Close** the table.

2 Import **External Data** from the **a09G_Customers** Excel file into a new table in the **9G_Monthly_Promotions** database. The **first row contains column headings**. Change the data type for the **Postal Code** field to **Text**. **Let Access add primary key**. Import to table **Lastname Firstname 9G Customers** It is not necessary to save the import steps.

3 Open the **9G Customers** table. Merge it with the existing Microsoft Word Office **a09G_Promotions_Letter**. The recipients will be selected from the existing list in the **9G Customers** table. Be sure the **Show/Hide** button is active. Place your insertion point at the beginning of the fifth blank line after the current date. Add the **Address Block**. Insert the **First Name** and **Last Name** fields between the space and the colon in the salutation line. Place a space between these fields.

4 In the closing of the letter, replace **Firstname Lastname** with your **Firstname Lastname Save** the document in your **Access Chapter 9** folder as **Lastname_ Firstname_9G_Letter_Main**

5 **Preview your letters** and **Complete the merge** for only the fifth record. **Save** the Word document in your **Access Chapter 9** folder as **Lastname_Firstname_9G_ Promotions_Letter** Unless you are required to submit your files electronically, **Print** the letter. **Close** the Word window, and then **Exit** Word, saving changes if necessary. Close the **9G Customers** table.

6 **Import External Data** from the text file **a09G_ Monthly_Promotions**. Import the source data into a new table in the current database. Use the **tab delimiter**. The **first row contains field names**. The data types are correct. **Let Access add primary key**. Import this text to **Lastname Firstname 9G Monthly Promotions** Do not save the import steps.

7 From the **9G Monthly Promotions** table, **Create** a report. In the **Title** of the report, move **9G Monthly Promotions** to a second line. Add the **a09G_Logo** to the report header. With the **Size Mode** property set to **Zoom**, resize the **logo control** until it reaches the **1.5-inch mark on the horizontal ruler** and the **0.75-inch mark on the vertical ruler**. **Save** the report as **Lastname Firstname 9G Monthly Promotions** and then **Close** the report.

8 In the **Navigation Pane**, right-click the **9G Monthly Promotions** report. **Export** the form as an **HTML document**. **Save** the document in your **Access Chapter 9** folder as **Lastname_Firstname_9G_Monthly_Promotions_ HTML** Open the destination file after the export operation is complete. In the **HTML Output Options** dialog box, click **OK**.

9 If you are instructed to submit this result, create a paper or electronic printout of the Web page. **Close** the Web browser window. In the **Export - HTML Document** dialog box, click the **Close** button.

10 **Exit** Access.

End **You have completed Project 9G**

Content-Based Assessments

GO! Fix It | Project 9H Customer Service

Project Files

For Project 9H, you will need the following files:

a09H_Customer_Service.accdb
a09H_Survey.xlsx
a09H_Liberty_Motors.accdb

You will save your files as:

Lastname_Firstname_9H_Customer_Service.accdb
Lastname_Firstname_9H_Survey_Results.rtf
Lastname_Firstname_9H_Survey.xlsx
Lastname_Firstname_9H_Survey_Results_HTML.html

Open the **a09H_Customer_Service** database, and Save as **Lastname_Firstname_9H_ Customer_Service** Update the data with information from the following sources:

- From the **a09H_Liberty_Motors** database, link the **9H Customers** table.

- Copy the chart from the **a09H_Survey** workbook to the Page Footer area in the **9H Survey Results** report. Add your **Lastname Firstname** to the beginning of the report title.

If you are instructed to submit this result, create a paper or electronic printout.

From the **a09H_Customer_Service** database, export the following documents:

- Export the **9H Survey Results** report to an RTF file. Save as **Lastname_Firstname_9H_ Survey_Results.rtf**

- Export the **9H Survey** table to Excel. Be sure all data is visible in the worksheet. Place your name in a header. Save as **Lastname_Firstname_9H_Survey**

- Export the **9H Survey Results** report to an HTML file. Save as **Lastname_Firstname_9H_ Survey_Results_HTML**

If you are instructed to submit this result, create a paper or electronic printout. If you submit this database electronically, also submit **a09H_Liberty_Motors** to view the linked objects properly.

End You have completed Project 9H ————————————

GO! Make It | Project 9I Sponsored Events

Project Files

For Project 9I, you will need the following files:

a09I_Sponsored_Events.accdb
a09I_Annual_Run.docx
a09I_Customers.docx

You will save your files as:

Lastname_Firstname_9I_Sponsored_Events.accdb
Lastname_Firstname_9I_Customers.txt
Lastname_Firstname_9I_Run_Main.docx
Lastname_Firstname_9I_Run_Letters.docx

From the student files that accompany this textbook, open the **a09I_Sponsored_Events** database file. Save the database in your **Access Chapter 9** folder as **Lastname_Firstname_ 9I_Sponsored_Events** Convert **a09I_Customers** to a tab-delimited text file, and save it as **Lastname_Firstname_9I_Customers.txt** Create a paper or electronic printout as directed. Import the text file as the **Lastname Firstname 9I Customers** table in the database. Be sure the Postal Code is imported as a text data type, and let Access create a primary key. Open the table, and add your information in **Record 25**. Create the set of merged documents for Records 24–25 using **9I Customers** and **a09I_Annual_Run.docx**. Save the main document as **Lastname_Firstname_ 9I_Run_Main** and the merged letters as **Lastname_Firstname_9I_Run_Letters** Create a paper or electronic printout of the letters as directed. Your completed documents will look similar to Figure 9.46.

Project Results

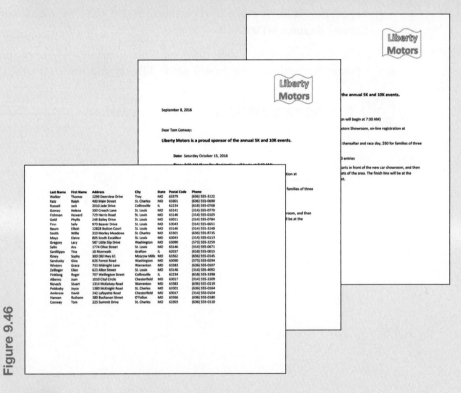

Figure 9.46

End You have completed Project 9I

Content-Based Assessments

GO! Solve It | Project 9J Sales Data

Project Files

For Project 9J, you will need the following files:

New blank Access database
a09J_Sales_Data.xlsx
a09J_Quarterly_Commission.txt
a09J_Congratulations.docx
a09J_Logo.jpg

You will save your files as:

Lastname_Firstname_9J_Sales_Data.accdb
Lastname_Firstname_9J_Congratulations.docx
Lastname_Firstname_9J_Main_Doc.docx

Phillip Garrett would like to combine data into one database, so he has asked you to import the files. Create a new Access database named **Lastname_Firstname_9J_Sales_Data** From the **a09J_Sales_Data** workbook, import the **9JQtrly Sales** worksheet as the **Lastname Firstname 9J Qtrly Sales** table. Do not import the field(skip) **Total**. Let Access add the primary key. Merge this table with the **a09J_Congratulations** Word document, replacing the word *Salesperson* with the Salesperson field and inserting the 3rd Qtr sales field after the dollar sign. Replace Firstname Lastname with your name. Save the main document as **Lastname_Firstname_9J_Main_Doc** and save the certificates as **Lastname_Firstname_9J_Congratulations** Create a paper or electronic printout of the certificates as directed.

Import the data from the **9J Quarterly Commissions** text file as the **Lastname Firstname 9J Qtrly Commissions** table. The first row contains column headings, and let Access add the primary key. From that table, create a report. Delete the 4thQtr sum from the Report Footer and page numbering from the Page Footer. Add the **a09J Logo** and edit the title: **Lastname Firstname 9J Commission**. Insert the chart from the **9J Qtrly Commission** worksheet into the Page Footer. Save the report at **Lastname Firstname 9J Commission** Create a paper or electronic printout of the letters as directed.

	Performance Element		
Performance Criteria	**Exemplary:** You consistently applied the relevant skills	**Proficient:** You sometimes, but not always, applied the relevant skills	**Developing:** You rarely or never applied the relevant skills
Import the 9J Qtrly Sales worksheet	Table created with correct fields and settings as directed.	Table created with no more than two missing fields or settings.	Table created with more than two missing fields or settings.
Create merged document with 9J Qtrly Sales and a09J_Congratulations	Merged documents created with correct fields and settings as directed.	Merged documents created with no more than two missing fields or settings.	Merged documents created with more than two missing fields or settings.
Import the 9J Quarterly Commissions delimited text file	Table created with correct fields and settings as directed.	Table created with no more than two missing fields or settings.	Table created with more than two missing fields or settings.
Create the 9J Commission report with a chart	Report created and formatted with chart pasted correctly.	Report created with no more than two missing formatting elements.	Report created with more than two missing formatting elements.

End You have completed Project 9J

Content-Based Assessments

GO! Solve It | Project 9K Advertisements

Project Files

For Project 9K, you will need the following file:

a09K_Advertisements.accdb

You will save your files as:

Lastname_Firstname_9K_Advertisements.accdb
Lastname_Firstname_9K_Advertisements_Workbook.xlsx
Lastname_Firstname_9K_Cost_Analysis.html

Jessie Pine, Auto Sales Manager of Liberty Motors, explores many different venues to advertise the business. Most of the data for the advertisements is kept in a database. Some of the employees would like to see the data arranged in a worksheet to create a what-if analysis. Open the **a09K_Advertisements** database, and then save it as **Lastname_Firstname_9K_Advertisements** Export the **9K Advertisements** table to an Excel workbook. Save the workbook as **Lastname_Firstname_9K_Advertisements_Workbook** Rename the sheet tab **9K Data** If necessary, autofit the columns. Copy the data from the **9K Cost Analysis** query to a second sheet in the same workbook. Rename this sheet **9K Analysis** Type **Lastname Firstname 9K Advertisements** as a header for each of the sheets. Unless you are required to submit your files electronically, print both worksheets in landscape orientation.

Export the **9K Cost Analysis Summary** query to an HTML file. Save the file as **Lastname_Firstname_9K_Cost_Analysis.html** Unless you are required to submit your files electronically, print the Web page.

		Performance Element		
		Exemplary: You consistently applied the relevant skills	**Proficient:** You sometimes, but not always, applied the relevant skills	**Developing:** You rarely or never applied the relevant skills
Performance Criteria	Export the 9K Advertisements table to Excel	Worksheet created with correct fields and settings as directed.	Worksheet created with no more than two missing fields or settings.	Worksheet created with more than two missing fields or settings.
	Export the 9K Cost Analysis query to Excel	Worksheet created with correct fields and settings as directed.	Worksheet created with no more than two missing fields or settings.	Worksheet created with more than two missing fields or settings.
	Export the 9K Cost Analysis Summary query to HTML	Web page created with correct fields and file type.	Web page created with no more than two missing fields or incorrect file type.	Web page created with more than two missing fields and/or incorrect file type.

End You have completed Project 9K

Outcomes-Based Assessments

Rubric

The following outcomes-based assessments are *open-ended assessments*. That is, there is no specific correct result; your result will depend on your approach to the information provided. Make *Professional Quality* your goal. Use the following scoring rubric to guide you in *how* to approach the problem, and then to evaluate *how well* your approach solves the problem.

The *criteria*—Software Mastery, Content, Format and Layout, and Process—represent the knowledge and skills you have gained that you can apply to solving the problem. The *levels of performance*—Professional Quality, Approaching Professional Quality, or Needs Quality Improvements—help you and your instructor evaluate your result.

	Your completed project is of Professional Quality if you:	Your completed project is Approaching Professional Quality if you:	Your completed project Needs Quality Improvements if you:
1-Software Mastery	Choose and apply the most appropriate skills, tools, and features and identify efficient methods to solve the problem.	Choose and apply some appropriate skills, tools, and features, but not in the most efficient manner.	Choose inappropriate skills, tools, or features, or are inefficient in solving the problem.
2-Content	Construct a solution that is clear and well organized, contains content that is accurate, appropriate to the audience and purpose, and is complete. Provide a solution that contains no errors in spelling, grammar, or style.	Construct a solution in which some components are unclear, poorly organized, inconsistent, or incomplete. Misjudge the needs of the audience. Have some errors in spelling, grammar, or style, but the errors do not detract from comprehension.	Construct a solution that is unclear, incomplete, or poorly organized; contains some inaccurate or inappropriate content; and contains many errors in spelling, grammar, or style. Do not solve the problem.
3-Format and Layout	Format and arrange all elements to communicate information and ideas, clarify function, illustrate relationships, and indicate relative importance.	Apply appropriate format and layout features to some elements, but not others. Overuse features, causing minor distraction.	Apply format and layout that does not communicate information or ideas clearly. Do not use format and layout features to clarify function, illustrate relationships, or indicate relative importance. Use available features excessively, causing distraction.
4-Process	Use an organized approach that integrates planning, development, self-assessment, revision, and reflection.	Demonstrate an organized approach in some areas, but not others; or, use an insufficient process of organization throughout.	Do not use an organized approach to solve the problem.

Outcomes-Based Assessments

GO! Think | Project **9L** Employee Recognition

Project Files

For Project 9L, you will need the following files:

    a09L_Employee_Recognition.accdb
    a09L_Birthday_List.docx
    a09L_Birthday_Card.docx

You will save your files as:

    Lastname_Firstname_9L_Employee_Recognition.accdb
    Lastname_Firstname_9L_Birthday_List.txt
    Lastname_Firstname_9L_Card.docx
    Lastname_Firstname_9L_Card_Main.docx
    Lastname_Firstname_9L_Birthday_List.html

Liberty Motors is a friendly workplace, and the employees treat each other as family. You have been asked to help with an employee recognition project. You will import the data from a Word table into a database table and then merge this table with cards created in Word. The birthday list will be uploaded to the company intranet, so it will need to be exported to HTML.

Open **a09L_Employee_Recognition** and save it as **Lastname_Firstname_9L_Employee_Recognition** Open **a09L_Birthday_List.docx**, and then convert the table to text. Save this text file as **Lastname_Firstname_9L_Birthday_List** and then import it into your database as a table named **Lastname Firstname 9L Birthday List** Add your name and birthday to the table, and merge it with **a09L_Birthday_Card** so the person's full name appears on the line after Happy Birthday and their favorite cake appears before the word "cake." Adjust the spacing as necessary. Merge your card only (Record 13), and save it as **Lastname_Firstname_9L_Card** Save the main document as **Lastname_Firstname_9L_Card_Main** If you are instructed to submit this result, create a paper or electronic printout of your birthday card.

Export **9L Birthday List** table to HTML. Save the file as **Lastname_Firstname_9L_Birthday_List.html** Unless you are required to submit your files electronically, print the Web page.

End **You have completed Project 9L** —————————————————

Outcomes-Based Assessments

GO! Think | Project **9M** Service Records

Project Files

For Project 9M, you will need the following files:

New blank Access database
a09M_Service_Records.xlsx
a09M_Logo.jpg
a09M_1stQ_Service.xlsx

You will save your database as:

Lastname_Firstname_9M_Service_Records.accdb

Liberty Motors takes great pride in its service department. It is important that accurate service records are maintained in a database. Many of the mechanics are more comfortable completing the service forms and reports in a Word table. You have been asked to import this information into an Access table, and then create a report to be used to display the activities of the service department.

Create a new database and save it as **Lastname_Firstname_9M_Service_Records** Import the **a09M_Service_Records** worksheet. Do not include a primary key, and save the table as **Lastname Firstname 9M Service Records** Open the table, and be sure all data is visible. Create a report from this table. Add the **a09M_Logo** to the title, and resize it to fit the area. Move 9M Service Records to the second line of the title and delete the date and time controls from the Report Header. Delete the page number controls from the Page Footer and the Count control from the Report Footer. Adjust the width of each column to fit the data, and adjust the width of the report so it is 7 inches wide. Copy the chart from **a09M_1stQ_Service.xlsx** to the Page Footer area. Save the report using the default name. Unless you are required to submit your database electronically, print the report.

End You have completed Project 9M ————————————————

Outcomes-Based Assessments

You and GO! | Project **9N** Club Directory

Project Files

For Project 9N, you will need the following file:

> Lastname_Firstname_8N_Club_Directory.accdb (your file from Chapter 8)

You will save your database as:

> Lastname_Firstname_9N_Club_Directory.accdb
> Lastname_Firstname_9N_Reminder_Letter.docx
> Lastname_Firstname_9N_Letters.docx
> Lastname_Firstname_9N_Letter_Main.docx
> Lastname_Firstname_9N_Activities.html

Create a personal database containing information about a club and its activities, if you do not already have one from Project 8N. Name the new database **Lastname_Firstname_9N_Club_Directory** If you do not have the database from Project 8N, create two related tables, one that lists the activities your organization has planned and the other to serve as the directory of the group. The Activities table should include information about the name (primary key field), date, cost, and location of the activity. The dates must all occur next year; consider attaching directions to the event to the table. The Directory table should include full name, address, phone number, e-mail, and an activity they are planning. If you have the database from Project 8N, save it as **Lastname_Firstname_9N_Club_Directory** in your Access Chapter 9 folder.

Open Word, and create a short letter to send to members about a special meeting that will be held a week from Tuesday. Save the letter as **Lastname_Firstname_9N_Reminder_Letter** Close Word. In the database, select the Directory table and merge it with 9N Reminder Letters. Save the letters as **Lastname_Firstname_9N_Letters** Save the main document as **Lastname_Firstname_9N_Letter_Main** Unless you are required to submit your database electronically, print the letters.

Export the Activities table to HTML. Save as **Lastname_Firstname_9N_Activities** Unless you are required to submit your database electronically, print the Web page.

You will be using this database in future chapters. Be sure to make corrections to your tables as necessary to prepare for the next chapter.

End **You have completed Project 9N** ⎯⎯⎯⎯⎯⎯⎯⎯⎯⎯⎯⎯

Business Running Case

Razvan CHIRNOAGA/Shutterstock

Front Range Action Sports is one of the country's largest retailers of sports gear and outdoor recreation merchandise. The company has large retail stores in Colorado, Washington, Oregon, California, and New Mexico, in addition to a growing online business. Major merchandise categories include fishing, camping, rock climbing, winter sports, action sports, water sports, team sports, racquet sports, fitness, golf, apparel, and footwear.

In this project, you will apply skills you practiced from the objectives in Access Chapters 7–9. You will create advanced forms and reports as well as a PivotTable to present data in different formats. You will also create macros to automate tasks and integrate Access data with other applications. Your printed results will look similar to Figure 3.1.

Project Files

For Project BRC3, you will need the following files:

- aBRC3_Company_ Operations.accdb
- aBRC3_Logo.gif
- aBRC3_Hours_Worked.xlsx
- aBRC3_Average_Prices.xlsx
- aBRC3_Advertising_Letter.docx

You will save your files as:

- Lastname_Firstname_aBRC3_Company_ Operations.accdb
- Lastname_Firstname_aBRC3_ Employee_Tabs.docx
- Lastname_Firstname_aBRC3_Main_Doc.docx
- Lastname_Firstname_aBRC3_Merge.docx
- Lastname_Firstname_aBRC3_Table_ HTML.html

Project Results

Figure 3.1

Business Running Case

Front Range Action Sports

1 **Start** Access. Navigate to the location where the student data files for this textbook are saved. Locate and open the **Lastname_Firstname_aBRC3_Company_Operations** file. If you did not add the **Front Range Action Sports** folder to the Trust Center, enable the content.

2 **Save As Lastname_Firstname_aBRC3_Company_Operations** in your **Front Range Action Sports** folder.

3 **Open** the **Navigation Pane**, if necessary. **Open** the **BRC3 Employees** table in **Design** view. Add four new fields between **Lastname** and **Availability**; name the first field **Address** the second field **City** the third **State** and the fourth **Postal Code** Select an appropriate data type for each field, and limit the size of **State** to **2** characters that should always be displayed in capital letters. Limit the size of **Postal Code** to **10** characters. **Save** the changes, and **Close** the table. **Rename** the table **Lastname Firstname BRC3 Employees Close** the **Navigation Pane**.

4 On the Ribbon, click the **Create tab**. In the **Forms** group, click the **Form Design** button to open an empty form in **Design** view. Use **BRC3 Employees** as the record source for the form. On the **Design tab**, click the **Tab Control** button. In the **Detail** section, align the plus (+) sign of the pointer with the **0.25-inch mark on the horizontal and vertical rulers**, and then click.

a. Extend the right edge of the **tab control** to the **5-inch mark on the horizontal ruler**. To the **first page** of the **tab control**, in the **Property Sheet**, add a caption of **Employee Information** From the **Field List**, add the **Empl ID, Firstname, Lastname, Address, City, State**, and **Postal Code** fields at the **1.75-inch mark on the horizontal ruler** and the **0.75-inch mark on the vertical ruler**. Widen the **Firstname, Lastname,** and **Address** text boxes to the **4-inch mark on the horizontal ruler**. To the **second page** of the **tab control**, add a caption of **Scheduling** In the same position as on the **Employee Information** page, add the **Availability, Start Date, Hourly Wage,** and **Max Hours** fields. Be sure all data is visible on both pages.

b. Add a **Logo** in the **Form Header** using **aBRC3_Logo**; resize it to **2 inches wide** and **0.75 inches tall**. Add a **Title** to the **Form Header**. It should read **Lastname Firstname BRC3 Employees** with *BRC3 Employees* on the second line. **Center** the title in the control.

c. **Save** the form as **Lastname Firstname BRC3 Employees Form** Switch to **Form** view. Enter the address information for each record as shown in **Table 1**.

d. Use the **Office Clipboard** and **Microsoft Word** to create a document displaying both tab controls of **Record 3**. **Save** this document as **Lastname_Firstname_aBRC3_Employee_Tabs** If you are instructed to submit this result, create a paper or electronic printout of the document. In Access, close the form.

5 **Open** the **Navigation Pane**. Open **BRC3 Suppliers Contact List** report in **Design** view. **Close** the **Navigation Pane**.

a. Edit the title of the report to read **Lastname Firstname BRC3 Inventory By Supplier** using your first and last names and placing *BRC3 Inventory by Supplier* on a second line.

b. Delete the **Date** and **Time** controls from the **Report Header**. Drag the **Page Footer section bar** down to the **2-inch mark on the vertical ruler**. In the **Detail** section, add a **Subform/Subreport** control, aligning the top of the plus (+) sign of the pointer with the **1-inch mark on the horizontal ruler** and the **0.5-inch mark on the vertical ruler**, and then click.

6 Using the **Subreport Wizard**, select the **BRC3 Inventory by Sport** report, and click **Next two** times. Name the subreport **Lastname Firstname BRC3 Inventory Subreport** Click **Finish**.

a. Right-click in the **Report Header** in the subreport, and click **Report Header/Footer** to remove it from the subreport. Click **Yes** to confirm the deletion of the controls.

Table 1

Empl ID	Address	City	State	Postal Code
1	241 Ridge Road	Redmond	OR	97756
2	400 Longview Drive	Bend	OR	97701
3	5 Button Court	Terrebonne	OR	97760
4	708 Ohmes Road	Sisters	OR	97759
5	2010 Frontier Drive	Redmond	OR	97756
6	100 Fernway Lane	Redmond	OR	97756

- - - ➤ (Return to Step 4-d)

(Business Running Case: Front Range Action Sports continues on the next page)

Business Running Case

b. Delete the **Sport text box control** from the **Sport Header**. Drag the **Detail section** upward until it meets the **Sport Header**. Scroll down, and delete the controls from the **Sport Footer**.

c. Delete the **subreport label control**. Reduce the width of the subreport until it reaches the **6.5-inch mark on the horizontal ruler**.

d. Click to select the subreport. On the **Format tab**, in the **Control Formatting** group, click **Shape Outline**. Point to **Line Type**, and then click the first option for **Transparent**. Resize the report so it is **7.5 inches wide**.

7 Switch to **Layout** view. Select the **text box controls** for **Company**, **E-mail Address**, and **Business Phone**. On the **Format tab**, change the **Background Color** to **Blue, Accent 4, Lighter 60%** and the font to **Bold**. **Save** the report. If you are instructed to submit this result, create a paper or electronic printout of the first page of the report. **Close** the report.

8 Create a macro to automatically open the **BRC3 Employees Form** for editing and display a security message that identifies the information as confidential (see **Table 2**).

9 **Close** the database. Reopen **BRC3_Company_Operations** to see the **Employees** form appear with the message box. **Close** the message box, and **Close** the form.

10 Open the **Database Documenter**. In the displayed **Documenter** dialog box, click the **Macros tab**, and then click the **Options** button. If necessary, clear the **Permissions by User and Group** check box, and then click **OK**. In the **Documenter** dialog box, click **Autoexec**, and then click **OK**. If you are instructed to submit this result, create a paper or electronic printout. **Close Print Preview**.

11 Design a query to display the **Company** from the **BRC3 Suppliers** table and **Category**, **Retail Price**, and **Sport** from the **BRC3 Inventory** table for all records. **Run** the query. **Save** the query as **Lastname Firstname BRC3 Inventory Data** Switch to **PivotTable** view.

a. From the **PivotTable Field List,** drag the **Sport** field to the **Drop Column Fields Here** area. Drag the **Company** field to the **Drop Row Fields Here** area. Drag the **Retail Price** field to the **Drop Totals or Detail Fields Here** area.

b. Auto calculate the **Average** for the **Retail Price**. Hide **Details** and **Drop Zones**.

c. **Save** the query. If you are instructed to submit this result, create a paper or electronic printout of the document with normal margins and landscape orientation. **Close** the query.

Table 2

Macro Name	Action	Arguments	Comment
Autoexec			Purpose: To open the Employees form for editing along with a message identifying the database as confidential
	DisplayHourglassPointer	Hourglass On: Yes	Displays the busy mouse pointer
	Echo	Echo On: No Status Bar Text: Macro is running	
	OpenForm	Form Name: BRC3 Employees Form View: Form Data Mode: Edit Window Mode: Normal	Displays the BRC3 Employees Form
	Echo	Echo On: Yes	
	DisplayHourglassPointer	Hourglass On: No	Restores normal mouse pointer
	MessageBox	Message: Confidential! For Use by Front Range Action Sports Management ONLY Beep: Yes Type: Warning! Title: Confidential Information	Displays a security message

(Business Running Case: Front Range Action Sports continues on the next page)

Return to Step 9

Business Running Case

Front Range Action Sports (continued)

12 **Open** the **Navigation Pane. Open** the **Inventory by Sport Report** in **Design** view. **Close** the **Navigation Pane**. If necessary, reduce the width of the report to **6.5 inches**. Resize the title text box control until it reaches the right edge of the report, and center the title in the control.

a. Drag the **Page Header section bar** down to the **1-inch mark on the vertical ruler**. Add a button below the title in the **Report Header** beginning at the **3-inch mark on the horizontal ruler**. This button should be called **Summary**. Embed a macro to display the **BRC3 Inventory Data** query in **PivotTable** view in **Data Mode Read Only. Save** the report. Switch to **Report** view to test the button, and then **Close** the report.

b. Open the **Database Documenter**, and view the object properties for the report. If you are instructed to submit this result, create a paper or electronic printout of page 3 only. **Close** Print Preview.

13 On the **External Data tab**, in the **Import & Link group**, click the **Excel** button. Locate and open the **aBRC3_Hours_Scheduled** file. Be certain **Import the source data into a new table in the current database** is selected. Use the column headings and field names and assign **Empl ID** as the primary key. Name the table **Lastname Firstname BRC3 Hours Scheduled Open** the table, be sure all data is visible, and then **Close** the table.

14 **Open** the **Navigation Pane**. Click the **BRC3 Suppliers** table. **Close** the **Navigation Pane**. Merge the table with the existing Microsoft Word document named **aBRC3_Advertising_Letter**. The recipients will be selected from the existing list in the table.

a. Delete the words *Inside Address* from the letter, and insert the **Address Block**. Be sure the blank line remains between the address and salutation. Insert the **Company** field after the space following *Attention*. In the closing of the letter, replace *Firstname Lastname* with your **Firstname Lastname Save** the main document as **Lastname_Firstname_aBRC3_Main_Doc**

b. **Preview your letters** and **Complete the merge** for **Record 3** only. **Save** the Word document in your **Front Range Action Sports** folder as **Lastname_Firstname_aBRC3_Merge** Unless you are required to submit your files electronically, **print** the letters. **Close** the Word window, and then **Exit Word**.

15 **Open** the **Navigation Pane**. Select the **BRC3 Average Prices Query** and create a new report. Switch to **Design** view.

a. Replace the report title with **Lastname Firstname BRC3 Average Prices** and make *BRC3 Average Prices* appear on the second line. If necessary, resize the **title control** so both lines are visible. Delete the **logo placeholder** in the **Report Header**.

b. Delete the controls in the **Page Footer** and **Report Footer**. Increase the size of the **Page Footer** section to the **2-inch mark on the vertical ruler**. Resize the report so it is **7.25 inches wide. Save** the report as **Lastname Firstname BRC3 Average Prices**

c. **Start** Excel. **Open** the **aBRC3_Average_Prices** workbook. In the worksheet, select the chart. **Copy** the chart to the Office Clipboard. In the **BRC3 Average Prices** report, **Paste** the chart in the **Page Footer. Save** the report, and then switch to **Report** view. If you are instructed to submit this result, create a paper or electronic printout. **Close** the report. **Exit** Excel.

16 In the **Navigation Pane**, right-click the **BRC3 Hours Scheduled** table. **Export** the report as an **HTML document. Save** the document in your **Front Range Action Sports** folder as **Lastname_Firstname_aBRC3_Table_HTML Open** the destination file after the export operation is complete. In the **HTML Output Options** dialog box, click **OK**. If you are instructed to submit this result, create a paper or electronic printout of the Web page. **Close** the Web browser window. In the **Export - HTML Document** dialog box, click the **Close** button.

17 **Close** the **Navigation Pane. Close** the database, and then **Exit** Access.

End **You have completed Business Running Case 3**

Administering Databases

OUTCOMES

At the end of this chapter you will be able to:

OBJECTIVES

Mastering these objectives will enable you to:

PROJECT 10A
Manage Access files.

1. Compact and Repair a Database (p. 671)
2. Back Up a Database (p. 672)
3. Convert Databases to an Earlier Version of Access (p. 674)
4. Replicate and Synchronize a Database (p. 675)

PROJECT 10B
Improve performance and customize Access.

5. Use Microsoft Access Analysis Tools (p. 680)
6. Add Action Tags (p. 687)
7. Modify Access Views and Behaviors (p. 689)

Rannev/Shutterstock

In This Chapter

After a database is created, a database administrator works to keep the database useful and efficient. Throughout the life of a typical organization's database, tables are added; design changes are made to queries, forms, and reports; and data is constantly added. Eventually, database performance can degrade. Fortunately, Access provides several tools to ensure database functionality. Analysis tools enable the administrator to identify potential problems and then fix them. File management tools rebuild databases into smaller, more efficient files. Understanding how to maintain a database is critical to the success of the individuals who rely on its data.

Located in the northern part of the greater New York metropolitan area, **Image MedTech** develops, manufactures, and distributes medical imaging equipment for the diagnosis and research of conditions and diseases. The equipment records images, processes and stores these images, and provides a means for printing and distributing them electronically. The company is a leader in state-of-the-art noninvasive diagnostic methods such as measurement of body temperature and blood flow. The company's products are used in a variety of healthcare environments, including hospitals, doctors' and dentists' offices, imaging centers, and pharmaceutical companies.

Project 10A Customers

myitlab
Project 10A Training

Project Activities

In Activities 10.01 through 10.05, you will use several tools in Access to manage database files. A file structure can be optimized, or the file can be backed up. Access 2010 supports many different file formats, and you may need to convert from one file format to another. Access also provides a tool that enables users to work with portable copies of the database that keep in sync with each other. Image MedTech needs you to administer its databases by applying several of these file management tools. As you work, you will create screen shots. Your finished screen shot document will look similar to Figure 10.1.

Project Files

For Project 10A, you will need the following files:

> a10A_Customers.accdb
> a10A_Customer_Service.accdb

You will save your files as:

> Lastname_Firstname_10A_Customers.accdb
> Lastname_Firstname_10A_Customers_2016-02-02.accdb (Your date will differ)
> Lastname_Firstname_10A_Customer_Service_2010.accdb
> Lastname_Firstname_10A_Customer_Service_2003.mdb
> Lastname_Firstname_10A_Replica.mdb
> Lastname_Firstname_10A_Screens.docx

Project Results

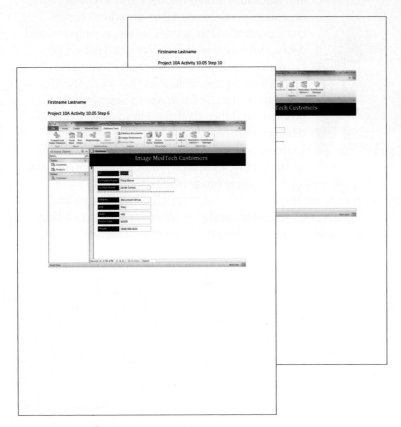

Figure 10.1
Project 10A Customers

Objective 1 | Compact and Repair a Database

Database files should be rebuilt routinely to ensure optimal performance. When working with a database, file sizes increase rapidly, especially as forms, queries, or reports are modified or deleted. Unlike most application files, when objects or records are deleted, the database file size does not decrease. Access provides a tool that rewrites database files so that the data and objects are stored more efficiently.

Activity 10.01 | Compacting and Repairing a Database

Compact & Repair is a process in which an Access file is rewritten to store the objects and data within it with less wasted space. Image MedTech has a database in which new forms, queries, and reports were created, and several old objects need to be removed from the database. In this project, you will delete the old objects and then use the Compact & Repair tool to optimize the Image MedTech database file.

1 **Start** Access. Navigate to the location where the student data files for this textbook are saved. Locate and then open the **a10A_Customers** file. Display **Backstage** view, and click **Save Database As**. In the **Save As** dialog box, navigate to the drive on which you will be saving your folders and projects for this chapter. Create a new folder named **Access Chapter 10** and then save the database as **Lastname_Firstname_10A_Customers** in the folder.

2 If necessary, enable the content or add the Access Chapter 10 folder to the Trust Center.

3 In the **Navigation Pane**, under **Queries**, click **Products Query**, and then press ⌈Del⌋. In the displayed message, click **Yes**. Using the same technique, delete the **Products** form and **Products** report.

4 At the beginning of each remaining database object name, add **Lastname Firstname** using your first and last names.

5 Click the **Start** menu, and then click **Windows Explorer**. In Windows Explorer, open your **Access Chapter 10** folder.

6 If necessary, click the **Change your view** button in the toolbar, and click **Details**. **Maximize** the **Windows Explorer** window, and then compare your screen with Figure 10.2.

Access database file sizes are commonly measured using bytes. The file size for the database is about 600 KB. *KB* is the abbreviation for kilobyte. A single *kilobyte* stores 1,024 bytes. A *byte* typically stores a single character, such as a digit or letter, and is used to measure storage sizes on disks or in computer memory. The other file with the same name is a temporary file that Access creates whenever a database file is open. Access deletes this temporary file when the database is closed.

Figure 10.2

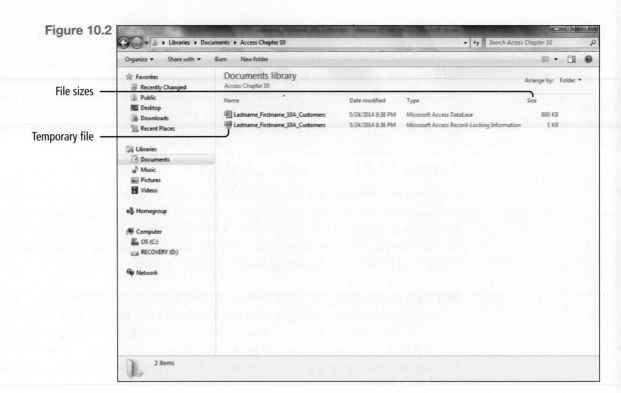

File sizes

Temporary file

7 Switch to **10A_Customers** by clicking the Access button on the taskbar. Display **Backstage** view, and click the **Compact & Repair Database** button.

8 Switch to the **Chapter 10 folder** window, and then observe the smaller file size.

9 Switch to the **10A_Customers** Access window for the next activity.

Objective 2 | Back Up a Database

Organizations often invest important resources to prevent the loss of their data. *Data loss* is the unexpected failure of information caused by such actions as hardware malfunction, accidental deletion of records, theft, or natural disaster. When data is lost in a database, it is usually recovered using a copy of the database. *Backing up* refers to the process of creating a copy of a file or files. Organizations typically back up their databases at least once a day and before making design changes or performing maintenance tasks. The collection of backup copies is used to recover data and provide a useful historical record of the organization's transactions.

Activity 10.02 | Backing Up a Database

Microsoft Access provides a tool to create backup copies of its databases. A *backup* is a copy of an original file that is stored in an alternate location. MedTech needs a daily backup of its database. The company will use its set of daily backups to recover data and as a historical record of its business activities. In this activity, you will back up the Image MedTech database.

1 Display **Backstage** view, click **Save & Publish**, and then double-click **Back Up Database**. Compare your screen with Figure 10.3.

The current date is placed at the end of the file name.

Figure 10.3

Current date appended to
file name; yours will differ

Another Way

You can also make
backups using Copy
and Paste. In Windows
Explorer, copy the
original file to the
Clipboard. In the remote
location, paste the file.
Care should be taken to
rename each backup
copy manually because
Copy and Paste will not
place the current date in
the file name of the
backup copy.

2. In the displayed **Save As** dialog box, click the **Save** button.

3. Switch to the **Windows Explorer** window. If necessary, double-click the line to the
right of the **Name** column header so that the entire file name for the backup displays.

4. Double-click the line to the right of the **Type** column header so that all of the text in
the Type column displays.

5. Compare your screen with Figure 10.4. Be sure that the text is not truncated in the
Name, Size, Type, and Date Modified columns.

   Depending on your settings and your operating system, the order of your columns may be
   different.

Figure 10.4

Columns widened to
display all information

6. **Close** Windows Explorer. **Close** the database.

Note | Back Up to an Alternative Location

In a business application, storing backup copies on the same computer is not recommended. If a data loss event
happens, the backup copy would probably be lost along with the original. Many organizations store their
backup copies on removable media and then store the media in a location that is safe from theft or natural
disaster. Many organizations store their backup copies on a separate hard drive located in another building.

Access | Chapter 10

Objective 3 | Convert Databases to an Earlier Version of Access

Microsoft Access 2010 supports databases that are saved in several different formats. Database file versions prior to Access 2002 - 2003 must be converted to the new Access 2010 file format before they can be opened. The Access 2010 file format, however, does not support all of the features found in the older Access 2002 - 2003 file format. If those features are needed, the database will need to be converted from the Access 2010 file format to the Access 2002 - 2003 file format. When working with an Access 2002 - 2003 file, Microsoft Access 2010 opens the file and adds the features supported by the older file format to the Ribbon. A database that utilizes features new to Access 2007 or Access 2010 cannot be converted to the 2002 - 2003 format.

Activity 10.03 | Converting to a 2002 - 2003 Database

Access 2010 can work directly with the Access 2002 - 2003 and Access 2010 file formats. The file format used by Access 2010 supports many features not found in older file formats. Conversely, the Access 2002 - 2003 file format supports several features that are not available when the database is saved in the Access 2010 file format. A summary of features for the two file formats is shown in Figure 10.5. Image MedTech would like to use a feature that is available only for databases saved in the 2002 - 2003 file format. In this activity, you will convert a database to the 2002 - 2003 file format.

Comparison of Supported Features

Feature	2002 - 2003 File Format	2010 File Format
File extension	.mdb	.accdb
Locked-down version	MDE file	ACCDE file
Replication	Yes	No
User-level security	Yes	No
Data access pages	Yes	No
Password protection	Yes	Yes (Enhanced)
Multivalued lookup fields	No	Yes
Attachment data type	No	Yes
Calculated data type	No	Yes
History tracking for Memo fields	No	Yes
Rich Text Formatting in Memo fields	No	Yes
Integration with Windows SharePoint Services	No	Yes
Integration with Outlook	No	Yes

Figure 10.5

1 Locate and then open the **a10A_Customer_Service** file from the location where the student data files for this textbook are saved. **Save** 🖫 the database in your **Access Chapter 10** folder as **Lastname_Firstname_10A_Customer_Service_2010** If necessary, click **Enable Content**.

2 Display **Backstage** view, click **Save & Publish**, and then double-click **Access 2002 - 2003 Database**.

> **Note** | Attempting to Convert a Database with Access 2010 Features
>
> Access will not convert a database to an older version if it contains features supported only with the Access 2010 file format. The features must be removed before converting the database.

3 In the displayed **Save As** dialog box, if necessary, navigate to your Access Chapter 10 folder. Change the file name to **Lastname_Firstname_10A_Customer_Service_2003** and then click **Save**. If a message displays, click **OK**.

4 **Close 10A_Customer_Service_2010**, and then **Open 10A_Customer_Service_2003**. If necessary, click **Enable Content**.

The application title bar displays *(Access 2002 - 2003 file format)*.

5 Click the **Navigation Pane arrow**, and then click **All Access Objects**.

6 Click the **Database Tools** tab, and then compare your screen with Figure 10.6.

The Administer group displays two buttons: *Replication Options* and *Switchboard Manager*. These two features are not supported in the Access 2010 file format. Microsoft Access 2010 displays these buttons only when an Access 2002 - 2003 file is open.

Figure 10.6

Access 2002 - 2003 file format

Administer group

> **More Knowledge** | Converting an Access 2002 - 2003 File to the Access 2010 File Format
>
> To convert a 2002 - 2003 file to the Access 2010 file format, use the Save As command and select Access 2010 for the file type. If the older version contains features that are not supported by the Access 2010 file format, Access will remove those features.

Objective 4 | Replicate and Synchronize a Database

Access provides a method to enable multiple users to work with multiple copies of a single database, and then share their changes with the original database and each other. A *replica* is a special copy of a database in which any changes that are made are sent to the original database and any other replicas that may exist. *Replication* is the process of creating a replica. Replication enables several users to work with the database without connecting to their organization's network. When they do connect to the original database, they can send their changes to the master (original) database.

Activity 10.04 | Creating a Replica of a Database

An employee at Image MedTech needs to work on the database while she is on a business trip. She will not be able to access the company database while away, so she will need to update the original database when she returns. In this activity, you will replicate the database, and then test the replica set. A *replica set* is composed of the original database and all replica copies. Replication is not supported with the Access 2010 file format, so you will use the Access 2002 - 2003 database that you created earlier.

1 If necessary, open **Lastname_Firstname_10A_Customer_Service_2003**, and then click the **Database Tools tab**.

2 In the **Administer group**, click the **Replication Options button**, and then click **Create Replica**.

3 Read the displayed message that the database must be closed, and then click **Yes**.

> In a replica set, design changes can be made to the Design Master only. A *Design Master* is the original database in a replica set. Design changes made in the Design Master are passed on to each replica.

4 The database closes, and a conversion message displays. Read the conversion message, and then click **No**.

5 In the displayed **Location of New Replica** dialog box, be sure that your **Access Chapter 10** folder is open. In the **File name** box, type **Lastname_Firstname_10A_Replica**

6 Select the **Prevent deletes** check box.

> Selecting the Prevent deletes check box prohibits others from deleting records.

7 Click **OK**. The database opens and a message with information about the replica displays. Read the displayed message, and then click **OK**. Compare your screen with Figure 10.7.

> In the title bar, *Design Master* displays next to the file name to indicate that the Design Master is currently open. In the Navigation Pane, the Replication icon displays next to each database object name.

Figure 10.7

Replication icons →

8 Open the **Customers** form. Click the **New (blank) Record** button, and then enter the following record:

ID	100999
Company Name	**Flora Stone**
Contact Name	**Javier Cortez**
Address	**341 Lincoln Drive**
City	**Troy**
State	**MO**
Postal Code	**63379**
Phone	**(636) 555-0121**

9 Switch to **Layout** view. On the **Design tab**, in the **Themes group**, notice all of the buttons are gray—inactive. Select the text box controls for the following fields: **ID, Company Name**, and **Contact Name**. Click the **Format tab**, and add a **hairline** outline to selected controls.

> Files saved in the Access 2002 - 2003 file format cannot display the Theme features used in later database formats; however, you can use other formatting options to enhance database objects.

10 Click **Save** 🔚, **Close** the form, and then **Close** the **Database**.

11 Open **Lastname_Firstname_10A_Replica**, and then open the **Customers** form. Navigate to the last record in the form.

> The replica does not yet reflect the changes that you made to the original. These changes will be updated in the next activity.

12 **Close** the form.

Activity 10.05 | Synchronizing a Database

Replicas enable Access to synchronize changes made to the Design Master and replicas. To *synchronize* is to update each member of a replica set by exchanging all updated records and design changes. In this activity, you will synchronize all of the changes that you made in the previous activity.

1 If necessary, open **Lastname_Firstname_10A_Replica**.

2 Click the **Database Tools tab**. In the **Administration group**, click the **Replication Options** button, and then click **Synchronize Now**.

3 In the displayed Synchronize Database dialog box, click **OK**.

4 Read the displayed message, and then click **Yes**. In the displayed message, click **OK**.

> The database closes, synchronizes the replica set, and then reopens.

5 Open the **Customers** form. Click the **Last Record** button, and then compare your screen with Figure 10.8.

> The formatting applied in the Design Master has been applied to the form in the replica copy. The record for Flora Stone, which was added in the Design Master, also has been added to the replica.

Figure 10.8

Record for Flora Stone added

Formatting applied

6 Press [Alt] + [PrtScr]. Create a new, blank Word document. In the **Word** document, type your first and last names, press [Enter], and then type **Project 10A Activity 10.05 Step 6** Press [Enter], and then **Paste** the screen shot. **Save** 🖫 the document in your **Access Chapter 10** folder with the name **Lastname_Firstname_10A_Screens** Leave the Word document open.

7 In **Access**, **Close** the form, and then **Exit** Access.

8 Return to the **Windows Explorer** window. In your **Access Chapter 10** folder, be sure that you are still in **Details** view and that all the files created in this project display. Be sure that the columns are wide enough to display all of the Name and Type descriptions.

9 Press [Alt] + [PrtScr], and then **Close Windows Explorer**.

10 In the **Word** document, press [Enter], and then press [Ctrl] + [Enter] to insert a page break. Type your first and last names, press [Enter], and then type **Project 10A Activity 10.05 Step 10** Press [Enter], **Paste** the screen shot, and then click **Save** 🖫. If you are instructed to submit this result, create a paper or electronic printout of the Word document.

11 **Close** the document, and **Exit** Word.

End **You have completed Project 10A** ————————————

Figure 10.10

Show introductory pages check box

---

5 Click the **Next** button. In the displayed wizard dialog box, read the directions. Be sure that the **Yes, let the wizard decide** option button is selected, and then click **Next**.

6 In the displayed wizard dialog box, read the directions, and then compare your screen with Figure 10.11.

The wizard suggests placing the product data into a related table currently named Table2. It suggests using Product ID as its primary key. In the proposal for Table1, a lookup field will be inserted to relate the two tables.

Figure 10.11

Table 2

Table 1

One-to-many relationship

Suggested primary key

---

7 Double-click the **Table1** title bar. In the displayed dialog box, type **Lastname Firstname Invoices** and then click **OK**. Widen the field list until the entire table name is displayed.

8 Double-click the **Table2** title bar. In the displayed dialog box, type **Lastname Firstname Product** and then click **OK**. Widen the field list until the entire table name is displayed.

9 Click the **Next** button, and then read the directions displayed in the wizard dialog box. In the **Invoices** table, click **Invoice #**, and then click the **Set Unique Identifier** button.

10 Press `Alt` + `PrtScr`. Create a new, blank Word document. In the **Word** document, type your first and last names, press `Enter`, and then type **Project 10B Activity 10.06 Step 10** Press `Enter`, and then **Paste** the screen shot. **Save** 🖫 the document in your **Access Chapter 10** folder with the name **Lastname_Firstname_10B_Screens** Leave the Word document open.

11 Switch to the **Access** window. Click **Next**, and then read the directions displayed in the wizard dialog box. Be sure that the **Yes, create the query** option button is selected, and then click **Finish**.

12 **Close** the displayed **Access Help** window, **Open** ⏵ the **Navigation Pane**, and then compare your screen with Figure 10.12.

The two tables have been created and the original table has been renamed Invoices_OLD. A query named Invoices is created and is opened in Datasheet view. This query is used so that the reports and forms that relied on the old Invoices table will still work.

Figure 10.12

Query in Datasheet view

Original Invoices table

New tables

New query

13 **Close** the query.

> **Note** | Preventing Accidental Deletion of Records During the Conversion Process
>
> Access creates the relationship between the Invoices and Product table with the Enforce Referential Integrity and Cascade Update Related Records options selected. The Cascade Delete Related Records is not selected so that you cannot accidentally delete any records.

Activity 10.07 | Using the Performance Analyzer

Poor database design impairs performance, especially when the database is used to store large amounts of data. Image MedTech needs to analyze its database to increase its performance. In this activity, you will use the **Performance Analyzer** to identify and fix problems with the database. The Performance Analyzer is a wizard that analyzes database objects and then offers suggestions for improving them.

1 If necessary, open **Lastname_Firstname_10B_Invoices**.

2 Click the **Create tab**. In the **Queries group**, click the **Query Design** button. Add the **Invoices** table that you created in the previous activity and the **Customers** table, and then **Close** the **Show Table** dialog box. If necessary, expand the field lists until all fields and table names display

3 From the **Invoices** table, add the **Invoice #** and **Date** fields to the design grid. From the **Customers** table, add the **Company Name** and **Phone** fields.

4 From the **Invoices** table, drag **Customer ID** and drop it over **Customer ID** in the **Customers** table. Compare your screen with Figure 10.13.

> An *indeterminate relationship* between the two tables is established using Customer ID as the common field. An indeterminate relationship is one that does not enforce referential integrity. The relationship applies to this query only and is not defined for the entire database.

Figure 10.13

Indeterminate relationship ————

5 In the **Results group**, click the **Run** button. Click **Save** 🖫, type **Lastname Firstname Sales** and then click **OK**. **Close** the query.

6 Click the **Database Tools tab**. In the **Analyze group**, click the **Analyze Performance** button.

7 In the displayed **Performance Analyzer** dialog box, click the **All Object Types** tab. Click the **Select All** button, and then click **OK**. Compare your screen with Figure 10.14.

> The Performance Analyzer provides three levels of suggestions: Recommendations, Suggestions, and Ideas. For this database, the Performance Analyzer has no recommendations, one suggestion, and several ideas.

Access | Chapter 10

Figure 10.14

Ideas

Suggestion

8 Under **Analysis Results**, click the suggestion **Table 'Lastname Firstname Invoices':Relate to table 'Customers'**. Click the **Optimize** button. Click the first item labeled with the **Idea** icon. Notice that the Optimize button is unavailable.

A one-to-many relationship between the two tables is defined, and the Performance Analyzer displays a check mark next to the item. Access fixes only those problems identified as a recommendation or suggestion.

9 Press Alt + PrtScr. In the **Word** document, press Enter, and then press Ctrl + Enter to insert a page break. Type your first and last names, press Enter, and then type **Project 10B Activity 10.07 Step 9** Press Enter, **Paste** the screen shot, and then click **Save** 📄.

10 Return to **Access**. Read through the remaining ideas, and then click the **Close** button.

Activity 10.08 | Viewing Object Dependencies

The Object Dependencies pane shows the dependencies between database objects. A **dependency** is an object that requires, or is dependent on, another database object. For example, several forms, reports, and queries may rely on a single table. Deleting that table would "break" those dependent objects. In this activity, you will use the Object Dependencies pane to determine whether any objects depend on the Invoices_OLD table. If not, you will delete the table.

1 Click the **Customers** table to make it active, and then click the **Database Tools tab**.

2 In the **Relationships group**, click the **Object Dependencies** button. If a message displays, click **OK**. On the right side of the Access window, notice that the Object Dependencies pane displays.

3 If necessary, in the **Navigation Pane**, click the **Customers** table, and then in the **Object Dependencies** pane, click **Refresh**. If a message box displays, click **OK**. Widen the pane so all object names are visible.

4 If necessary, click the *Objects that depend on me* option button. Compare your screen with Figure 10.15.

The Invoices table, Sales query, Customers form, and Customers report all depend on the Customers table.

Figure 10.15

Dependent objects

5 In the **Navigation Pane**, click the **Invoices_OLD** table, and then in the **Object Dependencies** pane, click **Refresh**. If a message displays, click **OK**. Notice that no database objects depend on the **Invoices_OLD** table.

6 **Close** the **Object Dependencies** pane, and then delete the **Invoices_OLD** table.

7 On the **Database Tools tab**, in the **Analyze group**, click the **Analyze Performance** button. In the displayed **Performance Analyzer** dialog box, click the **All Object Types** tab, click the **Select All** button, and then click **OK**.

With the deletion of the old Invoices table, only four ideas are given by the Performance Analyzer.

8 In the **Performance Analyzer** dialog box, click the **Close** button. **Close** ◀◀ the **Navigation Pane**.

Activity 10.09 | Using the Database Documenter

The *Database Documenter* builds a report with detailed information about all of the objects in a database. This detailed report is often referred to as a *data dictionary*. The data dictionary created by the Database Documenter should be printed periodically and stored in a secure location. Image MedTech needs to document certain database features. In this activity, you will create a report using the Database Documenter.

1 If necessary, open **Lastname_Firstname_10B_Invoices**.

2 On the **Database Tools tab**, in the **Analyze group**, cick the **Database Documenter** button. In the displayed **Documenter** dialog box, click the **All Object Types** tab, click the **Select All** button, and then click **OK**.

The Database Documenter displays the data dictionary report in Print Preview. This report cannot be saved as an Access object.

3 In the **Zoom group**, click the **Zoom** button, and then compare your screen with Figure 10.16.

Figure 10.16

4 Click the **Next Page** button to skim through a few of the pages.

In an organization, this report would be printed, bound, and stored in a secure location.

5 Click the **Close Print Preview** button. On the **Database Tools tab**, in the **Analyze group**, click the **Database Documenter** button.

6 In the displayed **Documenter** dialog box, click the **Options** button. Verify that only the **Relationships** check box is selected.

7 Under **Include for Fields**, click the **Nothing** option button. Under **Include for Indexes**, click the **Nothing** option button. Compare your screen with Figure 10.17.

Figure 10.17

8 Click **OK**. In the **Documenter** dialog box, click the **Tables** tab, select the **Lastname Firstname Invoices** check box, and then click **OK**.

9 Click the **Zoom** button, and then scroll as needed so that all of the report text displays in the window.

10 Press [Alt] + [PrtScr]. In the **Word** document, press [Enter], and then press [Ctrl] + [Enter] to insert a page break. Type your first and last names, press [Enter], and then type **Project 10B Activity 10.09 Step 10** Press [Enter], **Paste** the screen shot, and then click **Save** [💾].

11 In **Access**, click the **Close Print Preview** button. Recall that this report cannot be saved.

Objective 6 | Add Action Tags

Action tags enable the end user to perform tasks from Access that would usually require another program, such as Outlook, to be open. Action tags are assigned in a table's Design view by changing the field's Action Tags property. With action tags in place, the user can perform tasks within Access such as automatically adding a phone number to their Outlook Contacts.

Activity 10.10 | Adding Action Tags

The Marketing Department at Image MedTech would like to integrate the customer data in its database with Microsoft Outlook 2010. Outlook is a personal information management program that manages e-mail, contacts, tasks, and appointments. In this activity, you will assign an action tag to the Phone field in the Customers table.

1 If necessary, open **Lastname_Firstname_10B_Invoices**. **Open** [»] the **Navigation Pane**.

2 In the **Navigation Pane**, open the **Customers** table in **Design** view.

3 In the **Field Name** column, click **Phone**. Under **Field Properties**, click the **Smart Tags** box, and then click the **Build** button. In the Action Tags dialog box, select the **Telephone Number** check box, and then compare your screen with Figure 10.18.

The available action tags that could be applied to this field display.

Figure 10.18

Available action tags

4 Click **OK** to close the dialog box.

5 **Save** 🖫 your changes, and then switch to **Datasheet** view.

6 Scroll, if necessary, so that the **Phone** column displays. Place the pointer over any field containing a phone number, but do not click.

> A small, purple triangle indicates that an action tag is available. When you point to the field, the Smart Tag Actions button displays.

7 Click the **Smart Tag Actions button arrow**, and then compare your screen with Figure 10.19.

> If your computer is connected to a phone, Outlook will dial the number when the Call command is clicked. When the Add to Contacts command is clicked, Outlook starts and opens a new, untitled contact with the phone number already entered. Unless you have configured Outlook 2010 to work on your computer, do not try using any of the smart tag actions.

Figure 10.19

Add to Contacts command —

8 With the **Smart Tag Actions** menu still displayed, press [Alt] + [PrtScr]. In the **Word** document, press [Enter], and then press [Ctrl] + [Enter] to insert a page break. Type your first and last names, press [Enter], and then type **Project 10B Activity 10.10 Step 8** Press [Enter], **Paste** the screen shot, and then click **Save** 🖫.

9 In **Access**, **Close** the table.

Objective 7 | Modify Access Views and Behaviors

Access has many options that affect database views and behaviors. These options are changed using the Access Options dialog box. For example, there are options to alter colors and borders, options for how text is formatted, and settings that alter how windows display. The Access Options dialog box is also used to add and remove commands from the Quick Access Toolbar. You can create a custom interface by changing the options for the Navigation Pane. Hundreds of option settings are available to the database designer.

Activity 10.11 | Modifying Access Options

Image MedTech would like its database to have a unique look and feel. In this activity, you will use the Access Options dialog box to customize the appearance of all databases opened on this computer.

1 If necessary, open **Lastname_Firstname_10B_Invoices**.

2 Display **Backstage** view, and click **Options**. If necessary, click **General**. Compare your screen with Figure 10.20.

The left pane displays several option groups that, when clicked, display their settings in the larger pane. The settings for the General option group currently display.

Figure 10.20

3 Under **User Interface Options**, click the **Color scheme arrow**, and then click Blue.

4 Under **Personalize your copy of Microsoft Office**, in the **User name** box, type your first and last names. In the **Initials** box, type your first, middle, and last initials.

5 Click **OK**, and then observe the changes to the database color scheme.

These changes will affect every database opened on this computer as well as documents in the other Office 2010 applications.

6 Display **Backstage** view, and click **Options**. In the left pane, click **Datasheet**.

7 Under **Gridlines and cell effects**, clear the **Horizontal** check box.

8 Under **Default font**, click the **Size arrow**, and then click **9**.

9 In the left pane, click **Object Designers**. Under **Table design view**, in the **Default text field size**, replace the existing value with **50**

The default field size for new text fields will be 50 instead of 255.

10 In the left pane, click **Client Settings**. Scroll down to view the options under **Display**. Clear the **Show Action Tags on Datasheets** check box.

11 Click **OK**. Open the **Customers** table in **Datasheet** view. Scroll so that the **Phone** field displays. Place the pointer over any phone number and notice that the **Smart Tag Actions** button does not display.

Although the purple triangles still appears in the Phone field, the Smart Tag Action button does not appear. In addition, the font size is smaller for the entire table, allowing the columns to be smaller and still display the data.

12 **Close** the **Customers** table.

Activity 10.12 | Customizing the Quick Access Toolbar

Any Access command, including those not available on the Ribbon, can be added to the Quick Access Toolbar. Image MedTech would like to add its commonly used commands to the Quick Access Toolbar. In this activity, you will use two different methods to customize the Quick Access Toolbar.

1 If necessary, open **Lastname_Firstname_10B_Invoices**.

2 Display **Backstage** view, and click **Options**. In the left pane, click **Quick Access Toolbar**. Alternatively, on the **Quick Access Toolbar**, click the **Customize Quick Access Toolbar arrow**, and then click **More Commands**. Compare your screen with Figure 10.21.

Under *Choose commands from*, the commands from the Popular Commands group display. Under *Customize Quick Access Toolbar*, the commands on the current Quick Access Toolbar are listed. The *Customize Quick Access Toolbar* menu provides two options—the Quick Access Toolbar can be modified for all databases or just the current database.

Figure 10.21

Customizes all databases
or current database only

Current commands on
the Quick Access toolbar

3 In the list below **Popular Commands**, click **Close Database,** and then click the **Add** button.

Image MedTech wants this button added for all databases opened on this computer.

4 In the upper right corner, click the **Customize Quick Access Toolbar arrow**, and then click the path to the currently open database. In the list below **Popular Commands**, scroll down. Click **Quick Print**, and then click the **Add** button.

Image MedTech wants this change for the currently opened database only.

5 Click **OK**, and then compare your screen with Figure 10.22.

The Close Database and Quick Print icons have been added to the Quick Access Toolbar. Icons added to just one database are placed in a separate area to the right of the other icons.

Figure 10.22

Icons for all databases

Icon for this database only

Access | Chapter 10

6 Open the **Customers** table in **Datasheet** view. Press `Alt` + `PrtScr`. In the **Word** document, press `Enter`, and then press `Ctrl` + `Enter` to insert a page break. Type your first and last names, press `Enter`, and then type **Project 10B Activity 10.12 Step 6** Press `Enter`, **Paste** the screen shot, and then click **Save** 🖫.

7 In **Access**, **Close** the **Customers** table.

Activity 10.13 | Setting Current Database Options

The Current Database group provides several useful options you can change. These options enable the database designer to create the look and feel of a custom application. Image MedTech would like its database to have a unique look and feel, and the company does not want end users to make design changes. In this activity, you will create a custom application title and application icon for the database, and then disable Layout view.

1 If necessary, open **Lastname_Firstname_10B_Invoices**.

2 Display **Backstage** view, click **Options**, and then, in the left pane, click **Current Database**.

3 Under **Application Options**, in the **Application Title** box, type **Image MedTech**

The *application title* is the text that displays in the Access title bar when that database is open. If the Application Title box is left blank, the file name and application name display instead.

4 To the right of **Application Icon** box, click the **Browse** button. In the displayed **Icon Browser** dialog box, change the file type to **Bitmaps (*.bmp)**.

5 In the **Icon Browser** dialog box, navigate to where the student files for this project are stored. Locate and click **a10B_Icon**, and then click **OK**.

6 To the right of the **Display Form** box, click the down-pointing arrow, and select **Customers** to display this form when the database is opened.

This is an alternative to creating an autoexec macro that will simply display a form when the database is opened.

7 Under **Application Options**, select the **Compact on Close** check box.

With this option selected, the database will be compacted and repaired each time it is closed.

8 Clear the **Enable Layout View** check box.

9 Click **OK**, read the displayed message, and then click **OK** again.

10 Close the database, and then reopen **Lastname_Firstname_10B_Invoices**.

11 Close the **Customers** form. **Open** the **Customers** report in **Report** view, and then compare your screen with Figure 10.23.

The application title displays in the title bar. The application icon displays in the report's tab, in the upper left corner of the screen, and also in the application's taskbar button. If the database file or icon image file is renamed or moved to another location, the icon will no longer display.

Figure 10.23

Application title

Application icons

12 Close the report.

Activity 10.14 | Customizing the Navigation Pane

The database designer may choose to customize the Navigation Pane to create a custom interface for the end user. Image MedTech would like its users to see only forms and reports in the Navigation Pane. In this activity, you will customize the Navigation Pane by adding a custom category and two groups. You will then add the form and report to their respective groups.

1 If necessary, open **Lastname_Firstname_10B_Invoices**.

2 Display **Backstage** view, click **Options**, and then, in the left pane, click **Current Database**.

3 Under **Navigation**, click the **Navigation Options** button, and then compare your screen with Figure 10.24.

The existing categories for the Navigation Pane display on the left and the groups for each existing category display on the right. Categories and Groups are edited using the buttons below the two columns.

Figure 10.24

Existing Items

Groups for Tables and Related Views

Editing buttons

4 Click the **Add Item** button, type **Image MedTech** and then press [Enter].

Image MedTech displays as a category. A *Navigation Pane category* is a top-level listing that displays when the Navigation Pane arrow is clicked.

5 With the **Image MedTech** category selected, click the **Add Group** button. Type **Data Entry** and then press [Enter].

Data Entry displays as group. A *Navigation Pane group* is a second-level listing that displays when a Navigation Pane category is selected.

6 Click the **Add Group** button. Type **Reports** and then press [Enter].

7 Click **OK** three times to close the dialog boxes. If necessary, close and reopen the database, and then **Close** the **Customers** form.

8 Click the **Navigation Pane arrow**, and then click **Image MedTech**. In the **Navigation Pane**, under **Unassigned Objects**, drag the **Customers** form and drop it over the **Data Entry** group.

9 Drag the **Customers** report and drop it over the **Reports** group. Compare your screen with Figure 10.25.

The objects display as shortcuts within their respective Navigation Pane groups, and they are no longer listed under Unassigned Objects.

Figure 10.25

Shortcut to objects

Unassigned objects

10 Display **Backstage** view, click **Options**, and then under **Navigation**, click the **Navigation Options** button.

11 In the **Categories** column, click **Image MedTech**. In the Groups column, clear the **Unassigned Objects** check box, and then click **OK** three times. Close and reopen the database.

Only the two objects that you assigned earlier display in the Navigation Pane.

12 Right-click the **Customers** form, and in the displayed shortcut menu, click **Rename Shortcut**. Add your **Lastname Firstname** at the beginning of the object name. Use this same technique to add your last and first names to the **Customers** report name.

13 Press Alt + PrtScr. In the **Word** document, press Enter, and then press Ctrl + Enter to insert a page break. Type your first and last names, press Enter, and then type **Project 10B Activity 10.14 Step 13** Press Enter, **Paste** the screen shot, and then click **Save** . If you are instructed to submit this result, create a paper or electronic printout of the Word document.

14 **Exit** Word and return to Access. In the **Quick Access Toolbar**, right-click the **Close Database button**, and then click Remove from Quick Access Toolbar. Use this same technique to remove the **Quick Print button** from the Quick Access Toolbar.

15 Display **Backstage** view, click **Options**, and then click **General**. Click the **Color scheme arrow**, and then click **Silver**.

16 Click **Datasheet**. Click the **Default Font size button arrow**, and then click **11**. Under **Default gridlines showing**, select the **Horizontal** check box.

17 Click **Object Designers**, and then set the **Default text field size** back to **255**

18 Click **Client Settings,** scroll down, and then under **Display**, select the **Show Action Tags on Datasheets** check box.

19 Click **OK** to close the **Access Options** dialog box, and then **Exit** Access.

End **You have completed Project 10B** ————————————————

Content-Based Assessments

Summary

As databases collect more and more data, and database objects are added, modified, and deleted, performance begins to degrade. Access provides several analysis tools designed to improve database performance. Multiple copies of a database can be replicated so that individuals can work with the database away from work and then synchronize their changes with the design master when they return. You have practiced creating databases using several different file types, each with a specific purpose, such as creating a backup. Finally, you practiced customizing Access views by adding commands to the Quick Access Toolbar and by creating a custom Navigation Pane.

Key Terms

Matching

Match each term in the second column with its correct definition in the first column by writing the letter of the term on the blank line in front of the correct definition.

_____ 1. The process in which an Access file is rewritten to store objects and data more efficiently.

_____ 2. The abbreviation for a kilobyte.

_____ 3. A unit used to measure computer storage sizes; it typically stores a single character, such as a digit or letter.

_____ 4. The unexpected failure of information caused by such actions as hardware malfunction, accidental deletion of records, theft, or natural disaster.

_____ 5. The process of creating a copy of a file or files.

_____ 6. A special copy of a database in which any changes made are sent to the original database.

_____ 7. To update each member of a replica set by exchanging all updated records and design changes.

_____ 8. A wizard that analyzes all database objects and then offers suggestions for improving their design.

_____ 9. A relationship between two fields/tables that does not enforce referential integrity.

_____ 10. A tool that builds a report with detailed information about all of the objects in a database.

A Access Options

B Application title

C Back up

D Byte

E Compact & Repair

F Data loss

G Database Documenter

H Display Form

I Indeterminate relationship

J KB

K Navigation Pane category

L Performance Analyzer

M Replica

N Action Tags

O Synchronize

_____ 11. A tool that allows the user to perform tasks within Access such as automatically adding a phone number to their Outlook Contacts.

_____ 12. The text that displays in the Access title bar when a database is open.

_____ 13. A dialog box where adjustments can be made to give a database a unique look and feel.

_____ 14. An Access option that allows you to display a particular type of object when the database is opened; can replace an autoexec macro.

_____ 15. A top-level listing that displays when the Navigation Pane arrow is clicked.

Multiple Choice

Circle the correct answer.

1. What unit is used to measure storage sizes and equates to 1,024 bytes?
    A. Kilobyte   B. Megabyte   C. Terabyte

2. A copy of the database that is stored in an alternative location is called a:
    A. backup   B. background   C. back end

3. Which of the following tasks requires the database be saved in a 2002-2003 database format?
    A. Compact and Repair   B. Backup   C. Replication

4. Which wizard looks for repeated data in a table, and then splits the table into two or more related tables?
    A. Database Documenter   B. Table Analyzer   C. Object Dependency

5. An object that requires, or is dependent on, another database object is called a:
    A. dependency   B. requirement   C. normalization

6. Which tool builds a report with detailed information about all of the objects in a database?
    A. Database Documenter   B. Object Dependency   C. Table Analyzer

7. Which detailed report provides information about every aspect of a database?
    A. Report Details   B. Data Table   C. Data Dictionary

8. Which field property enables the end user to perform tasks from Access that would usually require another program like Outlook to be open?
    A. Communication   B. Action Tag   C. Index

9. A top-level listing that displays when the Navigation Pane arrow is clicked is a:
    A. Navigation Pane group   B. Navigation Pane category   C. Navigation Pane layout

10. A second-level listing that displays when the Navigation Pane arrow is clicked is a:
    A. Navigation Pane group   B. Navigation Pane category   C. Navigation Pane layout

Access | Chapter 10

Content-Based Assessments

Skills Review | Project **10C** Administration

Image MedTech needs to protect its database files and build several front-end databases using a single set of back-end tables. The company also needs to work with a database saved in Access 2003. One worker will need to work with that database at home and then synchronize the changes when he is at work. In this project, you will optimize the company database and then split it into two files. You will convert an old database, and then create a replica of the Design Master. You will document your work by creating screen shots. Your completed screen shots will look similar to Figure 10.26.

Project Files

For Project 10C, you will need the following files:

> a10C_Administration.accdb
> a10C_QC.accdb

You will save your files as:

> Lastname_Firstname_10C_Administration.accdb
> Lastname_Firstname_10C_Administration_2016-07-01.accdb (your date will differ)
> Lastname_Firstname_10C_QC_2010.accdb
> Lastname_Firstname_10C_QC_2003.mdb
> Lastname_Firstname_10C_Replica.mdb
> Lastname_Firstname_10C_Screens.docx

Project Results

Figure 10.26

(Project 10C Administration continues on the next page)

Content-Based Assessments

Skills Review | Project 10C Administration (continued)

1 Start **Access**. Locate and open the **a10C_Administration** file. Save the database in your **Access Chapter 10** folder as **Lastname_Firstname_10C_Administration** If necessary, click **Enable Content**.

2 In the **Navigation Pane**, under **Queries**, click **Salary Group C**, and then press (Del). In the displayed message box, click **Yes**.

   a. Repeat this technique to delete the **Salary Group D** and **Salary Group E** queries.

   b. Delete the following reports: **Salary Group C**, **Salary Group D**, and **Salary Group E**.

   c. For the remaining database objects, add your own **Lastname Firstname** at the beginning of each object's name.

3 Display **Backstage** view, click **Save & Publish**, and then double-click **Back Up Database**. Save the backup in your Access **Chapter 10 folder** using the name provided in the **Save As** dialog box.

4 Display **Backstage** view, and then click the **Compact & Repair Database** button.

5 From **Backstage** view, click **Close Database**.

6 From **Backstage** view, click **Open**. Navigate to where the student files for this project are stored, click **a10C_QC**, and then click **Open**.

7 Save the database in your **Access Chapter 10** folder as **Lastname_Firstname_10C_QC_2010** and then save it in your **Access Chapter 10** folder.

8 From **Backstage** view, click **Save & Publish**, and then double-click **Access 2002 - 2003 Database**. Name the file **Lastname_Firstname_10C_QC_2003** and then save it in your **Access Chapter 10** folder. In the displayed message, click OK.

   a. **Close 10C_QC_2010**, and then **Open 10C_QC_2003**.

   b. If necessary, click **Enable Content**.

9 Click the **Navigation Pane** arrow, and then click **All Access Objects**.

10 On the **Database Tools tab**, in the **Administer group**, click the **Replication Options** button, and then click **Create Replica**.

   a. In the first displayed message box, click **Yes** to close the database and create the replica.

   b. In the second displayed message box, click **No** to decline making a backup of the database.

   c. Name the file **Lastname_Firstname_10C_Replica** and then save it in your **Access Chapter 10** folder. Click **OK**, and then in the displayed message box, click **OK**.

11 In the original file, open the **Quality Control Form** in **Layout** view. Select the **Title** control, and change the font color to **Black**. **Close** the form, saving changes.

12 From **Backstage** view, click **Close Database**, and then click **Open**. Navigate to your **Access Chapter 10 folder**, and then double-click **Lastname_Firstname_10C_Replica**. If necessary, click **Enable Content**

13 Open the **Quality Control Form**. For the first record, change the **Serial Number** to **2981B** and then **Close** the form.

14 Click the **Database Tools tab**. In the **Administer group**, click the **Replication Options** button, and then click **Synchronize Now**.

   a. In the **Synchronize** dialog box, click **OK**.

   b. In the next message box, click **Yes** to close the database and synchronize the files. Click **OK**.

15 Open the **Quality Control Form**. Press (Alt) + (PrtScr). **Close** the form and then **Exit Access**.

   a. Open a new, blank **Word** document. In the **Word** document, type your first and last names, press (Enter).

   b. Type your first and last names, press (Enter), and then type **Project 10C Step 15** Press (Enter), and then **Paste** the screen shot.

   c. Save the **Word** document in your **Access Chapter 10** folder as **Lastname_Firstname_10C_Screens**

16 Open **Windows Explorer**, and then open your **Access Chapter 10** folder.

   a. If necessary, maximize the **Windows Explorer** window and switch to **Details** view. Be sure that all the files created in this project display and that the columns are wide enough to display all of the **Name** and **Type** descriptions.

   b. Press (Alt) + (PrtScr), and then **Close Windows Explorer**.

   c. In the **Word** document, press (Enter), and then press (Ctrl) + (Enter) to insert a page break. Type your first and last names, press (Enter), and then type **Project 10C Step 16** Press (Enter), and then **Paste** the screen shot.

   d. Click **Save**. If you are instructed to submit this result, create a paper or electronic printout of the **Word** document.

17 Exit **Word**. If you are to submit your work electronically, follow your instructor's directions.

End **You have completed Project 10C**

Content-Based Assessments

Skills Review | Project **10D** Marketing

Image MedTech needs to improve the performance of its marketing database. In this project, you will use the Access analysis tools to make several improvements to the database. You will then add action tags and change several Access options. You will document your work by creating screen shots. Your screen shots document will look similar to Figure 10.27.

Project Files

For Project 10D, you will need the following files:

> a10D_Marketing.accdb
> a10D_Icon.bmp

You will save your files as:

> Lastname_Firstname_10D_Marketing.accdb
> Lastname_Firstname_10D_Screens.docx

Project Results

Figure 10.27

(Project 10D Marketing continues on the next page)

1 Start Access. Locate and then open the **a10D_ Marketing** file. Save the database in your **Access Chapter 10** folder as **Lastname_Firstname_10D_Marketing** If necessary, click **Enable Content**.

2 From the **Database Tools tab**, in the **Analyze group**, click the **Analyze Table** button. If the introductory page displays, click **Next** two times.

a. Under **Tables**, click **Sales Reps**, and then click **Next**. Be sure that **Yes, let the wizard decide** is selected, and then click **Next**.

b. Double-click the **Table1** title bar, type **Lastname Firstname Sales Reps** and then click **OK**. Double-click the **Table2** title bar, type **Lastname Firstname Regions** and then click **OK**.

c. Click **Next**. With the **Regions table** still selected, click the **Add Generated Key** button—the button with the green plus sign and yellow key. In the **Sales Reps** table, click **Sales Rep ID**, and then click the **Set Unique Identifier button**.

d. Click **Next**, and then click **Finish**. **Close** the **Access Help** window, and then **Close** the **Sales Reps** query.

3 Select the **Sales Reps_OLD** table. On the **Database Tools tab**, in the **Relationships group**, click the **Object Dependencies** button. In the displayed message box, click **OK**.

a. In the **Object Dependencies pane**, check that no database objects depend on the **Sales_Reps_OLD** table. Press [Alt] + [PrtScr], and then **Close** the **Object Dependencies pane**.

b. Open a new, blank **Word** document. Type your first and last names, press [Enter], and then type **Project 10D Step 3** Press [Enter], and then **Paste** the screen shot.

c. Save the **Word** document in your **Access Chapter 10** folder as **Lastname_Firstname_10D_Screens**

d. In **Access**, delete the **Sales_Reps_OLD table**. Rename the **Customers** table with your **Lastname Firstname** before the object's name.

e. **Close** the **Navigation Pane**.

4 Click the **Create tab**. In the **Queries group**, click the **Query Design** button. Add the **Customers** and **Sales Reps** tables, and then **Close** the dialog box. Expand the field lists so all fields and table names display.

a. From the **Customers** table, add the **Company Name** field, and then from the **Sales Reps** table, add the **Firstname** and **Lastname** fields.

b. Relate the two tables by dragging the **Sales Rep-Sales Rep ID field** and dropping it on the **Customers-Sales Rep field**.

c. Click **Save**, type **Lastname Firstname Customer Query** and then click **OK**. **Close** the query.

5 On the **Database Tools tab**, in the **Analyze group**, click the **Analyze Performance** button. Click the **All Object Types tab**, click the **Select All** button, and then click **OK**.

a. Under **Analysis Results**, click the Suggestion with the green question mark. Click the **Optimize** button.

b. Press [Alt] + [PrtScr], and then **Close** the **Performance Analyzer** dialog box. In the **Word** document, press [Enter], and then press [Ctrl] + [Enter] to insert a page break. Type your first and last names, press [Enter], and then type **Project 10D Step 5** Press [Enter], **Paste** the screen shot, and then click **Save**.

6 Return to **Access**. On the **Database Tools tab**, in the **Analyze group**, click the **Database Documenter** button.

a. In the **Documenter** dialog box, on the **Tables tab**, check the **Customers table**, and then click the **Options** button. Under **Include for Table**, only **Relationships** should be checked. The **Include for Fields** option and the **Include for Indexes** option should be set to **Nothing**. Click **OK** two times.

b. In Print Preview, **Zoom** in and then scroll so that all of the report text displays. Press [Alt] + [PrtScr], and then click the **Close Print Preview** button.

c. In the **Word** document, press [Enter], and then press [Ctrl] + [Enter] to insert a page break. Type your first and last names, press [Enter], and then type **Project 10D Step 6** Press [Enter], **Paste** the screen shot, and then click **Save**.

7 **Open** the **Navigation Pane**. **Open** the **Customers** table in **Design** view. **Close** the **Navigation Pane**. Click the **Contact Name** field name, click the **Smart Tags** box, and then click the **Build** button. Check **Person Name**, and then click **OK**.

8 Click **Save**, and then switch to **Datasheet** view. In the first record, place the pointer over Scot Holloway, and then click the Smart Tag Actions button.

a. Press [Alt] + [PrtScr]. In the **Word** document, press [Enter], and then press [Ctrl] + [Enter] to insert a page break. Type your first and last names, press [Enter], and then type **Project 10D Step 8** Press [Enter], **Paste** the screen shot, and then click **Save**.

(Project 10D Marketing continues on the next page)

9 Return to **Access**, and then **Close** the **Customers** table. From **Backstage** view, click **Options**. If necessary, click **General**. Click the **Color scheme arrow**, and then click **Blue**.

10 Click **Current Database**, and then in the **Application Title** box, type **Image MedTech Marketing**

a. In the **Application Icon** box, browse to select **a10D_ Icon**, a bitmap file located within the student files.

b. Clear the **Display Status Bar** check box.

c. In the **Display Form** box, click the down-pointing arrow and select the **Customers Form**.

11 Under **Navigation**, click the **Navigation Options** button.

a. Click the **Add Item button**, type **Marketing**, and then press Enter.

b. Click the **Add Group button**, type **Customers** and then press Enter.

c. Click the **Add Group button**, type **Sales Reps** and then press Enter. Click **OK** two times to close the dialog boxes.

d. Read the displayed message, and then click **OK**.

e. From **Backstage** view, click **Close Database**, and then reopen the database. **Open** the **Navigation Pane**.

12 Click the **Navigation Pane arrow**, and then click **Marketing**.

a. Drag the **Customers** table and drop it into the **Customers** group. Drag the **Customer** query and drop it into the **Customers** group. Drag the **Customers** form and drop it into the **Customers** group.

b. Drag the **Sales Reps** table and drop it into the **Sales Reps** group. Drag the **Sales Reps** query and drop it into the **Sales Reps** group.

13 From **Backstage** view, click **Options**, and then click **Quick Access Toolbar**.

a. In the list of **Popular Commands**, scroll down, click **New**, and then click the **Add** button.

b. Click the **Customize Quick Access Toolbar arrow**, and then click the path for the current database. In the list below Popular Commands, click **Open**, and then click the **Add button**. Click **OK** twice to close the dialog and message boxes.

14 Press Alt + PrtScr. In the **Word** document, press Enter, and then press Ctrl + Enter to insert a page break. Type your first and last names, press Enter, and then type **Project 10D Step 14** Press Enter, **Paste** the screen shot, and then click **Save**. If you are instructed to submit this result, create a paper or electronic printout of the Word document.

15 Exit **Word**. On the **Quick Access Toolbar**, right-click the **New** icon and click **Remove from Quick Access Toolbar**. From **Backstage** view, click Options. Click **General**, and then change the **Color scheme** back to **Silver**. Click **OK**, and then **Exit** Access.

End **You have completed Project 10D** ────────────────

Content-Based Assessments

- **1** Compact and Repair a Database
- **2** Back Up a Database
- **3** Convert Databases to an Earlier Version of Access
- **4** Replicate and Synchronize a Database

Mastering Access | Project **10E** Management

Image MedTech needs to protect its database files. The company also needs to work with a database saved in Access 2003. One worker will need to work with that database while on a trip and then synchronize the changes when she returns. In the project, you will optimize the company database. You will convert an old database, and then create a replica set. You will document your work by creating screen shots. Your completed screen shots will look similar to Figure 10.28.

Project Files

For Project 10E, you will need the following files:

> a10E_Management.accdb
> a10E_Tubes.accdb

You will save your files as:

> Lastname_Firstname_10E_Management.accdb
> Lastname_Firstname_10E_Management_2016-07-01.accdb (your date will differ)
> Lastname_Firstname_10E_Replica.mdb
> Lastname_Firstname_10E_Screens.docx
> Lastname_Firstname_10E_Tubes_2003.mdb
> Lastname_Firstname_10E_Tubes_2010.accdb

Project Results

Figure 10.28

(Project 10E Management continues on the next page)

Mastering Access | Project **10E** Management (continued)

1 Start **Access**. Locate and open the **a10E_Management** file. Save the database in your **Access Chapter 10** folder as **Lastname_Firstname_10E_Management** If necessary, click **Enable Content**.

2 Delete the following queries: **FL Customers**, **HI Customers**, **VA Customers**, and **WA Customers**. Delete the following reports: **FL Customers**, **HI Customers**, **VA Customers**, and **WA Customers**. Do not delete the State Query or State Report.

3 For the remaining database objects, add your **Lastname Firstname** at the beginning of each object's name.

4 Create a backup copy of the database. Save the backup in your **Access Chapter 10** folder with the name suggested by Access.

5 Compact & Repair the database.

6 Close the database. Locate and open the **10E_Tubes** file. In your **Access Chapter 10** folder, **Save** the database as **Lastname_Firstname_10E_Tubes_2010**

7 In your **Access Chapter 10** folder, **Save** the database in the **Access 2002 - 2003** file format as **Lastname_Firstname_10E_Tubes_2003**

8 **Close 10E_Tubes_2010**, and **Open 10E_Tubes_2003**. Click the **Navigation Pane arrow**, and display **All Access Objects**.

9 Replicate the current database. Do not create a backup. Save the replica in your **Access Chapter 10** folder as **Lastname_Firstname_10E_Replica**

10 Open the **X-Ray Tubes Data Entry Form**, and add a white background to all of the text box controls. **Close** the form, saving changes.

11 **Close** the database, and then open **Lastname_Firstname_10E_Replica**. Open the **X-Ray Tubes Data Entry Form**. In the first record, change the **Coefficient** to **1.68** and then **Close** the form.

12 **Synchronize** the replica and Design Master databases. Open the **X-Ray Tubes Data Entry Form**. Press ⌊Alt⌋ + ⌊PrtScr⌋. **Close** the form, and then **Exit** Access. Open a new, blank **Word** document, type your first and last names, press ⌊Enter⌋, and then type **Project 10E Step 12** Press ⌊Enter⌋, **Paste** the screen shot. Save the Word document in your **Access Chapter 10** folder as **Lastname_Firstname_10E_Screens**

13 **Open Windows Explorer**, and then open your **Access Chapter 10** folder. If necessary, maximize the **Windows Explorer** window and switch to **Details** view. Be sure that all the files created in this project display and that the columns are wide enough to display all of the **Name** and **Type** descriptions. Press ⌊Alt⌋ + ⌊PrtScr⌋, and then **Close Windows Explorer**.

14 In the **Word** document, press ⌊Enter⌋, and then press ⌊Ctrl⌋ + ⌊Enter⌋ to insert a page break. Type your first and last names, press ⌊Enter⌋, and then type **Project 10E Step 14** Press ⌊Enter⌋, **Paste** the screen shot, and then click **Save**. If you are instructed to submit this result, create a paper or electronic printout of the Word document.

15 **Exit** Word.

End **You have completed Project 10E** ————————————

Content-Based Assessments

Mastering Access | Project **10F** Sales Reps

Image MedTech needs to improve the performance of its Sales database. In this project, you will use the Access analysis tools to make several improvements to the database. You will then add action tags and modify the database by changing several of its options. You will document your work by creating screen shots. Your screen shots document will look similar to Figure 10.29.

Project Files

For Project 10F, you will need the following files:

a10F_Sales_Reps.accdb
a10F_Icon.bmp

You will save your files as:

Lastname_Firstname_10F_Sales_Reps.accdb
Lastname_Firstname_10F_Screens.docx

Project Results

Figure 10.29

(Project 10F Sales Reps continues on the next page)

Access | Chapter 10

Mastering Access | Project **10F** Sales Reps (continued)

1 Start **Access**. Locate and open the **a10F_Sales_Reps** file. **Save** the database in your **Access Chapter 10** folder as **Lastname_Firstname_10F_Sales_Reps** If necessary, click **Enable Content**.

2 Use the **Table Analyzer** wizard to analyze the **Customers** table. Have the wizard decide how to split the table, and then rename the suggested tables as follows:

Suggested Table	New Name
Table1	**Lastname Firstname Customers**
Table2	**Lastname Firstname Sales Reps**

3 Click **Next**. In the **Customers** table, set **Customer ID** as the primary key. In the **Sales Reps** table, set **Sales Rep ID** as the primary key. Choose the option to create the query, and then **Finish** the wizard.

4 **Close** all open objects, **Open** the **Object Dependencies** pane, and then display all database objects that depend on the **Customers_OLD** table. Press [Alt] + [PrtScr], and then **Close** the **Object Dependencies** pane. Open a new, blank **Word** document, type your first and last names, press [Enter], and then type **Project 10F Step 4** Press [Enter], and then **Paste** the screen shot. Save the **Word** document in your **Access Chapter 10** folder as **Lastname_Firstname_10F_Screens**

5 Delete the **Customers_OLD** table. Rename the **Sales Directors** table as **Lastname Firstname Sales Directors** Rename the **Customers** query to **Lastname Firstname Customers Query**

6 Start a new query in **Query Design** view, and then add the **Sales Directors** and **Sales Reps** tables to the query. Resize the field lists so all fields and table names are visible. From the **Sales Directors** table, add the **Region** field. From the **Sales Reps** table, add the **Firstname** and **Lastname** fields. Create an indeterminate relationship between the **Director ID** fields in both tables, if necessary. Click **Save**, type **Lastname Firstname Regions Query** and then click **OK**. **Close** the query.

7 Run the **Performance Analyzer** wizard for All Object Types. Optimize the item with the Suggestion icon. Press [Alt] + [PrtScr], and then **Close** the dialog box. In the **Word** document, press [Enter], and then press [Ctrl] + [Enter] to insert a page break. Type your first and last names, press [Enter], and then type **Project 10F Step 7** Press [Enter], **Paste** the screen shot, and then click **Save**.

8 Start the **Database Documenter**. In the **Documenter** dialog box, select the **Sales Directors** table. Select the following options: under **Include for Table**, only **Relationships** should be checked. The **Include for Fields** option and the **Include for Indexes option** should be set to **Nothing**. Generate the report.

9 In **Print Preview**, zoom in and then scroll so that all of the report text displays. Press [Alt] + [PrtScr], and then click the **Close Print Preview button**. In the **Word** document, press [Enter], and then insert a page break. Type your first and last names, press [Enter], and then type **Project 10F Step 9** Press [Enter], **Paste** the screen shot, and then click **Save**.

10 Open the **Customers** table in **Design** view. For the **Phone** field, assign the **Telephone Number** action tag.

11 Click **Save**, and then switch to **Datasheet** view. In the first record, display the **Smart Tag Actions** for the phone number. Press [Alt] + [PrtScr], and then **Close** the table. In the **Word** document, press [Enter], and then press [Ctrl] + [Enter] to insert a page break. Type your first and last names, press [Enter], and then type **Project 10F Step 11** Press [Enter], **Paste** the screen shot, and then click **Save**.

12 Open the **Access Options** dialog box. Under **Object Designers**, change the default text field size in tables to **75** Change the **Query design** font size to **12** Press [Alt] + [PrtScr], and then **Close** the dialog box. In the **Word** document, press [Enter], and then insert a page break. Type your first and last names, press [Enter], and then type **Project 10F Step 12** Press [Enter], **Paste** the screen shot, and then click **Save**.

13 In the **Access Options** dialog box, under **Current Database**, change the **Application Title** to **Image MedTech Sales** For the **Application Icon**, assign **a10F_Icon**, a bitmap file located within the student files. Disable **Layout** view.

14 Edit the following Navigation Pane options: add a new item named **Sales** and then add a new group named **Sales Reps** In the **Navigation Pane**, display the **Sales** category. Drag the **Sales Reps** table and drop it into the **Sales Reps** category. Using the **Navigation Pane** options, do not display Unassigned Items in the Navigation Pane when the Sales category is selected.

15 For the current database only, add the following commands to the Quick Access Toolbar: **Import Access database**, **Import Excel spreadsheet**, and **Open**.

(Project 10F Sales Reps continues on the next page)

Mastering Access | Project **10F** Sales Reps (continued)

16 Close all open dialog boxes and database objects. Press [Alt] + [PrtScr]. In the **Word** document, press [Enter], and then insert a page break. Type your first and last names, press [Enter], and then type **Project 10F Step 16** Press [Enter], **Paste** the screen shot, and then click **Save**.

If you are instructed to submit this result, create a paper or electronic printout of the screen shots document.

17 **Exit** Word. Reset the default text field size in tables to **255** and the default Query design font to **8**. **Exit** Access.

End You have completed Project 10F —————————————

Content-Based Assessments

Apply 10A and 10B skills from these Objectives:

3 Convert Databases to an Earlier Version of Access

4 Replicate and Synchronize a Database

5 Use Microsoft Access Analysis Tools

6 Add Action Tags

7 Modify Access Views and Behaviors

Mastering Access | Project **10G** Products

Image MedTech needs to make various improvements to two of its databases. In this activity, you will use analysis tools and change options. You will then convert an old database and replicate it. You will document your work by creating screen shots. Your screen shots document will look similar to Figure 10.30.

Project Files

For Project 10G, you will need the following files:

    a10G_Products.accdb
    a10G_Rad_Levels.accdb

You will save your files as:

    Lastname_Firstname_10G_Products.accdb
    Lastname_Firstname_10G_Rad_Levels_2010.accdb
    Lastname_Firstname_10G_Rad_Levels_2003.mdb
    Lastname_Firstname_10G_Replica.mdb
    Lastname_Firstname_10G_Screens.docx

Project Results

Figure 10.30

(Project 10G Products continues on the next page)

Content-Based Assessments

Mastering Access | Project **10G** Products (continued)

1 Start **Access**. Locate and open the **a10G_Products** file. **Save** the database in your **Access Chapter 10** folder as **Lastname_Firstname_10G_Products** If necessary, click **Enable Content**. For all of the database objects, add your own **Lastname Firstname** at the beginning of each object's name.

2 In the **Navigation Pane**, open the **Product Line** query in **Design** view. Widen the field lists so all information is visible. Create an indeterminate relationship between the **Line ID** fields in both tables. Click **Save**, and then **Close** the query.

3 Run the **Performance Analyzer** wizard for **All Object Types**. Optimize the item with the **Suggestion** icon. Press [Alt] + [PrtScr], and then **Close** the wizard. Start **Word** to open a new, blank document, type your first and last names, press [Enter], and then type **Project 10G Step 3** Press [Enter], and then **Paste** the screen shot. Save the Word document in your **Access Chapter 10** folder as **Lastname_Firstname_10G_Screens**

4 Start the **Database Documenter**. In the **Documenter** dialog box, select the **Products** table. Select the following options: under Include for Table, only **Relationships** should be checked. The **Include for Fields** and **Include for Indexes** options should be set to **Nothing**. Generate the report.

5 In **Print Preview**, zoom in and then scroll so that all of the report text displays. Press [Alt] + [PrtScr], and then click the **Close Print Preview** button. In the **Word** document, press [Enter], and then press [Ctrl] + [Enter] to insert a page break. Type your first and last names, press [Enter], and then type **Project 10G Step 5** Press [Enter], **Paste** the screen shot, and then click **Save**.

6 Open the **Employees** table in **Design** view. For the **Phone** field, assign the **Telephone Number** action tag. **Save** the table.

7 Switch to **Datasheet** view. In the first record, place the pointer over the phone number, and then click the **Smart Tag Actions** button. Press [Alt] + [PrtScr], and then **Close** the table. In the **Word** document, press [Enter], and then insert a page break. Type your first and last names, press [Enter], and then type **Project 10G Step 7** Press [Enter], **Paste** the screen shot, and then click **Save**. Close the database.

8 Locate and open the **a10G_Rad_ Levels** file. **Save** the database in your **Access Chapter 10** folder as **Lastname_Firstname_10G_Rad_Levels_2010**

9 Open the **Access Options** dialog box, and then click **Current Database**. Under **Application Options**, click **Overlapping Windows**. **Close** and then re-open the database. **Open** the **CR1001** table in **Datasheet** view. Press [Alt] + [PrtScr] and then close the table. In the **Word** document, press [Enter], and then insert a page break. Type your first and last names, press [Enter], and then type **Project 10G Step 9** Press [Enter], **Paste** the screen shot, and then click **Save**.

10 Save the database in the Access 2002 - 2003 file format. Name the file **Lastname_Firstname_10G_Rad_Levels_2003** and save it in your **Access Chapter 10** folder. **Close 10G_Rad_Levels_2010**, and **Open 10G_Rad_Levels_2003**.

11 Replicate the current database. Do not create a backup, name the replica **Lastname_Firstname_10G_Replica** and then save it in your **Access Chapter 10** folder.

12 With the **CR1001** table selected, click the **Create tab**. In the **Forms** group, click the **Form** button. Click **Save**, type **Lastname Firstname CR1001** and then press [Enter].

13 **Close** the form. In the **Navigation Pane**, display **All Access Objects**. **Close** the database. **Open Lastname_Firstname_10G_Replica**. Synchronize the replica and Design Master databases. **Open** the **CR1001** form. Press [Alt] + [PrtScr]. **Close** the form, and then **Exit** Access. In the **Word** document, press [Enter], and then insert a page break. Type your first and last names, press [Enter], and then type **Project 10G Step 13** Press [Enter], **Paste** the screen shot, and then click **Save**.

14 **Open Windows Explorer**, and then open your **Access Chapter 10** folder. If necessary, maximize the **Windows Explorer** window and switch to **Details** view. Be sure that all the files created in this project display and that the columns are wide enough to display all of the **Name** and **Type** descriptions. Press [Alt] + [PrtScr], and then **Close Windows Explorer**.

15 In the **Word** document, press [Enter], and then insert a page break. Type your first and last names, press [Enter], and then type **Project 10G Step 15** Press [Enter], **Paste** the screen shot, and then click **Save**. If you are instructed to submit this result, create a paper or electronic printout of the Word document.

16 **Exit** Word.

End **You have completed Project 10G**

Content-Based Assessments

GO! Fix It | Project 10H Films

Project Files

For Project 10H, you will need the following files:

a10H_Films.accdb
a10H_Icon.bmp

You will save your files as:

Lastname_Firstname_10H_Films.accdb
Lastname_Firstname_10H_Films_2016-07-06.accdb (your date will differ)
Lastname_Firstname_10H_Screens.docx

Image MedTech needs various improvements made to its database. In this activity, you will use analysis tools, change options, and split a database into two files. You will document your work by creating screen shots.

- Create a backup copy of the database. Save the backup in your Access Chapter 10 folder using the name suggested by Access.

- Use the Table Analyzer wizard to analyze the Films table. Let the wizard decide how to split the table, and then rename the suggested tables as follows:

Suggested Table	New Name
Table1	**Lastname Firstname Films**
Table2	**Lastname Firstname Film Series**

- Assign Product ID as a primary key, and then finish the wizard using the wizard's suggested options.

- In the Object Dependencies pane, display all database objects that depend on the Films_OLD table. Capture the screen, and paste it into a Word document. Save the Word document in your Access Chapter 10 folder as **Lastname_Firstname_10H_Screens** Delete the Films_OLD table.

Open the Access Options dialog box, and make the following changes:

- Change the Color Scheme to Blue.

- Change the Application Title box to **Image MedTech** Add a10H_Icon as the application icon. Use as a Form and Report Icon.

- For the current database only, add the following commands to the Quick Access Toolbar: Open, Print Preview, and Quick Print.

- Capture the database window, and paste it into the Word document created above.

Compact & Repair the database.

Open Windows Explorer, and then open your Access Chapter 10 folder. Be sure that all the files created in this project display completely, including the Name and Type descriptions. Capture the screen, and paste it into the Word document created above. If you are instructed to submit this result, create a paper or electronic printout of the Word document.

Change the Access color scheme back to Silver, and then exit Access.

End You have completed Project 10H ————————————

Content-Based Assessments

GO! Make It | Project 10I Employees

Project Files

For Project 10I, you will need the following file:

> a10I_Employees.accdb

You will save your files as:

> Lastname_Firstname_10I_Employees.accdb
> Lastname_Firstname_10I_Employees_backup.accdb
> Lastname_Firstname_10I_Screens.docx

Create a backup copy of the database before beginning this assignment. Customize the options for the datasheet. Then, review the object dependencies for the **Employees** table to analyze the database design. Compact & Repair the database before capturing the file list from this assignment. You will document your work by creating screen shots. Your screen shot document will look similar to Figure 10.31.

Project Results

Figure 10.31

Content-Based Assessments

Apply a combination of the 10A and 10B skills

GO! Solve It | Project 10J Optimize

Project Files

For Project 10J, you will need the following file:

a10J_Optimize.accdb

You will save your files as:

Lastname_Firstname_10J_Optimize.accdb
Lastname_Firstname_10J_Screens.docx

Image MedTech needs to improve the speed of its database. In this project, you will use the Performance Analyzer to improve the database. To start, open **a10J_Optimize**, and then save it as **Lastname_Firstname_10J_Optimize**

Run the Performance Analyzer for all database objects. For all items marked Suggested, optimize the database. Capture the screen, and paste it into a Word document. Save the Word document in your Access Chapter 10 folder as **Lastname_Firstname_10J_Screens**

Select the Customers table, and run the Database Documenter with the following options: under Include for Table, only Relationships should be checked. The Include for Fields option and the Include for Indexes option should be set to Nothing. Generate the report, and zoom so the data is readable on the screen. Capture the screen, and paste it into the Word document created above.

For each database object, add your **Lastname Firstname** at the beginning of its name. Add the Close Database and Quick Print buttons to the Quick Access toolbar for this database only. Capture the screen, and paste it into the Word document created above.

Open Windows Explorer, and then open your Access Chapter 10 folder. Be sure that all the files created in this project display completely, including the Name and Type descriptions. Capture the screen, and paste it into the Word document created above. Submit the project as directed by your instructor.

	Performance Element		
	Exemplary: You consistently applied the relevant skills	**Proficient:** You sometimes, but not always, applied the relevant skills	**Developing:** You rarely or never applied the relevant skills
Run Performance Analyzer; capture in Word document	Analyzer complete with all suggestions optimized.	Analyzer complete, not all suggestions optimized.	Analyzer complete, none of the suggestions optimized.
Create Database Documenter report for Customers table; capture in Word document	Data dictionary created with correct object and all necessary components.	Data dictionary created with correct object or with missing components.	Data dictionary created using an incorrect object.
Add Close Database and Quick Print buttons to the Quick Access toolbar; capture in Word document	Correct buttons added as directed.	Incorrect buttons added or buttons added to wrong location.	Incorrect buttons added to the wrong location.

(leftmost column label, rotated: Performance Criteria)

End You have completed Project 10J

Content-Based Assessments

GO! Solve It | Project 10K Pipeline

Project Files

For Project 10K, you will need the following file:

a10K_Pipeline.accdb

You will save your files as:

Lastname_Firstname_10K_Pipeline.accdb
Lastname_Firstname_10K_Screens.docx

Image MedTech would like to make some changes to the 10K_Pipeline database. Begin by saving the file as **Lastname_Firstname_10K_Pipeline** Use the Table Analyzer to convert the Sales Pipeline table into several smaller, related tables. For each suggested table, assign an appropriate name that includes your **Lastname Firstname** Make sure each table is assigned an appropriate primary key. Ignore the wizard's suggestions for correcting typographical errors, and do not have the wizard create a query. Close the new tables, and then open the Relationships window. Rearrange the displayed tables so that the table names and relationships display clearly. Save the layout of the Relationships window. Capture the screen, and paste it into a Word document. Save the Word document in your Access Chapter 10 folder as **Lastname_Firstname_10K_Screens**

Check for object dependencies for the Sales Pipeline table. Capture the screen, and paste it into the Word document created above. Delete the Sales Pipeline table. Create a Navigation Pane category named **Pipeline** with two groups: **Customers** and **Sales Department** Display the Pipeline group, and assign each table to the correct category. Do not display the Unassigned Objects group. Capture the database window, and paste it in the Word document created above.

Submit the project as directed by your instructor.

	Performance Element		
	Exemplary: You consistently applied the relevant skills	**Proficient:** You sometimes, but not always, applied the relevant skills	**Developing:** You rarely or never applied the relevant skills
Run Table Analyzer, define table names and primary key fields	Analyzer run and tables created including all elements.	Analyzer run and tables created with no more than two missing elements.	Analyzer run and tables created with more than two missing elements.
Arrange tables in the Relationships window (screen capture)	Tables moved so relationships display clearly.	Tables moved, but relationships do not display clearly.	Tables not moved in Relationships window.
View object dependencies for Sales Pipeline table (screen capture)	Object dependency pane is created accurately and displays no object dependencies.	Object dependency pane is created with dependencies.	Object dependency pane is created with missing elements.
Create a custom Navigation Pane for Pipeline (screen capture)	Custom Navigation Pane is created to display database objects accurately.	Custom Navigation Pane is created with no more than two missing elements.	Custom Navigation Pane is created with more than two missing elements.

Performance Criteria

End You have completed Project 10K

Outcomes-Based Assessments

Rubric

The following outcomes-based assessments are *open-ended assessments*. That is, there is no specific correct result; your result will depend on your approach to the information provided. Make *Professional Quality* your goal. Use the following scoring rubric to guide you in *how* to approach the problem and then to evaluate *how well* your approach solves the problem.

The *criteria*—Software Mastery, Content, Format and Layout, and Process—represent the knowledge and skills you have gained that you can apply to solving the problem. The *levels of performance*—Professional Quality, Approaching Professional Quality, or Needs Quality Improvements—help you and your instructor evaluate your result.

	Your completed project is of Professional Quality if you:	Your completed project is Approaching Professional Quality if you:	Your completed project Needs Quality Improvements if you:
1-Software Mastery	Choose and apply the most appropriate skills, tools, and features and identify efficient methods to solve the problem.	Choose and apply some appropriate skills, tools, and features, but not in the most efficient manner.	Choose inappropriate skills, tools, or features, or are inefficient in solving the problem.
2-Content	Construct a solution that is clear and well organized, contains content that is accurate, appropriate to the audience and purpose, and is complete. Provide a solution that contains no errors in spelling, grammar, or style.	Construct a solution in which some components are unclear, poorly organized, inconsistent, or incomplete. Misjudge the needs of the audience. Have some errors in spelling, grammar, or style, but the errors do not detract from comprehension.	Construct a solution that is unclear, incomplete, or poorly organized; contains some inaccurate or inappropriate content; and contains many errors in spelling, grammar, or style. Do not solve the problem.
3-Format and Layout	Format and arrange all elements to communicate information and ideas, clarify function, illustrate relationships, and indicate relative importance.	Apply appropriate format and layout features to some elements, but not others. Overuse features, causing minor distraction.	Apply format and layout that does not communicate information or ideas clearly. Do not use format and layout features to clarify function, illustrate relationships, or indicate relative importance. Use available features excessively, causing distraction.
4-Process	Use an organized approach that integrates planning, development, self-assessment, revision, and reflection.	Demonstrate an organized approach in some areas, but not others; or, use an insufficient process of organization throughout.	Do not use an organized approach to solve the problem.

Outcomes-Based Assessments

Apply a combination of the 10A and 10B skills.

GO! Think | Project **10L** Image MedTech

Project Files

For Project 10L, you will need the following file:

> a10L_Image_MedTech.accdb

You will save your files as:

> Lastname_Firstname_10L_Image_MedTech.accdb
> Lastname_Firstname_10L_Image_MedTech_2016-02-27.accdb (your date will differ)
> Lastname_Firstname_10L_Screens.docx

Image MedTech would like you to redesign the database so it is easier for the staff to use. To start, open **a10L_Image_MedTech**, and then save it as **Lastname_Firstname_10L_Image_MedTech** Create a backup file for the database.

Customize some of the Access Options: add an application title of **Image MedTech: Company Information** disable the Layout view, and choose a color scheme. Display the Invoices Entry Form when the database is opened. Add the New, Open, and Quick Print buttons to the Quick Access toolbar for all databases opened on the computer. Customize the Navigation Pane displaying all objects in either the new Customers, Products, or Staff groups in the Image MedTech Category. Compact and Repair the database. Create a screen capture of the database window and the files created for this project.

Submit the project as directed by your instructor. Return all options to default before exiting Access.

 You have completed Project 10L ————————————

Apply a combination of the 10A and 10B skills.

GO! Think | Project **10M** Design

Project Files

For Project 10M, you will need the following files:

> a10M_Design.accdb
> a10M_Icon.bmp

You will save your files as:

> Lastname_Firstname_10M_Design.accdb
> Lastname_Firstname_10M_Design_2003.mdb
> Lastname_Firstname_10M_Replic.mdb
> Lastname_Firstname_10M_Screens.docx

Image MedTech would like you to redesign its database. Open **a10M_Design**, and then save it as **Lastname_Firstname_10M_Design**

Change the following options for the current database. Assign the icon named **a10M_Icon** located with the student files. Set the icon to display in all forms and reports. On the Quick Access Toolbar, add five tools that you think will be used frequently for all databases. Create a screen capture of the Access window, and paste it in a Word document.

Save the database in 2002 - 2003 format, adding 2003 to the file name, and then create a replica named **Lastname_Firstname_10M_Replica** Make two design changes to the Customers form in the Design Master, and then synchronize. In 10M_Replica, create a screen capture of the Customers form, and paste it into the Word document created above.

Submit the project as directed by your instructor. Reset the Quick Access Toolbar to its default buttons.

 You have completed Project 10M ————————————

Apply a combination of the 10A and 10B skills.

You and GO! | Project 10N Club Directory

Project Files

For Project 10N, you will need the following file:

> Lastname_Firstname_9N_Club_Directory.accdb (your file from Chapter 9)

You will save your files as:

> Lastname_Firstname_10N_Club_Directory.accdb
> Lastname_Firstname_10N_Club_Directory_backup.accdb

Create a personal database containing information about a club and its activities, if you do not already have one from Project 9N. Name the new database **Lastname_Firstname_10N_Club_Directory** If you do not have the database from Project 9N, create two related tables, one that lists the activities your organization has planned and the other to serve as the directory of the group. The Activities table should include information about the name (primary key field), date, cost, and location of the activity. The dates must all occur next year; consider attaching directions to the event to the table. The Directory table should include full name, address, phone number, email, and an activity they are planning. If you have the database from Project 9N, save it as **Lastname_Firstname_10N_Club_Directory** in your Access Chapter 10 folder.

Create a backup copy of the database before beginning to work with it. Name the backup copy **Lastname_Firstname_10N_Club_Directory_backup** Customize the database by creating a descriptive title to appear in the application title bar and customizing the Quick Access toolbar to allow for easy access to a few commonly used tools.

Run the Performance Analyzer on all objects in the database, and optimize any of the suggestions offered. Compact and repair the database.

End **You have completed Project 10N** ——————————————————

Securing Databases and Writing SQL Statements

OUTCOMES

At the end of this chapter you will be able to:

OBJECTIVES

Mastering these objectives will enable you to:

PROJECT 11A
Secure Access databases.

1. Utilize the Trust Center (p. 719)
2. Use the Database Splitter (p. 723)
3. Encrypt and Decrypt Databases (p. 725)
4. Create a Locked Database (ACCDE File) (p. 727)

PROJECT 11B
Write SQL statements.

5. Modify a Query in SQL View (p. 731)
6. Create a Query in SQL View (p. 733)
7. Create a Union Query Using SQL (p. 736)
8. Create Calculated Fields and SQL Aggregate Functions (p. 738)

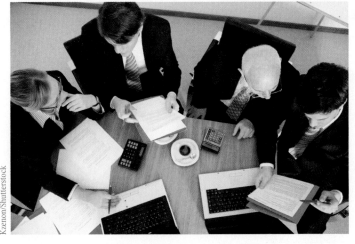
Kzenon/Shutterstock

In This Chapter

Organizations that store information in databases often limit who can view and change the design and the data. Design changes include adding and removing fields from a table; adding tables; and designing queries, forms, and reports. Access provides a mechanism whereby users must enter their user name and password before opening a database. Access also provides information and a means to ensure the security of a database that you plan on sharing.

Access provides a view for creating and modifying the SQL, or Structured Query Language, that makes all of its queries work. Certain types of queries must be designed using this view. For example, by using SQL, the results of two or more queries can be combined into one query. Database designers also use this view to learn how SQL works.

Attorneys at **Lacy-Rennier Law Partners** counsel their clients on a wide variety of issues, including contracts, licensing, intellectual property, and taxation, with emphasis on the unique needs of the sports and entertainment industries. Entertainment clients include anyone involved in creating or doing business in the entertainment industry. Sports clients include colleges and universities, professional sports teams, athletes, and venue operators. Increasingly, amateur and community sports coaches and organizations with concerns about liability are also seeking counsel.

Project 11A Lawyers

myitlab
Project 11A Training

Project Activities

In Activities 11.01 through 11.05, you will secure data using various methods. Lacy-Rennier Law Partners has a database that contains lawyer data, corporate client data, and corporate case data. To maintain attorney-client confidentiality, the partners must be sure that the data is seen only by authorized lawyers. You will encrypt a database saved in the Access 2010 file format, set security options in the Trust Center, lock the database, and split a database. Your generated printouts will look similar to Figure 11.1.

Project Files

For Project 11A, you will need the following files:

a11A_Recruitment.accdb
a11A_Lawyers.accdb

You will save your files as:

Lastname_Firstname_11A_Recruitment.accdb
Lastname_Firstname_11A_Lawyers.accdb
Lastname_Firstname_11A_Lawyers_be.accdb
Lastname_Firstname_11A_ACCDE.accde
Lastname_Firstname_11A_Screens.docx

Project Results

Figure 11.1
Project 11A Lawyers

Objective 1 | Utilize the Trust Center

Critical data is stored in a company database—a set of objects that depend on one another, especially the core data stored in tables. The security of this information is critical for doing business and keeping information safe. As discussed in Chapter 4, the Trust Center evaluates a database and contains security and privacy settings that can disable components in a database considered untrusted; enabling content or adding a location to the Trust Center allows you to once again use those components.

Activity 11.01 | Viewing Trust Center Options

Lacy-Rennier Law Partners has contracted with a recruiting firm to perform first-round interviews for potential employees. The recruiting firm has shared the database containing applicant information. In this activity, you will review the Trust Center settings to determine which components of the database are currently usable.

1 **Start** Access. Navigate to the location where the student data files for this textbook are saved. Locate and then open the **a11A_Recruitment** database. Display **Backstage** view, and click **Save Database As**. In the **Save As** dialog box, navigate to the drive on which you will be saving your folders and projects for this chapter. Create a new folder named **Access Chapter 11** and then save the file as **Lastname_Firstname_11A_ Recruitment** in the folder. Do not enable content or add the folder to the Trust Center. Compare your screen with Figure 11.2.

Notice the Security Warning displayed below the Ribbon. Access has not identified the Access Chapter 11 folder as a trusted location; therefore, the database is opened in *disabled mode,* meaning all executable content is turned off.

Figure 11.2

Security Warning

2 Double-click the **Print Report** macro to print the **Upcoming Events Report**. In the dialog box that is displayed, click the **Show Help** button, and then compare your screen with Figure 11.3.

The macro includes the Echo macro action, which, as you learned in Chapter 8, is not considered one of the trusted actions. Because the database content has not been enabled and the location has not been added to the list of trusted locations, the macro stops running when it comes to the Echo action. The status bar also explains why the macro stopped running.

Figure 11.3

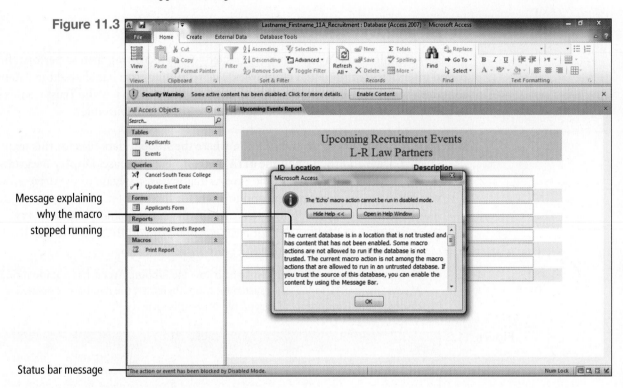

Message explaining why the macro stopped running

Status bar message

3 Click **OK** in the dialog box to close it. In the **Macro Single Step** dialog box, click **Stop All Macros**. Because the OpenReport macro action occurs before the Echo macro action, the action has executed and the report is open. **Close** ⊠ the report.

4 Double-click the **Cancel South Texas College** query to delete those records. Notice the message in the status bar. Double click the **Update Event Date** query to run it, and compare your screen with Figure 11.4.

Notice the status bar message: *The action or event has been blocked by Disabled Mode.* Action queries that add, update, or delete data are disabled when a database is not trusted.

Figure 11.4

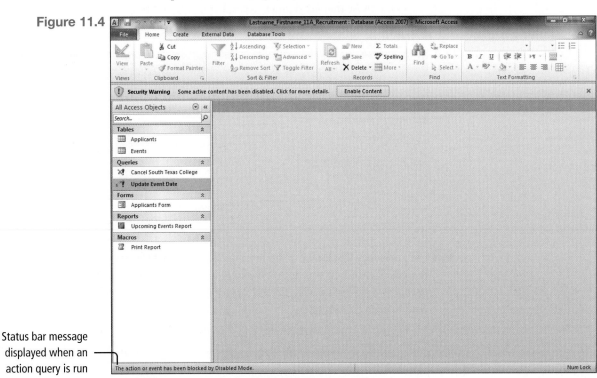

Status bar message displayed when an action query is run

More Knowledge | Disabling Actions in an Untrusted Database

As a security measure, Access displays an untrusted database in Disabled Mode, meaning all executable content is turned off. That includes VBA code and unsafe expressions, unsafe macro actions, and several types of queries that add, change, or remove data from the database.

---

5 Display **Backstage** view, click the **Enable Content** button, and then click **Advanced Options**. In the **Microsoft Office Security Options** dialog box, click **Open the Trust Center** in the bottom left corner. If necessary, click **Message Bar** on the left side of the **Trust Center** dialog box, and then compare your screen with Figure 11.5.

The default setting is responsible for the Security Warning Message Bar that appears when a database is opened from an untrusted location. This notifies the user that some content is disabled in the database and provides a button to enable the content.

Figure 11.5

Trust Center dialog box

Message Bar options for an untrusted database

6 On the left side of the **Trust Center** dialog box, click **Macro Settings**. Compare your screen with Figure 11.6.

The default setting does not allow any untrusted macro actions to run, but it does display a message notifying the user regarding why the macro cannot continue. The same setting can be selected without the error message. A tighter security setting is to disable all macros except those that are digitally signed. A less secure setting is also available, to enable all macros. Access does warn users that this setting is not recommended for security reasons.

Figure 11.6

Macro settings related to
untrusted databases

7 Click **Privacy Options** on the left side of the **Trust Center** dialog box. If necessary, clear the check boxes to the left of *Download a file periodically that helps determine system problems* and *Sign up for the Customer Experience Improvement Program*. Compare your screen to Figure 11.7.

The Privacy Options allow you to select security settings related to your personal privacy.

Figure 11.7

Privacy Options for Access

8 Click **Trusted Locations** on the left side of the **Trust Center** dialog box. In the **Trusted Locations** pane, at the lower right, click **Add new location**. In the **Microsoft Office Trusted Location** dialog box, click **Browse**. In the **Browse** dialog box, navigate to where you saved your **Access Chapter 11** folder, double-click **Access Chapter 11**, and then click **OK**. Click **OK** two more times to close the dialog boxes. **Close** the **11A_Recruitment** database.

Adding the file location to the list of Trusted Locations enables the content in the 11A_Recruitment database, allowing you to run the action queries and macros with untrusted actions.

9 **Open** the **11A_Recruitment** database. **Open** the **Upcoming Events Report** in **Design** view, and add your **Lastname Firstname** at the beginning of the report title. **Save** and close the report. Run the **Print Report** macro. If you are instructed to submit this result, create a paper or electronic printout of the macro result.

10 **Close** ✕ the report, and then **Close** the **11A_Recruitment** database.

Objective 2 | Use the Database Splitter

Business databases are often divided into two parts—a back end and a front end. The *back end* consists of the database tables and their data. The back end is typically placed on a server and is not directly seen by the end user. In Access, the *front end* comprises the database forms, queries, reports, and macros. The end users open the front end to work with the data stored in the back-end tables. Dividing the database enables the database administrator to maintain a single source of data while designing multiple front ends to meet the needs of various departments in the company.

Activity 11.02 | Splitting a Database

A *split database* is an Access database that is split into two files—one containing the back end and one containing the front end. Several departments at Lacy-Rennier Law Partners need their own forms, reports, and queries. Instead of trying to coordinate separate databases, the company would like to place all of the database tables on a network server. Each department will then have its own custom front end that links to the tables in the back-end file. In this activity, you will use the Split Database tool to create two separate files—one for the back end and one for the front end.

1 Navigate to the location where the student data files for this textbook are saved and open the **a11A_Lawyers** database. Display **Backstage** view, and click **Save Database As**. In the **Save As** dialog box, navigate to the **Access Chapter 11** folder, and then save the file as **Lastname_Firstname_11A_Lawyers**

2 Click the **Database Tools tab**, and then in the **Move Data group**, click **Access Database**. Compare your screen with Figure 11.8.

The Database Splitter dialog box displays to define the process. Access suggests backing up a database before splitting it.

Figure 11.8

Database Splitter explanation

3 In the displayed **Database Splitter** dialog box, read the message, and then click the **Split Database** button.

Notice the information regarding an encrypted database: the front end keeps the database, but a password will need to be added to the back end to secure it.

4 In the **Create Back-end Database** dialog box, if necessary, navigate to your **Access Chapter 11** folder. Notice the suggested file name, and then click the **Split** button. Read the displayed message, click **OK**, and then compare your screen with Figure 11.9.

In the Navigation Pane, the five tables display the linked table icon and the other objects display as before. Recall that a linked table is a table that resides in a separate database file.

Figure 11.9

Tables linked to the back end

Forms and reports reside in the front end

5 Press **Alt** + **PrtScr**. Open a new, blank **Word** document. In the **Word** document, type your first and last names, press **Enter**, and then type **Project 11A Activity 11.02 Step 5** Press **Enter**, and then paste the screen shot. **Save** the **Word** document in your **Access Chapter 11** folder as **Lastname_Firstname_11A_Screens**

6 Return to **Access**. **Close** the database, and then **Exit** Access. Click the **Start** menu, and then click **Computer**. In the **Windows Explorer** window, navigate to your **Access Chapter 11** folder. Double-click **Lastname_Firstname_11A_Lawyers_be**. Compare your screen with Figure 11.10.

The five linked tables reside in this back-end database file. Typically, the file containing the back end would reside on a network server that all departments can access. Notice that none of the front-end objects in the Lawyers database were copied to this back-end file.

Figure 11.10

Back-end tables

No reference to the front-end objects

7 **Close** the database.

> **More Knowledge** | Moving the Back End to a Microsoft SQL Server
>
> Instead of moving the back end into a separate Access database file, it can be placed on a Microsoft SQL Server. *Microsoft SQL Server* is a database application designed for high-end business uses. If a database contains thousands of records, or if it will be accessed by multiple users at the same time, moving the back-end files to a Microsoft SQL Server will dramatically improve performance.

Objective 3 | Encrypt and Decrypt Databases

The data stored in any company's database is one of that company's most valuable assets. If proprietary knowledge is made public, the company could lose its competitive advantage. Further, personal information stored in the database needs to be protected from unauthorized access. For these reasons, the data needs to be hidden until the correct password is entered. Only authorized users should know what that password is.

Activity 11.03 | Encrypting Databases with a Password

Lacy-Rennier Law Partners has a moral and legal responsibility to keep the data it collects hidden from unauthorized individuals. If one of the company computers or laptops is ever lost or stolen, the data should be unreadable to anyone outside of the company. In this activity, you will make an Access 2010 database unreadable until a password is entered.

1 Display **Backstage** view, and then click **Open**. In the **Open** dialog box, open the **Access Chapter 11** folder, and then click **Lastname_Firstname_11A_Lawyers** one time. In the lower right corner of the **Open** dialog box, click the **Open button arrow** (not the Open button), and compare your screen with Figure 11.11.

> Four additional open modes display. *Open Read-Only* opens the database so that all objects can be opened and viewed, but data and design changes cannot be made. *Open Exclusive* opens the database so that changes can be made, but no one else may open the database at the same time. *Open Exclusive Read-Only* opens the database in both Exclusive and Read-Only modes. *Show Previous Versions* searches for previous versions of the database.

Figure 11.11

Five open options

2 Click **Open Exclusive**.

> The database must be opened in exclusive mode before it can be encrypted. To *encrypt* means to hide data by making the file unreadable until the correct password is entered.

3 Display **Backstage** view, and click the **Encrypt with Password** button. Compare your screen with Figure 11.12.

Figure 11.12

Set and verify a database password

4 In the **Set Password** dialog box, in the **Password** box, type **2010GO! Series** In the **Verify** box, type **2010GO! Series** and then click **OK**. Access passwords are case sensitive, so be sure to capitalize exactly as shown. If a message box displays, click **OK**.

> *Strong passwords* are created so they will be hard to guess and the database is secure. They use a combination of upper and lowercase letters, special characters, numbers, and spaces in a character string. A *weak password* is a password that is easy to guess. Weak passwords may lead to costly losses of valuable data.

5 **Close** and then reopen the database. In the displayed **Password Required** dialog box, type **2010GO! Series** and then click **OK**. **Close** the database.

> With encrypted Access 2010 files, individuals must enter a password to access the database. There is no way to retrieve a forgotten password to be able to open an encrypted database. Be sure to store passwords in a safe place away from the data they protect, in case it is ever necessary.

6 Using the technique you just practiced, encrypt the **Lastname_Firstname_11A_ Lawyers_be** database with **GO! 11Abe**. If necessary, click **OK** to close the message box. **Close** the database.

Activity 11.04 | Decrypting a Database with a Password

Lacy-Rennier Law Partners periodically resets the passwords used for its database in order to make them more secure. In this activity, you will remove a password currently used to open the Lawyers database so it will be ready to reset later. When you no longer want a password to be required to open a database, you must *decrypt* the file or unset the password.

1 **Open** the **11A_Lawyers_be** database for exclusive use. Review the previous activity if you do not remember the password for this database. Display **Backstage** view, and click the **Decrypt Database** button to display the **Unset Database Password** dialog box, and then compare your screen with Figure 11.13.

> To prohibit an unauthorized user from removing the password encryption applied to a database, the password must be entered to discontinue the password requirement for opening the current database.

Figure 11.13

Enter password to remove encryption

2 Type **GO! 11Abe** and then click **OK**. **Close** the database.

3 Open the **11A_Lawyers_be** database. **Close** the database.

> Notice the database opened without asking you to provide a password.

Objective 4 | Create a Locked Database (ACCDE File)

A business may want to secure the design of certain objects in the database when providing a working copy of the database for staff. An *ACCDE file* is an Access 2010 file format that prevents users from creating forms and reports and making design changes to forms, reports, and macros while performing other regular database tasks. Because design changes might be necessary in the future, a copy of the original database should be stored in a secure place.

Activity 11.05 | Creating a Secure ACCDE File

Lacy-Rennier Law Partners wants to provide a locked-down version of their database so users cannot make any design changes. In this activity, you will create and test an ACCDE file.

1 **Open** the **Lastname_Firstname_11A_Lawyers** database. Review Activity 11.03 if you do not remember the password for this database.

2 Display **Backstage** view, click **Save & Publish**, and then double-click **Make ACCDE** in the right column under **Advanced**. Compare your screen with Figure 11.14.

The Save As dialog box displays, with the Save as type box showing ACCDE File.

Figure 11.14

File type

3 In the **File name** box, change the file name to **Lastname_Firstname_11A_ACCDE** Be sure that the path for your **Access Chapter 11** folder displays, and then click **Save**.

4 **Exit** Access. Switch to the **Windows Explorer** window, and then compare your screen with Figure 11.15.

The Type description for the ACCDE file is Microsoft Access ACCDE Database. A padlock is added to the icon to indicate the file's "locked-down" status.

Figure 11.15

Padlock added to the icon for an ACCDE file type

5 In the **Windows Explorer** window, double-click **Lastname_Firstname_11A_ACCDE** and type the password. Review Activity 11.03 if you do not remember the password for this database.

6 Click the **Create tab**, and then compare your screen with Figure 11.16.

The forms and reports creation tools are dimmed, indicating that new forms and reports cannot be created.

Figure 11.16

ACCDE file opened ————

Tools are unavailable ————

7 In the **Navigation Pane**, under **Forms**, right-click **Corporate Clients**, and notice that the Design View command is dimmed. Design changes cannot be made in an ACCDE file.

8 Double click the **Corporate Clients** form to open it in **Form** view. Add a new record using the following information. Replace **Firstname Lastname** with your first and last names. **Close** ☒ the form.

CorpID	**C0025**
OrgName	**Little Elm Community College**
Street	**2010 South Main Street**
City	**Little Elm**
State	**TX**
PostalCode	**75068**
Phone	**(214) 555-5011**
Representative	**Firstname Lastname**

The form can be used for normal database tasks as long as no Design view features are used.

9 If you are instructed to submit this result, create a paper or electronic printout of the current form only. **Close** the database, and then **Exit** Access.

10 In **Windows Explorer**, with the **Access Chapter 11** folder contents active, press Alt + PrtScr. In the **Word** document, press Ctrl + End to go to the end of the document. Press Ctrl + Enter to go to a new page, and then type your first and last names, and then press Enter. Type **Project 11A Activity 11.05 Step 10** press Enter, and then **Paste** the screenshot. **Save** the file. If you are instructed to submit this result, create a paper or electronic printout of the Word document. **Close** Word, and **Close** the Windows Explorer window.

 You have completed Project 11A ————————————

Project 11B Overdue Accounts

Project Activities

In Activities 11.06 through 11.11, you will write queries in SQL view, creating queries that cannot be created in Design view. Lacy-Rennier Law Partners stores billing information in two unrelated tables. It needs queries that combine the data from both tables so the company can call those clients who need to pay their bill. The only way to combine these two queries is to work in SQL view. The partners have given you several tables from their database, each with a small sample of data. Once the queries are working properly, they can be applied to the full data set. Your completed queries and report will look similar to Figure 11.17.

Project Files

For Project 11B, you will need the following file:

a11B_Overdue_Accounts.accdb

You will save your database as:

Lastname_Firstname_11B_Overdue_Accounts.accdb

Project Results

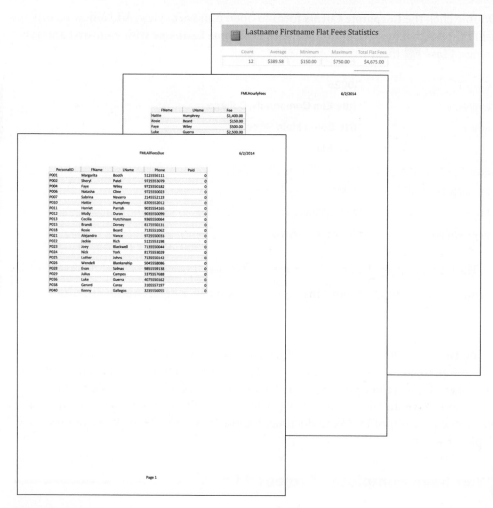

Figure 11.17

Project 11B Overdue Accounts

Objective 5 | Modify a Query in SQL View

SQL (often pronounced sequel), or *Structured Query Language*, is a language used by many database programs to view, update, and query data in relational databases. In Access, all queries use SQL; queries can be created in Design view and then modified in SQL view. Starting in Design view saves time and is a good way to become familiar with writing SQL statements.

Activity 11.06 | Modifying a Query in SQL View

Lacy-Rennier Law Partners needs a query that lists each client who was charged a flat fee and has not yet paid that fee. In this activity, you will create that query in Design view and then modify it in SQL view.

1 **Start** Access. Navigate to the location where the student data files for this textbook are saved. Locate and then open the **a11B_Overdue_Accounts** database. Display **Backstage** view, and click **Save Database As**. In the **Save As** dialog box, navigate to your **Access Chapter 11** folder, and then save the file as **Lastname_Firstname_11B_Overdue_Accounts**

2 Rename each table by adding **FML** to the beginning of each object name. Be sure to replace *FML* with your own initials, and do not use any spaces in the table names. **Close** « the **Navigation Pane**.

Note | Table and Field Naming Conventions

You will be creating queries by writing SQL. To simplify the SQL statements, database designers usually choose a naming convention where table and field names are abbreviated terms and do not contain any spaces. For this reason, this project follows what is known as the *Upper Camel Case* naming convention, and you will add your initials to the table names instead of your first and last name.

---

3 Click the **Create tab**, and then in the **Queries group**, click the **Query Design** button. Using the techniques you have practiced, add the **FMLPersonalClients** and **FMLFlatFeeBilling** tables to the query design workspace. **Close** the **Show Table** dialog box. Expand the field lists to display all data.

4 From the **FMLPersonalClients** table, add the following fields to the design grid: **PersonalID**, **FName**, **LName**, and **Phone**. From the **FMLFlatFeeBilling** table, add the **Paid** field to the design grid. In the **Criteria** box for the **Paid** column, type **No**

5 Click **Save**, type **FMLFlatFeesDue** using your own initials, and then click **OK**.

6 Locate the status bar in the lower right corner of the database window, and then click the **SQL View** [SQL] button. Click any blank area in the SQL workspace, and then compare your screen with Figure 11.18.

When you work in Query Design view, Access builds the equivalent SQL statement. An *SQL statement* is an expression that defines the SQL commands that should be performed when the query is run. SQL statements typically contain several SQL clauses that begin with keywords. *Keywords* are commands built into the SQL programming language. Keywords are typically written using uppercase letters. In SQL View, statements are edited in the design grid.

Figure 11.18

SQL statement

Design grid

SQL View button

SELECT FMLPersonalClients.PersonalID, FMLPersonalClients.FName, FMLPersonalClients.LName, FMLPersonalClients.Phone, FMLFlatFeeBilling.Paid
FROM FMLPersonalClients INNER JOIN FMLFlatFeeBilling ON FMLPersonalClients.PersonalID = FMLFlatFeeBilling.PersonalID
WHERE (((FMLFlatFeeBilling.Paid)=No));

7 In the SQL statement, click to the left of the keyword *FROM*, and then press Enter.

This SQL statement starts with a SELECT clause. A ***SELECT clause*** lists which fields the query should display. The second clause in this SQL statement is a FROM clause. A ***FROM clause*** lists which tables hold the fields used in the SELECT clause.

8 Click to the left of the keyword *INNER*, and then press Enter **two** times. Click to the left of the keyword *WHERE*, and then press Enter.

A ***JOIN clause*** defines the join type for a query. Recall that an inner join displays only those records that have a corresponding record in both of the related tables. A ***WHERE clause*** defines the criteria that should be applied when a query is run.

9 In the **WHERE** clause, remove all six parentheses.

These parentheses would be needed only if a more complex WHERE clause was written. Often, the SQL generated while in Design view will not be as efficient as the SQL written by a SQL programmer in SQL view.

10 Click **Save**. In the **Results group**, click the **Run** button. Click the **LName column arrow**, and then click **Sort A to Z**. Compare your screen with Figure 11.19.

> The results include each client who was charged a flat fee and has not yet paid that fee. Brandi Dorsey and Faye Wiley are each listed two times. This type of duplication may lead to duplicate phone calls being made to the client.

Figure 11.19

Duplicate listings

11 In the status bar, click the **SQL View** button. Click to the right of the keyword SELECT, press (Spacebar) and then type **DISTINCT**

> The **DISTINCT** keyword removes duplicates from query results. It always follows the SELECT keyword and is added only in SQL View.

12 **Run** the query and notice that duplicate records no longer display. Click **Save** 🔲, and then **Close** ☒ the query.

Objective 6 | Create a Query in SQL View

Many database designers find it easier to design their queries in SQL view than in Design view. The typical SQL query uses the same three-step sequence. Understanding this sequence removes much of the complexity of the typical SQL statement. Working in SQL view enables the designer to write more efficient SQL and also provides more control than Design view. Many types of queries can be created only when working in SQL view.

Activity 11.07 | Creating SQL Statements

Lacy-Rennier Law Partners needs a query that lists each client who was charged an hourly rate and has not yet paid the fee. Due to the nature of this query, you will need to work in SQL view to write a query not available in Design view. In this activity, you will create that query in SQL view.

1 Click the **Create tab**, and then in the **Queries group**, click the **Query Design** button. Close the displayed **Show Table** dialog box, and then in the status bar, click the **SQL View** button.

> Because you started with a select query, the SELECT keyword displays, followed by a semicolon. Semicolons are used to mark the end of SQL statements.

2 Click before the semicolon, press Spacebar and then type the following, substituting FML with your own initials: **FMLPersonalClients.PersonalID, FMLPersonalClients. FName, FMLPersonalClients.LName, FMLPersonalClients.Phone, FMLHourlyBilling.Paid** Compare your screen with Figure 11.20.

> In a SELECT clause, both the table name and field name are included and are separated by a period. Multiple fields must be separated by commas.

Figure 11.20

Period separates table and field names

Comma separates fields

Semicolon ends statement

3 Press Enter two times, and then type the following FROM clause, substituting your own initials: **FROM FMLPersonalClients, FMLHourlyBilling**

> All tables used in the SELECT clause must be listed in the FROM clause and are separated by commas.

4 Press Enter two times, and then type the following WHERE clause, substituting your own initials: **WHERE FMLHourlyBilling.Paid=No**

> Recall that in the WHERE statement, the criteria for the query is defined.

5 Click **Save** 🔲, and then, substituting your own initials, type **FMLHourlyFeesDue** Click **OK**.

6 Be sure that the semicolon is at the end of the query. Click the **Run** button, and then compare your screen with Figure 11.21. If you receive a message that the query has errors or the Enter Parameter Value dialog box displays, go back and check your typing very carefully.

> The result of this query is a cross join query. Recall that in a cross join query, every possible combination of records between two related tables will be returned. If no join type is defined or if there is a mistake in the WHERE clause, SQL returns a cross join query. When tables contain a large number of records, cross join queries will take a very long time to run. In this query, the join type needs to be defined.

Figure 11.21

7 Save 💾 your query, and then return to **SQL view**.

Activity 11.08 | Specifying the Join Type in SQL

The HourlyFeesDue query currently returns a cross join. Once a join type is specified in the query, it will display one record per customer. In this activity, you will add an SQL clause so that the two tables used in the query use an inner join.

1 In **SQL** view, in the **FROM** clause, click between *FMLPersonalClients* and the comma, and then press Spacebar.

2 Press Del to remove the comma.

3 Type the following JOIN clause, **INNER JOIN**

The ***INNER JOIN*** keyword instructs the query to use an inner join between two tables.

4 Click to the right of *FMLHourlyBilling*, press Spacebar, and type the following ON clause: **ON FMLPersonalClients.PersonalID = FMLHourlyBilling.PersonalID**

The ***ON*** keyword is used to specify which field is common to two tables. The combination of INNER JOIN and ON keywords creates a relationship between the two tables. In this query the PersonalID field is used to join the tables.

5 Click **Save** 💾, and then **Run** the query. Sort the **LName** column in alphabetical order, and then compare your screen with Figure 11.22.

Figure 11.22

Duplicate values

The tables are joined correctly, but customers with more than one outstanding bill are listed two or more times.

6 Return to **SQL View**. After the **SELECT** keyword, press [Spacebar], and then type **DISTINCT**

7 **Run** the query. Check that no customer is listed more than once. Click **Save** 🖫, and then **Close** ✕ the query.

Objective 7 | Create a Union Query Using SQL

Using SQL, the results of two or more queries can be displayed in one query. A *union query* combines the results of two or more similar select queries. The combined queries must have the same number of columns and the same data types in each corresponding column. Union queries are created only in SQL view.

Activity 11.09 | Creating a Union Query in SQL View

Recall that Lacy-Rennier Law Partners needs a list of all personal clients with amounts owed. In earlier projects, you built two separate queries, one for flat fees and the other for hourly fees. In this activity, you will use SQL to combine the results of both queries into a single query.

1 Click the **Create tab**, and then in the **Queries group**, click the **Query Design** button. **Close** the displayed **Show Table** dialog box.

2 In the **Query Type group**, click the **Union** button. Notice that the query switches to SQL view.

3 **Open** » the **Navigation Pane**. Open the **FMLFlatFeesDue** query, and then in the status bar, click the **SQL View** button. With the entire SQL statement selected, right-click anywhere in the design grid, and then click **Copy**.

4 **Close** the **FMLFlatFeesDue** query. In the union query, right-click anywhere in the design grid, and then click **Paste**. **Close** « the **Navigation Pane**.

5 At the end of the SQL statement, delete the semicolon, and then press [Enter] **two** times.

6 Type **UNION** and then press [Enter] **two** times. Compare your screen with Figure 11.23.

The *UNION* keyword is used to combine one or more queries in a union query.

Figure 11.23

UNION keyword

```
SELECT DISTINCT FMLPersonalClients.PersonalID, FMLPersonalClients.FName, FMLPersonalClients.LName, FMLPersonalClients.Phone, FMLFlatFeeBilling.Paid
FROM FMLPersonalClients INNER JOIN FMLFlatFeeBilling ON FMLPersonalClients.PersonalID = FMLFlatFeeBilling.PersonalID
WHERE FMLFlatFeeBilling.Paid=No

UNION
```

7 **Open** [»] the **Navigation Pane**, and then open the **FMLHourlyFeesDue** query. In the status bar, click the **SQL View** button. With the entire SQL statement selected, right-click anywhere in the design grid, and then click **Copy**.

8 **Close** the **FMLHourlyFeesDue** query. In the union query that you are building, right-click next to the insertion point, and then click **Paste**.

9 Click **Save**, type **FMLAllFeesDue** using your own initials, and then click **OK**.

10 In the **Navigation Pane**, notice the union query icon to the left of the query's name. In the **Results group**, click the **View button arrow**, and notice that Design view is not available for this query.

11 **Run** the query, and then compare your results with Figure 11.24.

Figure 11.24

12 If you are instructed to submit this result, create a paper or electronic printout of the query. Click **Save** [🖫], and then **Close** [✕] the query. **Close** [«] the **Navigation Pane**.

Objective 8 | Create Calculated Fields and SQL Aggregate Functions

SQL is a powerful language that does far more than create select queries. SQL provides commands to create calculated fields and summarize data using aggregate functions. Recall that an aggregate function performs a calculation on a column of data and returns a single value. When creating calculated fields, many developers prefer to work in SQL view because long expressions can be viewed without having to use the Zoom feature.

Activity 11.10 | Creating Calculated Fields in SQL

Lacy-Rennier Law Partners needs a list of total amounts due for the clients who were billed at an hourly rate. In this activity, you will write an SQL statement with a field that calculates fees by multiplying the number of hours by the hourly rate.

1 Click the **Create tab**, and then in the **Queries group**, click the **Query Design** button.

2 Use the displayed **Show Table** dialog box to add the **FMLPersonalClients** and **FMLHourlyBilling** tables, and then **Close** the dialog box. Expand the field lists so all field names are displayed.

3 From the **FMLPersonalClients** table, add the **FName** field, and then add the **LName** field.

4 In the status bar, click the **SQL View** button.

> Starting this query in Design view saves you from having to type the SELECT, FROM, and INNER JOIN clauses.

5 To the right of the entire SELECT clause, type a comma, press Spacebar, and then type the following: **FMLHourlyBilling.Hours * FMLHourlyBilling.Rate AS Fee**

> A calculated field with the caption *Fee* will display the product of the Hours and Rate fields for each record. The *AS* keyword creates captions for fields.

6 At the end of the SQL statement, click to the left of the semicolon, press Enter, and then type the following WHERE clause: **WHERE FMLHourlyBilling.Paid = No**

7 Click **Save**, type **FMLHourlyFees** using your own initials, and then click **OK**.

8 **Run** the query, and then compare your screen with Figure 11.25.

Figure 11.25

9 If you are instructed to submit this result, create a paper or electronic printout of the query. **Close** ☒ the query.

Activity 11.11 | Writing SQL Aggregate Functions

Lacy-Rennier Law Partners needs a report showing summary statistics for the amounts due from clients paying flat fees. In this activity, you will use SQL aggregate functions to calculate summary statistics and then create a report based on the query.

1 Click the **Create tab**, and then in the **Queries group**, click the **Query Design** button. **Close** the displayed **Show Table** dialog box. In the status bar, click the **SQL View** button.

2 In the design grid, delete the semicolon, press Spacebar, and then, substituting *FML* with your own initials, type the following: **Count(FMLFlatFeeBilling.Fee) AS Count**

Count is an SQL aggregate function.

3 Press Enter, and then type the following FROM clause: **FROM FMLFlatFeeBilling**

4 Press Enter, and then type the following WHERE clause: **WHERE FMLFlatFeeBilling .Paid = No;**

5 Click **Save** 🖫, type **FMLFlatFeesStats** using your own initials, and then click **OK**.

6 Click the **Run** button, and then compare your screen with Figure 11.26.

The number of records in the query displays in a column that has *Count* as its caption.

Figure 11.26

Caption

Number of records

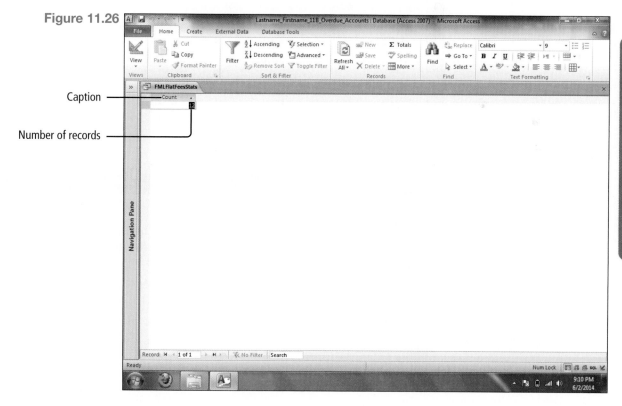

7 Return to **SQL View**. Click to the right of the entire **SELECT** clause, and then type a comma. Press Enter, and then type the following: **Avg(FMLFlatFeeBilling.Fee) AS Average,** Press Enter.

8 Continue adding to the SELECT clause by typing **Min(FMLFlatFeeBilling.Fee) AS Minimum,** and then press Enter. Type **Max(FMLFlatFeeBilling.Fee) AS Maximum,** and press Enter. Type **Sum(FMLFlatFeeBilling.Fee) AS [Total Flat Fees]**

> Because Total Flat Fees contains spaces, it must be enclosed in square brackets. In Access SQL statements, any table name or field name that has spaces must be enclosed in square brackets. If there are no spaces, then the square brackets are optional. After [Total Flat Fees], no comma is needed because it is the end of the SELECT clause.

9 Compare your screen with Figure 11.27, click **Save** 🖫, and then **Run** the query.

Figure 11.27

10 Close ✕ the query. **Open** ≫ the **Navigation Pane**, and then click to select the **FMLFlatFeesStats** query. Click the **Create tab**, and in the **Reports group**, click the **Report** button.

11 Click anywhere in the **Total Flat Fees** column to select the column. In the **Grouping & Totals group**, click the **Totals** button, and then click **Sum** to remove the second displayed total for that column.

12 In the **Report Header**, delete the **Date** and **Time** boxes. Change the report's title to **Lastname Firstname Flat Fees Statistics** Resize the textbox so the title fits on one line. If you are instructed to submit this result, create a paper or electronic printout.

13 Click **Save** 🖫, and then accept the Report Name by clicking **OK**.

14 **Close** ☒ the report, and then **Close** the database. If you are instructed to submit this result, create a paper or electronic printout.

End **You have completed Project 11B**

Access | Chapter 11

Summary

In this chapter, you practiced securing databases and writing queries in SQL. Databases saved in the Access 2010 file format protect data by encrypting the database, which makes the data unreadable to anyone who does not possess the correct password. You also practiced saving a database in a locked-down format, a format that uses the .accde file extension to protect forms, macros, and reports from design changes. Additionally, a database can be split to store the back end on a server and provide different areas of the company with department-specific forms, reports, and queries.

Writing your own SQL in SQL view provides options not available in query Design view. You used SQL view to write SQL to join two queries in a union query, create calculated fields, and provide aggregate statistics. Knowing how to modify SQL directly gives you greater control and flexibility when designing queries. The same SQL statements that you wrote in this chapter can also be used to query databases other than Access, such as Microsoft SQL Server or MySQL.

Key Terms

Matching

Match each term in the second column with its correct definition in the first column by writing the letter of the term on the blank line in front of the correct definition.

_____ 1. An open database with all executable content turned off.

_____ 2. To open the database so that all objects can be opened and viewed, but data and design changes cannot be made.

_____ 3. To hide data by making the file unreadable until the correct password is entered.

_____ 4. Passwords that use a combination of upper and lowercase letters, special characters, numbers, and spaces in a character string.

_____ 5. A password that is easy to guess.

_____ 6. The process used when you no longer want a password to be required to open a database.

_____ 7. An Access 2010 file format that prevents users from making design changes to forms, reports, and macros.

_____ 8. The database tables and their data stored in a separate file.

_____ 9. The database forms, queries, reports, and macros stored in a separate file.

A ACCDE

B AS

C Back end

D Decrypt

E Disabled mode

F DISTINCT

G Encrypt

H Front end

I Open Read Only

J SELECT

K SQL Server

L SQL statement

M Strong password

N UNION

O Weak password

_____ 10. A database application designed for high-end business uses.

_____ 11. An expression that contains several SQL clauses to define the commands that should be performed when the query is run.

_____ 12. The SQL clause that pulls the fields that should display.

_____ 13. An SQL keyword that removes duplicates from query results.

_____ 14. The SQL keyword used to combine one or more queries.

_____ 15. An SQL keyword that creates a caption for a field.

Multiple Choice

Circle the correct answer.

1. In disabled mode, which of the following would not work?
   A. delete query
   B. trusted macro action
   C. data entry on a form

2. Which command is used to open a database that you will encrypt?
   A. Open Read-Only
   B. Open Exclusive
   C. Open Exclusive Read-Only

3. A password that is hard to guess is considered a:
   A. storage password.
   B. strong password.
   C. suspend password.

4. What do you do to unset a database password?
   A. trust the database
   B. decode the database
   C. decrypt the database

5. An ACCDE file appears with a modified icon in Windows Explorer; it includes:
   A. a padlock.
   B. an X.
   C. an Access 2003 icon.

6. An Access database that is stored in two files—one containing the back end and one containing the front end—is called a:
   A. replica database.
   B. backup file.
   C. split database.

7. The end users open which file to work with data in a split database?
   A. back end
   B. front end
   C. ACCDE file

8. The SQL clause that specifies which tables are used is the:
   A. JOIN clause.
   B. WHERE clause.
   C. FROM clause.

9. The SQL clause that defines the criteria that should be applied when a query is run is the:
   A. JOIN clause.
   B. WHERE clause.
   C. FROM clause.

10. The SQL clause used to define which field is the common field between two related tables is the:
    A. JOIN clause.
    B. WHERE clause.
    C. FROM clause.

Content-Based Assessments

Apply **11A** skills from these Objectives:

☐ Utilize the Trust Center

☐ Use the Database Splitter

☐ Encrypt and Decrypt Databases

☐ Create a Locked Database (ACCDE File)

Skills Review | Project **11C** Paralegals

Lacy-Rennier Law Partners wants to secure the database tables used by its paralegals. You will encrypt the database using a secure password, create a locked ACCDE file, and split the database to allow Human Resources to design separate front-end databases to be used by various departments. Your completed documents will look similar to Figure 11.28.

Project Files

For Project 11C, you will need the following file:

a11C_Paralegals.accdb

You will save your files as:

Lastname_Firstname_11C_Paralegals.accdb
Lastname_Firstname_11C_Paralegals_be.accdb
Lastname_Firstname_11C_Paralegals_ACCDE.accde
Lastname_Firstname_11C_Screens.docx

Project Results

Figure 11.28

(Project 11C Paralegals continues on the next page)

Content-Based Assessments

1 **Start** Access. Locate and then open the **a11C_Paralegals** file. Save the database in your **Access Chapter 11** folder as **Lastname_Firstname_11C_Paralegals** If necessary, add the Chapter 11 folder to the Trust Center.

2 Click the **Database Tools tab**. In the **Move Data group**, click the **Access Database** button.

a. In the **Database Splitter** dialog box, click the **Split Database** button.

b. In the **Create Back-end Database** dialog box, be sure your **Access Chapter 11** folder is open.

c. Click the **Split** button, accepting the default name for the back-end file. Read the message, and then click **OK**.

3 Press Alt + PrtScr. Open a new, blank **Word** document.

a. In the **Word** document, type your first and last names, press Enter, and then type **Project 11C Step 3** Press Enter, and then paste the screen shot.

b. Save the **Word** document in your **Access Chapter 11** folder as **Lastname_Firstname_11C_Screens**

c. Return to the **11C_Paralegals** database.

4 In the **Navigation Pane**, double-click the **PersonalCasesForm**, and then enter the following new record:

PCaseID	ServiceCode	Description	LeadParalegal	Closed
PC00011	PS004	Employment Contract	P003	No

5 If you are instructed to submit this result, print the current form only. **Close** the form, and then **Close** the database.

6 Display **Backstage** view, and then click **Close Database**.

a. From the **Backstage** view, click **Open**. In the **Open** dialog box, open the **Access Chapter 11** folder, and then click **Lastname_Firstname_11C_Paralegals** one time.

b. In the lower right corner of the **Open** dialog box, click the **Open button arrow**, and then click **Open Exclusive**.

7 Display **Backstage** view, and click the **Encrypt with Password** button.

a. In the **Set Database Password** dialog box, in the **Password** box, type **11C HR paralegals** In the **Verify** box, type **11C HR paralegals** and then click **OK**. If a message box displays, click **OK** to close it.

b. Display **Backstage** view. **Close** and then reopen the **11C Paralegals** database. In the displayed **Password Required** dialog box, type **11C HR paralegals** and then click **OK**.

8 Display **Backstage** view, click **Save & Publish**, and then double-click the **Make ACCDE** button.

a. In the **Save As** dialog box, be sure that your Access Chapter 11 folder is open. Save the locked database as **Lastname_Firstname_11C_Paralegals_ACCDE**

b. **Close** the database, **Exit** Access.

9 Open **Windows Explorer**, and then navigate to and open your **Access Chapter 11** folder.

a. If necessary, maximize the **Windows Explorer** window and switch to **Details** view. Be sure that all the files created in this project display. Be sure that the columns are wide enough to display all of the **Name** and **Type** descriptions.

b. Press Alt + PrtScr, and then **Close Windows Explorer**.

c. In the **Word** document, press Enter, and then press Ctrl + Enter to insert a page break. Type your first and last names, press Enter, and then type **Project 11C Step 9** Press Enter, and **Paste** the screen shot.

d. Click **Save**. If you are instructed to submit this result, create a paper or electronic printout of the **Word** document.

10 If you are submitting this project electronically, submit all the files listed at the beginning of this project as directed by your instructor.

End **You have completed Project 11C**

Content-Based Assessments

Apply **11B** skills from these Objectives:

- 🔲 Modify a Query in SQL View
- 🔲 Create a Query in SQL View
- 🔲 Create a Union Query Using SQL
- 🔲 Create Calculated Fields and SQL Aggregate Functions

Skills Review | Project **11D** Top Accounts

Lacy-Rennier Law Partners wants a report that lists its top accounts. To build the report, you will create two queries using SQL view. You will join the two queries into a single query. You will then create a query that summarizes the data in the union query and build the report from this query. Your completed report will look similar to Figure 11.29.

Project Files

For Project 11D, you will need the following file:

a11D_Top_Accounts.accdb

You will save your database as:

Lastname_Firstname_11D_Top_Accounts.accdb

Project Results

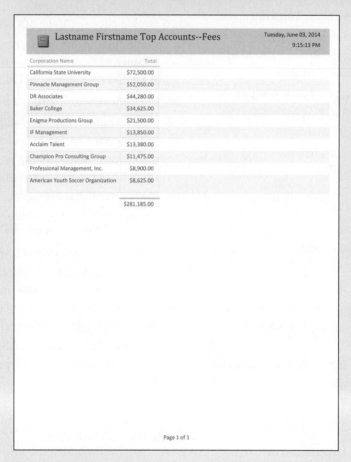

Figure 11.29

(Project 11D Top Accounts continues on the next page)

1 **Start** Access. Locate and open the **a11D_Top_Accounts** file. Save the database in your **Access Chapter 11** folder as **Lastname_Firstname_11D_Top_Accounts**

a. **Rename** the database tables by adding **FML** to the beginning of each table name, using your own initials.

2 Click the **Create tab**, and then in the **Queries group**, click the **Query Design** button.

a. In the displayed **Show Table** dialog box, add the **CorpAccounts** and **FlatFees** tables to the Design view. Resize field lists so all fields are visible.

b. From the **CorpAccounts** table, add the **CorpName** field to the design grid. From the **FlatFees** table, add the **Fee** field to the design grid.

3 In the **Show/Hide group**, click the **Totals** button.

a. In the **Total** row for the **Fee** column, change **Group By** to **Sum**.

b. **Save** the query with the name **FMLFlatFeesQuery** using your own initials.

4 In the status bar, click the **SQL View** button.

a. After the *AS* keyword, replace the text *SumofFee* with **Total**

b. In the **Results group**, click the **Run** button. View the results, and then click the **SQL View** button. **Save** and **Close** the query.

5 Click the **Create tab**, and then in the **Queries group**, click the **Query Design** button. **Close** the **Show Table** dialog box, and then click the **SQL View** button.

a. Replace the existing text with the following SELECT clause, using your own initials: **SELECT FMLCorpAccounts.CorpName, Rate * Hours AS Total**

b. On a new line, enter the following FROM clause, using your own initials: **FROM FMLCorpAccounts INNER JOIN FMLHourlyFees ON FMLCorpAccounts.CorpID = FMLHourlyFees.CorpID;**

c. Click the **Run** button to test the query. **Save** the query as **FMLHourlyFeesQuery** using your own initials.

6 Click the **SQL View** button. In the SELECT clause, replace the text *Rate * Hours* with **Sum(Rate * Hours)**

a. At the end of the SQL statement, delete the semicolon, press Enter, and then type the following clause: **GROUP BY FMLCorpAccounts.CorpName**

b. Click the **Run** button, view the results, and then click **Save**. **Close** the query.

7 Click the **Create tab**, and then in the **Queries group**, click the **Query Design** button. In the displayed **Show Table** dialog box, click the **Close** button, and then in the **Query Type group**, click the **Union** button.

a. Display the **FlatFeesQuery** query in SQL view. Select the entire SQL statement, right-click, and then click **Copy**. Display the union query that you are building, right-click, and then click **Paste**. Delete the semicolon, press Enter **two** times, and then type **UNION**

b. Display the **HourlyFeesQuery** query in SQL view, and then **Copy** the entire SQL statement. Display the union query, press Enter **two** times, and then press Ctrl + V.

c. **Save** the query with the name **FMLFeesUnion** using your own initials, and then click the **Run** button. View the results, and then **Close** all three open queries.

8 Click the **Create tab**, and then in the **Queries group**, click the **Query Design** button.

a. In the displayed **Show Table** dialog box, click the **Queries tab**, and then add the **FMLFeesUnion** query to the Design view. Add the **CorpName** and the **Total** fields to the design grid.

b. In the **Show/Hide group**, click the **Totals** button. In the **Total** row for the **Totals** column, change **Group By** to **Sum**.

c. Click in the **Sort** row for the **Totals** column. Click the displayed arrow, and then click **Descending**.

d. **Save** the query with the name **FMLTopFeeAccounts** using you own initials. Click the **Run** button and view the results. Autofit columns as necessary.

9 Click the **SQL View** button. After the SELECT keyword, press Spacebar, and then type: **TOP 10**

a. **Run** the query and view the results.

b. Click **Save**, and then **Close** the query.

10 In the **Navigation Pane**, click to select the **TopFeeAccounts** query. Click the **Create tab**, and then in the **Reports group**, click the **Report** button.

a. Change the report **Title** text box to **Lastname Firstname Top Accounts—Fees** Make adjustments so the title fits on one line. If necessary, adjust date and time control box widths to fit within right margin. Change the **CorpName** label to **Corporation Name**

(Project 11D Top Accounts continues on the next page)

Skills Review | Project **11D** Top Accounts (continued)

b. At the top of the **Totals** column, change the **SumofTotals** label to **Total** At the bottom of the **Totals** column, click the text box that calculates the grand total, and then apply the **Currency** format. If necessary, autofit the bottom to display the total amount.

c. **Save** the report with the name suggested by Access.

11 If you are instructed to submit this result, create a paper or electronic printout of the report. **Close** the report.

12 **Exit** Access. If you are submitting this project electronically, submit the database as directed by your instructor.

 You have completed Project 11D ————————————————

Content-Based Assessments

Apply **11A** skills from these Objectives:

1. Utilize the Trust Center
2. Use the Database Splitter
3. Encrypt and Decrypt Databases
4. Create a Locked Database (ACCDE File)

Mastering Access | Project **11E** Accountants

Lacy-Rennier Law Partners wants to secure the databases used by its accounting and marketing departments. You will split the database into front- and back-end files, encrypt databases with a password, and create an ACCDE file to lock the database design. Your screenshots will look similar to Figure 11.30.

Project Files

For Project 11E, you will need the following file:

    a11E_Accountants.accdb

You will save your files as:

    Lastname_Firstname_11E_Accountants.accdb
    Lastname_Firstname_11E_Accountants_be.accdb
    Lastname_Firstname_11E_ACCDE.accde
    Lastname_Firstname_11E_Screens.docx

Project Results

Figure 11.30

(Project 11E Accountants continues on the next page)

Mastering Access | Project **11E** Accountants (continued)

1 **Start** Access. Locate and open the **a11E_Accountants** file. Save the database in your **Access Chapter 11** folder as **Lastname_Firstname_11E_Accountants** If necessary, add the Chapter 11 folder to the Trust Center.

2 Split the database into a back-end and front-end file. Save the back-end file in your **Access Chapter 11** folder with the name suggested by Access.

3 Press [Alt] + [PrtScr], and then **Close** the database. Open a new, blank Word document, type your first and last names, press [Enter], and then type **Project 11E Step 3** Press [Enter], and then **Paste** the screen shot. **Save** the Word document in your **Access Chapter 11** folder as **Lastname_ Firstname_11E_Screens**

4 Open **11E_Accountants_be**. Press [Alt] + [PrtScr], and then **Clos**e the database. In the Word document, press [Enter], and then press [Ctrl] + [Enter] to insert a page break. Type your first and last names, press [Enter], and then type **Project 11E Step 4** Press [Enter], **Paste** the screen shot, and then click **Save**.

5 **Open** the **11E_Accountants** database using the **Open Exclusive** command. Encrypt the database using the password **11E GO! Series** Click **OK** two times, and then **Close** the database.

6 Open **11E Accountants** using the password. Create a secure ACCDE version of the database file. Save the ACCDE file in your **Access Chapter 11** folder as **Lastname_Firstname_11E_ACCDE**

7 **Close** the database, and **Exit** Access.

8 Open **Windows Explorer**, and then open your **Access Chapter 11** folder. If necessary, maximize the Windows Explorer window and switch to **Details** view. Be sure that all the files created in this project display and that the columns are wide enough to display all of the **Name** and **Type** descriptions. Press [Alt] + [PrtScr], and then **Close** Windows Explorer.

9 In the Word document, press [Enter], and then press [Ctrl] + [Enter] to insert a page break. Type your first and last names, press [Enter], and then type **Project 11E Step 9** Press [Enter], **Paste** the screen shot, and then click **Save**. If you are instructed to submit this result, create a paper or electronic printout of the Word document.

10 If you are submitting this project electronically, submit all the files listed at the beginning of this project as directed by your instructor.

End **You have completed Project 11E**

Content-Based Assessments

- **5** Modify a Query in SQL View
- **6** Create a Query in SQL View
- **7** Create a Union Query Using SQL
- **8** Create Calculated Fields and SQL Aggregate Functions

Mastering Access | Project **11F** Services

Lacy-Rennier Law Partners wants a report that describes the various services it provides to corporations and organizations. To build the report, you will create two queries using SQL view. You will join the two queries into a single query. You will then create a query that summarizes the data in the union query and build the report from this query. Your completed report will look similar to Figure 11.31.

Project Files

For Project 11F, you will need the following file:

    a11F_Services.accdb

You will save your database as:

    Lastname_Firstname_11F_Services.accdb

Project Results

Service	Average
Arbitration	$578.13
Contracts	$714.02
Copyright	$6,208.33
Licensing	$6,413.75
Litigation	$14,659.72
NCAA Compliance	$2,350.00
Risk Management	$3,496.04
Taxation	$1,371.88
Trademark	$1,022.50

Lastname Firstname Services — Wednesday, June 04, 2014 — 11:56:11 AM — Page 1 of 1

Figure 11.31

(Project 11F Services continues on the next page)

Mastering Access | Project **11F** Services (continued)

1 **Start** Access. Locate and open the **a11F_Services** file. Save the database in the **Access Chapter 11** folder as **Lastname_Firstname_11F_Services** At the beginning of each table name, add **FML** using your own initials and no space.

2 Start a new query in **Design** view. **Add** the **Services** and **FlatFees** tables to the query. From the **Services** table, add the **Service** field to the design grid. From the **FlatFees** table, add the **Fee** field.

3 In the **Show/Hide group**, click the **Totals** button. In the **Total** row for the **Fee** column, change **Group By** to **Avg**.

4 In SQL view, adapt the *SELECT* statement so that the calculated field's caption will display as **Average Run** the query and view the results. **Save** the query as **FMLFlatServices** using your own initials.

5 Start a new query in **Design** view, and then switch to **SQL** view. Add a **SELECT** statement that displays the **Service** field from the **Services** table.

6 Add a calculated field to the *SELECT* statement that multiplies the **Rate** and **Hours** fields from the **HourlyFees** table.

7 Add a **FROM** clause that joins the **Services** table to the **HourlyFees** table with an inner join that uses the **ServiceCode** fields from each table. If needed, use the **FROM** clause in the query created earlier in this project as your reference.

8 For the calculated field, add a SQL aggregate function that calculates the average (**AVG**) of the **Rate** field multiplied by the **Hours** field. Write the SQL needed so that the calculated field's caption displays as **Average**. Add a **GROUP BY** clause that groups the query by each **Service**. If needed, use the query created earlier in this project as your reference.

9 **Run** the query and view the results. **Save** the query as **FMLHourlyServices** using your own initials.

10 Create a new union query. **Copy** and **Paste** the SQL from the two queries created earlier and join them using the **UNION** keyword. **Run** the query, view the results, and then **Save** the query as **FMLServicesUnion** using your own initials.

11 Create a new query in **Design** view. In the displayed **Show Table** dialog box, click the **Queries tab**, add the **ServicesUnion** query, and then **Close** the dialog box. Add the **Service** field to the design grid, and then add the **Average** field.

12 In the **Show/Hide group**, click the **Totals** button. In the **Total** row for the **Average** column, change **Group By** to **Avg**. **Save** the query with the name **FMLServicesQuery** using your own initials. Click the **Run** button, view the results, and then **Close** all open queries.

13 In the **Navigation Pane**, click to select the **ServicesQuery**. Click the **Create tab**, and then in the **Reports group**, click the **Report** button.

14 Change the **Title** text box to **Lastname Firstname Services** Click the **AvgofAverage** label, and then change the label text to **Average** At the bottom of the **Service** column, click the text box that calculates the total number of services, and then press [Del]. Click the same box area again to select the placeholder for the calculated control and press [Del] again. Save the report using the name suggested by Access. If you are instructed to submit this result, create a paper or electronic printout.

15 **Close** the report, and then **Exit** Access. If you are submitting this project electronically, submit the database as directed by your instructor.

End **You have completed Project 11F**

Content-Based Assessments

Apply **11A** and **11B** skills from these Objectives:

- **2** Use the Database Splitter
- **3** Encrypt and Decrypt Databases
- **5** Modify a Query in SQL View
- **6** Create a Query in SQL View
- **7** Create a Union Query Using SQL
- **8** Create Calculated Fields and SQL Aggregate Functions

Mastering Access | Project **11G** Bonuses

The two lead partners, Lacy and Rennier, need to secure the front end of the database with a password before creating a confidential query that lists the four lawyers who have generated the most business. You will create two queries using SQL view, join them in a union query, and then build another query summarizing the union query. Your completed report will look similar to Figure 11.32.

Project Files

For Project 11G, you will need the following file:

    a11G_Bonuses.accdb

You will save your files as:

    Lastname_Firstname_11G_Bonuses.accdb
    Lastname_Firstname_11G_Bonuses_be.accdb

Project Results

Figure 11.32

(Project 11G Bonuses continues on the next page)

Content-Based Assessments

Mastering Access | Project 11G Bonuses (continued)

1 **Start** Access. Locate and then open **a11G_Bonuses**. Save the database in your **Access Chapter 11** folder as **Lastname_Firstname_11G_Bonuses** At the beginning of each table name, add **FML** using your own initials and no space.

2 Split the database using the name Access suggests for the back end to save it in your **Access Chapter 11** folder.

3 **Close** the database. **Open** the **a11G_Bonuses** database again in Exclusive mode, and then encrypt it using the password **11G Bonus!** If a message box displays, click **OK**. **Close** the database, and then **Open** it using the password.

4 Start a new query in **Design** view. Add the **Lawyers** and **FlatFees** tables to the query, expanding the field lists as necessary. From the **Lawyers** table, add the **FName** and **LName** fields to the design grid. From the **FlatFees** table, add the **Fee** field.

5 In the **Show/Hide group**, click the **Totals** button. In the **Total** row for the **Fee** column, change **Group By** to **Sum**.

6 In **SQL** view, change the caption for the calculated field to **Total** Run the query and view the results. **Save** the query as **FMLFlatFeesQuery** using your own initials.

7 Start a new query in **Design** view, and then switch to **SQL** view. Using the earlier query as your guide, write a SELECT statement that displays the **FName** and **LName** fields from the **Lawyers** table.

8 Add a calculated field to the *SELECT* clause that multiplies the **Rate** and **Hours** fields. Write the SQL needed so that the calculated field's caption displays as **Total**

9 For the calculated field, add an SQL aggregate function that calculates the total of the **Rate** field multiplied by the **Hours** field.

10 Add a **FROM** clause that joins the **Lawyers** table to the **HourlyFees** table with an inner join that uses the **LawyerID** fields from each table.

11 Copy the *GROUP BY* clause from **FlatFeesQuery** and **Paste** it into the current query. **Run** the query and view the results. **Save** the query as **FMLHourlyFeesQuery** using your own initials.

12 Create a new union query. **Copy** and **Paste** the SQL statements from the two queries created earlier and join them using the **UNION** keyword. **Run** the query, view the results, and then **Save** the query as **FMLUnion** using your own initials. **Close** all open queries.

13 Create a new query in **Design** view, add the union query, and then add the **FName**, **LName**, and **Total** fields to the design grid. Add the **Total row** to the design grid, and then in the **Total row** for the **Total** column, change **Group By** to **Sum**.

14 In the **Total** column, add a **Sort** type of **Descending**. Display the **Property Sheet**, and then, on the **General** tab, change the format to **Currency**.

15 In SQL view, after *SELECT*, add a space and then type **TOP 4 Save** the query as **FMLTopLawyers** using your own initials. **Run** the query, and then **Close** the query.

16 Create a report based on the **FMLTopLawyers** query to display all fields. Change the report title to read **Lastname Firstname Top Four Lawyers** on one line, removing the Date and Time controls. Change the **SumofTotal** caption to read **Total**, the **FName** caption to read **First Name**, and the **LName** caption to read **Last Name** Remove the **Count** total from under the **FName** field. If you are instructed to submit this result, create a paper or electronic printout. **Close** the report, saving changes using the default name. **Exit** Access.

17 If you are submitting this project electronically, submit the database as directed by your instructor.

End **You have completed Project 11G**

Content-Based Assessments

GO! Fix It | Project 11H Annual Dinner

Project Files

For Project 11H, you will need the following file:

a11H_Annual_Dinner.accdb

You will save your files as:

Lastname_Firstname_11H_Annual_Dinner.accdb
Lastname_Firstname_11H_ACCDE.accde
Lastname_Firstname_11H_Screens.docx

Lacy-Rennier Law Partners needs to be sure it has a locked-down version of the database for security reasons as it prepares for its annual dinner. In this project, you will create a guest list for the upcoming annual dinner using queries created in SQL view.

Open **a11H_Annual_Dinner**, and save as **Lastname_Firstname_11H_Annual_Dinner** At the beginning of each table name, add **FML** using your own initials and no spaces.

Create the following queries in SQL view to develop the guest list for the annual dinner:

- Start a new query in Design view. From the CorpAccounts table, add CorpName, Street, City, State, and PostalCode to the design grid. From the FlatFees table, add the Date field, but it should not display in the result. Display results where the date is after **12/31/2015** Save the query as **FMLFlatFees2016Query** using your own initials.

- Start a new query and switch to SQL view. Write a SELECT statement that displays CorpName, Street, City, State, and PostalCode from the CorpAccounts table. Add a FROM clause that joins the CorpAccounts table to the HourlyFees table with an inner join using the CorpID field. Add a **WHERE** clause to return those records with a date after **12/31/2015** Refer to the SQL view of the query created earlier in this project, if necessary. Save the query as **FMLHourlyFees2016Query** using your own initials.

- Create a new union query. Copy and paste the SQL from the two queries created earlier and join them using the UNION keyword. Run the query, view the results, and then save the query as **FMLDinnerGuests** using your own initials. Close all open queries.

- Create a report based on the DinnerGuests query. Resize each column to better fit its contents. Be sure all of the report displays on a single landscape page. Change the Title text box to **Lastname Firstname Dinner Guests** Save the report with the name suggested by Access, and then close the report. If you are instructed to submit this report, create a paper or electronic printout.

Secure a locked-down version of the database by creating a locked version of the database named **Lastname_Firstname_11H_ACCDE** Close the database.

- Open Windows Explorer, and then navigate to and open your Access Chapter 11 folder. Be sure that the files created in this project display completely, including the Name and Type descriptions. Capture the screen, and paste it into a Word document saved as **Lastname_Firstname_11H_Screens**

- If you are instructed to submit this result, create a paper or electronic printout of the Word document.

End You have completed Project 11H —————————

Content-Based Assessments

GO! Make It | Project 11I Seminar

Project Files

For Project 11I, you will need the following file:

a11I_Seminar.accdb

You will save your files as:

Lastname_Firstname_11I_Seminar.accdb
Lastname_Firstname_11I_Seminar_be.accdb
Lastname_Firstname_11I_ACCDE.accde
Lastname_Firstname_11I_Screens.docx

Open the **a11I_Seminar** database file. Save the database in your **Access Chapter 11** folder as **Lastname_Firstname_11I_Seminar** Rename all of the tables to include your initials and no space before the table names. Split the database, accepting the default name for the back end.

Using SQL, create a query that lists each lawyer's full name and phone number if they have seminars listed in the Seminars table. Add the necessary SQL command so that lawyers are listed one time in the query results. Save the query as **FMLPresenters** using your own initials. Create a report based on the query results including an appropriate title. Create a paper or electronic printout of the report as directed. Create a locked database named **Lastname_Firstname_11I_ACCDE**

Capture the screen displaying the files created in this project. Create a paper or electronic printout as directed. If you are submitting this project electronically, submit the databases as directed by your instructor. Your completed documents will look similar to Figure 11.33.

Project Results

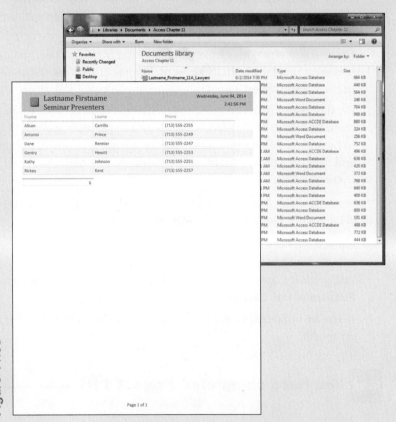

Figure 11.33

End You have completed Project 11I —————————

Content-Based Assessments

GO! Solve It | Project 11J Law Library

Project Files

For Project 11J, you will need the following file:

a11J_Law_Library.accdb

You will save your files as:

Lastname_Firstname_11J_Law_Library.accdb
Lastname_Firstname_11J_ACCDE.accde

Lacy-Rennier Law Partners wants to secure its Law Library database and use SQL view to create a query. To start, open **a11J_Law_Library**, and then save it as **Lastname_Firstname_ 11J_Law_Library**. At the beginning of each table name, add **FML** using your own initials and no space.

Create a query named **FMLTopServices** in SQL view. The query should display the top three services that are represented in the FMLLawLibrary table; display the count as **Resources** Create a locked file named **Lastname_Firstname_11J_ACCDE**, and then encrypt it using the password **11J GO!Library** Submit the databases as directed by your instructor.

		Performance Element		
		Exemplary: You consistently applied the relevant skills	**Proficient:** You sometimes, but not always, applied the relevant skills	**Developing:** You rarely or never applied the relevant skills
Performance Criteria	Create TopServices query in SQL view	Query created with correct syntax and format.	Query created with fewer than two missing elements.	Query created with more than two missing elements.
	Create 11J ACCDE database	ACCDE file created accurately.	ACCDE file created with an incorrect name.	No ACCDE file created.
	Encrypt the 11J ACCDE database	Back-end database is encrypted using the correct password.	Either the wrong database is encrypted or the wrong password is used.	The wrong database is encrypted with the wrong password or no database is encrypted.

End You have completed Project 11J

Content-Based Assessments

Apply a combination of the 11A and 11B skills.

GO! Solve It | Project **11K** Contracts

Project Files

For Project 11K, you will need the following file:

a11K_Contracts.accdb

You will save your database as:

Lastname_Firstname_11K_Contracts.accdb

Lacy-Rennier Law Partners needs a list of clients who have asked for assistance with contracts. Because the clients are listed in two tables, you will need to use SQL to return only one record per client and then combine the two queries in a union query. To start, open **a11K_Contracts**, and then save it as **Lastname_Firstname_11K_Contracts** At the beginning of each table name, add **FML** using your own initials and no space.

Using SQL, create a query that lists personal clients who have cases listed in the Cases table. List only the clients where the ServiceCode is equal to SC02. Include the Name, Street, City, State, and PostalCode fields. Add the necessary SQL command so that clients are not listed more than one time in the query's results. Save the query as **FMLPersonal** query using your own initials.

Using SQL, create a query that lists corporate clients who have cases listed in the Cases table. List only the clients whose ServiceCode is equal to SC02. Include the CompanyName, Street, City, State, and PostalCode fields. Add the necessary SQL command so that clients are listed only one time in the query's results. Save the query as **FMLCorporate** query using your own initials.

Create a union query that combines the two queries. Save the query as **FMLAllClients** using your own initials. Create a report based on the union query. Format the report to effectively present the results on one page with a descriptive title. Save the report as **FMLAllClients**.

Submit the database as directed by your instructor.

Performance Element			
	Exemplary: You consistently applied the relevant skills	**Proficient:** You sometimes, but not always, applied the relevant skills	**Developing:** You rarely or never applied the relevant skills
Create Personal query using SQL	Query created with correct syntax and format.	Query created with no more than two missing elements.	Query created with more than two missing elements.
Create Corporate query using SQL	Query created with correct syntax and format.	Query created with no more than two missing elements.	Query created with more than two missing elements.
Create AllClients union query using SQL	Query created with correct syntax and format.	Query created with no more than two missing elements.	Query created with more than two missing elements.
Create FMLAllClients report	Report created with correct syntax and format.	Report created with no more than two missing elements.	Report created with more than two missing elements.

Performance Criteria is printed vertically along the left side of the table.

End You have completed Project 11K

Outcomes-Based Assessments

Rubric

The following outcomes-based assessments are *open-ended assessments*. That is, there is no specific correct result; your result will depend on your approach to the information provided. Make *Professional Quality* your goal. Use the following scoring rubric to guide you in *how* to approach the problem and then to evaluate *how well* your approach solves the problem.

The *criteria*—Software Mastery, Content, Format and Layout, and Process—represent the knowledge and skills you have gained that you can apply to solving the problem. The *levels of performance*—Professional Quality, Approaching Professional Quality, or Needs Quality Improvements—help you and your instructor evaluate your result.

	Your completed project is of Professional Quality if you:	Your completed project is Approaching Professional Quality if you:	Your completed project Needs Quality Improvements if you:
1-Software Mastery	Choose and apply the most appropriate skills, tools, and features and identify efficient methods to solve the problem.	Choose and apply some appropriate skills, tools, and features, but not in the most efficient manner.	Choose inappropriate skills, tools, or features, or are inefficient in solving the problem.
2-Content	Construct a solution that is clear and well organized, contains content that is accurate, appropriate to the audience and purpose, and is complete. Provide a solution that contains no errors in spelling, grammar, or style.	Construct a solution in which some components are unclear, poorly organized, inconsistent, or incomplete. Misjudge the needs of the audience. Have some errors in spelling, grammar, or style, but the errors do not detract from comprehension.	Construct a solution that is unclear, incomplete, or poorly organized; contains some inaccurate or inappropriate content; and contains many errors in spelling, grammar, or style. Do not solve the problem.
3-Format and Layout	Format and arrange all elements to communicate information and ideas, clarify function, illustrate relationships, and indicate relative importance.	Apply appropriate format and layout features to some elements, but not others. Overuse features, causing minor distraction.	Apply format and layout that does not communicate information or ideas clearly. Do not use format and layout features to clarify function, illustrate relationships, or indicate relative importance. Use available features excessively, causing distraction.
4-Process	Use an organized approach that integrates planning, development, self-assessment, revision, and reflection.	Demonstrate an organized approach in some areas, but not others; or, use an insufficient process of organization throughout.	Do not use an organized approach to solve the problem.

Outcomes-Based Assessments

GO! Think | Project **11L** Case History

Project Files

For Project 11L, you will need the following file:

    a11L_Case_History.accdb

You will save your files as:

    Lastname_Firstname_11L_Case_History.accdb
    Lastname_Firstname_11L_ACCDE.accde

    Lacy-Rennier Law Partners needs to secure a database containing a list of past cases. At the beginning of each table name, add **FML** using your own initials and no space.

    Using SQL, create a query that lists corporate clients who have past cases listed in the PastCases table. List only the client name and how many cases they have had. Group the data by CompanyName, and then display the count as **Past Cases** Save the query as **FMLHistory** using your own initials.

    Create an ACCDE file named **Lastname_Firstname_11L_ACCDE**

    Submit the project as directed by your instructor.

 You have completed Project 11L _____

GO! Think | Project **11M** Phone List

Project Files

For Project 11M, you will need the following file:

    a11M_Phone_List.accdb

You will save your database as:

    Lastname_Firstname_11M_Phone_List.accdb

    Lacy-Rennier Law Partners wants a list of all names and phone numbers of clients with open cases. To start, open **a11M_Phone_List**, and then save it as **Lastname_Firstname_11M_Phone_List** At the beginning of each table name, add **FML** using your own initials and no space. Encrypt the database using the password **11MGO! Series**

    Create a query that lists the names and phone numbers of personal clients who have open cases listed in the CaseHistory table. Add the necessary SQL command so that clients are not listed more than one time in the query's results. Save the query as **FMLPersonalOpen** using your own initials.

    Using SQL, create a query that lists the names and phone numbers of corporate clients who have open cases listed in the CaseHistory table. Add the necessary SQL command so that clients are not listed more than one time in the query's results. Save the query as **FMLCorpOpen** using your own initials.

    Create a union query that combines the two queries. Save the query as **FMLAllOpen** using your own initials. Create a report based on the union query. Format the report to effectively present the results on one page with a descriptive title. Save the report as **FMLAllOpen** using your own initials. Submit the project as directed by your instructor.

 You have completed Project 11M _____

Outcomes-Based Assessments

Apply a combination of the **11A** and **11B** skills.

You and GO! | Project **11N** Club Directory

Project Files

For Project 11N, you will need the following file:

Lastname_Firstname_10N_Club_Directory.accdb

You will save your files as:

Lastname_Firstname_11N_Club_Directory.accdb
Lastname_Firstname_11N_Club_Directory_be.accdb

Create a personal database containing information about a club and its activities, if you do not already have one from Project 10N. Name the new database **Lastname_Firstname_11N_Club_ Directory** If you do not have the database from Project 10N, create two related tables, one that lists the activities your organization has planned and the other to serve as the directory of the group. The Activities table should include information about the name (primary key field), date, cost, and location of the activity. The dates must all occur next year; consider attaching directions to the event to the table. The Directory table should include full name, address, phone number, email, and an activity they are planning. If you have the database from Project 10N, save it as **Lastname_ Firstname_11N_Club_Directory** in your Access Chapter 11 folder.

Split the database to move the tables to the back end file using the default name provided by Access. Encrypt the front end file with the password **11N GO!Club**

Using SQL, create a query that displays the activity name, date, cost, and location for all items that have already occurred. Save the query as **FMLPastActivities** using your own initials. Create a second query using SQL to display the average cost of activities grouped by location. Save the query as **FMLAverageCost** using your own initials. If needed, use queries created earlier in this project as your reference.

 You have completed Project 11N ——————————————

Business Running Case

Front Range Action Sports is one of the country's largest retailers of sports gear and outdoor recreation merchandise. The company has large retail stores in Colorado, Washington, Oregon, California, and New Mexico, in addition to a growing online business. Major merchandise categories include fishing, camping, rock climbing, winter sports, action sports, water sports, team sports, racquet sports, fitness, golf, apparel, and footwear.

In this project, you will apply skills you practiced from the objectives in Access Chapters 10 and 11. You will perform file analysis and management tasks to create smaller, more efficient files. You will also encrypt a database with a password and create queries using SQL statements. Your results will look similar to Figure 4.1.

Project Files

For Project BRC4, you will need the following file:

>   aBRC4_Company_
>   Administration.accdb

You will save your files as:

Lastname_Firstname_aBRC4_Company_
    Administration.accdb
Lastname_Firstname_aBRC4_Screens.docx
Lastname_Firstname_aBRC4_ACCDE.accde

Project Results

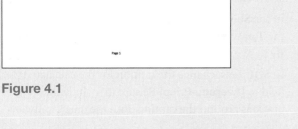

Figure 4.1

Business Running Case

Front Range Action Sports

1 **Start** Access. Locate and open the **aBRC4_Company_ Administration** database. **Save** the database in your **Front Range Action Sports** folder as **Lastname_ Firstname_aBRC4_Company_Administration**

2 Rename the following tables to keep them short and without spaces. Be sure to replace **FML** with your initials.

Original Table Name	New Table Name
BRC4 Hours Scheduled	FMLHoursScheduled
BRC4 Suppliers	FMLSuppliers
BRC4 Inventory	FMLInventory
BRC4 Employees	FMLEmployees

3 Open the **Suppliers** table in **Design** view, and change the following field names. Any field name not in this list should remain the same.

Original Field Name	New Field Name
Supplier ID#	SuppID
E-mail Address	Email
Business Phone	Phone
Postal Code	PostalCode

4 Open the **Inventory** table in **Design** view, and change the following field names. Any field name not in this list should remain the same.

Original Field Name	New Field Name
Item Name	ItemName
Retail Price	Rprice
Supplier ID#	SuppID

5 **Delete** the **Average Prices Query** and **Suppliers Contact List** report. **Close** the **Navigation Pane**.

6 On the **Database Tools tab**, in the **Analyze group**, click the **Analyze Performance** button. Click the **All Object Types** tab, click the **Select All** button, and then click **OK**. Under **Analysis Results**, review the Ideas with the yellow light bulb. Press Alt + PrtScr, and then **Close** the dialog box. Open **Word**, and in a blank document, type your first and last names, press Enter, and then type **Project BRC4 Step 6** Press Enter, **Paste** the screen shot, and press Enter again. **Save** the document as **Lastname_Firstname_aBRC4_Screens**

7 Return to Access. On the **Database Tools tab**, in the **Analyze group**, click the **Database Documenter** button. In the **Documenter** dialog box, on the **Tables tab**, check the **Suppliers** and **Inventory** tables, and then click the **Options** button. Under **Include for Table**, only **Relationships** should be checked. The **Include for Fields** option and the **Include for Indexes** option should be set to **Nothing**. Click **OK** two times.

8 In **Print Preview**, **Zoom** in and then scroll so that all of the report text displays. Press Alt + PrtScr, and then click the **Close Print Preview** button. In the **Word** document, type your first and last names, press Enter, and then type **Project BRC4 Step 8** Press Enter, **Paste** the screen shot, and then click **Save**.

9 Return to Access. From **Backstage** view, click the **Compact & Repair Database** button. **Close** the database.

10 Open **aBRC4_Company_Administration** in **Exclusive mode** so it can be encrypted. Display **Backstage** view, and click the **Encrypt with Password** button. In the **Set Database Password** dialog box, type **GO! FRAS** in the Password and Verify boxes. Click **OK**. If necessary, click **OK** to close the message box. **Close** the database.

11 **Open** the database using the password. From **Backstage** view, click **Options**. Under **Current Database**, change the **Application Title** to **Front Range Action Sports**

12 For the current database only, add the following commands to the Quick Access Toolbar: **Import Access Database**, **Import Excel Spreadsheet**, **Open Recent File**, and **Quick Print**.

13 **Close** all open dialog boxes and database objects. Press Alt + PrtScr. In the **Word** document, press Enter, and then press Ctrl + Enter to insert a page break. Type your first and last names, press Enter, and then type **Project BRC4 Step 13** Press Enter, **Paste** the screen shot, and then click **Save**.

14 Create a new query in **Design** view. Add the **Inventory** table to the query. Expand the field list so all data is visible. From the **Inventory** table, add the **Category** and **RPrice** fields.

a. In the **Show/Hide group**, click the **Totals** button. In the **Total** row for the **RPrice** column, change **Group By** to **Avg**.

b. In **SQL** view, change the caption for the calculated field to **[Average Price]** Be sure to include the square brackets around the caption. **Run** the query and view

(Business Running Case: Front Range Action Sports continues on the next page)

Business Running Case

Front Range Action Sports (continued)

the results. **Save** the query as **FMLAvgRetail** using your own initials. If you are instructed to submit this result, create a paper or electronic printout of the query results. **Close** the query.

15 Create a new query and switch to **SQL** view.

a. Write a **SELECT** statement that displays the following fields from the **Suppliers** table: **Company**, **Address**, **City**, **State**, and **PostalCode**.

b. Add a **FROM** clause that joins the **Suppliers** table to the **Inventory** table with an inner join using the **SuppID** field from each table.

c. Add a **WHERE** clause that returns only those records where the **Category** is **Shoes**.

d. Add the necessary SQL command so that companies are not listed more than one time in the query's results. Save the query as **FMLShoeSuppliers** using your own initials. **Close** the query.

16 **Open** the **Navigation Pane**. Create a report titled **Lastname Firstname Shoe Suppliers** based on the **FMLShoeSuppliers** query. Title the report **Lastname Firstname Shoe Suppliers** Make sure the title fits on one line. Format the report to effectively present the results on one page so all data is visible. **Save** the report

as **FMLShoeSuppliers** using your own initials. If you are instructed to submit this result, create a paper or electronic printout of the report. **Close** the report.

17 In **Access**, from **Backstage** view, click **Save & Publish**, and then double-click **Make ACCDE** to create a locked version of the database in your **Front Range Action Sports** folder. Save it as **Lastname_Firstname_aBRC4_ACCDE**

18 **Close** the database and **Exit** Access. Open **Windows Explorer**, and navigate to your **Front Range Action Sports** folder. If necessary, maximize the Windows Explorer window and switch to **Details** view. Be sure that all the files created in this project display and that the columns are wide enough to display all of the Name and Type descriptions. Press [Alt] + [PrtScr], and then **Close** Windows Explorer.

19 In the **Word** document, press [Enter], and then press [Ctrl] + [Enter] to insert a page break. Type your first and last names, press [Enter], and then type **Project BRC4 Step 19** Press [Enter], **Paste** the screen shot, and then click **Save**.

20 **Close** the **BRC4_Screens** document and **Close** Word. Submit the project as directed by your instructor.

End You have completed Business Running Case 4 ——————————

Glossary

ACCDE file An Access file format that prevents users from making design changes to forms, reports, and macros.

Action A self-contained instruction that can be combined with other actions to automate tasks.

Action query A query that creates a new table or changes data in an existing table.

Action Tag A field property that enables the end user to perform tasks from Access that would usually require another program, such as Outlook, to be open.

Address bar The bar at the top of a folder window with which you can navigate to a different folder or library, or go back to a previous one.

Aggregate functions Calculations such as MIN, MAX, AVG, and SUM that are performed on a group of records.

Alignment The placement of paragraph text relative to the left and right margins.

All Programs An area of the Start menu that displays all the available programs on your computer system.

Alphabetic index Grouping of items by a common first character.

AND condition A condition in which only records where all of the values are present in the selected fields.

Append To add on to the end of an object; for example, to add records to the end of an existing table.

Append query An action query that adds new records to an existing table by adding data from another Access database or from a table in the same database.

Appended When importing, data is added to the end of the existing table.

Application Another term for a program.

Application title The text that displays in the Access title bar when a database is open.

Argument A value that provides information to the macro action, such as the words to display in a message box or the control upon which to operate.

Arithmetic operators Mathematical symbols used in building expressions.

AS An SQL keyword that creates captions for fields.

Ascending order A sorting order that arranges text in alphabetical order (A to Z) or numbers from the lowest to highest number.

ASCII An acronym for American Standard Code for Information Interchange, also known as Plain Text.

AutoNumber data type A data type that describes a unique sequential or random number assigned by Access as each record is entered and that is useful for data that has no distinct field that can be considered unique.

AutoPlay A Windows feature that displays when you insert a CD, a DVD, or other removable device, and which lets you choose which program to use to start different kinds of media, such as music CDs, or CDs and DVDs containing photos.

Back and Forward buttons Buttons at the top of a folder window that work in conjunction with the address bar to change folders by going backward or forward one folder at a time.

Back end A file that consists of the database tables and their data, that is typically placed on a server, and that is not directly seen by the end user.

Back up A feature that creates a copy of the original database to protect against lost data, usually stored in an alternative location.

Backing up The process of creating a copy of a database or other files to prevent data loss.

Backstage tabs The area along the left side of Backstage view with tabs to display various pages of commands.

Backstage view A centralized space for file management tasks; for example, opening, saving, printing, publishing, or sharing a file. A navigation pane displays along the left side with tabs that group file-related tasks together.

Bang operator The exclamation (!) mark that tells Access that what follows it is an object that belongs to the object that precedes it in the expression.

Best Fit An Access command that adjusts the width of a column to accommodate the column's longest entry.

Between . . . And operator A comparison operator that looks for values within a range.

Blank database A database that has no data and has no database tools— you must create the data and the tools as you need them.

Blank Report tool An Access tool with which you can create a report from scratch by adding the fields you want in the order in which you want them to display.

Bound The term used to describe objects and controls that are based on data that is stored in tables.

Bound control A control that retrieves its data from an underlying table or query; a text box control is an example of a bound control.

Bound report A report that displays data from an underlying table, query, or SQL statement as specified in the report's Record Source property.

Byte A measurement for data that typically stores a single character, such as a digit or letter, and is used to measure storage sizes on disks or in computer memory.

Calculated control A control that contains an expression, often a formula, that uses one or more fields from the underlying table or query.

Calculated field A field that stores the value of a mathematical operation.

Caption A property setting that displays a name for a field in a table, query, form, or report other than that listed as the field name.

Cascade Delete An option that deletes all of the related records in related tables when a record in a table is deleted.

Cascade options Options that update records in related tables when referential integrity is enforced.

Cascade Update An option that updates records in related tables when the primary key field is changed.

Cell The small box formed by the intersection of a column and a row in a worksheet.

Center alignment The alignment of text or objects that is centered horizontally between the left and right margin.

Chart A graphic representation of data.

Click The action of pressing the left button on your mouse pointing device one time.

Clipboard A temporary storage area in Windows that can hold up to 24 items.

Column chart A chart used to display comparisons among related numbers.

Combo box A box that is a combination of a list box and text box in a lookup field.

Command An instruction to a computer program that causes an action to be carried out.

Common dialog boxes The set of dialog boxes that includes Open, Save, and Save As, which are provided by the Windows programming interface, and which display and operate in all of the Office programs in the same manner.

Common field A field in one or more tables that stores the same data.

Compact & Repair A process in which an Access file is rewritten to store the objects and data more efficiently.

Comparison operator Symbols that evaluate each value to determine if it is the same (=), greater than (>), less than (<), or in between a range of values as specified by the criteria.

Compound criteria Multiple conditions in a query or filter.

Compressed file A file that has been reduced in size and thus takes up less storage space and can be transferred to other computers quickly.

Condition A statement that specifies certain criteria that must be met before the macro action executes.

Conditional formatting A way to apply formatting to specific controls based on a comparison to a rule set.

Context sensitive command A command associated with activities in which you are engaged.

Contextual tabs Tabs that are added to the Ribbon automatically when a specific object, such as a picture, is selected, and that contain commands relevant to the selected object.

Control An object on a form or report that displays data, performs actions, and lets you view and work with information.

Control layout The grouped arrangement of controls on a form or report.

Convert To change data from one format to another, such as converting a Word table to a delimited text file.

Copy A command that duplicates a selection and places it on the Clipboard.

Criteria (Access) Conditions in a query that identify the specific records for which you are looking.

Cross join A join that displays when each row from one table is combined with each row in a related table, usually created unintentionally when you do not create a join line between related tables.

Crosstab query A query that uses an aggregate function for data that can be grouped by two types of information and displays the data in a compact, spreadsheet-like format.

Currency data type An Access data type that describes monetary values and numeric data that can be used in mathematical calculations involving data with one to four decimal places.

Cut A command that removes a selection and places it on the Clipboard.

Data Facts about people, events, things, or ideas.

Data dictionary A detailed report with information about the objects in a database that should be printed periodically and stored in a secure location.

Data entry The action of typing the record data into a database form or table.

Data loss The unexpected failure of information caused by such actions as hardware malfunction, accidental deletion of records, theft, or natural disaster.

Data source (Access) The table or tables from which a form, query, or report retrieves its data.

Data type The characteristic that defines the kind of data that can be entered into a field, such as numbers, text, or dates.

Data validation Rules that help prevent invalid data entries and ensure data is entered consistently.

Database An organized collection of facts about people, events, things, or ideas related to a specific topic or purpose.

Database Documenter An option used to create a report that contains detailed information about the objects in a database, including macros, and to create a paper record.

Database management system Database software that controls how related collections of data are stored, organized, retrieved, and secured; also known as a *DBMS*.

Database template A preformatted database designed for a specific purpose.

Datasheet view The Access view that displays data organized in columns and rows similar to an Excel worksheet.

Date control A control on a form or report that inserts the current date each time the form or report is opened.

DBMS An acronym for *database management system*.

Debugging A logical process to find and reduce the number of errors in a program.

Decrypt An action that removes a file's encryption or unsets a password.

Default The term that refers to the current selection or setting that is automatically used by a computer program unless you specify otherwise.

Default value A value displayed for new records.

Definition The structure of the database—the field names, data types, and field properties.

Delete query An action query that removes records from an existing table in the same database.

Delimited file A file where each record displays on a separate line and the fields within the record are separated by a single character called a delimiter.

Delimiter A character used in a delimited file to separate the fields; it can be a paragraph mark, a tab, a comma, or another character.

Dependency An object that requires, or is dependent on, another database object.

Descending order A sorting order that arranges text in reverse alphabetical order (Z to A) or numbers from the highest to lowest number.

Deselect The action of canceling the selection of an object or block of text by clicking outside of the selection.

Design grid The lower area of the Query window that displays the design of the query.

Design Master The original database in a replica set.

Design view An Access view that displays the detailed structure of a query, form, or report; for forms and reports, may be the view in which some tasks must be performed, and only the controls, and not the data, display in this view.

Desktop In Windows, the opening screen that simulates your work area.

Destination table (Access) The table to which you import or append data.

Detail section The section of a form or report that displays the records from the underlying table or query.

Details pane The area at the bottom of a folder window that displays the most common file properties.

Dialog box A small window that contains options for completing a task.

Dialog Box Launcher A small icon that displays to the right of some group names on the Ribbon, and which opens a related dialog box or task pane providing additional options and commands related to that group.

Disabled mode The format in which an untrusted database is opened; all executable content is turned off.

DISTINCT An SQL keyword that removes duplicates from query results.

Document properties Details about a file that describe or identify it, including the title, author name, subject, and keywords that identify the document's topic or contents; also known as *metadata*.

Double-click The action of clicking the left mouse button two times in rapid succession.

Drag The action of holding down the left mouse button while moving your mouse.

Drop zones The design area in a PivotTable to which fields are dragged.

Dynamic An attribute applied to data in a database that changes.

Edit The actions of making changes to text or graphics in an Office file.

Ellipsis A set of three dots indicating incompleteness; when following a command name, indicates that a dialog box will display.

Embedded macro A macro that is stored in the event properties of forms, reports, or controls.

Encrypt A process to hide data by making the file unreadable until the correct password is entered.

Enhanced ScreenTip A ScreenTip that displays more descriptive text than a normal ScreenTip.

Event Any action that can be detected by a program or computer system, such as clicking a button or closing an object.

Export The process used to send *out* a copy of data from one source or application to another application.

Expression (1) A combination of functions, field values, constants, and operators that produce a result.

Expression (2) The formula that will perform a calculation.

Expression Builder A feature used to create formulas (expressions) in query criteria, form and report properties, and table validation rules.

eXtensible Markup Language See *XML*.

Extract To decompress, or pull out, files from a compressed form.

Field A single piece of information that is stored in every record and formatted as a column in a database table.

Field list A list of the field names in a table.

Field properties Characteristics of a field that control how the field displays and how data can be entered in the field.

File A collection of information stored on a computer under a single name, for example a Word document or a PowerPoint presentation.

File list In a folder window, the area on the right that displays the contents of the current folder or library.

Fill The inside color of an object.

Filter by Form An Access command that filters the records in a form based on one or more fields, or based on more than one value in the field.

Filter by Selection An Access command that retrieves only the records that contain the value in the selected field.

Filtering The process of displaying only a portion of the total records (a subset) based on matching a specific value.

Find Duplicates Query A query that is used to locate duplicate records in a table.

Find Unmatched Query A query used to locate unmatched records so they can be deleted from the table.

First principle of good database design A principle of good database design stating that data is organized in tables so that there is no redundant data.

Flagged A highlighted word that the spelling checker does not recognize from the Office dictionary.

Flat database A simple database file that is not related or linked to any other collection of data.

Folder A container in which you store files.

Folder window In Windows, a window that displays the contents of the current folder, library, or device, and contains helpful parts so that you can navigate.

Font A set of characters with the same design and shape.

Font styles Formatting emphasis such as bold, italic, and underline.

Footer A reserved area for text or graphics that displays at the bottom of each page in a document.

Foreign key The field that is included in the related table so the field can be joined with the primary key in another table for the purpose of creating a relationship.

Form (Access) An Access object you can use to enter new records into a table, edit or delete existing records in a table, or display existing records.

Form footer Information at the bottom of the screen in Form view that is printed after the last detail section on the last page.

Form header Information, such as a form's title, that displays at the top of the screen in Form view and is printed at the top of the first page when records are printed as forms.

Form tool The Access tool that creates a form with a single mouse click, which includes all of the fields from the underlying data source (table or query).

Form view The Access view in which you can view the records, but you cannot change the layout or design of the form.

Form Wizard The Access tool that creates a form by asking a series of questions.

Format Painter An Office feature that copies formatting from one selection of text to another.

Formatting The process of establishing the overall appearance of text, graphics, and pages in an Office file—for example, in a Word document.

Formatting marks Characters that display on the screen, but do not print, indicating where the Enter key, the Spacebar, and the Tab key were pressed; also called *nonprinting characters*.

FROM clause An SQL statement that lists which tables hold the fields used in the SELECT clause.

Front end The database forms, queries, reports, and macros that end users open to work with the data stored in the back-end tables.

Gallery An Office feature that displays a list of potential results instead of just the command name.

Group footer Information printed at the end of each group of records; used to display summary information for the group.

Group header Information printed at the beginning of each new group of records, for example, the group name.

Group, Sort, and Total pane A pane that displays at the bottom of the screen in which you can control how information is sorted and grouped in a report; provides the most flexibility for adding or modifying groups, sort orders, or totals options on a report.

Groups On the Office Ribbon, the sets of related commands that you might need for a specific type of task.

Header A reserved area for text or graphics that displays at the top of each page in a document.

HTML Stands for HyperText Markup Language. The language used to display Web pages.

HyperText Markup Language See *HTML*.

Icons Pictures that represent a program, a file, a folder, or some other object.

Import The process of copying data from another file, such as a Word table or an Excel workbook, into a separate file, such as an Access database.

Indeterminate relationship A relationship between two fields that does not enforce referential integrity.

Index A special list created in Access to speed up searches and sorting.

Info tab The tab in Backstage view that displays information about the current file.

Information Data that is organized in a useful manner.

Inner join A join that allows only the records where the common field exists in both related tables to be displayed in query results.

Innermost sort field When sorting on multiple fields in Datasheet view, the field that will be used for the second level of sorting.

Input mask A field property that determines the data that can be entered and how the data displays.

Insertion point A blinking vertical line that indicates where text or graphics will be inserted.

Instance Each simultaneously running Access session.

Is Not Null A criteria that searches for fields that are not empty.

Is Null A criteria that searches for fields that are empty.

Join A relationship that helps a query return only the records from each table you want to see, based on how those tables are related to other tables in the query.

JOIN clause An SQL statement that defines the join type for a query.

Join line In the Relationships window, the line joining two tables that visually indicates the related field and the type of relationship.

Junction table A table that breaks down the many-to-many relationship into two one-to-many relationships.

KB The abbreviation for kilobyte.

Keyboard shortcut A combination of two or more keyboard keys, used to perform a task that would otherwise require a mouse.

KeyTips The letter that displays on a command in the Ribbon and that indicates the key you can press to activate the command when keyboard control of the Ribbon is activated.

Keyword Commands built into the SQL programming language.

Kilobyte A measurement for data that stores 1,024 bytes.

Label control A control on a form or report that contains descriptive information, typically a field name.

Landscape orientation A page orientation in which the paper is wider than it is tall.

Layout selector A small symbol that displays in the upper left corner of a selected control layout in a form or report that is displayed in Layout view or Design view; used to move an entire group of controls.

Layout view The Access view in which you can make changes to a form or report while the object is running—the data from the underlying data source displays.

Left outer join A join used when you want to display all of the records on the *one* side of a one-to-many relationship, whether or not there are matching records in the table on the *many* side of the relationship.

Legend Text that describes the meaning of colors and patterns used in a chart.

Library In Windows, a collection of items, such as files and folders, assembled from various locations that might be on your computer, an external hard drive, removable media, or someone else's computer.

Line chart A chart used to display trends over time.

Link A connection to data in another file.

Linked form A form related to the main form that is not stored within the main form; click on the link that is displayed on the main form to view the related form.

List box A box containing a list of choices for a lookup field.

Live Preview A technology that shows the result of applying an editing or formatting change as you point to possible results—*before* you actually apply it.

Location Any disk drive, folder, or other place in which you can store files and folders.

Logical operators Operators that combine criteria using AND and OR. With two criteria, AND requires that both conditions be met and OR requires that either condition be met.

Lookup field A way to restrict data entered in a field.

Macro A series of actions grouped as a single command to accomplish a task or multiple tasks automatically.

Macro group A set of macros grouped by a common name that displays as one macro object in the Navigation Pane.

Mail merge To combine a main document and a data source to create letters or memos.

Main document The document that contains the text of a letter or memo for a mail merge in Microsoft Word.

Main form A form that contains a subform.

Main report A report that contains a subreport.

Make table query An action query that creates a new table by extracting data from one or more tables.

Many-to-many relationship A relationship between tables where one record in one table has many matching records in a second table, and a single record in the related table has many matching records in the first table.

Merge Combining two documents to create one.

Message Bar The area directly below the Ribbon that displays information such as security alerts when there is potentially unsafe, active content in an Office 2010 document that you open.

Metadata Details about a file that describe or identify it, including the title, author name, subject, and keywords that identify the document's topic or contents; also known as *document properties*.

Microsoft Access A database program, with which you can collect, track, and report data.

Microsoft Communicator An Office program that brings together multiple modes of communication, including instant messaging, video conferencing, telephony, application sharing, and file transfer.

Microsoft Excel A spreadsheet program, with which you calculate and analyze numbers and create charts.

Microsoft InfoPath An Office program that enables you to create forms and gather data.

Microsoft Office 2010 A Microsoft suite of products that includes programs, servers, and services for individuals, small organizations, and large enterprises to perform specific tasks.

Microsoft OneNote An Office program with which you can manage notes that you make at meetings or in classes.

Microsoft Outlook An Office program with which you can manage e-mail and organizational activities.

Microsoft PowerPoint A presentation program, with which you can communicate information with high-impact graphics.

Microsoft Publisher An Office program with which you can create desktop publishing documents such as brochures.

Microsoft SharePoint Workspace An Office program that enables you to share information with others in a team environment.

Microsoft SQL Server A database application designed for high-end business uses.

Microsoft Word A word processing program, also referred to as an authoring program, with which you create and share documents by using its writing tools.

Mini toolbar A small toolbar containing frequently used formatting commands that displays as a result of selecting text or objects.

Modal window A child (secondary window) to a parent window that takes over control of the parent window.

Multi-page form A form that displays the data from the underlying table or query on more than one page.

Multiple Items form A form that enables you to display or enter multiple records in a table.

Multivalued fields Fields that hold multiple values.

Named range A range that has been given a name, making it easier to use the cells in calculations or modifications.

Navigate The process of exploring within the organizing structure of Windows.

Navigation area An area at the bottom of the Access window that indicates the number of records in the table and contains controls (arrows) with which you can navigate among the records.

Navigation Pane (Access) An area of the Access window that displays and organizes the names of the objects in a database; from here, you open objects for use.

Navigation Pane category A top-level listing that displays when the Navigation Pane arrow is clicked.

Navigation Pane group A second-level listing that displays when a Navigation Pane category is selected.

Nested subform A subform that is embedded within another subform.

Nonprinting characters Characters that display on the screen, but do not print, indicating where the Enter key, the Spacebar, and the Tab key were pressed; also called *formatting marks*.

Normalization The process of applying design rules and principles to ensure that your database performs as expected.

Object window An area of the Access window that displays open objects, such as tables, forms, queries, or reports; by default, each object displays on its own tab.

Objects The basic parts of a database that you create to store your data and to work with your data; for example, tables, forms, queries, and reports.

Office Clipboard A temporary storage area that holds text or graphics that you select and then cut or copy.

ON An SQL keyword that is used to specify which field is common to two tables.

One-to-one relationship A relationship between tables where a record in one table has only one matching record in another table.

One-to-many relationship A relationship between two tables where one record in the first table corresponds to many records in the second table—the most common type of relationship in Access.

Open dialog box A dialog box from which you can navigate to, and then open on your screen, an existing file that was created in that same program.

Open Exclusive An option that opens the database so that changes can be made, but no one else may open the database at the same time.

Open Exclusive Read-Only An option that opens the database in both Exclusive and Read-Only modes.

Open Read-Only An option that opens the database so that all objects can be opened and viewed, but data and design changes cannot be made.

Option button A round button that allows you to make one choice among two or more options.

Options dialog box A dialog box within each Office application where you can select program settings and other options and preferences.

OR condition A condition in which records that match at least one of the specified values are displayed.

Orphan record A record that references deleted records in a related table.

Outer join A join that is typically used to display records from both tables, regardless of whether there are matching records.

Outermost sort field When sorting on multiple fields in Datasheet view, the field that will be used for the first level of sorting.

Page footer Information printed at the end of every page in a report; used to print page numbers or other information that you want to display at the bottom of every report page.

Page header (Access) Information printed at the top of every page of a report.

Page number control A control on a form or report that inserts the page numbers when displayed in Print Preview or when printed.

Paragraph symbol The symbol ¶ that represents a paragraph.

Parameter A value that can be changed.

Parameter query A query that prompts you for criteria before running the query.

Paste The action of placing text or objects that have been copied or moved from one location to another location.

Paste Options Icons that provide a Live Preview of the various options for changing the format of a pasted item with a single click.

Path The location of a folder or file on your computer or storage device.

PDF (Portable Document Format) file A file format that creates an image that preserves the look of your file, but that cannot be easily changed; a popular format for sending documents electronically, because the document will display on most computers.

Performance Analyzer A wizard that analyzes database objects and then offers suggestions for improving their design.

Pie chart A chart used to display the contributions of parts to a whole amount.

Pivot The ability to rotate a table to swap row headings with column headings to display the data in a different way.

PivotChart A graphical view of the data in a PivotTable.

PivotTable An object view used to organize, arrange, analyze, and summarize data in a meaningful way.

Plain text A document format where text does not contain any formatting, such as bold or italics.

Point The action of moving your mouse pointer over something on your screen.

Pointer Any symbol that displays on your screen in response to moving your mouse.

Points A measurement of the size of a font; there are 72 points in an inch, with 10-12 points being the most commonly used font size.

Pop-up window A window that displays (pops up); usually contains a menu of commands, and stays on the screen only until the user selects one of the commands.

Populate The action of filling a database table with records.

Portrait orientation A page orientation in which the paper is taller than it is wide.

Preview pane button In a folder window, the button on the toolbar with which you can display a preview of the contents of a file without opening it in a program.

Primary key The field that uniquely identifies a record in a table; for example, a Student ID number at a college.

Print Preview A view of a document as it will appear when you print it.

Program A set of instructions that a computer uses to perform a specific task, such as word processing, accounting, or data management; also called an *application*.

Program-level control buttons In an Office program, the buttons on the right edge of the title bar that minimize, restore, or close the program.

Property Sheet A list of characteristics—properties—for fields or controls on a form or report in which you can make precise changes to each property associated with the field or control.

Protected view A security feature in Office 2010 that protects your computer from malicious files by opening them in a restricted environment until you enable them; you might encounter this feature if you open a file from an e-mail or download files from the Internet.

Pt. The abbreviation for *point*; for example when referring to a font size.

Query A database object that retrieves specific data from one or more database objects—either tables or other queries—and then, in a single datasheet, displays only the data you specify.

Quick Access Toolbar In an Office program, the small row of buttons in the upper left corner of the screen from which you can perform frequently used commands.

Quick Commands The commands Save, Save As, Open, and Close that display at the top of the navigation pane in Backstage view.

Range An area that includes two or more selected cells on a worksheet that can be treated as a single unit.

Read-Only A property assigned to a file that prevents the file from being modified or deleted; it indicates that you cannot save any changes to the displayed document unless you first save it with a new name.

Record All of the categories of data pertaining to one person, place, thing, event, or idea, and which is formatted as a row in a database table.

Record selector bar The bar at the left edge of a record when it is displayed in a form, and which is used to select an entire record.

Record selector box The small box at the left of a record in Datasheet view that, when clicked, selects the entire record.

Record source The tables or queries that provide the underlying data for a form or report.

Redundant In a database, information that is repeated in a manner that indicates poor database design.

Referential integrity A set of rules that Access uses to ensure that the data between related tables is valid.

Relational database A sophisticated type of database that has multiple collections of data within the file that are related to one another.

Relationship An association that you establish between two tables based on common fields.

Replica A special copy of a database where changes made are exchanged with the original database and any other replicas that may exist.

Replica set The original database and all replica copies.

Replication The process of creating a replica.

Report A database object that summarizes the fields and records from a table or query in an easy-to-read format suitable for printing.

Report footer Information printed once at the end of a report; used to print report totals or other summary information for the entire report.

Report header Information printed once at the beginning of a report; used for logos, titles, and dates.

Report tool The Access tool that creates a report with one mouse click, which displays all of the fields and records from the record source that you select—a quick way to look at the underlying data.

Report Wizard An Access feature with which you can create a report by answering a series of questions; Access designs the report based on your answers.

Required A field property that ensures a field cannot be left empty.

Ribbon The user interface in Office 2010 that groups the commands for performing related tasks on tabs across the upper portion of the program window.

Ribbon tabs The tabs on the Office Ribbon that display the names of the task-oriented groups of commands.

Right outer join A join used when you want to display all of the records on the *many* side of a one-to-many relationship, whether or not there are matching records in the table on the *one* side of the relationship. This should not occur if referential integrity has been enforced because all orders should have a related customer.

Right-click The action of clicking the right mouse button one time.

Run The process in which Access searches the records in the table(s) included in the query design, finds the records that match the specified criteria, and then displays the records in a datasheet; only the fields that have been included in the query design display.

Sans serif A font design with no lines or extensions on the ends of characters.

ScreenTip A small box that that displays useful information when you perform various mouse actions such as pointing to screen elements or dragging.

Scroll bar A vertical or horizontal bar in a window or a pane to assist in bringing an area into view, and which contains a scroll box and scroll arrows.

Scroll box The box in the vertical and horizontal scroll bars that can be dragged to reposition the contents of a window or pane on the screen.

Search box In a folder window, the box in which you can type a word or a phrase to look for an item in the current folder or library.

Second principle of good database design A principle stating that appropriate database techniques are used to ensure the accuracy of data entered into a table.

Section bar A gray bar in a form or report that identifies and separates one section from another; used to select the section and to change the size of the adjacent section.

Select To highlight, by dragging with your mouse, areas of text or data or graphics, so that the selection can be edited, formatted, copied, or moved.

SELECT clause An SQL statement that lists which fields the query should display.

Select query A type of Access query that retrieves (selects) data from one or more tables or queries, displaying the selected data in a datasheet; also known as a *simple select query*.

Serif font A font design that includes small line extensions on the ends of the letters to guide the eye in reading from left to right.

Shortcut menu A menu that displays commands and options relevant to the selected text or object.

Show Previous Versions An option that searches your computer for previous versions of the selected database.

Simple select query Another name for a select query.

Single stepping Debugging a macro using a process that executes one action at a time.

Single-record form A form that enables you to display or enter one record at a time in a table.

Sort The process of arranging data in a specific order based on the value in each field.

Source file When importing a file, refers to the file being imported.

Source table The table from which records are being extracted or copied.

Split button A button divided into two parts and in which clicking the main part of the button performs a command and clicking the arrow opens a menu with choices.

Split database An Access database that is split into two files—one containing the back end and one containing the front end.

Split form An object that displays data in two views—Form view and Datasheet view—on a single form.

Spreadsheet Another name for a worksheet.

SQL statement An expression that defines the structured query language commands that should be performed when a query is run.

Stacked layout A control layout format that is similar to a paper form, with label controls placed to the left of each textbox control. The controls are grouped together for easy editing.

Standalone macro A macro contained in a macro object that displays under Macros in the Navigation Pane.

Start button The button on the Windows taskbar that displays the Start menu.

Start menu The Windows menu that provides a list of choices and is the main gateway to your computer's programs, folders, and settings.

Static data Data that does not change.

Status bar The area along the lower edge of an Office program window that displays file information on the left and buttons to control how the window looks on the right.

Strong password A password that is difficult to guess and that uses a combination of upper and lowercase letters, special characters, numbers, and spaces in a character string.

Structure In Access, the underlying design of a table, including field names, data types, descriptions, and field properties.

Structured Query Language (SQL) A language used by many database programs to view, update, and query data in relational databases.

Subdatasheet A format for displaying related records when you click the plus sign (+) next to a record in a table on the *one* side of a relationship.

Subfolder A folder within a folder.

Subform A form that is embedded within another form.

Subreport A report that is embedded within another report.

Subset A portion of the total records available.

Synchronize To compare and update database objects in each member of a replica set by exchanging all updated records and design changes.

Syntax The spelling, grammar, and sequence of characters of a programming language; Access expects object names to be referred to in a specific manner, which is called the syntax.

System tables Tables used to keep track of multiple entries in an attachment field that you cannot view or work with.

Tab control A control that is used to display data on the main form on different tabs, similar to the way database objects, such as forms and tables, display on different tabs.

Tab order The order in which the insertion point moves from one field to another in a form when you press the Tab key.

Table (Access) The database object that stores data organized in an arrangement of columns and rows, and which is the foundation of an Access database.

Table Analyzer A wizard that searches for repeated data in a table and then splits the table into two or more related tables.

Table area The upper area of the Query window that displays field lists for the tables that are used in the query.

Tables and Related Views An arrangement in the Navigation Pane that groups objects by the table to which they are related.

Tabs On the Office Ribbon, the name of each activity area in the Office Ribbon.

Tags (1) Custom file properties that you create to help find and organize your own files.

Tags (2) Codes that the Web browser interprets as the page is loaded; begin with the < character and end with the > character.

Task pane A window within a Microsoft Office application in which you can enter options for completing a command.

Text box control The graphical object on a form or report that displays the data from the underlying table or query; a text box control is known as a bound control.

Text data type An Access data type that describes text, a combination of text and numbers, or numbers that are not used in calculations, such as a number that is an identifier like a Student ID.

Text string A sequence of characters.

Theme A predefined format that can be applied to the entire database or to individual objects in the database.

Theme A predesigned set of colors, fonts, lines, and fill effects that look good together and that can be applied to your entire document or to specific items.

Title bar The bar at the top edge of the program window that indicates the name of the current file and the program name.

Toggle button A button that can be turned on by clicking it once, and then turned off by clicking it again.

Toolbar In a folder window, a row of buttons with which you can perform common tasks, such as changing the view of your files and folders or burning files to a CD.

Totals query A query that calculates subtotals across groups of records.

Triple-click The action of clicking the left mouse button three times in rapid succession.

Truncated Refers to data that is cut off or shortened.

Trust Center An area of the Access program where you can view the security and privacy settings for your Access installation.

Trusted Documents A security feature in Office 2010 that remembers which files you have already enabled; you might encounter this feature if you open a file from an e-mail or download files from the Internet.

Trusted source A person or organization that you know will not send you databases with malicious content.

Unbound control A control that does not have a source of data, such as a title in a form or report.

Unbound report A report that does not display data from an underlying table, query, or SQL statement and has an empty Record Source property setting.

Unequal join A join that is used to combine rows from two data sources based on field values that are not equal; can be created only in SQL view.

UNION An SQL keyword that is used to combine one or more queries in a union query.

Union query A query type that combines the results of two or more similar select queries.

Unmatched records Records in one table that have no matching records in a related table.

Update query An action query that is used to add, change, or delete data in fields of one or more existing records.

Upper Camel Case The practice of writing phrases in which the elements are joined without spaces and the initial letter of each element is capitalized.

USB flash drive A small data storage device that plugs into a computer USB port.

Validation rule An expression that precisely defines the range of data that will be accepted in a field.

Validation text The error message that displays when an individual enters a value prohibited by the validation rule.

Views button In a folder window, a toolbar button with which you can choose how to view the contents of the current location.

Weak password A password that is easy to guess.

WHERE clause An SQL statement that defines the criteria that should be applied when a query is run.

Wildcard character In a query, a character that serves as a placeholder for one or more unknown characters in your criteria; an asterisk (*) represents one or more unknown characters, and a question mark (?) represents a single unknown character.

Window A rectangular area on a computer screen in which programs and content appear, and which can be moved, resized, minimized, or closed.

Windows Explorer The program that displays the files and folders on your computer, and which is at work anytime you are viewing the contents of files and folders in a window.

Windows taskbar The area along the lower edge of the Windows desktop that contains the Start button and an area to display buttons for open programs.

Wizard A feature in Microsoft Office that walks you step by step through a process.

Workbook An Excel file that contains one or more worksheets.

Worksheet The primary document used in Excel to save and work with data that is arranged in columns and rows.

XML Stands for eXtensible Markup Language. The standard language for defining and storing data on the Web.

XML presentation files Files that can be created so that the data can be viewed in a Web browser.

XML schema A document with an *.xsd* extension that defines the elements, entities, and content allowed in the document.

Zero-length string An entry created by typing two quotation marks with no spaces between them ("") to indicate that no value exists for a required text or memo field.

Zoom The action of increasing or decreasing the viewing area on the screen.

Index

F

Field List, 487, 488
  Design tab, 572
field list, definition, 119
Field Name, 258
  Data Type, 268, 280
  Description box, 279–280
  Design view, 292
  Field Properties, 285
  Priority field, 292
  Start Date, 296
Field Name column, Row Selector box, 269
field names, 55–58, 731
  : (colon), 327
  destination tables, 353
  Edit Relationships dialog box, 272
  spaces, 280
  [] (square brackets), 325, 327, 430
Field Options, Data Type arrow, 606
Field Properties
  Action Tags box, 687
  Default Value box, 292
  Description box, 281
  Field Name, 285
  Field Size box, 279
  Format box, 279, 289
  General tab, 299
  Indexed property box, 293
  Input Mask box, 285
  Lookup tab, 284
  Required box, 290
  Status field, 283, 290
  Validation Rule box, 294, 296
Field row
  Design view, 326, 330
  right-click, 326, 327
  shortcut menus, 327
fields. See also *specific fields or field types*
  adding, 472
  calculated fields, 325–330
  controls, 487
  default values, 292
  definition, 51
  deleting, 64–65, 472
  Is Null/Is Not Null criteria, 135–136
  modifying, 65–66
  PivotTable, 572
  properties, 65, 285–294
    testing, 297–299
  renaming, 58
  required, 290–292
  sorting records, 125–126
  tables, indexing, 293–294
Field Size box, Field Properties pane, 279
Fields tab
  Add & Delete group, 269
  Data Type, 269
  Field Validation group, 291
  Formatting group, 269
  Insert Merge Field dialog box, 630
Field Validation group, 291
files
  compressed, 44–45
  definition, 3
  extracting compressed files, 45

  finding, 3–6
  locations, trusted locations, 256–257
  management, Backstage view, 14
  names, dates, 255
  opening, 22–25
  printing, 18–20
  properties, Read-Only, 23
  saving, 13–18
    with new names, 22–25
  source
    definition, 61
    importing, 608
  storing, 14
File Conversion dialog box, 603–604
File list, 5
File name box, 17, 255
File tab, 8
fills, 12
filtering
  definition, 201
  PivotTable, 570
  records, 201–205
Filter By Form command, definition, 203
Filter By Selection command, definition, 201
Filter Name box, ScreenTips, 541
Filter & Sort
  AutoFilter, 571
  Design tab, 571
Find and Replace dialog box
  Cancel, 265
  Find tab, 264
  Find What box, 264
  Look In box arrow, 264
Find button, Home tab, 264
Find Duplicates Query Wizard, 339–342
Find Event, 564, 566
  _ (underscore), 560
  Form Header, 559
Find group, Home tab, 264
finding
  files, 3–6
  folders, 3–6
  unmatched records, 341–342
FindRecord, Submacro, 557
Find tab, Find and Replace dialog box, 264
Find Unmatched Query Wizard, 339–342
Find What box, Find and Replace dialog box, 264
first principle of good database design, definition, 52
First Record button, 485
Fixed, Format property, 281
flagging, spell checking, 269
flash drives, USB, 6
flat databases, definition, 51
folders
  creating, 13–18
  definition, 3
  finding, 3–6
folder window, 4–5
Folder window toolbar, 5
Font Color button, 36, 497
Font Color button arrow, 505
Font group
  Center button, 505
  Font Size button arrow, 505

SINGLE PC LICENSE AGREEMENT AND LIMITED WARRANTY

READ THIS LICENSE CAREFULLY BEFORE OPENING THIS PACKAGE. BY OPENING THIS PACKAGE, YOU ARE AGREEING TO THE TERMS AND CONDITIONS OF THIS LICENSE. IF YOU DO NOT AGREE, DO NOT OPEN THE PACKAGE. PROMPTLY RETURN THE UNOPENED PACKAGE AND ALL ACCOMPANYING ITEMS TO THE PLACE YOU OBTAINED THEM. *THESE TERMS APPLY TO ALL LICENSED SOFTWARE ON THE DISK EXCEPT THAT THE TERMS FOR USE OF ANY SHAREWARE OR FREEWARE ON THE DISKETTES ARE AS SET FORTH IN THE ELECTRONIC LICENSE LOCATED ON THE DISK:*

1. GRANT OF LICENSE and OWNERSHIP: The enclosed computer programs ("Software") are licensed, not sold, to you by Prentice-Hall, Inc. ("We" or the "Company") and in consideration of your purchase or adoption of the accompanying Company textbooks and/or other materials, and your agreement to these terms. We reserve any rights not granted to you. You own only the disk(s) but we and/or our licensors own the Software itself. This license allows you to use and display your copy of the Software on a single computer (i.e., with a single CPU) at a single location for academic use only, so long as you comply with the terms of this Agreement. You may make one copy for back up, or transfer your copy to another CPU, provided that the Software is usable on only one computer.

2. RESTRICTIONS: You may not transfer or distribute the Software or documentation to anyone else. Except for backup, you may not copy the documentation or the Software. You may not network the Software or otherwise use it on more than one computer or computer terminal at the same time. You may not reverse engineer, disassemble, decompile, modify, adapt, translate, or create derivative works based on the Software or the Documentation. You may be held legally responsible for any copying or copyright infringement which is caused by your failure to abide by the terms of these restrictions.

3. TERMINATION: This license is effective until terminated. This license will terminate automatically without notice from the Company if you fail to comply with any provisions or limitations of this license. Upon termination, you shall destroy the Documentation and all copies of the Software. All provisions of this Agreement as to limitation and disclaimer of warranties, limitation of liability, remedies or damages, and our ownership rights shall survive termination.

4.DISCLAIMER OF WARRANTY: THE COMPANY AND ITS LICENSORS MAKE NO WARRANTIES ABOUT THE SOFTWARE, WHICH IS PROVIDED "AS-IS." IF THE DISK IS DEFECTIVE IN MATERIALS OR WORKMANSHIP, YOUR ONLY REMEDY IS TO RETURN IT TO THE COMPANY WITHIN 30 DAYS FOR REPLACEMENT UNLESS THE COMPANY DETERMINES IN GOOD FAITH THAT THE DISK HAS BEEN MISUSED OR IMPROPERLY INSTALLED, REPAIRED, ALTERED OR DAMAGED. THE COMPANY DISCLAIMS ALL WARRANTIES, EXPRESS OR IMPLIED, INCLUDING WITHOUT LIMITATION, THE IMPLIED WARRANTIES OF MERCHANTABILITY AND FITNESS FOR A PARTICULAR PURPOSE. THE COMPANY DOES NOT WARRANT, GUARANTEE OR MAKE ANY REPRESENTATION REGARDING THE ACCURACY, RELIABILITY, CURRENTNESS, USE, OR RESULTS OF USE, OF THE SOFTWARE.

5. LIMITATION OF REMEDIES AND DAMAGES: IN NO EVENT, SHALL THE COMPANY OR ITS EMPLOYEES, AGENTS, LICENSORS OR CONTRACTORS BE LIABLE FOR ANY INCIDENTAL, INDIRECT, SPECIAL OR CONSEQUENTIAL DAMAGES ARISING OUT OF OR IN CONNECTION WITH THIS LICENSE OR THE SOFTWARE, INCLUDING, WITHOUT LIMITATION, LOSS OF USE, LOSS OF DATA, LOSS OF INCOME OR PROFIT, OR OTHER LOSSES SUSTAINED AS A RESULT OF INJURY TO ANY PERSON, OR LOSS OF OR DAMAGE TO PROPERTY, OR CLAIMS OF THIRD PARTIES, EVEN IF THE COMPANY OR AN AUTHORIZED REPRESENTATIVE OF THE COMPANY HAS BEEN ADVISED OF THE POSSIBILITY OF SUCH DAMAGES. SOME JURISDICTIONS DO NOT ALLOW THE LIMITATION OF DAMAGES IN CERTAIN CIRCUMSTANCES, SO THE ABOVE LIMITATIONS MAY NOT ALWAYS APPLY.

6. GENERAL: THIS AGREEMENT SHALL BE CONSTRUED IN ACCORDANCE WITH THE LAWS OF THE UNITED STATES OF AMERICA AND THE STATE OF NEW YORK, APPLICABLE TO CONTRACTS MADE IN NEW YORK, AND SHALL BENEFIT THE COMPANY, ITS AFFILIATES AND ASSIGNEES. This Agreement is the complete and exclusive statement of the agreement between you and the Company and supersedes all proposals, prior agreements, oral or written, and any other communications between you and the company or any of its representatives relating to the subject matter. If you are a U.S. Government user, this Software is licensed with "restricted rights" as set forth in subparagraphs (a)-(d) of the Commercial Computer-Restricted Rights clause at FAR 52.227-19 or in subparagraphs (c)(1)(ii) of the Rights in Technical Data and Computer Software clause at DFARS 252.227-7013, and similar clauses, as applicable.

Should you have any questions concerning this agreement or if you wish to contact the Company for any reason, please contact in writing:

Multimedia Production,
Higher Education Division,
Prentice-Hall, Inc.,
1 Lake Street,
Upper Saddle River NJ 07458.